HUMAN GEOGRAPHY
OF THE SOUTH

THE UNIVERSITY OF NORTH CAROLINA
SOCIAL STUDY SERIES

UNDER THE GENERAL EDITORSHIP OF HOWARD W. ODUM. BOOKS MARKED WITH *
PUBLISHED IN COÖPERATION WITH THE INSTITUTE FOR RESEARCH IN SOCIAL SCIENCE.

BECKWITH: *Black Roadways: A Study of Folk Life in Jamaica*............$3.00
BRANSON: *Farm Life Abroad*... 2.00
*BREARLEY: *Homicide in the United States*................................. 2.50
*BROWN: *Public Poor Relief in North Carolina*............................ 2.00
*BROWN: *The State Highway System of North Carolina*..................... 2.50
*BROWN: *A State Movement in Railroad Development*....................... 5.00
CARTER: *The Social Theories of L. T. Hobhouse*.......................... 1.50
CROOK: *The General Strike*... 6.00
FLEMING: *The Freedmen's Savings Bank*.................................... 2.00
GEE (ed.): *The Country Life of the Nation*............................... 2.00
*GREEN: *Constitutional Development in the South Atlantic States, 1776-1860*.. 3.00
GREEN: *The Negro in Contemporary American Literature*.................. 1.00
*GRISSOM: *The Negro Sings a New Heaven and a New Earth*................ 2.50
HAR: *Social Laws*.. 4.00
*HEER: *Income and Wages in the South*.................................... 1.00
*HERRING: *History of the Textile Industry in the South*..............*In Preparation*
*HERRING: *Welfare Work in Mill Villages*................................. 5.00
HOBBS: *North Carolina: Economic and Social*............................. 3.50
*JOHNSON: *Folk Culture on Saint Helena Island*.......................... 3.00
*JOHNSON: *John Henry: Tracking Down a Negro Legend*.................... 2.00
*JOHNSON: *A Social History of the Sea Islands*.......................... 3.00
JORDAN: *Children's Interests in Reading*................................. 1.50
KNIGHT: *Among the Danes*.. 2.50
LINDQUIST: *The Family in the Present Social Order*...................... 2.50
LOU: *Juvenile Courts in the United States*............................... 3.00
McCRACKEN: *Strike Injunctions in the New South*......................... 3.00
*METFESSEL: *Phonophotography in Folk Music*............................. 3.00
MILLER: *Town and Country*... 2.00
*MITCHELL: *William Gregg: Factory Master of the Old South*............. 3.00
*MITCHELL: *Textile Unionism and the South*.............................. 1.00
*MURCHISON: *King Cotton is Sick*.. 2.00
NORTH: *Social Differentiation*... 2.50
ODUM: *An Approach to Public Welfare and Social Work*................... 1.50
*ODUM (ed.): *Southern Pioneers*... 2.00
*ODUM AND JOHNSON: *The Negro and His Songs*............................ 3.00
*ODUM AND JOHNSON: *Negro Workaday Songs*............................... 3.00
*ODUM AND WILLARD: *Systems of Public Welfare*.......................... 2.00
POUND: *Law and Morals*.. 2.00
*PUCKETT: *Folk Beliefs of the Southern Negro*........................... 5.00
*RHYNE: *Some Southern Cotton Mill Workers and Their Villages*.......... 2.50
ROBINSON: *A Changing Psychology in Social Case Work*................... 2.50
ROSS: *Roads to Social Peace*.. 1.50
SCHWENNING (ed.): *Management Problems*................................. 2.00
SHERRILL: *Criminal Procedure in North Carolina*......................... 3.00
*STEINER AND BROWN: *The North Carolina Chain Gang*..................... 2.00
*VANCE: *Human Factors in Cotton Culture*................................. 3.00
*VANCE: *Human Geography of the South*.................................... 4.00
*WAGER: *County Government in North Carolina*............................ 5.00
WALKER: *Social Work and the Training of Social Workers*................ 2.00
WAY: *The Clinchfield Railroad*.. 5.00
WHITE: *Some Cycles of Cathay*... 1.50
WILLEY: *The Country Newspaper*... 1.50
WINSTON: *Illiteracy in the United States*................................ 3.00
*WOOFTER: *The Plight of Cigarette Tobacco*............................... 1.00

The University of North Carolina Press, Chapel Hill, N. C.; The Baker and Taylor Co., New York; Oxford University Press, London; The Maruzen Company, Tokyo; Edward Evans & Sons, Ltd., Shanghai; D. B. Centen's Wetenschappelijke Boekhandel, Amsterdam.

HUMAN GEOGRAPHY
OF THE SOUTH

A STUDY IN REGIONAL RESOURCES
AND HUMAN ADEQUACY

BY

RUPERT B. VANCE, Ph.D.

Research Associate, Institute for Research in Social Science,
University of North Carolina

CHAPEL HILL
THE UNIVERSITY OF NORTH CAROLINA PRESS
1932

PRINTED IN THE UNITED STATES OF AMERICA BY
THE SEEMAN PRESS, DURHAM, NORTH CAROLINA

FOR RHEBA

PREFACE

REGIONALISM and the new geography afford a point of vantage from which this volume views the American South as a test of human adequacy to master the resources of its region and to develop thereon a distinctive and competent culture.

However much he would have enjoyed it, the author has not written a regional sociology of the South. Nor does he contend that the relation of the resources of a region to the cultural adequacy of its population yet forms the subject matter of human geography. At such a point, however, converge the lines of force from geography, ecology, human biology, economics, and technology. Within this scaffolding of nature and culture has been erected the architecture of a region. With many a side glance at the historical development, this volume attempts to give a synthetic treatment of the interaction of men and nature in the American South.

Acknowledgment is due first of all to the multitude of scholars whose monographs, bulletins, and journal articles have been consulted in this treatment. They will be found cited in footnotes and bibliography. For careful reading of the manuscript and many helpful criticisms I am indebted to Dr. Ulrich B. Phillips of Yale, Dr. Erich W. Zimmermann, Professor of Economics and Resources, University of North Carolina, Dr. A. N. J. den Hollander, Geographer, University of Amsterdam, and Dr. Howard W. Odum, Director, Institute for Research in Social Science, University of North Carolina, and the Southern Regional Study of the Social Science Research Council. Possibly more than the author realizes the volume owes its style of approach to many stimulating contacts with Dr. Odum. Nor should the give and take with graduate seminars in Social Demography and Regional Sociology fail of acknowledgment. The arduous labors of editorial supervision have been shared by Dr. Katharine Jocher, while the manuscript has been read and the bibliography carefully checked by Rheba Usher Vance.

Chapel Hill
October 5, 1932

R. B. V.

TABLE OF CONTENTS

Introductory

CHAPTER I   PAGE

THE CONCEPT OF THE REGION.................................... 3

Physical factors of the region—Cultural factors of the region.

I. Backgrounds: Physical and Cultural

CHAPTER II

THE SOUTH'S PROFILE... 20

The South of many regions—Physiographic regions—Coastal plain—Florida—The Piedmont plateau—Appalachian highlands—Ozark-Ouachita highlands—The profile of culture——The valley section through North Carolina—The valley section through Tennessee—Population distribution in the valley section through Georgia.

CHAPTER III

POPULATION MOVES ACROSS THE SOUTHERN MAP................. 40

To the Revolution in the coastal plain—From the Revolution to the Civil War—Population depletion in areas of early settlement.

CHAPTER IV

THE HERITAGE OF THE FRONTIER............................... 59

The southern frontier—The frontier process—Traits of the southern frontier—Frontier and plantation in conflict—The frontier heritage.

II. Regions and Resources

CHAPTER V

THE SOUTHERN SOIL... 77

Physics of the soil—The soil as product—Soil areas of the South—Human geography of soils—Soil erosion—The social geography of erosion—Remedies for erosion.

CHAPTER VI

THE PINEY WOODS.. 109

Pioneers and the forests—Turpentining the piney woods—Lumbering in the piney woods—The future of the cut-over lands.

CHAPTER VII

LIVE STOCK IN THE SOUTH................................... 145

Beginnings—The frontier—The plantation—Grass in the South—The South and the tick—Cut-over pine lands—The biological factor—Dairying in the cotton belt—Present trends.

CHAPTER VIII

THE COTTON ECONOMY...................................... 177

Southern agriculture against the national background—Cotton and the plantation—The cotton system—Cotton culture complex.

CHAPTER IX

THE FRINGES OF THE COTTON BELT........................... 205

Tobacco—Rice—Sugar—Trucking regions in the South—Southern fishing fringe.

CHAPTER X

THE SOUTHERN HIGHLANDS, FRONTIER HERITAGE.............. 240

The southern highlands—Mountain culture—Cultural change—Towns—The Ozark-Ouachita highlands.

CHAPTER XI

THE DELTA, PLANTATION HERITAGE........................... 261

The delta metropolis—The delta of commerce—The delta of agriculture—Social incidence of flood.

CHAPTER XII

THE PIEDMONT CRESCENT OF INDUSTRY....................... 275

A Fringe Belt—Water power—Textiles in the Piedmont—Rayon emerges—The coal and iron district—Tobacco manufacturing—Furniture.

CHAPTER XIII

THE SOUTH MEETS THE WEST................................. 316

From frontier to ranch—From cattle to cotton—The Rio Grande valley——The industrial southwest—The Gulf Coast's monopoly of sulphur—The human geography of oil—The Texas gulf port area—Population elements.

III. Human Relations of Climate

CHAPTER XIV

THE SOUTHERN CLIME.. 351

The South as climatic province—The biology of climate—The significance of climate to the culture of the South—Historical development.

CHAPTER XV

CLIMATE, HEALTH, AND ENERGY................................. 375

The geography of disease—Climate, health, and energy—Hookworm and the South—The geography of the hookworm—Bio-social factors in hookworm—Malaria—Geography of the disease—Malaria and social resources —Relation to energy and efficiency—Eradication of malaria—Rural malaria control.

CHAPTER XVI

CLIMATE, DIET, AND HUMAN ADEQUACY.......................... 411

The geography of diet—The South's heritage of food—The biology of diet—The shifting American diet—The southern menu today—The share tenant—The small owner—The well-to-do farmer—Culture areas in diet —The South deviates from standards of nutrition—Cultural change in food habits—Regional diet and human adequacy.

IV. Prospect and Retrospect

CHAPTER XVII

THE STRUCTURE OF A REGIONAL ECONOMY....................... 442

The South's status—Regional resource areas—The basis in natural resources—Transportation in the South—Human adequacy in its biological aspects—Social adequacy and economic organization—Colonial economy and cultural status.

CHAPTER XVIII

RECONSTRUCTING THE REGION.................................. 482

Regionalism and regional planning—Regionalism and the South—The chamber of commerce movement—The proponents of agrarianism—The eclectic tasks of regionalism in the South—The reorganization of southern agriculture—Salvaging the marginal highlanders—The new flood control—The Florida beautification program—Guiding the urban trend— A folk renaissance for the South.

BIBLIOGRAPHY 512

INDEX 581

TABLE OF MAPS

FIGURE   PAGE

1. Agricultural Regions 13
2. Soil Regions 82
3. Soil Regions of the Cotton Belt........................... 88
4. Expenditures for Fertilizer by Farmers, 1924................. 96
5. Farms Reporting Expenditure for Fertilizer, 1924............. 96
6. Original Timber Regions 110
7. Forest, Cut-Over Land, and Woodland, 1920................. 134
8. Hay Acreage, 1924..................................... 153
9. Cattle and Calves on Farms, 1925......................... 166
10. Swine on Farms, 1925................................... 172
11. Average Value of Farms with Land, Buildings, Livestock
   and Equipment, 1925 180
12. Value of Farm Real Estate Per Acre, 1925................... 181
13. Farms Operated by Tenants and Croppers................... 188
14. Farms Operated by Croppers, 1925........................ 189
15. Farms Operated by Tenants Other than Croppers, 1925........ 189
16. Vegetables Grown for Home Use Only, Value, 1919........... 226
17. Seven Vegetables Grown for Sale, Acreage, 1924............. 228
18. Percentage of Improved Land............................. 228
19. Average Annual Precipitation............................. 354
20. Average Length of Growing Season........................ 358
21. Farms on Hard-Surfaced Roads, 1925...................... 456
22. Farms on Improved Dirt Roads, 1925...................... 457
23. Farms on Unimproved Dirt Roads, 1925.................... 457
24. Urban Population, 1920.................................. 458
25. Farm Population, 1925................................... 475
26. Farm Population Per Farm, 1925.......................... 478
27. Farm Population under 21 Years of Age, 1925............... 478
28. Farm Population under 10 Years of Age, 1925............... 480
29. Village Population, 1920................................. 505

LIST OF TABLES

TABLE   PAGE

1. The South and the Nation, 1920-1930 21
2. Outline of Factors Used in the Classification of Soils 81
3. Soil Provinces of the United States 83
4. Classification of Soils in the United States 84
5. Production and Consumption of Fertilizers in the South 97
6. Statistics of Cotton Culture in Eight Soil Regions of the South, 1909 100
7. Production of the Turpentine Industry, 1910-1930 123
8. Gum Turpentine Rosin Industry in the South 123
9. Area of Woodland, Restocking, and Cut-Over Lands, 1920 124
10. Classification of Southern Pine Lands, 1920 125
11. Milk Processing Plants in the South 169
12. Crop and Animal Ratios in the South 175
13. Farm Areas in the South, 1925 182
14. Farm Values in the South, 1925 183
15. Farm Incomes in the South, 1924-28 184
16. Farms in the South by Color and Tenure of Operators, 1930 191
17. Record of a 160 Acre Cotton Farm in Texas, 1894-1909 195
18. Farms Growing Specified Products in Ten Cotton States, 1920 .. 197
19. Economic and Social Status of Various Tenure Levels in a Tenancy Area 202
20. Tobacco: Acreage, Production, Value, 1910-1929 214
21. Rice: Acreage, Production, Value, 1924-1929 219
22. Cane Sugar Production in Louisiana, 1911-1929 224
23. Relation of Seasons to Soils and Trucking Areas 229
24. Farm Value of South's Commercial Truck Crops, 1926-1929 ... 236
25. The Southern Fishing Fringe 238
26. South's Manufacturing Progress By Decades, 1880-1920 280
27. Manufacturing in the South by States, 1927-1929 281
28. Power Installed in the South to 1927 288

[xiii]

TABLE   PAGE

29. Average Annual Wages in Cotton Textiles.................... 294
30. Spindles and Active Spindle Hours by Sections, 1921-1931..... 297
31. Cotton Manufacturing in Southern States..................... 298
32. Classification of South's Textile Industry, 1929............... 301
33. Southern Iron Output...................................... 307
34. Southern Coal Resources and Production, 1900-1929.......... 308
35. Manufacture of Tobacco in the South, 1929.................. 313
36. Petroleum Production by States and Fields................... 344
37. Petroleum Refining Industry of Southwest, 1929.............. 346
38. Death Rates in the South by States and Races, 1920-29........ 377
39. Malaria in Mississippi, 1914-1930.......................... 398
40. Deficiencies in Diet of 400 Georgia Farm Families............ 433
41. Comparative Rank of Dietary Surveys....................... 434
42. The South's Status, 1930................................... 442
43. Railways and Waterways in the South, 1929................. 454
44. Highway Mileage and Expenditures in South to 1929......... 459
45. Motor Vehicles Registration and Gasoline Tax Revenues
    in the South to 1929...................................... 460
46. South's Comparative Birth Rates by States and Races, 1920-1927 477
47. Excess of Births Over Deaths in the South, by States and
    Races, 1925-1929 479

HUMAN GEOGRAPHY
OF THE SOUTH

CHAPTER I

THE CONCEPT OF THE REGION

HERBERT SPENCER in the only interview granted the newspapers on his one visit to America analyzed American culture from the viewpoint of a sociologist. "In the first place," he said in 1882, "the American people have come into possession of an unparalleled fortune—the mineral wealth and the vast tract of virgin land producing abundantly with small cost of culture. . . . Then they have profited by inheriting all the arts, appliances, and methods developed by older societies, while leaving behind the obstructions existing in them. . . . Once more, there is inventiveness which, stimulated by the need of economizing labor, has been so wisely fostered. . . . The progressive incorporation of vast bodies of immigrants of various bloods has never occurred on such a scale before. . . . Then your immense plexus of railways and telegraphs tend to consolidate this vast aggregate of states in a way that no such aggregate has ever before been consolidated."[1]

In a series of thoughtful phrases Spencer suggested the factors of geography, material culture, technology, biological stocks, and communication that have served to give the United States the unity it possesses. In the adjustment of European culture to the American environment, the people themselves, certainly in the South, were more of a unity than the physical conditions they were to meet. The "customs, laws, languages, institutions which they brought with them, as well as their inherited tendencies, beliefs and prejudices; their intelligence, skill, knowledge of business methods and industrial processes and inventions"[2] were rather uniformly those held by the English common people. They thus formed a kind of culture complex. In their new American environment the people met two distinct sets of stimuli: the Indian culture and the physical

[1] *Essays, Scientific, Political, and Speculative,* III, 471-80.
[2] William A. Schaper, "Sectionalism and Representation in South Carolina," American Historical Association, *Report for 1900,* I, 246.

conditions. The Indians were both an obstacle to occupation and an aid to adjustment to the wilderness.[3] The adoption by the settlers of the Indians' forest folkways, as Turner convincingly shows us, created the frontier. The Indian, then, in a large sense made for the cultural unity of early America; and for a long time the frontier, North and South, was essentially the same.

PHYSICAL FACTORS OF THE REGION

In seeking to account for that diversity in our national culture which has made American history at once so interesting and so tragic, one is compelled to fall back on geographic factors. It will be wise, as H. H. Barrows holds, to view such a problem "from the standpoint of man's adjustment to the environment rather than from that of environmental influence."[4]   Only in this way can one avoid "assigning to geographic factors a determinative influence they do not exert."   In any study of the human geography of the region in America, the attempt should be made throughout to ascertain how European culture became, in seeking to conform to geographic conditions, American culture. Accordingly it will be useful to divide the geographic complex into its elements and to indicate some ways in which societies react to these elements.

For any given area at least eleven elements may be found to make up the geographic background: (1) Position; (2) area; (3) climate; (4) relief; (5) soil; (6) minerals; (7) waters of the land, including underground waters; (8) oceans; (9) coast and coast lines; (10) native vegetation; (11) native animal life.[5]   The importance of these elements may be accepted without question. Position exists in reference to other regions; it determines the accessibility or isolation of cultural groups. Area sets limits to the quantity of population that may be supported and thus aids in determining national strength. The relief, valley, plateau, mountain range, or plain, affects climate by means of altitude and influences communication. Like position it may make for exclusion. "The nucleus of population has its basis in the most accessible portions of a given physiographic area. From there it spreads along the lines of least resistance to the surrounding

---

[3] *Ibid.*, pp. 245-46.

[4] "Geography as Human Ecology," *Annals* of the Association of American Geographers, XIII, 3.

[5] Charles C. Colby, *Source Book for the Economic Geography of North America,* p. xiv.

hinterland."[6] Climate, itself, is composed of many factors: temperature, humidity, precipitation, cloudiness, and prevailing winds. Together with soils and minerals, climate furnishes the basis of the greater part of what we call natural resources. To these must be added those native avenues of transportation, the ocean and the waters of the land. Fronting on the ocean, the contour of coast lines, by affording or withholding harbor, influences the use that may be made of nature's waterways.

Growing out of the inorganic environment are the biological factors: native vegetation and animal life. Surface features, chief mineral resources, major types of soil, mean annual temperature and the annual range of temperature, the length of the growing season, the mean annual rainfall and the seasonal distribution of rainfall furnish nature's conditions for vegetation.[7] Not only is the plant complex conditioned by these physical factors, but plants themselves exist in what may be called communities. As the ecologists have shown, in every area exists a delicate equilibrium of plant contending with plant for a place in the sun and the soil. Animals subsist on plant life and on each other, so that we may think of man's organic *milieu* as an equilibrium of plants, animals, insects, bacteria, and parasites, all in contact and all interacting through natural biological processes. In passing to the realm of the organic, man's *milieu* has become increasingly complex.

The extent to which the principle of interaction in a complex unity ranges through the organic world is indicated in the geography of disease. Many human diseases are transmitted by microbes or bacteria which spend part of their period of growth incubating in an animal host. The range of this host is determined by climate, and the disease may accordingly become known as peculiar to, let us say, the torrid climate, although it would be perfectly possible for men to have the disease in other areas provided the carrier were present. The question of animal and vegetable life is thus so complicated that, as Marsh suggests, "we can never know how wide a circle of disturbance we produce in the harmonies of nature when we throw the smallest pebble into the ocean of organic being."[8]

[6] C. A. Dawson, "Population Areas and Physiographic Regions in Canada," *American Journal of Sociology*, XXXIII, 43.

[7] R. H. Whitbeck, "Fact and Fiction in Geography by Natural Regions," *Journal of Geography*, XXII, 86-94.

[8] Quoted from R. Mukerjee, *Regional Sociology*, p. 231.

The change of any factor in a region, as variation in rainfall or the introduction of a new plant or insect, is sufficient to establish a new equilibrium. In so far as animals prey upon vegetation and upon each other they may be regarded as the superstructure of this complex, but when man arrives on the scene he becomes the new superstructure.

Man's so-called conquest of nature accordingly has consisted in disturbing nature's equilibrium of flora and fauna. From native plants growing in a region man has developed the few at the expense of the many, outlawing them as weeds and attempting their extermination. He has artificially bred plants to points where nature could never have taken them and then he has introduced exotic vegetation. Cotton, corn, wheat, rye, oats, and fruits are pampered monstrosities created and kept alive by man. This alien complex he has maintained by force of plow, hoe, and fertilization against the encroaching wilderness and the weeds, which themselves have become domesticated outlaws. To the fauna offered by nature he has been no less arbitrary. Wild animals of the forest and field he has driven before him and exterminated. For the bison of the western plains he has substituted the cattle of Texas ranches. At so fast a pace has this new complex been substituted for an old one that in so new a country as America the ecologists find it well-nigh impossible to map the natural biotic zones. In no place, however, has man dominated the organic complex completely. One of the penalties of the artificial equilibrium is the introduction of fungi, parasites, and insect pests, before unknown, to prey upon man's pampered monstrosities.

The foregoing discussion has served to suggest that the legitimate approach to human geography lies not in a detached study of the social significance of geographic elements but in an analysis of interconnected wholes. In our modern workaday world the staple, artificially propagated and guarded from its rivals who would crowd it from the common table of light and soil, offers the key to the region. This complex unity of flora and fauna thus counts more in the world economy than native vegetation and animal life. These facts lead to a view of the region; and it is noteworthy that regionalism has been the revivifying influence in modern geographic studies.

L. G. W. Joerg has rightly termed the "recognition of regional geography as the ultimate goal and highest expression of geographic research."[9] Carl O. Sauer has expressed the opinion that regional geography offers the most urgent field of inquiry.[10] Such a study is not ready to announce generalizations but must describe, interpret, and analyze regions. The region must be accepted as an environmental type in which what we have called the geographic elements are combined in certain definite and constant relations. Even here we can distinguish between what may be roughly called the physical region and the region of the organic complex. The physiographic region is basically geological; in W. M. Davis' formula it is the product of structure, process, and stage; the organic is based on the uses to which plants and animals have put the stage of soil and climate furnished by nature.[11]

If each of the main geographic elements be used as criterion for plotting a region, it will be found that the regions so delimited vary greatly in size. Physiographic, thermal, rainfall, soil, and mineral regions do not necessarily coincide.[12] Of these the climatic region is the largest unit; the soil region the smallest; and the physiographic region occupies a position midway.

Such a physiographic unit has been defined by Neven N. Fenneman as "an area which is characterized throughout by similar or closely related surface features, and which is contrasted in these respects with neighboring areas."[13] Such an area would also possess a uniform physiographic history. Although the evidence for such regions is more distinct and the barriers between are more sharply defined than in other types of regions, the factors are infinitely complex. Basing their work on the immense number of studies completed by the United States Geological Survey, it took the committee of experts headed by Fenneman four months to produce a map of the physiographic regions of the United States. Even here many of the boundaries must be left indeterminate for regions merge into each other without perceptible change.

The physiographic area leads to the next stage, the natural life

[9] *Annals* of the Association of American Geographers, IV, 36.

[10] *The Geography of the Ozark Highlands,* p. vii.

[11] *Physical Geography, passim.*

[12] R. H. Whitbeck, *op. cit.,* p. 87.

[13] "Physiographic Boundaries within the United States," *Annals* of the Association of American Geographers, IV, 86.

area.   The result of geological and climatic processes, embodied in the soil, plus climate and weather, considered as habitat, furnish the background of the ecological community.   This biotic region may be defined as a climatic and physiographic province characterized by an assemblage of species differing from those found in adjacent areas.[14]   The most complete survey of the natural vegetation areas yet made of the United States proceeds on this assumption.   "The forms of vegetation here described are not merely aggregations of species but are biological communities characterized by certain similarity in their biological aspect, in their environment, in their past history, and in their ultimate development.   The biological is thus made the basis of classification and the environment is measured in terms of vegetation and not the vegetation in terms of temperature, moisture, evaporation, or any other factor.[15]   It will be remembered that Köppen's first classification of climate was in terms of vegetation.

In any settled region the natural distribution of plants and animals has long since been disturbed, and any attempt to reconstruct these natural life areas is likely to meet with failure. The one field in which natural plant areas can still be mapped is forestry.   *The Atlas of American Agriculture* furnishes a brilliant example of this type of research in its reconstruction of the natural forests of the United States.[16]   The United States is thus found to comprise roughly an eastern hardwood and pine forest province, a mid-western grass area, and a region of desert shrubs.[17]   The equilibrium of these societies of grasses, trees, and desert shrubs

[14] L. R. Dice, "Biotic Areas and Ecological Habitats as Units for the Statement of Animal and Plant Distribution," *Science*, LV, 335-38.

[15] *Atlas of American Agriculture*, "Natural Vegetation," Pt. I, Sec. E, p. 3.

[16] *Ibid.*, Map, pp. 3-4.

[17] The nine forest regions of the eastern United States beginning at the South are as follows: (1) Subtropical Forest: Mangrove; (2) Southeastern Pine Forest: Longleaf, Loblolly, and Slash Pines; (3) River Bottom Forests: Cypress, Tupelo and Red Gum; (4) Southern Hardwood Forests: Chestnut, Chestnut Oak, and Yellow Poplar; (5) Southern Hardwood Forest: Oak and Hickory; (6) Southern Hardwood Forest, Oak and Pine; (7) Northwestern Hardwood, Birch, Beech, Maple, and Hemlock; (8) Northeastern Pine Forest: Jack, Red, and White Pines; (9) Northern Coniferous Forest: Spruce, Fir.   Three desert shrub plant areas are given: (1) Southern Desert: Creosote Bush; (2) Salt Desert: Greasewood; (3) Northern Desert: Sagebrush.   The grass regions comprise about seven divisions: (1) Prairie: Tall Grass; (2) Plains: Short Grass; (3) Desert Grassland: Mesquite; (4) Desert Savanna: Mesquite and Desert Grass; (5) Pacific Grassland: Bunch Grass; (6) Alpine Grassland: Alpine Meadow; (7) Marsh: Marsh Grass.

has been disturbed by the uses to which man has put the region. Only some ten per cent of the eastern timber is in virgin condition; and seventy per cent of the grass land east of the 100th meridian has been planted to crops.

The interrelation of the organic and inorganic may be suggested by noting the effect of temperature and rainfall on the distribution of plants by areas. Distribution of plants and animals over the earth's surface according to Dr. C. Hart Merriam is governed not so much by an average of annual temperature as by the temperature during the period of growth and reproductive activity of the plant.[18] The various events in the life of the plant as leafing, flowering, and maturing of fruit take place when the plant has been exposed to a definite quantity of solar heat for a brief period. Plants, then, are restricted in their northward distribution by the total amount of heat received during their period of growth and by the amount of cold they can endure in winter. In their southward distribution they are restricted by the mean temperature of a brief period covering the hottest part of the year. On the basis of thermal means worked out along this line Dr. Merriam has mapped three life zones for the United States: Boreal, austral, and tropical.

"The position and density of forests," for example, are due to the peculiar distribution of rainfall in this country. The central portion of the continent, far from the moist ocean winds, find insufficient moisture to support a dense forest."[19] Roughly the United States may be divided into two rainfall areas: a moist east and an arid west which possesses a moist Pacific fringe. In mapping such areas the average annual rainfall should not be considered more important than the question of the distribution of precipitation throughout the year. Rain may fall at such a season as to be a detriment rather than a benefit to plant life. The United States has been divided into five general areas of precipitation depending on the type and source of rainfall:[20]

1. Pacific area with its source the Pacific Ocean has a long period of precipitation during midwinter and an almost total absence during late summer.

[18] "Laws of Temperature Control of the Geographic Distribution of Terrestrial Animals and Plants," *National Geographic Magazine*, VI, 229-
[19] "Natural Vegetation," *Atlas of American Agriculture*, p. 3.
[20] General A. W. Greeley, "Definition of Rainfall Types," *National Geographic Magazine*, V, 45-58.

2. Mexico, an area of light rainfall, originating in the Gulf of California, has its heavier period during July, August, and September with its lowest in February, March, and April.

3. Tennessee, Gulf states, the rainfall coming from the Gulf of Mexico, is heaviest during the last of winter and the first of spring with light precipitation in midautumn.

4. Missouri, Northern Mississippi Valley, find the source of precipitation in the Gulf of Mexico, the Great Lakes and Hudson Bay; highest precipitation is in winter with major quantity of rain in late spring and early summer.

5. Atlantic area is one of fairly heavy rainfall coming from the Atlantic Ocean with distribution fairly uniform throughout the whole year.[21]

"The notion of natural region," as Paul Vidal de la Blache writes, "is simply the expression of a fact brought more and more into evidence by the observations which have been carried on for a century: meteorological observations showing that the averages for temperature and rain hardly vary in a given region; botanical observations showing in the same climate the reproduction of the same types of plants; geological observations proving that if there is great variety in the construction of the soil, all is not disorder, and that the very way in which the sediments have been deposited, and the way in which the movements of the earth's crust have taken place, implies a certain regularity of behavior."[22]

Cultural Factors of the Region

The value to social science of these physical regions lies in the human uses to which they are devoted. "Man living on earth lives in relation to a corn belt, a wheat region, a trade or manufacturing region; to semi-arid pasture, or to some other natural region. Hence classification of region by human use is scientific method for the study of geography."[23] What counts is obviously not the native societies of plants and animals existing atop the physical complex of soil and climate but the artificial equilibrium of flora and fauna introduced and maintained by man. The *raison d'etre* is economic; these plants and animals are ones which may be con-

[21] See also *American Atlas of Agriculture,* Pt. II, Sec. A, "Precipitation and Humidity," by J. B. Kincer, Map, pp. 6-7.

[22] Quoted by R. Mukerjee, *Regional Sociology,* p. 237.

[23] J. Russell Smith, *Human Geography,* II, v.

sumed or given in exchange, but they also condition man's social and institutional interests. Le Play's famous formula is also regional: place conditions work, work conditions the family organization, and the family is the social unit which makes up society.[24] This formula of place-work-folk has received its most brilliant American demonstration in Turner's account of the evolution of frontier society in accordance with the conditions of the wilderness. According to this conception, physical and climatic *milieux* remaining constant, the regions change as the state of agriculture and of industry advance. Thus a frontier belt may become a hunting area, an Indian trading region, a ranching area, then a region of grain farming, and finally a dairying area.

In the uses that man, in the effort to clothe, feed, house, and defend himself, makes of the map furnished by nature, Jean Brunhes finds the scope of human geography.[25] These activities become permanently recorded on the soil and comprise the cultural landscape. He finds six essential series of social phenomena correlated with geographic factors: (1) Human habitations: inhabited areas, character of houses, roads; (2) plant conquest: cultivated fields; (3) animal conquest: domestication and breeding of animals; (4) exploitation of minerals; (5) devastation in plant life; (6) devastation in animal life.

To Brunhes many of the most important phases of society lie beyond the reach of geography to touch or influence. The forms of the family, political organization, social organization, the character of religion, of laws and literature exhibit little or no relation to geographic phenomena. In the phrase of C. Vallaux which he has quoted with approval: "The influence of geographic factors is negative, but not positive; they often may hinder a phenomenon, but they do not determine what it will be."[26] Man has not evolved in a vacuum, and it is obvious to point out in reply to Vallaux that when nature prevents she also determines. "Human geography," says Georges Gariel, and he is right, "is destined to review all the sociological theories that speculate about some sort of abstract man."[27]

[24] See Pitirim Sorokin, *Contemporary Sociological Theories*, pp. 66-73.
[25] *Human Geography*, pp. 36-41, 48-52.
[26] C. Vallaux, *Le sol et l'etat*, p. 106.
[27] Quoted by Mukerjee, *op. cit.*, p. 132.

It is with the human uses of the region in mind that Dr. O. E. Baker has mapped the agricultural areas of the United States.[28] Five plants, corn, wheat, cotton, oats, and hay occupy more than eighty-seven per cent of the total crop area of the country.[29]   In combination with livestock they make up the various types of farming. Dependent upon moisture conditions, length of the growing season, contour of the land, and physical, chemical, and bacterial conditions of the soil, they furnish the agricultural regions of the United States.[30]   In regard to climate the United States may be divided roughly into four overlapping areas: a cold northern, a warm southern, a moist eastern, and a dry western region.[31] The soils fall into three divisions: The East and South, largely light-colored forest lands; the central plains, dark-soiled grasslands; and the West, desert shrub and bush lands.[32] Using as his index the proportion of domesticated plants and animals used in each crop system, Dr. Baker lists the following agricultural regions of the eastern United States: (1) Subtropical Crops Belt; (2) Cotton Belt; (3) Middle Atlantic Trucking Region; (4) Corn and Winter Wheat Belt; (5) Corn Belt; (6) Hay and Dairying Belt; (7) Spring Wheat Area. The western United States he divides according to crops produced into the following areas: (8) Grazing and Irrigated Crop Region; (9) Columbia Plateau Region; (10) Pacific Subtropic Crops Region; (11) North Pacific Hay, Pasture, and Forest Region.[33] We have proceeded thus by inevitable stages from the region as laid down by geology to the region as transformed by the hand of man. Such human use areas are physiographic; they are also economic. Economic factors, such as values per unit of weight and distances to markets, may determine the extent and distribution of plant production.[34] The building of a railroad may thus transform the uses to which man puts a region.

The study of the cultural landscape shows man remaking the regional map and plots the distribution of his artifacts in space.

[28] U. S. D. A. *Yearbook*, 1921, Fig. 2, p. 416.

[29] W. J. Spillman, "Distribution of Types of Farming in the United States," *Farmer's Bulletin* 1289, p. 3.

[30] Oliver E. Baker, "Agricultural Regions of North America, Part I," *Economic Geography* (Oct. 1926), p. 460.

[31] *Ibid.*, p. 467.

[32] *Ibid.*, p. 466.

[33] U. S. D. A. *Yearbook*, 1921, Fig. 2, p. 416.

[34] W. J. Spillman, *op. cit.*, p. 3.

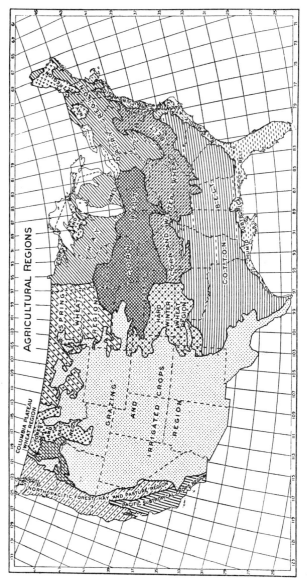

FIGURE 1.—The United States may be divided agriculturally into two parts, the East and the West, on the basis of the prevalent use of the land, whether for crops or for pastures. The dividing line approximates longitude 103°, except that it trends southeasterly in Texas and northwesterly in Montana. The East has a humid climate; the West an arid or semiarid climate, except in the north Pacific region, parts of the Columbia Plateau, and at the higher altitudes in the mountains. The East is divided into eight areas (excluding the forest and hay region) on the basis of the dominance of a certain crop or kind of farming, which is the result largely of latitude and temperature conditions. The West is divided into four regions on the basis of the use of the land for grazing or crops, which is determined largely by altitude and rainfall. (Courtesy of U. S. Department of Agriculture).

No less challenging is the study of the comparative cultural routines of social groups as conditioned by different agricultural regions. Here the seasonal demands of economic plants and animals set limits to the seasonal round of days and works and plot the distribution of man's activities in time. By no one can Le Play's formula of place, work, and folk be better tested than by one who should set himself to keep comparative seasonal graphs of the cultural activities of the family of a wheat farmer, a cotton grower, a truck gardener, a dairyman, and a tobacco farmer as they follow their plants and animals around nature's cycle of the season. That social factors beyond the obvious ones of seasonal diet and dress, family work in the fields, and recreation shape themselves in such a cycle is indicated by H. C. Brearley's findings that high homicide rates in South Carolina fell within the periods of slack work in cotton farming, August and December.[35] Thus occurs "the development of the cultural out of the natural landscape" and the region becomes the culture area characterized not only by common physical traits but by common culture traits. The region beginning as man's stage becomes in R. Mukerjee's phrase "his handiwork and his heritage." "The region thus conceived, registers the gain of trial and error for ages, and gives man handy tools and weapons, folkways or customs which make life easier and smoother for him."[36]

Again the United States can offer examples, roughly drawn, of culture areas based on regional facts. The New England states, superimposed on a fishing-small grain culture, developed with labor of an independent, individualistic type an urban-industrial culture manned by an immigrant proletariat. The South from a tobacco-indigo-rice culture made the transition first to a cotton-slave culture, then to a cotton-tenant culture, and is now in restricted areas in the first steps of industrial culture. The Mid-West made the transition from the cattle culture of the plains to grain culture ending in the development of the Corn and Wheat Belts. The Pacific has also made a transition from timber to grain-fruit culture. Such a view has recently been given popular currency by a philosophic if superficial foreign observer. "America is at bottom a new land of budding localisms, very much as Europe

[35] "Homicides in South Carolina: A Regional Study," *Social Forces*, VIII, 218.
[36] R. Mukerjee, *Regional Sociology*, p. 232.

was at the end of the migrations of the peoples," thinks Hermann Keyserling.[37] To him "America seems to be subdivided into large provinces of a comparatively unified character, provinces out of which there would undoubtedly have grown in earlier days and under different conditions separated cultures."[38] This is fortunate for "localism alone can produce in America a thoroughly authentic type of man, and this type alone can be the germ cell of an authentic American nation."[39] Keyserling cites examples of localisms producing authentic cultures. "It seems a providential thing that Minnesota has been colonized to such a large extent by Swedes, for the landscape is essentially Swedish." The atmosphere of Minneapolis he finds "Swedish at bottom and yet fundamentally American." "The only really cultural atmosphere one finds today in America is that of Virginia." "I should not greatly wonder," he adds, "if, after a few centuries Texas did not develop a very delightful original culture."

Variations in the cultural landscape, different customs for different regions, the cultural routine of man's days and works, all these offer materials for literary art. An adequate regionalism in literature has proved heir to the local color of the 1890's. The corn and wheat belts at the hands of Hamlin Garland, Willa Cather, Martha Ostenso, and O. E. Rölvaag have been presented in regional portraiture. Writers like Edgar Lee Master, Zona Gale, and Sinclair Lewis have risen to portray caustically the life of the trading center and the metropolis grown out of the hinterland of wheat.

The American South at last has promised a literature which shall be regional but not provincial. That the new regionalism evident in the works of Ellen Glasgow, Du Bose Heyward, Julia Peterkin, E. C. L. Adams, Howard W. Odum, T. S. Stribling, and Rose Wilder Lane is not entirely dependent upon a newer objective attitude toward the Negro can be shown by an appeal to *Barren Ground, Teeftallow,* and what is possibly the masterpiece of regional portraiture, Elizabeth Madox Roberts' *The Time of Man.* Out of the promise of Dorothy Scarborough's *The Land of Cotton,* Jack Bethea's *Cotton,* and Herbert Kroll's *Cabin in the Cotton,* na-

[37] "Genius Loci," *Atlantic Monthly* (Sept. 1929), p. 311.
[38] *Ibid.,* p. 303.
[39] *Ibid.,* p. 302.

tional literature may expect in some near future to be enriched by an epic of cotton comparable to the trilogy planned for wheat by Frank Norris. Nor should the literature of the southern mountains be overlooked. The realistic literature of folk close to the soil is now ripe for sociological analysis in terms of regional culture traits, social attitudes, and social values.

When it comes to the geography of politics more than one thinker has followed the lead of N. S. B. Gras in seeing a rise of regionalism at the expense of nationalism. Not that the old political forms will disappear; they will simply be forced to accommodate themselves to the rising demands of regions. The foundation of regionalism offered by the factors of physiography and natural resources are being tremendously strengthened by modern business. It may be safely said that economic exploitation of nature's treasures is at last to force regional policies upon the heedless state. Scattered towns with their small hinterlands have coalesced into larger areas each finding its nucleus in a great metropolis. "Metropolitan regionalism," writes N. S. B. Gras who has best investigated this field, "is the most likely to challenge the state in a way to be heard from because it represents rich, well-organized and somewhat self-sufficing communities."[40] America has ten or twelve great metropolitan regions either developed or developing. In the East, Boston, New York, and Philadelphia; in the West, Chicago, St. Louis, Twin Cities, and Kansas City; on the Pacific, Seattle, San Francisco, and Los Angeles. In the South, it is Gras' opinion that New Orleans has lost, that Cincinnati and Baltimore on the border have had indifferent success, and that, due to rapid industrial development, Atlanta is likely to become the center of the first metropolitan region in the South.[41]

The Federal Reserve Areas in the United States are traces made on the financial map by metropolitan regionalism. In the allocation of the water from Boulder Dam we find another regional complex that transcends state lines. The division of the United States in corps areas may be taken as delimiting provinces suitable for military defense. Reclamation and rivers and harbors projects are examples of regionalism in both the geographic and political sphere. There are two great economic complexes that may be ex-

[40] "Regionalism and Nationalism," *Foreign Affairs,* VII, 459.
[41] *Ibid.,* p. 461.

pected to force regionalism on the attention of the state. The first of these is the railroads, and the task is one of consolidation, elimination, and unification of systems until each natural crop and natural resource province shall be efficiently interconnected with metropolitan centers. The second is the pressing problem of electric power. Hydro-electric development based on the natural distribution of flowing rivers and water power demands coördination of large areas. In the expressive phrase of Robert W. Bruere, Giant Power is a Region Builder. On the basis of city planning and regional surveys of the hinterlands Patrick Geddes and Victor Branford have erected plans for the development of natural areas that are nothing short of social reconstruction.

The concept of region is giving a new direction to research. Practically every state has a geological survey which issues reports couched in the terms of the hardrock geologists. These reports, of interest mainly to mineralogists, make little use of the regional concept and furnish no data of use to either business men or social scientists. Kentucky, a state of great physical contrasts, clearly divided into natural regions, has, under the direction of Dr. W. R. Jillson, published the first complete series of regional geographic studies made for any state in our country. In the place of offering compendiums of facts the study attempts to express the individuality of the region as the site of a particular group with a particular culture. Chapters are found on rural culture patterns and the cultural landscape of towns. These studies while often partaking more of the physical than of the human and cultural factors have been said to rank with some of the best work done in Europe.[42]

Michigan has under way a Land-Economic Survey in coöperation with the United States Bureau of Soils, the Lake-States Forest Experiment Station, and the Michigan Department of Agriculture. "The outstanding difference between this undertaking and any other that approximates it," writes P. S. Lovejoy, "is in the effort to determine all the factors that will make for the intelligent use of land, to consider all the variables and to carry on the work

[42] Kentucky is divided into six clearly defined natural areas on which the following regional monographs have been issued: D. H. Davis, *The Jackson Purchase,* 1923; *The Mountains,* 1924; W. G. Burroughs, *The Coal Fields,* 1927, *The Knobs,* 1926; D. H. Davis, *The Blue Grass,* 1927; C. O. Sauer, *The Pennyroyal,* 1927. These monographs are called reconnaissance studies of the distribution and activities of men in particular regions.

with no prejudice for or against the possibly competing utilizations. Topography, types of growth, soils and uses of land are covered in field surveys. Intent in land ownership, assessed valuations, areas of tax delinquency, trade areas, and production areas are all to be mapped and so intensive is the survey that no variations of more than ten acres can escape record."[43] While primarily an economic survey for land utilization the analysis and interpretation by natural areas will have wide bearing on the human ecology of the state.

The survey of St. Helena Island, South Carolina, shows the suitability of a small natural area, homogeneous in its physical and ethnic features, to interpretation as a cultural unit.[44] The Department of Commerce has divided the United States into nine commercial regions for the purpose of study and in 1927 published its first survey, that of the Southeast. F. Stuart Chapin outlined before the American Sociological Society at its 1927 meeting plans of the University of Minnesota for a regional survey of the spring wheat belt which is to extend over two decades. The Institute for Research in Social Science at the University of North Carolina seeks to give to all its southern studies a definite regional slant based on background studies of rural areas. The Social Science Research Council has indorsed regional research as one of the major methods of promotion for the development of methods, personnel, new agencies of research, the securing of financial resources, the discovery of new research projects, and the collection of storehouses of regional information. One of the purposes of the Council is to bring together for conference regional groups to consider the problems of their areas. Two such areas have been designated: the Pacific Coast, composed of a small number of units, and the South, consisting of a large number of units. With coöperative effort between the students of physical backgrounds and the students of culture the new direction given research may in time be expected to produce results equal to the best work of the French School.[45]   *   *   *   *   *   *   *

[43] Harold Titus, "Michigan Takes Stock," *The New Republic,* August 28, 1929, pp. 39-41.

[44] T. J. Woofter, Jr., *Black Yeomanry.*

[45] This chapter does not comprehend the whole concept of the sociological region as much as it points out the social and demographic interrelations of the geographic region. There is an increasingly large bibliography on special aspects of regionalism,

The attempt to apply the method of regional interpretation to that historical entity known as the American South bristles with difficulty. The section has passed from frontier to plantation to a limited industrialism in the midst of a great cotton economy. Underneath the political and cultural unity superimposed on the South by its history will be found the texture of various physiographic regions. To define the limits and the characteristics of these physical areas and to point out their natural relations is our first task.

such as economic, industrial, regional planning, folk and regional society, as well as other sociological aspects. For example, see an unpublished bibliography being prepared for the Southern Regional Study; also chapters I, IV, V, and XIII of Franklin H. Giddings' new volume, *Civilization and Society,* edited and arranged by Howard W. Odum. Other titles are listed in: Howard W. Odum, "Folk and Regional Conflict as a Field of Sociological Study," *Publication* of the American Sociological Society, XXV, 1-17; "Notes on the Study of Regional and Folk Society," *Social Forces,* X, 164-175.

CHAPTER II

THE SOUTH'S PROFILE

THE SOUTH OF MANY REGIONS

THE THIRTEEN STATES called the South stretch from Virginia and Kentucky down the Atlantic to the Gulf, across the Mississippi to Texas and Oklahoma.[1] They cover an area of 863,250 square miles with a population in 1930 of 33,744,296 souls. With 28.5 per cent of the nation's area and 27.4 per cent of its population, the section's rate of population increase from 1920 to 1930 was just a trifle below the nation's. It has 32.4 per cent of its people living in towns and cities compared to 56.2 per cent for the nation. While its density of population falls but little below that of the nation, it is much below the density of the country east of the Mississippi. The thinly settled great plains bring down the nation's average. In wealth as estimated for 1928 by the National Industrial Conference Board, the South ranks $1,736 per capita compared to $3,000 for the nation. The South's percentage of Negro population in 1930 was 26.2; the nation's, 9.7; the South's percentage of total illiteracy was 9; the nation's, 4.3.

Practically every cultural and demographic characteristic for which statistical indices can be obtained serves to set off the South. Observers, travelers, and students have long been impressed by the individuality of the section. Not only to the popular mind does the South appear as a distinctive region, but to as notable a geographer as Carl O. Sauer "the South is a major cultural division of the United States, perhaps its most strikingly outstanding cultural unit." Common traditions, a similar ancestry, common economic interests, and similar climate help to account for its unity.

---

[1] The reasons for this selection, which no doubt appear somewhat arbitrary at the outset, will be presented in the course of the volume. In the Southern Regional Study, now being projected under the auspices of the Southern Regional Committee of the Social Science Research Council, the Southern Region is divided into two main divisions, the Southeast, comprising eleven of the states above mentioned, and the Southwest, comprising Texas, Oklahoma, New Mexico, and Arizona.

TABLE I
THE SOUTH AND THE NATION, 1920-1930

STATE	Area Square Miles	Population		Per Cent Increase 1920-30	Density 1930 Population Per Square Mile	Per Cent Urban		Per Cent Negro		Per Cent Gain or Loss Negro Pop. 1920-30	Per Cent illiteracy 1930	Estimated Wealth Per Capita—1928
		1920	1930			1920	1930	1920	1930			
nia.........	42,627	2,309,187	2,421,851	4.8	56.8	29.2	32.4	29.9	26.8	−5.8	8.7	$2,189
cucky........	40,589	2,416,630	2,623,668	8.6	64.7	26.2	30.6	9.8	8.6	−4.2	6.6	1,559
h Carolina....	52,426	2,559,123	3,170,287	23.9	50.4	19.2	25.5	29.8	29.0	20.3	10.0	1,837
essee........	42,022	2,337,885	2,608,759	11.6	62.2	26.1	34.3	19.3	18.3	5.7	7.2	1,970
h Carolina....	30,989	1,683,724	1,732,567	2.9	55.9	17.5	21.3	51.4	46.0	−8.2	14.9	1,475
gia..........	59,265	2,895,832	2,902,443	0.2	49.0	25.1	30.8	41.7	37.0	−11.2	9.4	1,380
da..........	58,666	968,470	1,466,625	51.4	24.9	36.7	51.7	30.4	29.4	31.1	7.2	2,046
ama........	51,998	2,348,174	2,646,248	12.6	50.8	21.7	28.1	38.4	38.3	4.9	12.6	1,284
issippi........	46,865	1,790,618	2,009,821	12.2	42.8	13.4	16.9	52.2	50.2	8.0	13.1	1,376
nsas........	53,335	1,752,204	1,854,482	5.8	34.7	16.6	20.6	27.0	25.8	1.3	6.8	1,474
siana........	48,506	1,798,509	2,094,496	16.5	43.1	34.9	39.7	38.9	37.1	10.9	13.5	1,973
homa.......	70,057	2,028,283	2,391,777	17.9	34.4	26.6	34.3	7.4	7.2	15.3	2.8	1,756
s...........	265,896	4,663,228	5,821,272	24.8	21.9	32.4	41.0	15.9	14.7	15.3	6.8	1,986
South........	863,250	29,551,867	33,744,296	14.2	39.9	25.4	32.4	28.5	26.2	4.3	9.0	$1,736
United States.	3,026,789	105,710,620	122,807,017	16.1	40.5	51.4	56.2	9.9	9.7	13.6	4.3	$3,000
South's percentage.....	28.5	27.9	27.4	88.2	98.5	49.4	57.6	287.9	270.1	31.6	....	57.9

"South of the Ohio a sense of continuity with the past persists because change has been slow and the tempo of life has not been much accelerated nor its measure syncopated."[2]　Lewis F. Carr may be taken as representative of those who feel the South is almost a different country:

ts ways are different, its conditions are different, its point of view is different. It has a character and personality all its own. The thoughts that we think are not the South's thoughts, and the mental habits that are natural to us must be dropped and stowed away for a while when we consider the South. Conditions that to our mind would indicate one type of development will not do so at all in a country that has a different racial condition, a different tradition, and measure of value. The South started from its own premise; it moved under peculiar conditions; it has arrived at totally different conclusions.[3]

The South, however, can be different without being a unit. Geography by the very nature of the science is disposed to be equally impatient of two dogmas that have arisen concerning the

[2] Carl O. Sauer, *Geography of the Pennyroyal*, pp. 5, 9-10.
[3] *America Challenged*, p. 165.

South. The implications of that ritualistic phrase, the "Solid South," can best be matched by its untenable counterpart, "No North, no South." History, not geography, made the solid South, and to the extent that the area has forgotten its history and allowed the geography of region and resource to assert itself, to that extent the section has fashioned its cultural landscape along many and varied lines. As Holland Thompson pointed out, not even the historic ante-bellum South can be treated as a cultural unity:

There was a South of the plantation, and of the upland farm; of the Coastal Plains and of the mountains; the South with lands almost incredibly fertile and the barren South where living was hard; the civilized South, and nearby the South, ignorant and rude; the austere Calvinist South, and the South of romance; the haughty aristocratic South and the democratic South.[4]

In a common touching devotion to the moribund democratic party and a certain attitude of condescension toward the Negro the South has been one. The South, unlike the Middle West, is not a single physical region but many.

An examination will serve to convince one that the section holds within its bounds many physiographic areas and many human use regions. As a matter of fact, the South possesses approximately all the characteristic physical areas of the United States. If it cannot approach the Rockies for mountain ranges, it possesses its share of mountain zone in the southern Appalachians. Of the original eastern forest the South owns its due proportion of heavily timbered areas. In swamp and overflow areas the region is possibly most unfortunate, possessing in Florida, the Mississippi, and Coastal swamps, much the major portion of undrained land in America. Of the unforested Central Prairies and the western semi-arid plains the South possesses the broad strips that dip into Texas and Oklahoma. Diversity of contour, moreover, is a factor making for diversity of culture. Russia, says Miss Newbigin, illustrates the "significance of the natural region negatively by showing how slow and difficult is the rise of a stable community where structure and relief are markedly uniform over wide areas, so that a human region has to be created where a natural region in the usual sense

---

[4] "The Coming of Industry to the South," *The Annals* of the American Academy of Political and Social Science, 153, p. 11.

scarcely exists."[5] Structure and relief thus form the basis for division into natural regions. The American South possesses enough diversity in the build of the land to justify its treatment as a complex of interrelated subregions. Accordingly, the first purpose of this chapter will be to trace out the physiographic foundations underlying the human use regions into which the area may be divided.

Physiographic Regions

Following the formula set forth by W. M. Davis, geologists have come to see the physiographic region as the result of three geological factors, the structure, the geological process operating, and the stage at which the process has arrived. Weathering, erosion, and the transporting of soils with resulting physical and chemical changes go to make up the geological process. Given the same type of structure subject to the same type of climate, weathering would in an infinity of time reduce the rocks to the same type of soils. Thus, theoretically, physiographic regions tend to become soil regions. That they do not is due, among other things, to the stage at which the geological process has arrived.

In the South are found at least seven of America's physiographic regions: the Atlantic Tidewater, Subtropic Gulf Coast; the Coastal Plain, the Piedmont, the Appalachian Highlands, the Mississippi Flood Plain, and the Ozark-Ouachita Highlands. Within these main divisions are many subdivisions of soil and topography. With each of these areas are associated certain groups of economic plants and animals, certain industries, certain modes of living, certain psycho-social types of people. Withal the likenesses will often be found greater than the differences, and those who attempt to force regionalism to fit any scheme of geographic determinism are riding to a fall. In many instances regional diversity has been smoothed out by cultural diffusion. We can do no better in presenting these areas as seen by the physiographer than to arrange them in what we shall call the cultural series of the regional profile.

Coastal Plain

Stretching from Cape Cod in the north to Mexico in the south, the Coastal Plain of the eastern United States varies in width from less than a mile to over 500 miles. This lowland has de-

[5] Marion Newbigin, *Regional Geography of the World*, p. xviii.

veloped from a "mass of soft sands, silts and clays disposed in strata that dip gently seaward."[6] The Coastal Plain continues under the sea 100 to 200 miles from the shore where it ends in a steep scarp, "the transition from the outer edge of the shallow continental shelf to the abysmal depths of the main ocean floor."[7] The true continental margin is as high as a mountain range and, if sea level were lowered to its foot, would be a region of ice and snow. It is not surprising then that, as Bowman says, the present position of the shore line upon this plain is purely accidental. That it is changing at a fairly rapid rate is evident to students of geology.

In its stretch around the eastern coast the Coastal Plain is broken by two variations, the Florida Peninsula and the lower alluvial valley of the Mississippi, both in the South. In the southern area Isaiah Bowman has marked out five subdivisions of the Coastal Plain.[8] From the Potomac River to the Neuse long arms of sea-drowned rivers reach as estuaries inward past terraced plains of loam. Broad sounds with long slender reefs fringe this coast. The Carolina-Georgia lowlands from the Neuse to the Suwanee show the same sloping plain, here covered with great stretches of pine-grown sands ending in swampy margins and fringed by sea islands and coastal reefs. Extending from the Suwanee River to the eastern bluffs of the Mississippi River is the most irregular area of the Coastal Plain. Its inner border has been dissected to form an interior lowland. On the seaward border are found characteristic broad lagoons, low coastal swamps, and level, wide-spreading savannas. On the coast line one finds long narrow keys, many of which are submerged and constitute shoals. The next area, bounded on the east by a continuous line of bluffs and on the west by the conspicuous Crowley's Ridge, is not a coastal plain but a combined delta and flood plain under the dominance of the Mississippi River. Lying practically at base level, from 30 to 60 miles wide and extending 600 miles, the Alluvial Valley is one of the most extensive low areas in the United States.

[6] Isaiah Bowman, *Forest Physiography*, p. 498. This work, is the only regional physiography of the United States yet published. Within its pages lie digested countless obscure geological monographs, and its felicitous phrasing in description can best be appreciated by the physiographer. The indebtedness of the present chapter to this work is heavy.

[7] *Ibid.*, p. 500.

[8] *Ibid.*, pp. 501-2.

Ill drained, occupied by a great meandering river, it displays in the form of bayous, lakes, cut-offs, meanders, and abandoned channels, a great maze of water spread upon a plain almost without a perceptible slope.

The fifth area, the Gulf Plain of Louisiana and Texas, extends from Atchafalaya River to the Rio Grande. Its coast line shows a sea advancing on a low shore with long sand reefs enclosing lagoons, drowned river courses, estuaries, and sea cliffs. Next occur broad savannas, clothed with coarse grass, scrub pine and palmetto alternating with swamps. Above follows a western sandy area and an eastern clayey region.[9] The Gulf Plain gradually rises in successive benches from the Gulf toward the interior. Much of the area was formed below the waters of the Gulf from the detritus worn from the land and deposited on the sea floor.[10]

The soils of the Gulf area are more fertile than those along the Atlantic Coast. The crystalline rocks of the Appalachian system have in the process of weathering and decay furnished the débris laid in place by stream action. Consequently the soils are siliceous, while the silt from the interior of the continent, derived from rocks of limey or clayey nature, are much richer. Shaler estimated that perhaps 50,000 square miles of soil have been brought into position by river currents. Much of this area is river bottoms and deltas of the highest fertility, hindered from the most efficient cultivation only by imperfect drainage.[11]

FLORIDA

Florida is not a coral reef but possesses an interior whose basis is a limestone of marine origin. This flat, low-lying sandy table extends south by east into the Atlantic Ocean. "A depression of 50 feet would cover all of southern Florida except the tops of sand hills and ridges while an elevation of 50 feet would extend the shore line westward 20 miles from Cape Romano and make dry land of Biscayne Bay and the Bay of Florida."[12] Less than a tenth of the Florida shelf lies above the ocean. From the viewpoint of geological structure Florida "is an elevated crust block modified by a number of minor folds."[13] On the basis of both topography

[9] *Ibid.,* pp. 529-30.
[10] N. S. Shaler, *The United States of America,* I, 89.
[11] *Ibid.,* I, 91-93.
[12] Bowman, *op. cit.,* p. 543. [13] *Ibid.,* p. 545.

and vegetation the region may be divided into pineland and swamp. The 30,000 square miles of pine land are set off by relief into dunes, rolling sand plains, flat land, and rock ridges. The dunes lie near the coast in ridges flanked by rolling sand plains. Between these and the Everglades lie the imperfectly drained pine flat lands. That great saw-grass morass, the Everglades, may be thought of as a huge series of shallow, connected sinks without either soil or surface drainage. In this region of "grassy water a difference of two feet in topography may mean the difference between a shallow lake and dry land for hundreds of square miles."[14]   The poor drainage of interior Florida is due to the youthfulness of its surface with lack of time for a system of drainage to become organized, the absence of relief or a dominating slope, and the dissolving effect of ground water on limestone in opening passages for underground drainage without regard to surface features.[15]

The Piedmont Plateau

The boundary between the Coastal Plain and the Piedmont Plateau has been called the Fall Line. According to Bowman the doubtful width of this dividing line makes the term "fall belt" more appropriate. The division, however, is clearly marked, and the "two provinces present some of the most strongly marked contrasts in the United States. The boundary is never a cliff and seldom ever a well-defined scarp, and the lowland hills are as rugged and more than half as high as the Piedmont hills, but the distinction stands out chiefly because of differences in soil."[16]   In the Piedmont all the details, topography, soils, and water courses reflect the character of the rock. "In coastal regions these features represent the work of streams born upon plains newly uplifted from the sea or reflect the general altitude of the lowland rather than its rock character. In the Piedmont Plateau the rocks are crystalline, the soils residual, the stream courses flow in narrow gorges with cataracts and rapids while in the Coastal Plain the soils are derived from clay, sand, and gravel deposits and the streams flow in shallow valleys and discharge into broad tidal estuaries or coastal swamps."[17] The Piedmont province were it otherwise situated would possibly never have been called a plateau; it is a plateau only by reference to the low flat Coastal Plain. It swings southwestward from

[14] *Ibid.*, pp. 548-49.
[15] *Ibid.*, p. 551.
[16] *Ibid.*, p. 449.
[17] *Ibid.*, p. 499.

northern New Jersey to Central Alabama where it finally passes beneath the sediment of the Coastal Plain. It varies in width from 50 miles in the northern sector to its maximum, 125 miles in North Carolina. Beginning at an altitude of 1,000 to 1,200 feet on the west it inclines seaward evenly at the rate of 20 feet per mile until it reaches 400 to 500 feet altitude on the east. It appears to the eye "not as a smooth plain but as a broadly undulating surface extending in every direction as far as the eye can reach: upon this general surface are low knobs and ridges rising above the general level of the plateau, while below the general level are numerous rather than deep and narrow streams, valleys, and channels."[18]

APPALACHIAN HIGHLANDS

Between the Mississippi Valley and the Piedmont Plateau lie three physiographic provinces of comparatively high altitude—the Appalachian Plateau, the parallel ridges of the Great Appalachian Valley, and the narrow Appalachian Mountains.[19] In the Appalachian Plateau the sandy soils lifted to a higher altitude have been deeply dissected. The Great Valley is the trough of a region telescoped. In the Appalachian Mountains and Piedmont Plateau the basis of crystalline rock, schists, gneisses, and granites are deeply decayed and manteled with residual soil. This great mountain system reaches from the St. Lawrence Valley to central Alabama. It is composed of the four central members of a series of six. The northern and southern belts of the Appalachians differ in rock type—the southern is crystalline and the northern chiefly sedimentary. The southern beds of insoluble rock material have resisted erosion, and their outcrops are marked by the highest ridges and mountain ranges of the series. The Blue Ridge extending northward as far as Pennsylvania forms the eastern escarpment to the southern Appalachians. At the north it is a true ridge; at the south it is a great scarp descending sharply to the Piedmont. This escarpment is not a sharp break but a labyrinth of coves, hills, and spurs, representing the work of erosion on a mass of highly irregular rock.[20] Within the Unakas, Great Smokey, and Blue Ridge on the east and the edge of the Appalachian Plateau on the west, lies the great Appalachian Valley—not a single river valley

---

[18] *Ibid.*, p. 624.
[19] *Ibid.*, pp. 586-89.   [20] *Ibid.*, p. 620.

but a series of many. The Coosa, Tennessee, Shenandoah, Cumberland, Middle Hudson, and Champlain valleys are in this series. The alternate ridges, some as long as 300 miles, run parallel. They have resulted from a folding of the region in which plane surfaces extending 153 and 81 miles have been telescoped to 65 and 55 miles.[21]

From the standpoint of human geography the most important features of this whole region are its basins, gorges, and coves. They range in size from tiny flat areas along streams to large plains such as the Asheville Basin. They occur at headwaters of streams, at their junctions where soil has been washed into the hollows, and in spots where soft underlying rock, has decayed. It is these areas that make the region, for these comparatively small and scattered coves and valleys contain the population. Accordingly, only one fourth of the land is under cultivation. It is, however, unsafe under the conditions of soil texture, rainfall, and slope to cultivate as much as 18 per cent of the surface of this area.

Ozark-Ouachita Highlands

Across the Mississippi lies one other highland area composed of the Ozark and Ouachita Mountains divided by the Valley of the Arkansas River. Bowman describes the "Ozarks as "a broad, relatively flat topped dome somewhat extensively dissected and consisting of three subdivisions, the Salem Platform, the Springfield structural Plain, and the Boston Mountains."[22] The region extends from near Jefferson City and St. Louis in the north to the Arkansas River in the south, from the Nesbo in the west to the Black River on the east. While the rest of the region was reduced by erosion, the sandstone beds possessing a differential uplift left the Boston Mountains standing out as a bold escarpment. The soils of the highlands are covered with flinty, angular scraps of chert left from the weathering of the overlying limestone. The finer soil particles thus produced have seeped down by action of water to the base of the weathered zone. Much of the region is thus unfitted for the average type of agriculture but produces a luxuriant forest. Trees standing in the midst of stony steep areas send their roots down to the finer soils. Thus the area is available for a high type of tree culture with forests, fine orchards, and nut-bearing trees.

[21] *Ibid.*, p. 672.   [22] *Ibid.*, p. 452.

The valley of the Arkansas River stands at a level of about 800 feet above the sea. The overlapping folds of rock strata have been levelled off by stream erosion so that they form a comparatively level plain, bounded near the Arkansas by characteristic river bottoms. The plain ascends by parallel small ridges to altitudes varying from 1700 to 2500 feet. Thus within a very small area agriculture runs the gamut from river bottom to hill lands.[23]

The Ouachita Mountains, a range 200 miles long, south of the Arkansas Valley, extend from Little Rock to Oklahoma. They nowhere rise more than a few thousand feet, and exhibit a regular development of ridges and valleys except for faults along their borders. In soils and general adaptability to human uses they may be classed as lesser Ozarks.

The Profile of Culture

This hasty survey of physiographic regions leaves us with two essential problems. The first has to do with the relation of the physical region to the types of civilization; the second deals with the natural sequence of contiguous and related areas. We shall be faced with the first problem throughout this volume. The underlying theory of human geography as bearing on this field has been well put by Carl O. Sauer.

The field of regional geography is not concerned with an encyclopaedic compendium of facts that are bound together simply by their occurrence in a particular region. . . . The dominant theme . . . is the expression of the individuality of the region as the site of a particular group of people and their work. To begin with there is the physical fact of the area characterized by a distinctive location, by a climate, and by a particular body of land. . . . This physical site has been occupied by a group of people or by successive groups. The occupation has led to a series of characteristic contacts with the area as cultural forms. Man's areal activities are expressed by the kind and distribution of his homes, storerooms, workshops, highways, fields, and other marks of his tenure.[24]

Thus the student arrives at the cultural landscape, leaving him the task of fitting his areas into a sequential array.

It is the task of human geography as a science of distribution to throw the physiographic elements into an ordered framework with meaning for cultural science. Such schemes will be both

[23] *Ibid.*, pp. 455-56.
[24] *Geography of the Pennyroyal*, p. x.

physical and cultural, and they must of necessity establish relationships between physical regions and social types. Building on the work of the LePlay School in developing the place-work-folk formula, Professor Patrick Geddes has suggested a sequential array of physiographic regions and characteristic modes of life. Studies by the LePlay School were able to point out relations between the steppes and pastoral economy, tundras and hunting and fishing, forest and hunting, plains and agriculture, and mountains and mining.[25] LePlay thus pointed out the simple but needed truth that mines produce not merely coal and ores, but, even more significant for civilization, a human type—miners; pastures not merely sheep but shepherds also.[26] The physical regions are thus correlated with forms of economy, of social organization—in short, of culture.

LePlay's scheme of distribution, it will be observed, remains on a plain surface of two dimensions. It is necessary to relate the distribution of culture to topography and thus make it three dimensional. When this is done it is found the regions fall into an ordered series—a natural sequence of regions which may be called the physiographic profile. This scheme as worked out by Geddes has been called "the most helpful key that has yet been fashioned for the elucidation of human geography."[27] With changes it may serve to interpret almost any series of regions. It furnishes the touchstone by which we shall try to relate the geology of the American South to its varied regions.

The most typical land form to be encountered on the globe is the physiographic profile as it slopes from the area's land core, represented by its highlands, to the sea. Geddes calls this sequence of regions the *valley section* and finds that it may be divided into six or seven *zones,* each serving as the habitat of a cultural type growing out of the resources and occupations incident to the region.

Beginning with the core of the area's land mass we have first the mountains' steep escarpment followed by the dip slope of the highlands. The third area, the uplands, levels out to the upland plains which slope down to central plains. Next follows the mari-

[25] P. Sorokin, *Contemporary Sociological Theories,* ch. ii.
[26] C. C. Fagg and G. E. Hutchings, *An Introduction to Regional Surveying.*
[27] *Ibid.,* p. 136.

time plain or tidewater and after that comes the seacoast and the sea. The distribution of social types along the valley section also follows a natural sequence. On the escarpment, that steep and rocky mountain ledge, is found the miner with his technology and life of the mining camp. In the forest of the higher mountain slopes lives and works the woodsman, while along the forest edge preys the hunter. The uplands furnish the native haunts of the shepherd with his pastoral arts. The upland plains, a deeply dissected plateau, is the home of poor peasants who wring a niggard livelihood from unfertile soil while the central plains with open fertile tracts harbor the rich peasants. The maritime plains, the alluvial and mild tidewater, afford the garden agriculture of the truck grower, while on its sea coast fringe the fisherman plies his net.[28] It cannot be contended that the generalizations of this scheme apply in all details to every physiographic profile. The essential fact remains, however, that regions are related in natural sequence. Be that as it may, the *valley section* follows at many points the contour of the South and serves both to interpret and explain its unity of diversity.

The South may be considered for the purpose of our analysis as consisting of three valley sections which come together at the apex of the southern Appalachians, forming what we may call a trihedral angle. One valley section slopes at right angles to the Appalachian chain from its apex to the Atlantic. This section reaches its greatest development across the state of North Carolina. Another slopes from this apex to the Mississippi River across the state of Tennessee. In this section the so-called Delta with its rich soils subsitutes for the sea. The third section from the apex continues parallel with the Appalachian chain across Georgia and Alabama until it reaches the Gulf Coast near the Mississippi's mouth. To the far South the valley section flattens out as we have seen until the whole of Florida is a subtropic maritime plain. Moreover, many of the zones of the Southeast swing around the southern terminus of the Appalachians in crescent or half-moon shape.

THE VALLEY SECTION THROUGH NORTH CAROLINA

One may best present these regions with their social types by giving social-economic cross sections of North Carolina and Tennes-

[28] *Ibid.,* pp. 135-40.

see. These two states in their profusion of zones are sufficient to demonstrate the South of many regions. In traversing their borders we shall be describing in terms of culture the areas already described in terms of physiography.

The apex of the valley slope in Kentucky and West Virginia furnishes the mining culture atop the mountain escarpment. It is here that the outcrop of minerals, mostly coal and iron, have furnished a new extractive culture based on an old frontier with its origins in hunting and forestry.

North Carolina's regional series begins with the dip slope. Here is the retarded frontier, much like the escarpment except in its absence of minerals. It too has passed through the hunting stage to arrive at the status of a small self-sufficing economy. As S. H. Hobbs points out the "region best illustrates farming as practiced before the era of commercialized agriculture."[29] The products sold from the farms represent a small proportion of the total value of their production, and the cash income per farm is as low as anywhere in the United States. Of all southern areas it ranks highest in percentage of white population, farm ownership, and in the number of meat and milk animals per farm. Its churches and schools are the poorest in North Carolina. Family ties are strong and the denizens of isolated communities are closely related. The illiteracy rate is the highest for white people in the United States.

Following the dip slope of the Carolina highlands come the uplands of the Piedmont Plateau. Here we find another area of small farms, a frontier yeomanry, which largely came down the great valley from Pennsylvania and lived separated by the fall line and sand hills from the early tidewater aristocracy. The Piedmont dweller, while not the stock raiser of the scheme, is a small landowning farmer growing much of his own living at home. He is in the cotton and tobacco economy but not in so deep as in other areas. This is the region in which, to use Geddes' phrase, the rustic type has assumed its urban disguise. An emerging industrial area, it possesses a monopoly of the main branches of tobacco manufacture and is the nation's leading textile area. At the southwest the zones curve in a crescent skirting the edges of the Appalachians from Birmingham to Danville, Virginia. For North Carolina over half of the Piedmont's population is urban and the zone

[29] *North Carolina Economic and Social*, p. 85.

has experienced the South's greatest increase in urban ratios. There are no great cities if one excepts Atlanta, but the area is one of the country's few places where small towns are flourishing. Every little town is the site, actual or potential, of a cotton mill to which the high tension lines bring the necessary power, stringing the mill villages together in the regional economy of a super-power zone.

The fall line with the narrow sand hills marks the transition to the coastal plains. In Geddes' series this is the central plains inhabited by the rich peasant type. The area is fertile enough to support such a type, but cultural and racial factors find the population divided into two types—landlords and tenants, neither of whom are as well off as they might be. Here is the seat of the ante-bellum cotton plantation, and today the cash crops of cotton and tobacco are cultivated by croppers, share tenants who pay either a half or a third or a fourth of their product to landlords. First in the nation in its combined production of cotton and tobacco, no other area produces cash crops of such value; no area has increased its tenancy rate so rapidly, and in no area do live stock, milk, and home-grown vegetables play so little part in farming. Sixty-eight percent of all farms are operated by tenants, and in this lower group is to be found the most abject rural poverty in America. This class owns no property, moves often, is highly illiterate, and forms few and tenuous connections with church and school. A succession of bad years in cotton and tobacco serves to threaten the landlords of the region with bankruptcy. The towns give evidence of the wealth to be gained by buying the raw products of the farm and furnishing the food, feeds, supplies, and fertilizers purchased but not produced in the commercial farming region. Dr. Hobbs well says that the cream of wealth produced in this section is skimmed off by the town traders and bankers.[30]

The five years between 1920 and 1925 were sufficient to point the trend of increasing differentiation between this plantation area and the yeoman farming of the Piedmont. In the twenty-one tobacco growing counties of Coastal North Carolina, 60 per cent and more of the farmers were tenants. In the nineteen tobacco counties of the Piedmont, 69 per cent of the farmers owned their own farms and homes. Moreover, between 1920 and 1925 the Coastal Plain

[30] *Ibid.,* p. 76.

showed a loss of more than 1,700 landowners, 5.3 per cent of the number in 1920, and an increase of 6,422 croppers, 4 per cent. In the same period the Piedmont counties gained 2,145 landowners, an increase of 5.3 per cent over 1920.[31]

The maritime plain in North Carolina extends inland as far as the effects of the tide are visible. As might be expected it contains both a fishing fringe and a truck gardening culture. Sluggish rivers flow through flat swampy areas. There is but one large city, and population has long been stagnant. Standards of living are largely based on live-at-home farming although cotton and tobacco are increasingly important in their corn, peanut, soy bean, and potato culture. The presence of numerous rivers and sounds together with the lack of banks and trade have served to restrict land transportation facilities. Inland waterways can be greatly improved, trucking is capable of increase, while the returns from fish, oysters, crabs, and scallops are but a promise of the zone's possibilities. It is this area which farther down the coast breaks into sea islands and at the tip flattens out to include all of Florida where it has developed into a tropical garden and orchard culture.

The Valley Section Through Tennessee

The preceding survey shows that the theoretical valley section applies surprisingly well to the series of regions sloping down the eastern tract from the mountains to the sea. It can also be adapted with variations for the slope from the highlands to the alluvial valley of the Mississippi. In fact the extent to which the series of physiographic regions of which we have spoken enters into the life-complex of a people is well shown in Tennessee. The basic geographic regions are six:

(1) The Appalachian Mountains, a narrow barrier on the eastern border; (2) the Great Valley of East Tennessee, a broad depression containing a succession of parallel ridges and valleys; (3) the Cumberland Plateau, a broad barrier region; (4) the Highland Rim or Plain; (5) the Central Basin or Plain; (6) the West Tennessee or Gulf Embayment Plain subordinate to which may be noted the western valley of the Tennessee River and the flood plain of the Mississippi.[32]

[31] Sidney D. Frissell, Unpublished MS in files of Institute for Research in Social Science, University of North Carolina.

[32] L. C. Glenn, "Physiographic Influences in the Development of Tennessee," *The Resources of Tennessee*, April, 1915, pp. 44-63, quoted in C. C. Colby, *Economic Geography of North America*, pp. 246-56.

The current of the South's common culture has always found the highland region a barrier. The isolation of this tract in colonial days led North Carolina both to ignore and irritate the settlers until they seceded and formed the short-lived state of Franklin. Likewise the migration of the cotton kingdom westward left the highlands and plateaus untouched. "Poor, untaught, but independent and self-assertive," writes E. E. Miller, "they saw in the rich slave owner of the cotton country a 'furriner' with whom they had neither tastes nor interests in common. They came to hate slavery and the wealth and culture it produced."[33] They volunteered in great numbers for service in the Union armies and made good fighters. The retarded Anglo-Saxon of the highlands is no myth; on the other hand, he is not a universal type even for that area. Proud, sensitive, self-reliant, untaught in the schools, often unchurched, untraveled, he is not unlearned in the ways of his world, and when one chances to leave for the outside world before his personality has become set in the mould of his culture he is likely to climb far. For if there be such a thing as good stock, these highlanders have it.

In the great valley society developed as a checkerboard in accordance with topography. In the fertile limestone valleys large and fertile farms were possible, and in some places slave-owning became profitable and the plantation culture developed. A slow process of social differentiation has taken place, "and the less energetic have been pushed into the poorer lands of the shale hills and chert ridges." The divisions in the Civil War were along the same lines, neighborhood against neighborhood. The Cumberland Plateau with its scanty soils belongs with the ridges and highlands. Over most of the plateau slavery was unknown. "During the Civil War the people either remained at home, or, if they entered the contest, they divided along lines of cleavage made possible by the existence of old family or neighborhood grudges and feuds, and a good part of the fighting was of a local or guerrilla character between bands of so-called home guards."[34]

In the center of the state, the Central Plain, lies the Bluegrass region, an area whose soil is made rich by a basis of disintegrating

[33] E. E. Miller, "Three Quarters of Bewilderment," *These United States,* E. Gruening, ed. I, 144.
[34] L. C. Glenn, quoted by Colby, *op. cit.,* p. 251.

limestone. Between this area and the Cumberland Plateau lies the Highland Plain whose soils varying widely partake of the characteristics of both its neighboring regions. Fine diversified farms, grazing lands, stock, and dairy farming characterize the bluegrass. Here are found, to quote E. E. Miller again, "the remains of an ante-bellum aristocracy, a country dwelling gentry, prosperous farmers who once raised speedy trotters and showy saddle horses."[35]

In ante-bellum days farms were often large, slaves profitable, and when the Civil War broke out the men enlisted in the Confederate Army. Now the Jersey and the Shorthorn have replaced the old régime, but the region is still rich. L. C. Glenn holds that conditions have been better here and the development of civilization has probably been more homogeneous than elsewhere in the state. The Bluegrass, one of nature's beauty spots, is loved by all who see it. "Its inhabitants are not always so loved. They have a certain sense of superiority that cannot always conceal itself."[36]

Next comes the real cotton belt, that portion of the Gulf Plain containing the alluvial valleys of the Tennessee and the Mississippi. Here one may as well be thrown into the Mississippi Delta or the Georgia Black Belt, for it is a region that has little in common with the highlands and plateaus. Spreading cotton fields on creek and river bottom, tenant shacks, Negro croppers, supply stores, and commissaries, all supervised by the supply merchant and the planter, go to make up the cultural landscape of the plantation.

All of these factors have gone over into political geography and have contributed toward making Tennessee the doubtful state of the democratic South. L. C. Glenn has well analyzed the political geography of the Commonwealth:

The features of the state lend themselves easily to a threefold division for political purposes that has long been recognized and observed. The division is into east, middle, and west Tennessee. The line separating the east and middle division crosses the Cumberland Plateau so that it is divided somewhat equally between them, while the line separating the middle and western divisions is approximately the lower or northwest portion of the Tennessee River. East Tennessee is Republican in politics and is interested in diversified agriculture, mining, and manufacturing, while middle and west Tennessee are Democratic politically, and interested primarily in agriculture. The two latter divisions with

[35] *Op. cit.,* p. 145.   [36] *Ibid.,* p. 254.

heir common politics and similar, though by no means identical, nterests, usually dominate in political matters.

n early days there was a land office and a treasurer for each of these hree divisions. The Supreme Court still sits in rotation in east, middle, and west Tennessee. There is a state normal school for each of the hree divisions and a state asylum for each division. In the constitution of political boards and committees it is usually specified that equal representation be given to each of these three divisions, so that in many ways the state comprises three separate communities more or less distinct and different from each other, and yet united under one system of government.[37]

Population Distribution in the Valley Section Through Georgia

One more example may be given. Lawrence La Forge[38] has written an analysis of the map of Georgia that well shows the influence of the profile of physiography on the distribution and density of population. The sparsest population of the state is found in the Coastal Plain where occurs a large proportion of swampy land. The valleys of the Savannah and Chattahoochee Rivers on he east and west, together with the wider belt forming the boundary between the Coastal Plain and the Piedmont Plateau, rank next in scattered population. The hilly, broken surface of these strips offers less level, tillable land. In the Highlands, also, he surface is too rough and the soil too poor to support a dense population.

The belt of densest population is a strip of the Piedmont stretched diagonally across the state. The climate has rendered this area more desirable; water power exists for moving the wheels of industry, and trade routes have converged to build up a great shipping center at Atlanta. Next in density will be found central and southwest portions of the Coastal Plain where are combined soil more fertile and topography more level than in the remainder of the plain.

The extent and distribution of towns and cities furnish an index of the natural resource ability of a region to support population in masses. "The number of cities and towns in the Coastal Plain and in Appalachian Georgia is almost the same, although

---

[37] Quoted by Colby, op. cit., p. 256.
[38] S. W. McCallie (ed.), "Physical Geography of Georgia," Geological Survey of Georgia, Bulletin 42, p. 157 ff.

the first division includes 60 per cent and the other, 40 per cent of the land area. The Piedmont, the Central Uplands, with only 31 per cent of the area, contains more than 42 per cent of the incorporated places, 80 per cent of which lie south of the Chattahoochee River. The influence of topography can best be seen in the size of area required for each town. In Georgia, as a whole, there is one incorporated town to about 100 square miles of area. In the different provinces this ratio ranges from one town to every 150 square miles in the Lookout Plateau, through one to 123 square miles in the Highland, one to 120 square miles in the Valley, and one to over 73 square miles in the Central Upland."[39]

In the Coastal Plains with their low lying land there are no towns except along the railroads, where they are strung like beads. La Forge notices that few of the cities are located on large streams. Geography here plays its rôle, for "in a large part of the state the level, well drained areas with plenty of room for future growth of population are on the uplands and not in the valleys, which are as a rule narrow with steep sides."[40] Macon, Augusta, and Columbus, however, have been enabled to take advantage of sites where streams have widened their river valleys into terraces that seem ideally formed for city growth.

Atlanta is the only Georgia metropolis surrounded by satellite towns and suburban areas that normally are attracted to large cities. That Savannah, Macon, Columbus, and Augusta are conspicuously surrounded by empty areas on the map is again due to topography.

Savannah is situated between tidal marshes on one side and the estuary of Savannah River on the other side, and for miles south and southwest of the city the surface is subject to occasional inundations and there are no good town sites. Macon, Augusta, and Columbus are situated in the belt of hilly country along the boundary between the Coastal Plain and the Central Upland, where the surface is much rougher, is less adapted to attract and support a dense population, and is less suitable for town sites than it is farther south in the Coastal Plain or farther north in the Central Upland.[41]

If we were to follow it out we should find that the South's third valley section runs parallel with the Cumberland range and diagonally transects northern Alabama, southern Mississippi, and

---

[39] *Ibid.*, p. 159.
[40] *Ibid.*, p. 160.   [41] *Ibid.*

southeastern Louisiana. It repeats the modes of life of the profile with interesting variations. The mining area is not found on the escarpment but where the dip slope passes under the Coastal Plains near Birmingham. In the Coastal Plain is found the piney woods belt which at one time occupied at least two zones in the valley slope of the old southeast. In addition to their trucking and fishing fringes, the maritime plains of the Gulf offer both a rice zone and a sugar bowl. In other respects the valley section reproduces many of the characteristics already noted in North Carolina and Tennessee.

Thus the South is not one region but many. Because "the varied relief of the earth's surface is the geographer's starting point, the fundamental fact,"[42] we have retraced its physiographic regions. For each area we have found that the mode of life practiced by its occupants showed some characteristic features. We have seen that these regions are not carelessly flung in disordered array but that they fit together in the unity of sequence. This concept of the valley section serves to relate the physiographic areas with what we may call the profile of the South. There yet remains much to explain of soil, crop belts, and climate before we can interpret the South. We shall meet these again in the consideration of regions and resources. Let us begin with man ascending the South's profile, slowly climbing up the valley section.

[42] The words are Marion Newbigin's.

CHAPTER III

POPULATION MOVES ACROSS THE SOUTHERN MAP

THE EASTERN SHORE of the United States faces the Atlantic Ocean, from whose depths it has recently arisen, with a series of gently sloping terraces. Sea islands fringing the Carolina coasts and drowned rivers up whose channels flow the tides characterize the tidewater slope. These shallow water boundaries fringed with reefs served to force settlements of that strip back upon the estuaries of the rivers.[1] Gently rising, the coastal plain extends some hundred to two hundred miles until it reaches the fall line. There the Piedmont foothills of the Appalachian ranges rise and break the smooth flow of the lowland rivers, setting a barrier of rough and shallow channels against navigation. The fall line coincides roughly with the line of 500 feet altitude above sea level. Ascending to a thousand, two thousand, three thousand feet, the shelf slopes up more sharply to the Appalachians whose crests in the Blue Ridge and Carolina mountains occasionally reach six thousand feet. Reaching, though discontinuously from Nova Scotia to Alabama and Georgia, the Appalachians form a fairly unified system of mountains.

It is up this valley slope, gentle at first, rugged and threatening at the last, that the old world peoples may be pictured as ascending by the avenue of tidal rivers and mountain valleys. The rush of population up the rivers from the coast furnished an aristocratic warp of settlement later to be crossed by a more plebian woof threaded down the valley from Pennsylvania. True, the first settlements on the southern coast appeared more as casual stragglers than as swarming hordes. Contour and topography, as might be expected, persuasively but firmly directed the spread of population over the southern map. Population tends to collect at the most accessible spots and to spread to the hinterland by lines of least

[1] Livingston Farrand, *Basis of American History*, p. 11.

resistance. The one check to this tendency—the lure of natural resources—may serve to deflect streams of population from smooth channels into more arduous paths. And always behind these streams of migration may be found forces driving them out and on. For man is by nature loath to leave the old home.

The most accessible spots were the natural harbors of the coast; the lines of least resistance were the rivers that led to the back country. When the mountains finally loomed, the passes and the valleys furnished the channels of migration. Lured at first by mythical gold, the new habitants of the region soon came to seek instead good land, fresh and almost free, for tobacco, cotton, and food. This chapter attempts to show how the South as a region was settled by such a process.[2]

On the broken Atlantic Coast at least three indentations of historical importance are found in the South. Chesapeake Bay, Albemarle and Pamlico Sounds, with later the Gulf of Mexico and all its branches, represent the land welcoming the sea and those it bore. From the Chesapeake to Florida the indentations while fewer, smaller, and shallower, are, as Farrand says, of great historical importance. The southern coastal plain is intersected with small, short rivers from the Appalachians to the sea. The Potomac, the James, the York, the Roanoke, Neuse, Yadkin, Cape Fear, Santee, Savannah, and Altamaha, are parallel streams draining down the coastal slope into the sea. Between these a network of creeks further aided the process of settlement.

Waiting as prizes after a race and serving to lure population further and further inland, were the undeveloped resources of the South. In obedience to society's call for goods and the individual's need for means of livelihood, men were to migrate in search of the region's "game, the basis of the fur trade; its pine forests yielding tar, pitch, turpentine, lumber and ship timbers so much in demand in England; its pastures affording fodders for herds of horses, cattle and hogs in great number; its fertile soils, which were to yield in time great quantities of rice, indigo, and cotton together with corn and small grain."[3]

[2] Ellen C. Semple from the point of view of the physiographic regionalist in her *American History and Its Geographic Conditions,* and Ulrich B. Phillips as historian of industrial processes in his *American Negro Slavery* and *Plantation and Frontier Documents,* have best generalized this field.

[3] William A. Schaper, "Sectionalism and Representation in South Carolina," American Historical Association, *Report,* 1900, I, 258.

The colonists found the pathways to these areas already in use when they arrived. The use of the entrances and exits provided by geology had been indicated by the Indians. Writes Turner in his illuminating manner:

The Indian trade pioneered the way for civilization. The buffalo trail became the Indian trail, and this became the traders' "trace," the trails widened into roads, and the roads into turnpikes, and these in turn were transformed into railroads. The same origins can be shown for the railroads of the South, the far West and the Dominion of Canada. The trading post, reached by these trails were on the sites of Indian villages which had been placed in positions suggested by nature; and these trading posts, situated so as to command the water systems of the country, have grown into such cities as Albany, Pittsburgh, Detroit, Chicago, St. Louis, Council Bluffs, and Kansas City. Thus civilization in America has followed the arteries made by geology pouring an ever richer tide through them, until at last the slender paths of aboriginal intercourse have been broadened and interwoven into the complex mazes of modern commercial lines, the wilderness has been interpenetrated by lines of civilization growing ever more numerous.[4]

References to early racial elements in the population will no longer serve to account for differences in the development of North and South. In culture, in economic status, and in social rank, the newly arrived immigrants of both areas were pretty much alike. The researches of T. J. Wertenbaker have shown that the Virginia aristocracy itself rose from the English merchant class.[5] Germans made up much of the later immigration to the South, but they came in great part from Pennsylvania. True, New England had her Puritans distinctive in culture and tradition, but the early South possessed a stock of a culture no less distinctive. The most notable contribution to southern population was a cultural group, less set off by physical traits of race than by their social heritage. The lowland Scotch, transplanted first to Ulster, then to America, were wrongly called Scotch-Irish. Intensely conditioned by their historic culture, the Scotch-Irish "carried with them," as Justin Windsor has pointed out, "all that excitable and determined character which goes with a keen-minded adherence to original sin, total depravity, predestination and election."[6] He was a "zealot as a

---

[4] *The Frontier in American History*, p. 14.
[5] *Patrician and Plebian in Virginia; The Planters of Colonial Virginia.*
[6] *The Westward Movement*, p. 12.

citizen and a zealot as a merchant, no less than as a Presbyterian. Thanks to his persecutors, he made a religion of everything he undertook and regarded his civil rights as divine rights. Thus out of persecution emerged a type of man who was high principled and narrow, strong and violent, as tenacious of his own rights as he was blind often to the rights of others, acquisitive yet self-sacrificing, but most of all fearless, confident of his own power, determined to have and to hold."[7]

On the other hand, these new entrants were an important colonial unifying force. Moving directly to the West, they had no loyalty to any individual colonial government. Colonial boundaries, even if known, were of little importance in the wilderness. Both the yeoman and the Scotch-Irish tended to follow the mountain valleys which ran north and south. They came to think of themselves only as Americans and not as inhabitants of some particular colony.[8]

These so-called racial streams consisted merely of national groups which settled together because of common culture. Their variety and yet their essential likeness is well shown by the five "racial" streams that entered North Carolina.[9] The English from Virginia, alleged by William Byrd and John Fiske to be "shiftless people who could not make a living for themselves in Virginia,"[10] settled around the Chowan River and Albemarle Sound from 1635 on to 1663. A few French Huguenots from Charleston, South Carolina, found their way to the neighboring province. Scotch Highlanders of the MacDonald clan, including the famous Flora herself, located on the Cape Fear River around 1729. By 1760 it was estimated that 40,000 Ulster Scotchmen, some having come 435 miles down the Great Valley from Pennsylvania, had settled on the Cape Fear River and in the Carolina Uplands. Following the same route from 1745 to 1775 Germans settled Western North Carolina in and about what is now Forsyth County.

In the settlement of America the curious-minded may perceive a geographic laboratory in which is worked out the interesting problem of how population disperses itself over a new map. We are not forced back to prehistory with speculations about primitive

[7] Constance Lindsay Skinner, *Pioneers of the Old Southwest,* pp. 5-6.
[8] Robert Riegel, *America Moves West,* p. 6.
[9] R. D. W. Connor, *History of North Carolina,* I, 178.
[10] John Fiske, *Old Virginia and Her Neighbors,* II, 271.

migrations; the settlement of America is almost contemporaneous, and it is well recorded. Neither do we have to wait for the slow processes of natural growth of population; the streams of migration are steadily pushed into the interior by increments from Europe. If there are to be found anywhere geographic influences, gross or subtle, upon population distribution they should be evident here. "The ordinary process of development of an American state," points out Carl O. Sauer, "involved the emergence on the frontier of a detached, vigorously growing center based on the discovery of valuable and coherent new country."[11] This well-defined nuclear area of superior fertility, easy accessibility, and early settlement organized and dominated the surrounding frontier. We shall find this process repeated in the relation of the Tidewater region to Virginia, the Charleston area to South Carolina, the Savannah area to Georgia, the New Orleans Delta to Louisiana, the Bluegrass to Kentucky, the Nashville Basin to Tennessee, and the Yazoo Delta to Mississippi. In the formation of states and the establishment of state boundaries Sauer points out that convenient lines of demarcation were often drawn through regions of lower attraction at the time sparsely settled so as to make dominant settlements central in position. Little counties in the tidewater and big counties in the back country attested to this dominance. A proportion which first indicated the relative population densities of the two areas was, after the back country filled up, retained by the dominant tidewater to the advantage of their proportional representation.

To the Revolution in the Coastal Plain

After the first shock of acclimation to a new area, debilitating diseases, and a strange staple of agriculture, population grew and spread itself abroad. And as always it followed the lure of resources by the geographic line of least resistance. The Chesapeake Bay and its tributary, the James, had offered the first invitation to settlement. "Twelve years after the founding of Jamestown, twenty-five miles from the mouth of the James River, the plantations extended up that water course for seventy miles, spreading out four to six miles from either bank.[12] The rivers lent themselves to use both as lines of least resistance to the incoming colonist and as avenues for transporting his staples. By 1624 planta-

[11] *Geography of the Kentucky Pennyroyal*, pp. 10-11.
[12] Ellen Semple, *American History and Its Geographic Conditions*, p. 33.

tions dotted the shores to the head of navigation at the present site of Richmond: by 1663 this area merged on the map to the north with the Maryland colony at the Potomac and reached south to Chowan Peninsula on Albemarle Sound.[13]

"The "stringtown" method of settlement served to push population further up the rivers, while at the same time increasing density enabled the settlers to fill up the areas of land interlaced with streams that were to be found between the larger rivers. Widely scattered population, few towns, and the use of rivers for transportation rather than the building of roads resulted. In addition, the staple agriculture led planters to act as immigration agents in recruiting indentured servants.

The first clearings on the York River had begun about 1630; the Rappahannock and the Potomac had come next. Already social differences between regions had begun to appear.[14] Tidewater peninsulas were held chiefly by planters; mainland and upland, south and west, offered settlement to men of little property. These farmers, living more within the bounds of domestic economy, "found it of no advantage to live within hail of ocean-going ships; and most of those who owned tidewater farms sold them to neighboring planters and moved inland."[15]

The coast and the rivers leading to it did not open the only avenue of advance into this area. The Great Valley lay as a trough between crests of Appalachian ridges. This continuous geological formation, reaching from eastern Pennsylvania, known as the Shenandoah in Virginia, led by easy stages to upland and back country. Thus, while the planters still clung to the tidewater and the most daring settlers of Virginia and Maryland had built their cabins within fifty miles of the Blue Ridge, a stream of immigration poured into the back country of North Carolina. "It was shortly before 1740 that this tide reached North Carolina. Coming down from Virginia it ran along the head waters of the Yadkin, Haw, Neuse, Tar, Catawba, and Deep Rivers until the whole country from what is now the vicinity of Raleigh in the east to the neighborhood of Morganton on the west was taken

---

[13] *Ibid.*

[14] U. B. Phillips, *Plantation and Frontier*, I, 76. Much of this account must follow with unreserved acknowledgment Dr. Phillips' analysis.

[15] *Ibid.*

up."[16] Governor Tryon reported that in the summer and winter of 1765 more than a thousand immigrant wagons passed through Salisbury. As Bassett says, they came by families, friendly bands or by congregations; Scotch-Irish, English, Germans and Pennsylvania Dutch, Moravians, and Welsh. The Great Valley thus became (as it remains today) "a stronghold of Scotch-Irish Presbyterianism, standing out in marked contrast, sometimes in sharp antagonism to the Anglican influence of the tidewater."[17]

In the meantime, a somewhat different population grouping had grown up in the tidewater of the lower South. Around Charleston on the Ashley and Cooper Rivers about 1670 and later at Savannah grew up a notable planter society in a rich indigo and rice district. Unlike early Virginia this region developed a town life which did much in giving cultural "unity and coherence to a heterogeneous mass of people in an undeveloped country."[18] Society here, to a much greater extent, was organized upon the basis of the planter and his plantation. The many swamps tended to keep population sparsely settled, and isolation must have encouraged their visits to Charleston. Moreover, the concentration of rice marketing in Charleston due to shallow rivers prevented the development of a "sylvan Venice" comparable to Virginia. "The Charleston-Savannah district," as Phillips remarks, "employing very few indented servants and attracting very few independent white laborers" did not furnish an industrial society calculated to send out either pioneers or frontier farmers.[19]

These were furnished by the Valley migration which by now had debouched into Piedmont South Carolina and Upland Georgia. These thinly settled groupings of backwoods farmers were of the true frontier stamp. That the inhabitants of the back country with its "broken region of red clay soil" kept so distinct from the tidewater was due to another topographical feature. Both the sandhills and pine barrens reaching from southern Virginia to upper Georgia formed a natural barrier between the Piedmont and the middle country. With an altitude as high as 600 to 700 feet, the

[16] John Spencer Bassett, "Regulators in North Carolina," *American Historical Reports* (1894), p. 145.

[17] Evarts Boutell Greene, *Provincial America,* p. 236.

[18] Schaper, "Sectionalism and Representation in South Carolina," American Historical Association, *Report,* 1900, I, 259.

[19] *Plantation and Frontier,* I, 82.

sandhills possessed a soil once thought to be utterly worthless. To reach the upland areas men from the coast would have to cross from fifty to one hundred fifty miles of "pine barrens" practically devoid of resources. Only a thin stream from Charleston crossed this natural barrier to join the full tide of immigration from the north.[20] The coastal régime in both the Carolinas thus came to be cut off from their important upland fringes and to lack touch with the needs and wishes of the frontier. Out of this fact of cultural geography grew struggles over representation in Virginia and both the Carolinas, the War of Regulation in North Carolina, and the abortive Regulators' Movement in South Carolina.

At the outbreak of the Revolution the South could show about three areas fairly well settled. The Chesapeake lowlands and surrounding hill regions boasted widespread rural communities based on tobacco and containing the promising towns of Baltimore, Annapolis, Norfolk, and Richmond. The back country, stretching from the Shenandoah Valley in Virginia to the Piedmont of the Carolinas, was thinly settled by frontier farmer folks. Besides the well-developed plantation section of the Carolina-Georgia lowlands there were to be found only a few "feeble garrisons and trifling posts for the Indian trade" at St. Augustine, Pensacola, Mobile, Biloxi, New Orleans, and Natchez.[21]

That the early American settlements fringed the coast was due to that stubborn fact of geography, the Appalachian barrier. It had a width of almost three hundred miles and from Maine to Alabama its tangled forests stretched without a break. "It was long before its geography was known" and as Shaler adds it must have seemed to civilized men almost as impassable as the Alps.[22] The Spanish dotted the country with detached settlements and the French tried to encompass a territory extending from the St. Lawrence and Great Lakes down the Mississippi. For a hundred and fifty years the colonists remained hemmed up against the Appalachians. Accordingly, "it was possible in 1700 to ride from Portland, Maine, to southern Virginia, sleeping each night in some considerable village."[23] The English had found, in Miss Semple's words, "a naturally defined area isolated enough to lend them protection

[20] Ibid.   [21] Ibid., pp. 83-84.
[22] N. S. Shaler, *Nature and Man in America*, p. 195.
[23] Ibid.

and cohesion. . . . The Appalachian barrier narrowed their horizon and shut out the great beyond; it transformed the hunter into the farmer and the gentleman adventurer into the tobacco grower."[24] "If our ancestors on the continents," speculates Shaler, "had secured a ready access to the interior, it is likely that a hundred years would have gone by before the colonies became sufficiently dense in population to permit the interactive life which prepared the way for the American Revolution."[25]

Before the end of the Revolution only three small areas of settlement were pushed across the Appalachians—two through the famous Cumberland Gap. To the west of the Yadkin River on the Watauga was established in 1769 the first settlement in the present Tennessee. Peopled largely by participants in the unsuccessful Regulators' Movement of North Carolina, the settlement possessed in handsome, well-educated John Sevier the most cultured man on the whole frontier. Judge Richard Henderson with the aid of Daniel Boone settled his Transylvania purchase from the Indians in the heart of the Kentucky Bluegrass around 1775. When the grant was invalidated the Judge received land on the Cumberland at the site of the present Nashville. There James Robertson with eight others started Nashborough and had five hundred settlers within a year.

From the Revolution to the Civil War

The eighty odd years from the Revolution to the Civil War were to see the resistless tides of peoples rise and fill the valleys and uplands of the South. As population became denser and the state of the arts advanced, culture came to count more than in the colonists' early struggles against nature undisguised and untamed. The forces pushing the Americans on in their westward trek across the map and the paths by which they advanced should be considered in accounting for population dispersal.

The pressure of immigration from England and other parts of Europe aided by the generous native birth-rate furnished the first incentive to expansion. Many of the immigrants were received within the folds of the prevailing system as apprentices, indentured servants or hired men. When they rose to independence their new status required the feel of good dirt of their own

[24] *American History and Its Geographic Conditions*, pp. 37-38.
[25] *Op. cit.*, p. 199.

under their feet. As apprentices they took up no room in the social system; as freemen they sought land and thus forced an expansion that was both spatial and social. Geographic expansion was thus an unavoidable concomitant of the natural process going on within society. The "stringtown" agriculture pushing its way along the river banks made the expansion less in breadth but greater in length. But this Virginia pattern cannot be applied to the whole South; by the time the tide of migration down the valley reached upland Georgia, the settlers were crossing streams without much regard for their potentialities either as barriers or as avenues for transport. Slavery was to make in course of time an aristocracy out of the frontier, pushing yeomen out of the developing black belts into the uplands. After the cotton gin made cotton a staple rather than a plant of doubtful value the untilled acres of the upland and Mississippi South continued to draw planters until the Civil War. The cyclical rise and fall of agricultural prices especially after the close of the Napoleonic Wars sent bankrupt farmers on a long trip to the West to escape debt and taxes by a new start. Soil exhaustion in the eastern area, first cropped to tobacco, pushed planters to seek the rich black lands of Alabama, Mississippi, and later Texas. Land and slaves for southern society of the first half of the nineteenth century were the supreme social value. Land ownership, as Miss Martineau well saw, was regarded as the solution for all individual and social ills. "The possession of land is the aim of all action, generally speaking, and the cure of all social evils among men in the United States. If a man is disappointed in politics or love he goes and buys land. If he disgraces himself, he betakes himself to a lot in the West. If the demand for any article of manufacture slackens, the operatives drop into the unsettled lands. If a citizen's neighbors rise above him in the towns, he betakes himself where he can be monarch of all he surveys. An artisan works that he may die on land of his own. He is frugal that he may enable his son to be a landowner."[26]

Writing of the American scene as it appeared in 1800, Henry Adams pointed out that "no civilized country had yet been required to deal with physical difficulties so serious, nor did experience warrant the conviction that such difficulties could be overcome." It was a thousand miles from New York to the nearest possible port

[26] Harriett Martineau, *Society in America*, I, 292.

on the Mississippi; it was twelve hundred miles from Washington to the site of Natchez. "If the Puritans and the Dutch needed a century or more to reach the Mohawk, when," he asked with reason, "would they reach the Mississippi?" But, as if the Revolution had been a restraining leash, at its close they broke through the mountain barrier and poured down upon the Mississippi plain which Jefferson had finally secured for them in 1803.[27]

The place of rivers as avenues of approach was now taken by, first, the mountain passes and trails, and next the traces and post roads to the lower Mississippi. While the first movements of note into the mountains occurred between 1720 and 1770, extensive transappalachian settlements were not made until after the Revolution. The parallel ridges of the Appalachians running roughly northeast and southwest enclosed a few streams like the Shenandoah, the New, and the Holston, but the great drainage streams cut across the grain of the mountains from west to east, or east to west.[28] In the stages of geology these rivers were older than the great ridges themselves, and they retained their ancient beds by continuous erosion. In so doing they created paths for the incoming flow of population. In their earlier wanderings Indian and buffalo had kept to the wind-swept crests of ridges free of dense timber and erosion, but the incoming white man lowered the trails from ridge tops to river valleys.[29]

Rounding the southern end of the Appalachians the level roadways of the Gulf and Coastal Plain, broken only by occasional swamps and rivers, led to the Mississippi Valley. It was barred, however, by the Indians, and until 1820 the Creeks and Cherokees were able to confine Georgia within the Altamaha and the Ocmulgee Rivers.[30] Over the mountains, however, at least four trails led the southerners to the West.[31] Trails from Winchester, Virginia, and Fredericksburg, Maryland, led to Cumberland Fort at the head waters of the Potomac where they connected with the Youghiogheny and Monongahela by the "Shades of Death" and Great Meadows. The Valley road which, by the Broad and Yadkin, led to the Carolinas and to Charleston by the New led through

[27] *History of the United States*, I, 16.

[28] Semple, *American History and Its Geographic Conditions*, p. 55.

[29] Archer B. Hulbert, *The Paths of Inland Commerce*, pp. 14-15.

[30] Semple, *op. cit.*, pp. 63-64.

[31] Hulbert, *op. cit.*, pp. 18-19; Semple, *op. cit.*, p. 65 ff.

western passes to the uplands of Tennessee. Continuing between the ridges, migrants found that the Cumberland Gap opened upon the Warriors Trail, a direct path to the dark and bloody grounds of Kentucky. To the southwest ran the old Rutherfordton Trail which the Southern Railway now follows through Asheville. By these paths the pack horse trade with the Indians first found its way; here the settlers poured down valleys and through passes, and by these trails traders supplied the needs of the white settlers on the frontier.

The line of the frontier as drawn at the time of the first census in 1790 shows most of New York, Pennsylvania, and Georgia vacant of citizens.[32] Population at its furtherest reaches extended from southwest Pennsylvania down the Ohio and between the parallel valleys of the Holston and the Clinch into upland Tennessee on the northeast. South of the great bend in the Ohio the present state of Kentucky consisted of clustered settlements along rivers and creeks cut off from Virginia by the rugged Cumberland Plateau.[33] The line marking the limits occupied by hostile Indians in 1790 pointed out the areas of immediate future expansion.[34] Practically all of present New York, Pennsylvania, and Kentucky were open to settlement. Accordingly, the map of 1800 shows South Carolina filled in and the Tennessee and Kentucky areas grown much larger, especially the space around Nashville.[35]

The spread of cotton culture to the uplands beginning in the early 1800's and the removal of Indian tribes after 1820, brought into prominence the paths to the lower Mississippi Valley. Already far-flung groups of settlers on the Tombigbee and between the Natchez district and the Yazoo suggested the beginnings of Mississippi and Alabama.[36] Travelers to these regions and the long prominent but lately acquired New Orleans came down the Ohio or Tennessee into the Mississippi. The first trails from Charleston and Savannah to Mobile and New Orleans were primitive

[32] *A Century of Population Growth,* 1790-1900, U. S. Bureau of the Census, 1909, map, p. 18.

[33] Semple, *op. cit.,* p. 72.

[34] *A Century of Population Growth,* 1790-1900, U. S. Bureau of the Census, 1909, map, p. 38.

[35] See Dixon Ryan Fox, *Harper's Atlas of American History,* p. 23.

[36] Semple, *op. cit.,* p. 157.

paths whose "forests, thickets, swamps, and innumerable water courses were sufficient to deter all but the most adventurous."[37]

The first passable land routes to the valley were developed out of the post roads established for carrying the mails. Congress created a post road from Nashville to Natchez in 1800 and after the acquisition of Louisiana the mail was sent on to New Orleans. By 1804 a mail route from Washington by way of Knoxville and Nashville to Natchez, a distance of 1,300 miles, could be traversed in twenty-four days.[38] Another route was proposed around the Appalachian through Virginia, the back parts of North Carolina and South Carolina to Jackson Court House in Georgia, thence by as level a route as possible to New Orleans. It led from Fredericksburg by Danville, Salisbury, Spartanburg, Greenville thence to the Tombigbee settlements about Mobile by an Indian trading path along a fine, high, level, sandy ridge, thence from Mobile to New Orleans.[39] There finally came to be suggested three roads leading from Washington to New Orleans: the eastern, middle, and western trails. The first led from Washington by way of Richmond, Raleigh, Columbia, Milledgeville via the Alabama River to New Orleans. The middle route went through the Piedmont either by Georgetown, Charlotte, Lynchburg, and Danville or by Alexandria, Fredericksburg, Cumberland Court House, and Greensboro. They joined at Salisbury and proceeded to Monticello, Georgia, where they united with the eastern route. The western trail led from Washington through Georgetown, Fairfax Court House, by Lexington in the Shenandoah Valley, to Knoxville, thence through Alabama to Natchez and on to New Orleans.[40]

By the time the culture of cotton became an established technology, migration pretty well followed isothermal lines. After attempts to establish cotton culture in Missouri failed, southerners from the eastern belt went to the southern west. Sir Charles Lyell thought he saw in the migrations of the 1840's an attempt of advancing settlers to secure the type of physical environment they had left behind. "They who go southward from Virginia to North and South Carolina and thence to Georgia and Alabama follow, as if by instinct, the corresponding zones of country. The

[37] Julian P. Bretz, "Early Land Communication with the Lower Mississippi Valley," *The Mississippi Valley Historical Review*, XIII, 3.
[38] *Ibid.*, p. 9.
[39] *Ibid.*, p. 17.   [40] *Ibid.*, pp. 24-25.

inhabitants of the red soil of the granitic region keep to their oak and hickory, the 'crackers' of the tertiary pine barriers to their lightwoods, and they of the newest geological formations in the sea-islands to their fish and oysters."[41]

The year 1820 found Georgia extended as far west as the Ocmulgee, where she was barred by the Cherokee and Creek Indians. The next area of settlement spread from Mobile up the Tombigbee and Alabama Rivers as far north as Muscle Shoals, connecting with the overflow from Tennessee. From lower Louisiana fringes of population extended up the Mississippi, the Red, the Ouachita and the Yazoo Rivers. Areas of sparse settlement were found in Arkansas along the Mississippi and extending up the Arkansas, White, and St. Francis Rivers. Louisiana had been admitted as a state in 1812. In a time of shifting politics Mississippi with fifty thousand souls, including slaves, was judged worthy of admission in 1817. Alabama followed in 1819 and Arkansas in 1836.

By 1840 all these areas had filled out, leaving sparsely settled sections in the interior swamps of southern Georgia, the flat coastal lowlands of Alabama and Mississippi, and the Ozark-Ouachita highlands and St. Francis bottoms of Arkansas. By 1850 the frontier line had passed Arkansas and pushed out a sector of southeast Texas. While Texas had been settled much earlier the census of its population distribution could not appear on our map before its annexation in 1845. The Pine Barrens, fringes of the Gulf and swampy lands, still stood out as regions of sparse population.[42]

The processes of population movement were characteristic of a changing frontier order. Phillips has spoken of a pell-mell régime in which a scrambling, scattered mass of planters, slaves, farmers, poor whites, and frontiersmen nearly all were concerned with getting cotton lands.[43] The vast impersonal processes of migration receive added illumination when viewed in the movements of individuals. The appearance made by migrating plantation forces is suggested by a sarcastic news item from a newspaper in the slowly depleting Eastern Belt: "Arrived in town last evening on his way to the Mississippi, Brigadier General Wade Hampton and suit, Commander in Chief of the Western Army, preceded by a divi-

[41] *A Second Visit to the United States,* II, 89.
[42] See maps Semple, *op. cit.,* pp. 152, 153. Fox, *op. cit.,* pp. 33, 56.
[43] *Plantation and Frontier,* I, 85-86.

sion of fifty ragged meagre looking negro infantry. Should his Excellency fail in obtaining laurels before Mobile, he will be able to make sugar at New Orleans."[44]

The ability to change habitat and occupation, developed in the frontier with its free lands and unrestricted migrations, is well shown in the *Autobiography of Gideon Lincecum*.[45] Born in middle Georgia in 1793 of parents who had moved from North Carolina, he taught school for a year at the age of 24, traded with the Indians in 1819, and served as surveyor and school commissioner at Columbus, Mississippi. He resumed Indian trading, was invalided for three years by a sunstroke, but cured himself after he had been given up by physicians. He managed a team of Choctaw ball players in a tour of the United States in 1830, and then began the practice of medicine. Discontented with prevailing systems he studied among the Indians and thereafter used their herb remedies. In 1834 he made explorations in Texas, returned to practice medicine at Columbus for seven years, and finally removed to Texas as a planter, physician, and a student of natural history.

The problems of an immigrant of higher economic status are given in the migrations of a Maryland slaveholder, Leonard Covington, from 1806 to 1812.[46] Covington, a member of Congress, after a period of depression in tobacco prices, found his Aquasco plantation deeply in debt. He received encouraging reports concerning Mississippi Territory from his brother, Alexander, who had removed thither. Accordingly, Covington organized a group of his neighbors as immigrants and directed his brother to purchase a parcel of public lands for their settlement. Unable to dispose of his Maryland plantation at a satisfactory price in a period of depression, he nevertheless sent thirty-six slaves down the Ohio to Mississippi. Twenty-six slaves, the remainder, he left to work the Maryland plantation under an overseer. Covington, himself, was appointed lieutenant-colonel in the regular army before leaving Maryland and served continuously until killed in Canada during the War of 1812.

[44] Augusta (Ga.) *Chronicle*, Nov. 15, 1811, quoted by U. B. Phillips, *Plantation and Frontier*, II, 196.

[45] Published in Mississippi Historical Society *Publications*, VIII, 443-519. Summarized by Phillips, *Plantation and Frontier*, II, 185.

[46] Summarized from his letters by Phillips, *Plantation and Frontier*, II, 201.

To a certain William C. Duncan, writing for Mr. De Bow in the fifties, the pell-mell régime in the Mississippi Valley seemed destined to be the highest development of the human race. "The Caucasians of the Valley are destined to be, if they are not now, the most mixed race which has ever existed. . . . Here in a new climate, intermarrying with the people of the country, their physical wants abundantly supplied, and under new moral, social, and political relations, their previous habits will in time be modified, and their physical peculiarities worn gradually away, until at last their descendants will be indistinguishable from the mass of the population."[47]   Already these lowlands had become regions of large slaveholdings for the production of cotton and sugar," "especially subject to spasms of inflation and depression."[48]   Of Louisiana in 1823 Timothy Flint wrote, the "people in the pine woods raise cattle by the hundreds and thousands—are poor, satisfied, and healthy. In the bottoms are the sugar and cotton plantations with wealth and sickness."[49]   The same held true for early Mississippi.

Florida lay outside the cotton belt, although after its purchase in 1819 it received some immigration in the northern part. Its settlement was so retarded, however, that it was barely admitted to statehood in time to withdraw with the Confederacy. Texas furnished the one remaining goal of the population advance. The prairies for ranching and the river valleys and black lands for cotton drew many settlers to what is now southeastern Texas. The establishments were more scattered, fewer slaves were carried into the region, and agriculture partook more of the nature of domestic economy.

The distribution of population in the South on the eve of 1860 may now be set forth. Tidewater Virginia had passed through a period of soil exhaustion at the hands of plantation economy in the raising of tobacco and was now being tilled in many instances by farmers using northern methods. Planters who failed to divide their estates up into smaller units for raising varied crops were living after a fashion, some partly on the proceeds of the sale of their slaves. The extension of cotton culture together with the erosion

[47] De Bow, *Resources of the Southern and Western States,* I, 8.
[48] Phillips, *Plantation and Frontier,* I, p. 87.
[49] In his *Last Ten Years in the Valley of the Mississippi,* quoted by Semple, *op. cit.,* p. 167.

to which the rolling hills, denuded of forest cover, proved peculiarly susceptible had left the Piedmont of the Carolinas in somewhat the same stage of soil exhaustion. In the Shenandoah Valley, however, attempts to introduce plantation economy had failed and the farmers followed northern methods, producing steady crops of hay, grain, and fruit.

The Charleston-Savannah region with its sea islands devoted to cotton and its swamps taken over for rice, remained possibly the most prosperous part of the eastern belt under the plantation régime.[50] The neighboring pine barrens and sandhills in the back country and Florida remained sparsely settled with a poor class of white farmers. Cotton had not been long introduced into the uplands of Georgia and South Carolina. Much of the area was cultivated by small farmers and all of it was fairly prosperous. But the area which for four decades had bought spare Negroes from the Eastern Belt and served as magnet for the migrant population of the South was composed of the Alabama Black Prairie, the Mississippi and Red River bottoms, and portions of east Texas. Here cotton was most flourishing and sugar estates existed in great plantations. Kentucky and middle Tennessee were regions of diversified agriculture with some industrial development, while the isolated mountain dwellers of Kentucky, West Virginia, and Western North Carolina remained completely out of the current of southern culture.

POPULATION DEPLETION IN AREAS OF EARLY SETTLEMENT

A final glance, before we close this brief survey, at the area first settled in America shows some surprising changes in population ratios. Some of the most flourishing of the early settled tidewater and coastal areas are more sparsely settled today than when the first census was taken in 1790. Population depletion can be found in northern New England, portions of eastern and western rural New York and Central Pennsylvania. In the South a strip of counties from Central Virginia to the eastern shore, in the north central area of North Carolina, scattered counties in the upper northwestern section of Georgia, in Middle Tennessee, and in fringes of northern Kentucky show less population now than in the first census after their settlement. In many cases this

---

[50] Phillips, *Plantation and Frontier*, I, 88-91.

can be shown to result from the tendency to subdivide large counties as the population grew denser.[51] Exactly how much the boundaries of these counties have contracted is a question involving difficult research into old maps and survey records. In Virginia, however, seven tidewater and three Piedmont counties without having undergone any change of boundaries showed smaller total population in 1920 than in 1790. The Institute for Research in the Social Sciences at the State University made a study of the contemporary processes of migration. They found among other things that in the proportion of migration Negroes exceeded whites, females exceeded males, and the children of farm owners exceeded the children of tenants. Sixty per cent of the white and only 27 per cent of the Negro migrants remained in the state. More women than men, more Negroes than whites went to cities. The prevailing trend, however, is from country to city. Only 12 per cent of the migrants went into farming as an occupation, while 21 per cent of those who remained depend on timber and fishing rather than on agriculture. The lure of the city and the decreasing importance of agriculture is sufficient to show how sharp a break exists between old forms of population movements and the new.[52] The same comparative decline appears to have taken place in first settled tidewater areas of South Carolina and Georgia. The passing of rice culture and the unhealthful climate and contour have left Savannah and Charleston almost without an agricultural hinterland. Around Savannah once proud estates have been broken up and sold to small Negro farmers who now make up the bulk of the yeomanry occupying the district.

In the settlement of the South it is to be seriously doubted that the contour of the land offered advancing colonials any obstacles more severe than those confronting the northern group. The South was particularly fortunate in her rivers, channels to the back country, and runways of commerce. The Appalachians, it is true, were a barrier, but a benevolent one for her early development. They served to prevent hasty expansion and to isolate the group in some measure from hostile Indians. When the time

[51] *A Century of Population Growth*, 1790-1900, U. S. Bureau of the Census, 1909, p. 73 ff.

[52] Wilson Gee and J. J. Corson, Jr., *Population Depletion in Certain Tidewater and Piedmont Areas of Virginia.*

came for the growth of population to force expansion, the barrier could be either crossed by natural trails or skirted around its southern tip on the route to New Orleans. Rivers, the crests of ridges, mountain passes, and valleys served as natural roadways for population movements up the valley section and beyond. In the population dispersal the frontier fringe led the advance. When an area of outstanding advantage was reached it became a densely settled plantation region which served as the nucleus for organizing and dominating the surrounding frontier zones. If different cultural developments occurred in the South during this era, as undoubtedly they did, they must be laid largely to what Ulrich B. Phillips has called "the combined and interacting influence of the frontier and plantation systems."

CHAPTER IV

THE HERITAGE OF THE FRONTIER

"To clear the forest, hunt the wild beasts, scatter the savage tribes, and rout the hordes of a less hardy race than their own; then to till the soil, dig in the mines and work out the rude ways of physical existence—these form the elements of American civilization. All the higher duties of human improvement are done for her. The exercises of lofty thought and the elegancies of art all come from Europe. She has no such indigenous standards of tastes and knowledge as that in which they have their source." Thus wrote an early English traveler and attempted to define the impress the frontier had already left on America.[1] Professor Boutmy said America was not so much a democracy as a huge commercial company for the discovery, cultivation, and capitalization of her vast territory of prairies, forests, and waste lands.[2] These two observers like many others have sensed not any peculiar genius of American people but the adjustment of European culture to the geography of the wilderness. It was the special task of Frederick Jackson Turner to present this interpretation of our society to the consideration of American historians.

The frontier is the initial stage in the settlement of new regions by representatives of more populous and advanced civilizations. Free land and virgin soils beckon large hordes of immigrants animated by motives of independence, escape, and adventure. With civilization behind and what we are pleased to call savagery before, the advancing pioneer belt is characterized by sparsity of population, self-sufficing economy, and a reversion to primitive modes of living.[3] In words of singular force and charm Turner has sketched the temporary triumph of geography:

[1] Thomas Calley Gratton, *Civilized America*, I, 6. Quoted in Nevins, *American Social History Viewed by English Travellers*, p. 249.

[2] Quoted by F. J. Turner, *The Frontier in American History*, p. 211.

[3] In R. T. Ely, et al., *Foundation of National Economy*, R. H. Hess discusses the economy of the frontier, pp. 100-8.

The wilderness masters the colonist. It finds him a European in dress, industries, tools and modes of travel and thought. It takes him from the railroad car and puts him in the birch canoe. It strips off the garments of civilization and arrays him in the hunting shirt and moccasin. It puts him in the log cabin of the Cherokee and Iroquois and runs an Indian palisade around him. Before long he has gone to planting Indian corn and plowing with a sharp stick; he shouts the war cry and takes the scalp in orthodox Indian fashion. In short at the frontier the environment is at first too strong for the man. He must accept the conditions which it furnishes or perish, and so he fits himself into the Indian clearings and follows the Indian trails. Little by little he transforms the wilderness, but the outcome is not the old Europe. . . . The fact is that here is a new product that is American.[4]

The Indian was not the frontier, he was an element in it. The Indian as a man was often a barrier in the settlers' advance across the map; his culture and techniques were aids. If the man as a hinderance has often been overestimated, his culture as an aid has more often been underestimated. And his culture was of the forest. That it was crude goes without saying, but that the culture of the white man who took his place became of necessity crude is equally true. Sparsity of settlement, with the wilderness arrayed against man in what appeared overwhelming odds, is the characteristic of the frontier. The United States Census adopted this measure as an arbitrary index of the frontier and drew the line of the frontier at a density of six persons per square mile.

The frontier took the culture patterns of a complex civilization and pruned and trimmed them to fit nature, open and undisguised. Man's modes of behavior thus underwent a forest-change, strange and yet natural. For it must be remembered that the folkways of the frontier were not only adjustments to conditions of crude culture, they were also expressions of human nature. Rough and tumble fighting was, it is true, the kind of fighting required for survival against Indians and rough men in an area of sparse settlement and magnificent distances, but it also served as outlet for impulses possessed by us all. A burly westerner who was "churched" for fighting showed an unrepentant face to his deacon-judges when they threatened him with civil prosecution and im-

---

[4] Turner, *op. cit.*, p. 4.

prisonment. "I don't want freedom," he is said to have replied bitterly, "I don't even want to live if I can't knock down a man who calls me a liar."[5]

THE SOUTHERN FRONTIER

In the popular mind the distinctive culture traits of the South are supposed to have been received as heritages from the plantation. The plantation in many respects developed a cultural super-structure at once complex and enlightened. It must be remembered, however, that the plantation throughout its existence remained in contact with the frontier, and, though it may in places have overcome and fused with the frontier, at no time did the plantation system wipe it out. The highly urbane types supposed to be characteristic of the plantation society are thus confronted by crude types characteristic of the frontier. Thus has arisen the popular paradox that the South is at once the most crude and the most courtly, the most promising, the most provincial, and the most backward area in the United States.

The South being the section the least urban and industrialized, its habits of rural life make up a comparatively large part of its culture. Rural life of today has received the heritages of the frontier. Moreover, its conditions strikingly partake of the nature of the frontier. Both agriculture and the frontier separate people spatially, leaving a population of low density; both bring them into close contact with wilful nature and set them at primitive tasks.[6] In both the frontier and the farm these primitive tasks are many and varied; for them there has developed no division of labor, no specialization, and no elaborate technology. Accordingly the farmer and the pioneer are jacks of all trades; they are suspicious of innovations and of experts. They believed in the good old phrase that a fool can put on his coat better than a wise man can do it for him. Just as the pioneer is by nature and necessity independent, the farmer is an individualist and a conservative, steeped in routine. A child of pioneer-farmer parents has written:

My father and mother were pioneers and I know that they had a sort of stubborn pride in doing things and meeting emergencies in their own way, perhaps because they had survived the test of a time when they

[5] A. B. Hulbert, *The Paths of Inland Commerce*, p. 87.
[6] A. O. Craven, *Soil Exhaustion, as Factor in the Agricultural History of Virginia and Maryland, 1606-1860*, University of Illinois Studies, XIII, 23-24.

had to rely upon themselves. . . . In later times when the country was settled, they still took pride in following their own peculiar methods, when it would have been easier and less expensive to seek the advice and experience of others.[7]

What in the individual persists as habit, in society remains as cultural survivals. The farmer is notoriously a conservative and agriculture a custom-ridden occupation. "Crops unsuited to the soils, poor tools and destructive methods are continued long after profits have ceased and the outside forces which compelled them in the beginning no longer operate."[8] Bronislaw Malinowski has advanced the view that no trait of culture persists as · a survival unless it serves some functional purpose in society. Man, however, does not live by logic alone nor do all the logics of men agree. Something must be left to the slow flow of time and the reverence for tradition. Cultural change has never been so uniform that some parts of our culture were not left behind in the transition. The transition between the frontier and agriculture with the cultural lag of coon hunting can be easily detected in this complaining comment on the state of affairs in early Missouri:

Until our people are educated up to the point where they can value a sheep higher than a dog and agriculture and manufactures better than opossum and coon hunting, I suppose our annual crops of nutritious grains will grow to waste their fragrance on the desert air, and our rapid streams send their babbling waters to cool the mean whiskey instead of making cheap clothing for our ragged people.[9]

The Frontier Process

It is hardly possible, however, to write of the frontier in the South as a timeless, dateless entity. As it fled before advancing density of population the frontier changed its character. It is possible to hold with some that the southern frontier passed through three stages characterized by the woods rover, the cattle raiser, and the farmer, and was merging into the fourth, the plantation, at the outbreak of the Civil War. The advancing fringe of the frontier as it penetrated the wilderness was furnished by the Indian Trader. Drab, bold, mercenary, adventurous, he spied out the

---

[7] A. H. Sanford, *Story of American Agriculture*, p. 283.
[8] A. O. Craven, *op. cit.*, p. 24.
[9] *First Annual Agricultural Report*, Missouri, appendix, p. 59.

land, charted the wilderness, and planted in the breasts of savages the passion for the fruits, good and evil, of civilization. Lacking the trader's access to Indian society the long hunter followed close behind. Next came the rangers and ranchers of the cane-brakes and cowpens, herders of cattle and drovers of hogs; more permanently attached to one spot, they furnished the first barriers against the Indians and paved the way for the incoming small farmer.[10] The farming system, however, formed the backbone of the frontier. Existing in contact with the plantation it gave tone to the whole South. Carl O. Sauer, among others, has suggested a more realistic view of the problem of frontier succession:

Apart from its essential self-sufficiency, the economy of the frontier showed considerable diversity according to time and place. Cultural succession is not uniform; the hunter followed by the stock raiser who in turn gave way to the farmer is a myth.[11]

In the Kentucky Bluegrass, Sauer is able to show that the first settlers were frontier farmers who became increasingly interested in grazing until the pressure of population caused a partial replacement of live stock by other interests. The Kentucky frontier developed cattle grazing on the plains, the foraging of hogs in the woods, tobacco patches in new forest clearings, and corn patches in the old.[12]

Following the lead offered in Peck's *New Guide to the West,* published in 1837, Turner has seen the farmers' advance on the frontier as a series of waves.

First comes the pioneer who depends for the subsistence of the family chiefly upon the natural growth of vegetation called the range and the proceeds of hunting. A squatter with a horse, cow, and one or two breeders of swine he strikes into the woods with his family and becomes the founder of a new county or perhaps state. He builds his cabin, gathers around him a few other families of similar tastes and habits and occupies till the range is somewhat subdued and hunting a little precious, or what is more frequently the case, till the neighbors crowd around, roads, bridges, and fields annoy him and he lacks elbow room.

[10] Archibald Henderson's *The Conquest of the Old Southwest* gives an illuminating interpretation.
[11] *Geography of the Pennyroyal,* p. 137.
[12] *Ibid.,* pp. 137-39.

Then he sells his cabin and clearing to the next immigrant and breaks for high timber.

The next class of immigrants purchase the land, add field to field, clear out the roads, throw rough bridges over the streams, put up hewn log houses with glass windows and brick or stone chimneys, occasionally plant orchards, build mills, school houses, court houses, etc. and exhibit the picture of plain, frugal, civilized life.

Another wave rolls on. The men of capital and enterprize come. The settler is ready to sell out and take advantage of the rise in property and push farther into the interior and become himself a man of capital and enterprize in turn.

A portion of the first two classes remain stationary amidst the general movement, improve their habits and rise in the scale of society.[13]

Going out as an advance guard of the back settlements the frontier fringe formed a "buffer state" against the Indians. If such a situation induced combativeness, its isolation also made for a domestic economy in which every man was a jack of all trades. That men might thrive under such conditions was shown by the comment in 1765 of a French traveler viewing a Roanoke River settlement in North Carolina:

. . . the lands back of the first of mountains, what they Commonly Call the blue ridge, are very rich, they are Inhabited by the scotch Irish, Germans, and Dutch, which were sent thither to Serve as a bariere betwixt the lower setlers and the Indians; this, however, turned out otherwise, lucily for the poor wretches, that were sent there to be butchered; necessity, and the great Distance from any seaport, or town, obliged them to be industrious in riseing all their necessaries within themselves, and at the same time to be watchful of the Indians and secure their little habitations with palisadoes and out works; the Soil answered beyond their Expectations, in So much that it is at present the plentifulest part of America. They have all sorts of Catle, grain, roots, and fruits buter, Chees, and beer. of their own brewing, they manufacture their own aparel and have Everything In short, Except salt and Iron: they Drive great Droves of Catle to the lower setlements, also butter, Chees and hemp which they Dispose of to advantage and a Considerable quantity of flower.[14]

---

[13] Turner, *The Frontier in American History,* pp. 19-21.
[14] *American Historical Review,* XXVI, 737.

Traits of the Southern Frontier

Regardless of the stages in the pioneer advance the underlying traits characteristic of the frontier make a coherent picture. Because of the scarcity of labor and the crude homemade utensils, the frontier farmer and his family were obliged to become accustomed to the hardest kind of manual labor. The Reverend John Urmstone, writing from North Carolina in 1711, indicated the self-dependence in manual tasks required of frontier industry.

Workmen are dear and scarce. I have about a dozen acres of clear grounds and the rest woods, in all three hundred acres. Had I servants and money I might live very comfortably upon it. . . .

I am forced to work hard with ox, hoe, and spade. I have not a stick to burn for any use but what I cut down with my own hands. I am forced to dig a garden, raise beans, peas, etc., with the assistance of a sorry wench my wife brought with her from England.

Men are generally of all trades, . . . carpenters, joiners, wheelwrights, coopers, butchers, tanners, shoemakers, tallow-chandlers, watermen, and what not; women, soap-makers, starch-makers, dyers, etc. He or she that cannot do all these things, or hath not slaves that can over and above all the common occupations of both sexes, will have but a bad time of it; for help is not to be had at any rate everyone having business enough of his own. This makes tradesmen turn planters, and these become tradesmen. There exists no society one with another when all study and live by their own hands of their own produce: and what they can spare, goes for foreign goods.[15]

The work routine of women on the frontier was likely to be even more devoted to manual toil. The utensils of the housewife were cruder and her day was long. A typical day has been thus described:

She "unkivered" the coals which had been smothered in the ashes the night before to be kept alive till morning and with kindling in one hand and a live coal held in the tines of a fork or between iron tongs in the other she blew and blew and blew until the splinters caught fire. Then the fire was started and the water brought from the spring, poured into the "kittle" and while it was heating and chickens were fed, the cows milked, the children dressed, the bread made, the bacon fried, and then coffee was made and the breakfast was ready. That over, and

[15] From F. L. Hawks, *History of North Carolina*, II, 215-16, quoted by Phillips, *Plantation and Frontier*, II, 271-72.

the dishes washed and put away, the spinning wheel, the loom, or the reel were the next to have attention. Meanwhile keeping a sharp lookout for the children and the hawks, keeping the chickens out of the garden, sweeping the floor, making the beds, churning, sewing, darning, washing, ironing, taking up the ashes and making lye, watching for the bees to swarm, keeping the cat out of the milkpans, dosing the sick children, tying up the hurt fingers and toes, kissing the sore places well again, making soap, robbing the bee hives, stringing beans for winter use, working the garden, planting and tending a few hardy blossoms in the front yard. . . . getting dinner, darning, patching, mending, milking again, reading the Bible, prayers, and so on from morning till night and then all over again the next day. It could never have been said of them that they had fed on roses and lain in the lilies of life.[16]

If the hunting-shirt, the leggings, the waggoner's frock, the leather breeches and moccasin borrowed from the Indians made picturesque garb for the frontiersman, it is to be doubted that the region did as well for woman's attire.

The women wore linsey [flax] petticoats and bed gowns [like a dressingsack] and often went without shoes in the summer. Some had bonnets and bed-gowns made of calico, but generally linsey; and some of them wore men's hats. Their hair was commonly clubbed. Once at a large meeting I noticed there were but two women that had on long gowns. One of them was laced genteely, and the body of the other was open and the tail thereof drawn up and tucked in her apron or coat-string.[17]

The dwellings which housed the family were equally an adaptation to the frontier. Log-pens were built in squares with a plastering of clay, a dirt floor, one door, possibly the luxury of a window and the ubiquitous smoking chimney. In dread of hostile Indians these cabins were arranged in clusters and surrounded by stockades. Monette writes of the frontier habitations in the Mississippi Valley:

The inside appearance of a frontier habitation was also unique and adapted to the circumstances of the times. . . . The whole furniture of a home consisted of one home-made bedstead and one trundle bed under it for children, both well furnished with bear-skins and buffalo

---

[16] John P. Arthur, *Western North Carolina, 1730-1913*, p. 256.

[17] Unpublished MSS. "In the Older Time" by General William Lenoir. Cited by Archibald Henderson, *op. cit.*, p. 41.

robes instead of blankets: a few split bottom chairs, and a few three-legged stools, a small movable bench or table, supported by two pairs of crosslegs for the family meals; a shelf and water-bucket near the door. The naked wood and clay walls, instead of the ornamental paper and tapestry of the cities, were embellished with the whole wealth of the family wardrobe. The frocks, dresses and bedgowns of the women, the hunting-shirts, pantaloons and arms of the men, all were suspended around the walls from wooden hooks and pegs, and served as a good index to the industry and neatness of the mistress of the house. The cooking utensils and table furniture consisted of a few iron pots, "pewter plates and dishes," spoons, knives and forks which had been transported from the east with their salt and iron; besides these, a few wooden bowls or "trenchers," "noggins and gourds," completed the list of cooking utensils. . . . As soon as the mechanic and merchant appeared, sashes with two or four lights of glass might be seen set into gaps cut through the side logs. Contemporaneously, old barrels began to consti-tute the tops of chimneys, and joists and planks sawed by hand, too, the place of puncheons.[18]

The very organization of the industrial routine and the sim-plicity of habitation on the frontier farm made it a fostering hab-itat of the family. Out of its domestic economy came the rapid and easy growth of the family. W. B. Weeden writes of the early New England family in terms that can be easily applied to the South:

The common people created self-sustaining families as readily as the banyan tree spreads a growth around the parent trunk. New land was easily obtained. A thrifty farmer could buy acres enough on which to settle his sons from the savings of a few years. The axe could create the log house anywhere and in most places sawmills gave a cheap supply of planks and deals. The splitting of shingles was an accomplishment almost as common as whittling. The practice of making this cheap and excellent roofing material was carried into the middle states by the New England emigrants. The homestead was often given to the younger son who provided for the parents in their old age, the elder brothers having acquired settlements of their own. Thus the teeming social soil was ready for the family roots which were constantly extend-ing. Unmarried men of thirty were rare in country towns. Matrons were grandmothers at forty; mother and daughter frequently nursed their children at the same time. Father, son, and grandson often worked together in one field and that field was their own.[19]

[18] John Wesley Monette, *Valley of the Mississippi*, II, 6.
[19] *Economic and Social History of New England, 1620-1879*, II, 860.

No immigrant went to the frontier for ease and idleness. "The climate was trying; fever was common; the crops ran new risks from strange insects, drought, and violent weather; the weeds were annoying; the flies and mosquitoes tormented him and his cattle."[20] There existed in a phrase, a frontier without soap with "nothing clean but birds, nothing industrious but pigs, and nothing happy but squirrels."[21]

The chance of being shot or scalped by the Indians was hardly worth considering when compared with the certainty of malarial fever, or the strange disease called milk sickness, or the still more distressing home-sickness, or the misery of nervous prostration which wore out generation after generation of women and children on the frontier and left a tragedy in every log cabin. Not for love of ease did men plunge into the wilderness. Few laborers endured a harder lot, coarser fare or anxieties and responsibilities greater than those of the western emigrant. Not merely because he enjoyed the luxury of salt pork, whiskey, or even coffee three times a day did the American laborer claim superiority over the European.[22]

It was in this crude labor expended in the exploitation of the frontier that Henry Adams saw the spirit of the frontier, a spirit that strangely perturbed his sensitive mind:

From Lake Erie to Florida, in a long unbroken line pioneers were at work, cutting into the forest with the energy of beavers and with no more express moral purpose than the beavers they drove away. The civilization they carried with them was rarely illumined by an idea; they sought room for no new truth and aimed neither at creating like the Puritans a government of saints nor like the Quakers, one of love and peace; they left such experiments behind them and wrestled only with the hardest problems of frontier life. To a new society, ignorant and semi-barbarous, a mass of demagogues insisted on applying every stimulant that could inflame its worst appetites, while at the same time taking away every influence that had hitherto helped to restrain its passions, greed for wealth, lust for power, yearning for the blank void of savage freedom such as Indians and wolves delighted in—these were the fires that flamed under the caldron of American society.[23]

[20] Henry Adams, *History of the United States*, I, 57-59.
[21] A. B. Hulbert, *Paths of Inland Commerce*, p. 87.
[22] Henry Adams, *op. cit.*, I, 58-59.
[23] *Ibid.*, I. 177-78.

The frontier was not all individualism and competition in exploitation of the wilderness. Out of family and kinship groupings, out of the very hardships and crude contacts of the pioneer belts grew spontaneous associations and methods of coöperation. Informal combinations, extra-legal and voluntary associations, impressed, because of their number and great variety, all of the early travelers to the United States. "The log rolling, the house raising, the husking bee, the apple paring, and the squatters' association whereby they protected themselves against the speculators in securing title to their clearings on the public domain, the camp meeting, the mining camp, the Vigilantes, the cattle raisers' associations, the gentlemen's agreements are a few of the indications of this attitude."[24]

Closely related to these attitudes is the trait of hospitality, a sort of mutual aid associated with a low density of population. A companion trait was frontier inquisitiveness. Not only is the granting of shelter to travelers a much more desirable practice in regions of sparse settlements but the contacts furnished by these travelers possess greater social value. On the frontier the hospitality of the home places put scant demands upon the larder and the regimen. There is but one fare, plain fare, and host and guest alike accept it. In sparsely populated areas of the South where the plantation had displaced the frontier the passion for hospitality was equally great.

So put to it for companionship were Virginia planters of 1800 that one plan was to send the Negroes round at nightfall to the nearest inn with a note to any lady or gentleman putting up there stating that if they did not like their accommodations, Mr. ———— would be happy to see them at his house close by, to which the black with a lantern would conduct them. In the morning the planter remunerated the landlord for any loss he may have suffered in the removal of a guest. John Bernard, the clever English actor who played in America, recounted another more drastic plan. Reclining in a wagon, dressed in a suit for bathing and surrounded by rifles, fishing tackle, bottles and obedient blacks, the planter was driven into the nearest ford. There by the aid of his slaves he combined the four enjoyments of bathing, fishing, shooting, and drinking with waiting for a guest. If at length the form of a stranger appeared, he sprang from his plank and shouted

[24] Turner, *op. cit.,* p. 343.

an invitation to alight and take a drop of something sociable. If the traveller refused up went the rifle to the shoulder and compliance was demanded in the tone of a European footpad. If the stranger yielded he might find himself carted to the mansion and there beset with nog, flip, sling, and toddy until he was lucky to escape by any desperate device. Bernard relates with relish how such a hospitable planter once caught as involuntary guest a New England preacher on a tour against slavery and was compelled to listen to an all night comparison between himself and Beelzebub.[25]

Personality no less than occupational types represents adjustments to the frontier folkways and *modus vivendi.* Such were those traders, the *coureurs des bois,* "half peddlers and half hunters with a little finish of the broker." Through their agency the goods imported from France were pushed from New Orleans "into the most remote settlements of the country and the Indian villages and exchanged for the production of the country." Long after the trade vanished decrepit men of that class, crippled, frost bitten, and old were found to retain a singular predilection for that wandering half savage life, still dressing in skins with leggings and moccasins.[26]

The pack-horse trade supplied the needs of the frontier settlements for guns, ammunition, knives, blankets, tobacco, hatchets, and liquor. The West sent to the East, "in addition to skins and pelts, whiskey that brought a dollar a gallon. Each pony could carry sixteen gallons and every drop could be sold for real money. On the return trip the pack-horses carried back chiefly salt and iron."[27] A passage from Doddridge's *Notes* best describes this trade:

In the fall of the year, after seeding time, every family formed an association with some of their neighbors, for starting the little caravan. A master driver was to be selected from among them, who was to be assisted by one or more young men and sometimes a boy or two. The horses were fitted out with packsaddles, to the latter part of which was fastened a pair of hobbles made of hickory withes—a bell and collar ornamented their necks. The bags provided for the conveyance of the salt were fitted with bread, jerked, boiled ham and cheese [which] furnished a provision for the drivers. At night after feeding the horses, whether

[25] John Bernard, "Retrospections of America," quoted by Allen Nevins, *American Social History as Viewed by British Travellers,* pp. 38-40.

[26] De Bow, *Industrial Resources of the South,* I, 411.

[27] A. B. Hulbert, *Paths of Inland Commerce,* p. 27.

put in pasture or turned out into the woods, were hobbled and the bells opened. The barter for salt and iron was made first at Baltimore; Frederick, Hagerstown, Oldtown, and Fort Cumberland in succession became the places of exchange. Each horse carried two bushels of alum salt weighing eighty-four pounds to the bushel, but it was enough considering the scanty subsistence allowed them on the journey. The common price of a bushel of alum salt at an early period, was a good cow and a calf.[28]

The river trade in the flatboat age about 1820 recruited another frontier type, "a lusty crew collected from the waning Indian trade and the disbanded pioneer armies." These river men of great strength, "alligator horses" as they called themselves, were rough in their work and their lives. Hulbert quotes the names and boasts in which they delighted. The Snag, the Snapping Turtle, the Salt River Roarer, "the very infant that turned from his mother's breast and called out for a bottle of old rye." "One squint of his eye would blister a bull's heel." He was a "genuwine double acting engine, can out-run, out-swim, chaw more tobacco and spit less, drink more whisky and keep soberer than any man in these localities."[29]

Frontier and Plantation in Conflict

The distinction between the frontier farm and the plantation as economic units has been clearly drawn by U. B. Phillips.[30] On the southern farm the laboring force was small, the devotion to staples was not marked, and a less regular routine was followed than on the plantation. Frontier industry furnished neither employers nor employees of labor; agriculture was often pursued as a side line for the production of certain necessities while the main business of life was hunting or Indian trading. The conflict of the system with the more stable and compactly organized plantation was inevitable.

The plantation followed after the frontier and located upon the central fertile lands. From these lands, "delta," "basins," river bottoms, black belts, and bluegrass as areas of dominance the planter societies organized the surrounding frontier zones. The process was well known; the explanation difficult. "The passage

---

[28] Quoted in Hulbert, *ibid.*, pp. 27-28.
[29] *Ibid.*, p. 71.
[30] *Plantation and Frontier*, I, 72-73.

of the years," writes Phillips, "witnessed a systemizing process in the cotton belt, and in some measure a segregating process which put the planters in control of most of the fertile and accessible areas."[31]   The white population of the district, says a writer in *DeBow's Review,* divides into three parts: One part, consisting of a few slaveholders, obtains possession of all the valuable cotton lands and monopolizes for a few white families all the advantages of the cotton demand.   A second part removes with its slaves, if it possesses any, from the district, while a third continues to occupy the sandhills or sometimes perhaps takes possession of the exhausted land which has been vacated by the large planters because they, with all their superior skill and advantages of capital, could not cultivate it with profit.   This last class remains ignorant of all luxury, having no higher aim than to procure the bare means of subsistence.[32]

It is on Frederick Law Olmsted, perhaps the most observant of all travelers in America, that we have to depend for pictures of this changing scene.   The following description from a place in Louisiana on the Texas Route in the fifties shows the plantation in full possession with a lazy ebb of the frontier:

The plantations occur, perhaps, at an average distance of three to four miles.   Most of the remaining inhabitants live chiefly, to appearances, by fleecing emigrants.   Every shanty sells spirits and takes in travellers. Every plantation has its sign, offering provender for sale generally curiously worded or spelled, as 'Corn Heare."   We passed through but one village, which consisted of six dwellings.   The families obtained their livelihood by the following occupations: one by shoeing the horses of emigrants; one by repairing the wheels of their wagons; one by selling them groceries.   The smallest cabin contained a physician.   It was not larger than a good sized medicine chest but had the biggest sign.   The others advertised "corn and fodder."   The prices charged for any article sold or service performed were enormous, full one hundred per cent over those of New Orleans.[33]

In the processes of competition the farm on the southern frontier seemed fated to yield possession of all fertile cotton lands to the

[31] *Ibid.,* I, 86.
[32] *De Bow's Review,* XVIII, 79.   Quoted by Olmsted, *Journey in the Back Country,* p. 310.
[33] Olmsted, *A Journey Through Texas,* p. 62.

advancing plantation. Many observers saw in this ever recurring fact a proof of the superiority of Negro labor over white workers in the semi-torrid climate of the South. Olmsted speculating on the chances of the plantation replacing the farm system of the hard-working German immigrant, laid it to the economies of large scale production practiced by the planter.

The planter was likely to win, due to the fact that his expenses for fencing on account of his larger fields and larger estate are several hundred per cent less than those of the farmer; to the fact that his expenses for tillage, having mules and plows and other instruments to use at the opportune moment, are less than those of the farmer, who in many cases cannot afford to own a single team; to the fact that he has from experience a better knowledge of the most successful method of cultivation; to the fact that he has a gin and a press of his own in the midst of his cotton fields to which he can carry his wool at one transfer from the picking, by which he can put it in order for market expeditiously and at an expense much below that falling upon the farmer, who must first store his wool, then send it to the planters' gin and press and having it prepared at the planters' convenience, paying perhaps exorbitantly therefor; and finally to the fact that the planter deals directly with the exporter, while the farmer, the whole profit of whose crop would not pay his expenses on a journey to the coast, must transfer his bale or two to the exporter through two or three middle men, carrying it one bale at a time, to the local purchaser.[34]

This is an explanation in the economist's terms of available capital and low overhead costs.

It cannot be denied that the two systems remained pretty much in conflict wherever found together. It was the desire of every planter, thought Olmsted, to get possession of the land of any poor non-slaveholding neighbor.[35] The ideal plantation was both large and isolated. As a Louisiana planter explained it to Olmsted the representative of a hangover frontier farm system had a bad effect upon the discipline of the plantation laborers. The contrast between the small farmer, "most of the time idle, and when working, working only for their own benefit and without a master—constantly offered suggestions and temptations to the slaves to neglect their duty and to run away." In some places low grog shops, owned by poor whites, grew up in which Negroes might

[34] Olmsted, *Journey in the Back Country*, pp. 350-51.
[35] *Ibid.*, pp. 449-50.

exchange chickens or a pig for spirits and no questions asked. If slavery tended to make an aristocracy out of the frontier, one of its concomitants was an habitual irritation which the planter could hardly escape feeling toward the lingering representatives of the frontier.

The plantation forced new westward marches of the frontier. The profitable crops, with the exception of sugar and rice, were those which exhausted the soil most quickly; the plantation had to expand to live. Before the day of fertilization there were no hopes of growing continuous crops of tobacco and cotton on the same tract. Lincoln's mild compromise to leave slavery where it existed appeared in reality a threat of extinction.[36] Wherever the plantation expanded it sent forward the frontiersman as its advance guard. Many of the pioneers locating their frontier farms on fertile soil were no doubt able to extend them into plantations. As cotton and the plantation advanced upon the back country, says F. J. Turner, free farmers were forced "either to change to the plantation economy and buy slaves or to sell their land and migrate."[37] Many in upland areas resisted this compulsion and remained as yeoman farmers in a plantation society. Religious beliefs and agricultural habits made the change to slavery distasteful to many. An advance guard of the frontier whom Sir Charles Lyell met was, it is possible, fated to become the progenitor of a dynasty of planters.

At one turn of the road, in the midst of the wood, we met a man with a rifle, carrying in his hand an empty pail for giving water to his horse, and followed at a short distance by his wife, leading a steed, on which was a small sack. "It probably contains," said our companions, "all their worldly goods; they are movers, and have their faces turned westward, a small detachment of that great army of emigrants, which is steadily moving on every year toward the Rocky Mountains. This young married couple may perhaps go down to the Mississippi, and buy, for a few dollars, some acres of land, near a wooding station. The husband will fell timber, run up a log cabin, and receive ready money from the steamboats, which burn the wood. At the end of ten or fifteen years, by which time some of their children

---

[36] Archer Butler Hulbert, *Frontiers,* p. 41.
[37] *The Rise of the New West,* p. 54.

will have become profitable servants, they may have put by 2000 dollars, bought a farm, and be living in a frame-house.[38]

Throughout the period the frontier continued to offer escape from the all-encompassing plantation.

THE FRONTIER HERITAGE

When the dominant plantation areas were established they were likely to be surrounded both by zones of sturdy yeoman farmers and by "poor whites." The yeomanry, occupying the upland areas, pointed to the passing of the frontier stage. The ebb of the frontier remained in the "poor white." Not an example of biological depletion, he retained in a meager environment the crude culture of the frontier. Poverty, whiskey, malaria, inadequate diet, and poor health came to aggravate his existence. It is possible to map fairly accurately the region occupied by the so-called poor whites of the Old South.[39] The Pine Barrens of south central Georgia, surrounded by a tier of black belt counties, were shown by the Census of 1860 to be far behind the average South in value of land, houses, farm products, and live stock. Similarly, the pine woods of Mississippi, east of the Pearl River, were poor, and the people were known as "hill billies," "sand hillers" and "clay eaters." In the unproductive sand hills, stretching through North and South Carolina, in the pine woods and clay bottoms of Alabama and Florida were found isolated communities of poor illiterate peoples living on unfrequented roads.

To De Tocqueville the influence of slavery united to the English character served to explain the manners and social conditions of the southern states.[40] In the South today it can safely be said that no flavor is stronger than that imparted by the frontier. No trait of the frontier can safely be neglected by the social historian as an antiquarian's item. The child born in the northern frontier would before its tenth year, Olmsted predicted, "be living in a well organized and tolerably well provided community; schools, churches, libraries, lectures, and concert halls, daily mails and printing presses, shops and machines in variety, having arrived within at least a day's journey of it; being always within influencing distance

---

[38] Lyell's *Travels in the United States, Second Visit,* II, 205-6.

[39] See article of that title by P. H. Buck in *American Historical Review,* XXX, 41-54.

[40] De Tocqueville, *Democracy in America,* I, 36.

of it."[41] Whether or not the instance proved Olmsted's optimism justified, the frontier did not recede so quickly in the South.

When it did recede it gave way to a rural society which contains many elements in common with the frontier.

The frontier is transitional: hunter, fur trader, Indian fighter, freighter, prospector, scout, river pilot, lumberjack, stagecoach driver, cowboy have their day; and the farmer survives. The last of the pioneers holds fast to the earth; the vanguard of the conquest is gone and the army of occupation is entrenched.[42]

The South still possesses the largest number of practically self-sufficing farms to be found in any comparable area in the nation. Its rural life is characterized by isolated farmsteads in the open country. If southern conditions of living have often appeared crude to the critics, it is for the reason that they have retained not only the usages but often the conditions of the frontier. More than any other section except the sparsely settled western range it has remained a pioneer belt, and the common man living in the open county faces much the same situation with the cultural heritage left by the frontier. While they were formative the folkways of the South got the stamp of the frontier. From the frontier, part of the area passed to the plantation, but the plantation area retained many of the frontier traits. Institutions and customs are still tinged with the shades of the forest, whether as survivals or as adjustments to ruralism.

[41] *A Journey in the Back Country*, p. 414.
[42] E. Douglass Branch, *Westward*, p. 593.

CHAPTER V

THE SOUTHERN SOIL

To THE human geographer the soils of the United States should possess special interest. In Europe one hardly knows when or how the soil was first used and accordingly many of the lessons of a beginning agriculture are lost. We have here, however, the transplantation of a previously developed agriculture to a soil prepared by nature and left largely untilled for centuries. N. S. Shaler has well said that American agriculture has been conditioned by the "possession of a virgin soil, of fields in which the natural processes had for ages been accumulating the stores of nutriment which the crops remove. So far our agriculture has rested almost altogether upon these ancient accumulations of fertility. By a swift and unending process of tillage we have been gathering in this harvest and sending the products away to foreign lands."[1]

Because the natural fertility of land, stored by long geological processes, had remained unexhausted by planting, the differences in fertility of various regions were not so soon discovered by the early settlers. The test of the soil came when a series of crops had been planted. Of the two important new crops tobacco rather than corn had the quality of first affecting the fertility of the soil. Patrick Sheriff in his *Tour Through North America* held that Indian corn had a peculiar trait in that it was capable of being grown for several years on the same land without the application of fertilizer.[2] This gave rise to unfounded hopes in the breasts of early settlers that their soils possessed an inexhaustible fertility. The experience of the eastern cotton and tobacco belts with soil exhaustion and of the highland and plateau regions with erosion can be examined to show how baseless were these hopes.

"Human civilization," C. F. Marbut points out, "has not en-

[1] *United States of America,* I, 401.
[2] Published in Edinburgh, 1853, p. 394. Cited by Jane Louise Mesick, *America as Viewed by British Travellers, 1785-1835,* p. 153.

dured for a sufficient length of time to enable us to trace the development of the soil on any one spot from infancy, through youth, to maturity, much less to old age."[3]   Man's occupancy of the soil, however, has enabled him to point out cycles in the development of fertility—the most important soil quality. For the purposes of society the materials from which soils originate, the processes by which they develop, and the structure which they attain must coalesce in fertility. The presence of soil fertility has been especially related to social factors in an area like the South. "In regions where there is little mining, manufacturing, fishing, or foreign commerce, the population gets its living pretty directly from the soil, whether through lumbering, grazing, or raising crops, the number of inhabitants is pretty closely correlated with soil fertility."[4]

PHYSICS OF THE SOIL

The main constituents determining the fertility of a soil are its levelness, depth, fineness, mellowness, and amount of available plant food. How level and how deep any given soil region is found to be, results mainly from its development in a physiographic region. A soil is mellow if it can be broken with ease. Its fineness and mellowness depend on the kind of rock from which the soil was formed. The amount of plant food available is determined largely by soil origin and the part the climate plays in the process of the disintegration of plants.

From the standpoint of agriculture the structure of the soil is its most important quality. Soils with poor structure are hard and refractory to cultivate when dry, and plastic but intractable when wet. The lack of plant foods in soils of favorable texture may be remedied by fertilization.[5] With the exception of certain mineral constituents, most of the body of plants are drawn from water and the atmosphere. It is the texture of the soil that determines both its adaptability to tillage and the circulation of water. Water, which the soil retains by absorption and surface attraction even to 10 to 20 per cent of its own weight, clings to the surface of soil particles as an envelope, and thus tends to distribute itself evenly throughout

[3] In H. L. Shantz and C. F. Marbut, *The Vegetation and Soils of Africa*, p. 129.

[4] R. M. Harper, "Resources of Southern Alabama," Alabama Geological Survey, *Special Report No. 11*, p. 17.

[5] Louis A. Wolfanger, "Major World Soil Groups and Some of Their Geographic Implications," *Geographical Review*, XIX, 95.

a uniform texture. If wilting is to be prevented, water must be supplied to plants as fast as it is lost. The rate of supply of soil water is simply the speed at which water can move in the soil. This is a function of the texture of soil particles and the structure into which they have coalesced.

By mechanical analysis in the laboratory, soil particles can be classified according to size, and each type of particle shown to fill a definite function in soil structure.[6] The following measurements are standard in Great Britain:

Fine gravel.....................above 1 mm. in diameter
Coarse sand.............................1 to 0.2 mm.
Fine sand.............................0.2 to 0.4 mm.
Silt.................................0.4 to 0.01 mm.
Fine silt..............................01 to .002 mm.
Clay ....below .002 mm.

No element in the soil is "more necessary in proper proportions or more harmful in excess" than clay. It acts as a plastic colloid in the presence of water and its adhesive properties bind the soil together. "Soil without clay would be very much like a sand heap." Clay impedes the movements of air and water in the soil and serves to keep water layers within reach of plant roots. Coarse sand on the other hand keeps the soil open and tillable and increases drainage. As the amount of sand increases beyond this point of moderate drainage and evaporation the soil becomes less suited to cultivation. The fine silts and sand ranges in function somewhere between the clays and the coarse sands. Fine gravel exaggerates the effect of sand in the soil. In addition decomposed plant residues become incorporated in the soil in the form of humus. This complex mixture possesses the property of withdrawing ions from the soil; it swells when wetted and thus increases the water-holding capacity of soils. Unless replaced humus slowly disappears from the soil.

How these various elements in the soil function together in promoting plant growth is well shown in Milton Whitney's analogy of the soil as a living organism.[7] The structure of small rock

[6] This analysis of soil factors is from the work of Edward J. Russell in *Soil Conditions and Plant Growth;* pp. 53-113, cited in E. G. Nourse's *Agricultural Economics,* pp. 161-67.

[7] *Soils and Civilization,* pp. 27-33.

fragments and the hard pan which serve as supporting walls furnish the skeleton of the soil. Soil colloids such as clay act as a coating to withdraw from active solution mineral, organic, and gaseous substances which otherwise would be readily washed out of the soil by rainfall. The processes of bacteria, enzymes, and oxidation which digest and break down organic débris in the soil may be said to make up its digestive system. The soil breathes frequently and deeply to depths of fifty feet and more, interchanging its gaseous products with fresh air to bring about oxidation. In addition to this respiratory system the soil possesses a circulatory system by which waste products and nutrient materials are carried in solution through larger channels and soil capillaries. The way in which the various systems of the soil function together may be used to distinguish and describe various soil types.

The Soil as Product

The story of the formation of soil patterns both in their internal structure and in the distribution of soil types in space as regions is one of the most fascinating topics with which the geographer has to deal. The soil is the product of original materials and natural processes which have arrived at a particular stage. Studies by Russian scientists of the great soil belts of their country have shown that, given time to arrive at maturity, soil areas tend to coincide with climatic regions.

Soils are developed from soil material consisting of geological deposits of various kinds directly through the operation of climatic forces, of which rainfall seems the most important, and indirectly through the influence of native vegetation. The development is through the various stages of infancy, youth, maturity, and old age and can take place only when erosion is relatively inactive. The broad general characteristics of the soil at any time are due to the climate of the locality if the soil is mature. If the soil is immature it will be influenced by the nature of the geological formation and the immaturity may be due to the topography.[8]

Shale and sandstone, limestone and marl, crystalline rock and organic matter furnish the original materials of soil. By means of stream action, atmospheric reaction, weathering, glaciation, and plant growth the region's climate and rainfall reduce these mate-

[8] H. L. Shantz and C. F. Marbut, *The Vegetation and Soils of Africa,* pp. 128-29.

rials to a texture fine enough for the formation of soil. The resulting product can then be classified on the basis of its specific properties such as color, natural drainage, content of organic matter, of lime carbonate, of plant food, and the arrangement of the soil in sections. This last, called the soil profile, shows normally three divisions: the "A" horizon, the portion cultivated, the "B" horizon, the subsoil where soluble and unsoluble materials are deposited by seeping waters, and the "C" horizon, the unweathered or parent soil material. Swamp, muck, and desert soils are generally found without profiles. A final classification of the soil as to texture is made on the basis of the size of the particles. The following table makes clear the relation of physiographic region to climatic areas in the production of soils.

TABLE II

OUTLINE OF FACTORS USED IN THE CLASSIFICATION OF SOILS*

I. Region — Temperature	1. Frigid 2. Temperate 3. Subtropical 4. Tropical
II. Section — Precipitation	1. Humid 2. Semiarid 3. Arid
III. Province — Agency of Formation	1. Weathering 2. Biology a. Streams 3. Water..........b. Lakes 4. Atmosphere c. Ocean 5. Glaciation 6. Gravity
IV. Group — Kinds of Material	1. Acid crystalline rock 2. Basic crystalline rock 3. Shales and sandstone 4. Limestone and marl 5. Organic matter
V. Series — Specific Properties	1. Color 2. Natural Drainage 3. Content and condition of organic matter 4. Content of lime carbonate 5. Content of plant food 6. Arrangement of soil in section
VI. Class — Texture	1. Size of particles.

*From T. L. Lyon, E. O. Flippin, H. O. Buckman, *Soils—Their Properties and Management*, p. 721.

Soils range in stage from infancy and youth through maturity to old age. The nearer to maturity different geological formations

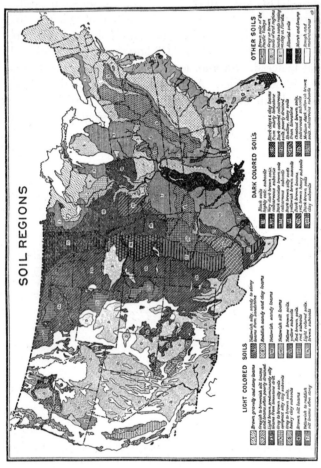

FIGURE 2.—Soils originally or at present covered with forest are normally light colored and are likely to be less fertile than soils in regions of lower rainfall, Grassland soils, in general, are dark colored, the humid prairie soils being commonly almost black and highly fertile, the subhumid prairie soils blackest of all, while the semiarid short-grass plains soils are dark-brown or chocolate colored, the color gradually fading to medium brown in areas of lesser rainfall, and to light brown or even ashy gray in desert areas. The light-colored forest soils in the United States total about 800,000,000 acres, the dark-colored grassland soils about 600,000,000 acres, and the light-colored arid soils about 500,000,000 acres. (Map prepared by C. F. Marbut and associates, Bureau of Chemistry and Soils). (Courtesy of U. S. Department of Agri-

come the more likely are they to be found crumbled together in great tracts of soil, possessing similar characteristics and corresponding to climatic belts.[9] Soils are thus mature when they show an absence of geological features and a great predominance of characteristics acquired by weathering and organic accumulations. This condition can be attained only on smooth surfaces where the soils have lain undisturbed for a long period of time. Soil on slopes may remain perpetually immature by having its upper cover removed as rapidly as it advances in age. The influence of climatic zones and of topography on the development of soil belts will be of peculiar value in explaining certain areas in the South.

SOIL AREAS OF THE SOUTH

The foregoing discussion has served to clear the ground for the presentation of the soil areas of the South on the basis, first of provinces of geological origin and, second, of zones of climatic maturity. By 1913 the United States Soil Survey[10] had mapped and described thirteen definite soil regions and provinces in this country.

TABLE III
SOIL PROVINCES IN THE UNITED STATES

PROVINCE	Estimated Area in Acres
1. ATLANTIC AND GULF COASTAL PLAIN	218,362,000
2. PIEDMONT PLATEAU	47,214,000
3. APPALACHIAN MOUNTAIN AND PLATEAU	84,837,000
4. LIMESTONE VALLEY AND UPLAND	67,870,000
5. RIVER FLOOD PLAINS	75,247,000
6. GREAT PLAINS	331,968,000
7. ARID SOUTHWEST	81,148,000
8. LOESSIAL AND GLACIAL PROVINCE	385,083,000
9. GLACIAL LAKE AND RIVER TERRACE	42,788,000
10. GREAT BASIN	118,034,000
11. ROCKY MOUNTAIN	265,575,000
12. NORTHWEST INTERMOUNTAIN	75,984,000
13. PACIFIC COAST	109,180,000

In the first five regions listed are found most of the soil tracts of the South. In addition a comparatively wide belt of loessial soils parallels the eastern bank of the Mississippi, and Western Texas encroaches on the Great Plains and Arid Southwest regions.

The newer soil science restricts its classification to normally mature types. It seeks to make distinction, not on the basis of the

[9] Wolfanger, *loc. cit.,* p. 100.
[10] C. F. Marbut, H. H. Bennett, J. E. and M. H. Lapham, "Soils of the United States," *Bulletin 96,* Bureau of Soils, Washington, 1913, p. 8.

characteristics of the geological material from which the soil comes, but of the soil itself. Origin does not tell much of the agricultural properties of soil. For example, a residual soil formed from limestone does not necessarily contain any lime. The soils of the United States in this classification are divided into two major groups on the basis of whether or not they accumulate lime.[11] West of about the 100th parallel of longitude are found the Pedocals, soils which accumulate in the "B" horizon a higher percentage of lime than is found in their parent materials. Similarly the eastern area of the Pedalfers is characterized by a predominance of iron and alumina rather than lime in the subsoil. Except for the prairies which belong with the Pedalfers, the distinction is roughly that between semi-arid western grass lands and humid eastern forest lands. The Pedocals are much more fertile but lacking rainfall are not so tillable. The following soil areas are found in the United States. Here the great bulk of the South falls in the red-and yellowerths which range through eleven states. The South possesses that fraction of the gray-brownerths which make up the limestone basins of Virginia, Kentucky, and Tennessee. All the laterites may be found in Florida and South Georgia. The tall grass eastern sections of Oklahoma and Texas are prairyerths while their western areas are blackerths.

TABLE IV*

CLASSIFICATION OF SOILS OF THE UNITED STATES

PEDOCALS: The West	PEDALFERS: The East
1. Blackerths—Subhumid: heavy grass cover	1. Podsols—Cold-humid: coniferous forests
2. Brownerths—Subhumid: medium grass cover	2. Gray-Brownerths—Cool-humid: deciduous forests
3. Chestnuterths—Semiacid: light grass cover	3. Prairyerths—Subhumid: heavy grass
4. Grayerths—Desert: scant vegetation	4. Red-and-Yellowerths—Warm-humid mixed oak-pine forest
	5. Ferruginous Laterites—Hot-humid: equatorial forest

*See C. C. Huntington, F. A. Carlson, *Environmental Basis of Social Geography*, p. 307. Also L. A. Wolfanger, *The Major Soil Divisions of the United States*, pp. 18-33.

A valuable measure of the worth of southern soils may be taken by comparing them with others of the eastern group.[12] In terms of abundance of rainfall and length of growing season the Pedalfers rank in the following order:

[11] Louis A. Wolfanger, *The Major Soil Divisions of the United States*, p. 14 ff.
[12] *Ibid.*, p. 95.

1. Ferruginous laterites
2. Red-and-yellowerths
3-4. Gray-brownerths and Prairyerths
5. Podsols

Measures of soil favorability and economic utilization coincide. When account is taken of the soil's natural fertility, the perfection of its physical features, and the proportion under cultivation, the groups rank thus on each count:

1. Prairyerths
2. Gray-brownerths
3. Red-and-yellowerths
4. Ferruginous laterites
5. Podsols

It will be seen that when measured in terms of maturity under the influence of climate and vegetation the soils of the South are neither the best nor the worst in the country. Because of slope, topography, rainfall, and stream action many of the South's soils have been transported before maturity. It is necessary, accordingly, to consider factors of geological origin.

With the exception of highland and plateau areas, it is found, for example, that southern soils are not native to their homeland. In fact upwards of 90 per cent of the soils surveyed in the United States have been deposited in their present localities by moving water, moving ice, or moving air.[13] The materials of the Gulf and Coastal plain were originally laid down in the shallow water of the Atlantic Ocean by rivers. Their velocities varying with the slope, the rivers deposited coarse sands on sloping areas and fine silts on level places. The plateau and mountain regions have remained young as soils go, because erosion has removed soil covers before geological processes of disintegration were completed. The soils of the limestone valleys and uplands have been formed from limestone rather than crystalline rocks. Receiving material from the various soil provinces, the great rivers extending like fingers through the South have deposited fine, rich silts as valley filling to form the bottom lands of the Flood Plains region. The great variety of soils in the plains of the South is thus explained by J. Russell Smith as due to the varying velocities of the streams which deposited them.

[13] *Bulletin 96*, U. S. Bureau of Soils, p. 10.

The movements of the water that placed these deposits were sometimes swift carrying away everything but the coarser sand. In other
places the less swift current left finer sand; and in yet other places it
left clay or nearly pure clay. Sometimes there was deposited an abundance of shell, giving a high lime content, and again fossil beds (marl)
were formed. So rich in plant food were the marl beds that they were
quarried for fertilizer. In other places the lagoon behind the barrier
beach has been filled by a mixture of humus from river mud, animal
and plant remains, and sand from the barrier beach. This makes soil
of the finest kind. In many places, especially in the South, the sea
retreating across the plain left its legacy of ancient beaches, which makes
the surface very sandy. There are also areas of upland marshes, characteristic of level lands having abundant rainfall.[14]

Differences in methods of deposit followed by varying conditions of drainage, which account for different types of erosion, have
resulted in complicated mixtures of soil plaques on which have
been accumulated the effects of climate and the débris of vegetation.
Coastal Plains, Piedmont and Blue Ridge, alluvial strips, the Loess
Belt, and limestone basins and prairies furnish the bases of distinctive soil types in the South.[15]

The Coastal Plain is largely a region of mature soils, red-and-
yellowerths and laterites, with a large proportion of the soil pre-
vailingly sandy. The soils are leached of plant foods by constant
rains, and organic matter is oxidized before it can form humus in
the laterites which C. F. Marbut has called the end stage or death
stage of soils. Their texture, however, is surprisingly tractable to
tillage, and fertilization performs wonders on truck soils with long
growing seasons. Pine can grow on the sandy coastal flats because
shedding their needles only after several years they make no
great demands on fertility. Such slow shedding, however, in turn
builds up soils lacking humus—poor soils fit only for more pines
or wiregrass. The early settlers called these lands pine barrens.[16]

The lean ground of the Piedmont and Blue Ridge possesses
enough plant food to support a hardwood forest. The soils of the
Piedmont are reddish brown, chocolate brown, dark gray, light
gray, and whitish. They range in quality through good, bad, and
indifferent, the lowest grades being those formed from the wear

[14] *North America*, p. 139.
[15] U. B. Phillips, *Life and Labor in the Old South*, pp. 6-16.
[16] E. E. Huntington and F. E. Williams, *Business Geography*, p. 49.

of quartz rock with a little admixture of plant foods. Soils with such sandy bodies as characterize the Piedmont make good corn and pea land, and can be reclaimed for cotton by the addition of humus or fertilizer. To offset their disadvantages the Piedmont soils possess the merit of being cheaply cultivated as compared with sticky clay soils.

The alluvial strips and pockets of southern rivers possess soils of rich silt but are often water-logged. The make-up of alluvial lands with their loams and clays may be represented by the conditions found in the Yazoo Delta as presented by E. N. Lowe.[17] The loam lies in ridges five to six feet deep along the streams by which it was deposited by a process of over-slopping. The soils are deep, rich, quick, and easy to work. These loam belts, because they are elevated and dry, are preferred as building sites and frequently serve as levees. They are often found curving about in the alluvial plain, thus indicating where the streams once ran. Sometimes they enclose crescent-shaped lakes which rest in bends made by the now departed rivers.

Between the loam ridges where the surface has received less deposit are found the swamps and the clay soils. The popular term "buckshot lands" well characterizes the clay soils of the color of lead, which when wet feel like soft soap. If plowed wet the soil dries in bits like buckshot and looks extremely unpromising for agriculture, but as it dries the soil falls to pieces and becomes loose and light in texture. As a result of the combination of these two soils with a hot, moist climate, the Delta is burdened with animal and vegetable life. Somewhat related is the unique Loess Belt on the east bluff of the Mississippi from Memphis to Natchez. Here silt from the dried mudflats of the river has been deposited by west winds as a thin veneer on this portion of the coastal plain. The soil is rich but extremely liable to erosion.

Most fertile of all areas in the South are the limestone soils—limestone prairies in the coastal plains and limestone basins in the mountains. Limestone dissolves rather than disintegrates with rainfall leaving its phosphate impurities to enrich the soil and its parent material, the "C" horizon, to hold moisture like a sponge. Outstanding of these favored black lands are the Alabama Black

[17] "Mississippi: Its Geology, Geography, Soils, and Natural Resources," Miss. Geological Survey, Jackson, 1915, *Bulletin 12*, pp. 265-68.

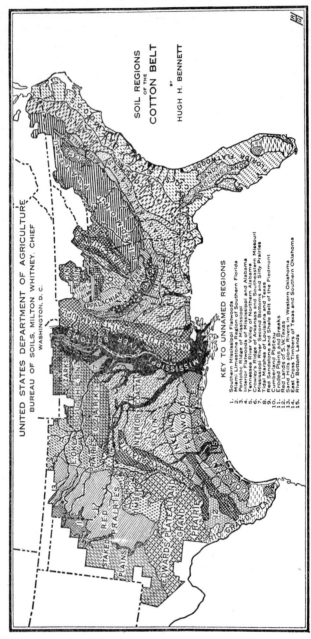

FIGURE 3.—Excepting in southern Florida, only cotton-growing counties of some importance are included. The most productive soils are the bottoms of the Mississippi and tributary rivers, the black prairies of Alabama, Mississippi, and Texas. Fertilizer makes the upper Coastal Plain and the Piedmont Plateau of Atlantic Coast States very productive. (Courtesy of U. S. Department of Agriculture).

Belt and the Texas Black Waxy, both notable in southern annals as producers of cotton and corn. Further northward, separated by long spurs of the Cumberland Plateau, lie the three great limestone basins, the Nashville Basin, the Kentucky Bluegrass, and the Great Valley of which the Shenandoah is a part. Here in rich soils diversified farming has reached its southern zenith. In grass, grain and dairying, fine horses, fine cattle and fine folks these regions excel. "A full century ago," Phillips remarks, "they were saying in the Bluegrass that Heaven could only be another Kentucky, and they are saying it yet."[18]

The South is fortunate in that its soils have been studied in more detail than those of other regions in the United States.[19] In his work on the soil regions of the Cotton Belt, Hugh H. Bennett has classified these regions still further. Differences in soil colors and native vegetation are very noticeable. Many of the names given these regions are applied locally and the change from one area to another can be noted by the casual traveler. For a rough index of the fertility of these subregions we may take the average yield of cotton per acre as worked out in the *Cotton Atlas* in the period before the advent of the boll weevil. Due allowance must be made, however, in the Southeast for the use of fertilizers.

ATLANTIC COASTAL PLAIN:

The Atlantic Coast Flatwood reaching in a narrow strip along the tidewater region of the Carolinas and Georgia with an elevation from 6 to 150 feet contains 21 million acres. Its soils are mainly dark and grayish sands and sandy loams underlain by mottled sand and clays. The native vegetation is the typical open forest of long leaf pine with undergrowth of gall bushes and grass. The yield of cotton has averaged with fertilization 200 pounds per acre, but a definite shift has been made in this area to tobacco and truck crops.

The Flatwoods of Florida and Southern Mississippi with 15 million acres belong to the same type. Their soils of dark grayish to white sands support long leaf pine with some palmetto undergrowth. Little cotton is grown and the area is definitely subtropic.

[18] *Life and Labor in the Old South,* pp. 12-13.
[19] Hilgard's *Report on Cotton Production,* Vols. V, VI, 1880 Census. H. H. Bennett, "Soils and Agriculture of the Southern States," Cotton Section of the *American Atlas of Agriculture.* O. E. Baker, "The South," *Economic Geography.* III, 50-86.

The Middle Coastal Plain in the Carolinas, Georgia, and Northern Florida ranges from 100 to 400 feet in elevation and comprises over 20 million acres of gently rolling land. Its grayish sandy loams over yellow sandy clay subsoils have an original covering of long leaf pine and wire grass. Cotton yields 205 pounds per acre due to fertilization.

The Upper Coastal Plain with over 28 million acres possesses an altitude of from 200 to 500 feet with rolling surface. Grayish to reddish sandy loams over sandy clays furnish the soils which are covered by long and short leaf pines with some oak and hickories. Cotton yields 190 pounds per acre.

The Sand Hills form a narrow belt of loose, deep, grayish sandy land in rolling hills. The region contains but three and a half millon acres with a native vegetation of long leaf pine and blackjack oaks. Cotton yields 180 pounds with extensive fertilization.

EASTERN UPLANDS AND HIGHLANDS:

The Piedmont Plateau which extends from New York to Alabama has over 26 million acres in the South. Its altitude ascends from 100 to 1500 feet giving the region a surface rolling and hilly. The soils are loams of red clay or grayish sand over clay subsoils. The vegetation is largely oak, short leaf pine and hickory. With the use of fertilizer cotton averages 180 pounds per acre.

The Blue Ridge Mountain Area ranges in elevation from 1000 to 6000 feet. The soils are grayish to reddish sandy and clayey loams with red clay subsoils. The native forests are of hardwood with some pine and undergrowth of rhododendron and mountain laurel.

The Cumberland Plateau through eastern Tennessee and northern Alabama has an elevation of 1000 to 3000 feet. The soils are grayish to yellowish sandy, silt and shale loams with yellowish subsoils. The prevailing trees are chestnut, oak, and yellow poplar.

The Southern Ozarks comprise 15 million acres in Arkansas of mostly rough land with steep stony slopes, ranging in altitude from 500 to 2900 feet. The soils are light brownish sandy and stony loams, and the vegetation is oak and hickory.

The Limestone Valleys and Uplands are parts of the Appalachian system underlain by limestone.

The Blue Grass Region of Kentucky, The Central Basin of Tennesee, and *The Appalachian Valley* which stretches from Pennsylvania to

Alabama are characterized by brown soils of silt loam and clay loam with reddish brown subsoils. Their altitudes vary from 500 to 3000 feet.

The Highland Rim of Tennessee belongs to the upland division with an altitude of around 1000 feet. Its soils are silt loam, gravelly and clay loams. About 50 million acres are found in the limestone valleys of the South.

GULF COASTAL PLAIN:

The Gulf Coastal Plains of Louisiana and Texas comprise a flat imperfectly drained area of low lying black, brown, and gray clays devoted mostly to rice, grazing, and corn.

The Interior Flatwoods reach from the Mississippi bottoms of Louisiana into Texas with 13 million acres at an elevation of 100 to 500 feet. Long leaf pine and post oak occupy soils, mainly of gray sandy loam, silt loams and clays with compact mottled subsoils. The surface is flat and poorly drained. Cotton yields 175 pounds.

The Interior Coastal Plain consists of about 29 million acres of rolling lands, mainly grayish, brownish or reddish sandy loams with long and short leaf pine in the east and oak and prairie grass in the western part. The production of cotton has been around 165 pounds.

The Mississippi Bluffs and Silt Loam Uplands form a long strip east of the great river of almost 17 million acres with an elevation of from 100 to 600 feet. The surface is level to undulating, badly gullied in places, and the soils, loessial in origin, are of brown silt loams on which grows a native vegetation of oak, sweet gum, and poplar. Cotton yields about 200 pounds.

The Clay Hills reach from western Georgia through Alabama and Mississippi containing 8 million acres. The surface is hilly and the subsoils are stiff clays. Cotton yields 145 pounds.

The Black Prairies extend in crescent shape from Alabama into northeast Mississippi containing 4 million acres at an elevation of 200 to 500 feet. The soils are dark gray and brown limey clays with greatly rolling surface. The land is rich but due to cultural factors the yield of cotton is as low as 150 pounds. The advent of the boll weevil has led to the abandonment of cotton in much of this area.

The Black Waxy Prairies of Texas contain over 13 million acres of flat to undulating lands of good drainage with soils of black limey clays. The elevation is from 100 to 600 feet. The cotton yield is about 175 pounds.

ALLUVIAL PLAINS:

Mississippi and other River Bottoms include the flood plains of the Mississippi from Missouri to the Gulf. Much of the area of 16 1-2 million acres with altitude of 0 to 300 feet and level surface is subject to overflow. The soils are brown or mottled clays, silt loams, and fine sandy loams with a vegetation of cypress, red gum, and oak. The Yazoo Delta with the highest yield of cotton in the South is one of the most fertile soils in the world. There are more alluvial soils in the South than in any other region in North America.

The Second Bottoms and Silty Prairies of the Mississippi, although laid down by the river, are now above overflow. The soils are brown and gray, silt and sandy loams with mottled subsoils.

WESTERN PRAIRIES AND PLAINS:

Eastern Oklahoma Prairies contain 11 million acres at an elevation of 800 to 1200 feet. The surface is gently rolling with soils of brown, black, and reddish loams, clays and stony loams with clay subsoils. The vegetation is prairie grass interspersed with post and blackjack oak and red cedar. The area yields something over 180 pounds of cotton to the acre.

The Red Prairies extending across western Oklahoma into north central Texas contain over 31 million acres. With an elevation of 1000 to 2000 feet, its surface is rolling with some eroded areas. Its soils, red and brown in color, are fine sandy loams, silt and clay loams with clay subsoils. Prairie grasses furnish the native vegetation.

The Staked Plains include all Texas to the west of the Red Prairies, an area of about 12 million acres. The elevation is 2500 to 4000 feet and the surface is level. Soils are mainly light brown to chocolate brown silty clays and sandy loam underlain with heavy subsoils. Grazing is giving way to cotton in this area.

The Edward Plateau and Grand Prairie extend from central Texas to the Rio Grande and have a combined area of almost 14 million acres. The surface is rolling to hilly and elevation from 1000 to 2000 feet. The soils, black, brown, gray and red are limey silt and clay loams supporting a vegetation of prairie and plain grasses with post oak and cedar.

HUMAN GEOGRAPHY OF SOILS

The above classification of soil areas in the South, the result of many patient labors by soil inspectors and analysts of the Bureau of Soils, will serve throughout this work as a basis for the consideration of the southern map in both its physical and cultural aspects. It will be of value in this chapter to glance at some of the ways in which different soil types have aided in influencing the distribution of human population and their modes of earning a living.

Given such soils it would not have been difficult for the geographer to predict their treatment at the hands of pioneer farmers, cotton and tobacco planters before the day of commercial fertilizers. The greatest influences of the southeastern areas on the historical development of the region have been exercised through the medium of soil exhaustion. Here is the force, neatly balanced against the call of fertile western lands, that caused the extension of both frontier and plantation. We have evidence especially from the ubiquitous pen of Olmsted that erosion and soil exhaustion prevailed to a large degree under the conditions of slavery. It is likely, as southern students have contended, that much waste of land was due to inefficiency of Negroes recently inducted into southern civilization. On the other hand soil exhaustion resulted from the organization of the plantation around one staple. Neither slavery nor the plantation *per se* forced soil exhaustion as much as did the type of crop culture, extensive and lacking adequate cover crops and animal husbandry. Expansion thus became the mode of escape, the planter migrated with his slaves or as in Virginia sold them down the river. "Exhausted" fields were turned out to become the prey of erosion.

The early history of land utilization in Virginia as shown in Avery O. Craven's excellent history reveals "(1) a steady cropping of lands in tobacco followed by Indian corn with ever lowering yields; (2) the general absence of meadows and stock with only here and there an exceptional farmer making use of manure to prolong the fertility of his lands; (3) and everywhere a tendency to abandon tobacco under the pressure of necessity in favor of wheat," whose yields rarely ran above ten bushels to the acre.[20] He traces the cycle thus:

Throughout the colonial period and afterward, agriculture was based upon a single crop produced by exploitive methods which caused yields to decline and lands to reach a condition in which the planters declared them "exhausted." Abandonment took place on a wide scale and the planters always accepted expansion as a matter of course. An

[20] *Soil Exhaustion in Virginia and Maryland*, p. 82.

agricultural life was developed which was based upon the exploitation of the soil's natural fertility. To the evil of a single crop was added insufficient plowing and shallow cultivation, which, on loose soils and rolling lands and under heavy concentrated rainfall, invited destructive erosion; a constant replanting of the same crop in the same soils rapidly depleted the available plant food materials and encouraged soil toxicity and the development of harmful soil organisms; and the failure to add organic matter or artificial fertilizers prevented recovery or even the checking of the work of destruction. Expansion was the only escape, and expansion from the small to the large unit and from the older to the newer regions became a normal part of life in the section; and when expansion became difficult, lowering standards of living, hardening of social lines, and conflict between the various agents in social, economic and political life developed.[21]

Craven has shown that this process of soil wastage was checked in Virginia even before the Civil War by the appearance of the small farmers, by diversified farming, and by intensive utilization of land as in trucking. Between 1830 and 1850 the planters of this area improved their methods and conserved their soils to such an extent that Craven feels that "in no section of the nation and in no period of its history were greater agricultural advances made or greater difficulties overcome."[22]

While the record has not been so thoroughly examined for the other states of the Southeast, Professor R. H. Taylor shows that by 1840 the opinion had become general in South Carolina that the system of agriculture was ruinous to the soil and the planters. Through every agricultural address delivered in the state between 1840 and 1860 runs the burden of soil exhaustion and its remedies. The gradual deterioration of the soil was laid at the door of shallow plowing, meagre use of manures, lack of rotation and of diversification of the plantation. "Tens of thousands of acres of once productive land are now reduced to the maximum of sterility" ran a typical complaint. Another predicted in 1850: "The period is fast approaching when no more forest lands can be cut down and put into cultivation and the choice must be made between improvement and migration."[23] North Carolina was not so much under

[21] *Ibid.*, p. 162.

[22] *Ibid.*

[23] See R. H. Taylor, "Commercial Fertilizers in South Carolina," *South Atlantic Quarterly*, (April, 1930), p. 178.

the domination of the plantation, being liberally sprinkled with Lutherans, Moravians, Quakers, and Scotch Presbyterians who with other yeomanry were devoted to small and self-sufficing farming. Portions of both North Carolina and Georgia must have gone through the cycle of soil exhaustion attendant upon cotton, however, if one is to judge by present-day consumption of commercial fertilizers.

It was finally commercial fertilization which came both to repair the ravages of soil exhaustion and to extend to further reaches its primary cause, the culture of cotton. The first Peruvian Guano was imported at Baltimore in the early 1840's whence its use spread to Virginia and the Carolinas. First mentioned in South Carolina in 1845, it was regarded mainly as a costly form of experimenting. From 1850 to 1860 sporadic experiments were tried and controversies about its use raged in the agricultural papers. The peak of its use was reached about 1865, after which phosphates, first secured from Baltimore, were, beginning in 1868, mined from native beds in the state. The output had increased from 20,000 tons in 1868-70 to 355,000 in 1883. By 1890 the use of commercial fertilizers had become general throughout South Carolina. In all the southeast it brought again under cultivation thousands of acres of worn-out lands and carried cotton culture to the very foot of the Blue Ridge. It accounted for a revival of agriculture in an area of exhausted soils and limited financial resources for improvement. Its results, Taylor points out, could be seen in the rise of trucking on the coast, in the abandonment of cultivation of alluvial lands where ditching costs more than fertilizers, and in increased specialization in cotton and tobacco.[24] Cover crops and the growing of food and food stuffs were further neglected so that by 1890 E. C. Brooks estimated that "very few of the southern states were growing as much food as in 1860."[25]

The extent of soil exhaustion under a one crop system is best shown by figures of fertilizer consumption. Germany, the United States, and France in 1928 used 56 per cent of the world's commercial fertilizer. It is significant that the country of virgin soils should be a close second to Germany, cropped before medieval days. When attention is turned to the areas of use, it is found that of

[24] *Ibid.*, pp. 183-89.
[25] *Story of Corn*, pp. 214-15.

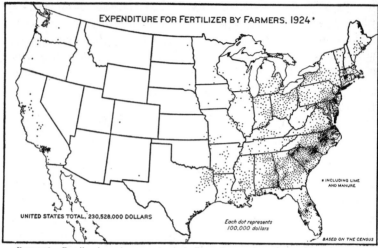

FIGURE 4.—Fertilizer is used at present principally on the more intensively cultivated crops, particularly cotton, tobacco, fruit, and truck, including potatoes, and almost wholly as yet in the Eastern and Southern States, where the rainfall is heavier and soils more leached. About half of the expenditure in 1924 was in the coastal plain and piedmont portions of Georgia, the Carolinas, and Virginia. Minor territories are the trucking districts of New Jersey and Long Island, the tobacco-onion district of the Connecticut Valley, the Aroostook potato district in Maine, and the fruit-trucking district in Southern California. Significant and prophetic is the considerable expenditure shown in Ohio and Indiana and even in Illinois, Iowa, and Minnesota. (Courtesy of U. S. Department of Agriculture).

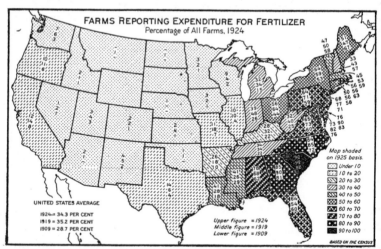

FIGURE 5.—Ninety per cent of the farmers in South Carolina bought fertilizer in 1924 and about 85 per cent in Georgia and North Carolina. In Delaware, Maryland, and Alabama about three-fourths of the farmers bought fertilizer; in Pennsylvania, New Jersey, Virginia, and Florida about two-thirds; in New England, New York, and Ohio about one-half; in Michigan, Indiana, West Virginia, Kentucky, Tennessee, Mississippi, and Louisiana one-third to two-fifths; in Wisconsin, Illinois, Missouri, and the Pacific Coast States about one-tenth. The use of commercial fertilizer is moving west, and although it is used mostly on intensively cultivated crops that have a high value per acre, its use on the general farm crops, even in the fertile Corn Belt, has proven profitable. (Courtesy of U. S. Department of Agriculture).

the 7,843,236 tons consumed in the United States in 1929, the thirteen southern states took 5,503,953 tons, comprising 70.2 per cent. North Carolina, using about a million and a third tons, leads the nation, followed by Georgia, South Carolina, Alabama, and Florida which altogether consume over half. The farmers of South Carolina, who account for one eighth of the country's consumption, spend for fertilizer each year approximately one fourth to one third of the value of the state's cotton crop, 20 to 25 million dollars.[26] The great variation in the amount of commercial fertilizer used in the South is due largely to the cycle of cotton prices. The soils of the newer southwestern areas are commonly thought free from this drain, but from 1919 to 1929 Texas increased her consumption fourfold, from 46,000 to 187,215 tons, mainly in the northeastern section bordering on Arkansas. The following table indicates the extent to which both production and consumption of commercial fertilizers centers in this area.

TABLE V

PRODUCTION AND CONSUMPTION OF FERTILIZER IN THE SOUTH, 1927

	No. of Establishments	Total Persons Engaged	Cost of Materials etc. in thousands of dollars	Value of Products in thousands of dollars	Consumption in tons as indicated by sale of tags		
					1925	1928	1929
Virginia..........	44	2,296	11,291	15,272	451,656	437,709	429,886
Kentucky.........	2	118	789*	1,120*	93,000	90,500	90,500
North Carolina....	84	2,212	14,027	18,423	1,217,822	1,349,360	1,293,573
Tennessee........	9	695	3,557	4,923	142,174	150,726	142,745
South Carolina....	49	1,823	9,405	11,739	873,255	788,293	760,053
Georgia..........	114	3,091	17,389	22,093	778,808	883,274	868,911
Florida..........	24	1,306	9,253	14,807	358,463	468,907	416,885
Alabama.........	55	1,273	7,818	9,497	598,115	681,100	675,150
Mississippi.......	11	360	2,017	2,792	258,028	333,350	327,806
Arkansas.........	5	128	754	910	123,387	126,391	156,582
Louisiana.........	11	594	3,013	4,142	110,784	143,693	174,278
Oklahoma........	...	.....	......	......	5,000	8,203	14,045
Texas............	6	98	555	811	101,008	144,643	192,133
Total South (Inc. Md.).....	461	16,921	99,795	133,702	3,111,500	5,606,149	4,934,547
Total the Nation..	621	22,711	138,142	190,304	7,311,063	7,883,521	7,843,236

*Includes one establishment each in Missouri and West Virginia.

Other soil influences may be pointed out. Archer B. Hulbert[27] has recently devoted a volume to the subject. From the ability of

[26] "The Fertilizer Problem in South Carolina," Clemson Agricultural College, *Circular 107*, p. 1.

[27] *Soil: Its Influence on American History.*

streams to lay down stratified deposits of alluvial soil and to coat the inland lagoons and river terraces with rich silt this historian sees important social results in the way of settlement and the planting of towns and cities. He has pointed out the rôle of stream and soil in the historic process of settling this country.

Excellent soils at all deltas had a direct bearing on making such spots choice land for the squatter or prospector. The bars in the main river added to the strategic character of the mouths of streams as sites of settlement. . . . The bars in the main stream decreased its depth and made fording safer. The main fords were located by the larger game animals at such points, and men, following their well-laid paths, found and used these fords. Frequently high water rendered the ford impassable, especially after vehicles came into use. Thus the ferry boat was needed, and the business of ferrying was a profitable one. Ownership of land at such points was, therefore, doubly advantageous, giving the owner a lucrative employment at odd hours. As vehicle travel became common, the ferry was usually moved to a part above the shifting bars, where there was a steady depth of water. Railways came later, following streams with monotonous regularity, and bridged streams on the site of the ancient ford. Hundreds of farms in these strategic locations became hamlets in the era of the stage and wagon and blossomed into cities on the advent of the railways. Beyond this interesting evolution we see its secret of the soil-transporting power of water.[28]

The importance of the quality of the soil to the student of society is well shown in the influence of soils derived from limestone upon the politics of Kentucky.

When, in 1861, it was to be determined whether Kentucky should go with the South or North, the question turned in the main on the occupations of the population. Where the soils were rich, the plantation system was possible, the slave element was large, and in general the voice of the people was for union with the South. Where the soils were thin, the people had no interest in slavery, for they owned no negroes. Old frictions with the slave-holding portions of the state existed, and consequently the people of this sterile land were generally devoted to the Union. A soil-map of Kentucky would in a rude way serve as a chart of the politics of the people in this crisis of the nation's history. If Kentucky possessed a soil altogether derived from lime-

[28] Archer B. Hulbert, "The Increasing Debt of History to Science." *Proceedings,* American Antiquarian Society, n. s., 29, pp. 29-43.

stone, there is no question but that it would have cast in its lot with the South.[29]

Before the boll weevil destroyed regional crop balances, distribution of races and types of agriculture could be shown to follow closely the pattern of soil belts. Ellen C. Semple made such an analysis of the Southeast on the basis of the Census of 1900. In Georgia, the rich alluvial soil of the swampy coast, given over to the production of rice and sea island cotton contained a population 60 per cent Negro. In the Flatwoods, a border zone of sandy pine barrens, the number of Negroes dropped to 20 or 30 per cent of the total. The Interior Coastal Plains, a rich area devoted to upland cotton, contained from 35 to 60 per cent Negroes. Alabama showed a similar distribution of soils and population from north to south over its level surface. In the deep calcareous soils of the Tennessee River Valley devoted to cereals, Negroes comprised 35 to 60 per cent of the inhabitants. The mineral belt covering the low Appalachian foothills contained the densest population of the state with less than 17 per cent Negroes. Further south the deep black loams of river bottoms and the crescent-shaped Black Prairie contained 60 per cent Negroes. Next the Coastal Flatwoods, sandy timber land, showed a decline in both quality of soils and proportion of Negro inhabitants.[30]

The extent to which fertile soils have attracted the plantation, cotton culture, and the Negro may be gleaned from the following figures bearing on eight soil regions in 1909. The census year 1909 has somewhat arbitrarily been taken as typical of the distribution of cotton culture before its disturbance by the spread of the boll weevil. Since these figures were compiled acreage has abandoned on the Eastern Belt with a greater concentration in the Delta and an extension to new areas in West Texas. In traits characteristic of the plantation and cotton culture it will be observed how consistently the Black Prairies and the Delta rank near the top and the Atlantic Flatwoods and Interior Coastal Plains may be found at the other extreme.

SOIL EROSION

Fertilization has saved the South from dire threat of soil exhaustion. The threat, however, remains in another form, soil erosion.

[29] N. S. Shaler, *Nature and Man in America*, p. 244.
[30] *Influences of Geographic Environment*, p. 48.

TABLE VI

STATISTICS OF COTTON CULTURE IN SELECTED COUNTIES OF EIGHT SOIL
REGIONS OF THE COTTON BELT IN 1909*

	Atlantic Coast Flat-Woods	Upper Coastal Plain	Sand Hills	Piedmont Plateau	Black Prairie of Alabama and Mississippi	Yazoo Mississippi Delta	Black Prairie of Texas	Interior Coastal Plain of Tex. and Louisiana
Number of counties selected..........	7	16	9	20	7	10	10	9
Per cent of land area in farms.........	47.4	65.7	62.2	84.3	68.9	52.6	86.1	62.0
Per cent of land area improved........	13.5	33.3	23.6	44.9	46.5	37.1	62.2	31.8
Per cent of land area in cotton.........	3.5	13.3	9.0	20.4	23.9	21.5	31.6	10.2
Per cent of land area in corn..........	4.3	9.6	6.8	10.0	8.2	6.5	14.5	8.5
Per cent of total farm land in "Plantations"....................	6.8	28.6	24.6	28.7	64.2	85.2	14.5	13.9
Per cent of total improved land in "Plantations"....................	2.5	16.4	9.3	15.3	45.1	56.6	10.6	7.8
Per cent of farms operated by:								
Negro tenants....................	23.3	44.8	31.5	40.8	78.7	86.1	9.5	24.3
Negro owners.....................	26.5	9.8	8.5	3.7	7.2	5.0	2.5	12.2
White tenants....................	13.7	16.7	24.0	28.9	5.2	5.1	55.7	25.9
White owners.....................	36.2	28.2	35.4	26.4	8.6	3.3	31.9	37.4
Acres per farm:								
Negro tenants....................	26.4	44.9	38.6	47.7	33.2	21.6	54.2	44.8
Negro owners.....................	49.6	82.5	86.7	79.1	75.7	59.3	67.8	94.3
White tenants....................	90.8	63.7	65.3	54.8	95.7	55.3	83.2	56.2
White owners.....................	195.4	159.5	156.5	107.3	196.0	223.4	124.9	133.6
Acres of improved land per farm:								
Negro tenants....................	19.2	35.7	28.1	31.7	29.0	21.0	49.0	35.4
Negro owners.....................	20.8	41.0	33.9	40.0	41.6	33.8	47.8	50.0
White tenants....................	29.6	40.2	30.9	31.9	56.6	34.0	66.9	35.4
White owners.....................	43.1	57.8	44.9	45.4	90.7	79.2	77.1	56.6
Farms reporting cotton, per cent of all farms:								
Negro tenants....................	83.6	89.5	90.0	91.8	91.6	76.6	87.3	82.9
Negro owners.....................	70.1	92.4	92.7	94.2	95.3	92.5	88.3	93.4
White tenants....................	71.0	83.0	83.5	89.1	77.3	70.0	88.3	71.3
White owners.....................	76.1	86.7	86.7	81.0	75.4	64.2	81.0	81.3
Work animals per farm (average of all tenures)........................	1.1	1.4	1.4	1.3	1.4	1.3	3.4	1.8
Acres per work animal:								
Cotton, corn, oats, wheat; total.....	16.3	22.9	18.9	19.8	18.5	14.5	15.7	15.0
Cotton............................	6.9	12.6	10.1	12.1	13.5	11.1	10.1	8.1
Corn.............................	8.5	9.1	7.6	5.9	4.6	3.4	4.6	6.7
Oats.............................	0.9	1.2	1.1	1.1	0.4	0.3	0.8	0.2
Acres of cotton per farm reporting:								
Negro tenants....................	9.6	20.5	17.1	20.2	20.6	17.2	36.7	20.3
Negro owners.....................	8.7	18.3	15.0	19.6	21.4	19.6	30.6	19.8
White tenants....................	11.0	19.3	14.8	16.9	24.7	21.4	41.2	16.7
White owners.....................	11.9	19.8	14.7	16.8	27.7	54.3	41.1	19.9

*Atlas of American Agriculture, Part V, Section A, "Cotton," pp. 12-13.

Of the rainfall on the soil, the greater part, after circulating through
plant organisms, returns to the air by evaporation, and about one

hird flows to the sea. It is this one third that changes the surface of the earth by means of erosion. Erosion involves the scouring of channels, the sapping and undermining of banks and strata, and the transportation and removal of soil materials in suspension and in solution. Other factors constant, the rate of erosion tends to vary in geometric ratio with the slope of the surface—the slope determining the swiftness of the stream.

In the state of nature a balance is reached between vegetation and land forms so that the soil cover is disturbed but slightly and slowly. Primitive agriculture often served only to stimulate the growth of the native arrangement of plants in local patches, leaving production to natural processes. In long settled areas an effective agriculture brings about changes in the natural balance existing between a soil and its covering. By the processes of plowing and cropping the mulch is dissipated, humus diminished, the soil grows harder, and after each rain there is more surface run-off and less water soaked into the subsoil. Crops substituted for native vegetation cover the soil imperfectly and for only part of the year; accordingly the soil is subject to evaporation directly rather than through the medium of young plants. Rain drops with their force unbroken by foliage sludge the soil into slime at its surface and pack down the soil beneath. The natural drainage is affected by the resulting channels cut in the surface, and the water level is lowered.[31]

It is perfectly true that the surface soils of all lands are moving slowly but surely down to the sea. The small particles, the last to be deposited, are the first to go. Normally under the cover of native vegetation this movement of soils is a slow process permitting the regeneration of soils from rock material almost equally as fast as it is carried away.[32] N. S. Shaler has estimated that a particle of mud which escapes from the Mississippi to the Gulf of Mexico is likely to have been more than five thousand years on the journey from its original site in the bed rock.[33]

The displacement of surface soils takes two forms, gully erosion and sheet erosion. Such movements of soil may be checked but they cannot be stopped. In gully erosion water runs off in streams,

[31] W. J. McGee, "Soil Erosion," U. S. D. A. Bureau of Soils, *Bulletin* 71, 1911, pp. 19-27.
[32] E. N. Lowe, Mississippi Geological Survey, *Bulletin* 42, p. 276.
[33] *The United States of America*, I, 378.

creating channels which grow deeper and wider, finally rendering the land nearly worthless. In sheet erosion the soil removal is nearly uniform, the flowing waters carry off particles from every part of the field. The process may continue until the development of incipient gullies, parallel to each other, known as shoestring gullies.[34] Sheet erosion "goes on wherever there is enough slope for rainwater to run down hill, even in desert countries where the precipitation is only three or four inches."[35]

The results of erosion are both physical and chemical. The development of gullies means ruin to the contour of the land. This is also accompanied by a deterioration in soil structure, since erosion, in removing the finer particles, leaves behind the skeleton of the soil, the fine gravel and heavier sands. The land between gullies drains too rapidly, and by lowering the water table for the good land renders it difficult for plants to obtain enough circulating soil water for proper growth. The chemical counterpart of erosion is leaching, the process whereby plant food, such as salts, is taken out in solution. Leaching goes on in all soils but the process is especially accelerated in regions of high rainfall as the tropics. Since leaching proceeds by percolation through the soil, sloping is not a necessary condition and erosion may not be present.

The baneful effects of erosion do not stop with the soils from which the cover is removed. The fertility of neighboring bottoms may be affected by deposits of sand in layers left by the flow of waters. Channels of rivers and waterways may be choked and diverted in their courses by silting. The rivers of the Southeast which now run thick with red clay mud were reported by earlier travelers as being peculiarly clear and limpid. Such have been the results of cultivation and the loss of forest cover. Erosion has assumed a new importance in the development of hydro-electric power. If water power development is to be permanent and coordinated, the great reservoir sites created by large dams should retain their capacity. As it is now, the life of a water power system is definitely limited by the number of years it will take the soil removed by erosion to fill up the reservoirs. There already

[34] R. O. E. Davis, "Soil Erosion in the South," U. S. D. A. *Bulletin* 180, p. 9.
[35] H. H. Bennett, "The Increased Cost of Soil Erosion," *The Annals* of the American Academy of Political and Social Science, CXLII, 172.

xist in the South "many reservoirs which have silted shut so that
nothing remains except the channels of the stream."[36]

The South is more susceptible to erosion than any other section
of the country. Erosion is favored by deforestation, slopes, shallow
soils, and heavy rainfall. The South possesses the highest annual
rainfall in the United States, averaging around 50 to 60 inches.
Grass and humus serve to protect the soil but southern crops such
as cotton and corn require that grass be weeded out. Iowa has
an annual rainfall of 30 inches, and during the winter her soils
are frozen impervious to rainfall. The southern climate is practically frostless and her denuded cotton and corn fields remain exposed to leaching and erosion the year around. Sloping surfaces
are found in the regions of the Piedmont, Appalachians, Ozarks,
limestone valleys, and clay hills. It is unsafe to cultivate over 18
per cent of the surface of the Appalachians. About 74 per cent of
the area is estimated to be forested and this is too small for the
preservation of slopes from erosion. Here three types of erosion
have been pointed out. On sodded "balds" overgrazing and tram-
pling by cattle have broken turf and started landslides that developed into gullies. On slopes where forests held the balance between
erosion and the accumulation of humus, timbering has removed
the protective covering and started the accelerating process of rain
wash. In the third place, slopes cleared for agriculture and now
abandoned have proved especially susceptible to caving and undercutting.[37]

Shallow soils are furnished by the thin veneer of upland loess
on the bluffs of the Mississippi. In this area, covering almost half
the width of Mississippi, special names have been given common
erosional features. A "break" is the head of a small retrogressive
ravine; a "gulf" is a large break with precipitous wall of great
depth and breadth; a "gut" is merely a road cut deepened by
storm wash and the effects of passing travel.[38]

In 1909 W. W. Ashe wrote, "there are in the dissected upland
areas of the South more than 500,000,000 cultivated acres all now
idle" because of soil exhaustion and erosion.[39] No less than

---

[36] W. W. Ashe, "Soil Erosion and Forest Cover in Relation to Water Power
in the Southeast," *Engineering World*, XXIII, 73.

[37] Isaiah Bowman, *Forest Physiography*, pp. 610-15.

[38] *Ibid.*, p. 524.

[39] "The Waste from Soil Erosion in the South," *Review of Reviews*, 39, p. 439.

50,000,000 tons of fertile earth are borne from upland farms by the rivers of the South each year. The Alabama River, he estimates carries three million tons of soil yearly to the sea; the Tennessee carries eleven million, and the Roanoke which carries four million discolors the waters of its sound for forty miles.[40]   Hugh H. Bennett, leading expert on erosion of the Bureau of Soils, has estimated "at least 513 million tons of suspended soil material and 270 tons of dissolved matter are carried out to tidewater every year. The Mississippi alone holds 428 million tons of this traffic in wastage."[41] Chemical analysis has enabled experts to estimate the amount of potential plant food contained in this erosional débris at 126 billion pounds or 21 times the yearly net loss removed by the crops. The value of the phosphorous, nitrogen, and potash removed in solution is approximately $2,000,000,000. The extent of erosion as shown by Bennett is startling. In one county in the southern Piedmont 90,000 acres of land once cultivated have been mapped as rough, gullied land unfitted for cultivation. In a southern coastal plain county 73,000 acres have been thus struck out on the map. In one Piedmont county it seems clear that a soil layer ranging from four to eighteen inches deep has been removed. North Carolina county agents estimate on an average only ten crops are secured from steep land from its clearing until abandonment of cultivation.[42]   The red plains of Oklahoma and Texas, practically a new region for farming, have become one of our most severely washed areas. Out of 17 million acres in the southern Brown Loam Belt, the Mississippi bluffs and loessial soils, eight millions have lost soil to a depth of four to twenty inches. J. Russell Smith is willing to assert that since 1880 erosion has destroyed an area of the Cotton Belt equal to that of Belgium.[43]

THE SOCIAL GEOGRAPHY OF EROSION

Hand in hand with physical factors of erosion go social factors that condition soil exhaustion. "Men may because of ignorance or habit ruin their soils, but more often economic or social conditions entirely outside their control lead or force them to a treatment of

[40] *Ibid.*, p. 441.

[41] "The Increased Cost of Erosion," *The Annals* of the American Academy of Political and Social Science, CXLII, 170-72.

[42] J. Russell Smith, *Tree Crops*, p. 4.

[43] *North America*, p. 253.

their land that can end only in ruin." Two such situations have been found in the South in the condition of the frontier and the plantation. The frontier finds its population too sparse to use its available land supply intensively. The standards of living of frontiersmen have been acquired in more highly developed regions. The domestic economy of the frontier proves insufficient to meet the needs and the new settlers are forced to the excessive cultivation of a staple that will furnish a surplus for exchange demanded by money economy. The production of this staple makes demands upon a sparse population that cannot be met by normal returns from the soil. Excessive distance from the market renders intensive agriculture unprofitable. Agricultural tools and technique are also likely to be crude and wasteful. All these factors point to one conclusion: the native fertility of the soil is forced to carry the load of the frontier. "The object has been," wrote a contemporary, "to cultivate as much land with as few hands as possible, to exhaust the soil and turn it common, and then to remove and pursue the same course again, upon new land."[44] As soon as a field grew unprofitable it was likely to be thrown out of cultivation and another area cleared. Left bare of native vegetation the abandoned fields become subject to erosion—the waste of land.

From the long time view of physical resources this was hopeless exploitation. From the viewpoint of the human factors such exploitation of soil resources was doubtless desirable. It hastened the development of the frontier into a densely populated more complex society. "The destruction of a little land amid such an abundance was a matter of small consequence compared to the rapidity with which wealth and luxury were replacing privation and simplicity."[45] By the use of no other resources could the frontier have developed cities and towns, laid out lines of transportation, and acquired the economic surplus necessary to foster education.

It is true, however, that even in the midst of the frontier environment certain national groups retained the cultural practices of old-world agriculture and thus protected their fields against erosions. This was true of the German farmers in the early settlement of the Ozark hillsides.

[44] John L. Williams' *The Territory of Florida*, 1837, quoted in Phillips, *Plantation and Frontier*, I. 131.
[45] A. O. Craven, *Soil Exhaustion in Virginia and Maryland*, p. 38.

Whereas the pioneer American farmer often ruined the river-hill farms in a little while, the German settlers built up the most valuable plantations. Much of the hill land was veneered with loess, but had been avoided by the Americans because of its uneven surface. The Germans, however, who were accustomed to careful farming on a small scale were able to cultivate the hill soil, so as to avoid erosion and were willing to expend upon it the additional labor which its topography required. Properly tilled the bluff lands yielded excellent regular returns.[46]

The abolition of slavery and the change to tenancy and the modern plantation has left the situation in the South much the same as regards erosion. The same staples are cultivated, but the remedy for soil exhaustion is fertilization rather than migration to new areas. A shifting tenancy with no permanent interest in the land does not find landowners with long-time plans for preventing erosion. There exists only one method of interesting tenants in the care of land rather than production of crops. That is to pay them extra for all work done in preserving land. The owner looks after both production and conservation; the transient tenant cares only for production.

REMEDIES FOR EROSION

Remedies for erosion are briefly four in number: terracing, intensive cultivation, an agriculture of grass, forestry and tree cropping. Terraces have been used in parts of the old southeastern states for 75 years. The sloping valleys of Virginia contain some of the best examples of terracing known. Says Dean I. O. Schaub of North Carolina State College: "If you go from Raleigh to New Orleans you can almost pick out the counties that have county agents by observing the localities where the fields are terraced. To me this is the most outstanding visible monument of the county agent in the South."[47] There are now over 494,000 acres terraced in Texas.[48] Closely akin to terracing is intensive cultivation by the hand and knee farmer working on plots and patches. It is by such method that the Chinese have retained their soil covering through long centuries. Both of these remedies are dependent upon densely crowded populations and high land values. J. Russell Smith quotes a southerner as saying that it would be a boon to

[46] Carl Sauer, *Geography of the Ozark Highlands,* p. 169.
[47] *Fertilizer Review,* February 1929, p. 8.
[48] H. H. Bennett, *loc cit.,* p. 175.

the nation if land could become worth one hundred dollars an acre, so that people could not afford to destroy it and then move on and buy more for ten, twenty or thirty dollars an acre, to be in its turn destroyed.[49] Intensive cultivation, of course, conserves land at the expense of labor and men. The present agricultural surplus will, it seems likely, operate to further land abandonment rather than land conservation on all except the special purpose soils. Saving soil by means of grassy meadows seems at first sight an extensive use of lands. This is true, for a greater area is required with less cultivation. At the same time, however, the marketing of products of a meadow agriculture, milk, cream, and butter fat, is correlated with a density of population in urban centers. Accordingly an agriculture with grass and humus as a means of soil conservation in the South waits on the growth of dairying to become profitable.

There remains one other remedy applicable to the present situation, forestry and tree cropping. In the Appalachians and the Ozarks the South has thousands of sloping acres in meadow or under the plow that are slowly washing away. In a recent book on *Tree Crops,* J. Russell Smith after ransacking the agricultural experience of many climes urges the permanent planting of such slopes to nut and fruit trees. A new use of so large an area would demand changes in habits of consumption of a large part of the American public. To plant denuded and eroded areas to forests would demand no such changes, since the United States is now replanting only one fourth as much timber area as it clears for consumption each year. In the South it is observed that old field pine has a tendency to take possession of worn-out fields. Because of its much more rapid growth in the South these pines soon furnish a canopy of foliage and a mat of needles to break the force of rainfall. With the aid of Bermuda grass and wild honeysuckle the spread of roots may finally block gullies and stop washing. This, however, is a rather haphazard method of leaving the rebuilding of soils to nature. With the process of land abandonment going on as at present much of the poorer land has reverted to the state for taxes. The state by holding this land off the market may thus form the nucleus of a state forest reserve. The adoption of

[49] *North America,* p. 254.

such measures as a state policy would go far toward arriving at a solution of the dual problems of soil wastage and deforestation.

The soils of the South, it may be said in conclusion, do not rank in fertility with the blackerths and the prairyerths of say, the Corn Belt. Few soils do. On the other hand the native fertility of the Alabama Black Belt, the Texas Black Waxy, the limestone valleys and basins of Tennessee, Virginia and Kentucky, and the alluvial soils of the Mississippi system have seldom been excelled. In terms of the soil cycle it may be said that the soils of the highland areas because of removal by erosion have never reached maturity while the leached soils of the flatwoods have already passed into that stage. Many of these leached sandy soils have, however, the advantage of good physical constitution; they are tractable and take fertilization easily. The South possesses more plentiful rainfall and a longer growing season while the West has more fertile soil. It has been said that the South's advantage is permanent while the West's is temporary. This overlooks the fact that the prairie lands by an agriculture of meadows and livestock may have their fertility replenished, while clean cropping and heavy rainfall may further deplete southern soils. The soils of the eastern South have been cropped longer than any other section of equal size in the United States. Some of their areas have been passed through a cycle of soil exhaustion and have been saved from its dire threat only by the advent of commercial fertilizers. They now use more fertilizer than the rest of the nation, a fact which has begun to tell in favor of western areas in differential costs of cotton production.

CHAPTER VI

THE PINEY WOODS

THE PINEY WOODS of the southern states furnish a native plant complex, distinctive and far-reaching in the social adjustments it has occasioned. The ways in which men have ordered their lives in relation to the forests among which they have lived have furnished an interesting theme for geographers of all countries. Nowhere has the forest experience of a society been more enlightening than that of the settlers of the South as they cleared the land for pioneer farms, bled the pines for turpentine, distilled pine wood for naval stores, recklessly logged off the softwoods for timber, and finally came face to face with the problem of lumber shortage and unwanted cut-over lands. Obvious to the native, enigmatic to the outsider, difficult of depiction by the human geographer, the piney woods possess a life and language of their own.

The great Atlantic forests of North America, divided from the Pacific forests by a central area of prairie grasses and desert shrubs as though by a vast body of water, originally contained one million square miles of trees in unbroken array. After over one hundred and fifty years of settlement there remained in 1923 not more than 260,000 square miles of merchantable forest. Over 500,-000 square miles have been cleared for settlement and the remainder has been shorn of its timber, devastated by fire, and grown up in brushwood. The southern states, it is estimated, have left 90,000 square miles of coniferous forests. The southern forest region is characterized by four extended biotic communities. Least in importance is the subtropic forest of mangrove found mainly in coastal Florida of the Everglades, Louisiana of the Delta, and Texas of the Rio Grande. Along the southern rivers stretch the second group, the bottoms and bayou forests of mixed cypress, tupelo, and red gum. Third and more important in commerce is the more extended area of the southern hardwood forests. The oak, hickory

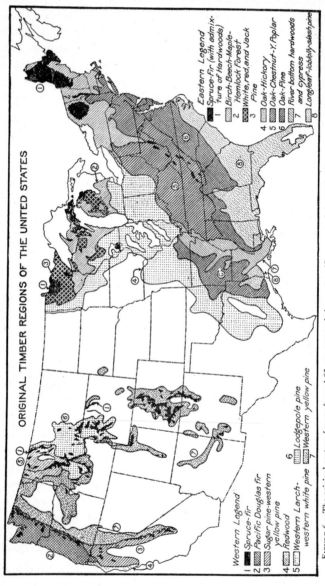

FIGURE 6.—The original eastern forests formed 83 per cent and the western 17 per cent of the total. Of our present forest land the East has 75 per cent and the West 25 per cent. But the West now has 61 per cent of the remaining saw timber supply. (Courtesy of the U. S. Department of Agriculture).

forests are found in the Ozarks and in parallel strips in central Texas. The major oak, short-leaf pine forest follows the Piedmont from New Jersey to Georgia with strips through northern Alabama, slanting southwestward through Mississippi. The oak, chestnut, yellow poplar forest group, in so far as it touches the South, comprises almost the whole of Kentucky and Tennessee with strips in northern Mississippi and Alabama.[1]

Fourth, the southeastern pine forest, largest and most important forestry area, covers the wide strip of the coastal plain from Virginia to beyond the Mississippi River. The chief of the United States Forestry Service has said:

The virgin pineries of the South covered 130 million acres and contained probably 650 billion board feet of saw timber. They formed one of the richest reservoirs of softwoods on the earth's surface and for the past thirty years they have been the mainstay of the eastern and central lumber markets of the United States. The production of southern timber passed its peak in 1916 and the last great migration of American sawmills is under way across the Great Plains to the virgin forests of the Pacific Coast.[2]

The southern pine forest untouched by human hand offered one of the most beautiful spectacles of nature. "A drive through the virgin long-leaf pine forest," wrote F. V. Emerson, "will be long remembered. The stately trunks rise forty to sixty feet and then spread out their dense foliage which joins above like the arches of a cathedral. There is little or no undergrowth, and the view fades into a maze of the column-like tree trunks."[3] To stand amid the still whispering of an illimitable forest of long leaf pine as twilight fades into dusk is to encounter in imagination the pioneer's thrill of fear in his forest experience with panthers and Indians. And apart from memories the piney woods possess a grandeur all their own.

While at least ten species of pine are found in the belt but four are of importance; short-leaf, long-leaf, loblolly, and slash pine. Short-leaf and loblolly pine grow farther inland extending through the Piedmont up to the hills. Long-leaf and slash pine hug the

[1] "Natural Vegetation," *American Atlas of Agriculture*, pp. 3, 11; map, pp. 4-5.
[2] W. B. Greely, "Relation of Geography to Timber Supply," *Economic Geography*, I, 7.
[3] "Southern Long Leaf Pine Belt" *Geographical Review*, VII, 81.

low coastal plain. It is they whose exuding oils and gums form the basis of the naval stores industry. Long-leaf grows in deepest sandy soils and withstands fire to an uncommon degree. In the relatively infertile sands of the "pine barrens" it excels all other trees in its ability to grow because of a long, stout tap root. Its scant foliage indicates to the lumberman a large heart with small waste from branches. It is valuable because of its great strength proved under pressure and strain of all kinds; moreover, owing to the resinous matter which permeates its fibers, the long-leaf is extremely durable. The virgin forests of slash pine were confined originally to poorly drained flat lands and the borders of swamps, but, with the cutting of the forests, slash pine is observed by students of ecology to be spreading inland over the southern map. It, however, does not grow on the soils of dry deep sandy ridges, the typical "pine barren hills." It furnishes the heaviest, hardest, strongest wood of all the commercial conifers in the United States. Loblolly pine, a tree of the lowlands, follows the coastal plain and river courses. It grows well on land too poor for other crops, and furnishes the most prolific seed producer among pines, bearing a full crop about every third year. Because it grows faster than either short or long-leaf pine, it furnishes the bulk of second growth timber and has been given the name of "old field pine." Short-leaf pine is the tree of the uplands with a preference for clay soils. It furnishes a large though not a tall tree and possesses a large proportion of sap wood.

Hints at the fertility of the soils underlying southern forest communities are furnished in some observations made by E. W. Hilgard.[4] If cotton is grown continuously on long-leaf pine areas the early settlers observed that the yield decreased over a half from the first year to the third. Where short-leaf pine is found intermingled with long-leaf production held out from five to seven years. On soils supporting hickory intermingled with oak steady crops could be grown as long as twelve years.

Regardless of the uses to which the southern timber belt has been put one is compelled to agree with John M. Hager that "its soil, climate, labor supply, transportation facilities and general economic position place it among the best regions of the world for the development of both hardwood and softwood timber

[4] *Soils*, p. 314.

growing."[5] The pine, one of the fastest growing species known, there meets ideal conditions for rapid growth. Heavy rainfall and long, warm summers with a minimum of cloudy days furnish nature's laboratory for making trees. Measurements by the United States Forestry Service show that while in a period of seventy years red spruce in Maine grew to a diameter of 1.8 inches, hemlock in New York to 3.3 inches, loblolly pine in Texas reached 24.0 inches. One lumber company in Texas has been able to cut its pines every five years, if it keeps down fires and takes no trees under 15 inches.[6] For example, no eastern species of conifer equals the slash pine in its rate of early upward growth. In its first year's growth it reaches as high as eight to twelve inches; by the fifth year it will be from six to ten feet high; and from its fifth to eighteenth year it grows two or three feet yearly. After twenty years its rate of upward growth slackens perceptibly.[7] Loblolly pine grows faster than either short or long-leaf. For the first twenty years its growth is slower than slash pine, but in the period from twenty to sixty its growth is not exceeded by any tree in the South. The best specimens grow as high as 170 feet with diameters of 65 to 70 inches. Its growth in diameter is also good, as witness the record of one tree that grew 12 inches in diameter in as many years.[8]

Up to certain density pines exhibit the desirable quality of growing better in thick stands. Indeed, pines grown in open space develop into what is known as bush or "bull pines," running to large branches reaching nearly to the ground. Grown under proper conditions of density the pines reach up in a slim, straight trunk of a diameter practically uniform until it branches near the very top.

PIONEERS AND THE FORESTS

Human settlement may be regarded as advancing upon the southern forest in a series of frontiers. As each frontier advanced, the forest gave way to the approach of man in another form of exploitation. First came the pioneers with the task of clearing the

[5] *Commercial Survey of the Southeast,* Domestic Commerce Series 19, p. 76.

[6] J. Russell Smith, *North America,* pp. 267-68.

[7] W. A. Matoon, "Slash Pine Primer," U. S. D. A. *Farmer's Bulletin* 1256, 1922, p. 8.

[8] W. A. Matoon, "Loblolly Pine Primer," U. S. D. A. *Farmer's Bulletin* 1517, pp. 3, 4.

ground for cultivation. For them land was the goal and the earth's unwanted garment of timber the wasted by-product. Next in the pineries developed the naval stores industry with resin and turpentine as end products and trees again the by-products. Low density of population conspired with increasing scarcity of timber to change this frontier to one of exploitation of yellow pine leaving the cut-over lands as a wasted by-product. The fourth frontier appears when these abandoned wastes are used for free range for grazing stock of the region. The process ends with timber shortage and the South is brought face to face with the next stage in prospect—agriculture or reforestation.

The early records of timber utilization in the South are either lacking or so confused that the best evidence is to be found in the forests themselves. The experience of the pioneer with the forest gives the clue to much of the country's later policies. The first act of man in claiming an area for cultivation is to remove the forest cover and so destroy the factor which throughout the ages has been most potent in enriching the soil. The pioneer regarded the forest as a goal to be reached because to him forested land meant fertile land, but the trees he regarded as an enemy to be destroyed because they retarded civilization.

Everywhere the pioneer sought the forest though he could not tolerate it; hailed it with delight only to destroy it; and accepted of its shelter and its generous bounties only to repay it with the axe and the grub hoe. In many cases the settlers crossed fertile prairies that they might locate upon less fertile forest lands. If his demands for the products of the forest did not keep pace with the amount removed to make way for agricultural purposes, the surplus was destroyed by fire. In the central valleys the pioneer sought the forest because he found there the building material for the construction of his rude palace, the log hut, which was the result of his first effort to build a home; he found there the fuel with which he might prepare his meals and temper the biting cold of the dreary winters; he found bubbling springs and sparkling streams, which furnished necessary water; he found abundant game for his table, which was more easily secured under cover of the forest; and finally he brought with him from the East the conviction that only forest lands were fertile. He failed to observe that the forest grew on the poorest land, on the clay and gravelly hills of loess and drift and on the sandy-bottom lands, that the rich surface soil of the forest was a product of the forest itself and constituted a veneer which was swept away from both hillside and

ttom-land by the first freshets which followed the clearing of the
rest, and that on the other hand the prairies teemed with plant life
milar to that upon which he depended for his crops, the prairie
asses being closely related to his cereals in both structure and habit.

hese were the first reasons which prompted the pioneer to settle in the
rest; but there were soon added two others. One was the fury of the
airie fires which periodically swept the great plains and he congratu-
:ed himself that he enjoyed the cover of the forest. Again he felt his
ter helplessness before the terror of the swirling, blinding blizzard
om which the forest protected him.[9]

he Black Prairie of Alabama, for example, was not settled before
30.[10]

Before the pioneer the Indian had already by the use of fire
ade large clearings in the eastern forests for patches of corn.
or the colonists, faced with the sheer overwhelming luxuriance
 vegetation, these clearings were greatly to be desired and many
ere the raids and forays carried on over their possession. The
oneer's first advance upon the forest partook of the same checker-
ard arrangement of alternating clearings and forests. A rude
rden, fields of a few acres situated in a circle of girdled and
:adened trees, reclaimed the squatter's human establishment from
e forest. Further south in his "cowpens" the family of the fron-
:ersman lived upon the range and the hunting in the shadow of
e wilderness. Backwoods settlements in the pine barrens of
outh Georgia were thus described in 1831:

he people were poor, unenterprising, and unenlightened, but contented
 their lowly circumstances. The pine woods stretched for scores of
iles unbroken save by an occasional corn or cotton patch. The wire
ass beneath the pines, and here and there a few wild oats furnished
stenance for ill-kept cattle. Few wagon roads existed, but bridle paths
d from cabin to cabin. The State of North Carolina was dubbed the
ip Van Winkle of the South, but Emmanuel and Tatnall counties
d their neighborhood in Georgia could easily surpass any other section
 sleeping ability. The people did not struggle against the enervating
fluence of their climate and surroundings. Without ambition or stim-
us of any kind the life history of each generation was a repetition of
at of the preceding one.[11]

[9] Bohumil Shemik, "The Pioneer and the Forest," *Proceedings,* Miss. Valley
st. Assn., III, 97, 98.

[10] T. P. Abernathy, *The Formative Period in Alabama History,* p. 37, 41.

[11] U. B. Phillips, "Georgia and States Rights," Am. Hist. Assn. *Reports,* II,
01, p. 141.

If the methods of the pioneer were wasteful he might be pa
doned. There existed, it must be remembered, no direct co
sumption of timber but the consumption of land, the desired ne
grounds. The forest was limitless and grew too rapidly. Su
direct consumption of timber as occurred was directed to the be
species and most desirable trees for the use of private shipbuilde
and the British and American navy. The extent to which su
culling of the woods proceeded must have been small compar
to the timber triumphantly given to the flames in the log-rollir
bees of the frontier. For on the frontier the use of fire and tl
axe to open clearings and dispose of their débris was not regardo
as waste but as victory over an encroaching enemy.

Trees grew rapidly and when cultivated lands were abandoned tl
forest returned again after a few years. Travellers passing through wh
appeared to be virgin forests were often surprised to discover the sca
of former cultivation and to learn that they were crossing what son
twenty years earlier was a tobacco field. Such conditions added mu
to the problem of labor but afforded some compensation in the for
of protection to neglected soils against washing and in the addition
organic materials in the form of falling leaves.[12]

Furthermore, the least that can be said is that the pioneer
first experience with forest conservation was unfortunate. Tl
English crown had reserved much of the best timber for the roy
navy and the Federal Government was to continue this polic
In 1799 the first Federal law was passed regarding timber for tl
navy. Live oak and cedar trees were to be reserved for nav
timbers at the discretion of the president in 1817. Further enac
ments were passed in 1822, 1827, 1828, and 1831. In all abo
200,000 acres were covered by these laws while the act of 1831 in
posed heavy fines for cutting timber reserved for the navy. The
acts served to irritate the pioneers. The laws showed ignoran
of the great extent of the forest reserves and they deprived mar
settlers of their legitimate timber resources. Accordingly, tl
prohibitions and their penalties came to be universally disregarde
on the frontier.[13]

---

[12] A. O. Craven, *Soil Exhaustion as a Factor in the Agricultural History of Vi
ginia and Maryland,* 1806-1860, p. 27.

[13] Gifford Pinchot in *The South in the Building of the Nation,* V, 259.

Turpentining the Piney Woods

Exploitation of the piney woods began as an industry of the
ontier. Wooden vessels and sailing ships found great need for
e pitch and tar, and the traditional name of naval stores by
ich the industry became known has never been lost. Naval
ores comprised the first industry to be developed in the south-
st, pitch and tar being staple since before 1700. The first men-
n of turpentining is found in a manuscript in the Public Rec-
d Office, London, dated 1610: "Instruction for Suche Things as
e to be Sente from Virginia."

ne trees or ffirre trees are to be wounded wth in a yarde of the
ounde, or boare a hoal with an ogar the thirde pte into the tree, and
t it runne into anye thinge that may receyve the same, and that which
sues oute wilbe Turpentyne worthe 18 L Tonne. When the tree
ginneth to runne softelye yt is to be stopped up agayne for p^{re}servinge
e tree.[14]

The demands of her shipping and the deficiency of all other
untries in these raw materials early secured the interest of Eng-
nd in the colonies of the South as an independent source of the
val stores, produced by dry distillation of wood. They were
cond only to tobacco as exports of the colonies of Virginia and
aryland with Norfolk as the chief shipping point. In 1700 they
rnished the chief exports of both North and South Carolina, the
tter shipping 60,000 barrels a year. The utilization of trees was
rried on mainly along navigable streams and inlets. Just before
e Revolutionary War the exports reached the total of 200,000
rrels of turpentine, pitch, and tar with an estimated value of
25,000 in present currency. Up until 1820 the use of turpentine
d rosin was limited to the demands of domestic industry. In
34 the copper still was perfected and the industry advanced
uth of the Cape Fear River. Rectified spirits of turpentine in
42 came into general use as an illuminant and led to the over-
oduction of rosin as a by-product. Perfection in technical meth-
ls was followed by the transfer of the still from the place of
ipment to the forest. The British Free Trade Act of 1846 greatly
imulated production until the Civil War served to depress the

[14] Cited in A. W. Schorger and H. S. Betts, "The Naval Stores Industry," U. S.
. A. *Bulletin* 229, p. 2.

industry.[15] The advantageous position, however, which souther
naval stores secured in the world markets during colonial day
has been retained up to the present. It is threatened today no
by competitors but by its vanishing virgin stands and its ow
crude techniques.

It was not until the turn of the century that the operators i
turpentine orcharding faced an adequate realization of the limi
set by nature to the supply of virgin timber. "Up to the middl
nineties the large supply of yellow pine stumpage, the prejudic
against lumber cut from turpentine trees, and the lack of ad
equate transportation facilities in many regions where turpen
tine operations were conducted caused large bodies of turpen
tine timber to be abandoned and left to be destroyed by fire, wind
and decay."[16] In each of the six large pine states such losses ra
from three to ten billion board feet of lumber. "There is n
more deplorable sight to the man who has a sense of the value o
trees than the abandoned turpentine orchard—a grim array o
mutilated trunks, scorched and charred where the box is made
broken by the wind, infested by insects, and worthless except t
illustrate the futility of killing the goose that laid the golden egg
The South is full of such pictures."[17]

The fundamental forces and processes of nature everywher
underlie and condition the adjustments of society. Necessary to
an understanding of life in the shifting pine belt is a comprehen
sion of the biological processes of the pine tree. Long-leaf and
slash pine are peculiar among trees in that during the transforma
tion of their food materials such as starch into woody tissue there
is formed a by-product known as resin. Contrary to popular be
lief resin is not the sap nor "life blood" of the pine tree. It i
stored in a system of ducts beneath the bark, and cutting the bark
serves to increase the number of ducts and stimulates the flow
of resin. The formation of resin accompanies the rising of the
sap, beginning about March and continuing until October or No
vember.[18]

The method of obtaining turpentine from standing pine re
mained traditional and unchanged from colonial until com

[15] Gifford Pinchot, "The Naval Stores Industry," U. S. D. A. *Bulletin* 229, p. 3
[16] *Idem.*
[17] O. W. Price, "Saving Our Southern Forests," *World's Work*, V, 3214.
[18] U. S. D. A., *Bulletin* 229, pp. 10, 17.

aratively recent times. The method of chipping the bark and
utting the "boxes," deep holes at the base, described by "an old
and in the business" for *DeBow's Review* held good for two hun-
red years.

ox the tree after the sap is gone down and stop before it rises; there-
ore it will require more hands to box than it will to work the trees.
A good hand will cut from 50 to 60 quart-boxes a day; some expert
xemen in practice, may cut 100, but it is very seldom such hands are
o be found. Care should be taken to cut the box on the straight side
f the tree. Some trees will contain from 1 to 4 boxes, owing to the
ze of it [*sic*]. Care should be taken to leave from 4 to 6 six inches of sap
nd bark between faces, so as to preserve the life of the tree. Cut the box
rom 4 to 4½ inches deep, about 8 inches wide. Go down the stump
o the tree so as to cut the heart as little as possible. Clean out the
hips and bark from the boxes that your turpentine may be free of
hem. The next work, after the box is cut, is to gauge or corner, by
. few chops, commencing in the edge of the box, running up the tree
videning it at the same time, so as to make a channel for the turpen-
ine to run into the boxes. If the face is nearly a foot wide, say from
en to eleven inches, then your boxes, or at least a part of them, will fill
quickly, and you should have your barrels ready so as to dip as fast
as the boxes fill. The next work, after the cornering is done, is to be
done with a hatchet made for the purpose; then comes the round shave.
Never go into a tree more than 2½ or 3 grains of the wood, and that
should be repeated every eight or nine days, never going up the tree
more than one-eighth of an inch at a chipping, that is with the round
shave, the only object is to keep the old cut fresh, you may go over
every seven days as many persons do. A hand can chip over his task
in five days, some will in less time. Twenty-five hundred is a task
for a good hand, then he has two days to dip; if his trees run well
and are thick, he can dip three barrels a day, if not, from two to two
and a half. The timber for barrels should be got in the winter, staves
32 inches long, the heading wide, so as to make, when round, 17½
inches across; a common cooper will make from four to six good barrels
a day. An average to the hand is two hundred barrels per year which
varies in price from $2.50 to $4.00 per barrel, as prices current will
show.[19]

The boxes are filled with gum every three or four weeks and
are dipped about seven times a season. A portion of the gum loses

[19] J. D. B. DeBow's *Resources of the Southern States*, III, 252.

about half its turpentine by evaporation and hardens on the face
It is called "scrape" from the method by which it is removed.

The one marked change from ante bellum methods has been
in the gradual replacement of boxing by a system of cups and
gutters for catching the gum. The box made a crude receptacl
open to chips, bugs, and dust which lowered the grade of th
gum. The box itself was a permanent wound to the tree which
left it liable to windfalls and invited fire by leaving a surface cov
ered with gum and unprotected by bark close to the inflammabl
wire grass. It also left the tree unprotected against insect pest
and threatening parasites. Moreover, the fact that cups can b
placed higher up the tree leaves less scrape. An experiment with
cups after the French methods by M. A. Pudgin at Monck'
Corner, South Carolina, was abandoned in 1868. W. W. Ashe in
1894 also tried out this method at Bladenboro, North Carolina
It is, however, to the untiring efforts of Dr. Charles H. Herty o
the United States Forest Service that the adoption of cupping
in turpentine is due.[20] His problem was to find a substitute fo
boxing "that would be simple enough to be used by Negro laborers
cheap enough to command the attention of operators and renters
and efficient enough to secure a maximum flow of resin." Herty
became one of the experts of the Bureau of Forestry under Gifford
Pinchot and proved the efficiency of the new methods by an ex
tensive experiment on a tract of pine land near Ocilla, Georgia
He also showed that trees when chipped lightly yielded more tur
pentine of good quality and left the tree in better condition for
lumbering. Gradually the improved technology won its way
with intelligent turpentine men, and the Negroes under capable
direction lost some of their contempt for the gutters and "flower
pots" hung on pegs. Pottery plants have gone into the manufac
ture of cups for the trade. Tin boxes have lately replaced many
of the flower pots. The system has offered the one hope of re
viving an industry that seemed destined to pass and it has already
added millions of dollars annual value to the turpentine industry

The southern pine belt now produces over 70 per cent of the
total world supply of naval stores, representing an invested capital
of over $50,000,000.

[20] "The Turpentine Industry in the Southern States," *Journal of the Franklin Institute*, March 1916; Edwin Mims, *The Advancing South*, pp. 87-92.

eorgia and Florida now predominate and account for about 50 per
nt of the world production, with their respective products for the
op year, April 1, 1925, to March 31, 1926, valued at $17,966,970 and
4,110,363. The value of Alabama's output was $3,180,064, which
mpares with $4,010,022 for Mississippi and $2,078,968 for Louisiana,
e other principal producing States. For the first three States the aver-
ge number of wage earners were, respectively, 12,961, 10,890, and
166; and total wages were $6,371,616, $5,864,038, and $1,145,788.[21]

For certain areas naval stores offer the main source of income.
ltogether pine chemicals furnish raw material going into a great
umber of industries such as paints, soaps, greases, belt dressing,
oofing, etc. The demand has possibilities of wide expansion at
1e hands of scientific research were there any guarantee of in-
reasing the supply of pine products.

Naval stores furnish an industry with a routine of labor, lan-
uage, and a life distinctly individual and picturesque. The hu-
1an factors in turpentining are most influenced by the fact that
1e industry has proved to be a migrating one. Turpentining has
1oved across the map as a kind of industrial frontier preceding
umbering. The process is called in expressive southeastern phrase
turpentining ahead of the cut," and consists of bleeding the trees
o the limit from two to four years before felling them for lumber.
n 1849, for example, North Carolina produced 91 per cent of the
1aval stores; in 1879 the lead went to South Carolina; from 1889
o 1899 it fell to Georgia; in 1909 and 1919 it was taken by Florida,
1nd North Carolina produced only one half of one per cent of
he crop in that last year.

Secretary Meredith in 1920 in a report to the Senate called at-
ention to these facts:

The naval stores industry of the South has migrated from state to state,
ollowing the timber. South Carolina has been practically abandoned
oy the industry for more than 20 years. In from four to six years under
oresent demands, Georgia will take its place with North and South
Carolina as an insignificant factor in production. . . . Florida has been
the mainstay of the naval stores production during the past ten years,
out the end of its supply is definitely in sight. Much of the long leaf
oine and slash pine of Alabama has already been worked. . . . Mississippi will show an increase in production during the next four or five

[21] *Commercial Survey of the Southeast,* p. 77.

years. The timber, however, both here and in Louisiana and Texas, i largely owned by lumbermen who will force a rapid exploitation fo naval stores in order that lumbering may not be delayed.[22]

TABLE VII

PRODUCTION OF THE TURPENTINE INDUSTRY, 1910-1930

YEAR	Spirits of Turpentine (In Thousands of Barrels)	Gum Rosin (In Thousands of Barrels)
1909–10	600	2,000
1914–15	560	1,900
1919–20	400	1,330
1924–25	530	1,765
1927–28	650	2,165
1928–29	560	1,865
1929–30	625	2,065

TABLE VIII

THE GUM TURPENTINE ROSIN INDUSTRY IN THE SOUTH

	1914	1925	1927	Percentage Increase and Decrease 1925–1927
Number of establishments	1,394	1,007	1,149	14.1
Wage earners, average for year	34,817	29,413	37,913	28.9
Wages paid*	$ 8,583	$15,190	$16,953	11.6
Cost of materials, supplies, fuel, power*	5,536	11,887	12,173	2.4
Value of products*	20,990	42,364	39,902	–5.8
Value added by manufacturing*	15,454	30,447	27,729	–9.0

*In Thousands of Dollars.

The pressure of the market for rosin and turpentine has no served the interests of conservation, but has hastened the process of exploitation and given rise to the chipping of trees too immature for lumber. Since an area is worked out and abandoned within a few years at most, the still locations or turpentine camps are temporary affairs and the equipment and processes remain crude by compulsion. The type of labor and the standard of living are also lowered. That the status of the worker is not even lower than it is may be laid to the fact that turpentining while migratory is not seasonal in the same sense as wheat.

The number of laborers employed remains much the same over the entire year because the operations in the woods incidental to the actual gathering of the crop cover all the intervening months. This obviates the irregularities attendant upon a floating labor supply and holds intact

[22] Quoted in *American Forestry,* 30, p. 406.

definite population units. In general the labor is of a semi-skilled character, consisting largely of Negroes. Wages are commonly paid on a piecework basis, ranging from $1.50 to $2.50 a day, varying with the season, nature of the timber being worked, prices, locality, and availability of labor. Current purchases are facilitated at the commissaries, and settlements are usually made semimonthly, the workers receiving in cash the difference between the amount of the total wage and purchases or advances for the period.[23]

If owned by planters, the pine lands may be leased by operating companies who work the turpentine. Stumps on cut-over lands are also blasted out and processed for naval stores. Many of the tracts, however, are owned by lumber companies who supervise the extraction of naval stores before beginning lumbering. The supervision in the field is in the hands of a mounted woods rider who is able to oversee the work on a number of crops of a thousand faces each.

LUMBERING IN THE PINEY WOODS

Even more than turpentining the lumber industry has migrated over the map. The reason is the obvious fact that it takes timber more than a generation to grow. Accordingly it has been treated as a mine to be exhausted rather than a crop to be regrown. Up until about 1880, however, more trees were cut for the sake of clearing land than for lumber. It is in part due to the social heritage of the pioneer's experience with timber as a by-product of free land that the United States has the highest per capita consumption of lumber in the world. Increasing demands for timber since that period have caused land to be logged more rapidly than it could be claimed for agriculture.[24] "For a hundred years the lumber industry has been in the process of migrating from one forested region to another" in search of virgin timber. In American lumbering operations there have occurred four great migrations.

The first lumbering took place along the Atlantic Coast from Maine southward to the Royal colonies in Virginia and the Carolinas. But lumbering as we know it did not get under full headway until nearly the middle of the last century, with the introduction of improved forms of

[23] *Commercial Survey of the Southeast*, p. 78.
[24] W. B. Greely, et al., "Timber: Mine or Crop?" Separate 886, U. S. D. A. *Yearbook*, 1922, p. 86.

machinery and large merchant mills. As the first cut of pine in the more thickly settled coast regions drew near its end the exploitation of the white pine forests of the Lake States began and the hardwood regions of the central Appalachians were opened to the market. As the cut of the Lake States drew to its close many manufacturers of that region removed their operation to the South and began the attack upon the great belt of long-leaf pine stretching from Virginia to Texas. Each of these moves increased the distance between the centers of production and the centers of consumption. Now four-fifths of the original southern pine is gone, and there is in progress a marked drift of lumbermen from the Southern States to the Pacific Coast and to the northern part of the Rocky Mountains, known as the Inland Empire.[25]

The exploitation of the third reserve of America's timber supply has occurred apace in the South. In 1920 every southern state, if we except the three border states of Kentucky, Missouri, and Oklahoma, showed a surplus of timber produced over timber consumed. Only five other states could be found in this group.[26] In 1920 the cut-over area lacked only some 43 million acres of reaching the present wooded area while the restocking area was

TABLE IX

AREA OF WOODLAND, RESTOCKING, CUT-OVER LANDS 1920
(IN MILLIONS OF ACRES)

	Original Wooded Area	Present Wooded Area	Cut-over Area	Restocking Area
1. Virginia	24.9	12.0	11.0	10.5
2. Kentucky	24.3	9.4	7.3	7.2
3. North Carolina	30.0	18.0	16.3	15.0
4. Tennessee	25.6	12.0	10.0	9.8
5. South Carolina	17.9	10.0	9.3	.7
6. Georgia	36.4	20.0	18.8	13.7
7. Florida	28.8	19.0	7.3	2.0
8. Alabama	32.0	20.0	18.0	11.4
9. Mississippi	28.8	17.0	12.0	8.7
10. Arkansas	32.0	21.5	17.3	15.5
11. Louisiana	25.6	17.3	12.6	8.8
12. Oklahoma	12.0	8.0	6.0	4.5
13. Texas	30.0	15.0	10.0	6.7
The South	348.5	199.2	156.1	121.3
The United States	822.8	469.4	331.3	250.1

[25] R. V. Reynolds and Albert H. Pierson, "Lumber Cut of the United States, 1870-1920," U. S. D. A. *Bulletin* 1119, p. 11.

[26] W. B. Greely, "Relation of Geography to Timber Supply," *Economic Geography*, I, 6.

227 million acres short of the original wooded area. The Capper report to the United States Senate in 1919 showed the South's comparative ranking as regards virgin stands of timber as follows:

	Acres
Pacific Northwest	77,115,000
Southern States (11) Virginia to Texas.......	39,135,000
Lake States	10,100,000
Northeastern States (9)	3,896,000
Central Hardwood Region	7,150,000

The Southern Pine report for January 1927 shows a startling decrease in the stand of southern virgin timber to 12,650,000 indicating a loss of 26,350,000 acres in less than eight years. The total stand of virgin timber in the South was placed at 75,750,000,000 board feet and the yearly cut at 8,500,000,000 feet. A 1928 United States Forest Service Bulletin reports: "The end of virgin timber in the South is definitely in sight, while already the younger timber is being cut as fast as it grows."[27]

For a long period now the southern pine states have held the center of the stage in lumber production. The first adequate census of forest products, that of 1870, found them in the lead and the census of 1920 was the first to show that lead seriously threat-

TABLE X

CLASSIFICATION OF SOUTHERN PINE LANDS 1920

	Total Net Pine Area (In Millions of Acres)	Area Old Growth (In Millions of of Acres)	Restocking Saw Timber (In Millions of Acres)	Merchantable Pine Stand (In Millions of Board Feet)
Virginia...........	4.0	...	1.5	8,698
Kentucky.........	...	...	..	......
North Carolina.....	10.7	.5	3.6	15,300
Tennessee.........	...	..	...	......
South Carolina.....	8.0	.6	2.5	13,889
Georgia...........	15.5	.7	3.8	21,807
Florida...........	18.0	11.0	.7	36,429
Alabama..........	15.5	1.5	3.5	25,316
Mississippi........	12.0	3.0	5.0	40,476
Arkansas..........	9.5	1.5	3.5	23,316
Louisiana.........	11.7	2.5	4.5	47,348
Oklahoma.........	2.0	.5	.5	4,791
Texas.............	7.4	...	1.5	8,698
The South......	114.3	23.4	29.3	257,526

[27] See Major George P. Ahern, "Deforested America," *Senate Document* 216, 1929, p. 3, for facts here presented.

ened. In that year southern pine stands were classified as in Table X. The peak of production of the lumber industries of the United States was reached in 1907, and the curve of timber output started on a long decline in the face of high prices and increased demands for building. The peak of southern production was reached in 1909, when almost 20 billion board feet were cut in the eleven pine states, and another peak was reached in 1917 with approximately nineteen and a half billion feet. The year 1920 was the first in which the western states threatened the eight states of the long-leaf pine belt. For that year eleven western states and only one eastern state were able to increase production, while in the other thirty-six states, including all southern states, production declined. The figures for 1929 showed that the Pacific states have, for the first time, come within some 1,316 million board feet of the production of the complete southern pine belt of eleven states.[28] The great timber reserve of the South has been exploited, and lumbering has reached its last frontier in the Pacific Northwest.

Transportation and type of sawmill offer the two keys to the technology of the lumber industry. Because of the exaggerated ratio which bulk and weight of timber bears to its value, transportation has always loomed large in the industry. Logging in northern and mountainous regions has been able to make use of hard packed snows in sledding out logs and of rivers in floating them to markets. This of course has served to decrease the expenses of lumbering operations except for the fact that the place of entry and exit of the logs must be owned and controlled by the company. In the pine flatwoods the first lumbering took place along rivers and railroad lines. Thus early the Piney Woods were pretty well stripped as far back of these lines of communication as ox-teams and mule teams could reach. The method was expensive and slow, and in the interior stretched unbroken regions of pine forests. The lack of snow, the sluggishness of the rivers of the flatwoods, and the level nature of the country all suggested one recourse—logging by railway. F. V. Emerson wrote in 1919:

Twenty to thirty years ago, when the northern forests were approaching exhaustion professional lumbermen bought these virgin pine forests at nominal prices. We have seen that the transportation problem of getting

[28] *Statistical Abstract, 1931,* p. 756.

the logs to mills and then getting the lumber to market had limited local development, for local companies possessed small capital. To locate large mills on a railroad and then haul the logs ten or fifteen miles or more required well-built tram roads, which are expensive. The large scale exploitation of pine timber, therefore, passed to companies possessed of ample capital, and the lumbering industry in this belt, like so many other industries, is largely in the hands of capitalists and strong companies, many holdings including tens of thousands of acres. Fortunately the level and rolling surface offers few obstacles, and thousands of miles of well-built railroads now traverse these forests. Most of these railroads are of standard gauge. After the timber has been cut, the owners are reluctant to abandon the expensive railroads and so maintain some train service, with the hope that the country will develop and make the roads profitable or that some trunk line will buy them as feeders. Many of the abandoned tram roads are now used as public highways, and they will be an important factor in the development of cut-over lands.[29]

It can be seen that the mere presence of natural resources has not been sufficient stimulus to insure their development. The lack of large aggregations of capital, of technical skill, and of acquaintance with economic opportunities involved have served largely to take the exploitation of the piney woods out of the hands of their original owners. An observer wrote of the spread of lumbering to the pine belt of southern Alabama in the early 1900's:

A few southerners told me, on my recent trip along the Gulf Coast, of the golden opportunities which they failed to grasp, of the numerous successes of Northern and Eastern men and lamented the passing of the old school of gentlemen, the midday mint juleps, and the easy-going business methods. Others looked prosperous and were working shoulder to shoulder with the Yankees.

Enterprising men from North Carolina have tapped the stately pines of Alabama's virgin forests, which only a few years ago were to be had for fifty cents an acre, lumbermen from the North and East have sawed these trees and shipped the products to every country in the world. . . . And the owners of the land, most of them residents of Mobile, have cheated themselves out of millions of dollars by failing to see the opportunities within their grasp and by not being sufficiently well informed as to intrinsic values to charge a fair price for the turpentining and lumbering rights.[30]

[29] "Southern Long Leaf Pine Belt," *Geographical Review,* VII, 81-90.
[30] R. W. Woolley, "Lumbering Around Mobile, Alabama," *Review of Reviews,* 33, pp. 191-92.

Sawmills range in type from the portable class I mill cutting less than 500,000 board feet to the large class V mills turning out over 10,000,000 board feet a year. Class I which contains almost 70 per cent of the mills in the United States produces only 10 per cent of the cut as compared to class V comprising four per cent of the mills but producing nearly 60 per cent of the annual lumber cut.[31] In 1920, 43 per cent of all mills and 40 per cent of class V mills were located in the South. The large mill, backed by plentiful capital, situated in great tracts of virgin timber, may employ a labor force of more than a thousand men. These are the old mills, representing the concentration of lumbering in strong hands. They have possessed heretofore something of the quality of permanency, have used more efficient and conservative logging and forestry technique, and have been forced to do less dumping on the market in order to meet the fixed charges of taxes and interest. As the large operators cut out their virgin stands the increasing trend is toward smaller mills. Between 1919 and 1920 it is estimated that over one eighth of the class V mills in the South either cut out or reduced their cut to class IV limits.[32]

The cutting of odd lots, small tracts, and second growth has of necessity fallen to the small portable mill. These "woodpecker mills" have come to be regarded by lumbermen as having about the same relation to good lumbering practices as sheep have to good grazing. One critic has called the portable sawmill "a small but insatiable monster which moved from place to place leaving mutilated spots where it rested and destroying more timber than it sawed."[33] Many owners after having overworked their turpentine stands have been forced to call in these small mills to salvage the immature timber before its death and decay. Much of the lumber produced by these mills is poorly manufactured, improperly seasoned, and dumped on the market. Lacking sufficient capital, forced to clean up with inefficient methods and to dump improperly seasoned lumber on the market to meet fixed charges, these mills constitute a marginal threat to the lumbering industry of the South.

The difference between large and small mills is the contrast

[31] U. S. D. A. *Bulletin* 1119, Plates I, II.
[32] *Ibid.,* p. 26.
[33] O. W. Price, "Saving Our Southern Forests," *World's Work,* V, 3215.

between moving timber to the mill and moving the mill to the timber. The large companies make their mills stationery and bring the logs to them by means of improved tram roads reaching the forest anywhere within a large radius. Thus the labor supply may live at home in communities and yet be transported to any part of the company's timber holdings. "The old time isolated lumber camp is thus disappearing. Its place is being taken by a more permanent and useful type of community."[34] It must be remembered, however, that it does not pay to lay rails unless the operations in virgin timber can be expected to last for twenty years. Unless the corporation owns the land outright it can hardly be expected to lay tracks. When it comes to the logging of second growth and small tracts the problem of transportation is solved, as has been suggested, by making the mill portable. Small companies buy cut-over lands at low price, and, by the employment of portable mills and transient labor, attempt to make hurried profits from quick turnover of second growth.

The clean-up of third growth, poles and wasted timber, usually undertaken by the portable mills, goes into the wood pulp industry. Heretofore, the South, in spite of its available raw materials, has not profited to a large extent from the paper industry. Instead of following lumbering into the South, paper mills first turned to Canada for their supplies.[35] Due to the great expense of installing wood pulp plants, they have largely remained in the North and East where they were first erected. The South, however, possesses the cheapest pulpwood in the nation, averaging, in 1929, $7.56 per cord for the rough wood.[36] But the pines streaked with pitch have heretofore been processed for the sulphate or kraft pulp. The South dominates the field of kraft pulp, producing from her pitch-pine woods paper bags, wood boards, and brown wrapping papers. In 1929, 36 plants with one million tons' capacity were located in this area, while the country normally imports 1,200 tons of kraft paper daily. The problem of diversification into fine and bleached papers is primarily one of developing chemical processes for treating pine pulp. The pulp

[34] Huntington and Williams, *Business Geography*, pp. 185-86.
[35] W. B. Greely, "Relation of Geography to Timber Supply," *Economic Geography*, I, 9.
[36] J. H. Pratt, "Lumber and Forest Products Industry in the South," *The Annals of the American Academy of Political and Social Science*, 153, pp. 70-71.

plant at Canton, North Carolina, the largest in the country, is devoted to fine papers. The United States Forest Product Laboratories at Madison, Wisconsin, have developed a process for producing a bleached pulp from yellow pine.[37]   Dr. C. H. Herty now of New York has announced that newsprint pulp can be made from slash pine and contends that farmers should grow more pines for the incoming industry.

Southern lumbering has not developed the lumberjack, that migratory worker, living in bunk houses without women and children and addicted to all the masculine vices and exploits. To a large extent it has made use of the stable native labor supply. L. C. Glenn writes that some of the lumbering companies operating in the Cumberland Plateau "permit and even encourage the original inhabitants to remain upon the land in what practically amounts to a system of free tenancy, since they consider their presence desirable for the protection that they may afford against forest fires and depredations by timber thieves or other trespassers as well as to furnish a source of labor for the operation of mines, logging camps, and lumber mills."[38]

The explanation of the lumber town is found in the fact that the industry has proved, in the phrase of Colonel W. B. Greely to be both pioneer and nomad. Though temporary in the South, timbering is not transitory and has not trained its workers in mobility. Lumbering furnished in 1920 employment for about a quarter of a million men and the support of a million people. Most of the population is housed in lumber towns that, in spite of their temporary nature, are often well developed.

The lumber towns are as a rule, up to date, with electric lights, city water, often gas, and sometimes paved streets. The schools are always good. These towns are necessarily more or less temporary, yet the modern method of extending tram roads for a considerable distance insures the town's existence for ten to twenty years until the timber of the tributary territory is cut. They are far from resembling the shack towns which grow up around small mills. These mill towns are serving and will serve as nuclei for the rural population which occupies the cut-over lands as the timber is removed.[39]

[37] *Ibid.*

[38] In *Physiographic Influences in the Development of Tennessee,* cited by C. C. Colby, *Economic Geography of North America,* p. 251.

[39] F. V. Emerson, *loc. cit.*

There are, however, many temporary camps and not all of the permanent camps can be so well characterized.[40]

However modern and up to date many of these lumber towns have become they are in danger of one common fate, a fate that has already happened to many. When the merchantable timber is cut out, operations cease. The lumberman is not an agriculturist; for him the land is a residue to be sold so that he may move on to new fields of timber exploitation. The region is dotted with abandoned towns and mill sites left stranded by the passing of the naval stores and timber supplies. "In every case the cessation of operations has left in its wake people released from remunerative employment who had the alternative of seeking a new community or deriving a meager subsistence from a patchy agriculture pending efforts to clear and improve the land."[41] "Their villages," writes a competent observer, "are nameless towns, their monuments huge piles of sawdust, their unwritten epitaph: *The mill cut out.* Locally the catastrophe has already arrived of a vanquished industry, unreplaced by any new industry remotely adequate to redeem the situation."[42] In Louisiana, for example, when the average mill cuts its last log, the whistle blows and 77 men are out of a job.[43]

In the pine belt, an area as large as Texas, stretching from Virginia to Mississippi, many such cases of abandoned lumber towns are to be found.

One lumber company with a chain of mills in the South lost one mill, burned: decided not to rebuild, and the town which it had created forthwith curled up and died. The country in which the firm was situated got to doing a little figuring and discovered that 85 per cent of its assessed values were derived from the lumber industry. . . . Whatever excuse there may be in excessive taxation, hostile legislation, etc. for the 'get from under' policy of many of the South's foreign owned (regionally speaking) lumber corporations, the fact that these companies are not conducted or financed by men who expect to remain in the South any longer than their timber lasts has operated powerfully against their practice of forestry. . . . To these men a large acreage of cut-over land was no doubt an annoyance rather than an opportunity.[44]

[40] Abraham Berglund, et. al., *Labor in the Industrial South,* ch. vi.
[41] *Commercial Survey of the Southeast,* p. 83.
[42] R. D. Forbes, "The Passing of the Piney Woods," *American Forestry,* 29, p. 134.
[43] *Ibid.*
[44] R. D. Forbes in *Lumber World Review,* November 10, 1921, cited in *Deforested America,* p. 32.

The migratory nature of the lumber industry, forced to move in search of its supply of timber, is shown in the history of McNary, Louisiana. A great lumbering corporation wished to keep its laboring force intact, and McNary, unlike other lumber towns, refused to "curl up and die."

The tragedy of the timberland was symbolized Monday when the last of the population of McNary, La., moved away in a 21-coach train bound for the new village of McNary, Arizona.

Two months ago, Louisiana had this thriving town of 3,000 persons. As the forests became denuded of pines the employers of the villagers began looking about for a new site. They found it in Arizona.

In two long special trains half the town was started westward to build a new village. Today the last of the inhabitants left. In 52 hours they will be at a point 80 miles from the new activity. Thence they will travel over a railroad just built into the heart of the timber country, and they will be back home in McNary.[45]

There is nothing to be gained, as R. D. Forbes has said, by blaming the southern lumberman.[46] From the viewpoint of the natural economic processes involved he is the agent through which the American public has carried out a policy prevailing in all fields, the quick exploitation of natural resources. If he has hastened the cutting of immature stands, he has often been forced to it by heavy turpentining operations which threatened trees with death. Often he has come into a southern community as the representative of a "foreign" corporation to run counter to the folkways of the free range. He has been burned out time and again by cattlemen using his forest as free pasture. Cutting trees prematurely is one means of escape from fire. Moreover, the lumberman has been forced to cut by merciless taxation. Lumber under the general property tax is forced to pay revenues as though it were an annual crop. When it is considered that twenty to forty years is none too long a time in which to mature timber, the injustice of such measures can be seen. It is generally agreed by students of public finance that the only method of taxation which promotes forestry is the severance tax—levied only when the crop

[45] H. H. Chapman, "Why the Town of McNary Moved," *American Forestry,* 30, p. 589.
[46] "The Passing of the Piney Woods," *American Forestry,* 29, p. 136.

s harvested. Lastly the lumberman's answer to the charge that he has not cut the forest clean must be that he has cut it as clean as the market demanded. When it is shown that scientific forestry and methods of conservation pay as profitably as the like investment in other forms of business enterprise, then the lumberman or someone else will adopt them.

THE FUTURE OF THE CUT-OVER LANDS

The metamorphosis of valuable timber holdings into typical cut-over lands brings the piney woods to a new frontier stage. Of the 125 million acres originally in pine forests, comprising 23 per cent of 12 southern states, 100 million acres have been cut-over. Up to the present 10½ million acres have been absorbed into agriculture. Over 33 million acres remain without new growth of trees.[47] The change is viewed with interest and apprehension by many people in the South. The state and local governing agencies are concerned, for, with the passing of timber, tax values suffer decreases so great that civic and educational services cannot be adequately supported. "In most of the counties of the pine country the improvements in the way of graveled roads, consolidated schools, and public institutions came in a large way from taxes on standing timber which is now gone or is fast disappearing. The present farming population cannot long hold up the burden of taxation when it is all thrown upon them."[48] Railroads fear decreases in freight traffic that will curtail their revenues below operating costs. Towns and cities which have grown up as trading and service centers for timbered areas are faced with loss of payrolls, falling real estate values, bankruptcy of mercantile establishments, and the forced migration of leading members of their professional classes. The solution is to be sought in the satisfactory disposal of the cut-over lands. In many cases the owners are but too glad to be free of cut-over lands at almost any price. They are lumbermen and if they are to remain in business feel they must be off to forests new. Many publicists have seen in these lands the nation's substitute for the free lands of the West. Obviously these cut-over lands must find their outlet in one of three forms of use: agriculture, grazing, or forestry.

[47] R. D. Forbes, *ibid.*, pp. 131-36.
[48] S. W. Greene in *Proceedings* of Fifth Southern Forestry Congress, p. 48.

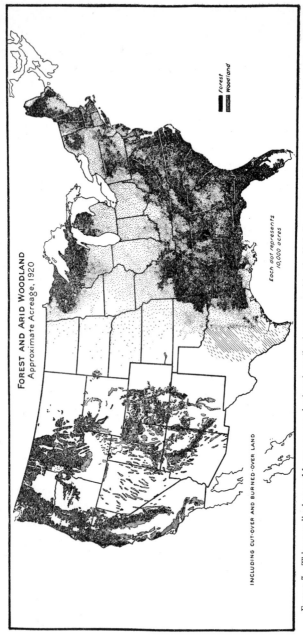

FIGURE 7.—This generalized map of forest, cut-over land, and woodland was prepared by the U. S. Department of Agriculture in cooperation with the Forest Service. The estimates for the States in the originally forested eastern portion of the United States, except for several States in which forest surveys have been made, are based largely on deductions from the statistics of the 1920 census. Of the 483,000,000 acres of forest and cut-over land in the United States about one-half is in the South, one-eighth in the Northeastern States, one-eighth in the Lakes States, and nearly one-quarter in the West, mostly in the Rocky Mountain and north Pacific regions. However, over half of the 137,000,000 acres or less of virgin saw timber is in the West. (Courtesy of U. S. Department of Agriculture).

For the purposes of agriculture these soils do not rank among the most productive in the South. They were avoided by emigrants on the westward trek who gave them the name of "pine barrens." It has been found that with the aid of commercial fertilizers their scanty crops of cotton, corn, and wheat can be measurably increased. In a period of agricultural surpluses, however, the increased cost of fertilization has operated to leave these lands outside the margins of cultivation. Moreover, with the expansion of cotton acreage in Western Texas, "abandonment of cotton farms is going on rather rapidly along the eastern Gulf Coast and the South Atlantic Coast."[49] Since these soils are "warm" and drain readily they make good truck soils. In certain areas immigrant groups like the Italians have with characteristic thrift and energy drained and built up soils for the production of strawberries and trucking crops until land values have risen from $10 to $100 an acre.[50] At present, however, the market is well supplied with early vegetables, fruit and truck crops, and yet hardly two per cent of the arable land is given to these crops. It is evident, holds O. E. Baker, that for the next 50 years at least 97 per cent of the newly added land supply must be used for other purposes than trucking.[51] These soils, however, are exceedingly productive of cowpeas, peanuts, and velvet beans, all plants valuable for stock feed and for enriching the soil.

The last thing that should happen just now in regard to these lands is their alienation to small owners in small tracts. "Reasonable expectation of immigration to the South for the next thirty years does not justify a belief that more than one fifth of the yellow pine lands can be sold advantageously prior to 1950. Yet a hundred million acres will be for sale during that period."[52] In the opinion of S. W. Greene: "There are not enough surplus farmers in the United States to farm the Piney Woods and there will not be for two generations."[53] Colonization has failed and will continue to fail "as long as land is sold at high prices in small tracts to clerks, conductors, mechanics, and other city people who know little about farming. The capital of such people is usually taken

[49] W. J. Spillman, *Balancing the Farm Output*, p. 49.

[50] F. V. Emerson, *loc. cit.*, p. 243.

[51] *Economic Geography*, III, 60.

[52] J. B. Woods, "Problem of Southern Pine Lands," *American Forestry* 29, p. 539.

[53] *Proceedings*, Fifth Southern Forestry Congress, p. 48.

up by the first payment and they have no means left to develop
the farm."[54]

Utilization either as cattle ranches or reforestation is indicated.
For such utilization it is necessary that cut-over lands be held
together in large tracts. Questionnaires sent out by the Department of Agriculture in 1921 indicated that the holdings of southern
lumber companies average 29,000 acres.[55] Large tracts under
unified control have suggested to some students of the problem
a return to the ranching conditions of the early West. Under
present conditions this is impossible, for without extensive pasture
improvement 600 acres of these lands will carry but 60 head of
cattle.[56] No purchase of less than a section, and that at low terms,
justifies entering the cattle business. Land sale companies which
buy large stretches of cheap lands with the intention of making
handsome profits by subdivision and resale have, accordingly,
hindered the development of the region. Ultimately the cut-over
lands of the South will be largely absorbed into the nation's agricultural production. At present, however, the situation in both
trucking and staple crops suggests that the "development of the
lands as a whole must be in large tracts consisting of several
thousand acres."[57] Needless to say, to reassemble small tracts from
the hands of agricultural colonists who have failed into large
holdings would be a hopeless task. The future for a long time will
remain with forestry and stock raising. It will be found profitable
to discuss proposals for grazing the cut-over lands in the chapter
on stock raising.

Development of reforestation in the South waits upon the development of a national attitude toward forestry. A Department
of Commerce report on conditions in the Southeast holds that the
tendency among lumber millmen is toward perpetual operation.
"The principle is to build smaller sawmills and have sufficient
timber available each year to keep the mills running at capacity."[58]
Needless to say such conditions have not yet been realized. The
shift in timber from a mining to a cropping system of utilization
has hardly made a start.

[54] U. S. D. A. *Bulletin* 827, p. 17.
[55] *Ibid.*, p. 16.
[56] *Ibid.*, p. 18.
[57] *Ibid.*, p. 17.
[58] *Commercial Survey of the Southeast*, p. 83.

D. L. Mason points out three periods of private forestry in America.[59] Before 1905 the Bureau of Forestry had worked out plans for forest management. A few private owners evinced no more than a mild curiosity and none of the plans was put into effect. From 1905 to 1918 the emphasis was placed on national forests and the view became current that cut-over lands were to pass into Federal or state hands for reforestation. Accordingly private owners began to regard the movement with more seriousness. Beginning with 1918 the situation changed greatly. The war, the aircraft and rayon industries, and the use of the Panama Canal increased the demands for timber, led to larger profits for lumbermen, and focused attention on a national forestry policy.[60] Hearings were held on reforestation, "mandatory" and "coöperative" forestry, paving the way in 1924 for the passage of the Clark-McNary bill which provided for Federal coöperation with the states in protection, conservation, and regrowth of forests. By 1920 a few private owners mostly in the redwood and southern pine districts had adopted the principle of perpetual operation with reforestation. Such firms have come to realize that without a new growth of timber coming on, their investments in sawmills, railways and towns, amounting in some cases to millions, were doomed.

On the other hand, there are many experts who hold that the point has not yet been reached where private forestry will pay. Until very recently, the theory is, the country has had too much wood and too many forests. Cheap wood and timber growing are directly opposed. No form of timber growing can survive competition with virgin stands. When the scarcity of lumber becomes so great that the public is willing to pay for orchard-grown wood fiber, forestry will offer a sound business opportunity. At present it is a race between annual rings and compound interest in the bank. When the annual rings beat the compound interest no such business opportunity will be allowed to go begging. It is pointed out that growing trees in government forest reserves is not a commercial but a public project. And just so far as it is supported by taxation, public forestry serves to interfere with the interaction of supply and demand. To this extent it may handi-

[59] *Journal of Forestry*, Feb. 1926, cited in Major George P. Ahern, *Deforested America*, Senate Document 216, 1929, p. 30.

[60] D. L. Mason and C. M. Stevens in *Lumber World Review*, December 10, 1923, cited in *Deforested America*, p. 29.

cap private growers of timber who operate without such aid. The plain truth of the matter is that forestry does not as yet produce 6 to 10 per cent dividends and manufacturing does. European forest projects operated as state subsidies show no such profits as would be necessary for private enterprise. Forestry investments stretch over too many generations. They "go against the grain of human nature, and nowhere on earth today is there any private forestry comparable to private investment in railroads, liberty bonds, or chemical concerns, and United States Steel."[61]

Reforestation, it must be remembered, is itself a natural process. "Throughout most of the eastern portion of the United States," says an authority, "the forest rather than grass or brush is the ultimate type of vegetation."[62] When abandoned, these areas will in course of time be recaptured by forests similar to the ones originally found on their soil. The classic example of the process is the large acreage of cotton land in Virginia and North Carolina, abandoned during the Civil War, later found reclothed in second growth timber. Moreover, early lumbering conditions were much more favorable to reforestation. Before lumber became high and before the day of the steam skidder "there was never any dearth of small trees left on the land after logging." It did not pay to cut the small timber, and logging with animals did not break many down. Subsequently these trees bore abundant seed, and reforestation was swift and complete.[63]

To recapture abandoned agricultural land, trees must possess seeds that may be easily transported, be able to grow in the open, and be capable of rapid growth. To insure regrowth of the original forest trees something like the same forest situation must prevail. To cut out a forest, however, is to destroy the natural environment of the seedlings of the species. If no "seed trees" are left standing the chances for regrowth are made much less. A Louisiana law requires that two seed trees per acre be left after cutting. The practice of cutting all timber leads to what is called "succession," that is the trees that spring up are not necessarily of

[61] See for theory of this type C. M. Stevens, in *Journal of Forestry*, May and June 1925; C. A. Schenck, *Journal of Forestry*, November 1926, January 1927, cited in *Deforested America*, pp. 30-32.

[62] P. L. Buttrick, "Forest Growth on Abandoned Agricultural Land," *Scientific Monthly*, V, 80-91.

[63] R. D. Forbes, "Passing of the Piney Woods," *American Forestry*, 29, p. 135.

the same variety as those cut. When a white pine forest is cut it is succeeded by such hardwoods as maples, beech, hemlock, and yellow birch. This is because their seedlings, more "tolerant" of shade than pine seedlings, are already established in the soil. However, when a hardwood forest is cut off and burned over poor trees such as birch and ash spring up. They are better able to live in the relatively poor soil.[64] "Old field trees" are accordingly in most areas inferior varieties of subordinate importance in commerce. In this respect, however, the South is more fortunate. "Loblolly pine, a tree of naturally limited distribution seeds in abundantly on abandoned fields in that section to the almost entire exclusion of the long-leaf itself."[65] In some soils scrub oak replaces the virgin pine, but loblolly pine, of more commercial importance than any other old field stand in the country, can hardly be regarded as an inferior tree.

Approximately one-fourth as much land is planted to trees each year as is cut over. Up until 1924 about one and a half million acres had been planted in the United States while 81 million acres of barren and fireswept land that once grew trees remained to be reforested.[66] All signs point to the South as the premier scene of this activity when it comes. "Three to five years of fire protection," writes Henry C. Wallace, "in the cut-over pine country of South Georgia is sufficient to start a healthy young forest beyond the threat of fires and pigs that will put our unplowed acres to work growing a profitable crop for which there is not a glutted market; repopulate our deserted forest regions and give the earth and the people something to do."[67] The South may be expected to lead in forestry for several reasons. First, yellow pine furnishes a type of lumber well established in channels of commerce and proved capable of many uses. Second, in the South all the climatic requirements for rapid growth come to focus in the pine, the fastest growing tree outside the tropics. Moreover, the South seems the only area in which forestry can be operated alongside other paying ventures. Grazing for the first cycle of growth while the trees are yet young, followed by thinning for poles and pinewood,

[64] Huntington and Williams, *Business Geography*, pp. 183-84.
[65] P. L. Buttrick, *loc. cit.*, p. 84.
[66] U. S. D. A. *Farmers' Bulletin* 1417, p. 13.
[67] "Forestry and Our Land Problem," *American Forestry*, 29, p. 15.

can be followed by turpentining at intervals after the trees reach a growth of 15 years, followed finally by cutting of timber.

Unless the pasture is overcrowded cattle graze among young pines without molesting them. Cut-over lands covered with young trees are thus dual purpose lands. Reforestation and hog raising are admittedly impossible companions. Because of his peculiar fondness for the juicy tap root the roaming razorback is the greatest enemy of the young long leaf pine. The goat, however, because of his hardihood in keeping down the briars and brambles that spring up on cut-over land is claimed by the forester as his principal ally. A goat, in the opinion of one forester, would rather have blackberry briars than candy to eat.

Real conflicts of interest have arisen in the pine belt where the cattle belong to the native farmers and the lands to lumber companies. Again the South faces a frontier heritage. Whether the land is forested, cut-over or reforested, the native farmers burn off the growth each year. The situation is well described by S. W. Greene in an address before the Southern Forestry Congress.

Under the present conditions in most sections the ideas of the forester and the cattleman are at odds. The forester says the range must be fenced and protected from fire for another crop of pines and the stockman says it must be left open and burned annually for his use. The difference is largely an economic one. The man who undertakes to grow another crop of timber owns a large tract of land, and has a permanent interest in its future development, while the man who favors open range and annual burning, as a rule pastures his cattle on land that does not belong to him and in which he has no future interest. The cattleman is represented by practically every citizen in the community and altho their [sic] individual holdings of cattle are very small it is a real asset to them [sic].

The native stockmen have known nothing but open range for generations. The range has been free for all since the land was public domain. The owner of the land bought it for the timber and until that was gone and he wished to put the land to some productive use, there was no question as to the right of the local people to use the range. Long established customs are hard to change and it takes time and education to accomplish it. You can't legislate against custom. The lumberman does not want his skidder legislated out of existence and a great many people look at reforestation as a fore-runner of a stock law which would close the open range. It would be best to go easy on the matter and establish some middle ground if possible. It will take a general country-wide sentiment against fires to stop them. The state troops couldn't do it under martial law. It is a problem of getting the cattlemen to see that they can raise stock without burning the woods and getting their help to control fires in return for the use of the pasture.[68]

Farmers believe that burning the woods each spring improves the pasturage and reduces the menace from boll weevils and ticks.

Many methods have been tried in the effort to reconcile grazing and forestry. The Crossett Lumber Company has successfully secured the coöperation of the native population in its program of reforestation by appointing thirty native farmers living in their respective areas to act as fire wardens. An even better method of avoiding the conflict is for the lumbering company to buy up the native cattle and operate the ranch themselves. The experience of the Southern Pine Lumber Company of Texarkana, Texas, is illuminating in this connection.

About ten years ago we started a grazing proposition, fencing into pastures approximately 35 thousand acres of cut-over land. . . . When we started the grazing undertaking we had an antagonistic native element to deal with. They had been running their cattle and hogs on this free range for many years besides feeling free to hunt and fish on the premises at their will. To overcome as much of their antagonism as possible we proposed to the cattlemen to buy their cattle, but told those who were running hogs that we were not interested in the razorback hogs and that they would have to come out. The cattlemen, in the main, sold us their cattle which constituted the foundation herd. Soon after our fences were built, they were cut half way between every post for perhaps a distance of half a mile. No efforts were made to apprehend the perpetrators because we were certain that a large number were implicated and that they were prepared to secure an alibi [sic] if necessary. We simply repaired the fences and shipped in bloodhounds. We still keep the bloodhounds, but there has never been any more fence cutting. Some of the owners of the hogs came and with our assistance gathered and took the hogs out. The hogs belonging to those who did not do this were gathered and turned out. Then came the question of stopping the hunting and fishing practice. This was necessary because of depredation and damage resulting from this practice. We tried to keep the hunters out by peaceable means, but wherever this failed we

[68] *Proceedings*, 1923, pp. 48-49.

resorted to injunction proceedings against different individuals and this has proven effectual to a large extent.[69]

Cattle grazing on the cut-over lands of this firm is found to be established on a paying basis. The enterprise, however, according to Mr. Gilbert, would not show any profit if the firm had to charge to the cattle ranch a rental on the land.

Grazing pays in the early stages of forestry. Unless the pastures are seriously overstocked the cattle do not damage the young pine seedlings. Moreover, the range riders also serve as fire wardens to keep fire out of the pineries and pastures. Grazing on lands devoted to reforestation, however, has its days limited. The mature pine forests, whether virgin or second growth, is practically clear of all undergrowth. As soon as the timber gets big enough to shade the ground there is much less grass. Thus while it may be possible to use grazing to defray in the South some of the cost of the early stage of growing young trees, forestry and grazing will not go hand in hand. A discussion of the use of cut-over lands for beef production is found in Chapter VII.

When forestry is once put on a permanent basis the pine belt will possess the advantage of profitable by-products of its timber such as can be found in no other region. As soon as slash and long-leaf pine reach a growth ranging from 15 years on they can be worked for rosin and turpentine. By use of the new technology the trees can be turpentined for periods of 30 to 50 years without injuring their lumber qualities. Mr. O. L. H. Wernicke, of the Pine Institute of America, has estimated that the annual yield of gum from 100 thrifty second growth pines will at current prices bring $30 per acre.[70] The cost of gathering should not exceed $20 per acre thus leaving an income of $10 per acre over a long period of time. No other timber belt can offer such easy or consistent returns to reforestation. In addition, the process of thinning for a good stand furnishes poles and pulpwood that find ready sale. At the close of the period of turpentining the forest land will be covered with lumber trees to the amount of 10,000 to 15,000 board feet per acre. At present prices the stumpage value of such lumber

[69] L. D. Gilbert, General Manager, before Ninth Southern Forestry Congress, *Proceedings,* 1927, pp. 86-87.

[70] In "Growing Pine Timber for Profit in the South," Forest Service, U. S. D. A. *Miscellaneous Publication* 24, 1928, pp. 9-10.

is over $10 per thousand. By the time the timber matures its monetary value will undoubtedly be much greater.

Instances may be cited to support the opinion of Forest Chief W. B. Greeley that the South is leading the country today in industrial forestry.[71] The Crossett Lumber Company of Crossett, Arkansas, after establishing a forestry department undertook a survey of all their logged-over lands.[72] Reserving for sale the lands most suitable for farming they divided the land suitable for timber into five classes: severely burned type, seed-tree type, pole type, old-field type, and hardwood type. A definite policy suitable for each type has been worked out and will be applied. The Southern Railway began in January 1925 a forestry demonstration on 12,000 acres of its lands near Pregnall and Ridgeville, South Carolina. A forester with three assistants began a program of fire protection, cutting off all merchantable trees in order to replant with slash and long leaf. A moderate profit has been secured from both turpentining and lumbering operations and the stage is now set for planting with fire-resistant carpet grass, and gum producing long-leaf and slash pines.[73] The Great Southern Lumber Company of Bogalusa has 140,000 acres, mostly well stocked with young pine. Recently they purchased 80,000 acres of second growth timber to mature in 10 to 20 years. They have reforested 18,000 acres by setting out small nursery-grown pine trees, a thousand per acre. Says the forester for the company:

We can see pictured for the future in the South reconstructed forests on sound business administration supporting permanent and prosperous industries. The sawmills, paper mills, creosote plants, naval stores production, and woodworking factories of every description, have already begun to take the place of speeding up the cut and then moving away.[74]

Three frontiers have passed in the piney woods. Long ago the day ceased to be when timber was deadened, cut and burned only for the sake of the land. The exploitation of naval stores with crude and reckless technology has had its limits set by nature. To no less extent has the frontier of inexhaustible areas of virgin timber been reached and passed. The nation has come to the point where

[71] U. S. D. A. *Miscellaneous Publication* 24, p. 2.
[72] J. W. Watzek in U. S. D. A. *Miscellaneous Publication* 24, pp. 10-13.
[73] J. C. Williams in U. S. D. A. *Miscellaneous Publication* 24, pp. 2-3.
[74] J. K. Johnson, U. S. D. A. *Miscellaneous Publication* 24, pp. 8-9.

forests must be regarded not as a mine but as a crop. While the rugged individualism of the frontier may have proved competent to exploit virgin stands, it has not solved the problem of those perennials whose periods of growth exceed the natural span of human life. The experience of Europe in first destroying and then being forced to replace many of her forests suggests that the task may better be delegated to the state, that corporate entity endowed with immortality. The state, however, owes the forester the immediate duty of revising taxation that penalizes reforestation. Once a forest policy, private or public, is adopted, the natural advantages of the South will assure it a foremost place. No other area can match the region's climatic resources with the possibilities of multi-level forestry. Grazing, the utilization of pulp wood, turpentining, and naval stores can be combined in the pine woods to divide the overhead costs of timber growing. By planting in cycles a large lumber company can stabilize the annual cutting activities to fit in with the multi-level forestry. It remains with the business man, the lumberman, and the forestry experts of the nation and the South to show whether the pine belt stands at the frontier of an adequate industrial forestry. If they prove unequal, the state will sooner or later take over the task.

CHAPTER VII

LIVE STOCK IN THE SOUTH

BEGINNINGS

EARLY AMERICA was unique in its lack of animals fitted for domestication. Although the Indians of the plains based their material culture to a large extent upon the buffalo, no Indian societies in North America possessed any domesticated animal except the dog. To the Spanish must be traced the introduction of live stock in America. In all their explorations along the Gulf of Mexico they took droves of animals, many of whom were lost or were stolen by the Indians. De Soto carried with him into Florida (1539-41) "thirteen sowes and had by this time (about one year later) three hundred swine."[1] Other dispersed herds became the foundation of herds of wild cattle, horses, and droves of wild pigs in the Southwest. Native cattle on the border still show strains of Spanish blood, and the famous Texas long horn was an adaptation of that stock to the wild range. The Jesuit Missions introduced animals and their husbandry. As early as 1773 five missions in California possessed 205 head of cattle, 94 sheep, 67 horses, and 77 mules.[2] Cattle grazing early became a leading industry of Mexico, Cuba, and southwest United States, which shipped great stores of hides and tallow to Spain.

The domestic animals brought to Virginia in the early Colonial days were turned out to shift for themselves and multiplied rapidly. In 1609 they had "six Mares and a Horse; five or six hundred swine; as many Hennes and Chickens; some Goats some Sheepe."[3] The animals were probably small and the lack of care probably conduced to inferior quality.[4] Wild animals made away with some, but Indians and settlers made away with even more. Ex-

---

[1] Lyman Carrier, *Beginnings of Agriculture in America*, p. 109.
[2] *Ibid.*, p. 110.
[3] Quoted by Carrier, *op. cit.*, p. 120.
[4] *Ibid.*, p. 134.

porting of all hides was prohibited in 1631 and an embargo was laid on sheep and mares in 1657. By 1668 horses had become plentiful and the law was repealed.

THE FRONTIER

The whole trend of cattle raising in America was modified by its forced adjustment to that socio-geographic complex, the frontier. In what might be called the hunting stage of early settlement the presence of wild game both gave the pioneers an abundance of meat in their diet and obviated the necessity of raising stock for slaughter. Meat eating long remained a marked trait in the food habits of Americans, partly no doubt as a survival from frontier conditions. Any frontier encompassed by Indians, hostile or friendly, was further restricted in stock raising by their depredations on cattle. An historian writes of early Kentucky:

Though cattle could easily have been raised by grazing them on the natural pastures in the summer and upon the extensive canebrakes in the winter, if the inhabitants had been living in a state of peace, yet such was not their condition. Surrounded by a savage foe, who was ever on the watch to seize upon the property or take the lives of the settlers, if they had raised cattle to any extent it would only have been for the use of the enemy, and the better to enable him to prolong his predatory incursions, and thereby do them the greater mischief. Thus situated they could rear no more cattle than they could secure within their stockade forts in time of danger. A few cows for milk and butter, and as many of the young as was necessary to keep up the stock and to supply the emigrants were as much as they could aim at, in the early period of our history. But game was plenty and the same rifle which was necessary for their protection, was amply sufficient to afford an abundant supply of bear, deer, and buffalo meat.[5]

Where comparatively free from hostile Indians, the southern frontier furnished a favorable locale for cattle raising. The poor roads and the great distance to markets made cattle especially important to frontiersmen, for live stock were self-transporting. John Pinkerton, traveling through North Carolina in 1747, was much amazed at the extent and manner of cattle grazing on the frontier:

Black cattle have mightily increased since the first settling of the colony. About forty years ago it was reckoned a great deal to have three or four

[5] De Bow, *Resources of the South*, II, 403.

cows, now some people have a thousand head; and for one man to have two hundred is very common. The cows graze in the forest, and the calves being separated and kept in pastures fenced in, they return home at night to suckle them; they are first milked, then shut up in a fold all night, milked again in the morning and then turned out into the woods. Here are hogs in abundance; they go daily to feed in the woods, where they rove several miles, feeding on nuts and roots; but having a shelter made at home, to keep them warm, and something given them to eat, they generally return in the evening. The beef and pork that are raised here find a good market in the sugar islands.[6]

Cattle production increased at a rapid pace in the South, and the cowpens came more or less to dominate the agricultural map. A cowpen was a partly cleared area in the forest, often a large acreage in canebrakes and peavines.[7] The resemblance of the cowpens to the ranching system which later prevailed on the great plains area is significant. "There were annual round-ups and branding of calves, conflicts between overlapping interests, and long drives of herds to tidewater markets. Cattle rustlers plied their trade and were summarily dealt with when caught. Might was the law of the range then as later. These cattlemen ever alert, always armed, fearless and resourceful, were an effective protection to the tidewater planters against attacks from the Indians of the Mississippi region."[8]

In the back country along the headwaters of the Susquehanna, Potomac, James, and the Broad, "men as rough as the wilderness they occupied" engaged in cattle raising. An officer under Braddock has given us our best picture of these frontier ranchers:

From the heart of the Settlements we are now got into the Cow-pens; the Keepers of these are very extraordinary kind of Fellows, they drive up their Herds on Horseback, and they had need do so, for their cattle are near as wild as Deer; a Cow-pen generally consists of a very large Cottage or House in the Woods, with about four-score or one hundred Acres inclosed with high Rails and divided; a small inclosure they keep for Corn, for the family, the rest is the Pasture in which they keep their Calves; but the manner is far different from anything you ever saw; they may perhaps have a stock of four to five hundred to a thousand Head of Cattle belonging to a Cow-pen, these run as they please in the Great

[6] John Pinkerton, *Travels*, II, 345; quoted by Carrier, p. 197.
[7] Turner, *Frontier in American History*, p. 16.
[8] Carrier, *op. cit.*, p. 215.

Woods, where there are no inclosures to stop them. In the month of March the Cows begin to drop their Calves, then the Cow-pen Master with all his men, rides out to see and drive up the Cows with all their newly fallen Calves; they being weak cannot run away so as to escape therefore are easily drove up and the Bulls and other Cattle follow them and they put these Calves into the Pasture and every Morning and Evening suffer the Cows to come and suckle them which done they let the Cows out into the great Woods to shift for their Food as well as they can; whilst the Calf is sucking one Tit of the Cow, the Woman of the Cow-pen is milking one of the other Tits, so that she steals some milk from the Cow, who thinks she is giving it to the Calf; soon as the Cow begins to go dry and the Calf grows Strong, they mark them, if they are Males they cut them and let them go into the woods. Every year in September and October they drive up the Market Steers, that are fat and of a proper age, and kill them; they say they are fat in October, but I am sure they are not so in May, June and July; . . . they reckon that a cowpen for every 100 Head of Cattle brings about 40 pounds Sterling per Year. The Keepers live chiefly upon milk, for out of their vast Herds they do condescend to tame Cows enough to keep their Family in Milk, Whey, Curds, Cheese and Butter; they also have Flesh in Abundance such as it is, for the lot of the old Cows and the lean Calves that are like to die. The Cow-Pen Men are hardy People, are almost continually on Horseback, being obliged to know the Haunts of their Cattle

You see, Sir, what a wild set of Creatures our Englishmen grow into when they lose Society, and it is surprising to think how many advantages they throw away, which our industrious country-men would be glad of: out of many hundred Cows they will not give themselves the trouble of milking more than will maintain their Family.[9]

The very ease and cheapness of cattle raising on the frontier placed its stamp on the breed. The free range placed the value of cattle on the number rather than the quality of live stock. In the winter cattle were driven into the canebrakes to range for themselves. The cost of feed was thus saved, but in the spring they turned up half starved and it took the summer for them to put on normal weight. Cow drivers from the South and the back country took their droves to Charleston, Philadelphia, and New York to market. At the close of the War of 1812 herds of more

[9] *Extracts of Letters from an Officer,* quoted in A. B. Hulbert, *Paths of Inland Commerce,* pp. 22-24.

1an a thousand cattle, were met going to Pennsylvania to fatten
or the Philadelphia market.[10]

What is meant by the survival of frontier practices in the case
f cattle is well shown in a comment found in the *First Annual
Report* of the Missouri State Board of Agriculture:

'he method has been to let cattle run through the summer and get fat;
:ll off what can be spared and keep the rest on the least possible amount
f roughness that will subsist an animal and keep strength enough in the
ody to begin with in the coming spring; in this way it takes one third
f the summer to recover the losses of winter starvation. I have no doubt
ut one-half of the entire neat cattle of this country with horses, mules,
1eep and hogs go through the winter season with no more food than
'ould be required to feed them well two weeks. As a result cows weigh
75 pounds and four year old steers reach 475 pounds. The Pointer is
1e universal hog here and a meaner one can not be found in any
•untry.[11]

The passing of frontier conditions in some respects injured the
1use of stock raising. In hilly areas the rougher uplands had been
sed for pasturage. Later they were planted to corn and put under
llage by the plow for which they were in no wise fitted by topog-
1phy. The result was erosion and the injury of fair grazing
nds. Close grazing is held in some regions to have killed the
.ue stem grass while in others the cessation of fires resulted
1 the growth of weeds, prairie grass, sassafras sprouts, and post
1k runners which took the place of native pasturage.

Well fitted to the frontier type of agriculture in the deep South
the mule. To that Virginia farmer, George Washington, must be
ven the credit of foreseeing the adaptation of the mule to southern
griculture. A "pair of Jacks" of the Andulusian breed presented
him by the king of Spain at the solicitation of Lafayette were
'obably the first asses imported into the South for breeding pur-
ses. In 1832 Henry Clay, "gallant Harry of the West," imported
e first blooded Catalonian Jack into Kentucky. The adoption of
e mule admirably suited to the climatic and labor conditions as
e general work animal was an important step in the beginnings
southern agriculture.[12]

[10] Turner, *op. cit.,* p. 16.
[11] Quoted by C. O. Sauer, *Geography of the Ozark Highlands*, p. 161.
[12] *The South in the Building of the Nation*, V, 82.

THE PLANTATION

Frontier farming as a rule expended very little care on improving the quality of its animals. At the same time the pioneer environment produced from the original stock types which, like
the long horn steer and razorback hog of minstrel song and story,
were adapted to survive in the wilderness and canebrake. The
stock also developed some qualities of acclimation which enabled
them to survive after a fashion diseases fatal to imported cattle.
If the frontier, however, did little to improve the quality of its animals it was kinder to their quantity.

It, in fact, seems a safe conclusion that the spread of the plantation caused a decline in the number of live stock in the South. Between 1850 and 1860 there was an absolute decline in the total number of cattle found in the states of Virginia, South Carolina, Georgia,
Mississippi, and Louisiana; and a less than normal increase occurred in North Carolina, Tennessee, and Alabama. On the other
hand, Arkansas, Texas, and the border states of Maryland and
Missouri showed notable increases with Texas far outstripping the
rest.[13]   The area of declining cattle follows in rough outline the
plantation regions. This trend has been a continuous one. Statistics
of live stock production in such a southern state as North Carolina show that there has been a progressive decline in the number
of swine, horses, and cattle per inhabitant since 1870.[14] This trend
fits in with the urbanization of the South, the one crop system of
agriculture, and the decreasing use of meat in the American diet
as well as the westward trend of ranching. It is true, of course,
that none of these factors played significant rôles in the advance
of the plantation. The decreasing importance of live stock in the
1850's must then be sought in the characteristics of the plantation
system itself.

The plantation was not fitted for stock raising. It was primarily an industrial organization for the employment of servile
labor in the routine production of staple crops, mainly cotton. That
slaves, however valuable for cotton and sugar, were of little use
in handling live stock was argued by such a pro-slavery Democrat

---

[13] *South in the Building of the Nation*, V, 254.

[14] H. M. Smedes, *Agricultural Graphics*, University of North Carolina Extension
Bulletin, pp. 42-47.

s Jacob De Cordova.[15] It is notable that slaves were not introduced in the stock ranges of Western Texas.

The care of blooded stock and dairy cows is admittedly a task
or experts, and slaves were not trained to expertness in this field.
Olmsted's *Journeys* are full of accounts of neglect and brutalities
lavished upon live stock by the slaves who tended them. Here
we have one instance where he comes near blaming the Negro
s a Negro rather than slavery as a system for a deplorable state
of affairs. He accounts for the prevalence of the mule in southern
agriculture in a characteristic passage:

So, too, when I ask why mules are so universally substituted for horses
on the farm, the first reason given, and confessedly the most conclusive
one, is, that horses cannot bear the treatment that they always *must* get
from negroes; horses are always soon foundered or crippled by them,
while mules will bear cudgelling, and lose a meal or two now and then,
and not be materially injured, and they do not take cold or get sick if
neglected or overworked. But I do not need to go further than to the
window of the room in which I am writing, to see, at almost any time,
treatment of cattle that would insure the immediate discharge of the
driver, by almost any farmer owning them at the North.[16]

It is true, however, that under slavery, cattle, hogs, and sheep
were to be found upon the vast majority of plantations. Many
slaveholders "took a great deal of pride in having a few well-bred
cattle of the Devon and Shorthorn breeds on their plantations,
and the blood of these cattle is still found in the native southern
herds in a few rich-red, big-framed cows."[17] We know that improved Shorthorns were imported into Virginia by a Maryland
firm, Miller and Gough, as early as 1783. In 1817 Colonel Lewis
Saunders imported his famous herd of Shorthorns into Kentucky,
and in the same year Henry Clay imported Herefords for his estate near Lexington.[18] The border state of Kentucky is regarded
by some students as having taken the lead in production of fine live
stock from 1840 to 1870. Kentucky, it must be remembered, had
her blue grass and was not a true plantation state. Fine horses

[15] *Texas: Her Resources and Public Men*, pp. 189-90.
[16] Olmsted, *A Journey in the Seaboard Slave States*, I, 51.
[17] F. W. Farley, "Growth of the Beef-Cattle Industry in the South," Separate
49, U. S. D. A. *Yearbook*, 1917, p. 4.
[18] *The South in the Building of the Nation*, V, 254.

were the pride of slaveholders in Virginia and Kentucky, and horse racing was regarded as the true sport of kings—and planters. The exploits of the troublesome "instantaneous cavalry" units in the Confederate Army are a tribute to the blood and breeding of their steeds. For example, the great Kentucky horse, Gaines Denmark, was ridden for two years in Morgan's command. Weakened by the hard military service, he died in 1864. On the whole, the conclusion seems justified that the plantation turned the emphasis in frontier farming from live stock to staple crops, decreased the number of cattle grown, and at the same time improved the blood of a small upper class of equine and bovine aristocracy owned by the planters.

The Civil War left the live stock industry of the South prostrate.[19] Thousands of sheep, hogs and cattle had been sacrificed for the needs of the warring armies or seized by foragers. Although the best blooded horses of Kentucky and Virginia were used as mounts in the cavalry units, enough of them escaped battle and raids to enable those regions to continue the breeding of fine stock. In western Texas, beyond the range of hostilities, cattle ranching continued undisturbed except for occasional depredations by Indians. The earliest recovery was found in the border states such as Kentucky and Virginia. In the economic and political disorganization following the break-up of the plantation there could be little provision for stock raising. In such a period of poverty former slaves while seeking to find a place in the new order were often reduced to the point of preying upon anything edible. A report of the United States Commissioner of Agriculture for 1867 on live stock in the South says: "Little has been done in this direction; the predatory character of a portion of the population has, in many respects, reduced the stock of hogs and sheep to a minimum. . . . Of the entire stock of domestic animals, in certain sections of the cotton states, less than one pound in every hundred is furnished by the care of man.[20]

GRASS IN THE SOUTH

The Cotton Belt in 1919 contained almost as much live stock as the Corn Belt, about 15,000,000 units. This is due to its large acreage, for the Corn Belt possesses 94 animal units per square mile

[19] *The South in the Building of the Nation,* VI, 136.
[20] *The South in the Building of the Nation,* VI, quoted p. 137.

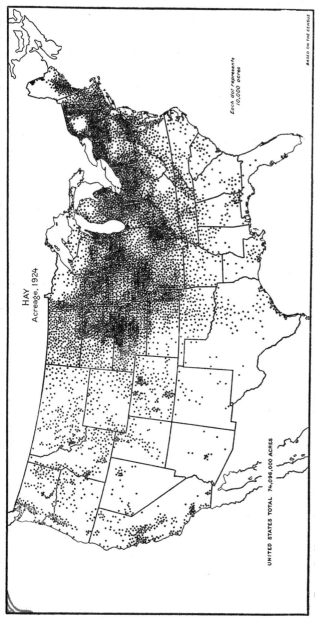

HAY
Acreage, 1924

Each dot represents
10,000 acres

BASED ON THE CENSUS

UNITED STATES TOTAL 74,096,000 ACRES

FIGURE 8.—No crop is so widespread as hay in the United States, largely because so many plants with varying climatic requirements, are made into hay. Although a little hay is grown everywhere, it is an unimportant crop in the Cotton Belt and in the southwestern country, except in the irrigated districts. Most of the hay is produced in the hay and dairy belt, in the Corn Belt, particularly around its margins, and in the corn and winter-wheat belt. Timothy and clover are the dominant hay crops in these regions. Locally hay (mostly alfalfa) is very important in the irrigated districts of the West, and a considerable quantity is grown in the spring-wheat region (mostly wild hay). (Courtesy of U. S. Department of Agriculture).

to the South's 34.[21]   This situation testifies to the lack of forage
crops in the South.   There are only six states in the Union with
less than ten per cent of their crop land planted to hay and forage.
They all belong to the southern South.   Only three others have
less than 15 per cent; they are South Carolina, Arkansas, and
Oklahoma.   North Carolina ranges between 15 and 20 per cent;
Tennessee and Kentucky, 20 to 30.[22]   Moreover, in the South
horses and mules constitute a larger proportion of the live stock
than in any other agricultural region.   This is partly due to the
heavy demand of cotton culture for horse and mule labor.

The one crop system does not furnish a complete explanation
of this state of affairs.   The South has never been a good grass and
hay country.   Those early explorers who wrote of the "goodly
meadows" near the southern coasts did not know how inferior
are the salt marsh grasses for forage.[23]   In the Middle Atlantic
States early settlers found the native vegetation of broom straw
"which is as dry as a stick and as yellow as straw, insomuch that
nothing will taste it."[24]   Further south in the pine barrens "the
most natural grass on this soil," wrote an observer before 1775
"is of a very harsh nature, and the cattle are not at all fond of it;
it is known by the name of wire grass; and they only eat it while
young; for the procuring it young or renewing this kind of pasture the woods are frequently fired."[25]

In 1883 a Mr. Charles Mohr of Mobile had collected in South
and Middle Alabama alone, 132 species belonging to 53 genera of
native grasses.[26]   The South, however, is not naturally a grass
country, and the possibility of forming a permanent close turf, except in the limestone regions of Kentucky, Tennessee, and the
Valley of Virginia, has long been seriously doubted.[27]   The farther north one goes in the United States the more likely is one to
find good grass, densely sodded.   Grass thrives best in cool, moist

[21] U. S. D. A. *Yearbook*, 1923, pp. 328-29.

[22] *Ibid.*, p. 33.

[23] Lyman Carrier, *Beginnings of Agriculture in America*, p. 26.

[24] John Mitchell, *The Present Status of Great Britain and North America*, p. 153,
quoted by Carrier, *op. cit.*, p. 29.

[25] Bernard Romans, *Natural History of East and West Florida*, p. 16; quoted by
Carrier, *op. cit.*, p. 29.

[26] John L. Campbell, and W. H. Ruffner, *A Physical Survey in Georgia, Alabama,
and Mississippi*, p. 14.

[27] Lewis F. Carr, *America Challenged*, p. 113.

climate and the grasses of the South are neither strong nor abundant enough to support dairy herds in full production or fill out grass-fed beef cattle.[28] The leached and eroded soils of the southeastern slopes are hardly fitted for producing good forage crops unless pains are taken to increase the fertility of the land.

Another fact of geography must be taken into account. The higher rainfall for all the areas of the Cotton Belt except its extreme western end results in autumn showers that make the raising of hay hazardous. From North Carolina to Louisiana many farmers attempt to produce hay, but a large part of the crop is lost each year in the curing and much of the rest is damaged by untimely rains. More dependable autumn weather is found in states farther from the Atlantic and the Gulf, particularly Arkansas, Oklahoma, and parts of Texas, all of which have larger acreages of hay. Accordingly, in most of the cotton states, not enough hay is produced for home use and much has to be imported from the Middle West. Since the freight charges often equal the original cost, southern planters pay a high price for this. If methods of curing suitable to the climate were worked out, hay would be more generally grown. It would not, however, be valuable as a cash crop in the South except where a few farmers in each community grew it for the local market.

The great drawback to forage crops in the South, however, is not excessive rainfall so much as lack of grasses adapted to southern conditions. The high producing crops of the North, timothy, red clover and blue grass, have little use as forage in the South. It is not probable, says the United States Department of Agriculture, that any hay grass possessing in the South an importance corresponding to timothy in the North will ever be discovered.[29]

Of the native grasses Johnson grass makes a heavy yield of excellent hay, but it is such a pest in fields where it is not wanted that its planting in clean fields is not ordinarily recommended. Furthermore, after the first two or three years, the thick, heavy rootstocks become so matted as to cut down its yield.[30] Crab grass is another native grass used as a volunteer hay crop. It grows on especially sandy soils but is also a great nuisance to

[28] Ibid.
[29] S. M. Tracy, "Forage for the Cotton Belt," Farmers' Bulletin 1125, 1920, p. 5.
[30] Ibid., p. 9.

crop lands. Many of the failures of crimson clover in the South are due to lack of proper inoculation, but this clover is not likely to succeed farther west than Louisiana because of dry periods.[31] Of the introduced forage plants alfalfa is undoubtedly the best legume for permanent meadows but does well in only a small part of the Cotton Belt. The rich soil with the abundance of lime that it demands is found in the black prairies and certain well-drained alluvial regions. Alfalfa has definitely failed on dry clay uplands, in the pine woods, and in the Gulf Coast region.[32]

The need for forage and hay in the South is shown by the fact reported by Lewis F. Carr that every year thousands of young cattle are shipped from the old South to the North and West for better growth on stronger grasses.[33] The old trails from Texas to the North and from the Southwest to Wyoming were both used for driving stock to better pastures.

A good hay plant is one that makes a large growth, is leafy, has fine and tender stems, is palatable, and grows tall and erect enough to be cut with a machine. The South possesses one grass suitable for permanent pastures that ordinarily does not fit the requirements for hay, Bermuda. "The Bermuda grass," wrote an enthusiast in 1883, "will take fast hold on the most hopeless looking gullies and in barren soils where no other grass will grow. And once lodged it holds on and spreads, even under hard pasturing . . . bears any amount of drought and close pasturing; is very sweet and nutritious when young . . . furnishes a grass sod which for density and freedom from foreign growth we have never seen surpassed."[34] That the enthusiasm is not misplaced is shown by more scientific and restrained language from the Department of Agriculture:

Bermuda grass is the foundation of the best permanent pastures in the South, especially on clayey soils. It endures severe drought and long flooding by water and makes excellent grazing from late spring until heavy frost. On rich and fairly moist clayey soils it grows large enough to be cut for hay, the quality of which is excellent. It is one of the best grasses for creek and river bottom lands for binding levees and ditch banks and for lawns which have good care.[35]

[31] *Ibid.*, p. 33.
[32] *Ibid.*, p. 29.   [33] *America Challenged*, p. 113.
[34] Campbell and Ruffner, *op. cit.*, p. 114.
[35] *Forage for the Cotton Belt*, pp. 5-6.

Bermuda has its drawbacks. For good growth it requires lands of high fertility which in the Cotton Belt are better used for cash crops. Even on many fertile soils it does not grow tall enough for hay. It cannot be used in a rotation of crops for it is a "poisonous" grass that once it takes the land resists all but the most skillful efforts to eradicate it.[36] In the northern parts of the Cotton Belt winter plowing will kill the plant by exposing its roots to frost. Further south the grass must be killed by smothering, planting at least two other heavy crops over it during the year.[37] Giant Bermuda grass, recently introduced from Brazil, is said on rich soil to grow runners twenty feet long and stems two feet high. For the light sandy soils near the Gulf Coast, carpet grass is fitted as Bermuda grass to the heavier and richer soils. It comes in very quickly where the land is heavily pastured and trampled and because of its creeping habit of growth can bear close grazing. It makes little growth after the first frost and cannot be used for winter grazing unless the stock are removed from the field in July or August. When this is done the grass makes a growth of six to twelve inches by November.[38]

The most widespread and most valuable self-seeding legume throughout the whole cotton region is a grass introduced from Japan, lespedeza or Japanese clover. It grows on all soils except the sandy soils of southern Florida, reaches its greatest growth in clayey soils with a fair amount of lime; on thin sandy soils it grows so low and spreading as to be valuable only for grazing. At its best it may reach a height of thirty inches and yield three tons of hay an acre.[39] Lewis F. Carr writes:

It is a true clover but it will grow on sour soils. It is typically Japanese in its morphological characteristics, its stems and leaves being very fine and delicate—resembling maidenhair fern. It is as good a feed as alfalfa but the leaves shatter freely so that much of the plant is lost in feeding. On good land it will make a ton and a half to two to the acre; but on poor soil it will not grow tall enough to be cut with a mowing machine. It grows so close to the ground that in the early part of the season it resembles the nap of a Turkish rug. . . . By the latter part of August the nap usually becomes ankle deep and sometimes deeper. I have seen

[36] Carr, *op. cit.*, pp. 113-14.
[37] *Forage for the Cotton Belt*, p. 8.
[38] *Ibid.*, p. 8.
[39] *Ibid.*, p. 34.

it grow so thick that it would not fall down after it was cut. . . . But though lespedeza offers an answer to the problem of grass in the South it is at best a very small plant for real hay making and its use is limited to very rich soils.[40]

Like Bermuda, lespedeza has a giant cousin, Korean clover, introduced by the Department of Agriculture about 1923. Its future is still uncertain. Though it grows higher, it does not grow so rank and fails to resist drought.[41] Sudan grass, imported from Africa, offered great promise. Although it can be cut two or three times a year it has not been successfully adapted to southern conditions. Napier grass is still in the experimental stage. Soy beans will grow on land too poor for corn and are less injured either by drought or moisture. Velvet beans furnish an important grazing crop for cattle and hogs in autumn and winter.

Cowpeas make good hay and are grown more widely than any other cultivated legume in the South. They must, however, be planted every year and are especially difficult to cure for hay in the uncertain weather of the South. The mower may be run from the time the dew dries until noon. The vines should be turned as soon as the upper surface wilts, and may be put into small cocks the following afternoon. There it should be left for three days until hauled to the barn. If the pitching is done by hand rather than by a tedder it requires a week of fair weather to cure a field of pea hay.[42]

In the grasses then, exists one of the main differences between southern and northern farming. Some day a grass that will thrive in the South, producing both hay and permanent pastures that may be plowed up, may be discovered or developed. Cotton and corn culture, agriculture without grass, have in the South met hardy grasses that persist in spreading and resist uprooting. The result is that southern farmers must wage war on grass. Just after the Civil War, a planter near Greenville, Mississippi, sowed grass on his land and was sued by a neighbor. The lack of grass fitted to southern soils and climate is well shown by methods of keeping lawns in the eastern coastal plains. Even for many of the better houses the yard is kept bare of vegetation, carefully sanded, and swept

[40] *Op. cit.,* p. 114.
[41] *Ibid.*
[42] *Forage for the Cotton Belt,* pp. 35-36.

several times a week. Certain grasses such as carpet or Bermuda might be grown on these yards, but the farmer rightly fears they may "take the place." Unless an all purpose grass such as timothy in the North is found in the South it must be realized that the section will continue to be handicapped in the pursuit of dairying and the production of fine beef cattle.[43]

The South and the Tick[44]

The climatic distribution of disease and disease parasites has furnished an additional handicap to live stock production in the South. The Texas tick fever may be counted as one of the factors of the complex of warm, moist climate. A minute parasite living within the blood cells of cattle causes tick fever. The life cycle of this parasite is dependent upon its host, the cattle tick. The stages of the tick from the vegetation on which it is hatched to its unwilling host, the cow, and back again demands a mild winter. Part of the penalty which any mild, moist region pays for its fertility is the fecundity of its insects, parasites, and obnoxious plants.

It has long been known that "murrain," "redwater" or "bloody murrain" killed many cattle brought into the South. The disease, without being understood, caused losses year after year in the early history of the South. It was first described scientifically by a Dr. T. Pease around the 1790's. He showed that a severe outbreak of disease and death among cattle in Lancaster, Pennsylvania, had followed the shipment of some North Carolina cattle into the region. Observation showed that practically all excessive deaths of northern cattle along roads and in pastures followed the transportation of southern cattle over those routes. At the same time the southern cattle remained perfectly healthy. Also northern cattle brought into the South usually succumbed. The danger of sending southern cattle to the North during hot weather, although mysterious, was firmly established. The affected area was located in 1885, and in 1891 the first Texas fever quarantine line was drawn by Dr. D. E. Salmon.

[43] Carr, *op. cit.,* p. 115.
[44] John R. Mohler, "Texas or Tick Fever," U. S. D. A. *Farmers' Bulletin,* No. 569, Nov. 1928. W. F. Ward, "Production of Beef in the South," U. S. D. A. *Yearbook,* 1913, pp. 259-82. *The Story of the Cattle Fever Tick,* U. S. D. A. *Yearbook* (3), 1922.

The means by which diseases like yellow fever and malaria are transmitted to men were first made known by a study of tick fever, the work of Smith and Kilborne. These men, both from the Bureau of Animal Industry, went to work with zest on experiments in laboratories and the cattle fields of Texas. In 1889 Smith was able to isolate protozoa in the blood stream and to recognize them as causes of Texas fever. In 1890 Kilborne proved by experiment with actual herds of cattle that the disease was carried not by contagion among cattle but by an intermediary host, the tick. Without its presence the protozoa cannot perpetuate their generations. The parasitism of the tick itself is so perfect that in case no cattle and horses are at hand the seed tick dies without further development. Thus was furnished the first experimental proof that certain diseases regarded as epidemic are carried from one organism to another by an intermediary host.

When these facts were made known two methods of combating the disease were suggested, one biological, the other regional. The first was based on the known facts regarding serum treatment and immunization. Experiments of the Bureau of Animal Industry in 1893 indicated that a mild, non-fatal attack of tick fever produced in northern cattle served to protect those cattle when carried South. From 1895 to 1897 further experiment showed the possibility of producing immunity in northern cattle by injections of blood from southern cattle. While these methods prepared certain cattle for standing exposure to ticks, the better plan seemed to lie in an attack on the region itself. Accordingly efforts were expended toward perfecting a method that would free meadows, fields, and farms of the ticks. Experiments finally developed a chemical solution strong enough to kill ticks without injuring cattle. This solution was applied by dipping, that is forcing cattle to swim for short distances through narrow vats containing the solution. Field experiments showed that regular dipping of all cattle in a definite area accompanied by quarantine of cattle from infected areas served to rid regions of the tick in a short time. Accordingly in 1906 the weight of the Federal Department was shifted from the immunization plan to the regional attack. An ambitious but scientific program for the complete eradication of the fever tick from the United States was boldly planned, and Congress made the first appropriation of $82,500 on July 1, 1906.

At the beginning of the work there were 741,515 square miles of infected territory, comprising 966 counties under quarantine in thirteen southern states. By November 1, 1913, 198,802 square miles had been freed of the tick at a cost of less than $10 a square mile to the Federal Government. In Mississippi, one of the worst infested states, eradication work was being carried on in 26 counties, by 1913, and dipping vats were being built in 15 others. Virginia, South Carolina, Kentucky, and Tennessee were tick free by 1922. North Carolina, Georgia, and Oklahoma were infested only on their eastern fringes. Texas, Arkansas, Louisiana, and Florida appeared the most hopeless. By June 30, 1930, there remained under quarantine 184 counties in five states. Alabama, Oklahoma, North Carolina, and Georgia had been added to the tick free areas. Cattle to the number of 16,136,527 were dipped during the year ending July 1, 1930. By December 1, 1931, only the lower tier of southern states remained dangerous territory. Texas with 52, Louisiana with 42, Florida with 25, and Arkansas with 8, accounted for the 137 counties still under quarantine.

Throughout its course the tick eradication campaign has run afoul of the folkways of the frontier. The coöperation, supervision, and paternal regimentation exercised by Federal inspectors and county agents have cut square across the individualism of owners of scrub stock. Many stockmen were openly contemptuous of the "tick theory," and the Department of Agriculture experts were much put to it at first to prove they knew what they were talking about. In many rural districts the opinion has held ground that dipping killed cows or ruined their milk. Dipping is too much trouble; it is not worth while to keep cattle if they have to be dipped. Owners in some places have had cows butchered rather than dip them. In certain rural areas dipping vats have been dynamited in the dead of night, and public opinion has blocked any serious effort to discover and punish those guilty. Dipping has been favored by those prepared to regard stock raising as a large scale industry capable of using scientific methods. It is opposed by those who raise a few scrub stock, preferably on a free range as did the frontiersman, as a kind of by-product of general farming. This type of farmer expects his stock to cost him nothing and is not disappointed if they yield him little. To him the fact that his scrub stock runs at large and spreads ticks abroad is nobody's business.

Cut-Over Pine Lands[45]

As a by-product of lumbering there were in the piney woods section of the South in 1921, 100,000,000 acres of cut-over land, an area equal to the combined acreage of Georgia, Alabama, and Mississippi. Since 1921 the area of the cut-over pine lands has been increased about 10,000,000 acres annually and is expected ultimately to reach 250,000,000 acres.

The disposition of these lands in our national economy presents a serious problem. They remain much as the lumbering crews left them, covered with stumps, logs, and timber débris. Taxes are mounting on non-productive tracts, and with prevailing agricultural surpluses there exists little market for the oversupply of land. It is known that much of the land possesses agricultural value, and yet there is danger that it may revert to the state for taxes. Interest in the question led to the Cut-Over Land Conference of the South, held in New Orleans in April 1917.

The improvement of the native pastures is among the most important problems facing beef cattle production in the cut-over piney woods. The abundance of grass on the range, mainly wire grass and broom sedge, furnishes good grazing for only a short time before it becomes dry and withered. In addition, these native pastures in the pine woods have been burned over almost every year since the country was settled. While burning makes for ease of grazing because the cattle do not have to pick out the green from the dead grass, it undoubtedly retards the growth of the range. The most serious injury has been to prevent the formation of humus in the land since all the organic matter is destroyed before it is incorporated with the soil. Some of the soils are so devoid of humus as to "check crack" in dry weather, much as does a dried mud puddle. These frequent fires have also had the effect of keeping out desirable pasture grass. Thus have been perpetuated wire grass and broom sedge which, although possessed of an uncanny ability to withstand fire, are not able to stand up under heavy grazing. Carpet grass, on the other hand, a valuable perennial that stands close grazing is not able to withstand the

[45] F. W. Farley and S. W. Greene, "The Cut-Over Pine Lands of the South for Beef-Cattle Production," U. S. D. A. *Bulletin*, 827.

frequent forest fires. In spite of these facts southern cattle owners have persisted in burning off the range each year much to the disgust of turpentine operators and lumbermen. While lespedeza may have proved adapted to these conditions in its suitability to various soils and ability to spread rapidly, there exists, however, no grass exactly suited to conditions on cut-over lands. E. B. Ferriss of the McNeil, Mississippi, Experiment Station has reported:

Many of the best pasture crops do not thrive as they should on the wild lands until the lands have been plowed and sweetened—at least to a limited extent. To plow and mow these lands with stumps still on them is almost out of the question.[46]

The Biological Factor[47]

Geographic factors, the presence of the tick, and the relative lack of good forage have retarded growth of southern cattle. Cattle heavily infected with ticks have been lowered in vigor and vitality to such an extent that they have not been able fully to utilize the grazing. Exclusive reliance on summer pasture has left many animals exposed to annual periods of starvation during winter. Thus they lose a large part of the gains made during the more favorable season and become so stunted that they require one to two years longer to reach mature size. Cultural methods of handling stock, survivals of the frontier, also retard their development. Until recently, for example, cattle have been left to graze at large on the "public range." With no segregation of bulls, breeding of under-aged and under-sized heifers seriously retards their growth and eventually, it is thought, reduces the size of the animals in the herd.

Factors of blood and breeding, however, have been as important as those of geography. Throughout the South, owing possibly to the low grade of the cattle, the practice has been to "top" rather than "cull" the herd for sales. This means that by selling the better rather than the poorer animals, owners have caused their herds progressively to deteriorate. An outstanding example is

[46] *Mississippi A. and M. College Bulletin,* 180. Cited U. S. D. A. *Bulletin* 827, p. 28.
[47] F. W. Farley, "Growth of Beef-Cattle Industry in the South," U. S. D. A. *Yearbook,* 1917. W. F. Ward, *op. cit.* F. W. Farley and S. W. Greene, *loc. cit.* Arthur T. Semple, "Beef Production in the Cotton Belt," U. S. D. A. *Farmers' Bulletin* 1379, 1923.

found in Florida where for many years bulls were topped for export to Cuba for bull fighting. The loss of better breeding stock has produced a marked effect on native cattle of Florida; they are small and of a quality inferior to those of other sections of the Piney Woods.

As shown the foundation stock introduced by the Spanish was composed of small animals. They have largely remained of inferior quality because of failure to introduce new blood. At the same time, the native stock has become adapted to its environment. Their thrift in utilization of sparse pastures, partial immunity to tick fever, and their general hardiness have become fixed to such a degree that there is little doubt among cattle men that they are transmitted to their offspring. There seems no doubt, on the other hand, that their unfavorable biological qualities are also fixed. For instance, it was found that the average weights of the type of cattle slaughtered in 1918 were 462 pounds at Jacksonville, 600 pounds at New Orleans, and 745 pounds at East St. Louis. Two biological qualities help account for the fact that native southern cattle are from 100 to 200 pounds lighter than western beef. In terms of the stockman they are "cold blooded," that is, do not respond readily to feed. Secondly, although they become compact when fattened, their weight is too much forward. This results in a small percentage of the valuable cuts and reduces the price received for southern cattle. There seems, accordingly, to be little foundation for the theory once widely held in the South, that the poor size and quality of native cattle is due only to lack of feed and care.

On the other hand, there exists the belief that pure bred animals put under southern conditions will rapidly degenerate to a type approximating the native cattle. This belief has received apparent confirmation in the extreme susceptibility of imported cattle to tick fever. While individuals sicken and die, the breed does not degenerate as cattlemen now well know.

The improvement of the two factors of environment and breed must go hand in hand. Since neither can be changed over night, it is best to keep them balanced. And until forage conditions are changed the hardiness of the native stock must be regarded as a quality valuable enough to be retained. If it were not for that quality, the strain of native cattle would have run out long ago because of the ravages of the cattle tick, seasonal starvation, breeding of immature animals, and inbreeding. It is better, says the Department of Agriculture in recognition of these facts, "to grow into the cattle business than to buy into it." This holds true, first, because of the heavy cost of a pure bred herd and, second, because of the dangers to which it is exposed in the South.

The method of "growing into" fine stock raising is fairly simple. It has been used with native Texas cows, possibly inferior to Piney Woods stock, and a superior grade of cattle has been developed from the Texas Longhorn by the use of Shorthorn and Hereford Bulls. The biological strain is improved simply by the use of a pure sire of proved prepotency and the herds are culled 10 to 15 per cent each year instead of topped. Lower prices are obtained from the sale of culls than of toppers but results are soon apparent in herds that possess the native hardiness plus qualities of fine stock. First cross calves from pure bred sires out of native cows of all types and colors are uniform in color and are built closer to the ground. They have shown a marked change in width, depth, and size of bone. Accordingly, there remains no doubt as to the value of the native southern cow for foundation herds. Cases of successful mixed beef herds in the South can be multiplied.

In Alabama one breeder has been grading up by the use of a pure-bred bull for the last 15 years and his herd of 178 head of grade Herefords now ranges from one half to fifteen sixteenths pure-bred. Practically half his herd could hardly be distinguished from pure breds. The records of these cattle have been followed closely. The yearlings now produced from high-grade cows weigh 200 pounds more than native yearlings under the same conditions as to pasturage and feed.

A Florida breeder has been grading up the native cows with pure-bred Shorthorn bulls for 15 years and his present herd is uniformly good. In his herd he has the original first-cross cow, called old Blue, and her granddaughters and great-granddaughters and the last could not be picked out from his pure bred heifers.[48]

One additional factor of the southern map as related to cattle raising is distance to market. The nearest markets and packing plants from the center of the Piney Woods cattle area are: New Orleans, 300 miles; Jacksonville, 420 miles; St. Louis, 582 miles;

[48] F. W. Farley and S. W. Greene, *op. cit.,* pp. 12-13.

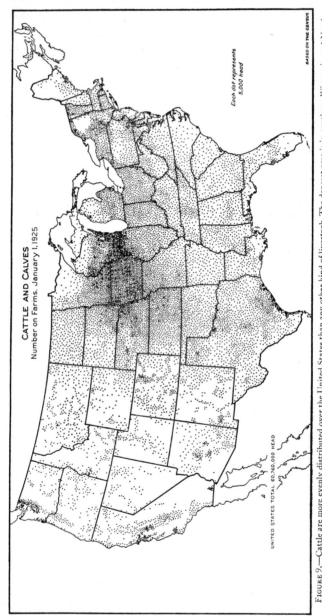

CATTLE AND CALVES
Number on Farms, January 1, 1925

Each dot represents
5,000 head

BASED ON THE CENSUS

UNITED STATES TOTAL 60,760,000 HEAD

FIGURE 9.—Cattle are more evenly distributed over the United States than any other kind of livestock. The densest area is in southern Wisconsin and Northern Illinois, Iowa, northern Missouri, eastern Nebraska, southeastern South Dakota, and southern Minnesota. On January 1, 1925, there were about 13,000,000 cattle in the Corn Belt, or 55 to the square mile; 11,000,000 in the hay and pasture region, or 34 to the square mile; 9,000,000 in the corn and winter-wheat belt, or 30 to the square mile; 7,000,000 in the Cotton Belt, or 17 to the square mile; and 8,000,000 in the two wheat regions, or about 20 to the square mile. The Western regions had about 11,000,000 cattle, an average of 9 to the square mile. In Iowa there were nearly 80 cattle to the square mile. (Courtesy of U. S. Department of Agriculture).

Fort Worth, 790 miles; and Baltimore, 860 miles. This, however, is more an economic than a geographic factor and will be remedied only with the development of cattle raising. As one lumberman has expressed it: "We would not build our sawmills and wait for the timber to grow, and we cannot expect to have big packing plants until we raise the cattle."[49] Already small packing plants have been located at Chipley, Florida; Moultrie and Macon, Georgia; Andulusia, Mobile, and Birmingham, Alabama; Natchez and Vicksburg, Mississippi; and Baton Rouge, Louisiana.

DAIRYING IN THE COTTON BELT

In 1919 the only five states in the Union having an average milk production of less than 2,000 pounds per dairy cow were cotton states: Alabama, Mississippi, Louisiana, Arkansas, and Texas. In addition to forage and fever conditions dairying in the South faces other factors involved in the Cotton System. Dairy cattle, for instance, are well adapted for using the by-products of cotton raising; cottonseed meal, cottonseed hulls, and legumes grown to enrich the soil. Many cotton plantations, moreover, have large acreages of abandoned fields, woodlands, and unimproved lands, that fencing, cutting of brush, improvement of water supply and shelter with sowing of grass seed would put in line for dairying. Dairying, on the other hand, is an all the year round routine, requiring steady and unremitting attention. Cotton production has a cultural routine with heavy peaks of human labor at two definite seasons of the year, chopping and harvesting. It is a hopeless task to accommodate the routines of cotton culture to full-fledged dairying. Moreover, the shift from cotton production to dairying is difficult because of large initial outlays required for stock, shelter, and equipment. The abundance of workers of low economic status has been fitted, however haphazardly, into the southern economic system by means of share tenancy. Custom has evolved a method by which workers without land or capital can till the soil for a share of the product. Although the rule of the "third and fourth" has been applied to staples such as cotton and corn, no method has been successfully set by custom under which tenants may engage in live stock raising and dairying. Not only are landlords afraid to trust stock to the tenants, but dairying is a new and arduous

[49] *Ibid.*, p. 49.

technique distasteful to the southern farmer. The close attention to duty, the habits of steady, skillful routine accepted by
butter fat producers of Wisconsin as a matter of fact, are traits not
yet present in southern culture.

Dairying is also dependent upon density and distribution of
population. By far the largest part in the grand total of milk
production is sold as market milk for household consumption in
nearby cities. Raw milk for family consumption commands a
higher price and takes precedence over all other dairy products.
The great dairy regions of New England, southern New York,
and eastern Pennsylvania have developed their industries along
the line of producing milk for the large eastern cities. The area
of butter and cheese production, for instance, has been pushed
back year after year by the higher price paid for market milk until
milk is shipped into New York City from the farthest parts of
the state. Conversely the larger the percentage of rural population the smaller the demand for milk, mainly because farm folks
are either self-supplying or go without. The lack of great cities in
the South has thus rendered it inadvisable to develop dairying
beyond a minimum point. In addition, primary markets for milk
are restricted by the fact that milk consumption does not play as
large a part in the food habits of the South. The industrial population uses milk to a much less extent than the same groups in
northern cities. The southern consumption of butter per capita
is 12 pounds a year; the national consumption is 17 pounds. Accordingly, the development of dairying in the southern states while
awaiting increased urbanization will necessarily be dependent
upon secondary markets.

The leading methods of selling milk in distant markets are, of
course, by processes which preserve part of its food qualities. Thus
as butter, cheese, ice cream, casein, milk sugar, or in powdered,
condensed, or evaporated forms, milk is prepared for secondary
markets. How far the South lags behind the nation in the processing
of its milk is clearly evident from the following tables which
show that thirteen southern states account for only 6.9 per cent
of the volume of such milk products as butter, cheese, ice cream,
and condensed milk.

It is noteworthy that outside of the bluegrass areas as Kentucky and Tennessee and the ranching areas as Texas and Okla-

TABLE XI

MILK PROCESSING PLANTS IN THE SOUTH, 1927
Butter, Cheese, Condensed Milk, Etc.

	Number of Establishments	Persons Engaged	Cost of Materials (In Thousands of Dollars)	Value of Products (In Thousands of Dollars)
1. Virginia.................	29	219	$2,411	$3,161
2. Kentucky...............	16	798	9,130	10,687
3. North Carolina..........	16	74	798	1,013
4. Tennessee...............	36	543	6,774	8,231
5. South Carolina..........	6	23	163	205
6. Georgia.................	10	130	1,100	1,362
7. Florida.................	..	...	.....	.....
8. Alabama................	13	67	780	1,035
9. Mississippi..............	22	235	4,746	6,059
10. Arkansas................	8	22	378	460
11. Louisiana...............	..	...	.....	.....
12. Oklahoma...............	40	533	10,049	12,134
13. Texas..................	40	600	8,665	11,035
The South...............	236	3,244	$44,999	$55,385
The United States........	6,721	43,307	$897,804	$1,057,544
The South's Percentage....	3.5	7.5	5.0	5.5

ICE CREAM PLANTS IN THE SOUTH, 1927

	Number of Establishments	Persons Engaged	Cost of Materials (In Thousands of Dollars)	Value of Products (In Thousands of Dollars)
1. Virginia.................	33	418	$2,045	$3,781
2. Kentucky...............	51	378	1,417	2,780
3. North Carolina..........	43	442	1,088	3,890
4. Tennessee...............	44	386	1,695	3,128
5. South Carolina..........	12	109	520	1,067
6. Georgia.................	25	310	1,376	2,681
7. Florida.................	62	472	2.060	3,834
8. Alabama................	28	304	1,268	2,227
9. Mississippi..............	41	248	1.026	1,857
10. Arkansas................	36	194	838	1,452
11. Louisiana...............	22	247	789	1,686
12. Oklahoma...............	41	352	1,536	3,071
13. Texas..................	103	872	3,114	6,291
The South...............	541	4,732	$ 19,576	$ 37,752
The United States........	2,961	31,065	$150,602	$301,644
The South's Percentage....	18.3	15.2	12.9	12.5

homa, the state to make the greatest advances in processing dairy products is Mississippi, the heart of the Cotton Belt. How this came about furnishes an interesting case study.[50] The fifteen years from 1913 to 1928 saw in the state a period of development in milk production and marketing that could not have been predicted.

[50] J. C. Holton, *Dairy Prosperity Dawns for Mississippi,* Leaflet, Miss. Dept. of Agr., 1928.

In the beginning there was no plant in the state to furnish a market for milk. Butter production was the foundation on which Mississippi constructed her dairy industry in the beginning. In 1909 the state sold only 3,334 pounds of butter; in 1919 it sold 1,864,595 pounds; by 1927 it sold 8,147,166 pounds. In 1912 there was only one creamery in the state: by 1923 the output of creameries in Mississippi was greater than the combined output of Virginia, North Carolina, South Carolina, Georgia, and Florida. The voice of Mississippi as of one crying in the wilderness was heard in Chicago and New York. Armour and Company established a creamery, first at Jackson and then another at Meridian. In 1927 their combined output amounted to two and a quarter million pounds of butter. The Brookhaven Creamery Company was the first in the South to inaugurate glass lined tank car service in transporting fluid milk. As a result the city of New Orleans now draws a large part of her milk supply from south Mississippi. In 1928 the state legislature followed suit with the passage of modern dairy and creamery laws insuring a high quality of sanitation.

The presence of dairying has served to attract other means of secondary marketing. "Saw mills go where the trees are." In 1925 there was not a single milk condensary south of the Mason and Dixon line. The Borden Company built the first at Starkville. Following closely were the Carnation Milk Company located at Tupelo, and the Pet Milk Company built at Kosciusko. These three plants in 1928 were receiving daily 300,000 pounds of milk. The Borden Company began the construction of its second plant at Macon in 1928 and others were promised. The first cheese plant was constructed in Mississippi in 1926; in 1928 there were fourteen in operation and three under construction. They included plants operated by local capital and by such national manufacturers as Kraft-Phoenix and A. H. Barber. In 1928 they were receiving about 300,000 pounds of milk daily. Another extensive market for milk is furnished by the ice cream industry. Mississippi had in 1928, 73 ice cream manufacturing plants and herself consumed annually a million and a half gallons. Other milk utilizing plants of recent origin in the state are: three dried buttermilk plants, three dried skim milk plants, five wholesale milk shipping plants, eleven whole milk distributing plants and one semi-solid buttermilk plant. In the five years from 1923 to 1928 the state witnessed an increase of 179 plants. They are classified as follows:

Cream Buying Stations	86
Ice Cream Plants	77
Creameries	27
Cheese Plants	14
Whole Milk Distributing Stations	13
Whole Milk Shipping Stations	6
Condensaries	4
Condensed Skim Milk Plants	4
Dried Buttermilk Plants	3
Dried Skim Milk Plants	3
Semi-Solid Buttermilk Plants	1
	238

This development, revolutionary though it seems, rests on solid foundation. Territories outside the two hundred mile radius of large eastern cities formerly produced the cheese, condensed milk, and butter supply of the whole country. But, as the growing cities have encroached upon these areas with the demand for more fluid milk, manufacturers have been forced to consider poverty-stricken cotton areas as a dairy frontier. Mississippi may thus be regarded as typifying an almost unexpected southern trend in which Kentucky, Tennessee, and Texas have taken part. These four southern states increased their production of condensed and evaporated milk from a blank zero in 1920 to 105 million pounds, 6 per cent of the nation's production, in 1929. During the same period cheese production in all the southern states increased from 170,000 to 13,897,000 pounds. Cheese factories increased from 10 to 54, so that, with the erection of a plant in South Carolina in 1930, every southern state is now producing cheese. Strange as it may sound the logical approach of a dairy frontier area is through dairy manufacturing. With the growth of urbanization and rising standards of living will come an increasing demand for fluid milk. Into these channels some of the secondary milk supply will easily flow.

Present Trends

In conclusion it is no great task to show that southern agriculture's greatest disparity with northern agriculture rests on this

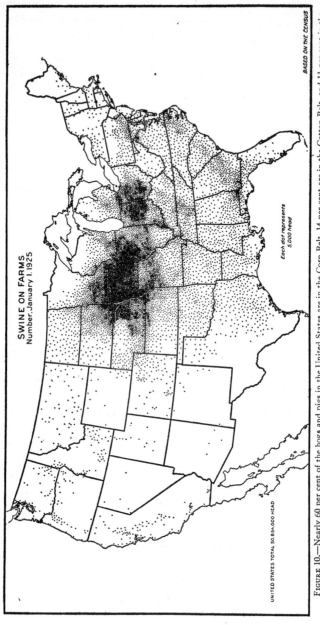

SWINE ON FARMS
Number, January 1, 1925

Each dot represents
5,000 head

BASED ON THE CENSUS

UNITED STATES TOTAL 50,854,000 HEAD

FIGURE 10.—Nearly 60 per cent of the hogs and pigs in the United States are in the Corn Belt, 14 per cent are in the Cotton Belt, and 11 per cent in the corn and winter-wheat belt. In 1919 there were, on the average, 108 swine per square mile in the Corn Belt, 18 in the Cotton Belt, 21 in the corn and winter-wheat belt, 12 in the hay and dairy region, and about 5 per square mile in the remainder of the United States. Just as the cool hay and dairy region finds the best outlet for its crops in feeding dairy cows, so the warm, fertile Corn Belt finds the growing of corn and feeding of beef cattle and hogs its most profitable system of farming. (Courtesy of U. S. Department of Agriculture).

matter of animal production. For the five year average from 1924 through 1928, crop incomes per farm for thirteen southern states reached 97.6 per cent of the nation's average. The South's cash income per farm from live stock products was only 25.4 per cent of the nation's while its gross income from live stock per farm was only 38.6 per cent of the national average.[51] Thus the South's disparity in agricultural incomes was largely due to the absence of livestock production. Almost 48 per cent of the South's cattle are found in Texas and Oklahoma and, outside these areas and the grass sections of Kentucky, Virginia, and Tennessee, the South has never contributed extensively to the commercial supply of beef. Moreover, the area's disparity in live stock production is increasing. The recent increases in swine production have occurred in the western Corn Belt at the expense of the South. From 1920 to 1929 swine production on southern farms underwent declines ranging all the way from 23.8 per cent in Oklahoma to 52.4 per cent in Tennessee. In that same period, aided by a decline in beef prices, the number of cattle in the entire South was reduced 24 per cent. The main losses were in beef cattle, for the number of cows and heifers kept for milking purposes declined only 6.3 per cent.[52] Increasing production per cow in many developing herds has demonstrated that climatic conditions do not prohibit high milk production in the South if other factors are regulated. The South's great handicap remains lack of improved pastures. Pastures are shown to be an absolute necessity for profitable production of cattle because of their negligible labor costs. Studies by the Department of Agriculture show the labor cost per ton of digestible cattle feed to be $21.21 for silage, $15.94 for grain, and 66 cents for pasture. Moreover, while natural or unimproved pastures support only one animal unit for each ten acres, improved pastures support one for each two acres at practically double the rate of gain. The census of 1920 showed only 20 per cent of pasture land in the eight southern states of Alabama, Arkansas, Florida, Georgia, Louisiana, Mississippi, North Carolina, and South Carolina to be improved. On this basis the 1925 census showed for these states a surplus of 1,500,000 animals above the

[51] See Table XIV, p. 183.
[52] See *The Agricultural Outlook for the Southern States 1930-31*, U. S. D. A. *Miscellaneous Publications*, 102, 1930, p. 51.

optimum pasture requirements.[53]   As pointed out the decrease in cattle has continued since 1925.

If Mississippi in some aspects has managed to take the lead, it is the coastal plain of the Southeast that remains the most backward. From 1879 to 1919 its acreage in harvested crops doubled, but in 1924 it was one third less than in 1919. Two per cent of its acreage was in hay or forage and 21 per cent in pasture compared to 17 per cent in forage and 41 per cent in pasture for the rest of the United States outside the Cotton Belt. Swine were found one fourth as numerous in 1924 as in 1919 and the area had one half as many milk cows per 100 acres in crops as in the nation outside the Cotton Belt. Milk production per cow was one half of that in the rest of the country, while the per capita production was only one fourth. Yet after presenting this dismal picture the Department of Agriculture was able to assert: "There are more live stock in the coastal plain than can be adequately provided for on the improved pastures available for them."[54]

To recount the story of live stock raising in the South is to tell the story of a struggle against odds. The frontier heritage of careless ways and scrub stock, nature's handicap of animal parasites, and grasses too delicate or too agressive here met a system of agriculture that seemingly left little place for live stock except the mule and the razorback hog. The average value of live stock on the farm in thirteen southern states for 1928 was $35.58. For the nation it was $76.25. The South averaged 43 acres for pasture per farm to 64 for the nation. And this figure is too high, for it includes the great ranch areas of Oklahoma and Texas. No other southern states rank as high as Kentucky with 30 pasture acres for each farm. North Carolina and South Carolina average less than ten. The fifteen states where wealth per country dweller is greatest produce $81.30 worth of animal products for each $100 worth of crops. Only four southern states, Kentucky, Virginia, Tennessee, and Florida exceed the United States average for 1929 of 224 animal units per 1,000 acres in crops. Florida ranks here only because much of her crop acreage is in intensive orchards or trucking farms. In eleven cotton states in 1928 the average value of animal products for each $100 of crops was placed at $27.12. The

[53] See U. S. D. A. *Yearbook*, 1931, pp. 423-24.
[54] *Ibid*.

TABLE XII

CROP AND ANIMAL RATIOS IN THE SOUTH

		Animal Units Per 1000 Acres in Crops	Value of Animal Products per $100 in Crops
1.	North Carolina	144	$21.90
2.	Tennessee	226	43.30
3.	South Carolina	107	21.80
4.	Georgia	121	27.70
5.	Florida	365	18.00
6.	Alabama	144	23.70
7.	Mississippi	191	22.00
8.	Arkansas	184	25.80
9.	Louisiana	173	18.90
10.	Oklahoma	154	42.60
11.	Texas	204	36.60

figures for separate states are given in Table XII. The South will be able to overcome the handicaps inherent in geography and breeds sooner than its competitive disadvantages with relation to other areas.

Nevertheless, a dairying industry adequate for local markets is becoming increasingly possible for the South. Already the section possesses 26.1 per cent of the nation's cows two years old and over kept for milk. This is but slightly under its proportion of the national area and population. The annual production of milk per milk cow in selected herds kept by crop correspondents of the Department of Agriculture during 1930 was 5,188 pounds for the United States and 6,002 for the western states. For eight South Atlantic states it was 4,007, for eight South Central 3,529. From 1925 to 1930, average production for the nation on this basis increased 8.4 per cent, for the South Atlantic section only 3.2 per cent, but for the South Central, 9.3 per cent.

Tick eradication has made possible the live stock industry in the South, and the steady establishment of markets will conserve it. For example, since the lifting of quarantine, South Carolina, by no means a well developed cattle state, has imported thousands of head of pure bred sires and has shipped blooded cattle to northern and western markets. In the earliest days in the creamery industry the South had her share of premature starts and failures, but in many areas that day of pioneering is past and the farmer may tie up with well-established milk lines and creameries. The idea once so often heard that because of climate the South could not produce good commercial butter is also passing. In the Dixie butter scoring contests of September, 1930, 53 southern creameries entered creamery butter. Sixty per cent of it scored between 90 and 93.5, considered high. The channels for marketing the southern butter are not yet well developed and the area still consumes four times as much butter as it puts in the channels of commercial distribution. As much as anything else in the South, however, the live stock industry is conditioned upon the cotton system. To it accordingly we next devote our attention.

CHAPTER VIII

THE COTTON ECONOMY

IT IS POSSIBLE that some varieties of each of the eight basic types of agriculture practiced in America exist in the South.[1] Extensive mechanized one crop farming, well typified by wheat growing, can be found in southern rice culture. The market garden with its highly intensive horticulture of the hand and knee type with occasionally a foreman bossing a gang of Mexicans weeding onions can be found along the Gulf from the Rio Grande Valley to Florida and along the Atlantic from Florida to Norfolk. Sheep and cattle ranches with saddle supervision of a bunch of cowboys raising stock still remain in our Southwest. The all-around animal farm with corn for hogs, hay for kine, and milk, butter, and cheese for the cities is more likely to be found in the Corn Belt or in Wisconsin than in the South. What Smith calls "The independent kingdom of my own," self-sufficing farming where the farmer and his sons grow all possible products for home use, is to be found at its lower backwoods levels in the Southern Highlands. The all-round diversified farmer with a fair balance between meat and plant products, food and cash crops, is still comparatively rare in the South. In an unmechanized but coördinated large scale farming by directed labor gangs the South offers a unique type for America in its sugar plantations of Louisiana. But small scale unmechanized farms devoted to a cash staple and loosely held together by the supervision of landlords and suppliers of credit furnish the one type of agriculture best known throughout the South. A sequel of the old plantation, this form of agriculture is now applied to tobacco and cotton. All these types of southern farming except cotton will receive consideration in later chapters.

After passing through a series of changes and adaptations in its equilibrium of plants and animals each natural region finally

[1] Huntington and Williams, *Business Geography*, p. 340. J. R. Smith, *North America*, pp. 301-2.

settles down to a crop system more or less standardized for the area. The adoption of a region's crop system is due to many factors already suggested such as qualities of the soil and the climate's relation to the optimum conditions of growth for plants and animals. The distribution of insect pests, parasites, fungi, rusts blights, scourges, etc., has also been pointed out as somewhat incidental to climate. Transportation, the location and character of markets, are obviously important economic factors. A factor in introducing and perpetuating a crop system that the human geographer has found to be especially important is the cultural habits of farmers. Entering a new region, farmers first attempt to reproduce the crop systems of the old country; having worked out an adaptation to the area, they hand down agricultural technique tools, and organization. To such an extent is this true that it has been maintained in many instances that culture in the anthropological sense conditions the choice of crops and of areas for settlement The English, for example, first planted wheat and root crops in the United States; the Germans introduced intensive farming in Pennsylvania; Italians habitually set out vineyards, and plant both trees and crops in a single field; Scandinavians go in for dairying and Mexicans prefer cattle ranching.[2] Russians from the lower Volga Basin introduced dry farming in the Columbia Basin. We shall need to recall these facts when we come to consider the plantation and the heritage of cotton culture.

Southern Agriculture Against the National Background

To obtain a clear perspective of the agriculture of the South one must view it as projected against the trends of the nation and of the times.[3] From 1920 to 1925 agriculture began a downward movement which the period 1925 to 1932 showed no evidence of checking. Farmers compose some 27 per cent of the nation's population but today receive a little over seven per cent of the national income. From 1920 to 1925 their average return on investment was 1.7 per cent; in 1920-21 the average farm operator suffered actual loss. Expressed in returns on investment the American farmer of all our classes seems to be in business for his health. During

[2] See Huntington and Williams, op. cit.

[3] The National Industrial Conference Board has made a valuable analysis in it Condition of Agriculture in the United States and Measures for Its Improvement See Evans Clark in New York Times, Jan. 2, 1927, whose analysis is here followed

this same period the average farmer's income from labor and management varied from $412 to $804 but this included the value of food, fuel, and shelter supplied by the farm. After these are deducted the average farmer in the best year had $170 available. In leaner years he had literally less than nothing.

To suggestions that he sell and get out from under, it can be replied that values of farms shrunk thirty per cent, losing twenty billion dollars in six years. Increasing bankruptcies, indebtedness, and bank failures in farming areas have reflected these trends. From 1921 to 1925 there were chalked up a total of 21,000 farm failures increasing the rate from 20 per 100,000 farms in the ten years before 1920 to between 93 and 123 since then. When one realizes how unusual it is for a farm to go into bankruptcy, the figures assume new significance for an era in which no increases in business failures occurred. Between 1890 and 1910 the burden of mortgaged debt on American farms did not increase faster than their value. From 1910 to 1920 the value of farm property rose 90 per cent while the mortgaged debt rose 217 per cent. It is estimated that, in 1890, 20 per cent of the farms were under mortgage, in 1920, 40 per cent, while in 1926 the indebtedness reached $8,500,000 covering 42 per cent of the value of property involved. That it rose no higher must in part be attributed to an increasing disinclination of capital to accept farms as financial risks. The personal indebtedness of American farmers rose from $1,000,000,000 in 1909-10 to $3,250,000,000 in 1924-25, accounting for an interest charge estimated to range from $70,000,000 to $112,000,000 annually. The records for 1925-26 of 433 bank failures in the Middle West and 312 in the South to only 18 for the Industrial East reflect the post-war deflation of agriculture. "At the close of 1925, the best year the farmer had had since 1920, the labor earnings of the average farm owner were $573—less than the value of the food, fuel, and rent enjoyed by the average farmer, a little more than the wages paid to hired labor without board, and less than half the average labor earnings of workers in other occupations." Accompanied by widespread drought and financial depression these tendencies have not slacked in downward trends.

Against this background of national agriculture we may project the cotton economy of the South. The South's farm problem resembles the nation's in that both have seen agricultural production

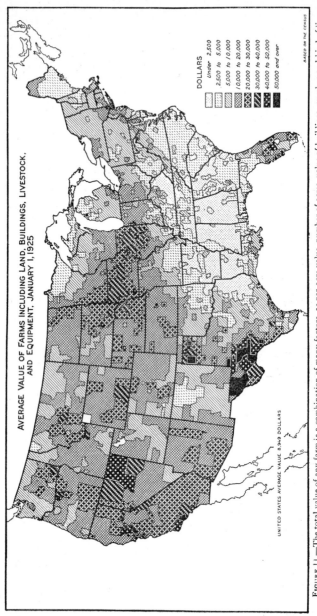

AVERAGE VALUE OF FARMS INCLUDING LAND, BUILDINGS, LIVESTOCK, AND EQUIPMENT, JANUARY 1, 1925

DOLLARS
Under 2,500
2,500 to 5,000
5,000 to 10,000
10,000 to 20,000
20,000 to 30,000
30,000 to 40,000
40,000 to 50,000
50,000 and over

BASED ON THE CENSUS

UNITED STATES AVERAGE VALUE 8,949 DOLLARS

FIGURE 11.—The total value of any farm is a combination of many factors, as per-acre value, number of acres, value of buildings, number and kind of livestock, equipment, and other items. Hence a high valuation of farm property may arise from a few acres of very high-priced land, as in certain sections of California, or from a large holding of cheap land, with considerable livestock, as in parts of the Rocky Mountain region. The average total value of an Iowa farm land, buildings, livestock, and equipment) on January 1, 1925, was $26,240, and of a California farm $25,107. Similar figures for the several census divisions range from $2,881 in the east South Central to $18,686 in the Pacific States. (Courtesy of U. S. Department of Agriculture).

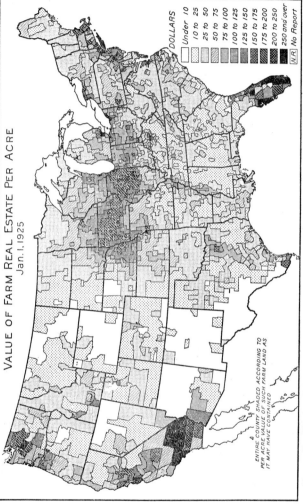

FIGURE 12.—The Corn Belt, California, and certain States on the Atlantic coast are conspicuous for their high average value per acre of farm real estate. There is great variation within practically every State, many of the Western States having small districts of highly valued irrigated land. Note the low values per acre of several of the Rocky Mountain States in comparison with high average value of farms for the same States as indicated in Figure 11. In the Cotton Belt, on the other hand, the value, both per acre and per farm, is small, but it should be recalled that many of the farms, as classified by the census, are the small holdings of croppers on plantations. (Courtesy of U. S. Department of Agriculture).

overdeveloped. In many other respects the South's agriculture presents a distinctive complex of its own. Clarence Heer's authoritative study of *Income and Wages in the South* contrasts the ten states most often regarded as characteristically southern with the rest of the nation. Over a period of some thirty years southern agriculture has furnished its farmers just over half the per capita returns received by farmers in the rest of the nation. In 1927 this ratio was 50.7 per cent; in 1924, 50.1. In periods of agricultural prosperity the South's percentage was a little higher, being 56.2 per cent in 1899, 53.4 per cent in 1909, and 55.3 per cent in 1919.[4]

It is these abnormally depressed rates of income that the student of southern agriculture must seek to explain. The most obvious explanation has to do with the size of farms. When the averages of thirteen southern states are compared with national averages for 1925, the southern farms are found to be 71.6 per cent as large with only 63.1 per cent of the crop acreage of the average farm of the nation and only 67.2 per cent of the pasture acreage. Table XIII points out these differences.

As might be expected values per farm are inclined toward an even lower level. The Southern farm was worth, in 1925, 46.4 per

TABLE XIII

FARM AREAS IN THE SOUTH, 1925 AGRICULTURAL CENSUS

STATES	Number of Farms	Land in Farms 1,000 Acres	Size of Average Farms in Acres	1,000 Acres in Crop Land	Crop Acres Average per Farm	1,000 Acres in Pasture	Average per Farm
1. Virginia	193,723	17,210	88.8	5,368	27.7	5,284	27.3
2. Kentucky	258,524	19,913	77.0	6,827	26.4	7,746	30.0
3. North Carolina	283,482	18,593	65.6	6,856	24.1	2,817	9.9
4. Tennessee	252,669	17,901	70.8	7,588	30.0	4,697	18.6
5. South Carolina	172,767	10,638	61.6	5,035	29.1	1,637	9.5
6. Georgia	249,095	21,945	88.1	10,695	42.9	3,848	15.5
7. Florida	59,217	5,864	99.0	2,022	34.1	1,489	25.1
8. Alabama	237,631	16,739	70.4	7,691	32.4	3,544	14.9
9. Mississippi	257,228	16,053	62.4	6,708	26.1	4,291	16.7
10. Arkansas	221,991	15,632	70.4	7,323	33.0	3,064	13.8
11. Louisiana	132,450	8,837	66.7	4,279	32.3	1,709	12.9
12. Oklahoma	197,218	30,868	156.5	15,837	80.3	13,015	66.0
13. Texas	465,646	109,674	235.5	29,368	63.8	75,067	161.2
South	2,981,651	309,872	103.92	115,606	38.77	128,216	43.00
Nation	6,371,640	924,319	145.1	391,459	61.44	407,935	64.02
South's Percentage	46.8	33.5	71.6	29.57	63.1	31.4	67.2

[4] Clarence Heer, *Income and Wages in the South*, pp. 12-22.

cent of the national average, its buildings came to 41.6 per cent of the national average for farm buildings, its implements were worth 41.9 per cent, and its live stock 46.8 per cent of those on the nation's average farm. As an evidence of the part played by the smaller sizes of farms, the value of land per acre in the South was 67.6 per cent of the nation's average, the region's highest comparative figure.

TABLE XIV

FARM VALUES IN THE SOUTH, 1925 AGRICULTURAL CENSUS
(Total Values in Millions of Dollars)

States	Number of Farms	Total Value	Average Per Farm	Value of Land	Value Land Per Acre	Value of Buildings	Per Farm	Value of Implements Machinery	Per Farm	Value of Live Stock	Per Farm
Virginia......	193,723	$999.4	$5,159	$600.6	$34.90	$286.1	$1,477	$40.0	$20.65	$72.6	$37.49
Kentucky.....	258,524	963.5	3,727	616.2	30.95	231.2	894	30.6	11.84	85.5	33.08
North Carolina	283,482	1,050.0	3,704	686.4	36.92	239.6	845	46.4	16.38	77.5	27.36
Tennessee.....	352,669	883.6	3,497	555.9	31.06	203.4	805	40.7	16.13	83.4	33.04
South Carolina	172,767	523.0	3,028	247.0	32.62	110.5	639	23.1	13.37	42.3	24.52
Georgia.......	249,095	686.6	2,757	433.6	19.76	153.9	617	26.9	10.85	72.1	28.96
Florida.......	59,217	513.8	8,678	415.8	70.91	63.0	1,065	14.5	244.92	20.4	34.51
Alabama.....	237,631	500.7	2,107	308.6	18.44	106.1	446	23.8	10.04	62.0	26.01
Mississippi....	257,228	550.5	2.140	347.0	21.62	112.1	435	28.3	11.01	63.1	24.54
Arkansas.....	221,991	628.8	2,833	420.7	26.91	119.9	540	31.2	14.05	56.8	25.61
Louisiana.....	132,450	385.9	2,914	251.7	28.49	72.9	550	21.3	16.11	39.8	30.12
Oklahoma....	197,218	210.1	6,736	879.3	28.49	169.4	859	58.3	29.60	102.9	52.23
Texas........	465,646	471.8	7,436	2,625.1	23.94	420.1	902	141.8	30.47	284.6	61.10
South.......	2,981,651	$12,375.7	$4,150	$8,488.5	$27.59	$ 2,288.7	$ 767	$527.4	$17.69	1,063.7	$35.68
Nation......	6,371,640	$57,017.7	$8,949	$37,721.0	$40.81	$11,746.6	$1,843	2,691.7	42.25	4,858.3	76.25
South's Percentage.	46.8	21.7	46.4	22.5	67.6	19.5	41.6	19.6	41.9	21.9	46.8

When the inquiry is shifted to incomes from farm production the story remains the same. The study of the five year average from 1924 through 1928 shows the average southern farm to have a cash income amounting to 63.7 per cent and a gross income of 68.5 per cent of the national averages. On incomes from crops the South shows up much better with about 97.6 per cent of the national average. Where the region loses, as has been pointed out, is in the low ratios of live stock production per farm, only 38.6 per cent of the national average.

The South is facing agricultural difficulties which represent one phase of the nation's agricultural problem. This complex includes

Table XV

Cash and Gross Incomes from Farm Production, Average, 1924-1928

STATES	CASH INCOME				GROSS* INCOME			
	Crops $1000	Livestock $1000	Combined $1000	Average Per Farm	Crops $1000	Livestock $1000	Combined $1000	Av Per
1. Virginia........	$103,244	$47,470	$150,714	$ 770.99	$131,373	$82,435	$213,808	$1,1
2. Kentucky......	91,625	67,936	159,561	611.20	118,675	113,479	232,154	8
3. North Carolina.	256,403	29,692	286,096	1,009.22	295,587	77,996	372,583	1,3
4. Tennessee.....	107,322	51,011	158,333	626.64	137,045	95,426	232,472	9
5. South Carolina.	121,619	10,481	132,100	764.61	142,732	37,005	179,737	1,0
6. Georgia.......	175,692	27,298	202,990	814.91	207,842	75,834	283,675	1,1
7. Florida.......	88,026	15,494	103,520	1,784.15	93,769	22,073	115,842	1,9
8. Alabama......	158,275	18,371	176,646	743.36	186,706	57,934	244,640	1,0
9. Mississippi.....	191,947	23,051	214,998	853.83	214,484	53,436	268,020	1,1
10. Arkansas......	160,716	26,622	187,338	843.90	183,614	59,396	243,010	1,0
11. Louisiana......	124,055	16,347	140,402	1,060.04	134,609	32,467	167,076	1,2
12. Oklahoma.....	227,179	71,802	298,981	1,515.99	240,298	109,139	349,436	1,7
13. Texas........	596,299	148,896	746,197	1,602.03	623,128	225,343	848,472	1,8
The South.........	$2,402,402	$554,471	$2,957,876	....	$2,709,962	$1,041,963	$3,750,925	....
South's Average per Farm......	$805.73	$185.96	....	$992.03	$908.87	$349.45	....	$1,2
The Nation........	$5,261,368	$4,659,288	$9,920,656	....	$5,928,638	$5,770,544	$11,699,192	....
Nation's Average per Farm......	$825.73	$731.25	....	$1,557.00	$930.48	$905.66	....	$1,8
South's Percentage .	97.6	25.4	....	63.7	97.7	38.6	....	

*Gross Income includes cash income plus values of materials consumed on the farm.

low prices on agricultural products, increase of mortgage debt and of tenancy, drift of population to the cities—especially of the young and vigorous—and depletion of soil fertility.

Conditions of the Southeast favorable to agriculture include a long growing season, adequate rainfall, fertile soils or soils highly productive if adequately fertilized, nearly flat or gently rolling land, nearness to markets, good transportation facilities, and low land values. These advantages have not been adequately utilized on account of the one crop system, small acreage per farm, absentee ownership, prevalence of tenancy, drift of population from the land, abandonment of farms, impoverishment of the soil, shortage of local food crops, lack of self-sustaining farms, inadequate marketing facilities for diversified agriculture, and unattractive rural environment. Plenty of advice and information are available to enable the remedying of these defects, but it is difficult under existing conditions for the advice to be followed. The habits and knowledge of those actually on the land, the existing credit policies, and the lack of organized markets handicap change.[5]

Cotton and the Plantation

Adapted to a great variety of plant life, the South has curiously enough come to be dominated by the cotton plant.[6] With all its economic, political, and social ramifications, the fact has basic foundations in the geography of a wide area.

The limits of the Cotton Belt are drawn by lines of temperature and rainfall. On the north it follows the summer average temperature of 77 degrees; on the south the belt has its bounds set along the Gulf and Atlantic Coast by an average rainfall limit of over 10 inches during the autumn. Beyond the northern temperature boundary the growing season is too short; below the southern limits the picking season is likely to be ruined by rains. Cotton production is found throughout the southern states extending from eastern North Carolina to western Texas. The Belt is 1,600 miles long and varies from 125 to 500 miles in width, the average width being 300 miles. In an area of 295,000,000 acres, less than 3 per cent of the world's land area, is grown about 55 per cent of the world's cotton.[7] Within the boundaries set by climate the density of cotton production varies according to soil areas, factors of technology, and economic organization.

Natural and economic forces have made the South peculiarly dependent upon cotton. Cotton may be grown only under certain climatic conditions which restrict its production in the United States to the southern states, whereas grain and forage crops which are grown to some extent in these states are grown in other parts of the United States under climatic conditions as favorable or even more favorable for their production. Since cotton will grow on practically all well-drained soils, is drought resistant, and yields well on light sandy soils to which fertilizers have been applied it is better suited to many of the soils of the South than are other staple crops. Furthermore, the South has a denser agricultural population and cheaper labor than other parts of the United

[5] The case of southern agriculture has been well summed up in the "Report of Special Advisors on Reclamation and Rural Development in the South." *House Document* No. 765, Part I, 1927, p. 5.

[6] Much of the documentation on which this chapter is based will be found in the author's *Human Factors in Cotton Culture*.

[7] O. E. Baker, *Economic Geography*, III, 65.

States, both of which circumstances favor the production of cotton as it requires a large amount of hand labor and yields high returns per acre.[8]

Cotton occupied some 42 per cent of the crop land in the Cotton Belt in 1920 and produced a value equal to the combined value of all other crops in the Belt. The value of cotton lint is exceeded by the values of corn, hog, and wheat crops for the whole United States but, when the value of cotton seed is included, cotton usually ranks second only to corn. Cotton and "cawn" are supposed to divide the South between them but in the ten cotton states cotton occupies some 44.5 million acres to 25.6 for corn. Only North Carolina, Tennessee, and Georgia have larger acreages planted to corn. In our export trade cotton's value exceeds that of any other agricultural commodity. It is the chief source of income to a large proportion of southern farmers and as a matter of course occupies the best land in the Belt and determines the time devoted to other crops.

Historically cotton fastened its hold upon the South through the plantation. The plantation made its appearance in America before either cotton or slavery. The first southern colonies were called plantations and the promoters expected no doubt that the returns of their venture would come from some sort of adaptation of feudal land tenure to America. The first organizations of labor in agriculture worthy of the term plantation included indentured servants and was applied to the growing of tobacco. Well known as it is in the tropics, the plantation would in the course of time have given way to a frontier yeomanry had it not been for the fortuitous introduction of the Negro slave and the cotton plant. The plantation according to Phillips has demanded four factors: land, fertile, plentiful and level; a labor supply, docile and of low status; management involving social as well as economic supervision; and a staple crop. In the South it has found five staples: tobacco, rice, indigo, sugar, and cotton, but cotton has outdistanced them all. Cotton early commanded an enviable place in the world's commerce. It also fitted into a regular and easily supervised routine of tasks to be accomplished by plow gangs, hoe gangs, and picking gangs, in all of which, except the plowing, women and children could participate. Technology came to the plantation's aid when

[8] O. C. Stine and O. E. Baker, *Atlas of American Agriculture,* Part V, Section A, "Cotton," 1918, p. 11.

he system seemed about to wane, and the invention of the cotton gin insured on the one hand cheap fabrics, on the other the extension of the cotton kingdom and the perpetuation of slavery.

How the plantation contended with the frontier and how it made an aristocracy, America's first, out of part of that frontier has been recounted. How the plantation, staggered by the shock of the abolition of slavery, after a brief hiatus reorganized its labor into a tenancy and share cropping system is more important for our chronicle. A stricken upper class possessing nothing but lands met a servile population possessed of nought except the labor of their hands. In what must have been an era of primitive barter, a system was arrived at whereby labor was secured without money wages and land without money rent. Up and down the Cotton Belt southern states after 1865 vied with one another in passing crop lien laws. Accepted as the temporary salvation of a wrecked economic structure, the system has increasingly set the mode for southern agriculture. Under the crop lien system the unpropertied farmer mortgages his ungrown crop for the supplies necessary to grow it. He also pledges a portion, third, fourth, or half of his crop, for use of the land. The most outstanding commentary one can make on the South is to point out the fact that from that day to this the percentage of those who must secure their year's livelihood by crop liens has steadily increased. Many of the enfeebled aristocracy saw their once proud acres go on the block for ridiculously low prices; but the hopes for the rise of a vigorous yeomanry to take their places never materialized. The crop lien system was developed to readjust the Negro to cotton production on terms more fitting a modern economy than slavery. Its success was so great as to be disastrous. Congregated on its original fringes, the unpropertied poor white farmers poured into the new scheme and helped to make temporary expediency a permanent arrangement. Southern states which possessed a rate of 30 per cent tenancy in 1880 now rank over 50 per cent, while long since the whites have come to produce the majority of the crop. The Census of 1900 showed that of all farmers to whom cotton offered the chief source of income 67.7 per cent were tenants. In 1910, although Negro farmers cultivated 52 per cent of the total cotton acreage, the white farmers produced 67 per cent of the total crop. In ten chief cotton states in 1920, 55 out of every hundred

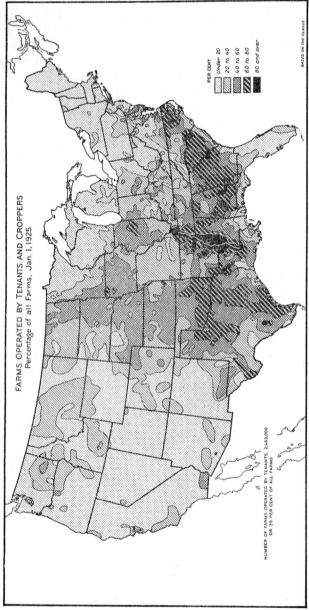

FARMS OPERATED BY TENANTS AND CROPPERS
Percentage of all Farms, Jan. 1, 1925

NUMBER OF FARMS OPERATED BY TENANTS, 2,463,000
OR 39 PER CENT OF ALL FARMS

PER CENT
Under 20
20 to 40
40 to 60
60 to 80
80 and over

BASED ON THE CENSUS

FIGURE 13.—Including cropper-operated farms with tenant farms, the percentage of all farms that are tenant-operated is high throughout most of the Cotton Belt and is highest on the most productive lands, notably in the alluvial districts along the Mississippi River. Outside the Cotton Belt the percentage is high only on the best land of the Corn Belt and in the moister portions of the wheat regions. It is low in the long-settled Northeastern States, in the Lakes States, and in the far West. Dairying, fruit and vegetable growing, and livestock ranching are less adapted to tenancy than cotton, corn, and wheat production, partly because of the greater investment, the greater technical skill, or greater permanence of tenure required of the farm operator. (Courtesy of U. S. Department of Agriculture).

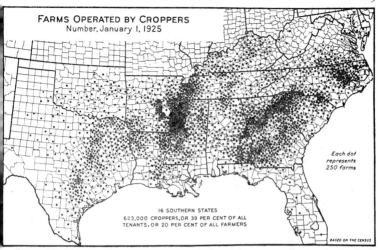

FIGURE 14.—This map shows croppers separately from other tenants. Croppers in the South generally grow cotton or tobacco for a share of the crop. They use work stock furnished by their landlords, they themselves owning little or no equipment, and in many States are by law classed as laborers and not as tenants. The territory of greatest density is in the Yazoo (Miss.) Delta, which is nearly all tillable and is largely devoted to cotton production. In parts of the old Cotton Belt, notably in South Carolina and Georgia, croppers have increased recently, because many renters lost so much that they could not furnish work animals and equipment with which to farm. Most of the croppers in Kentucky and Virginia grow tobacco. (Courtesy of U. S. Department of Agriculture).

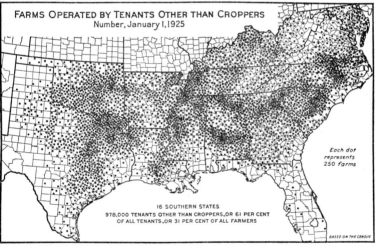

FIGURE 15.—This map indicates the number of tenants who own their work animals. Frequently, however, such tenants in the Southern States are so in debt that they only nominally own this stock. Comparison with Figure 14 shows a much more uneven distribution of croppers than of other tenants. In Oklahoma and in most parts of Texas, Arkansas, Alabama, and North Carolina, Tennessee, Kentucky, and Virginia the croppers are greatly outnumbered by the other tenants. Both classes of tenants are numerous in the strip of rich cotton-growing country along the Mississippi River, in the black prairie of Texas, and in South Carolina and Georgia. In the Yazoo delta and in southern Georgia there are many more croppers than other tenants. (Courtesy of U. S. Department of Agriculture).

farmers were tenants; and, out of every hundred tenants, 21 were cash renters, 37 were croppers, and 42 were share tenants. By 1925, 57.7 per cent of the farmers were tenants. The number of cash tenants among the renters had fallen to 11.2 per cent while the croppers had risen to 48.7 per cent. In 1930 the percentage of tenancy for these states was 61.5. Out of every 100 tenants there were 45 croppers, 42.3 share and other tenants, and 12.7 cash renters. Table XVI shows the distribution by states and races with the addition of the non-cotton states of Virginia, Kentucky, and Florida.

The following biased interpretation of the function served by the crop lien shows the point of view of the tenant:

When the landlord's lien law was passed every acre of agricultural land in North Carolina was immediately multiplied in value from three to ten times its actual market money value.

The landlord's lien law was originally introduced for the purpose of keeping the Negro in slavery. It not only accomplished its purpose in large measure but it has gradually made slaves of an increasing number of white people.

Viewed from one angle, the landlord's lien law has created and sustained a landed gentry, getting their income out of the labor of others . . . an income entirely disproportionate to the value of the crops produced if any reasonable allowance is made for the labor of men, women and children going to make the crop.[9]

It is doubtful that such a view will sustain economic analysis. A. E. Cance holds that the system of tenancy in the South merely gives a fictitious dignity to a low grade of unskilled farm laborers who would under other forms of agriculture be engaged as hired men. Southern courts have held that cropper farming is a method of paying wages in produce rather than a form of tenancy. Cance has said:

Tenancy attracts many farm operators who otherwise would not be engaged in farming at all. The tenant has no expenses of upkeep of land or buildings. With some notable exceptions he spends little or no time improving the farmstead or making it attractive. Rented farms left to the care of tenants are almost sure to "run down" in buildings, fences, ditches, lawns, roadsides and shrubbery if not in soil, for the period of

[9] F. M. Shannonhouse, letter in *Charlotte Observer*, March 26, 1922.

TABLE XVI

FARMS IN THE SOUTH BY COLOR AND TENURE OF OPERATORS, 1930

	IN THOUSANDS					PERCENTAGE OF TOTAL TENANCY BY STATES			
	All Farms	Owners and Managers	TENANTS Total	Cash	Croppers	Share & other tenants	1910	1920	1925	1930
Virginia..........	......	....	......	......	......	......	26.5	25.6	25.2	28.1
White..........	130.9	98.1	32.8	5.5	10.4	16.8	....	....	....	....
Colored........	39.6	24.5	15.1	1.7	6.7	6.5	....	....	....	....
Kentucky..........	......	....	......	......	......	......	33.9	33.4	32.0	35.9
White..........	237.3	53.8	83.5	8.7	27.1	47.6	....	....	....	....
Colored........	9.1	4.2	4.9	.1	3.1	1.6	....	....	....	....
North Carolina.....	......	....	......	......	......	......	42.3	43.5	45.2	49.2
White..........	202.8	122.4	80.4	6.6	34.2	39.4	....	....	....	....
Colored........	76.8	19.7	57.1	2.5	34.8	19.7	....	....	....	....
Tennessee..........	......	....	......	......	......	......	41.1	41.1	41.0	46.2
White..........	210.5	124.3	86.2	9.3	33.7	43.1	....	....	....	....
Colored........	35.1	7.9	27.2	2.8	16.5	7.8	....	....	....	....
South Carolina.....	......	....	......	......	......	......	63.0	64.5	65.1	65.1
White..........	80.5	39.1	41.4	6.5	17.8	17.0	....	....	....	....
Colored........	77.4	16.1	61.3	11.7	31.0	18.5	....	....	....	....
Georgia............	......	....	......	......	......	......	65.6	66.6	63.8	68.2
White..........	168.8	70.1	98.7	17.0	51.4	30.3	....	....	....	....
Colored........	86.7	11.1	75.6	10.5	49.4	15.6	....	....	....	....
Florida............	......	....	......	......	......	......	26.7	25.3	21.3	28.4
White..........	47.9	36.5	11.4	4.6	3.4	3.2	....	....	....	....
Colored........	11.0	5.7	5.3	2.4	1.4	1.4	....	....	....	....
Alabama...........	......	....	......	......	......	......	60.2	57.9	60.7	64.7
White..........	163.5	75.0	88.5	16.6	37.5	34.3	....	....	....	....
Colored........	93.8	16.0	77.8	32.0	27.5	18.2	....	....	....	....
Mississippi........	......	....	......	......	......	......	66.1	66.1	68.3	72.2
White..........	129.7	64.3	65.4	8.7	32.3	24.3	....	....	....	....
Colored........	182.8	22.7	160.1	18.3	102.9	38.8	....	....	....	....
Louisiana..........	......	....	......	......	......	......	55.3	57.1	60.1	66.6
White..........	87.6	43.3	44.3	6.1	17.2	20.9	....	....	....	....
Colored........	73.3	10.5	63.2	6.6	32.2	24.3	....	....	....	....
Arkansas...........	......	....	......	......	......	......	50.0	51.3	56.7	63.0
White..........	162.7	78.2	84.5	8.8	29.5	46.1	....	....	....	....
Colored........	79.5	11.4	68.1	6.1	45.4	16.5	....	....	....	....
Oklahoma..........	......	....	......	......	......	......	54.8	51.0	58.6	61.5
White..........	180.9	70.2	110.7	16.5	16.4	77.7	....	....	....	....
Colored........	22.9	8.4	14.5	1.0	4.5	8.9	....	....	....	....
Texas.............	......	....	......	......	......	......	52.6	53.3	60.4	60.9
White..........	409.4	173.1	236.3	15.4	68.8	151.9	....	....	....	....
Colored........	86.0	19.7	65.3	1.3	36.2	27.6	....	....	....	....
South.............	......	....	......	......	......	......	....	....	....	....
White..........	2,213.2	1,149.5	1,064.7	131.1	380.4	553.4	....	....	....	....
Colored........	875.2	179.1	696.1	97.9	392.3	206.4	....	....	....	....
South.............	......	....	......	......	......	......	....	....	....	....
Total...........	3,088.4	1,328.6	1,760.8	229.0	772.7	759.8	....	....	53.3	57.3
United States.......	6,228.6	3,624.2	2,664.3	489.2	Peculiar to South 99. X	2,175.1*	37.0	38.1	38.6	42.4
South's Percentage..	49.6	36.7	66.1	46.8		**70.4	....	....	....	....

*Includes standing renters, croppers, and share tenants.
**Percentage of all tenants exclusive of cash tenants.

tenure is short and the tenant cannot afford the necessary time and money to keep up a place he does not own.[10]

In short, the owners take part of the risk of production by taking the rent in a fraction of the yield. If the tenant is a cropper the owner also bears all the depreciation in tools and the risk of death of work stock. Lack of a rational form of tenancy has thus operated to perpetuate the low-standard farmers.[11]   Anything that tends to discourage or restrict the entrance into farming of low grade laborers will greatly simplify competitive conditions and raise the standards of agricultural proprietorship.

The traditional scapegoat for all the agricultural ills the South is heir to has long been the Negro. Because he has furnished the majority of tenant labor within the cotton system he has had to bear the brunt of the blame for the system. This characteristic attitude is well set forth in a public address of a southern governor near the turn of the century:

We have not diversified our crops because the Negro has not been willing to diversify. We have not used improved machinery on our farms thereby economizing expenses because the Negro is not willing to use such implements. We have not improved our soil because the Negro is not willing to grow crops to be incorporated into the soil, nor leave his cotton seed to be returned to the fields that he has denuded of humus and all possible traces of fertility. Because he is unwilling to handle heavy plows we have permitted him to scratch the land with his scooter just deep enough for all the soil to be washed from the surface, leaving our fields practically barren and wasted. We have not raised stock on the farm because the Negro is cruelly inhuman and starves the work animals we put in his hands for his personal support. We have accepted his thriftless and destructive methods simply because under our present system we have not been able to do without him. If this be true our present system in this relation is absolutely ruinous and it will not invite the residence of intelligent settlers from the outside."[12]

THE COTTON SYSTEM

It is but a partial answer to this criticism to suggest that the winning of the South was largely the work of the Negro and the pioneer. "Without the Negro the development of the southern

[10] In Dwight Sanderson (ed.), *Farm Income and Farm Life,* p. 77.

[11] *Ibid.,* p. 81.

[12] Governor Northen of Georgia, quoted by George K. Holmes in *Publications, American Economic Association,* 1904, pp. 122-23.

states," C. C. Stack points out, "would have been retarded half a century longer until the great tide of immigration had flowed over the Appalachian watershed and covered the fertile reaches of the great Northwestern territory."[13] The expansion westward of the plantation system was due to nothing so much as the unremitting, back-breaking toil of Negro labor gangs. Bolstered by his tropical origin, his imagined immunity to malaria, he felled the forests, cleared canebrakes and thick underbrush, drained marshes and subdued to cultivation alluvial areas in a humid subtropic clime. With the area left to the normal processes of immigration, the pioneers who filled the upland forests would have left untouched much of this unhealthful lowland so well fitted for the cultivation of indigo, rice, sugar, and cotton.

More pertinent is the assertion that the characteristics of the cotton system and of the cotton growers can be traced to origins other than Negro shortcomings. To lay the blame for the "whole miserable panorama of unpainted shacks, rain-gullied fields, straggling fences, rattletrap Fords, dirt, poverty, disease, drudgery, and monotony that stretches for a thousand miles across the Cotton Belt"[14] on the inherent traits of a minority and once subject race is to claim too much. Opposed to the naïve biology which thus accounts for the agriculture of a great domain is a rounded cultural interpretation. The geography, the seasonal cycle of plants, the economics of production and marketing, the social organization of a region—none of these things remains without influence and imprint upon its human denizens. Habits and attitudes which these factors condition are often attributed by those who disapprove to inherent willfulness or original sin. That cotton culture first on the plantation and afterward in the tenancy system conditioned and perpetuated the traits of which the governor speaks may be inferred from the fact that similar habits and attitudes are held by white croppers, tenants, and small farmers.

An analysis of the cotton system and the cotton complex is sufficient to show this. A definite set of practices surrounds the crop. Cotton is produced with (1) a large proportion of expensive credit, (2) in connection with a small percentage of other crops, (3) under

[13] In *Publications,* American Economic Association, 1904, p. 155.
[14] Robert H. Montgomery's phrases in his *The Coöperative Pattern in Cotton,* . 351.

a system of supervision and regimentation as in plantation and tenancy, (4) calling for a maximum amount of manual labor much of which is furnished by women and children. Moreover, (5) in prosperity cotton creates a vested interest in credit institutions to maintain it, (6) in times of depression, it enables failing farmers to continue in the cotton system by receding to the lower levels of tenure, and (7) at all times it encourages speculation, over-expansion, and over-production. Finally, (8) the crop is sold in a marketing system which the growers do not understand and over which they exercise little or no control.

The cotton system may be defined as the complex organization of financing, growing, and marketing cotton. It thus includes croppers, tenants, small farmers, and planters who comprise the growers, plus the banks, supply merchants, factors, and fertilizer dealers who finance the crop, and the local buyers, general buyers, coöperatives, shippers and exporters who assemble and classify cotton for sale to the mills or for export. As far as it is integrated the cotton system is organized around the method by which it is financed. In periods of prolonged depression this system tends to break down, only to reorganize in periods of rising cotton prices.

Deeply rooted in the cotton economy is the element of risk. As a Secretary of Agriculture once pointed out this is implicit in all farming:

The farmer supplies the capital for production and takes the risks of his losses; his crops are at the mercy of drought and flood and heat and frost to say nothing of noxious insects and blighting diseases. He supplies hard, exacting, unremitting labor. . . . Then there is the risk of over-production and disastrously low prices. From beginning to end the farmer must steer dextrously to escape perils to his profits and indeed to his capital on every hand.[15]

For cotton there exists a cycle of production initiated by acreage planted and determined in its outcome by the weather and the weevil. The yield per acre averaged over the whole belt has varied from 124.5 pounds of lint in 1921 to 222 pounds in 1897. Within the last fifty years the average income per cotton acre has ranged from $10.78 in 1898 to $60.62 in 1919, while the farm price per bale has explored the ranges between $25 and $155. Seven times

[15] James Wilson, U. S. D. A., *Yearbook*, 1910, p. 26.

between 1890 and 1928 a decrease in American production has occurred, and five times it has resulted in an increased total money value of the shorter crop. For the seven years a total decrease of 22,900,000 bales has meant an absolute increase of $406,800,000 in crop values. A decrease in production of 23.4 per cent then brought a 12.9 per cent increase in total value of the seven crops. To put it another way, eight low-price bumper crops since 1890 have been followed by eight attempts to cut acreage. For these years an average reduction of 11 per cent in acreage has resulted in an average of 25.2 per cent reduction in crops with a 33 per cent rise in cotton prices. Thus the original variation of eleven per cent has been tripled in the final price effect. Conversely the increases in production caused equally violent downward movements in the market.[16]

To the farmers of the South these cycles result in incomes subject to great vicissitudes. The danger to credit institutions and to standards of living lies not so much in the low incomes as in tragically irregular incomes. The averages in Table XVII show for example crop incomes not greatly below national standards. Robert H. Montgomery offers the following record of the income

TABLE XVII

RECORD OF A 160-ACRE COTTON FARM IN MENARD COUNTY, TEXAS, 1894-1909*

YEAR	Number of Bales of Cotton	Average Price per Pound in Cents	Total Money Income in in Dollars	Percentage of Income of Previous Years
1894	9	4.50	202.50	...
1895	5	8.25	247.50	122
1896	5	7.00	184.03	75
1897	16	5.00	412.25	224
1898	15	4.60	405.37	91
1899	13	6.50	628.75	155
1900	51	6.50	1982.50	315
1901	23	7.00	1039.00	53
1902	19	8.50	1059.50	102
1903	25	9.75	1738.30	164
1904	23	8.35	1332.25	77
1905	16	9.75	1194.60	90
1906	28	9.60	1588.80	133
1907	7	10.00	350.00	22
1908	41	8.25	1832.57	575
1909	8	13.55	772.80	42

*From Robert H. Montgomery, *The Cooperative Pattern in Cotton*, p. 251.

[16] Carl Geller, "Fewer Acres and More Dollars," *Commerce and Finance,* January 12, 1927, p. 123. Vance, *op. cit.,* pp. 122-23.

of a family with eight boys and three girls on a Texas cotton farm. The acres in cotton were gradually increased from forty in 1894 to eighty in 1899 where it remained.

After the total of eighty acres came into cultivation (1899-1909) the income varied from $350.00 to $1,982.50. It dropped in one year from $1,588.80 to $350.00, then rebounded to the second highest figure of the period, $1,832.57, only to fall again the following year to 42 per cent of that amount.

We may reduce the whole story to one figure if we are addicted to quoting averages. Considering the income of each year successively as 100, the average deviation of each year as compared to the previous one was 82 per cent. The American Locomotive Company regarded by experts as showing a maximum of variability in corporation income possessed, as Montgomery shows, an average variation of 32.6 per cent in income for the same period.[17]

Cotton, moreover, is grown in connection with a small proportion of other crops. Thus the hardships of irregular income are made greater by the lack of home-raised supplies on cotton farms. Diversification in the Cotton Belt has been consistently preached in and out of season but it has never been attained. Basing her estimates on standard products excluding extras and luxuries, Miss Henrietta R. Smedes found in 1920 that Mississippi, Alabama, South Carolina, and Georgia purchased over half their food and stock feed from outside the state. Other southern states can be pointed out which rank but little higher. Some index of the extent of diversification of the 2,550,407 farms in ten cotton states in 1920 may be found in Table XVIII. These figures are manifestly inconclusive in that they do not point out whether such farms produce less or more than enough for their needs.

This excessive reliance on one crop in an area suited to many is due in part to the peculiar fitness of cotton as a money crop in credit economy. The South is situated at some distance from the market centers of the world. Because cotton is non-perishable and combines the advantages of high value in small bulk it can bear transportation to distant world markets. It fits no less into the crop lien system. It is food for neither man nor beast and can be devoured neither by the tenants' mules nor his children. It must be ginned

[17] Robert H. Montgomery, *op. cit.*, pp. 251-52.

TABLE XVIII

FARMS GROWING SPECIFIED PRODUCTS IN TEN COTTON STATES, 1920

RANK	Number of Farms on Which Produced	Per Cent of Farms
All Farms............................	2,550,407	100
1. Corn................................	2,250,580	88
2. Eggs................................	2,049,996	80
3. Home Gardens.......................	1,953,160	77
4. Cotton..............................	1,872,326	73
5. Milk Cow...........................	1,605,074	67
6. Chickens...........................	1,599,427	67
7. Butter.............................	1,377,681	54
8. Hay and forage.....................	1,167,489	46
9. Pigs...............................	1,111,863	44
10. Sweet potatoes.....................	1,069,110	42
11. Cane for Syrup.....................	607,962	24
12. Irish potatoes.....................	545,014	21
13. Oats...............................	364,901	14
14. Pure bred animals..................	134,441	5

before sale and in the check up of neighborhood gins the landlord may protect himself against theft before settlement. A stock farm may suffer loss from ill treatment of animals but "any fool can grow cotton." Thus when no credit is forthcoming for diversification or mixed farming, landlords and supply merchants can always be found to stake the cotton farmer from cropper to planter.

Then again the peak loads of man labor in cotton come exactly at times when other crops need attention. Cotton is not yet adequately mechanized and its planting, chopping, and picking cannot be shifted or speeded up by machinery. The National Association of Farm Implement Manufacturers estimated in 1924 that modern machinery had saved American farmers 1,382,000,000 days of work in one year. These figures, if accepted, provide for the 10,953,158 persons listed as engaged in farming in 1920 an average saving of 127 days a year. But a small fraction of this saving fell to the lot of the cotton growers. Depending on yield, it requires 30 to 100 hours of human labor to pick an acre of cotton. The amount of farmer's time required to pick an acre of cotton would grow three acres of corn in Iowa or four acres of wheat in Kansas. Hand picking is the neck of the bottle which retards the application of machinery to planting and chopping. The machine does the work of many men and pays their labor return to its owner. Cotton's hitherto successful defiance of the machine has kept the cost of production extremely high and has drafted women and children to work in the field. According to 1920 figures, 19.8 per cent of all females ten years of age and over on farms in ten cotton states served as field laborers. The Census of Occupations probably underestimates the number of women engaged in agriculture. Of the 1,084,128 women so listed, in the United States in 1920, eighty per cent were found in ten cotton states. Of every hundred women field laborers 68 were Negroes and 32 white.

Add to this fact that the crop is produced with a large proportion of expensive credit. A Federal Reserve study in 1923 found that only 12 per cent of the cotton producers were able to finance the entire growing process without aid. From 50 to 90 per cent, depending on the locality, "borrow in the spring and continue until the cotton is marketed." The forms of security most used are, first, personal notes with one or more endorsements, second, mortgages on live stock, and, third, crop liens. Bank credit at interest rates averaging around 8.5 per cent is available for only the upper groups. Much of this comes to the growers at second hand through fertilizer dealers, landlords, and supply merchants. An examination of the studies available in this subject indicate that tenants and croppers may expect to pay around 25 per cent interest for this credit. Thus the grower's standard of living is lowered by the fact that one fourth of his expenditure during four to eight months goes into interest charges rather than consumers' goods. On the other hand the creditor has assumed in a single crop system both the production hazards and the market risks of the cotton grower. His extension of credit verges on pure speculation and high interest rates are his only protection.

It can easily be seen that in time of prosperity the credit institutions possess a vested interest in the cotton system which tends to perpetuate it. What is not so often realized is that in times of depression and failure the same system provides for the survival and perpetuation of the failing cotton farmer. He may fall to a lower level but he survives as a cotton producer. Croppers can enter the system empty-handed and compete against owners. They will have houses, lands, teams and tools furnished. Growers may fail and pass their losses on to merchants, landlords, and creditors but they will be furnished somehow and grow cotton the next year. The workers comprise the first charge on the industry. The cotton system like the Lord will provide, and under the "benevolent feudalism" of plantation and tenancy the inadequate producers will continue to overproduce cotton. The dire want following the initial devastation of the boll weevil furnished the first great exception to this condition and is held to account for a general exodus of Negro farmers from the eastern belt.

At all times there exists in the cotton system a tendency to expansion and overproduction. The lure of the cash crop meets a simple routine to which workers have been trained by long habituation. When new lands open up as in West Texas there is a completed culture complex with its human factors ready to occupy for the cotton system. The attitude ranges all the way from the simple desire of the farmer for more land to grow more cotton to make more money, to plans like the following for an unassailable monopoly for the South.

This threefold increase of the crop (to 30 million bales) can be brought about by increasing, by means of improved agriculture, the productivity of the land, and by reclamation of land along the Mississippi Valley. If this increase could be accomplished; if the labor could be found to handle it; if the markets for it could be secured in such volume that the price could remain near to its present standard; and if our capacity to spin and weave our share of the increase could be maintained, the Southern States would become the richest portion of the earth. The opportunity to develop the potentialities of cotton in field and in mill, to train and handle the labor involved in the development which would cover the whole field of the poor white, the immigrant and the Negro, to evolve the financial genius to move and market his world staples, makes of the Southern States a field for industrial talent and industrial leadership unsurpassed in the world.[18]

Such a view ignores the competing cotton areas of the world, areas which in the opinion of many students are becoming of increasing importance.

Cotton Culture Complex

In the expansion of cotton cultivation the Southwest has gained at the expense of the old Cotton Belt. The area west of the Mississippi first forged ahead of the eastern areas in 1920 while the only eastern state to show consistent gains in cotton acreage is Mississippi. In speaking of the cotton culture complex we have confined our

[18] James A. B. Scherer, *Cotton as a World Power*, pp. 312-13.

attention to the Southeastern, Gulf, and Delta sections where practices are more nearly standardized, leaving other developments to
be treated in a chapter on the Southwest. We shall also find the
traits in cotton culture more nearly uniform in regard to the
small farmer so often characterized by twenty acres and a mule.
Average cotton acreages per farm growing cotton in the Southeast
are small, ranging, for example, from 13 for Tennessee to 20 for
Georgia. We shall find that characteristic traits of cotton culture appear as responses to environment rather than responses to race. Croppers, tenants, and small owners, whether white or black, have developed pretty much the same practices and ways of living in the eastern portion of the Cotton Belt. The one exception to be found is the
plantation zones of the Mississippi Delta which deserves special treatment in a later chapter.

To focus attention on a specific area will serve to make definite
the picture of the common man of the South as cotton farmer.
For 1924-26 the Department of Agriculture made a most illuminating study of the living conditions of white cotton farmers in a
Piedmont county of Georgia.[19] There can be found on a comparable basis within this area 52 counties in the old Cotton Belt
none of which has a population less than 75 per cent white. The
Department estimates that perhaps 100,000 families in and along
the borders of the southern Piedmont live no better than those here
described. Here in a population six sevenths native-born white,
we find that two thirds of the farmers are tenants on farms valued
at less than $2,000 each. The average farm family consisting of
five members consumed for family living, goods to the amount of
$687.14 in value. Their cash expenditure for food during the year
was about $22 per person. On the average, 57.6 per cent of the
living, $396.07, was supplied from the farm. Their average net
cash income was $424 per family. This was made from farms
which averaged eight acres in cotton, thirteen in corn, and four
in other crops. Croppers, who made up one fourth of the farm
population, cultivated on the average 24 acres; tenants, 26 acres;
and the landlord with his tenants, 48 acres. Only one work animal
was found on 40 per cent of the farms and only 14 per cent had

[19] Howard A. Turner and L. D. Howell, "Conditions of Farmers in a White
Farmer Area of the Cotton Piedmont," 1924-1926, U. S. D. A. *Circular* 78, 1929,
p. 47.

over two. After they had paid ordinary living expenses averaging $291 per family, these farmers had left $133 to be applied to debts or added to their capital.

Although these people have developed but meager wants, their needs easily exceed their incomes. Thirty-four per cent of the families live in houses of one thickness of lumber while only 26 per cent possess automobiles or have their houses screened against flies. The expenditures of the average family for books, magazines, recreation, amusement, education, and religion amounted to $24 per year. It was almost equalled by their only luxury, $15 per year for snuff and tobacco. In the use of automobiles for private purposes farm owners spent fourteen dollars, renters, six dollars, and croppers less than one dollar a year. Most of these farmers attended churches whose ministers were farmers, themselves, serving practically without remuneration. Their wants would be much more scantily supplied but for the fact that 92 per cent of the housewives have cheap sewing machines and make part of the clothing for the family. The exodus of young people from these farms is increasing. Forty-seven per cent of owners' sons who have grown up have left the farm to go into other occupations besides agriculture. Only 29 per cent of croppers' children leaving home, however, have deserted agriculture.

A study of conditions in a cotton area of North Carolina reënforces the conclusions arrived at in the Piedmont county of Georgia. It vividly points out differences between land owning and landless classes, white or black, in cotton culture. In many instances the small cotton grower falls short of attaining standards of comfort or even decency. For those who possess a gift for figures, Table XIX compiled by Carl C. Taylor will afford, at a glance, a clear cut picture.[20]

The socially developed traits in this complex are well known. Out of this background one may expect a high degree of mobility. A study by the Department of Agriculture in 1922 estimated a shifting of occupants on 19 per cent of all farms in the United States, 27.7 per cent of tenants and 6 per cent of owners moving. In eight cotton states, however, 30 to 40 per cent of all farms showed a change of occupants. Having nothing to lose, tenants

[20] Given in Dwight Sanderson (ed.), *Farm Life and Farm Income*, p. 148.

TABLE XIX

TABLE SETTING FORTH ECONOMIC STATUS AND RESULTANT SOCIAL STATUS
OF DIFFERENT ECONOMIC CLASSES IN TYPICAL TENANT CROPPER AREA*

	OPERATOR LANDLORDS		OWNER OPERATORS		TENANTS		CROPPERS	
	White	Black	White	Black	White	Black	White	Black
Equity per family............	$14,494	$8,974	$3,998	$3,908	$886	$226	$352	$126
Equity per person...........	$2,750	$1,019	$889.00	$597.00	$177.40	$37.68	$ 72.15	$24.83
Per cent who are insolvent....	0	0	0	0	6.5	28.5	24.2	18.75
Annual cash income per individual...............	$425.65	$226.82	$253.82	$253.03	$174.45	$118.51	$143.13	$125.64
Average number of rooms per home....................	5.6	3.8	4.5	3.8	4.2	4.0	4.1	3.4
Per cent of homes with running water...........	6.6	0	0	0	0	0	1.7	0
Per cent of homes with lights other than oil lamps.......	10.2	0	0	0	3.5	0	1.7	0
Per cent of homes with kitchen sinks.............	10.2	20.0	0	0	1.3	0	0	0
Per cent of births at which doctor was in attendance...	76.0	33.3	72.5	28.6	57.5	8.3	48.0	14.6
Per cent of parents who can... read and write...........	81.8	80.0	80.0	90.0	86.5	35.8	70.8	42.3
Per cent of families who take.. papers and magazines......	83.4	60.0	65.0	60.0	55.4	7.4	50.0	17.9
Average number of books in homes...................	15.2	0.8	1.4	20.2	2.69	1.5	2.24	0.6
Number of times members of family have participated in recreation during year.....	3.04	.79	1.73	1.97	1.40	.25	.92	.88
Per cent of families who own automobiles.............	92.9	60.0	45.0	60.0	49.4	14.3	34.5	16.96
Per cent of parents in favor of consolidated schools, road bonds, college education, etc......................	59.4	36.7	46.7	73.5	45.3	14.3	41.1	17.4

*Data from *Economic and Social Conditions of North Carolina Farmers*, Carl C. Taylor and C. C. Zimmerman, Bureau of Economics and Social Research, North Carolina State College of Agriculture, Raleigh, North Carolina, 1922.

are easily led to move by a desire to secure better land or more agreeable landlords. Tenants, however, usually move within their own immediate neighborhoods. Only a fifth of 1,370 moves in a Georgia county were found to involve distances of ten miles or over, while 29 per cent were for less than two miles.

The lack of ownership in house or farm encourages shiftlessness as well as mobility. Possessing by law no right in his tenancy and no claim for improvements made, the cotton renter has acquired a shiftless attitude toward the place in which he lives. This is borne out by the common complaint by landlords of houses started on the road to ruin, fences torn down for firewood, and lands lacerated by erosion. With nothing to lose and all to gain, the tenant may adopt a policy verging on exploitation and expropriation.

Cotton has created another culture pattern for the South. The seasonal and cyclical nature of his money income not only serves to give the cotton grower a shifting standard of living but throws him back upon credit and prevents his acquiring habits of thrift. After a season of deprivation and close living on niggardly credit comes the sale of the crop and cash income to be husbanded if possible until the sale of next year's crop. The income of the cotton grower has its peaks of high prices but these peaks are not planned for and they do not serve to level up the general standard of living. In the Cotton Belt luxuries are likely to be bought on the spur of the moment during a good season in cotton and to be paid for in the poverty of next year's living. One can neither exercise a systematic thrift, budget expenses, nor indulge in installment buying on irregular returns from cotton.

The Cotton Belt, it may be concluded, offers the spectacle of a region in which the culture of a plant has deeply impressed the mode of life and characterized the habits and activities of its people. The cotton plant lays down an annual cycle of activities concerned with planting and cultivating, gathering and marketing of the crop which in turn has its effect upon social life and institutions. Thus the school, the church, and the community agencies find their seasons of intense activity during the two respites of cotton culture, for a few weeks in the late summer between the last chopping and the first picking and for two or three months in the winter between the last picking and the preparation of the ground for the next crop. The demands for hand labor perpetuate the field work of women and children, place a premium on a high birth rate, and otherwise affect the standards of domestic life. The demands of the cotton crop are greatest at precisely the period required for tending other crops and thus impede diversification. Furthermore, since cotton is food for neither man nor beast and cannot be disposed of except through the local gin, it furnishes an excellent basis for the crop lien system of credit which in turn further fixes the tradition of the one crop system upon the Cotton Belt and tends to limit the diet of the cotton farmer to the deadly monotony of meat, meal and molasses.

The cotton farmer is peculiarly subject to speculative risks of the market since his is one staple grown in America that can contribute nothing directly consumable by the farm family. Thus without adequate diversification, the risks of the market combine with the risks of the weather and the weevil to make the climb to ownership all the more difficult, to encourage speculation, to perpetuate tenancy and its attendant evils, inadequate housing, inefficient methods of agriculture, isolation, dependence on credit, backward community institutions, illiteracy, mobility, shiftlessness, and lack of thrift. Chained by inability to finance experiments and diversification, southern agriculture seems bound today to landlords, supply merchants, and credit institutions who hold the economic keys but are powerless to unloose the captive.

Devotion to cotton, belief in its expansion, lack of coöperation in planting and production programs continue. It cannot be claimed that by nature southern farmers are inept and shiftless. It is, for instance, the experimental activities not of technical agriculturists but of farmers themselves that introduced rice production on the Louisiana and Arkansas prairies, the culture of bright tobacco into South Carolina, and Spanish peanuts into the cornfields of Georgia.[21] Moreover, southern farmers have led many excursions in trucking, orcharding, and specialized farming only to witness local production expand beyond local markets and pull ruin down upon their heads. There is a needed and necessary place for cotton as a cash crop in southern agriculture. It is also possible that cotton can in the future be sufficiently mechanized to still its voracious demands for hand labor. If so, the unique features of cotton culture may be pruned off and the plant may come to occupy a normal and a legitimate niche in a balanced economy. Any adequate discussion of the rationalization of cotton must, however, be postponed to our chapter on regional reconstruction.

[21] H. H. Bennett, *Soils and Agriculture of the Southern States,* p. 13.

CHAPTER IX

THE FRINGES OF THE COTTON BELT

Tobacco

IF IN ITS SOCIAL effects tobacco is surprisingly like cotton, in its geographic conditions it differs greatly. In relation to tenancy, share cropping, and "furnishing," the two crops have developed similar conditions, oftentimes as complementary crops. In their demands upon soil and climate and in cultural routines the plants differ widely. The significant botanical fact about tobacco is its surprising variability. When other plants, because of change in soil or climate, would refuse to grow, tobacco proceeds to develop new variations. It is these variations in size, structure, delicacy of fibre, fragrance, porosity, color, and secretion of resinous substances that give the leaf its commercial values of quality and flavor. In hardly any other product is it found that variations in quality meet with such wide ranges in price. In the field of consumption a sophisticated market leading to secret buyers' grades meets in production technical methods of curing and variations produced by soil, breeding, and fertilization.

Possessing a much greater geographic range than cotton, tobacco adapts itself to climate, soils, and cultural situations. Valuable tobacco can be grown farther north than most grain crops. "In New England, Pennsylvania, and Wisconsin tobacco is ready for the harvest within eight weeks from the time of transplanting to the fields, but in Virginia, Kentucky, Tennessee and North Carolina from 110 to 140 days are required to ripen the leaves."[1] A northern climate tends toward the growth of leaves of large size, thinness, and weak aroma suitable for cigars. The sun of southern latitude produces a smaller more aromatic leaf of heavier body. The three main types in the United States are the cigar leaf of the

[1] J. B. Killebrew, "Tobacco," *Publications* American Economic Association, 1904, p. 136.

Connecticut Valley, burley of the Kentucky Blue Grass, and bright tobacco of the southeastern slope. The last two are of importance in southern economy.

The variegated checkerboard of soil plaques furnishes the foundation of tobacco qualities. The choice seed from Cuba and Sumatra planted in a given area will in the course of time, it is said, run into the one variety best suited for soil and climate. The chewing, smoking, cigarette, and snuff tobaccos thus each have a special locality. In each section there will be found only a small area of the soil that produces a quality of highest commercial value. A stone's throw from a strip of soil growing the finest quality will be found lands producing plants, luxuriant but practically worthless to the trade. The introduction of seed from fancy varieties soon finds the plants breeding to the level of the soil type, while the use of fertilization may serve only to accent the original qualities of the soil, and beyond certain definite limits it increases quantity at the expense of aroma and color.

White burley, which has changed sections of the Kentucky Blue-grass into a tobacco region, represents a remarkable variation due both to climate and soil. A soil, gray in color, rich in humus and the débris of disintegrated limestone, produces a leaf of low nicotine content and porous enough to absorb juices used in making plug. The most striking variation of species produced by soil, however, is that of yellow tobacco in the Bright Belt on which hinges the popularity of the cigarette. The story goes that in 1852 two brothers planted a crop of tobacco on a sandy ridge in Caswell County, North Carolina. The soil was thin, light in color, poor in plant nutrition, but porous and friable. The plants of the dark, heavy type when set out grew very slowly, changed from green to golden yellow and developed when cured a lemon hue and an unusually sweet aroma. At the market the tobacco brought a fancy price and soon sprang into demand by northern manufacturers for the best plug. It spread to whitish and yellowish sterile sandy soils first in the border Piedmont and after 1880 into the Carolina Coastal Plain. The relation between color of soil and of tobacco is distinct. Pale soils grow a yellow leaf; reddish or chocolate clayey soils furnish the rich, dark, heavy export tobacco; while on the gray soils of Kentucky is found the white burley. To fertilize the plant heavily is to make the leaves darker and stronger.

The theory in growing the best type of yellow tobacco is that the soil is a sponge, which must have the capacity to receive and retain just enough fertilizing matter to support the plant until it reaches a proper size. After that it is best that the fertilizer be exhausted so that the plant may go into a gradual decline in its vitality, like the hickory leaf in autumn growing more and more yellow, more and more delicate in tissue, more and more beautiful and storing up more and more sweetness until it is harvested. It was soon discovered that too much manure applied to the soil would destroy the best qualities of the leaf, vitiate its fragrance and diminish its brightness of color.[2]

The initial effect of the introduction of bright tobacco was to revive the social economy of a worn-out soil belt in North Carolina. Border counties of Virginia and North Carolina, covered for years with dwarf oaks, broomsedge and pines, were reclaimed by the use of commercial fertilizers and became the choicest lands for growing bright tobacco. Land sterile and abandoned which could be bought for fifty cents an acre in 1875 advanced to fifty dollars an acre in 1905. In good years $150 to $300 might be made from one acre of high quality tobacco. Manufacturers of tobacco products sprang up, the network of railways was extended, and centers of trade like Lynchburg, Richmond, Winston-Salem, and Durham were born or gained new growth. As the area extended, overproduction lowered the price. At the same time consolidation of small tobacco manufacturers enabled the larger units to store up reserves for curing and thus to be freer than growers from the exigencies of competition and the market. For many reasons, tobacco culture has not made its farmers permanently prosperous. So far short of improving the cultural landscape of the southeast has it fallen that an acute student and observer like J. Russell Smith can well write:

The tobacco territory is a disheartening sight to the traveller who is accustomed to well-kept fields and a neat countryside. The first impression is that everyone has recently moved away save a few who cultivate a patch of corn and tobacco here and there. This is so because of the system of cultivation. The man who may own 100 acres of land will derive all his money income from three to eight acres of tobacco. This with a patch of corn for his work animals, comprises his entire cultivated area. After a few crops the land is so impoverished and gullied that it is allowed to rest.[3]

[2] *Ibid.*, pp. 137-38.　　　　[3] *North America*, pp. 183-84.

In tobacco culture quantity is gained at the expense of quality, and quality brings the higher returns. The plant requires intensive cultivation and this serves to keep the acreage per farm exceptionally low. According to the 1920 Census, tobacco acreage represented 8 per cent of the total improved land on tobacco farms in Kentucky, 11 per cent in Virginia, and 17 per cent in North Carolina. The cultural routine is year around and so emphatic in its demands of hand labor that, according to a folk saying, it takes thirteen months a year to grow tobacco. The hand labor of minute and varied detail required to nurture this temperamental plant has descended as a heritage from slave women and children to the farmer's family of today. Olmsted quoted an observer who held "men are worth too much for growing corn to be employed in strolling through tobacco looking for worms" and concluded that tobacco continued to be cultivated because a class of labor good for nothing else can be put to work growing the leaf.[4]

The intensity of cultural routines in tobacco is shown by the extent of man labor in the crop. Horse and man labor furnish the greater part of the cost of growing tobacco, ranging from 45 to 65 per cent. Records secured and averaged by the Department of Agriculture show that 262 hours of man labor produce an acre of Kentucky dark, 375 hours, an acre of Kentucky burley, and 403 hours, an acre of Georgia bright tobacco. An idea of the comparatively small use of even simple horse-drawn machines may be gained from the average of horse labor required per acre: only 89 hours in the dark, fire-cured area, 98 hours for burley, and 90 hours in Georgia bright.[5]

The endless care required in tobacco culture is suggested by the fact that no general principles of cultivation can be worked out. The best adviser to the tobacco farmer in cultivation and curing may be an old settler who knows the local soil and growing conditions. The chief drawback in the introduction of the culture to new regions is the lack of such local knowledge; and in many new areas an experienced tobacco man must be engaged to instruct the farmers. In new Georgia areas the demonstrator receives as high as ten per cent of the crop or $8 per acre. Pains-

---

[4] *Journey Through the Back Country*, pp. 339-40.
[5] "History and Status of Tobacco Culture," U. S. D. A. *Yearbook*, 1922, Separate 885, pp. 426-27.

taking care in tobacco culture is confronted by the large number of operations requiring hand labor. Care of the plant bed, preparation of the field, transplanting, cultivation, topping, worming, suckering, spraying, harvesting, curing, stripping, and marketing make up an almost endless round of toil.

The picture of cultivation here presented, true in the main, is a composite from several localities and will fit no one given area. It serves to outline, however, the cultural routine of those who work in tobacco fields. The seed are so small they cannot be sown broadcast. First, the seed bed must be prepared, its soil pulverized and fertilized, possibly brush burned upon it to destroy bacteria, and then weeded by hand. The growth of plants, requiring six to eight weeks, demands about twenty hours labor per acre and furnishes, say, 3 per cent of the cost of production. The preparation of the field in parallel ridges, rows, and mounds to receive the plants, also requires about 20 hours. The transplantation of the plants, an operation requiring much care and back-bending labor, accounts for 25 to 30 hours. Transplanting begins about March 21 in South Georgia and starts a month later in the Carolina fields. In the border belt it starts about May 1; in burley, by May 11 to 21. The six cultivations which may be needed, together with constant weeding, will take another 25 to 40 hours. In order to concentrate the strength of the plant in fewer leaves the top buds must be pinched off. The lower leaves more likely to spoil, are cut off for the same reason. Sprouts called suckers grow out from the axis of the plant and these must also be cut off. This must be done in June or early July. Horn worms appear in great droves to devour the leaves and are to be killed or picked off by hand. In bright tobacco these processes together with spraying will use over sixty hours of the farmer's time for each acre in tobacco. The great variations in labor routine come in process of harvesting, curing, stripping, and marketing. In bright tobacco the leaves are plucked from the stalk as they ripen while in burley and dark the stalks are cut. In general, tobacco is ready to be cut and housed three months after transplanting. In the Coastal Carolinas the process begins as early as July 11, in other sections from August 20 to September 14. In Georgia areas harvesting thus requires over 10 hours while in Kentucky it ranges from 25 to 60.

In its perishable nature tobacco partakes of the characteristics of a trucking crop. Accordingly, a unique and important task requiring skill and care falls to the southern farmer in the curing of his tobacco. It requires the use of a specially constructed building, the tobacco barn, and accounts for an average of 59 work hours per acre. This process saves the crop from spoilage and imparts to the leaf those peculiar qualities on which depends the value of the farmer's year-around toil. Curing represents a nice excursion into plant physiology in which the tobacco leaf is forced to undergo a process of gradual starvation without being prematurely killed. The leaf must be harvested just at the time when an adequate balance has been reached in the replacement of green coloring matter by starchy food supply. The leaf after harvest continues to live on the reserve food supply until the drying process is completed. To kill the leaf by drying before the process of digestion is completed or to allow the reserve food supply to become exhausted before the leaf is dry is to spoil the tobacco in curing. The living cells are killed by excessively low or high temperature and by loss of water. The loss of water in drying is determined by heat and humidity; hence the necessity for barns and careful handling of flue heating and ventilation. In the bright belt the leaves are strung on sticks, suitable for arranging tier by tier in the curing barn. The heat is furnished by sheet iron flues leading from small furnaces at one end of the barn, and ventilation is provided. The yellowing process is started slowly at 80° since care must be taken not to kill the leaf by drying too rapidly. As the leaf begins to yellow, the humidity must be decreased by raising the temperature and increasing the ventilation until there comes the critical period called "fixing the color." This is done by removing the moisture as fast as it is given off by the leaf, for moisture retained after the leaf is yellowed leads to splotches of red and brown called "sponging." If heat is increased while the leaf remains full of sap a greenish black color develops known as "scalding" or "blistering." If the curing stage is passed successfully the tobacco is held at home until time for its conditioning for the market.[6]

The methods developed in marketing are again unique, and here the tobacco farmer is at a greater disadvantage than the cotton

[6] W. W. Garner, "Tobacco Curing," U. S. D. A. *Farmers' Bulletin* 523, 1928, pp. 3-9, 16.

grower. Cotton possesses grades of uniform standards for which there exist world-wide prices known to every farmer who glances at his paper. The tobacco farmer cannot grade his product by uniform standards, and, if he did, he would find no quotations to guide him in its sale. Nor can the tobacco farmer hold his product off the market in the face of unfavorable prices. Even after curing, his product remains perishable and must be soon subjected to redrying processes by the manufacturer if it is to be saved. The cotton grower hauls his bales to market and there his expenses cease. Tobacco in the South, however, is sold under an auction system in which the farmer pays the charges.

He prepares the leaves as soon as cured into soft, pliable condition and assorts them roughly as to quality, length, and color. This is a form of guess work, for the grower knows neither to what grades his product belongs nor for what uses it is fitted. The leaves are tied into bundles and the bundles hung on laths to prevent tangling and breaking of the fibres. It is then conditioned for market by exposure to moisture, sometimes by sprinkling with water. About 70 hours of work per acre, only 18 per cent of the total labor, in the Georgia area went for preparing and hauling the crop to market.

At the warehouse the loose leaves are arranged on the floor in piles and the buyers for large companies inspect the product to find within which of the private grades of his company it falls. The warehouse system gives the buyer the convenience of centralized public market where he may have choice among assorted grades. It gives the seller the advantage of open competition among buyers. Having roughly determined the grade, the buyer knows the limit his company allows him to bid on the lot. The auctioneer conducts the bidding at breakneck speed in a singsong jargon from pile to pile. In some markets, it has been stated, the rules require an auctioneer to sell as many as 240 lots of tobacco an hour. The price, name of buyer, and grade are tagged on each lot. If disappointed in the price offered, the farmer may refuse it and have the lot put up for auction a second time or removed to another warehouse. If he accepts the offer, he receives a check for the amount less an auction fee, a weighing charge, and a commission for selling. Meyer Jacobstein has estimated that with a storage fee of $1.50 and sampling fee of $1.00 on each hogshead, an auction fee of 25 cents per sample, an insurance fee of one half per cent value, and a warehouse commission of three per cent, with freight and drayage included, the warehouse may get as high as ten per cent of the gross selling price.[7]

With tobacco ranging in price from one cent to two dollars a pound, the farmer who receives, say, a flat rate of 30 cents per pound, has no conception of tobacco grades and remains ignorant of what portions of his crop brought a high price. The tobacco farmer sees his market but once a year. Being so constantly employed with his farm duties, he takes no time to determine whether or not he is making a saleable product. Possessing no standard grades or market quotations, he gains his idea of the value of tobacco from his neighbor's experiences without knowing the quality of his neighbor's crop. To a large extent it is true that the small farmer markets his crop in the dark. The United States Bureau of Markets of the Department of Agriculture is now conducting experiments which will, it is hoped, lead to the acceptance of uniform grades. The fact that tobacco must be stored several years for aging, and this charge must be borne by the manufacturer, does not necessarily operate to the farmer's benefit. In fact it may give the tobacco manufacturers a reserve supply that makes them temporarily independent of a short crop with its higher prices.[8]

Such is the labor routine and the seasonal drill of the farmer who follows after tobacco. It is truly a crop which wears out men and land. In such a culture the hand labor of women and children is accepted as a matter of course. In rural areas of tobacco counties in Kentucky, Virginia, and South Carolina studied by the Children's Bureau, farm work caused from one half to three fifths of all absences from school. Of 563 children in Kentucky and 606 children in Virginia and South Carolina working more than twelve days, over one third had worked three months in tobacco fields. Few worked less than eight hours a day and almost half worked ten hours. More than one fourth of the boys had worked four months, beginning with spring plowing and following the crop through until the last task was finished in early winter. Children kneel, sit, and stoop while their hands are busy at the

[7] *The Tobacco Industry,* p. 74.
[8] See T. J. Woofter, Jr., *The Plight of Cigarette Tobacco,* pp. 39, 71-74, 75-77.

tasks of transplanting, suckering, and worming.[9] Worming is to many the most disagreeable task of all and parents occasionally pay children five or ten cents for each hundred worms gathered. After the harvest children often stay up late into the night watching fires at the barn during the curing process.

These are the demands that soil, climate, the biology of a plant grown within the confines of a complex economic system make on the lives of men. That tobacco culture remains much the same regardless of changing political institutions and vanishing slavery systems is indicated by a letter to Lord Baltimore in 1729.

In Virginia and Maryland Tobacco is our Staple, is our All, and Indeed leaves no room for anything Else; It requires the Attendance of all our hands, and Exacts their utmost labour, the whole year around; it requires us to abhor Communities or townships, since a Planter cannot Carry on his Affairs, without Considerable Elbow room, within his plantation. When All is done, and our Tobacco sent home, it is perchance the most uncertain Commodity that Comes to Markett; and the management of it there is of such nature and method, that it seems to be of all other, most lyable and Subject to frauds, in prejudice to the poor Planters.[10]

Over-expansion and over-production in tobacco, a natural tendency in all crops, is not a mere matter of acreage and total volume of the crop. Variation in soil, fertilization, and curing work unexpected variations in quality. Ignorance of the market due to secret buyers' grades and lack of quotations joins these factors of nature to lead to the over-production of certain grades at the expense of others.

This risk is hidden, masked by hand tasks, executed by family labor. The raising of tobacco, to an even greater extent than other agricultural products, is subsidized by family labor. In no other way could it absorb the shifting cycle of depressed prices and survive. The farmer has never developed enough of a cost accounting system to assign to himself and family wages for their work. Like his brother, the farmer in cotton, he expects a living and possible "profits" from his crop, but in his rough and ready

[9] Harriet A. Byrne, "Child Labor in Representative Tobacco-Growing Areas," Children's Bureau *Publication* 115, 1926, pp. 41-42.

[10] Letter of Benedict Leonard Calvert, Annapolis, Md., Oct. 26, 1729, to Charles Lord Baltimore, published in the Maryland Historical Society's *Fund Publication*, No. 34, p. 70. Quoted by U. B. Phillips, *Plantation and Frontier*, I, 282-83.

accounting rent is real while family labor is given as a matter of course. Accordingly it is often true that crops on which the producer claims to have "made good" would show on any kind of balance sheet that assigned to family labor its customary outside wages, an actual loss. Hand cultivated crops sold in a fluctuating market have their losses masked by a traditional attitude toward the labor of women and children and leave the farmer, more often than he realizes, in the position of paying for the privilege of growing a crop.

It is this crop which is regarded as offering economic salvation to new areas of the Southeast. Its spread to a hitherto untried region is attended with risk and expense. Until the vagaries of soil, climate, and curing in relation to the locale and the type of tobacco become known, loss is to be expected even with the employment of expert help. Such expansion as that into South Georgia fastens a new routine of hand labor upon the women and children of the family and leads again to over-production.

TABLE XX

TOBACCO: ACREAGE, PRODUCTION, VALUE, 1910-1929

	ACREAGE		PRODUCTION (Thousand Pounds)		FARM VALUE (Thousand Dollars)	
	1910	1929	1910	1929	1910	1929
Virginia..................	185,427	170,000	132,979	118,320	$12,169	$20,706
Kentucky...............	469,795	473,000	398,482	361,845	39,868	65,856
North Carolina...........	221,890	764,000	138,813	508,060	13,847	93,991
Tennessee................	90,468	129,300	68,756	102,664	5,661	17,761
South Carolina...........	30,082	133,000	25,583	82,992	2,123	13,279
Georgia..................	2,025	110,000	1,485	89,870	293	65,856
Florida..................	3,987	12,300	3,505	11,070	1,025	3,454
Alabama*.................	211	......	90	......	14	......
Mississippi*..............	49	......	18	......	3	......
Arkansas*................	758	......	316	......	40	......
Louisiana................	519	1,000	172	378	42	151
Oklahoma*...............	82	......	50	......	5	......
Texas*...................	324	......	161	......	26	......
Total South.............	1,005,617	1,792,600	707,416	1,275,199	$281,054	$75,121
The Nation..............	1,294,911	2,016,400		1,560,891	104,303	285,583

*Produce small quantities mainly for home use.

RICE

Unlike tobacco, two southern staples, rice and sugar, stand definitely outside cotton culture. Both are grown in the humid subtropical belt fringing the Gulf Coast. A strip of coastal prairies, 25 to 50 miles wide and stretching 250 miles through southwest Louisiana and southeast Texas, furnishes the region for rice. In its 9 million acres this belt possesses definite geographic conditions which help to rank it among the most efficient rice growing areas yet developed. In addition, a coastal plain area in Arkansas has proved suitable for the crop.

The discovery and utilization of this splendid area was one of those historical accidents which occasionally change the cultural landscape. The production of rice in the Carolinas by the tide flow system under the routine of slavery had in the Civil War met a destruction of capital and a change in labor régime which it was vainly trying to overcome. The present rice district was the home of great cattle ranches, some of which remain along its swampy coastal margins. In 1884 and 1885 a few farmers from the wheat states of the Northwest settled on these southern prairies so like their own. They found rice grown for home consumption by their neighbors who used Oriental methods. It was but a step to the adaptation of the machinery of the wheat belt, the gang plow, disk, harrow, drill, broadcast seeder, and finally the twine binder to the needs of rice culture. By means of small levees and interior ditches the intersecting creeks could be diverted to flood the level prairies. These levees were cheaply constructed and little attention was paid to drainage. The prairies, however, were free of injurious grasses, and even if cultivation, spading, stacking and threshing were carelessly done, large crops could be grown. "The rice fields were handled like bonanza wheat farms of Dakota, and fortunes were made." Such conditions could not last. Droughts occurred, the creeks failed, and the rice farmers were faced with the necessity of providing a permanent water supply. Pumping plants for lifting the water 15 to 25 feet from stream bed to fields were developed in connection with a system of main and lateral surface canals.

By 1890 the irrigating canals were started in a small way in Acadia Parish, Louisiana. Hardly had the system supplied by large pumping plants been accepted as a success when it was discovered that the strata of gravel underlying the surface held the underground flow demanded by artesian wells. A six-inch pipe driven 200 feet to this water level, it was found, would furnish irrigation for 60 to 80 acres of rice. In other sections pipes may be sunk to depths of 400 to 600 feet where pressure insufficient to bring the water over the top brings it near enough the surface to be pumped. Wells may be put down 30 to 40 feet apart, united just below ground level and run by one engine and one pump. Eight 4-inch wells, for example, united within twenty feet of the surface, run by one 16-inch pump and a 50 horsepower engine will flood 500 acres of rice.[11]

A fortunate complex of geographic factors thus made possible the adjustment of the steel robots of the wheat field to an aquatic plant in a startling agricultural development. The prairies are far enough from the coast to be comparatively free from disastrous wind storms and the ravages of birds. They are near enough to partake of the coastal rainfall, the sea's gift to the rice plant. Rainfall ranges from 40 inches to 55 inches annually, and half of the precipitation falls during the growing season. Accordingly only about one half of the water used need be artificially supplied. The long frostless season of nine months lasts from March first to December first and for periods of maximum plant growth, the three summer months, the temperature averages 82°.[12] It is the soil, above all, which has conditioned this alternation of the vegetation of the marsh with the machine cultivation of dry land. Underlying the prairie is a subsoil of clay which forms a hard pan. The fields during flooding thus form a well-nigh perfect basin through which little water penetrates. When drained the fields dry soon and completely because water has seeped to no appreciable depth through the tight formation. The top soil of medium loam with about fifty per cent clay forms a perfect balance between sand and humus which are too porous and clay which is too compact. The best rice lands are said to be the buckshot soils—so stiff they can hardly be plowed unless first flooded to soften their texture.[13]

Other rice lands in the South are notably inferior in adaptation to irrigation and machine cultivation. The Tidal Deltas of South Carolina and Georgia, formerly flooded from rivers at high tide and drained at low, possess a soil which refuses to take power ma-

[11] S. A. Knapp, "Rice Culture," *Farmers' Bulletin,* 417, 1910, pp. 27-29.
[12] O. E. Baker, "Agricultural Regions of North America," *Economic Geography,* III, 62-63.
[13] S. A. Knapp, *op. cit.,* p. 8.

chinery. The alluvial lands of eastern Louisiana, many formerly used as sugar plantations, are similarly handicapped by soil factors. The inland marshes of Georgia and South Carolina are really high lands easily drained. Their water supply from streams is unreliable in dry periods and too cold during freshets.

The labor routine in this type of amphibian machine farming offers a significant contrast to methods of rice culture of the Orient. As soon as the seed is planted the "sprout" flooding may be applied 6 to 12 inches deep. Its purpose is to produce germination, and the water is allowed to remain until sprouts push through the hulls. When the pointed single leaves of the rice plant appear, the "point" or "stretch" flooding is applied to force growth ahead of the weeds. When the plant reaches six inches growth the water is lowered to four inches in depth and held from two weeks to a month. A period of dry growth of 40 to 50 days ensues until the plants begin to joint. Then the "harvest" flow is released over the fields and is held four to five inches deep until just before the time to harvest.[14] When drained the ground dries rapidly offering firm support to machines which sweep through the rice as though it were wheat of the Dakotas. The influence of topography cannot be exaggerated. The level prairie not only allows machine cultivation and harvesting but conditions the equitable maturing of the grain. Unequal depths of water would cause rice to mature at varying periods and such rice harvested together would possess the commercial value of the lowest grade in the mixture.

The geographic complex, complete mechanical devices, virgin lands, and intelligent management have here met to array American rice culture against Oriental cultivation in the world-wide battles of the industries. For the same reasons the level prairie section in east Arkansas between Crowley's Ridge and the Mississippi, when once it was discovered to possess a tight clay subsoil and water available for pumping, became a great rice-growing area. Accordingly, the southern rice fields can supply much of America's demands and, after paying the freight of its product halfway around the globe, undersell Japanese and Chinese rice at home. Figures compiled by S. A. Knapp and quoted by O. E. Baker interpret this paradox.

[14] C. G. Haskell, "Irrigation Practice in Rice Growing," U. S. D. A., *Farmers' Bulletin* 673, 1915, pp. 11-12.

ACRES PER LABORER IN RICE

Country	Acres per Laborer
Japan	½ to 1
China	½ to 2½
India	3
Egypt	4
Italy	5
United States	
Carolinas	8
Mississippi Delta	10
Louisiana-Texas	80

"The use of machinery and superior farm organization enables a man on these coastal prairies to cultivate perhaps 100 times as much land and produce probably 60 or 70 times as much rice as a man in Japan or China. The laborer can earn 15 to 20 times as large a wage and yet produce rice at one-half as great labor cost."[15]

It seems but just to say that the future of rice farming in the South will find its limits to exist in the demand and food habits of the people. While, for example, the 1919 Census showed that rice furnished three fourths of the value of the crops in the rice sub-region, the crop occupied only six per cent of the land area. Other crops occupied another six per cent. Furthermore, there exist "vast tracts of land along the Atlantic and Gulf Coasts and in the interior that cannot be used for any other agricultural purposes without expensive drainage and aeration of the soil."[16] Rice will thus remain an important factor, actual or potential, in all semi-tropical zones because of its ability to thrive under conditions of humidity. Changes in food habits of the American people such as might follow upon the diffusion of more palatable methods of cooking rice would find this region ready. There are about 10,-000,000 acres of land in the five states bordering the Gulf of Mexico well suited to rice culture. Only 3,000,000 acres of this can be successfully irrigated under present methods from surface and artesian flows. The balance of the area can be brought into cultivation only when prices justify such a step. If the crop were allowed to ripen by aging, as is done in the Orient, if brown rice retaining the essential oils and protein of the kernel's surface could be pop-

[15] Quoted by O. E. Baker, loc. cit., p. 63.
[16] Baker, ibid.

ilarized, the rice market might be expanded. The startling spread between wholesale and retail prices, ranging from 2½ to 4 cents a pound and often amounting to 50 per cent of the seller's price, also serves to reduce consumption. The method of milling for toll, moreover, by neglecting to sort and mill rice in uniform grades and styles, has tended to restrict consumption. If the rice millers did as the manufacturers in other industries—buy the raw product and handle the output as their own—brands and grades in rice having been introduced on the market could be supplied with certainty. This task is coming more and more to be regarded as the rightful field of the growers' coöperatives and they have done much.

Here is the contrast with cotton culture. Twenty acres and a mule, share tenancy and mobile croppers living on fatback and sirup have no place in this economy. It is rather an expanse of great farms, of machine agriculture and hired labor. If the tradition of slavery once clung to the rice farming of the Carolina coasts it was long since removed by wheat farmers from the Northwest.

TABLE XXI

RICE: ACREAGE, PRODUCTION, VALUE, 1924-1929

	Acreage (in thousand acres)		Production (in thousand bushels)		Farm Value (in thousand dollars)	
	Average 1924-1928	1929	Average 1924-1928	1929	Average 1924-1928	1929
Louisiana.............	472	472	16,944	18,833	$19,316	$18,399
Texas.................	160	144	6,952	7,416	7,752	7,254
Arkansas.............	175	156	8,097	7,956	9,149	7,772
The South.............	807	772	31,993	34,205	$36,219	$33,418
The United States.........	940	868	39,137	40,462	$44,603	$39,536

	(In thousand bushels)		
	1924	1928	1929
Exports (Including to Alaska, Hawaii, Porto Rico).............	12,763	24,728	20,987
Imports................	2,076	1,325	1,124
Net Balance of Exports....	10,687	23,403	19,773

SUGAR

On the southerly fringe of the Cotton Belt is found that alien to our geography, the sugar cane. Were it not for the fact that the protective tariff enables Louisiana sugar to be sold for two or three times what it costs to produce sugar in Cuba, this exotic plant would be grown in the southern United States only for its sirup.[17] It is safe to say that the difficulties which attend the transfer and cultivation of a tropic plant in the semi-tropic climates of Louisiana and Texas are reflected in the economic, cultural, and political life of the people. The soil of the Mississippi delta in southern Louisiana, ranking among the richest in the world, is almost ideal for sugar cane, a fact which somewhat compensates for its climatic drawbacks. High natural fertility, a top soil that retains water, and a subsoil permitting rapid drainage provide for the growth of cane. Such characteristics are found mainly in sandy loams or clays where laid down as alluvial lands. The cane demands during its period of growth large quantities of water; yet suffers from lack of aeration if the water is held stagnant near the surface by a tight subsoil. The soil, in short, should be such as affords the plant the best advantages of humid tropical conditions, heavy rains followed by steaming dazzling sunshine. In the sugar areas the summer temperature averages 81° F., the annual rainfall is about 60 inches, and the frost free season extends for some 250 days. Dry weather ripening increases the sugar content which in periods of excessive rain tends to be "watery."

The chief handicaps offered by the Louisiana climate in sugar production are the threat of frost in early winter and the alternation with the growing season of a dormant period unknown in the tropics. Cane in Louisiana must be allowed to stand until the last minute for the increase of sugar content; but at that it is always harvested immature. A warning of low temperatures of 26° F. from the Weather Bureau will serve to send a large force of men to fields for windrowing the seed and mill cane. This process consists of cutting, piling, and covering the cane in great rows. With such methods cane crops valued at $10,000,000 have been saved by timely warnings. If allowed to freeze, the cane bursts at its joints, fermentation sets in, and inversion or "souring" of the sugar results. In the tropic home of cane sugar, planting is not urgent and may extend over a period of five months. In Louisiana, however, either planting or protection by windrowing the cane must, because of the dormant season, be carried on at

[17] See Philip G. Wright, *Sugar in Relation to the Tariff*, pp. 244-53.

the same time as the processes of cutting, transporting, and hauling. If cane is planted before harvest it may sprout prematurely
and be killed by the winter's cold.[18] Cane for sirup can be grown
much farther north because the non-crystallizable sugars found in
immature cane are to be desired in sirup.

The unique labor routine in Louisiana sugar cane has been
analyzed by the economists of the Department of Agriculture.[19]
The crop is characterized by large requirements of heavy manual
labor. Its chief variations from the cultural routine of most field
crops inheres in the speeding-up process demanded by harvesting
and the additional fact that the material for planting constitutes a
considerable and bulky part of the cane of the previous crop. If
undertaken in the fall, planting conflicts with harvest and the
sprouting cane may be winter killed. If undertaken in the spring,
planting encounters the expense of windrowing and the disagreeable work in fields made quagmires by spring rains.

We may follow an average acre of sugar cane around the season
with its work crews. If planted in the fall the tasks of harvesting,
transporting, and covering seed cane require 11.21 days of man
labor; if planted in the spring, harvesting, windrowing, removing
from storage, and planting account for 15.67 labor days. Cultivation accounts for 12.04 more days, fertilization at least half a day,
and harvesting 10.97 days. Each acre demands from 34 to 39 days
of man labor and from 20 to 23 days of mule labor. "The American
farmer, accustomed to the use of labor saving machinery, is loathe
to perform the large amount of hand labor necessary for successful
growing of sugar crops."[20] The fact that during the rush period
all laborers receive a daily wage from 25 to 75 per cent higher
than that paid during the other seasons does not solve the problem.
A recourse to small farm production by owners instead of day
labor under supervision, while solving one problem, would place
insuperable difficulties in the way of coördination for large scale
production.

By the very nature of its task the sugar plantation possesses a
large-scale, closely integrated, capitalistic organization. Many plantations are very large. The company which owns one or more planta-

[18] E. W. Brandes, et al. "Sugar," U. S. D. A. *Yearbook,* 1923, Separate 893, pp.
8-15.
[19] Brandes, *loc. cit., Yearbook,* 1923, pp. 18-30.
[20] *Ibid.,* p. 98.

tions may also own a central sugar mill. From two thousand to five thousand acres in cane planted within distances of easy communication are required to supply such a mill. Both the mill and the plantation represent an overhead of fixed costs which must be met by efficient processing of the cane. Upon being cut the cane because of the activity of microörganisms in warm climates, is liable to rapid inversion. Cutting, stripping, topping, and transportation to the mill must be done in the shortest possible time. A network of private railways is thus necessary to draw the fields closer to the mills, and the cane is hauled in freight cars. Investments in mills and tracks are likely to range from half a million to a million dollars. The necessity for speed when once harvest has begun has brought about an organization of transportation and a rigid discipline in mill, railway, and field comparable to the efficiency of the supply service of an army. A manager of traffic must keep loaded trains moving in orderly procession to the mill and see that empties are provided wherever needed. The orders for cutting are received by field superintendents from a field manager who must keep in touch with the mill administrator and traffic manager. If, for example, the machinery of the mill breaks down, the fact must be communicated to all departments of the plantation and be followed by an instant cessation of activities in order to prevent an accumulation of loaded trains in the mill yards.[21] The organization, the labor routine, and the pattern of activity is that of the factory. The sugar plantation and mill must employ wage labor and in many other respects run counter to the traditional picture of southern agriculture.

It is at this point of the labor routine that the impact of an alien climate on a tropic plant is felt. A large plantation will employ perhaps 100 to 150 wage hands working the year around. During the combination season of planting and harvesting, through November and December, three or four times that many are needed, and even then the "best efforts of all hands fall short of accomplishing the tasks in a satisfactory manner." A similar, though less acute, situation obtaining in the harvesting of cotton is met by tenants attached to the soil who furnish family labor during emergency. Sugar culture demands too much centralization and integration for the typical plantation organization of share tenancy.

[21] *Ibid.*, p. 35.

The rush work of harvest is too heavy for women and children; accordingly no comparison with cotton picking is feasible. Among the Louisiana sugar planter's many problems, his chief difficulty is securing seasonal labor supply. Since slavery the recurring phases of the labor shortage have successively grown more acute. Northern industry and near-by oil fields can offer a year around routine that leaves the planter without help. The ability to triple the labor supply at a seasonable demand presupposes migratory workers or a large labor reserve. The last the South has possessed in a measure in unemployed and under-employed Negroes. With the shutting off of immigration, the reserve, much to its own advancement, is rapidly being depleted. The one way out for the planter, the invention of labor saving machinery, especially a giant cane harvester, has not yet been achieved.

In area the sugar cane delta contains about 5,200,000 acres. In 1924 less than one third of the region was included within its farms. A little over one ninth of the area was in crops and the average farm had 54 acres under cultivation.[22] The expansion of this area is not limited by consumption. During the last 100 years the per capita consumption of sugar in the United States has increased from 10 to over 100 pounds, the highest in the world. Cane and sugar beets together furnish hardly one fourth of the sugar consumed, while the production from sugar cane is about one fourth that from beets. Only 0.2 per cent of all acreage in crops in 1927 was planted to sugar. Of the 800,000 acres so planted, 575,000 were beet lands.[23]

Unless new varieties of cane are developed, the crop seems permanently restricted to the soil and climate offered by the Louisiana sugar bowl. The one exception is offered by new areas being open to cane in the Florida Everglades. Development of new cane varieties is rendered especially difficult by the fact that, as it normally reproduces by sprouting rather than from seed, the plant does not readily lend itself to the cross-fertilization necessary in growing hybrids. An adequate cane harvesting machine would solve the problem of harvest labor supply, lower costs, and expand acreage within the bowl. Such a machine in its operation will be faced by the fact that the best cultural practice in growing cane

[22] O. E. Baker, *loc. cit.,* pp. 52, 64.
[23] *Yearbook,* 1929, pp. 3, 7.

demands that the plants develop in close formation so that the heavy shade may both retard weeds and conserve moisture.

Fortunately the problems of the industry have lately proved less baffling. The flood of 1927 may be regarded as marking a definite break with the older type of sugar culture. The spread of cane disease had reduced the per acre yield one third to one half so that in 1927 the acreage was one third of that a decade before and the production about one fourth. Disease resistant varieties since developed and introduced by the Department of Agriculture have shown as high yields as the old ribbon cane. Especially successful in resisting disease is the variety known as PJO introduced from Java. Since its acceptance the production of sugar cane in Louisiana has doubled. This variety has proved the greatest single factor in restoring a threatened industry. It has produced an average of over 20 tons per acre in all sections of the area and shows, moreover, an almost abnormally high sucrose content. It reaches 14 per cent in many cases, yielding over 270 pounds to the ton. Purchase from cane growers on the basis of sucrose content has become almost universal, thus allowing the small farmer to share in the profit from exceptionally sweet cane.

Other significant trends in the processing of sugar are a tendency towards mergers and the development of by-products. Operating companies are being organized to take over and manage several plantations. One such company successfully operated during the

TABLE XXII

CANE SUGAR PRODUCTION IN LOUISIANA, 1911-1929

	Acreage (Thousand Acres)	Production (Thousand Tons)	Factories Operating	Refined Sugar (Tons)	Molasses (Thousand Gallons)
1911......................	310	5,887	188	328,879	35,062
1915......................	183	2,018	136	128,200	12,743
1920......................	182	2,492	122	157,626	16,856
1926......................	128	864	54	44,000	6,614
1929......................	155	2,918	65	186,000	19,619
Sugar in U. S..............	1911	1915	1920	1926	1929
			(1000 Short Tons)		
Beet Sugar Produced.......	600,000	874,000	1,089,000	897,000	1,018,000
Cane Sugar Produced.......	328,879	128,200	157,626	44,000	186,000
Production in U. S. and all Dominions.............	1,856,530	2,404,018	2,779,413	2,923,225	3,700,358
Additional Imported.......	1,845,279	2,689,067	3,228,279	3,968,880	2,823,175

928 season four plantations under one head; another, five. In
he field of by-products a technique has been evolved of making
)uilding board from sugar cane refuse. Cane cream developed
)y the chemists of the United States Department of Agriculture
s expected to attain popularity. A cream-like substance, it looks
ind tastes like caramel and may be used as icings or as a spread
'or breads.[24] Compared with its position not so many years ago
he sugar industry is improving. Whereas 55 mills with a grind-
ng capacity of 32,000 tons of cane every twenty-four hours operated
n the 1928 season, 65 mills produced 200,000 tons of sugar in 1929.

TRUCKING REGIONS IN THE SOUTH

The growing of fruits and vegetables has given the United
States a new billion dollar industry. The spread of truck growing
)n the edges and within the Cotton Belt is not so much a proof
)f diversification within the cotton system as it is of the rise of a
1ew specialization on its fringes. Diversification implies home
gardens whose products in the main do not enter the market.
Trucking crops, however, are grown entirely for the market and
heir interaction with the cotton system must be confined to the
1creage and men they take from cotton culture. Less than two per
:ent of the tillable land in the United States is required to pro-
luce the needed truck crops. The importance of trucking in rela-
:ion to area, however, far outdistances that of other forms of agricultural production, and the industry in the South deserves presenta-
:ion on its own account. The trucking industry is important
enough to the South and the Atlantic Coast Line Railway to justify
:he oft-told story, true, by the way, of a trainload of millionaires
en route to Palm Beach run off on a siding to wait for a train of
:abbages to pass.

Two types of areas are found in the South devoted to these
:rops: interior and coastal. Only the coastal strip can be said to
form any connected trucking region. Inland market gardening
1as grown up in limited districts around large cities. The land occupied is relatively high priced because of its urban proximity,
and the production is diversified. These crops hit the peak of production rather than the peak of prices. Accordingly such growers
survive simply because they are freed of much of the expense of

[24] A. W. Dykes, "Sugar," *Blue Book of Southern Progress*, pp. 104-5.

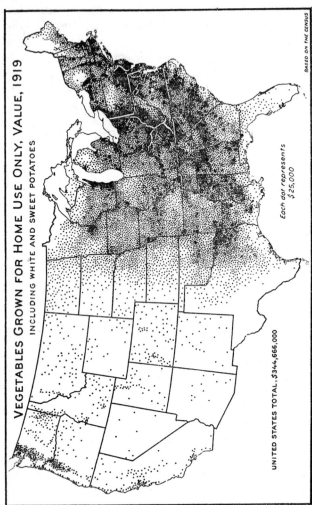

VEGETABLES GROWN FOR HOME USE ONLY, VALUE, 1919

INCLUDING WHITE AND SWEET POTATOES

UNITED STATES TOTAL, $344,666,000

Each dot represents
$25,000

BASED ON THE CENSUS

FIGURE 16.—The census of 1920 was the first to separate vegetables grown for home use from those grown for sale, and the census of 1925 obtained the returns only of the commercial crop of seven vegetables. The areas of greatest acreages of vegetables for home use are southeastern Pennsylvania, the upper Ohio Valley, the mountainous districts of eastern Kentucky and Tennessee and of northern Alabama, the upper piedmont of the Carolinas and Georgia, and much of Mississippi, the Lake Michigan shore counties of Wisconsin, southeastern Michigan, and central New York—districts of small farms owned by frugal people. The average size of the farm garden, however, is greatest, apparently, in Virginia and Massachusetts (about one-half acre), and smallest in the prairie and Plains States (about one-fifth acre). (Courtesy of U. S. Department of Agriculture).

transportation, packaging, refrigeration, and grading. Proximity also enables them to deliver fruits and vegetables in the natural state of ripeness rather than ripened artificially.

Five specialized long distance trucking areas can be pointed out in the United States, three of them in the South. The Pacific Coast, the Northern States east of the Rocky Mountains, the Gulf Coast, the Atlantic Coast, and the Inland South stand out as distinct trucking regions.[25] In some respects Florida deserves separate treatment as the most distinct trucking community in America. The extent of truck crops, when measured either in acreage or bushels, is not a true index of their agricultural importance to the South. These fruits and vegetables are available at periods when the market demands early products and their value is likely to be much greater than either acreage or bulk would imply.[26]

Soil and climate of the coastal strips are suited to give growing fruits and vegetables what they most need, water and sunshine. Areas of level topography fronting either on the Gulf or the Atlantic possess mild and equable temperatures. Sandy soils and heavy rainfall absorb the warmth and hold the moisture needed for watery products. Texture of soil is intimately related to warmth which hastens the maturity of growth. "Soil," says O. E. Baker, "supplies little more than sunshine, showers, and support— the plant is fed fertilizer with a precision based on scientific knowledge."[27] The earliest crops of vegetables come from light, porous, well-drained, warm, dry soils. The swing of the trucking season up the Atlantic Coast lasts six months from January to June. The influence of soil texture and the advance of the season has been summarized by Milton Whitney in six periods.

Each of the localities can in normal seasons count on from two to three weeks advance in crop maturity over the locality North, and this is the period in which they can market their crops at the greatest profit. Furthermore, there is about the same interval of two or three weeks in the time of maturity of crops on the several grades of soil. . . . The yields from the very early sandy soils are light; the quality of vegetables is not

[25] Fred J. Blair, "Development and Localization of Truck Crops in the United States," U. S. D. A. *Yearbook,* 1916, pp. 1-2.

[26] William Stuart, "Potato Production in the South," U. S. D. A. *Farmers' Bulletin* 1205, 1923, pp. 3-4.

[27] In *Economic Geography,* V, 44.

FIGURE 17.—The most important area of commercial vegetable production extends from New York City to Norfolk, Va. In this area about one-fifth of the Nation's commercial crop is produced. This commercial crop includes cabbage, cantaloupes and muskmelons, lettuce, onions, (dry) sweet corn, tomatoes, and watermelons. A second important area extends from Utica, N. Y., west to Buffalo, Erie, and Toledo. Another belt surrounds the southern half of Lake Michigan and extends southward into Illinois and Indiana. Several important districts have developed in Minnesota, Iowa, Missouri, and Texas. Florida, southern Georgia, and South Carolina, where perhaps one-third of the winter vegetables are grown, constitute an outstanding area. California has three important districts—the Sacramento-Stockton district, the Los Angeles district, and Imperial Valley. In California the winter crop is very important. Smaller centers of production adjoin most of the large cities. (Courtesy of U. S. Department of Agriculture).

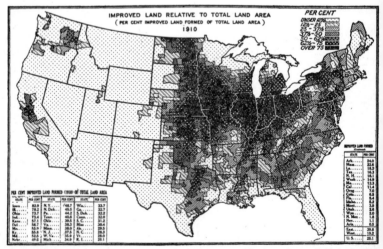

FIGURE 18.—The percentage of improved land relative to total land area, last available in the 1910 Census, offers a valuable index to the lay of the land, soil fertility, and economic structure. The South stands midway between the well-tilled Corn Belt and the practically unimproved stretches of the arid West. The amount of waste, swamp, and untilled land shows surprisingly large in portions of Georgia, Florida, Louisiana, and Texas. (Courtesy of U. S. Department of Agriculture).

TABLE XXIII*

RELATION OF SEASONS TO SOILS AND TRUCKING AREAS

LOCALITY	First Period	Second Period	Third Period	Fourth Period	Fifth Period	Sixth Period
Long Island........	......	....	....	....	....	Sand
Maryland-Delaware .	......	....	....	....	Sand	Fine Sand
Virginia...........	......	....	....	Sand	Fine Sand	Sandy loam
North Carolina.....	......	....	Sand	Fine sand	Sandy loam	Fine sandy loam
South Carolina......	......	Sand	Fine sand	Sandy loam	Fine sandy loam	Loam
Georgia-Florida.....	Sand	Fine sand	Sandy loam	Fine sandy loam	Loam	Silt loam

*See Milton Whitney, "Use of Soils East of the Great Plains Region," U. S. D. A. Bureau of Soils, *Bulletin 78*, pp. 15-17.

as a rule the best; they are very perishable and do not stand transportation well. They usually bring high prices, however, because of the great demand and limited supply on the market.

The crop from the fine sand maturing about two weeks later gives a larger yield of better quality in every way, which compensates for the lower market price and for the competition from the more sandy soils of the next northern localities. Georgia, for example, cannot compete in the northern markets with truck grown on her heavier soils simply because at the time it matures there is such a wide range of soils in more northern localities rushing vegetables over an ever-decreasing length of haul to the great markets.[28]

"When strawberries, for example, are ready to move from Louisiana, Florida shippers know that their season must close. Louisiana in turn must usually stop shipping when Tennessee and Arkansas begin in earnest."

All the factors of geography, economics, and technology are conditioned by the one important fact in trucking—the perishable nature of the product. The question in trucking is not how much may be grown on an acre but how much during a certain period of time. The shipping of vegetables from the South had to wait on fast train or boat service, the refrigerator car, and the artificial manufacture of ice. It was in 1854 that the steamer Roanoke carrying the first shipment of 200 barrels of garden truck from the Eastern Shore, Virginia, arrived in New York. The refrigerator car, first proved practicable in 1872, became influential in the trade ten years later. The first artificial ice in the South was made in

[28] *Ibid.*, pp. 15-17.

Norfolk in 1892, ending shipments of ice from Maine.[29]   The local manufacture of ice brought the whole South within reach of northern markets at once.

Thus it came about that trucking in the South passed through the pioneer stage to full bloom industry within a generation. Great stretches of cheap land within easy hauling distance of railroad facilities encountered cheap Negro labor used to hand tasks in picking and chopping cotton, pulling fodder, and caring for tobacco. Commercial or chemical fertilization had been worked out to take the place of manure in a cotton crop system without live stock. Such methods were already found for trucking which on sandy soil needed its stimulus to force early growth and produce full bodied plants. The local ice plant and the truck haul completed the picture.

All the cheap friable sandy plots on the southern coastal strips became potential truck land. The new revival did not proceed unchecked by the demands of an intensive agriculture. The products from an acre of truck land brought more than the value of the land, but the expense of production was also greater than the cost of the acre. For trucking counties on Long Island, to take an example cited by J. Russell Smith, the average expense per cultivated farm acre is $40 for fertilizer and $50 for labor.[30]   Compare with this the returns of $12 to $15 which the wheat grower expects from his acre. In such an economy, accordingly, the land offers no adequate security for the necessary investment. Neither local bankers nor the typical "furnishing" régime of the Cotton and Tobacco Belt were able to back truck growers. Many of them, especially in Florida, were well educated men who came from the North with their own capital. Many more came to be financed by the commission merchants who handled their fresh products. Others set themselves up in business with the heavy returns of one or two lucky years.

All the hazards found in other crops and more are augmented in truck by the perishable nature of the crop and its intensity of cultivation. Trucking and orcharding are attended with heavy risks, yielding the grower bountiful returns in money one year and providing an almost total loss the next. Even more than

[29] Wells A. Sherman, *Merchandising Fruits and Vegetables*, pp. 7, 26-44.
[30] *North America*, p. 165.

other farmers the fruit and vegetable grower lives in daily fear of weather. His is a product easily damaged by frosts, freezes, droughts, excessive moisture, and floods. Replanting, a costly operation in trucking, is sometimes necessary several times before a crop is secured. Delays and changes due to the weather count. To be slightly delayed in relation to other crops swinging up the coast ruins the market for truck. Grades count immensely, and for fruit and vegetables to be off size, off color, or slightly damaged makes them a drug on any but a famine market.

The whole business of over-expansion has not received adequate attention. The startling rise of the use of fresh products is one instance where an industry rather than waiting for demand in consumers created it by furnishing the supply. The increasing market has borne no relation to the slow increase of population. It has been rather a function of rapid urbanization with the passage of the old-fashioned cellar, the rising standard of living, and changing food habits. The acreage devoted to truck has been developed at an accelerating speed. This has been due partly to the surplus in all staple crops after the World War. Unlike the situation in cotton, increases in acreage produce no reaction on fruit and vegetable prices until the products actually appear in the market. An especially disturbing factor is the operation of real estate interests which, by planting bare plots with orange trees or truck gardens, are often able to subdivide at profit for themselves while creating future market gluts for an entire industry. Vested interests meet community pride, and towns from Florida to California are loath to admit there can be too many strawberries, heads of lettuce, or bunches of asparagus grown. The fault is with the consumer and he must be educated. "Food weeks" and "eat more" advertising financed by growers is suggested as the remedy. Such thinking overlooks the fact that urban America is already well-fed and that advertising will do no more than transfer groups of consumers from one product to another and back again. Variety and novelty will always win its way with the American housewife without the aid of advertising. Thus the alligator pear and the grape fruit were able to overcome the handicap of misleading names and to win a place on the table. "No historian has," says Sherman of the United States Marketing Bureau, "recorded the Georgia Peach Rush, the Texas Onion Rush, the Northwestern

Apple Rush, the California Prune Rush, the Grape Rush, the Asparagus Rush, the canning Cling Peach Rush, the Lettuce Rush, and the Mexican Tomato Rush. . . . Each, however, has left its own trail of bleaching financial skeletons to sober the thought of the student of our unparalleled development."[31]

An important trend in the development of the industry has been the specialization of area. The South is its own worst customer, due both to the lack of urbanization and to the presence of home gardens. With areas developed mainly in reference to long distance markets, it has paid growers of a locality to become proficient in one type of produce. Thus the district around Hastings, Florida, is devoted to Irish potatoes, three fourths of which are dug and shipped before the end of May. Plant City, near Tampa, is devoted to strawberries. Around Sanford, Florida, lies the celery delta, a triangular area of 30,000 acres, drained by tiles, irrigated by artesian wells, heavily fertilized and intensively cultivated. The Virginia Eastern Shores are noted for kale and spinach growing. The advantages of local specialization extend beyond the obvious one of making up shipments in carload lots. Soil plays some part in selecting areas for specialization, although the Norfolk fine sandy loam called cabbage soil in the vicinity of Charleston, South Carolina, is regarded as prime for lettuce at Wilmington, North Carolina, and is selected for Irish potatoes in other parts. Tradition and social heritage have much to do with retaining specialization after it is once adopted in an area. The growers come to possess and hand down the knowledge of the particular culture, the labor is skilled in its details, the stores handle the packing and crating supplies, and everybody possesses at least an elementary knowledge of packing and grading. Finally, cooperative associations of producers are formed which among other things tend to stabilize and perpetuate the practices of the culture. Such associations may buy and keep supplies, run packing houses and icing plants, and do the grading for their members.

In a summary such as this the important distinction between trucking and orchard culture must be pointed out. It is essentially the difference between the cultivation of annuals and perennials.[32]

[31] *Op. cit.,* p. 462.

[32] Erich W. Zimmermann, "The Resource Hierarchy of World Economy," *Weltwirtschaftliches Archiv,* XXXIII, 449-51.

Tree cropping requires much more capital to enter than trucking and one must wait periods of varying years for the trees to begin bearing. Tree culture is thus much more difficult to get into and to get out of than trucking. Many of the highly capitalized orchards in the South have thus been responsible for effecting the importation of large blocks of capital from the North. Again over-expansion in any truck crop is noticeable within a year and may be checked. The price of fruit, however, does not respond to new planting of orchards but goes down, say, six years later when the fruit actually reaches market. By that time the orange or peach grower has made an investment that can be revoked only by cutting down his orchard. Thus it has happened that an orchard may bankrupt several successive owners before it goes out of business itself.

The Southeastern states make a good showing in tree culture. Florida in 1924 possessed 33 per cent of the orange trees and 83 of the grape fruit trees of bearing age in the United States. Of the trees not yet bearing she possessed 69 per cent of the orange and 58 of the grape fruit.[33] Polk, Orange, and Valusia counties each have over 500,000 bearing trees. Of all peach trees in the country six southeastern states possessed 28.9 per cent in 1924. Georgia led the area with over 16 per cent. In several years the total farm value of the Georgia Peach crop has exceeded $10,000,000. In Macon, Houston, Peach, and Crawford counties peaches are grown by corporations in tracts of 800 acres or more. These same southeastern states possessed, in 1924, 37 per cent of the pecan trees then bearing and 47 per cent of those not yet mature. Almost 25 per cent of all American pecan trees were found in Georgia.

When fruits and vegetables are grown for canning their treatment differs largely from trucking practices. In the first place the areas are different. Florida at one extreme, earliest and highest price trucking area, has very little canning except that developing in tomatoes and grape fruit. The canning industry for the South Atlantic Coastal strip centers in Baltimore, the greatest canning city in the United States. Crops for canning are grown under contract with the factories which must have regular supplies. The grower need not bother with watching the market quotations; the price is determined upon by group bargaining between canners

[33] See *Commercial Survey of the Southeast*, pp. 48-55.

and truck growers before the gardens are planted, and contracts are signed a year in advance. The practice is much like the collective bargaining of labor unions with employers. Steamboats go up the bays and rivers which indent the Eastern Shores and make possible easy water transportation to canneries. For this reason there are still ten tidewater counties in the Eastern Virginia peninsula without railroads. Contrary to the popular view, canning and the trucking market are not likely to compete for the same crops. Truck produce is a forced growth out of season, while produce for canning is grown in the favorable season at less cost. On the other hand except in specific products canning cannot be regarded as an outlet for the growers' culls. The can possesses a time and form utility, as the economist would say, of its own. No crop, however, can be shifted from marketing to canning at a moment's notice. In the future it is possible, however, that methods of quick freezing which have proved of value in the fishing industry may be applied to early fruits and vegetables. Firms with processing equipment built on truck bodies may find it profitable to follow the seasonal swing up the coast. Foods thus treated retain their flavor in the frozen package and the process further removes trucking from the hazards of the perishable crops.

At present, however, fruits and vegetables show all the characteristics to be expected in marketing a perishable product. The system of cotton marketing is the result of 150 years' evolution in the distribution of one staple, non-perishable crop. Truck marketing has developed amid a bewildering variety of fruits and vegetables, all perishable and difficult to grade, within one hectic generation. Difficulties inhere in the very nature of produce and fruit. There are four sets of conditions, for instance, that affect Bermuda onion prices: the physical difference inherent in a given lot of Bermudas, the factors primarily determining the variations between seasons, those factors influencing price fluctuation within a given season, and the factors influencing prices at any given point.[34] These factors thus range all the way from quality of product, the carry-over, the volume and steadiness of shipments, to gluts in local markets.

In no other field, Mr. Sherman points out, has so great a volume of business been done on honor under conditions which make it

---

[34] W. Mackenzie Stevens, "The Marketing and Distribution of American-Grown Onions," U. S. D. A., *Bulletin* 1283, 1926, p. 53.

necessary for one party to trust so largely to the good faith of another.[35] Abuses have arisen at this point largely because of the sudden expansion of the industry. First dealers and commission merchants early in the development tended to neglect the local growers for the shippers with whom they could make greater profits. Then, when the same individual mixed the functions of the carload dealer with those of the commission merchant, he inevitably tended to dispose of his own goods before clearing produce shipped on consignment. The greatest weakness from the grower's viewpoint inheres in the fluctuation of the seasonal cycle. Early in the season when supplies are scarce and prices are high dealers are on hand with their services. When prices fall with the advance of the season buyers leave the section or receive goods only on consignment.[36] Thus, when the grower most needs the expert selling services of a representative in the market, he is likely to be left without them. In no other field has the agent acquired so much power over his principal. The tendency has existed until recently for the agent or buyer to throw the risks of a falling market upon the grower. This he has been able to do by refusing a shipment on the grounds of either defective grades or condition, thus forcing a readjustment in price. Earlier in the game he was able to attract shipment by sending out individual price quotations for his market area. These prices could not and did not stand up under the impact of the shipments they attracted.

But if market chaos ever existed in the industry, Sherman feels those days are passed. It is likely the abuses mentioned were never practiced by the outstanding dealers. Most of the problems about which honest differences of opinion might arise have been solved by government intervention. United States grades, accepted by all the trade, have been proposed and standardized. Inspectors have been trained who examine shipments at points of origin and receipt, and issue certificates of grade and condition. Such certificates are accepted as *prima facie* evidence in courts. Government representatives stationed at leading markets send out quotations on which the trade may rely. The quotations are now published in leading papers and broadcast daily over the radio. Under such conditions the danger of purely local gluts is largely imaginary.

[35] *Op. cit.,* p. 3.
[36] Stevens, *op. cit.,* p. 53.

With quotations from a whole region at hand a dealer can divert a car in transit from its designated market to a market en route. The one great danger that exists in the market remains over-expansion. The hope existing for this situation is that strict grading in seasons of surplus will be used to curtail the supply, while in periods of scarcity much produce of lower quality will be permitted to pass.[37]

TABLE XXIV

ESTIMATED FARM VALUE OF THE SOUTH'S COMMERCIAL TRUCK CROPS
PRODUCED FOR MARKET AND CANNING
(MILLION DOLLARS)

	1926	1927	1928	1929
Maryland	12.9	14.9	8.2	13.6
Virginia	19.3	28.8	14.4	21.4
North Carolina	10.3	14.1	7.9	8.2
South Carolina	10.0	8.9	6.5	9.1
Georgia	4.0	4.5	4.0	5.2
Florida	37.0	29.7	37.4	36.0
Alabama	3.7	4.3	4.5	3.6
Mississippi	7.0	6.7	4.6	5.3
Louisiana	16.7	12.5	15.3	15.0
Texas	18.9	17.2	18.4	19.0
Inland States				
Kentucky	2.2	2.8	2.0	2.7
Tennessee	5.8	6.5	4.6	5.6
Arkansas	6.0	5.7	4.5	5.4
Oklahoma	2.4	3.2	.7	1.4
The South	$156.9	$160.5	$133.7	$151.9
The Nation	$341.1	$343.1	$331.9	$369.7

SOUTHERN FISHING FRINGE

The outermost fringe of the Cotton Belt, furthest removed both in space and mode of life, is the coastal strip devoted to fishing.

Good fishing grounds extend along the entire seaboard, but most of the catch is taken from deep holes and inlets near the better markets. Southern fish differ from those taken in North Atlantic waters largely because of the climate and the Gulf Stream. Cape Hatteras furnishes the southern limit for many northern fish and the northern limit for many southern fish. North Carolina, says J. H. Matthews, has the most remarkable coastal section of any

[37] Wells A. Sherman has written in *Merchandizing Fruits and Vegetables* the best exposition of this field. The indebtedness of this section both to his facts and interpretation is cheerfully admitted.

state bordering on the Atlantic seaboard.[38] Its great sounds, Currituck, Albemarle, Roanoke, Croatan, Pamlico, Core, Bogue, and others, constitute a series found in no other state. Albemarle, said to be the largest fresh water sound in the world, furnishes spawning ground for migratory fish. It possesses resources exceeding any other sound and practically all the neighboring male population participates in fishing. Instead of the great sand banks of North Carolina, Georgia and South Carolina possess the sea islands which offer less protection to fishing. Accordingly, of the some 16,298 persons engaged in South Atlantic fishing in 1923, North Carolina furnished 9,308 together with almost half of the invested capital of eight million dollars. In that year the total catch amounted to 228 million pounds worth five million dollars. Shrimp leads in value, followed in order by menhaden, shad, oysters, mullet, and Spanish mackerel. The period from 1918 to 1925 showed an increase of 8.3 per cent in the number of persons engaged, a 14.6 per cent increase in investment, a 31.2 per cent decrease in quantity of catch with a 4.7 per cent increase in value. In 1928 some 11,882 fishermen caught over 258 million fish worth over six million dollars. The decreases in production can be traced to failures in the catch of menhaden. That vile fish, fit for only fertilizer, should not be named in the same breath with the many food fish of this coast.

With a longer coast line, 6,875 miles counting the principal indentations, the Gulf States comprise a much less important fishing sub-region. Florida stands out in importance in this area of low shores, sterile beaches, swamps and shallow bayous. Key West, settled in 1822, and still using a type of fishing equipment and methods of distribution practically identical with that fifty years ago, represents an all fishing community. In Florida the specialized sponge, clam, and shrimp industries are important. In 1925, at the sponge exchange of Tarpon Springs, Florida, 434,672 pounds of sponges were sold at a value of $715,097. It is estimated that an additional 50,000 pounds of sponges were sold outside the exchange. The largest bed of clams in the United States, 40 miles long and 5 miles wide, is to be found off the Florida coast in the vicinity of the Ten Thousand Isles. The clams may be either dug from the mud by workers who shovel them into flat bottomed boats or

[38] "Fisheries of the South Atlantic and Gulf States," *Economic Geography,* IV, 323-48.

removed by dredges. These clam dredges are two-storied boats with a power driven chain belt running along the bottom.

The social economy of the fishing fringe follows naturally from the conditions of its occupational routine. The catch is sold to dealers at prices fixed in advance of the season. "In dividing the profits as well as meeting the expenses all of the crew share alike. The captain receives no more than any one of the crew and his duties are equally laborious. The boat and seine which are generally owned by the captain or some relative or friend count for one share. The seine is kept in good order by the crew and the owner pays for such expenses as repairing the boat and keeping it painted."[39]   In mullet fishing on the southeast coast an observer sits on the beach in a kind of high chair until he observes a school of fish plying landward. By means of signals he then directs boats which put out, enclose the fish with nets, and draw them up on the beach.

TABLE XXV

THE SOUTHERN FISHING FRINGE

	Fishing vessels engaged	Fishing boats engaged	Vessels for transport	Production (Million Pounds)	Value (Million Dollars)
Maryland and Virginia (1925).........	574	16,895	523	333.2	$13.9
South Atlantic States (1927)..........	177	7,223	115	260.6	5.6
Gulf States (1927)..................	499	8,539	68	195.7	9.9
Mississippi River States (1922)........	...	15,538	13	105.7	4.5
South............................	1,250	48,195	719	895.3	$34.1
Total for Nation: Various Years					
(Excluding Alaska)...............	3,650	72,960	1,219	2,213.6	$94.6
PRODUCTION BY STATES 1927					
Virginia..				27.62	9.0
North Carolina....................................				144.4	2.7
South Carolina....................................				8.3	2
Georgia..				47.6	6
Florida...				138.4	6.4
Alabama..				11.3	4
Mississippi.......................................				37.8	1.4
Louisiana...				66.6	3.4
Texas..				21.2	1.0
Arkansas...				22.7	7
Tennessee..				5.4	1
Total The South..................................				$780.4	$26.4
The Nation.....................................				2,912.3	$112.7

[39] Matthews, loc. cit., p. 342.

As a rule the fisherman is not familiar with nor does he follow
ther occupations. In the southeast the fishermen, Americans of
ld stock, make no attempt to follow farming as a sideline. They
ind the life of the fisher too arduous and full of toil for variation.
)ff Florida and the Gulf, 90 per cent of the fishing is done in the
vinter. Many of these fishermen have inherited their vocation
y direct descent through many generations and know no other
alling. Surprisingly few of the Gulf fishermen are of native stock.
'rom Apalachicola through Texas natives of Italy, Sicily, Greece,
nd Mexico who once fished for the markets of Palermo, Naples,
'era Cruz, or Tampico, man the industry.[40]

[40] *Ibid.*

CHAPTER X

THE SOUTHERN HIGHLANDS: FRONTIER HERITAGE

FROM GRANDFATHER MOUNTAIN to the Father of Waters one travels from the heights of Dixie to the heart of Dixie. In the seven hundred and more miles from the southern highlands to the Mississippi the southern traveler passes from zenith to nadir. It needs but a customs barrier and a varying language to mark the limit of two cultures. Here are two American provinces, the Delta and the Highlands, that contradict that blanket term, the Solid South. If we accept the frontier and the plantation as the foundation stones of the South, these two regions show forth the elements that went into its making. Here are its starting points and its trend of development. To their contrast in geographic foundations may be added a contrast in institutional framework. The Highlands, a lingering frontier, and the Delta, a plantation zone projected into the present, stand as social laboratories reminding us of the elements from which the South was fashioned.

Abstract in presentation the concrete distinction between frontier and plantation comes to hand in an enlightening incident from social history. A scion of ante-bellum society, recently removed with his slaves from a Virginia plantation to a freshly settled section of the Mississippi Delta, was invited by his farmer neighbors to attend a log-rolling. Anxious to ingratiate himself with the pioneer community, he came with all his slaves and directed them at the task of housebuilding. One by one the yeomen drifted away from the task leaving the slaves to finish. Here are implicit many nice distinctions between two modes of society.

Both areas are rural and southern, and both have been subjected to missionary influence of outside culture. Otherwise the contrasts are startling. From an all staple cash economy to the self-contained domestic economy of the true frontier farm, from supervised tenant labor in a pseudo-feudal organization to an area of freeholds of patriarchal families, from overwhelming ratios of Negroes to no Negroes at all, from population density to isolation, comprise some of the transitions from Delta to Highlands. River towns and mountain courthouses, rich soil and poor soil, Negro Dialect and Elizabethan English, level flood plains and rugged mountains, river transportation and horseback trails epitomize these differences. The Delta followed the sectionalism of Calhoun and Davis, the Highlands knew no politics more recent than Washington and fought for the Union or not at all. From the same stock they came to follow diverse trails. If the flood menace of the Mississippi presents the South's greatest study in social incidence, the Highlands present its outstanding study in isolation.

THE SOUTHERN HIGHLANDS

The significance of this mountainous zone, among the highest inhabited areas in the United States, is obscured by the fact that it is divided among eight different commonwealths. Were this area thrown into one it would doubtless constitute America's one unique commonwealth. According to Campbell the Southern Highlands in 1910 comprised a region of 112,000 square miles, one half in the Allegheny-Cumberland Belt, over a fourth in the Blue Ridge, and less than a fourth in the greater Appalachian Valley, credited in all with a population of 5,330,111.[1] In 1920 Estabrook estimated the three areas at 100,000 square miles in which lived six million people.[2] The steepness of the region is shown by the fact that in the Blue Ridge 60,500 acres are found over 5,000 feet high.

From west to east these areas are called by geologists, the Plateau Belt, the Younger Folded, and the Older Folded regions. They possess contrasts of prime importance. Cumberland Plateau in the west, underlain with horizontal rocks of sandstone and shales, finds its surface rolling or rugged and covered with but a thin soil. In about forty per cent of this area are found workable deposits of coal; the remainder is better suited for agriculture. The plateaus of western North Carolina and eastern Tennessee rank among the most thickly settled rural communities in the South. In the Younger Folded region the underlying layers of porous limestone rather than hard sandstone have dissolved, creating deep and fer-

[1] John C. Campbell, *The Southern Highlander and His Homeland,* pp. 10, 13.
[2] Arthur H. Estabrook, "Is There a Mountain Problem?" *Mountain Life and Work,* April, 1927.

tile valleys which alternate with rocky and eroded ridges. "It is
on the ridges," writes Dean Charles D. Lewis "that poverty, poor
schools, and a population deprived of its intellectual leadership are
found in the greatest abundance."[3]

The Older Folded region, more resistant to dissection, has thus
remained higher. Sandstone, shales, and limestone here give way
to gneiss, schist, slate, marble, and granite. The rock heart of the
uplift is more exposed and thus furnishes a terrain often adapted
only to forest cover. Mineral wealth offers a basis for the economic
structure of the region and the rock is available for road construction. To keep in mind the ever present contrast between ridge and
valley will serve as an antidote against regarding the southern
mountaineer as a uniform and stable type.

The basins, gorges, and coves vary in size from many small
"flats," gently rolling areas along small rivers, to such large basins
as the site of Asheville. Small plains are found perched well up
on the mountain slopes where the headwaters of branches unite.
Elsewhere basins are formed where land waste has been washed
into the hollows of mountain slopes. From the high coves to the
river valleys these basins step down in a series of benches. The
streams descending the mountains have cut out channels of steep
valleys and deep gorges. The distribution of these basins, valleys,
and gorges determines the location of population. Only one fourth
of highland tracts can be said to be under cultivation, the population being as scattered as the flat lands they occupy.[4]

Here topography bears down in ruthless fashion upon human
life and its round of activities. E. A. Ross sketches the geographical
terrain bounding the horizon of social routine. "The mountains
come down to a point like the letter V. Adown this crease brawls
a petty river; leading into this from a smaller valley will be a
creek; into the creek, a branch, and into the branch, a fork. Each
settlement is a shoestring along one of these water courses and constitutes a world within itself, for it is insulated from its neighbors
by one or two thousand feet of steep wooded ridge. The only
wagon trails lie in the bed of a stream which you may have to
ford twenty times in a mile."[5] In one section, for example, Horace

[3] "The Changing Mountains," *Mountain Life and Work*, July, 1928, 15-19.
[4] Isaiah Bowman, *Forest Physiography*, pp. 610-11.
[5] E. A. Ross, "Pocketed Americans," *New Republic*, XXXVII, 170.

Kephart found that a straight line journey of fourteen miles took the traveler up and down eight transverse ridges each around 2,000 feet high. In another forty mile journey as the crow flies ten distinct mountain chains must be scaled and descended.[6]

It is a true saying that "cream sinks and the skim milk rises in the sociological milk pan of the mountains." Best of all are the valley farms, made rich by overflow and the decomposition of limestone, followed by the cove farms found in the hollows of the hills. Higher up are the ridge farms, poor, scarred and cobblestoned with rock. Where a people multiply and population pressure is strong upon the land, fertile farms are for a period divided among heirs. Finally a time comes when fields are too small to offer subsistence and young sons hoping to found families must push out. Ambitious sons have pushed out beyond the mountain rim; others have retreated back up the slopes to the shelter of a cabin and a cleared patch.

Bold is he who in any account of regional patterns would attempt to describe and interpret the culture of the southern mountain. About no section of equal magnitude, it seems, has there raged such a storm of controversy over mere social description. Unlike the Negro, that other victim of the literary exploiter of things southern, the mountaineer has struck back and struck back hard at criticism and misrepresentation. Neither he nor those closely acquainted with him have been content to hear the mountaineer called a peculiar people. Howard Mumford Jones' facetious presentation of the southern mountain tradition strikes a deserved note of satire:

The simple southern highlanders converse among themselves in sentences impartially compounded of "hit," "you uns" and "tote," a vocabulary which they find sufficient for all ideas. The cultivation of four rows of corn supplies all their needs and their babies cry for moonshine as soon as they are born. By day their chief occupation is to sit; by night they sleep seven in a bed, though they will promptly vacate the bed on the approach of a furriner and migrate to the floor which they prefer. They never wear nothing but sun bonnets and blue jeans. None of them has even seen a train, and in the intervals of singing ballets they ejaculate from time to time, "Yeh ain't done right by our little Nell," and immediately shoot everybody in sight with a rifle which saw service at Kings Mountain.[7]

[6] Horace Kephart, *Our Southern Highlanders,* pp. 20-21.
[7] H. M. Jones, "The Southern Legend," *Scribners,* May 1929, pp. 538-42.

The over-emphasis on the unusual was natural and to be expected. Much of the reporting on the mountains has been done by uncritical travelers and by mission schools engaged in raising funds for their enterprises. A mountain man once told Bishop John M. Moore: "You missionary people do not treat us right. You come with your cameras and photograph our worst houses and our lowest people and then throw them on the screens to be seen. You never tell of our good people nor of the substantial things of the community. But I reckon you have to do that in order to get money out of your members."[8]

Especially futile has been the controversy raging about the origin of biological stocks found in the Highlands. A homogeneity of physical type, striking to the anthropologists, with traits varying through blondness to huge rangy frames, has proved a paradox when subjected to social interpretation. The mountain stocks have been hailed on the one hand as the apotheosis of the Anglo-Saxon; on the other, as the decadence of poor whites. Admired by Henry Cabot Lodge and Theodore Roosevelt they have been shown to come from the loins of Scotch-Irish and the strictest of Presbyterians. Mr. John Fiske on the other hand comes dangerously near to assigning as their ancestors indentured servants and "shiftless people who could not make a place for themselves in Virginia society including many of the 'mean whites.' "[9] In this he had to witness Virginia's Governor Spottswood who held, "It is fully well known what morals such people bring with them hither." Against the view that the mountains were peopled by a population pushed out from developed areas or left behind in the westward trek can be placed the more tenable view that pioneers sought fertile soil, range for cattle, spring water, and "coverts that might hide deer in sightly valley and comely plateaus of their own deliberate choice."[10]

So much Governor Spottswood did admit, if allowed his slur that "such people . . . settle themselves where land is to be taken up . . . that will produce the necessarys of life with little labor." The plain truth is, of course, that the mountains then exercised no

[8] John M. Moore, *The South Today*, p. 132.
[9] *Old Virginia and Her Neighbors*, II, 311-21, 897.
[10] Marion Y. Rambo, "The Submerged Tenth Among the Southern Mountaineers," *Methodist Review*, July, 1905, p. 265.

such selective influence on early settlers as an observer reads into the contemporary situation. If one were to become a frontier farmer the mountains were no more cut off from markets than any wilderness clearing. To expect the frontiersmen to foresee that surfaced highways, railways, steamboat navigation, power lines, and modern industrialism would develop and pass by his sons is to read history backward with a vengeance. No more was the original old man of the mountain a criminal fleeing from the justice of Virginia settlements. There is no mystery necessarily inherent in the settlement of Appalachia; its coves and creek valleys were admirably fitted for the domestic economy of hunter and frontier farm. Yet "the retardation of the Appalachian Region is an outstanding fact in American life. When men of the type found have settled elsewhere this retardation has not been observed."[11] A publication of its state geological survey said of the Kentucky mountains: "The stock is in all probability in a large part the same as that of the Blue Grass but it has been modified by long isolation in an area of lesser opportunity."[12] This statement can well be applied to the whole area.

The paradox of highland portraiture is to be explained as the result of attempting to force varied regions and differing social classes into one rigid frame. Many people live here under average rural conditions, many urban, and some isolated and backward. Urban, rurban, rural, and super-rural, according to Arthur H. Estabrook "are terms that should be applied to conditions that range from those found in well-developed areas with good roads and schools such as the East Tennessee Valley to isolated cabins located in the fastnesses of the hills."[13]

If Richmond and Norfolk be excluded, Estabrook found that proportionately as many people in the mountains of Virginia pay income taxes as throughout the state. Greenbrier County of West Virginia in the average value of farm lands and buildings exceeded state levels in 1925 by almost $3.00 per acre. A Kentucky county without railroad or improved highway, considered the most backward area in the mountains, has 60 graded schools, three high

[11] John P. McConnell, "Retardation of the Appalachian Region," *Mountain Life and Work*, April, 1922, pp. 21-22.

[12] D. H. Davis, *Geography of the Kentucky Mountains*, pp. 157-58.

[13] "Is There a Mountain Problem?" *Mountain Life and Work*, April, 1927, p. 7.

schools, two hospitals, and eight public health nurses.[14]   In the Arkansas Ozarks many of the small cities, Springfield, Rogers, Fayetteville, and Siloam Springs, surpass the educational, social, and economic levels of the state.   Three of these counties have a per acre value of farm land greater than that for the state of Arkansas as a whole.[15]

Isolation in an almost barren mileau can be, however, a very real thing.   In mountain parlance the poverty stricken fall into three classes.   There are the Lord's poor, destitute by misfortune; the devil's poor, stranded by their own follies; and poor devils from worthless stock who never were nor could be otherwise.   We are fortunate in having the detailed analysis of the 83 families in an isolated border township in the southern Appalachians of 1910.[16] "Life," as Isaiah Bowman has said, "is largely a struggle against distance whose vertical and horizontal elements loom increasingly large."   Such distances loom large in terms of barriers to social and institutional contacts.

For these families the average distance to a church and to school was $2\frac{1}{4}$ miles; to a store, $3\frac{1}{8}$ miles; to a doctor, 4 miles; to a post office, $4\frac{1}{2}$ miles; to the county seat, $15\frac{1}{3}$ miles.   Further interpretation came from the portraiture of the average family.   With $5\frac{1}{2}$ members the family cultivated $7\frac{3}{8}$ acres of its 27 acre farm.   With $1\frac{1}{4}$ windows to the house, two beds, and $4\frac{1}{2}$ sleepers to the room, 44 families occupied log houses, 24, frame, and 15, box structures. Our average family made $161 from crops and spent $35.42 for clothes and $53.47 for food.   Their flour for a year cost $18.30, coffee $8.66, sugar $6.90, and tobacco $12.56.   For taxes they paid $2.46, while 56 men in the 83 families worked the road.   Variations were found within these families.   Forty-five raised their pork, 38 bought it; 40 raised molasses, 16 purchased, 27 used none; 13 raised their tobacco all or in part; 68 families had cook stoves while 15 cooked in the fireplace; 69 had meals regularly while 14 set no regular meal time.   Of the parents, one sixth were illegitimate, of the children eight per cent.   Poor ventilation, unsanitary practice, insufficient clothing and monotonous diet were the chief conditions

[14] *Ibid.,* pp. 7-8.

[15] A. H. Estabrook, "The Population of the Ozarks," *Mountain Life and Work,* April, 1929, p. 25.

[16] Reported in Samuel H. Thompson, *The Highlanders of the South,* pp. 51-53

affecting health. But eight toilets were found and the most prevalent diseases were tuberculosis, hookworm, and venereal disease. No picture can be regarded as typical, but if one keeps in mind class and locality this is not an overdrawn picture of poverty in mountain isolation.

MOUNTAIN CULTURE

As late as 1900 President Frost of Berea held that two million native Americans lived in Southern Appalachia on the level of colonial conditions. As in the Cotton Belt one may select traits clustering around the cotton plant; here we may describe the passing culture that was conditioned by topography. It has been often recognized as unique. "Bring us your northern culture," said a mountain dweller to a visiting professor, "but leave us our civilization." A teacher of success and charm wrote: "We who know intimately the life of the southern mountains long to preserve the old standards of courtesy and behavior, the dignity and simplicity of the hills."[17] One likes to think of Silar McDonald of North Carolina, who died in 1879, as a native product of this culture. Sturdy, uneducated, poor, his only heritage, a Negro boy from his grandfather, was his constant companion until death in old age. He acquired a taste for letters and early attracted attention by his writings for the state papers. He contributed to *Harper's,* corresponded with Maury, Henry of the Smithsonian Institute, and Longfellow, none of whom he ever met. In the *United States Agricultural Reports* for 1861 he proposed the theory of thermal belts in the mountains now established by climatologists.

Domestic economy is the *modus vivendi* of isolation. One can cross continents to find no more vivid contrast than the mountains afford with the nearby cash crop system of cotton and tobacco not two hundred miles away. Samplings from North Carolina show interesting facts. The cash incomes were three to five times as high for farmers in Coastal Plains as in Mountain counties yet the average mountain farmer used $10.00 worth of credit to $436.00 for the farmer in the Coastal Plains. The average highland farmer owned half as much property yet grew a much higher total of food supplies than his lowland colleague. Mountain landlords, for example, raised $627 worth of food and bought only $13 worth. The area ranked best in home produced meal and molasses and

[17] Ethel De Long in *The Survey,* XXXVII, 627.

was the only section to produce consistently more than a quart of milk per day per individual. For every $100 of cash income the average Ashe County farmer paid $65.50 in taxes. Expenses of the average Johnson County farmer were $261 of which $67 for taxes were the highest item.[18] Difficulty in meeting tax demands in cash is characteristic of domestic economy.

"It's a great life for dogs and men but it's hard on women and steers." In such a phrase DuBose Heyward let a character sum up the position of mountain women. Your true man mountaineer was a patriarch. The pattern of the field work of women is no deeper laid in the tenancy of cotton belts than in the corn fields and cow pens of the hillside. When there is a "passel" of men to be fed women wait to the last table as a matter of course. The boy child is the young autocrat; he lords it over his older sisters and too soon ignores the women folks of the family. Woman's task is made more onerous by repeated childbearing. To match mountain birth rates, says Ross, one must go to the Balkans and French Canada. Miss Harriette Wood who spent six years as a worker in a settlement school in the shut-off mountain region of Kentucky well portrays the place of women in this culture.

The status of women in this mountain culture has been much misunderstood and severely criticised because much of the outdoor work is done by them. A fact that is usually overlooked is that this is a corollary to primitive conditions everywhere. In pioneer periods the father and sons cut and hewed logs for buildings, split fence rails and shingles, secured wild game for the table and cleared and broke the new ground. Lighter tasks such as planting, hoeing, carrying water and milking could be, and very properly were, done by the mother and daughters if they contributed their share to the making of the home and were an asset rather than a burden. That women often did these tasks, and still do them, both for love of their husbands and families and also because in many cases they enjoy the outdoor work more than the household tasks is seldom considered by the critics.

It is true, however, that in the large the custom is an example of cultural lag. And that there is an undesirable by-product in a general attitude on the part of men to permit women to do this kind of work unneces-

[18] "Farm Income and Taxation" in North Carolina Agricultural Experiment Station, *Bulletin* 267, North Carolina State College, 1929, pp. 58-60. *Economic and Social Conditions of North Carolina Farmers,* North Carolina Tenancy Commission, 1922, pp. 31, 18.

sarily while they themselves engage in pursuits more to their liking and less essential. . . . This attitude is largely offset by a very real and fundamental respect for womanhood on the part of the mountain man. It is well known that it is absolutely safe for even young and attractive women to travel either on foot or on horseback in sections in which there are none but the native men. Crimes of violence against women are very rare, indeed, but occasionally a woman is shot by her lover or husband in a fit of jealousy. The mountain man's code as expressed by a native is: "No man in the mountains says an insulting thing at a woman unless she first throws the banter."

In general it may be said that the average woman submits unquestioningly to her lot of hard work, excessive childbearing, and the rule of her husband. It is something of a paradox, however, that when she becomes an old woman with a large family of grown-up children she comes into her own and assumes somewhat the character of a matriarch. She is often consulted, looked up to, loved, and respected.[19]

While the new moonshining is a capitalistic venture undertaken at the behest of lowland consumers, the old moonshining was more characteristic of the locale and deserves attention as an indigenous trait of mountain culture. Those to whom the drinking habit seems utterly at variance with the religious fundamentalism of the highlanders should realize that here were the mores of colonial America. The deadly dull monotony of the mountain menu leaves intoxicants the only invigorating article of diet. Mountain topography has completed the task of making permanent the imprint of this pattern on culture. Corn is the chief economic plant; distilling has long been a household technology; transportation is a baffling problem. Thus, instead of conveying corn on crude wagons over rocky gulches, its essence has long been conveyed by jug on horseback to bring many times the price of corn or forage.

In religion the hill dweller is a fundamentalist. It never pained an orthodox New Englander to contribute to the cause of missions in the southern highlands, for here, he recognized, were transplanted Puritans—Scotch Presbyterians of the South who had espoused the union cause. Just as isolation prevented the changes in southern sentiment from reaching their ears before the Civil War, so has it shut them out from revisions in the old-time religion. Here ig-

[19] Harriette Wood, "The Kentucky Mountains," unpublished M.A. thesis, University of North Carolina, 1930, pp. 54-55, 58.

norance preening on biblical texts is not humble as among the Scotch but self-confident and dogmatic. So Professor Ross felt on his journey through the highlands.

The once famous feuds, often cited as the hallmark of the highlands, were traits neither of mountain depravity nor clan alignments and animosities transferred from Scotland. Waiving the plausible contention that upland feuds were never more gruesome or numerous than black belt mob outbreaks, their old feud pattern is a beautiful example of culture as adaptation. From geography and history it was imposed. Stimuli to homicide were many where lands were settled by the squatter process and titles were so obscure that litigation often ended in what the community regarded as unfair dispossession of worthy old settlers. In no culture is the dog more prominent; and poisoned dogs, stolen dogs, sheep killing dogs offered a starting point for many a falling out. Moonshining, a precarious undertaking, lends itself to spite informing. Such incidents as in other areas would lead to lawsuits used here to occasion feuds. A certain feudal and fatalistic attitude, sometimes closely involved with a philosophy of personal honor, characterized their southern attitude toward homicide. Most important, the mountaineer lived in a milieu where litigation could not be trusted. Intermarriage within the confines of their coves left the population connected in a net of kinship groupings. Aggression, insults, and injuries found, because of kinship ties, the community divided into two hostile camps with no neutral buffer group. All who came to act as legal umpire, judge and jury, were regarded as assuming the mask of impartiality in order to protect a kinsman or wreak vengeance on an enemy. There remained the resort to feud, and judges, thought to be partisans, were sometimes shot down on the bench. The interesting social evolution from feud to legal process is concomitant with the breaking down of closed barriers of geography and close kinship. With the widening of the physical horizon has come the third group, neutral, unrelated, and thus able to satisfy two conflicting groups.[20] It may be mentioned in passing that advanced society finds itself in the same plight in litigation between capital and labor. Having developed no large neutral group, society

[20] Compare Ellsworth Faris' theory of punishment in "The Origin of Punishment," *International Journal of Ethics*, XXV, 54-67.

inds that labor trials have tended to cast aspersions on the imparﬁtiality of judges and the jury system.

CULTURAL CHANGE

Conditions have been no more static in the mountains than elsewhere. That we have here a picture of social organization arrested at a certain level is less true today than it ever was. The modern world is advancing at an ever increasing pace upon the highlands and bringing with it new adjustments. The remaking of agriculture, the extension of the network of railroads and hard surfaced highways, the new integration of education, and industrialism with its labor exploitation of large families are factors making a new highland society. The development of coal mining in Kentucky marked the passing in 1912 of the largest mountain area in the United States untouched by railroads. The Ford enterprises now own 125,000 acres of coal lands in Kentucky, possibly the largest single land holdings in the South. The spread of highways lost this region the reputation of possessing the largest horseback area in America. When Professor Ross attended a mountain church ten miles from town he heard, it is true, an unchanged gospel, but he found twenty-one Fords and only one saddled horse.[21]

The effects of highland industrialization on the region can be marked down in neither black nor white. The unfavorable effects, however, cannot be denied. The net profits of mining do not remain in the mountains; they go to outside capitalists. One of America's simplest ways of getting rich, says J. Russell Smith, has been to find distant, inaccessible coal lands, buy them from the scanty population for a few dollars an acre and build a railroad to the spot. Such development not only brings no wealth to native inhabitants but it increases tenancy. The original owners may now become renters and laborers on their old homesteads, now worth $50 an acre. Nor is the native labor supply immediately industrialized in order to receive the advantage of steady employment. Perry County, Kentucky, possessing, in 1910, 8,000 population underwent in 1912 a development in railways and bituminous coal sufficient to raise its population to 40,000. Of the present population 20 per cent moved in from neighboring counties while 35 per cent moved in from outside the mountains. Nor does the proc-

[21] "Pocketed Americans," *New Republic,* XXXVII, 171.

ess necessarily bring the region permanent communities and a con
structive citizenry.

The absentee and invisible corporation sends its men into the green and
peaceful wilderness where they build little houses for two or three hundred workers; put up a power house to pump and ventilate the mine
and run the electric cars; erect a barn for the mine mules, and get everything ready for the arrival of superintendents and mine bosses, the time
keepers and foremen.

The typical mining community, therefore usually consists of a few superintendents who have some education and several hundred employees
who are able to dig coal. In many cases these miners know little of the
English language and practically nothing at all of American customs and
ideals.

Towns in the Cumberland Plateau are, however, often filled with mountaineers who have come from the isolation of their mountain farms to
experience the crowded conditions of a mining town where the valley is
so narrow that the houses must be perched up on the side of the hill like
bleacher seats around an athletic field. It is not difficult to see why the
individualistic, independent feudist mountaineer with the point of view
of the mountaineer cannot become at once a public-spirited townsman.
When a community changes from a land of cabins to a mining town the
change is sudden and violent.[22]

The greatest suffering in this upheaval will be found among
those who, cast out from the community of self-sufficing households,
have not yet found a permanent place in a super-imposed industrialism.

Population once frozen has become fluid. Hundreds of the poorer type
of mountain people will be found in the worst sections of industrial
towns in these and neighboring states. The lowest of types of mountain
population are also found skirting many mining camps, living in houses
much inferior to those provided by the companies and enjoying none of
the advantages of the workers.[23]

Mary Verhoeff, wrongly or not, in 1911 regarded the highlander
as unfitted by his culture for participation in industry.

To work when the larder is empty and to rest when it is full has always
been his economic ideal. Accustomed to work in his own way he is

[22] J. Russell Smith, *North America*, pp. 226-27.
[23] Charles D. Lewis, *loc. cit.*, p. 19.

quick to resent dictation or interference and with little sense of the value of time or the moral obligation of a contact, will forsake his task regardless of consequence to employer and industry. Without disposition to coöperate he is at once the menace and despair of the labor union.[24]

Equally impressive are the favorable trends industrialization has given the region. It first must be recalled that when once attracted by mineral deposits railroads have occasioned the development of hitherto unsuspected resources. Then many stable and intelligent native owners do retain possession of their properties and receive royalties from mining enterprises. Mining towns offer markets for produce and encourage an agriculture of orchards and gardens to which the region is more adapted than the production of staple crops. Miners, moreover, spend for the benefit of the local merchants, thus building up a stable commercial class. The permanent improvements of industry furnish a basis of taxation, providing for schools, roads, and public services hitherto unattainable by local groups.[25]

Towns

Future development in the highlands is bound up with the emergence of urban centers. Urban growth in the mountains, holds D. H. Davis, will probably be characterized by the development of a relatively large number of centers of relatively small size rather than by the growth of a few major cities of large population. This is largely because topography divides the area in small hinterlands. Cities on the highlands' margins, however, have more favorable conditions for extensive growth.

Mountain cities are likely to be located in creek bottoms where the lines of drainage furnished the early facilities for communication. Here are found level plots for town development, and the focus of principal valleys offers an important hinterland. On level ridge tops where the surface has not been dissected railroad lines offer the relative advantage necessary to locate towns. Short distances set by topography have helped to multiply the cross roads and country store development beyond that usually found in districts of similar density.[26]

The county seat is centrally located and occupies an important

[24] *The Kentucky Mountains, Transportation and Commerce, 1750-1911*, pp. 34-35.
[25] See Carl O. Sauer, *Geography of the Ozark Highlands*, p. 209.
[26] See D. H. Davis, *Geography of the Mountains of Eastern Kentucky*, pp. 138-42.

place in the life of highland people. Court day was once a holiday in Kentucky and Virginia when the "settlers met upon the court-house green to trade and discuss public affairs." With the increasing complexity of society court week now retains its pristine importance only in rural and mountain counties. Highlanders are great experts in litigation and follow the legal intricacies of favorite attorneys with the zest they pay their favorite preachers of doctrinal sermons. Some, but not the majority, of the county seats follow a plan which has come to be accepted as a trait of the culture south of the Ohio. This pattern places the courthouse square in the center and builds the town around it. The automobile tourist is likely to find himself routed around the square that he may view the edifice.

In rugged coal and iron areas the industrial towns are often linear by force of topography. Breaking through the mountain barrier the river winds on the lowest level. On a second plane the railway follows its course; on a third runs the highway. Above in the sides of sloping hills are the coal mines whose tipples often overhang the roadway. An industrial stringtown stretches down the highway which its dwellers use for a footpath. The traveler by auto rushes past two rows of houses dangerously near; on one side the house stands on stilts; on the other they are set back into the hills. Thus has the cultural landscape developed guided by the demands of topography.

Industry, education, and communication are the driving forces for change in the mountains. One hundred forty-nine mountain schools are maintained in eight southern states by denominational and independent agencies. Through the girls many of them attempt to teach a science and an art of homemaking. Through the boys they teach an agriculture that will reach back into mountain coves and homesteads. In Georgia the Berry Schools have achieved national recognition. At Brasstown, North Carolina, Mrs. John C. Campbell has founded an institution patterned after the Danish folk schools. At Pine Mountain, Kentucky, the school has succeeded in merging itself with the life of the community. At Raeburn, in North Georgia, a school has worked out a family plan of training. The institution moves the family to the school farm and educates their children while the adults are operating the farm under direction. The knowledge of agriculture thus gained is afterwards put into practice on the home farm. In startling contrast the Kingston School at Iberia, Missouri, in the Ozarks has stuck strictly to the classics, teaching four years of Latin and two of Greek. Seventy-five per cent of its pupils go to college but few of these, it is safe to say, have returned to aid in reconstructing the region.

The equalization of state educational funds is proving the most important factor in the development of mountain public schools. In 1928 Tennessee spent $800,000 to equalize educational opportunities in poor counties; North Carolina, in the same year, spent $200,000 more for this purpose than was spent for all elementary education twenty years before. In ten plateau counties of Kentucky this program has meant in twenty years a 476 per cent increase in the value of school plants, 296 per cent increase in the cost of maintaining schools, 60 per cent increase in attendance, and a 100 per cent increase in teachers' salaries. Log school houses decreased from 184 to none. The ten poorest counties of the Tennessee mountains showed during the same period increases of 296 per cent in teachers' salaries, 333 per cent increase in high school enrollment, and 100 per cent increase in average length of school term.[27]

Only twenty years ago there could be found few permanently passable roads in the mountainous ends of the southern states. Today "roads to fulfillment" in Miss Harriet Berry's phrase have made possible schools, public welfare officials, school attendance laws, mothers' aid, and county and home demonstration agents.[28] Dean Charles D. Lewis has written of North Carolina:

Today every mountain county seat is reached, in most cases from two or more directions, by hard surface, state-maintained highways. In Virginia only two or three counties are not so served; and while Kentucky is lagging behind somewhat, great improvement has been made in road construction. In 1928 the ten poorest counties of Virginia had an aggregate of 310 miles of improved highway built and maintained by state and federal aid, Tennessee's ten poorest counties have 225 miles of such road, while North Carolina first to start its road-building program has constructed 500 miles in its ten poorest mountain counties. This total mileage of 1,035 represents a cost of at least twenty-five million dollars. This investment is bringing good interest by providing marketing facili-

[27] See C. D. Lewis, *op. cit.*, p. 15.
[28] See *Mountain Life and Work*, January, 1928, pp. 2-8.

ties for farm and forest products by affording work during construction and in maintenance, and more than all, in attracting tourists into this beautiful region for summer vacations and week-end trips.[29]

The development at Biltmore, the Vanderbilt estate near Asheville, first introduced modern dairying and trucking, along with spinach and celery culture to the mountains, and thus foreshadowed changes in highland agriculture. On the whole progress on the farm had lagged behind other changes. The opening of new contacts by means of roads, the rural mail delivery, parcel post, and the telephone have increased wants beyond the range of simple family agriculture that formerly produced 75 to 90 per cent of the living. Yet the farmer has no great cash crops like his brother of the plains.

Money must be obtained to buy the refinements and luxuries of life of the outside world. To secure these, cattle, sheep, and hogs were driven to market, timber was cut and rafted down the streams, men and boys went to the incoming railways, the opening mines, the sawmills that came further and further up the rivers, for work that would bring in cash to meet the growing family needs. This brought about a neglect of the old type of farming and the deterioration of the farm. Markets were developing nearby, but the demands were for products widely different from the crops the farms had been producing. Vegetables, small fruits, poultry and milk had been produced, but chiefly by the women; they were not men's crops. So passed the old order in many sections without the coming of the new. . . . It is only the story of rural life everywhere, but much exaggerated by the poorer land, worse roads and less efficient schools. These conditions were worse in the Plateau belt than elsewhere, for in the Folded region there were alternating belts of better soil than kept a fair degree of prosperity among the farming peoples.[30]

Older farmers spend spare time on public works as lumbering, roadmaking, and all outside activities are called. Boys saw no chance on the farm and many left it. Only one half of Berea's students return to their communities and that half is found largely among those who do not graduate. At the same time the presence of mining towns, lumber camps, vacation resorts, and hotels have led certain sections to advance in poultry production, dairying, and the growth of fruits and vegetables.

[29] *Op. cit.* p. 17.
[30] Charles D. Lewis, *ibid.,* p. 18.

Among the most encouraging trends, the creation of a native cheese industry furnishes a case study. The cheese industry has long proved a resource to the plateaus of Switzerland and the mountain districts of France and Italy. The making of cheese had been a home industry in some mountain areas a generation or more ago. The climate was fitted to the processes, and the product possessed the qualities essential for preservation and transportation. Labor, plentiful and cheap, was utilized because of lack of paying industries. Every family possessed a few cows and almost every house was built near a spring already used for keeping milk cool. Poverty offered an obstacle in the fact that no community was able to employ a trained high-priced cheesemaker. This problem was met by the proposal that each coöperative company hire and train a bright young man from the community in the art of making cheese. The industry would thus be established as a purely local enterprise and the wages paid cheesemakers would not be prohibitive.

The first coöperative cheese factory was organized by dairy extension specialists at Cove Creek, Watauga County, North Carolina, in the spring of 1915. The building was small, 14 by 16 feet, and its cost complete was only $400. Another was opened at Grassy Creek, North Carolina, six months later at a cost of $375. The reluctance of skeptical farmers was overcome by demonstrations which proved the cheese to be equal to the "store-bought" product. The first year after completion each factory returned almost $1,500 to its patrons. The year before the total sales from butter had averaged less than $300. Two other factories were erected before the end of the year and the demands on the demonstration agents became greater than they could meet. Larger factories have been built costing $1,000 each, subscribed jointly by 30 to 40 local stockholders. In 1917, two years after the campaign was under way, more than $125,000 worth of cheese was made in 34 factories in the mountain districts of North Carolina, Virginia, Tennessee, and West Virginia. The cost of milk and operation of the cheese factory amounted to about one fourth, leaving about $90,000 as newly created wealth. Such a successful home industry has reacted with beneficial effects on the community. In its pastoral industry, for instance, better care, more skillful feeding, more regular milking routines, and occasionally purchase of better stock have resulted.

Great pride is taken in efficient operation of factories; waste i guarded against, and by-products such as whey are carefully used in the feeding of hogs. A sign tacked over the whey barrels at on factory shows the earnestness with which efficiency is motivated "Don't spill the whey. Spilled whey creates filth, filth breed germs, germs cause disease, disease sometimes results in death, and death will lead to eternal hell for the man who takes more whey than belongs to him." The higher standard of living has resulted in better community standards. Farm houses are improved and remodelled, roads improved, school houses built, school term lengthened and better teachers employed.[31]

Industrial reconstruction can be set off against reconstruction i agriculture. On the Holston River a great printing company knitting mills, cement works, and a branch of the Eastman Kodak Company have transformed a rural mountain village. Kingsport Tennessee, offers an interesting case study in mountain industrializa tion—so interesting in fact as to have had a book written about itself.[32] It is a city deliberately planned and engineered by eastern bankers and industrialists. Thirteen years old in 1928 it had 15 indus trial plants employing 5,000 workers and a total population of 18,000 Its city planning was done by Dr. John Nolen of Cambridge, Massa chusetts. A level meadow was laid off for plants, an area o higher altitude for residences, and a level tract between reserved for the business section. All three sections are convenient ye distinct. To guide its development along lines of natural beaut the town engaged a municipal landscape artist. Moreover, it charter embodying the city manager plan was submitted to th Bureau of Municipal Research which eliminated some details and added others. The community represents a studied grouping o industries of 15 plants, independent as to ownership, manage ment, and marketing, yet clustered around the resources of th highlands. The Kodak concern uses every scrap of a tree from sawdust to distilled liquors from wood. Spent chestnut chips from a tannery are sold to a paper mill and converted into pulp. Th whole process from wood chips to the bound book has been known to take only 96 hours in Kingsport. In a surprisingly brief period

[31] C. F. Doane and A. J. Reed, "Cheesemaking Brings Prosperity to Farmers c Southern Mountains," U. S. D. A. *Yearbook*, 1917, Separate 737.

[32] Howard Long, *Kingsport*.

of time Tennessee mountaineers have developed into skilled laborers. Nor have eastern industrialists had occasion to regret their selection of location. Kingsport has invited industry and for the decade before 1930 had acquired over a plant a year. These two instances in diverse fields epitomize the process of change in the highlands and offer contrast to earlier levels of isolation.

The Ozark-Ouachita Highlands

The Ozark-Ouachita Highlands furnish a replica of the Appalachians. If they deserve separate treatment, it is because they are smaller, less rugged, and younger in settlement.

The highlands of the mid-continent comprise 91 counties which have been settled by a rural, native white, Protestant population for over 115 years. Its outer hills furnished the site of the first permanent white settlement east of the Mississippi. It area of 63,470 square miles—over half the area Campbell assigned to Appalachia—had in 1920 a population of 1,742,393, distributed in the three states of Arkansas, Missouri, and Oklahoma. No less than the Appalachians, the culture of the Ozarks is a derivative of the frontier.[33]

As a matter of fact the area received the greater part of its population from the southern highlands, 1820-1840 being the period of greatest migration. Arthur H. Estabrook traces the course of a typical migrant who, born in 1801 in the mountains of Virginia, married a wife born in 1805 in Tennessee, had children born in Kentucky in 1825, 1827, 1829, 1832, 1834, 1836. His last child was born in Newton County, Arkansas, in 1838.[34] Unlike the Appalachias there has been a continuous but fluctuating immigration to the Ozarks since the first settlement. Like Appalachia, however, mining has fostered a continuous movement of population to areas of development.

Industrial development in the southern Ozarks will not parallel that of Appalachia. The northern Ozarks, however, produce 60 per cent of Missouri's mining output, lead and zinc being found there exclusively. The area is relatively lacking in coal and iron and remains undeveloped in water power. Hay-pasture-dairy farm-

---

[33] Vance Randolph, *The Ozarks;* Carl O. Sauer, *Geography of the Ozark Highlands.*

[34] "The Population of the Ozarks," *Mountain Life and Work,* April, 1929, pp. 2-3, 25-28.

ing must be substituted for the poorly adapted grain farming of the Ozark. That the region is not perpetually doomed to poverty and sparse settlement is shown by progress in power, forestry, growth of resorts, as well as of a new type of agriculture.

Within the last year these hills have become the fifth ranking grape region of America, shipping large quantities of grape juice, jelly, preserves, and 14,000 tons of fresh grapes yearly. They are now the center of a tomato canning industry producing $2,500,-000 annual returns. Twenty of these counties produce every seventh quart of strawberries eaten in the United States, returning $600,000 to their highland growers. The dairy industry has reached a beginning in the hills producing 30,000,000 pounds of butter and 200,000 pounds of cheese in a recent year. In 1929, 865 carloads of cream were shipped to the Atlantic seaboard. Poultry products brought $55,000,000 into the Ozarks in 1928, eggs accounting for $22,000,000. The recency of the awakening in the hills can be shown by a reference to peaches. In 1928 from 5,000,000 trees the Ozark and Ouachita highlands shipped 4,000 cars of peaches. In 1920, eight years before, Arkansas shipped only 57 cars to outside markets. Highland, Pike County, Arkansas, is exceeded as a peach shipping center by only three carloading points in the United States.

CHAPTER XI

THE DELTA: PLANTATION HERITAGE

FROM CAIRO at the Ohio's mouth to the Gulf, the Mississippi River flows through a flood plain—a flood plain which it must have created by filling an ancient inland sea. To the bird's-eye observer this Delta, so-called, appears as a forest covered plain with the bank of the water courses as the highest point in the landscape. This is so true that each river has been said to have its bed in the axis of a ridge that accompanies it throughout. Through the course of ages the Mississippi must have flooded thousands of square miles in hundreds of overflows. J. Russell Smith explains: "As the water swings out of the main channel into the still backwaters its speed is checked. It drops part of its load of silt and mud. This makes the river bank higher than the back swamp."[1] Crooked and full of turns, this great river which is always building banks is also engaged in the work of cutting its banks away. The outer banks of this great carrier are always being under-cut and this process with the resulting cave-ins leads the river to discover lower courses and new channels in the back swamps and bayous.

By air line the distance from St. Louis to the Gulf of Mexico is 800 miles; by the tortuous route of the Mississippi it is 1,270 miles. Possessing a fall of only four inches to the mile this great sluggish stream spreads its width abroad, meanders, turns and returns, undercutting its banks and overflowing. Thus A. B. Hulbert points out that the Mississippi never remains the same:

It is said to bring down annually four hundred million tons of mud, but its eccentricity in deciding where to wash away and where to deposit its load is still the despair of river pilots. The great river could destroy islands and build new ones overnight with the nonchalance of a child playing with clay. It could shorten itself thirty miles at a single lunge. It could move inland towns to its banks and leave river towns far inland.

[1] "Plan or Perish," *Survey*, LVIII, 370.

It transferred the river town of Delta from three miles below Vicksburg to two miles above it. Men have gone to sleep in one state and have wakened unharmed in another because the river decided in the night to alter the boundary line. In this way the village of Hard Times, the original site of which was in Louisiana found itself eventually in Mississippi. Were La Salle to descend the river today by the route he traversed two and a half centuries ago, he would follow dry land most of the way for the river now lies practically everywhere either to the right or left of its old course.[2]

THE DELTA METROPOLIS

New Orleans, metropolis of this area, exemplifies the problems peculiar to the city in the Delta environment.[3] It arose a hundred miles up stream on the Mississippi at the point where goods were transferred from small river boats to ocean-going vessels. When railroads came to take the place of river craft, the operations begun in 1875 to make the channel accessible to modern ocean steamers were attended with success. Thus the city maintained its standing as an ocean port though a hundred miles from the Gulf.

New Orleans was built on the natural raised banks of the river and its growth, like that of all Delta cities, caused expansion into the swamp area back of the river. Many parts of the city thus came to lie below the river at high stage, and artificial levees had to be built atop the natural banks. These protective areas are now occupied by wharves, warehouses, and tracks. To complete communication with New Orleans is so difficult that the railroads are compelled to use ferries across the river. Shifting foundations of river mud and sand, with a river whose depths vary from 40 to 200 feet and whose width ranges from 1,500 to 3,000 feet, afford baffling obstacles to bridge construction. Until the recent completion of the bridge at Vicksburg, Memphis possessed the only crossing between St. Louis and the Gulf. Moreover, in an area overlaid with delta mud and sand, modern metropolitan architecture has proved almost as impossible as bridge construction. Building stone is lacking and must, therefore, be transported down stream. In addition, it is almost impossible to reach the bedrock foundation necessary to support great buildings. Consequently New Orleans did not possess a modern skyscraper until 1920. Its pavement program

[2] A. B. Hulbert, *Paths of Inland Commerce*, p. 177.
[3] Adapted from W. D. Jones and D. S. Whittlesey, *Economic Geography*, I, 215-17.

is also a recent development. Before 1890 the city possessed only
a few stretches of pavement, made of cobble stone brought in as
ship ballast.

Furthermore, its Delta location has given New Orleans unique
problems in relation to water supply, drainage, and sewage disposal. The soil cannot absorb the run off since water level is so
high as to prevent underground burial. The city's natural slope
would, if allowed, convert the area back of the river into a stagnant
lake. There are no clear springs and any well dug soon fills with
contaminated seepage. The Mississippi itself bears sediment and
bacteria from a hundred river towns. New Orleans was accordingly forced for a long period of its history to save for drinking
water the run-off from roofs in cisterns, open and above ground.
From these sources came repeated visitations from malaria and
yellow fever until finally the cisterns were closed by law. Early
in the twentieth century arrangements were made to take city water
from the Mississippi. In a great settling basin located above the city
water is now purified by chemical and mechanical means. Until
1900 New Orleans possessed open gutters for sewage and a few
sluggish canals which drained into Lake Ponchartrain, which is
lower than the city. The canals were covered, other covered drains
installed, and eight pumping plants force the drain water into the
Lake and two bayous. Another drainage and pumping system lifts
the sewage into the river. These are the conquests in municipal
engineering man has been forced to make of nature in order to
prosper in the Delta environment.

The mountains owe their distinctive quality of life to the conflict with space, especially in its vertical aspect. The Delta is as
much a region ruled by water. Its level contours, its fertile soils,
its former commerce, its present agriculture, and its perennial threat
of disaster all hail from the waters. Every Delta dweller must be
prepared to embark as did Noah while it rains forty days and forty
nights. Running through the center of the mighty trough which
cuts through the middle of North America from the Arctic Ocean
to the Gulf of Mexico, the river has created in its southern reaches
a distinctive region, an area of commerce and an area of agriculture.

The Delta of Commerce

The Mississippi system bade fair in its heyday to make the
Delta the artery of commerce of the nation. "Kick a barrel of flour

at Minneapolis," once said James J. Hill, "and it will roll to the Gulf." Certainly nature had done everything possible to open the Kentucky-Tennessee area and the expanding old Northwest toward the South. As Miss Semple points out, the convergence of the Ohio, Tennessee, and Cumberland rivers guided the incoming hordes of settlers toward the great central stream. Many and varied were the types of flatboats which the difficulty of overland traffic directed down its currents. The boatsmen floated their produce-laden crafts down to early New Orleans, there broke up their barges to sell both goods and timbers, and returned overland with the proceeds. Keel boats, however, were often pulled back up stream. Afoot or on horseback, the traders usually preferred to return overland rather than to face the river current. Voyage on the river of a thousand miles and overland of five hundred were commonplace in those hardy days.[4]

The innovation of the steamboat changed the Mississippi from a one-way artery of traffic and ushered into the Delta the continent's most flourishing era of internal commerce before the railroads. In 1807 Livingston and Fulton built a shipyard at Pittsburgh and launched the first steamer on the Ohio, the *New Orleans*. In the following winter it descended to New Orleans, but it was not until 1815 that a steamboat was able to ascend the river from New Orleans to Louisville, the trip requiring twenty-five days. By 1825 some 125 steam craft were plying the Ohio-Mississippi and their number increased by 1860 to over a thousand. The flush times of valley expansion had set in before 1837; by 1860 Mississippi, Alabama, and Louisiana raised over half the cotton crop. Rates of freight transportation were sliced in half, and the time from New Orleans to Pittsburgh decreased from 100 to 30 days. The old flatboats began slowly to disappear from the river, being replaced by stern wheelers and side wheelers of shallow draft which carried the farmers' produce to market at what was then regarded as a dizzy rate of speed. Memphis, Mobile, Vicksburg, and New Orleans rose to stations of commercial importance, while Charleston and Savannah languished. In the decade from 1850 to 1860 New Orleans handled almost half the cotton crop of the country.

Moreover, the old Northwest became the hinterland for the

[4] Ellen C. Semple, *American History and Its Geographic Conditions,* pp. 84-92; 152-55.

plantation area, supplying much of its grains and meats. Any river system, as Miss Semple points out, is a unifying force connecting in the bonds of commercial interests settlers at its navigable sources with dwellers at its mouth. The Delta could by no means absorb the bulk of the products of the great valley, so that many cargoes had to be transhipped at New Orleans for the ocean traffic. Thus while the Northwest became the granary of the lower plantation area it looked abroad for other markets. The trend of political combination failed to follow the drift of commercial intercourse.[5] The Erie Canal was opened in 1825 and the old Northwest became in course of time firmly bound to New York through the Erie, for the distance to the sea was shorter this way than through either the Mississippi or St. Lawrence. The Erie Canal in the words of *DeBow's Review* "made the Mississippi river to flow backward." In this era the palatial and luxurious steamboats came to present a vivid contrast to the semi-frontier regions through which they voyaged. The famous races between crack river steamers like the *Natchez* and *Robert E. Lee* lasted well into the post-bellum period.

The Civil War and the railroads were to finish the work begun by the canal. By the time the traffic on the river had recovered from the shock of war, parallel railroads had come to take its place. The river has never again reached the highwater mark, set in 1880, of one million tons received and transhipped at St. Louis for the lower South. The greater speed of the railways, the prevalence of many well-located branches, undermined the greatest historic internal waterway systems developed in the United States. A survey in 1925 showed that the old time packets had been pushed off the river.[6] No through steamers from St. Louis now make runs to Memphis, Vicksburg, or New Orleans. Five boats out of St. Louis and several out of Memphis remain to carry excursions or local freight connecting with trunk lines. The fact that the crisis of the World War gave the railroads more freight than they could well handle led to the establishment of a line of power barges for heavy traffic. These proved successful and at the close of the struggle were turned from government to private management. It cannot be said that they have made serious inroads on the railways,

[5] *Ibid.,* pp. 256-68.
[6] C. A. McCombs, "Present Status of Navigation of the Lower Mississippi," *Journal of Geography,* XXIV, 17-19.

and they offer no promise of return to the days when the Mississippi River was the commercial artery of a nation. However New Orleans and the Delta may have failed to organize the valley as its hinterland, the Crescent City retains its position as the second port of the nation. The Delta of commerce is thus not wholly a thing of the past, though the river is no longer its main artery of traffic.

The Delta of Agriculture

The Delta has always been, even in its palmiest days of commerce, predominantly a region of agriculture. "A land of low ridges, flats, cypress swamps, canebrakes, sloughs, and bayous, covered everywhere with great hardwood forests," it appears almost primeval.[7] Soils of surpassing depth and richness have accumulated silt at each overflow. Cotton obsessed, Negro obsessed, and flood ridden, it is the deepest South, the heart of Dixie, America's superplantation belt. The Delta, so-called, consists of a series of basins of rivers which flow into the Mississippi. In Arkansas the delta counties are clustered in the St. Francis Basin with Memphis as its metropolis and at the junctions of the White and Arkansas with the Mississippi. In Mississippi the Yazoo River marks off a delta area with Greenville and Vicksburg as commercial capitals. In Louisiana the Ouachita, Red, and Atchafalaya Basins are outstanding. Together with the alluvial lands of the great river, these basins form the Delta.

Here are the river bottom areas. The brown and mottled clay soil characterized by cypress, red gum, and oak growths produced before the boll weevil a smooth, silky staple as long as 1¾ inches and of exceptional strength. Old buyers have given special names to the best cotton grades. "Benders" are grown in the bends of the Mississippi, "rivers" on the banks of tributaries, and "creeks" along the smaller streams. Hubbard writes of old time photographs displayed in many cotton offices showing a planter on horseback in his field with the animal almost hidden in the foliage. Very little fertilizer is found necessary on many of the alluvial farms. The so-called second bottoms which lie above overflow also produce good yields.

Plantations in the alluvial valleys are more numerous and larger

---

[7] Fern Ellison Dorris, "The Yazoo Basin in Mississippi," *Journal of Geography,* XXVIII, 72-81.

than elsewhere. In the Yazoo Delta 70 per cent of the improved land is in cotton, 85 per cent of the farm land is operated according to the plantation system, and 86 per cent of the farms are operated by Negro tenants. The largest plantation in the world at Scott, Mississippi, in this Delta contains 37,000 acres. The average tenant's holding in this region is about twenty-three acres with around twenty acres in cotton. The Yazoo Delta has averaged at one time the highest yield of cotton in the cotton belt, 265 pounds to the acre. The land is flat and the rows stretch far away. On viewing the region for the first time one is likely to be oppressed by the lowness of the country and the innumerable tenant shacks each with its cotton house, that stretch far away into the distance.[8]

Slavery carried the Negro to the Delta; and mosquitoes, malaria, floods, and the high price of river bottom land have helped to keep yeomen white farmers out. Three types of plantations are discernible: the small plantation managed by the landlord who lives on it and directs to some extent the work; the large plantation owned by a capitalist or possibly a corporation and run by a managerial staff; and the plantation bought as a speculation by one engaged in another business who attempts to operate it as an absentee landlord. The 1910 Census of Plantations which also covered areas outside the Delta found the average plantation to contain 724 acres of which 425 were in improved land. The average value of lands and buildings was $17,322. The average plantation possessed an acreage five times and a value three times as great as the average for farms in the United States. The landlord retained for his own cultivation an average farm valued at $6,564, containing 330 acres, 26 per cent of which was improved. The average tenant farm contained 38.5 acres of which 81 per cent was improved. The tenant's farm, slightly over one tenth as large as the landlord's farm, was composed of richer and better cleared land. The total value of the average tenant's farm, however, was under $1,000 with buildings worth only $179.[9]

The Delta plantation is a unified economic organization with a system of management and a program of supervision of its work stock, implements, and Negro labor. To the owner or general manager falls this difficult task of financing the plantation by keeping

[8] Rupert B. Vance, *Human Factors in Cotton Culture*, pp. 20-22.
[9] *Ibid.*, pp. 70-71; 1910 Census, V, 881 ff.

up connection with credit institutions, by purchasing supplies, marketing products, and overseeing with the aid of a bookkeeper the accounts of all the tenants. Next in authority comes the farm manager. This successor to the ante bellum overseer has risen in intelligence, social status, and managerial ability. He directs the planting and cultivating of crops and the operation of the gin and the supply store. A gin mechanic is kept only during the active ginning season, but, if the plantation is fairly large, a commissary manager is kept the year around. In order to avoid losses, the manager supervises the tenant's financial dealing so that his living expenses advanced do not exceed his productive capacity. The work stock, tools, and crop, whether belonging to landlord or tenant, must be looked after. Tenants may desert at critical times, leaving debts unpaid and crops untended. All these contingencies require in the plantation manager a skillful blend of tact and firmness in dealing with the human element on the plantation. The average salary for plantation managers in 1920 was $2,100 a year and included as extras, free house rent, food for the family, and pasture for live stock. Assistant managers and overseers received $1,550 and $1,000 respectively with perquisites. The average cost of management on cotton plantations was approximately $1.83 per acre in crops.[10]

The production of cotton throughout the whole Delta is organized around the system of credit whereby it is financed. The plantation owners are forced to furnish their tenants not only material for working the crop but living expenses until the crop is harvested. To do this the owner is himself forced to borrow from at least four principal sources: banks, wholesale merchants, cotton factors, and local merchants. A study of conditions in 1922 showed that varying with locality, from 40 to 80 per cent of the planters' advances came from local banks.[11] Wholesale grocery companies operating in the Delta estimate that about 50 to 90 per cent of their business is done with plantation commissaries to whom they extend a line of credit amounting from 10 to 20 per cent of the total credit secured by the planters. In turn the owner gives the tenant a line of credit at his supply store, based on the tenant's cotton

[10] C. O. Brannen, "Relation of Land Tenure to Plantation Organization," U. S. D. A., *Bulletin* 1269, pp. 12-27. Vance, *op. cit.,* pp. 71-73.

[11] W. J. Corson, *Financing the Production and Distribution of Cotton,* Federal Reserve Bulletin, 1923.

acreage and secured by a crop lien. Each month the tenant is allowed to draw a part of his credit allowance in goods priced usually 10 to 25 per cent higher than the cash prices. The cotton factors to whom the crop is consigned for sale once furnished much of the credit but have recently suffered heavy losses. In 1922 some 5 to 10 per cent of planter advances in certain areas came from factors. The figure has declined since then. Such is the credit system by which the Delta plantations are kept functioning.[12]

To what kind of region does the Delta soil, cotton production, the Negro, and the ever-present plantation give rise? We may best answer this question by comparing the social-economic characters of 33 Delta counties: nine in Arkansas, twelve in Louisiana, and twelve in Mississippi with their state levels.[13] The Delta area is more rural than its rural states. An overwhelming proportion of its population is Negro, much above state average. In the Arkansas Delta the percentage of Negroes in the population is 73.8 as compared to 27 for the state; in Louisiana, 59.1 compared to 38.9 for the state; in Mississippi, 79.8 to 52.2 for the state. Two Mississippi counties show over 90 per cent Negro population and one has only 682 white persons in the county. The natural increase of population is lower for the river counties than for their states and the infant mortality rate is much higher.

The percentage of land in farms in the Delta is above the state levels for Mississippi, slightly above for Arkansas, and below state levels for Louisiana. The size of Delta farms is much less than for the state, being half or slightly over. This is due to the fact that the census counts tenant farms rather than plantations. The tenancy ratios, both white and black, are much higher than in the states. The value of Delta farm property except in Mississippi is lower than state levels. Value of farm buildings, land, and machinery also rank below state levels, indicating small size and lack of improvements of tenant farms. Only half of the farms in the Arkansas and Mississippi Delta and less than a fourth in the Louisiana have milk cows. This is far below the levels for their states and is paralleled by the Delta's low ranking in hogs and poultry reported. Mules comprise three fifths of the value

[12] *Ibid.*, pp. 174-75.
[13] This has been done by Virginia Denton in "Social Economic Characteristics of the Mississippi Delta," Master's thesis, University of North Carolina, 1930.

of all live stock reported in the Delta in 1925. With regard to income from farms, only the Mississippi Delta exceeds its state average in the ratio of $834 to $645. In Arkansas their incomes are approximately equal while the Louisiana Delta ranks lower than its state averages. In the value of crops the Arkansas Delta ranks $30 per farm lower than the state, the Louisiana Delta is $80 lower, while the Mississippi Delta farm ranks $270 above the state average. The percentage of Delta farms mortgaged is considerably higher than for the whole state: for Arkansas 47.8 to 32 per cent; for Louisiana 39.6 to 27.3 per cent; and for Mississippi 49.9 to 33.1 per cent. In all three instances the Delta counties outrank their states in illiteracy by large margins. In each case, however, the percentage of white illiteracy in the Delta is lower than in the states as a whole. The Negro illiteracy rate is much higher in the Delta counties of Louisiana and Mississippi than in those of Arkansas. These facts indicate that the white population of the Delta is a selected population, selected by that process by which the plantation vanquished the frontier.

With regard to resources, the Delta still represents the highest economic range the South with its peculiar social organization of black and white may be expected to attain without industrialization. Nowhere are ante bellum conditions so nearly preserved as in the Yazoo Delta. From the plantation mansions with their colonial architecture to the planter type, the Delta harks back to a proud agrarian tradition. Affable and courteous with equals, commanding and forceful with inferiors, the Delta planters composed Mississippi's aristocracy; and, as long as they held control, state politics preserved at least the form of dignity and decorum. Conversely, here the Negro is to be found at his lowest levels in America. The percentages of croppers and of illiteracy, valuable economic and social indices, are greatest in the Delta. Mississippi remains the one commonwealth whose population is over one half Negro, and ugly rumors of occasional peonage and the whipping of runaway tenants still come out of the Delta.

The vicissitudes of the plantation owner and his tenants caught in the cycles of crop production and the gyrations of the market have veritably proved the folk-saying that cotton is dynamite. The following report of a district manager of the Mississippi Staple

Cotton Coöperative Association tells its own story. Mules and human beings find themselves reduced to the same level of livelihood.

There is very little that we can comment on at this writing, other than to paint a picture of depression and general business stagnation. All planters within the district are greatly concerned as to how they will go through the winter, take care of their live stock and labor, until such time as furnishing is started again in February. Every planter that we know is very much concerned with feeding his stock and tenants at a minimum cost, not only throughout the winter but throughout the entire growing period of next year's crop. We know of one concern who has a schedule by which he [sic] believes he can take care of his live stock for 15c a day and his tenants for $4.50 per month per head. If any planter in the Delta is interested in securing this formula, we shall be glad to send it to him upon request.[14]

SOCIAL INCIDENCE OF FLOOD

Flood is an ever-present threat that gives the Delta many of its distinctive regional traits. In the face of a hundred difficulties, dwellers in the Delta have kept at the task of building and maintaining levees. "Like the Dutch in Holland," observed Edward King in 1880, "they assert their right to the lowlands in which they live, always braving inundation."[15] The desperate nature of the crisis and the magnitude of the task has made for detached attempts at control rather than for coöperation. Along the great river and various tributaries, state laws have provided that a group of citizens may come together, organize a drainage district, and plan to combat floods according to their own ideas. This means the erection of levees "to crowd the water out of the neighborhood" which according to J. Russell Smith must mean "to get it onto somebody else." In the conflict of local districts any general program has been overlooked. In times of danger, levees are often patrolled by armed guards to prevent their being dynamited by dwellers behind the levees on the other side. Such are the lengths to which men will go to relieve the danger to their own homes and farmsteads.[16] This atmosphere of suspicion and distrust has been engendered by repeated failures of the levee program in the past. In addition, landowners in these districts are weighted down by extra

[14] *Staple Cotton Review* (Nov. 1930), p. 5.
[15] *The Great South*, p. 67.
[16] See J. Russell Smith's "Plan or Perish," *Survey*, LVIII, 370-77.

levee taxes, unknown in more favored sections. These taxes not only seem perpetual, they appear futile. The bonds issued for erecting a great levee project are not paid off before another flood has made necessary new tax levies for repair and reconstruction. To the perpetual drain of taxation on the propertied classes in the Delta is added the recurring crises of flood which touch all Delta people, rich and poor, in their property and lives.

These disasters have occurred so often that a typical description may be undertaken.[17] When the gauge at Cairo shows the river at the 51 foot stage it is time to sound the signal for a desperate fight for life and property along the lower thousand miles of the river. In six days the crest of the flood will reach Memphis; in twenty-one it will flow past the mouth of the Red River; in thirty it will arrive at New Orleans. Within this period the levee boards of each district go into action. They organize their forces, charter boats, order and place at convenient points millions of sand-filled sacks. Guards are ordered to patrol the levees night and day on the lookout for the first signs of a break. Men and materials are rushed to the point of seepage. A crib may be built outside to confine the seeping water and thus equalize pressure on both sides of the embankment. If the levee is sloughing off on the inside thousands of sand bags are packed on each side. If the water rises to the levels of the retaining walls several tiers of sand bags are laid to hold back the flood while emergency calls are sent out, warning all in the area to save property and live stock.

These measures in all too many cases serve to delay rather than to prevent the threatened break. The waters, however, do not emerge in a great wall as when a crumbling dam releases a great reservoir down a mountain gorge. In the alluvial plains the great basins fill slowly. The waters creep up gradually but relentlessly, always seeking the lower levels, the swamps, the bayous, and parallel streams which will finally some hundred miles below conduct them back to the river. Many chances are accorded people for seeking higher ground and many retreat to upper stories or roofs of houses. The chance of saving human life is thus exceptionally good, and it is noted that not a single death was reported as due to drowning in the great floods of 1897, 1903, 1912, 1913, and 1922.

[17] John A. Fox, *Mississippi River Flood Problems,* Memphis River Levee Association, 1915, cited by Jones and Whittlesey, *op. cit.,* pp. 211-15.

The levees are always the highest spots on the landscape and serve as headquarters for rescue parties with their small boats. Live stock are, however, not so easily saved. Marooned on hillocks and high ground, they take fright at the approaching waters and are likely to lose their lives in attempts to swim out, often blindly undertaking distances of twenty to thirty miles. Small farmers in the flooded area are likely to lose all their household goods. Houses are usually left standing, although plastered with river mud, much water damaged, and smelling for a long time of the stagnant river stench of retreating floods.

Civilization itself has made these recurring floods more disastrous, for it has placed more of man's artifacts in their oncoming path. In the thirty-five years from 1880 to 1915, the 29,000 square miles of the Delta had seen its railroad network increase from just over 200 miles to 3,800 miles spreading in every direction. The floods of 1912 and 1913 thus suspended operations on four great transcontinental lines. One road, the old St. Louis, Iron Mountain and Southern, shows the extent of damage. This line had, in 1912, 352 miles of trackage under water up to five months; 512 miles were incapacitated, accounting for a total damage of $415,000 expended in repairs. In addition, the road lost $550,000 worth of traffic, representing approximately $5,500,000 in commerce. The recurrence of the flood in 1913 led to further damage of $440,-000 to the lines and a $196,000 loss in traffic. An inventory for one Arkansas county showed a loss in physical properties amounting to $988,800. In this flood, governmental agencies fed 272,753 refugees and issued seven and a half million rations. They were able moreover to save 54,500 head of stock. After the disaster the farmers of the Yazoo and St. Francis basins returned home in time to plant crops only to have them ruined by the flood of 1913.

It required the historic flood of 1927 to show of what devastation the great river system is capable. In one of the innumerable backwashes of the Mississippi stands a tree on which some native of scientific bent has nailed markers for six previous floods. Lowest on the tree is that of 1912, after which came 1922, 1887, 1884, 1882, and the highest of all 1927. In this flood 26,000 square miles, distributed in 170 counties in seven states were affected. Protecting levees along the Mississippi and its main tributaries broke in 195 places threatening 4,459,283 people. Almost 30 per cent, or 931,159 of the population were actually in the flooded area. Of the suf ferers 53.8 per cent were Negroes. The great height and force of the flood was shown in the exceptional loss of life, 246 having been reported drowned. Many believing themselves safe in areas which floods had never reached before must have found themselves in exorably trapped in the early stage of the disaster.

The flood's wide expanse and the material advancement of the Delta contributed to make the property loss the greatest in the re gion's history. Seeded and growing crops to the extent of 5,289,570 acres, or 28.2 per cent of the agricultural areas of the Delta, were destroyed to an estimated value of $101,562,395. Live stock and other forms of property amounting to $23,086,150 were lost ac cording to estimates of the Weather Bureau. These losses included according to Red Cross records, 165,298 head of live stock and 1,010, 375 of poultry. Impossible to estimate were the losses in the wiping out of thousands of wild animals valuable for game and trapping. Moreover, 162,017 homes were flooded and 8,947 destroyed along with 32,540 other buildings. A million people were thrown out of their occupations, normal habits, and daily routines. Of these 65,005 families lost their household goods, 23,566 lost their farm implements, and 38,506 their live stock. It was necessary for the Red Cross to care for 325,554 people in refugee camps and to feed 311,922 others in such temporary shelters as public buildings and second stories of flooded homes. Damages to public utilities and business were impossible to estimate. The railways bore a loss estimated at $10,000,000 and the Red Cross expended $17,000,000 in relief and rehabilitation.[18]

Here in brief review have passed two of the Southland's dis tinctive regions. In the transition from the Highlands to the Delta we have passed from the South's frontier to its plantation zone. Each has its problems whether it be of poverty levels and isolation or of over-specialization and the threat of floods. In the chapter on regional planning we shall glance at some of the programs and suggestions for the reconstruction of these regions.

In the Piedmont of the southeastern states we shall find another distinctive region. Having passed through the frontier stage and avoided the plantation, the Piedmont is definitely entering the stage of industrialization. Here the South is making her first coherent break with the agrarian tradition.

[18] The American Red Cross, *The Mississippi Valley Flood Disaster of 1927*, ch.

CHAPTER XII

THE PIEDMONT CRESCENT OF INDUSTRY

THE INDUSTRIAL AREA of the new South stretches in crescent from its southernmost tip at Birmingham, Alabama, to its northern end near Danville, Virginia. It passes through Alabama, Georgia, South Carolina, North Carolina, and Virginia. For its southern and eastern boundary it hugs the fall line, for its northern and western boundary it encroaches on the southern highlands. Its total area may be estimated at 50,000 square miles.

A FRINGE BELT

The Piedmont may simply be taken as the pioneer fringe of an industrialism that is advancing upon the whole South. Those on the ground lack perspective while many people in the North fail to realize the size and importance of the industrial transformation under way. "The South," writes Broadus Mitchell, "furnishes the continent's latest land boom, develops giant power to rival Niagara, finds its industrial stocks bought and sold on the New York stock exchange with those of Pittsburgh and Detroit. . . . It is becoming economically a part of the nation by reason of the movement to it of industrial plants from North and West." It comes as a distinct surprise to many to hear that North Carolina, for example, has the largest hosiery mill in the world, the largest paper pulp mill in the United States, the second largest aluminum plant in the world, and that Alabama ranks as the third state in the number of blast furnaces. Once the prophet, Henry W. Grady is now the patron saint of a new order. "Every skyscraper which rises in those astonishing cities of the new South," says a journal of national circulation, "is in a real sense a monument to Grady and his genius."

The Piedmont owes the impetus which furnished its early start in industrialization to its characteristics as a fringe belt. Bordering on the mountains and the coastal plains, its fringes—the breaks where one physiographic province undergoes the transition into another—have proved important factors in the localization of industry. The fall line played its part in the distribution of cities. Small boats making their way up the coastal rivers were unloaded of their freight at the approaches to rapids, and at these breaks in transportation grew up trading centers afterwards to become cities. Richmond, Raleigh, Macon, Columbus, Montgomery, and Little Rock thus arose at the fall line on southern rivers. Ellen C. Semple's generalization in regard to cities in Piedmont areas may well be applied to the South:

Piedmont belts tend strongly toward urban development even where rural settlement is sparse. Sparsity of population and paucity of towns within the mountains cause main lines of traffic to keep outside the highlands but close enough to their base to tap their trade at every valley outlet. On the alluvial fans or plains of these valley outlets, where mountain and piedmont roads intersect, towns grow up. Some of them develop into cities.

Piedmont cities draw their support from plains, mountains and transmontane regions, relying chiefly on the fertile soil and level country to feed their large population. Sometimes they hug the foot of the mountains. . . . Sometimes they drop down into the plain but keep the mountains in sight. They flourish in proportion to their local resources, in which mineral wealth is particularly important; and to the number and practicability of their transmontane connections. Hence they often receive their stamp from the mountains behind them as well as from the bordering plain.[1]

In material and energy resources the Piedmont is also a fringe belt. Minerals of the Appalachian ranges either find their outcropping on its borders or nearby. Coal, iron ore, limestone, and dolomite reach their maximum surface development at Birmingham, the end of the great valley. Chattanooga and Knoxville are in commercial proximity to the Piedmont if not tributary. To an even greater extent power resources are conditioned by the transition from province to province. The streams flowing through the Piedmont receive their "head" from sources in the mountains, and find their flow leveled to tamable slopes by the Piedmont incline. The slant of the Piedmont also furnishes reservoir sites whose back

---

[1] *Influences of Geographic Environment*, pp. 527-28.

flow does not cover disproportionate areas. After passing the fall line the streams level out on the coastal plain until they possess no more than enough momentum to wend their sluggish courses to the sea. Water wheels in the early stages of southern industry offered important sources of power and thus argued for the location of mills in the Piedmont. With the development of hydro-electric power the mills are now strung up and down the crescent-shaped fringe within tapping distance of the high-tension power lines.

In the important matter of reaching markets with the products of industrialism the Piedmont is again in the position of a fringe belt. In some respects it represents the entering wedge of the North going South and deserves the phrase, the "North of South and the South of North" by which it has been designated.

The one instance in which climate might have proved a definite drawback was found to be a matter amenable to technology. The absence of humidity in this area of the South was expected to afford an obstacle to the beginning of textile manufacturing. Both England and New England, areas of dampness and fog, afforded the high natural humidity needed in textile manufacture. The best manufacturing conditions, however, are now obtained by artificial humidification which can be regulated to the varying demands imposed by carding, roving, spinning, and weaving. Even in the mills of England and New England it has long been found advisable to use the self-regulating humidifiers.[2]

The problem of humidity in textile manufacturing serves to give point to the belief of many students that in the large the delayed industrialization of the South was not the result of geographic factors. The South possessed, if not its third, at least a fair share of the resources of raw material of mines and agriculture. And raw materials can be moved to centers of industry more easily than such centers can be moved to resources. The original location of such centers is again a matter of capital, technology, and skill that may be handed down, and of trained and aggressive leadership. Unless furnished in the cultural and economic background of a region, capital and technology are slowly and painfully acquired, ofttimes through dearly bought experience. The first impetus, to be successful, may necessarily come from outside.

[2] *See* Jefferson Bynum, "Piedmont North Carolina and Textile Production," *Economic Geography*, IV, 234-36.

It may be that the demoralization incident to southern leadership from thwarted hopes and frustrated efforts deserves much of the comment given it. E. Merton Coulter's picture of a thwarted Georgia plantation owner at the close of the Civil War is suggestive. "He became secretary and treasurer of the community Sunday school, calling the roll each Sunday and adding up the pennies—how different from the ante bellum gentleman calling the roll of his slaves and counting his bales of cotton. Instead of buying his gallons of wines and whiskeys he now wrote and delivered temperance lectures."[3]

The indecision, the baffled state of mind of a leadership trained in one field, lacking the traditions of the new technique, was encountered by Walter Hines Page in a tour of the South many years later.

Men spoke of the burden imposed by Reconstruction; they talked about the difficulties of developing the country without capital. Many men you would expect to be well-informed spoke with a sort of hopeless ignorance of economic forces; and you would often hear allusions to the North as if it were a foreign country and a country where men somehow prospered at the expense of the South. I do not recall bitterness in this undertone of conversation so much as loneliness—an isolation and a sense of despair. The South somehow seemed doomed to poverty for a long time to come.[4]

A shift in southern leadership from the plantation industry, theology, and politics to industry and the arts of commerce was to be expected. The traditional valuation of the professions in the South had to be reversed with the rise of industry.

My grandfather was a mighty man in theology in his day. He knocked out his opponents and he battered the devil. My father was a lawyer and a soldier. He fought the United States by argument and in war. I notice that the devil and the United States are both doing business yet. I made up my mind, therefore, that I would change the family job and do what I can to build mills and roads in Georgia.[5]

This is the way a student in a technical college answered the question of Walter Hines Page as to why he had abandoned the profes-

---

[3] "A Century of a Georgia Plantation," *Agricultural History*, III, 159.

[4] Walter Hines Page, "A Journey Through the Southern States," *World's Work*, XIV, 9004.

[5] *Ibid.*

sions of his fathers. The fact must be noticed, and it may be more important than realized, that the South for a long time stood outside the tradition of business enterprise. Its leadership occupied a field outside the range of the heritage and training implicit in the modern demands of business, finance, and engineering. The first southerners to become captains of industry learned the technique in northern factories and counting houses. Some like D. A. Tompkins returned, but many were lost to their section as leaders.

If, after 1880, the South may have been trying to lift itself into industry by its bootstraps, by 1900 the industrialization of the South had become largely a case of capital seeking labor supply. Closely related to the Piedmont's position as the fringe belt of southern resources has been the marginal status of its labor supply. Cheap labor, it must be candidly admitted, has outweighed other factors in developing industry southward. Cotton textiles, chief of the labor-orientated industries, has followed cheap man-power the world over. It is not necessary to speak of exploitation to account for the status of southern labor. It exists on the margin of two great industrial empires, agriculture and manufacturing. The small farmer exists on the borders of agriculture in the southeast because the cotton system, suffering from plethora, is expelling many of its tenants and small farmers. Low prices and competition with the Delta and the West in which the West has all the advantages of level topography, machine cultivation, comparative freedom from fertilizer costs and boll weevils have left the southeastern farmer seated on the edge of a decadent cotton industry. The Piedmont has been in a strategic position to tap the supplies of this marginal labor. In earlier times it drew upon the rural dweller from the disorganized cotton and tobacco areas. Recently it has drained the highlands of their labor reservoir sustained by a comparatively low-level domestic economy.[6] No adequate balance has yet been reached in southern areas. The Negro, kept out of practically all establishments except the coal and iron of Birmingham, has suffered a change in his age-old habits and has suddenly become the most mobile factor on the southern map. The shutting off of immigration and the resultant high wages, a residuum of war industries, have reallocated marginal black tenants bewilderingly contending with the gyrations of weather, weevil, and cotton prices

[6] Broadus Mitchell, *Rise of Cotton Mills in the South, passim.*

in Alabama and Georgia black belts. Southern labor remains a problem—a problem of oversupply that has not yet been met.

In yet another sense southern labor exists on the fringes. It stands at the outer entrance to industrialism but it has not yet penetrated far enough within the inner temple to gain its full rewards. Compared to their brothers in highly industrialized areas, southern workingmen have yet to become skilled. In textiles the finer weaves are done in large proportion in Eastern mills. In iron and steel the more complex fabrications and higher grade moldings are the products of Pittsburgh and Gary. This situation cannot be laid at the door of the southern laborer. To some he seems steeped in routine, afflicted with monotony and inferiority complexes. To many observers, however, including northern investors, he has seemed alert, intelligent, and capable of learning involved techniques. "The southern factory operative," says Broadus Mitchell, "is fit for a wider diversity of employments, he merits greater leisure

TABLE XXVI

SOUTH'S MANUFACTURING PROGRESS BY DECADES

	CAPITAL INVESTED* (Millions of Dollars)				VALUE OF PRODUCTS (Millions of Dollars)			
	1880	1899	1909	1919	1880	1899	1909	1919
Virginia.............	$26.9	$92.2	$ 216.3	$463.6	$21.7	$108.6	$219.7	$643.5
Kentucky...........	45.8	87.9	172.7	276.5	75.4	126.5	223.7	395.6
North Carolina......	13.0	62.2	217.1	669.1	20.0	85.2	216.6	943.8
Tennessee..........	20.9	63.1	167.9	410.2	37.0	92.7	180.2	556.2
South Carolina......	11.2	62.7	173.2	374.5	16.7	53.3	113.2	381.4
Georgia.............	20.6	79.3	202.7	448.7	36.4	94.5	202.8	693.2
Florida.............	3.2	25.6	65.2	206.7	5.5	34.1	72.8	213.3
Alabama...........	9.6	60.1	175.1	455.5	13.5	71.2	145.9	492.7
Mississippi.........	4.7	22.7	72.3	154.1	7.5	33.7	80.5	197.7
Arkansas...........	2.9	25.3	70.1	138.8	6.7	39.8	74.9	200.8
Louisiana..........	11.4	100.8	221.8	462.2	24.2	111.3	223.9	676.1
Oklahoma..........	....	4.0	38.8	277.0	....	8.1	53.6	401.3
Texas..............	9.2	63.6	216.8	585.7	20.7	92.8	272.8	999.9
The South.........	$179.9	$750.3	$2,011.8	$4,931.1	$285.8	$953.3	$1,881.3	$6,796.0
The Nation........	$2,790.2	$8,975.2	$18,428.2	$44,569.5	$5,369.5	$11,406.9	$20,672.0	$62,418.0
South's Percentage of the Nation's Manu- facturing........	6.4	8.4	10.9	11.1	5.3	8.4	9.1	10.9
Percentage Increase South...........	....	417.1	268.1	245.1	....	333.5	197.3	361.2
Percentage Increase Nation..........	....	321.6	205.3	241.8	....	212.4	181.2	301.9

*Capital Invested is not returned in the Census of Manufactures after 1919. Value of Products for 1929 will be found in Table XXVII

TABLE XXVII

MANUFACTURS IN THE SOUTH BY STATES, 1927-1929

| STATES | Number of Establishments | | Wage Earners Average for Year | | IN MILLIONS OF DOLLARS | | | | | |
| | | | | | Wages | | Cost of Materials, Fuel, and Power | | Value of Products | |
	1927	1929	1927	1929	1927	1929	1927	1929	1927	1929
Virginia.......	2,432	3,274	114,918	118,399	110	116	346	358	671	727
Kentucky......	1,851	2,227	74,912	76,201	83	87	250	262	447	490
North Carolina.	2,984	3,792	204,590	208,068	158	159	560	614	1,154	1,301
Tennessee......	2,098	2,846	114,968	126,921	101	114	351	387	614	706
South Carolina.	1,059	1,658	108,992	108,600	74	73	206	227	358	385
Georgia........	3,175	4,178	154,168	158,280	108	109	360	430	609	718
Florida........	1,912	2,214	61,219	64,936	56	54	91	97	218	232
Alabama.......	2,355	2,848	119,093	120,064	105	102	317	299	550	560
Mississippi.....	1,333	1,912	50,569	52,039	40	42	105	113	196	220
Arkansas.......	1,146	1,731	40,032	44,073	35	39	103	115	182	208
Louisiana......	1,624	1,986	82,415	87,511	79	83	427	441	638	684
Oklahoma......	1,373	1,651	27,932	31,279	35	40	269	307	371	452
Texas.........	4,065	5,187	116,763	131,503	130	147	842	998	1,206	1,450
The South.....	27,398	35,504	1,270,571	1,327,874	1,120	1,171	4,234	4,654	7,221	8,139
The Nation....	191,866	210,710	8,353,977	8,807,536	10,849	11,649	35,133	38,293	62,718	70,137
The South's Percentage...	14.3	16.8	15.2	15.1	10.3	10.1	12.1	12.2	12.3	11.6

and self direction, requires to be included in social councils, and will repay a higher standard of life."[7] That he has not arrived at higher skill is so far merely evidence that he has not yet had the opportunity. More skilled branches of textiles and steel have lagged in southern development and the southern workman has remained to a large extent on the outer margin of the skilled industrial group.

Both the capital invested and the value of products manufactured in the South have doubled decade by decade from 1880 to 1920. In that period the South increased its share of the country's capital in manufacturing from 6.4 per cent to 11.1. From 1880 to 1929 the section's share of the value of fabricated products increased from 5.3 to 11.6 per cent.

WATER POWER

Water power may be selected as the one unifying force underlying industrial development in the Piedmont Crescent. Over fifty

[7] "The Industrial Revolution in the South," *American Labor Legislation Review,* XVIII, 25.

per cent of the industry is electrified. High voltage lines stretch for over 3,500 miles and serve an area of over 120,000 square miles,—an area much larger than the Piedmont. In the Carolinas alone these lines reach 160 industrial communities, besides many isolated mills and factories. As have many others, this region has gone through the cycle from water power to coal and back to water power. The trend is definitely away from the small isolated power stations first adopted by individual mills and operated by either steam or water power. As sources of power they are being replaced by large central stations. Water and fuel still compete with each other for supremacy in cheapness, and yet equally important is their ability to supplement each other in the production of electrical energy. Steam power is held in reserve to bear its portion of peak loads and to compensate for stream shortage. In comparison to other regions "in these states a very high proportion of electric power is derived from water wheels rather than steam plants, although one of the important advantages of the Southeast in the generation of electrical energy is the abundance of fuel within short-haul distance for supplementing water power."[8] The presence of coal, as Raoul Blanchard points out, instead of retarding water power development in this region has expedited it.[9] Hydro-electric power, suitable for light manufacturing, cannot displace coal in industries requiring heat, as steel and brick-making.

The Southeast possesses more than 20 per cent of the developed hydro-electric horsepower of the United States, although within its borders are found only 7.6 per cent of the country's potential power. Thorndyke Saville, prominent expert in southern power resources, holds that with the exception of the Tennessee basin 60 per cent of the South's water power resources susceptible of economic development are now harnessed.[10] Alabama, South Carolina, and North Carolina rank with the leaders in possessing over 10 horsepower per 50 miles of flow. Only in New England and the Carolinas has water wheel capacity per square mile come near equaling the water resources per square mile available 90 per cent of the time. This

---

[8] *Commercial Survey of the Southeast*, p. 111.

[9] "Geographical Conditions in Water Power Development," *Geographical Review*, XVI, 97.

[10] "Power Situation in the Southern Power Province," *Annals* of the American Academy of Political and Social Science, 153, pp. 94-123.

high degree of development has taken place within a quarter of a century—dating its beginnings from about 1904.

The geographic layout for water power in the Piedmont has in fact proved more favorable than at first realized. Water power is the resultant of two factors, rainfall and altitude. Rainfall furnishes the volume, altitude accounts for the velocity of water. The greatest altitude in the United States is found along the Rocky Mountains while the highest rainfall, up to 100 inches a year, and the greatest amount of annual run-off, over 20 inches, is found along the Atlantic. The run-off of the great Mississippi System below Cairo, Illinois, is lost because of lack of slope and momentum. The ideal conditions for water power—a great upland gathering ground for water, which when accumulated falls rapidly to the sea —is met in the Southeast.[11] The Columbia, Colorado, and the St. Lawrence systems alone excel this area in America. The lack of the large lakes, marshes, and melting snows found along northern rivers led to the belief that southern rivers in the summer come perilously near running dry. Records kept by the United States Geological Survey over a long period of time showed, however, that the minimum flow of rivers throughout the Carolinas and Georgia are larger per square mile of drainage basin than in the rivers of New England or the Middle States. Such favorable run-off is due to the remarkably even distribution of the area's high rainfall throughout the year.[12] Porous soils and forest cover also serve to equalize flow. Moreover, as W. H. Voskuil has remarked, the peculiar contour of mountains and valleys on the eastern slope have served to make development comparatively inexpensive.[13]

The southern area has kept pace in the exploitation of energy resources. Since 1908 the South has tripled its water power development while the rest of the country was doubling its horsepower. For the three years from 1926 to 1929 one half of the gains made were in the South and, in 1926, 61 per cent of the gains were southern. In 1930 the South possessed 25.7 per cent of the hydro-electric generating capacity in the United States. The South has thus been overhauling its late start in the development of its energy resources.

[11] Herman Stabler, "Nation's Water Power," *Economic Geography*, III, 434-42.
[12] Henry A. Pressey, "Water Power of the Southern States," *Forestry and Irrigation*, January 1906, pp. 32-33.
[13] Cited Walter H. Voskuil, *The Economics of Water Power Development*, pp. 80-81.

The first long distance transmission line in the South was built by M. C. Whitener in 1896 from a small power plant on the Catawba. The hydro-electric development of the Piedmont got under way when J. B. Duke and W. S. Lee organized the Southern Power Company in 1904. The story of how Mr. Duke, suffering from erysipelas, was instructed by his physician in the intricacies of power dams, turbines, and transmission lines has been recounted elsewhere.[14]

In Alabama, development was started by Captain W. P. Lay in 1907 and got well under way by 1912. The Alabama Power Company with several hundred millions of capital has become the largest single enterprise in the state. This corporation was the original owner of the Muscle Shoals site which it sold to the government during the war for one dollar. By 1928 the Southeast was served by the following companies with a total annual output of about 5,000,000,000 kilowatt hours: Southern Power Company of North and South Carolina; Carolina Power and Light Company of North Carolina; Georgia Railway and Power Company, Georgia; Central Georgia Power Company, Georgia; Columbus Power Company, Georgia; Alabama Power Company, Alabama; Tennessee Power Company, Tennessee.

While the greatest potential water resources of the area are to be found in the Tennessee River system, the highest actual development has been reached on the Catawba River. The potential power of these states was estimated in 1924 at 2,944,000 horsepower available 90 per cent of the time and 5,056,000 horsepower available 50 per cent of the time. The present capacity of the Catawba development—combined water and steam plants—reaches 953,200 horsepower, soon to be increased to 1,103,200. From the pool at Bridgewater to the tailrace at Wateree, a distance of 300 miles, this river has a drop of 1,058 feet. Under the financial guidance of J. B. Duke and the engineering skill of W. S. Lee its development has proceeded so rapidly as to approach the spectacular. At times the amount of power available ran ahead of the market, but the demands of industry soon caught up and forced new construction. So well planned has been the utilization of stream flow that at many places the tailrace of one pond flows practically into the head of the next storage basin down the river. A drought in 1911

[14] J. W. Jenkins, *James B. Duke, Master Builder*, pp. 172-84.

rought the Catawba River so low that 152 mills shut down for ack of power, throwing 70,000 operatives out of work. Such poradic flow accentuated by lack of natural lakes is best overcome by the construction of storage reservoirs. In this manner the flow has been equalized along the whole system not only for seasonal but or daily uses. The Bridgewater reservoir at the head of the system possesses a storage capacity of 12½ billion cubic feet and regulates o a large extent seasonal flow. During the rainy season until September 1 it is filled, and by January 1 it is practically emptied. All other reservoirs along the system are used for storage over week-ends and when the load is light. By this means a normal 24 hour low is changed to a higher level flow for the 15 to 18 hour period when industrial and consumers' demands are highest. The water is thus utilized when the full load is on the system.

The most important stream of the Southeast in relation to energy resources is the Tennessee River and its tributaries. The Tennessee River Valley has been pertinently called the Ruhr of America. The expenditure of $750,000 in a detailed survey by the Board of Engineers of the United States Army of the power and navigation possibilities of the river and its tributaries is hardly an adequate index of the importance of this area. The total power stretch from Knoxville to Muscle Shoals is 392 miles. Effective development, however, must also include the river's tributaries, the Powell, Clinch, Holston, Watauga, French Broad, Hiwassee, and Oconee. The preliminary report by army engineers estimated over 2,000,000 horsepower of undeveloped hydro-electric energy. This is more than three times the ultimate power to be reached on the Muscle Shoals project and twice the primary horsepower developed by 1923 east of the Mississippi and south of the Ohio. The system, moreover, must be harnessed as a whole. Continuous flow at a high level can be secured only by interconnected series of storage reservoirs. Continuous power is always much more valuable than part time power. Moreover, if adequate planning is neglected, highways, railroads, habitations and towns will grow up in reservoir basins so that the expenses of expropriation will forestall development. The economic factors in the utilization of the Tennessee system are favorable; but the market for all its potential energy resources does not yet exist. Cheap power, however, tends to create its own market and rising industrialism points the way.

Super-power is well called a region builder. The Piedmont Crescent is fortunate in the possession of interconnected power systems which bid fair to foster and unify its regional interests. Super-power in the Southeast, however, does not exist as an organized system but as potential interconnection of systems. Each separate unit had expanded its power resources and extended its high voltage transmission lines until the interlacing of the system was a matter of building a few short connecting lines. A super-power zone is not created by fiat; it must come as the result of a gradual evolution. The wonders it can accomplish in the production of cheap power by tying several central stations into one system have no doubt been overestimated by the public. Such interconnections have nevertheless made possible economies in overhead and utilization of power. Capital invested is saved; the load factor can be increased for the whole system by smoothing out the diversity in peaks; operations can be carried on with less equipment in reserve; and more efficient stations are operated at maximum, while less efficient plants are called into service for secondary power.[15] The greatest contribution of super-power lies in its ability to distribute power evenly over a region in case of local shortage. The use of transformers has effected the transmission of currents of high voltage and low intensity for comparatively long distances. The loss of current in transmission ranges from 10 to 20 per cent, increasing as the distance of transmission increases. In passing it is noteworthy that the Duke lines were the first to engineer the transmission of power as high as 100,000 volts. While water power cannot be efficiently transmitted in the form of electric current over stretches of more than 200 or 300 miles, each unit in the interconnected system is able to relay its power to the next link in the chain. In this way a severe shortage resulting from a drought in North Carolina in 1921 was met by power from Muscle Shoals relayed through the Alabama and Georgia systems to the Carolina consumers.

The integrating and unifying effect of cheap and regular service is being felt throughout the southeastern super-power zone. The practice of manufacturers in generating their own power is on the decline. From 1924 to 1927 in this region the ratio of water power developed for their own use by manufacturers in this area

[15] Walter H. Voskuil, *The Economics of Water Power Development*, p. 21.

ell from 13.2 per cent of such total in the United States to 10 per cent. Moreover, Thorndike Saville holds that power projects developed ahead of their markets and under the necessity of drawing customers from other areas have created industrial rates that are as low or lower than in other states. Preston S. Arkwright, President of the Georgia Power Company, has pointed out that the industrial power rate for the South was 1.359 cents per kilowatt hour compared to 1.544 for 68 cities scattered over the United States.[16]

One advantage of power to the Piedmont Crescent is found in the even distribution of industry it has fostered throughout the region. Hydro-electric transmission has allowed in this zone the use of power at practically any point where labor, raw materials, and markets make the construction of a factory advantageous. Here we have the application of electricity to an industry capable of regional diffusion.

Coming into action late the industrialism of the South, unhampered by tradition and unencumbered by obsolescent power establishments, took over the practice best suited to its needs. Thus while the northeastern states form an illustration of centralized industry, establishing itself first in New England and migrating later to the Central Atlantic States and thence westward, the South displays a regional development of industry nowhere intensely focused but spread, on the contrary, in diluted form over a large area. The contrast is suggestive; for permanence, for national well being, for the common good, it would appear that a balanced economic life in which each section manufactures, in large measure its own products is preferable to a highly intensified manufacture setting up its own interests in opposition to the more extensive producing areas. The South presents an example of a power supply disposed to create a normal development from within, with minimum detraction from the opportunities peculiar to other sections.[17]

The next logical step in the distributive process as applied to power is rural electrification. Dependent at first upon increased returns in agriculture it may be expected to lead the way to great cultural and economic developments in farm life. In Switzerland, for example, under a government ownership system in which the

---

[16] "Power Situation in the Southern Power Province," *The Annals,* American Academy of Political and Social Science, 153, pp. 94-123.

[17] C. G. Gilbert and J. E. Pogue, *America's Power Resources,* pp. 136-37.

user pays royalties to the state, water power goes into the hous
and barn of the peasant, thrashes his grain, churns his butter, pump
his water, and prepares his cattle feed. The Columbus (Georgia
Electric and Power Company has lines with over 300 rural cu
tomers with special rates and has worked out a plan for joir
financing of rural lines by consumers and the company. Rura

TABLE XXVIII

POWER INSTALLED IN THE SOUTH TO 1927

STATES	PRIMARY HORSE POWER IN MANUFACTURING (In Thousands of Horse Power)			
	1899	1909	1925	1927
1. Virginia	136	283	441	503
2. Kentucky	144	230	257	318
3. North Carolina	154	378	800	810
4. Tennessee	130	242	447	475
5. South Carolina	112	276	423	478
6. Georgia	136	298	523	563
7. Florida	36	89	144	177
8. Alabama	173	357	697	779
9. Mississippi	65	206	211	214
10. Arkansas	79	173	117	183
11. Louisiana	190	346	410	415
12. Oklahoma	11	71	156	185
13. Texas	116	282	572	635
Total South	1,487	3,136	5,264	5,741
The Nation	10,097	18,675	35,772	38,825

STATES	TYPES OF PRIMARY HORSE POWER 1927				
	Steam Engines	Steam Turbines	Water Wheels Motor	Internal Combination Motors	Electric Motor Run b Purchased Current
1. Virginia	118,805	100,499	34,062	9,670	240,690
2. Kentucky	83,796	52,261	1,522	6,820	174,356
3. North Carolina	205,752	54,463	35,427	9,982	505,174
4. Tennessee	158,538	67,163	3,337	6,521	239,684
5. South Carolina	133,369	53,836	38,184	2,226	250,630
6. Georgia	159,678	52,691	29,142	9,421	314,967
7. Florida	68,572	18,152	795	14,421	75,640
8. Alabama	266,860	102,590	5,478	13,882	390,346
9. Mississippi	122,604	42,420	90	12,126	36,992
10. Arkansas	104,881	25,795	75	6,709	45,581
11. Louisiana	207,297	78,766	2,724	18,754	108,041
12. Oklahoma	48,951	46,045	......	20,257	70,227
13. Texas	190,448	96,446	1,711	46,351	300,499
Total South	1,869,551	791,127	152,597	177,140	2,732,827
The Nation	10,140,381	6,783,550	1,598,660	1,170,774	19,132,310

nes in Alabama increased from 38.9 miles with 240 customers in 924 to 183.3 miles serving 1,796 farm homes in 1926. The total, ompleted and authorized, will reach 350 miles to serve 3,618 cusomers. In Texas the Central Power and Light Company furnishes ural current for the electrical irrigation of more than 112,500 acres f rice lands, onion, spinach, and winter gardens. Many cotton ins in this area now operate with power from high tension lines. ust as electric power has aided in the even distribution of textile iills throughout the villages of the Piedmont, it may create a ew type of domestic economy on the isolated farm.

TEXTILES IN THE PIEDMONT

The industrial mainstay of the Piedmont crescent is cotton extiles. The first industry to arise in the Southeast remains the ading exponent of southern manufactures. Historically, it dates rom the days of household industry when Hamilton's report on nanufactures in 1791 estimated that in some districts of the South rom two thirds to four fifths of all the clothing of the inhabitants vas made at home. Power spinning was known in three South Carolina localities, Charleston, Williamsburg District, and Statesury as early as 1790. North Carolina's first mill, the Schenck Iill, was built at Lincolnton in 1813. Harriet L. Herring has ointed out three periods of increased activity in the construction f mills in the ante bellum period: during the War of 1812, the decde after 1820, and from 1845 to 1852.[18] Revival after the Civil Var and the flurry of Reconstruction began the vigorous upward wing in textiles that was fated to surpass the rest of the nation 1 physical production by 1921 and in value of product by 1925.

This startling rise of a new-old industry has often had its story ld.[19] Civil War and Reconstruction, however much they have een overplayed in southern apologetics, squandered the sections' esources and left its leadership in a state of shock. It required ie rise of many successful enterprises after the seventies to exorcise ie belief that only Yankees could manage cotton mills. Against ie counsel of northern advisers like Atkinson, southern colonels, lanters, doctors, and lawyers began to organize, build, and manage actories so that their towns might have mills and poor whites might

[18] *The Annals,* American Academy of Political and Social Science, 153, pp. 1-10.
[19] Broadus and George Mitchell, *The Industrial Revolution in the South.*

have work. Installment plans opened small savings to these amateur organizers, while machinery houses and commission firms granted long-time credits and subscribed for stock in order to gain new patrons. Claudius T. Murchison has written:

To establish a mill it was only necessary for the promoter to enlist the support of a few local friends to the extent of making available a sum which would assure a beginning equity in the venture of from $50,000 to $100,000. For the remainder of the capital a part could be secured via the loan route from bankers and a part from the machinery manufacturers. It was not uncommon prior to the war for the machinery manufacturers to accept, as a considerable part of their payment, stock in the proposed corporation which would later gradually be liquidated as the business became established. The character and layout of the plant and equipment would be left to the specialized mill engineer and to the machinery manufacturers. All that remained to be done was to import works manager, two or three mechanics, choose the labor force from the army of applicants which crowded the gates, open the selling account with a New York commission house who advised as to the character of the output and the project was under way.[20]

"An industry of these specifications," he adds, "was to the South of ten or twenty years ago like manna from heaven."

The rise of a successful and aggressive industry in the low price goods began to cut into the competitive earnings of New England mills. This was reflected by a threefold migration southward of units of the industry. First, southerners started mills of their own. Large corporations established southern branch mills for the production of low-count fabrics, while continuing to produce fine goods in the North. Then other mills losing in the competition were picked up and moved South. This last process might result in actual moving of equipment or it might mean the closing of a northern factory and the opening of one in the South. To the Piedmont chambers of commerce enticing outside mills became a greater sport than promoting local factories. A mill a week is said at one time to have been the motto of such an organization in the Southeast's largest textile district. Moreover, when depression came it appeared to hit New England harder than the South, and thus even in the periods of falling prices southern expansion continued.

[20] *King Cotton Is Sick,* pp. 131-32.

Back of this historical development are to be found the elements of regional geography and national economy. Compared to other southern industries, textiles furnish a far flung network of units. Unlike mining, the industry is not anchored to a fixed natural resource. Power lines distribute the energy to every hamlet. As for the location of the industry, the presence of near-by cotton fields carried no more weight than the presence of markets. Textiles in the South is thus a village, even a country-side, industry as compared to many others. The congestion and the crowding found in so many manufactures are here of no utility. Yet with every encouragement to scatter, it is remarkable that all down the southeastern tier of states the cotton mills are bunched compactly in the Piedmont crescent. Approximately three fourths of these mills are in the two Carolinas, and Gaston County boasts as many as a hundred.[21] Seventy-seven counties in 1931 contained more than 80 per cent of the nation's spindles. Of these 77 counties which possessed more than 100,000 spindles each in 1931, 21 are found in North Carolina, 15 in South Carolina, 13 in Georgia, 6 in Massachusetts, and 5 in Alabama. The other counties are found in eight states.[22]

It is the narrow, little streams, red from the erosion of clay hills, that first anchored the mills in the Piedmont. These streams, once thought useless because they would not float a boat, came to be dotted here and there with small mills in the days when water wheels vied with steam engines as sources of power. Here again the fall line served as a zone of demarcation beyond which the streams flattened out so as to possess no impetus. Here then in the Piedmont the power revolution found the mills and here it built others. Much more widely distributed, by virtue of its reliance on electric power, than other southern industries, textile manufacturing is surprising in its comparative confinement to the Piedmont.

The increasing localization of cotton mills in the South has often been explained in geographic terms as the movement of an industry seeking the source of its raw material. The explanation is not adequate. Freight rates are much higher on finished goods than on raw cotton. Compared to other industries, there is little loss

---

[21] Robert M. Brown, "Cotton Manufacturing: North and South," *Economic Geography*, IV, 74-87.

[22] Cotton Production and Distribution, *Bulletin* 168 Bureau of Census, 1931, p. 33.

of weight in textiles in the transition from raw material to the finished product. Accordingly, proximity to markets is of more avail than proximity to raw material. The North and East, moreover, furnished greater purchasing power than the South. In addition, at first much of the goods turned out in the South had to be sent to New England for dyeing, bleaching, and finishing before they were returned and sold in the South. Under these circumstances, no comparative advantage of location could be said to obtain even for the southern market. Both parties, mill operators and cotton growers, have proved so indifferent to this factor of resource location that southeastern mills buy a majority of their cotton from the Delta and the West. The upland staple has been getting shorter each year, so that much of it has to be exported to cheaper foreign markets. Only South Carolina, by virtue of the work of Clemson College and D. R. Coker in seed breeding, and the coöperation of the mills, has been able to improve her staple. On future contracts 96.6 per cent of the South Carolina crop is tendable. In 1930 South Carolina had 48 per cent of her crop in the 15/16 to 1-1/16 inch staple class; North Carolina 39.5 per cent; Georgia 15.6 per cent; Alabama 5.4 per cent.[23] As long as this situation obtains the southeastern mill loses as much as it gains by the logic of location.

Textiles, while using the raw materials of the cotton states, have imported a fair portion of their productive capital—how much no one knows—and market largely outside the region. The competitive advantage unquestionably obtained by southern textiles must, therefore, be sought elsewhere. They are to be found in special tax inducements, encouragements by railroads and communities, abundance of fuel and water power, and a cheap and plentiful labor supply. The cotton textile industry, to use Weber's terms, is oriented toward labor supply rather than toward markets or raw materials.[24] In addition, the recency of the development has operated to the cumulative advantage of southern mills. The newer installations have provided them with up-to-date plants and machinery while their housing, routing, and layout are planned in accordance with the latest technology. Equipment and processes are thus found better adapted to local conditions and modern requirements than in old and conservative New England mills. It must

[23] Press Release, Bureau of Agricultural Economics.
[24] C. J. Friedrick, *Alfred Weber's Theory of the Location of Industries.*

not be thought, however, that these technical improvements have implied more than a slow invasion of New England's superiority in fine goods. Such proficiency slowly gained requires workers whose aptitudes are the heritage of generations of skill and tradition.

This brings us at once to the consideration of labor as the decisive factor in the shifting of the industry. Here we are embarking upon the most controversial phase of the situation. Cotton milling has since its early beginnings demanded an unusually large number of workers for a mechanized industry. Moreover, the tasks of many of the machine tenders are so automatic that they may be said to border upon the perfunctory. Many of the details can be executed equally well by children after a little training. Accordingly, the workers have a low wage status and, after the passing of the idyllic days when Lucy Larcom was a New England mill girl, a kind of indefinable stigma has become attached to the cotton mill worker. Discussion of the mill village as a segregated community and the mill worker as a social type has been particularly vigorous in the South.

That a comparison of money wages shows the advantage to rest overwhelmingly with northern operatives is well known. Bureau of Labor figures computed for a year show the following weekly wage scales:

	Men	Women
North Carolina	$17.19	$14.06
South Carolina	15.01	12.05
Georgia	15.28	12.52
Massachusetts	22.05	17.95
New Hampshire	25.27	20.90
Rhode Island	22.13	18.64

Such figures which may be taken as typical if not average show a differential in favor of the North, ranging from $3.89 to $8.85 per month.[25] Clarence Heer, in his *Income and Wages in the South,* found the South's textile wage to be 66 per cent of that paid elsewhere. This differential increases the deeper one goes into the agricultural South. Thus, a United States Bureau of Labor Bulletin shows average hourly wages in 1926 to range thus:

[25] See Margaret Scattergood, "Facts About the South," *American Federationist,* XXXV, 826-29.

North Carolina .... .332
· South Carolina .... .261
Georgia .... .258
Alabama .... .245

Table XXIX is arranged to show these regional differences.

TABLE XXIX

AVERAGE YEARLY WAGES IN COTTON TEXTILE MANUFACTURE*

STATES	1921	1923	1925	1927	1929	Hours per Week†
Maine..................	$1000.06	$1012.01	$887.49	$959.39	$869.64‡	54
New Hampshire..........	884.39	929.95	925.15	1027.32	901.89	54
Massachusetts...........	906.84	1011.08	954.06	969.63	926.10**	48
Connecticut..............	943.21	1025.81	1028.19	1051.07	933.96	55
Rhode Island............	994.57	1073.42	1007.73	1045.61	997.49	54
New England Average.....	945.83	1010.45	960.52	101.060	937.81	
Virginia.................	872.80	940.45	821.52	837.63	748.37	60
North Carolina..........	624.25	676.73	641.26	691.23	661.93	60
South Carolina...........	645.41	651.98	631.60	657.84	651.86	55
Georgia.................	586.19	588.43	594.78	652.02	632.67	60
Alabama................	568.12	600.30	615.96	641.59	608.71	No limit
Average in Cotton Growing States.............	659.35	691.58	661.02	696.06	660.71	
Difference between New England and Cotton Growing States........	286.48	318.87	299.50	314.54	277.10	

*Based on compilation by Russell T. Fisher, secretary National Association of Cotton Manufacturers, from the latest U. S. Census statistics, in Henry P. Kendall. "Cotton Textiles: Where a Minority Blocks Concerted Planning," *The Survey*, LXVII, p. 593.
†Legal limit for employment of women and minors.
‡Includes 3 establishments in Vermont.
**Drop from 1927 due in part to strike in New Bedford ($700,000 loss in wages).

By many, these differentials have been taken merely as an indication of skilled processes of New England operatives as compared to the increasing lack of skill further South. There is, of course, truth in this contention, but it fails to account for the drift southward of the manufacture of fabrics requiring the least skill in processing. The other side of the shield is, of course, found in the fact that the typical industrialized community of the East by the very multiplicity of its activities competes for its labor supply, and thus offers it a higher wage.

The claim is often made that the differential in money wages is smoothed out in real wages. That the southern mill worker possesses real advantages as a consumer is undeniable. As so often

ointed out, his house is given him at a nominal charge of some
5 cents per room per week. Thus, for the average four-room
ungalow he pays a rental of $4.00 a month. Studies by the Na-
onal Industrial Conference Board, however, have shown fuel costs
o be no lower for southern than for New England textile operatives.
y virtue of the climate his clothing need not be so substantial nor
o costly. It is also claimed that living in an agricultural area the
outhern worker finds the cost of food cheaper. A family budget
tudy found food costs 6.3 per cent higher in Fall River, Massachu-
etts, than in Winston-Salem.

The southern industrial labor supply may be regarded as affected
y many factors: location, rural-urban population ratios, tenure lev-
ls, and income levels. The rural areas have not begun to be de-
leted of their man power. Over three fourths of the population
f the five southeastern states live outside cities of less than 2,500
nd more than half the total population lives on farms. In 1920 the
arm population ranged from 54 per cent of the total for Tennessee
o 63 per cent for South Carolina, but of the 820,192 white farmers
i these states in 1924, 348,444 or 42.5 per cent were tenants. With
o stake in the land, compelled to pay high interest rates and from
ne half to one fourth of their products as rent, these tenants and
reir families furnish a potential labor supply for any mill that will
pen its gates to unskilled labor. Moreover, a family wage of
30 or more a week affords returns sufficient to call from the farm
rousands of small owners whose vicissitudes with cotton, tobacco,
r highland farming have left them on the verge of failure. For
long time to come the southern labor supply bids fair to exceed
re industrial demand. If the mill jobs were open, if the mill houses
vere vacant, moving time in the cotton belt would find thousands
f sorely-driven farm families seeking haven in the mill villages,
o slender and so precarious are the returns from the one crop
ystem.

The further one penetrates into the deep South, the less indus-
rialization, the greater supply of potential operatives, and the lower
re wages one will find. It was with these classes in mind that
). A. Tompkins, one of the South's industrial pioneers, wrote:

he greatest benefactors of the South are those who have formulated
lans for the industrial development of the South, and have accomplished
re maintenance of regular work and regular cash pay rolls. Whoever

finds the way to keep people employed at profitable wages may depend upon it that these employed people will in time be more instrumental than anybody else in their own betterment.[26]

This not ill-considered view accounts for the high esteem in which the South early held her industrial pioneers.

We have not the complete data for a final judgment, but one is forced to the conclusion that the basic resources of the southern cotton textiles is not management, not nearness to raw materials, not necessarily improved technology, but labor that works long hours for low wages. The differential between New England and the Southeast is then the labor differential between a highly industrialized area and an area of decadent agriculture. The extent to which manufacturers sense this fact can best be shown by the deadly intensity with which they engage in conflict with labor unions which carry the implicit threat of higher wages. But unionization itself seems powerless at this stage to cope with the excess labor supply that besieges factory doors as potential strike breakers.

Textiles in the South have grown rapidly—perhaps too rapidly. Within about fifty years they have passed from vigorous youth through maturity to the disorganization of an overdeveloped industry. Well over a billion dollars are invested in southern textiles. New England in 1909 possessed half again as many active spindles as the South. By 1914 the advantage had declined to a third, by 1919 to a fourth, and by 1927 the South was 3,192,030 ahead. From 1921 to 1927 the cotton states increased their percentage of the nation's total cotton yardage from 54 to 67. In the same period the value of the product increased from 44 to 56 per cent, showing that growth in values practically kept pace with the physical output.[27] With a decline in the value of the nation's total product from 1923 to 1925 the South saw an increase of 8,000 in the number of wage earners. In 1927 the South possessed 52 per cent of the nation's spindles, a majority of the active looms, and used 72 per cent of the cotton processed in the nation. In 1930 the cotton states had 59 per cent of the country's textile wage earners, 59 per cent of the spindles, and 72 per cent of active spindle hours. Table XXX shows the trends.

[26] Quoted in G. T. Winston, *A Builder of the New South, A Biography of D. A. Tompkins*, p. 373.

[27] See *The Annals*, American Academy of Political and Social Science, 153, especially Broadus Mitchell, pp. 21-29, and Claudius T. Murchison, pp. 30-42.

TABLE XXX

SPINDLES IN PLACE AND NUMBER OF ACTIVE SPINDLE HOURS, 1921-1931,
BY SECTIONS (YEARS ENDING JULY 31)*

	SPINDLES IN PLACE (In Thousands)					
	1921–22	1923–24	1925–26	1927–28	1929–30	1930–31
New England	18,856	18,575	17,946	15,463	13,478	12,167
Other States	2,014	2,002	1,765	1,568	1,423	1,396
South	16,074	17,226	17,874	18,508	19,122	19,108
Total	36,945	37,804	37,586	35,539	34,024	32,673
South's Percentage	43	45	47	52	56	59
	ACTIVE SPINDLE HOURS (In Millions)					
New England	36,783	30,102	31,541	27,862	23,038	18,757
Other States	4,684	3,658	3,881	3,316	2,598	2,024
South	47,841	50,598	58,517	65,272	61,878	54,482
Total	89,308	84,359	93,941	96,451	87,515	75,263
South's Percentage	53	59	62	67	69	72

*See *Bulletin* 168, Bureau of Census, "Cotton Production and Distribution", 1930-31, pp. 42-45.

Textile management in the South has rested content to exploit the comparative advantage of a cheaper labor supply, and until recently has not looked elsewhere for opportunities of efficiency and coördination. With few alternative avenues of employment the southern labor supply must take its choice of agriculture or the cotton mill. The specialization is, of course, in the Southeast, where two thirds of the industrial workers in South Carolina, one half in North Carolina, and 35 per cent in Georgia are in textiles. The nature of the differentials in labor costs is such that they lead to the establishment in the deep South of many factories whose only chance for profits lies in underselling. This in turn probably epitomizes the process by which mills were brought South. It is discouraging to proponents of stability in the industry to realize that Texas and the Southwest now look at the Piedmont in the same light in which the Piedmont once looked at New England and are prepared to wage aggressive chamber-of-commerce warfare to invite the mills to their cheaper labor. The labor advantage has tended to mask in the balance sheets the symptoms of disorganization in the industry, and its factors of decadence thus have passed unnoticed and uncorrected.

These elements, accentuated by the depression of 1930-32, have been pointed out with vigor and clarity by C. T. Murchison of the University of North Carolina.[28] Briefly stated, his thesis is that cotton manufacturing is an industry caught between two speculative complexes—the price of raw cotton and the rapid changes in styles. Small units incapable of effective consolidation overproduce in the competition incidental to attempts to keep up with both style changes and the gyrating prices of raw cotton. This overproduction brings price levels low enough to result in failure of many marginal mills. These mills are bought up at depreciated values and reënter production with the necessity of making returns only on the marked down values—say fifty cents on the dollar. The remedy is to be sought in horizontal and vertical combinations creating concerns that will be able to exercise a restraining influence on production. The most cheering work in the industry has been the establishment of the Textile Institute with its accent on research improved technique, more orderly production, and a unified social plan.

TABLE XXXI

COTTON MANUFACTURING IN SOUTHERN STATES, 1927-1929

	Number of Establishments	Persons Engaged 1927	Cost of Material, Fuel, Power, etc. 1927 (Thousand Dollars)	Value of Product 1927 (Thousand Dollars)	Cotton Consumed 1929 (Thousand Bales)	Active Cotton Spindles 1929 (In Thousands)	Operating Spindle Hours 192 (In Millions)
Virginia........	11	8,552	$14,177	27,295	209	679	1,584
North Carolina.	383	98,482	184,930	311,155	1,642	6,129	22,143
South Carolina.	163	76,427	135,085	231,272	1,302	5,562	22,559
Tennessee.....	21	7,412	13,589	21,956	275	610	2,350
Georgia........	139	57,764	106,882	180,509	1,288	3,079	11,318
Alabama......	68	25,391	49,850	80,833	622	1,778	6,035
Florida........	..	......	......	......	......	......	......
Mississippi.....	14	2,822	3,682	6,563	43	147	......
Louisiana......	..	......	......	......	44	87	......
Arkansas......	3	325	576	949	22	59	......
Texas.........	26	5,700	11,675	21,125	149	255	797
Oklahoma.....	..	......	......	......	16	32	......
Total South....	828	282,875	520,449	$881,661	5,637	18,423	66,789
South inc. Ky. Md., and Mo.	840	286,418	$527,204	$893,559	5,733	18,613	68,360
The Nation....	1,610	504,688	915,206	1,659,518	7,970	32,417	99,604

[28] *King Cotton Is Sick.*

Rayon Emerges

No longer is it possible to regard the South's emerging rayon industry as an appendage of cotton textiles. Rayon differs so much in its geographic, technological, and economic implications that it points to a very different development.

The capital requirements for entering rayon production are very high. A rayon plant requires an original investment of from three to five millions while larger units are known to take eight and ten millions of capital. After the plant is built it is necessary to wait for months of labor to secure essential technical adjustments before beginning production. Thus while cotton mills were started in the South after 1880 by local capital and initiative, rayon production is open only to interests in command of large blocks of capital along with patent rights to certain technical processes.

Nevertheless, outside capital, much of it from Europe, is seeking the South as a locality for rayon mills. Developments in Virginia, Tennessee, and North Carolina are well known. In 1927 alone fifty millions were invested in rayon production in the South. The American Textile Directory of 1929 lists 35 plants devoted in whole or in part to the production or processing of rayon. Geographic and economic analysis will serve to make clear the reasons for such location. Lockwood, Greene and Company, industrial engineers, have estimated the production costs in rayon as follows: labor, 45 per cent; salaries, 9 per cent; raw materials, 25 per cent; taxes, insurance, and depreciation, 10 per cent; supplies and repairs, 6 per cent; and fuel, light, power, and water, 5 per cent.[29] These factors have been transplanted into terms influencing plant location by a large rayon producer somewhat as follows:

1. Topography of site: a level tract of sixty to eighty acres.
2. Altitude: 1,200 feet or more above sea level.
3. Position: distance from New York not more than 16 to 18 hours by train.
4. Transportation: at least one railroad to connect the site.
5. Water supply: a soft water system with a minimum flow of 50 million gallons daily. For disposal of wastes: site to adjoin a river with not less than 500 to 600 square miles of drainage area above site.

[29] *Rayon a New Influence in the Textile Industry,* Metropolitan Life Insurance Company, p. 11.

6. Labor supply: near city of not less than 10,000, lacking other industries competing for labor.

7. Tax exemptions, etc.: local inducement comparing favorably with others.

It should be pointed out that these specifications do not mention the lowered freight costs to be secured by proximity either to markets or to raw materials. Rayon wood pulp, for example, is shipped all over the world, the International Paper and Pulp Company in 1927 supplying from its Canadian mills 90 per cent of the American and 45 per cent of the world demand by rayon producers.[30] As spruce stands are cut out, chemical research is indicating that the industry may look to sugar cane waste, bagasse, and to the whole cotton plant for its supply of cellulose.

It has been suggested in some quarters that rayon is fated to destroy the whole economy of the cotton belt as well as those of all other cotton producing areas. As yet the industry is too young for anyone to predict with assurance the effect of rayon upon the consumption of cotton. In the short trend from 1923 to 1927 the consumption in the United States of three important fibres increased in the following ratios: cotton, 13.5 per cent; silk, 51.7 per cent; and rayon, 137 per cent. From 1927 to 1930 the production of rayon in the United States increased 43 per cent. The 110 million pounds produced in the United States in 1930 represented the industry's first recession, a decrease of 12 million pounds from 1929. It has been claimed that the increasing use of rayon has not decreased the demand for cotton. While it is known that an increasing number of cotton mills are using rayon in large quantities, it is held that the incidental displacement of cotton by rayon fibres has been compensated for by the increased sales of the more attractive cotton-rayon mixtures. This process of substitution, whether at the expense of silk or cotton, must somewhere reach an equilibrium. Just where it will tend to stabilize the demand for cotton remains a problem for the future when the trends shall become more clearly discernible.[31]

[30] *Rayon*, p. 12.

[31] *Rayon*, p. 22. Consult also: *Artificial Silk Handbook;* M. Avram, *The Rayon Industry;* N. H. Casson, *The Story of Artificial Silk;* United States Tariff Commission, *Information Survey on Artificial Silk*, 1925; Annual Numbers of the *Textile World.*

TABLE XXXII

CLASSIFICATION OF THE SOUTH'S TEXTILE INDUSTRY—1929
American Textile Directory

	Total Plants *	Cotton Mills	Knitting Mills	Woolen Worsted	Rayon Mills	Silk Mills	Dyeing Finishing	Miscellaneous **
Virginia............	102	20	30	15	1	22	2	11
Kentucky..........	45	11	11	8	1	1	3	13
North Carolina......	691	430	189	12	23	30	29	26
Tennessee..........	141	31	79	9	1	6	8	15
South Carolina.....	224	184	15	3	4	6	16	13
Georgia............	242	162	51	7	1	3	9	26
Florida............	8	..	..	..	..	..	..	8
Alabama...........	126	99	22	..	2	1	..	7
Mississippi.........	21	16	3	..	1	1	..	3
Arkansas..........	16	7	2	..	..	..	..	8
Louisiana..........	17	6	2	..	..	..	1	8
Oklahoma..........	16	7	2	..	..	..	..	8
Texas.............	75	36	6	2	1	..	1	33
The South.........	1,724	1,009	412	56	35	70	69	179
The Nation........	9,125	2,104	2,480	1,232	310	1,905	830	1,244

*Mills manufacturing more than one kind of goods are listed under all classifications but count as one mill in total.
**Includes flax, linen, lace, jute, batting waste mills, etc.

THE COAL AND IRON DISTRICT

The southern tip of the South's industrial crescent will be found where the Appalachian ridges gradually slope to the level of the coastal plain of Alabama. There at the end of the great valley, in the development around Birmingham, geology has provided the framework of industrialism in coal and iron. Geography has here interlaced three raw materials: iron ore, coking coal, and fluxing dolomite and limestone. J. Russell Smith writes of this area:

The Alabama iron district is one of the cheapest, if not the cheapest, iron district in the entire world. It possesses a phenomenal natural equipment. Jutting out of the hillsides that flank one side of the broad open valley are thick deposits of iron ore. On the other side of the valley are the coal mines and the coke ovens, and the limestone is at hand. Instead of carrying ore a thousand miles, as at Pittsburgh and the English furnaces, or fuel 600 miles, as at Lake Champlain, the raw materials for these southern furnaces are shifted across the valley by switching engines, and the local supply of cheap black labor helps to give a wonderfully low cost.[32]

[32] *The Story of Iron and Steel,* pp. 66-67.

The extent of nature's resources in this field have been analyzed by Langdon White.[33] The Birmingham district is an elliptical area 75 miles long and 40 miles wide. In its topography, long, narrow, canoe-shaped troughs parallel each other, separated by well defined ridges. In the center of the ellipse lies the city. Through the ridges at distances of two and three miles natural gaps are cut reaching to the valley's level. Through these natural portals enter and depart the railways which serve the city. Within this ellipse are contained the elements fitted to foster and sustain a range of industrial development in the South paralleling that of Pittsburgh and Gary. Lake Superior now furnishes 85 per cent of the iron ore produced in the United States. Birmingham ranks second with reserves estimated to be equally large. At their present rate of exploitation they may be expected to last more than three centuries.

Not all the advantages of iron ore lie with Birmingham. In the Lake Superior field the ore lies at the surface, and great steam shovels scoop up three to five tons at every swing. Ore at Birmingham is underground, costly, difficult and slow to mine. The beds of red hematite ore which outcrop at the surface slant downward with uniform dip and thickness and must be mined by slopes. The best area, the Big Team outcrop of Red Mountain, extends for over 25 miles. Its beds range in thickness from 15 to 28 feet and average 30 to 40 per cent of metallic content. The brown ores are so irregularly spaced in pockets with clay gravel and sand that their development hardly pays. There is a saying that no workman knows a brown ore bank beyond the length of his pick. At best the red ore of this field is low grade, containing less metallic ore per ton than ore of the Mesabi range by some 37 to 50 per cent. In addition, its high ratio of phosphorus has served to render its manufacture into steel a more difficult process.

One would expect to find iron and the limestone of the Great Valley together since iron in solution is precipitated in the limestone strata through which it trickles. Birmingham ore is self fluxing, that is, it contains sufficient limestone for its own reduction. That coal should be found in close proximity is, however, one of the happy accidents of nature. Of the 3,500 square miles in the area more than half are coal-bearing lands of some type. Of the three

[33] "Iron and Steel Industry of the Birmingham, Alabama, District," *Economic Geography*, IV, 349-65. Also *Economic Geography*, V, 327-34.

great coal fields, the Warrior, Cohaba, and Coosa, only the Warrior field is used for coke. The strata lie nearly flat, but faults at right angles operate to make mining difficult. The Pratt seam which has proved the best development lies just west of Birmingham. The Warrior field has enough coking coal to reduce all available ore, a supply estimated in excess of three and a third billion tons. The price of coke is lower in Alabama than at other centers. Since iron making must be carried on, in one story buildings, the process of necessity requires a great deal of space. The geology of iron ore deposits on the other hand usually indicates a rugged topography. In comparison with Pittsburgh, however, Birmingham is favored with plenty of level space for the assembly and reduction of raw materials. Vast quantities of water are required for cooling linings and other parts of the furnace. For this purpose the Birmingham field lacks the natural water supply such as furnished by Pittsburgh's rivers, and its metallurgy must be served by pumping plants and reservoirs.

On the east iron ore, on the west coking coal, in the valley bottom between, fluxing dolomite; such ideal juxtaposition means lower costs. United States' averages require for the production of 100 tons of pig iron, 183 tons of iron ore, 40 tons of limestone, 3 tons of scrap, and 102 tons of coke reduced from 151 tons of coal. Likewise, the production of 100 tons of steel consumes 90 tons of pig iron, 18 tons of scrap, 4 tons of ore, and 120 tons of coal.[34] The assemblage of such bulky materials accounts for much of the cost. In 1926 the freight costs of assembling were $5.58 per ton for Chicago, $4.73 for Pittsburgh, and $2.65 for Birmingham. Entering the cost of production per ton is the wages of the Negro labor of the South which is cheaper than that of any other iron making area and yet comparatively skilled. Langdon White estimated the cost of raw materials per ton in 1926 to be $15.10 at Chicago, $14.50 at Pittsburgh, and $11.27 at Birmingham. Thus in relative costs of assembling and manufacturing its materials Birmingham occupies the most strategic position in the pig iron industry. The city's handicaps, however, show up in steel production.

Because of their great bulk and weight, freight costs enter largely into the ultimate price of iron and steel products to con-

[34] Richard Hartshorne, "Iron and Steel Industry of the United States," *Journal of Geography*, XXVIII, 133-53.

sumers. While the tonnage of steel is less than half that of the iron ore and the coal required as raw materials, the freight cost of shipping is twice as great. Nearness to great centers of industrial and building activity is thus one of the prime factors in creating a great steel area. Birmingham, for instance, has lost the trade it once held north of the Ohio and along the Atlantic seaboard because of increases in transportation costs. The region can, however, compete successfully with Chicago and Pittsburgh in about one third of the United States where dwell one third of the people—roughly all the South and much of the far Southwest. The city, however, is its own best market, 86 per cent of its pig iron and 50 per cent of its steel being absorbed in local manufactures.

In foreign commerce the city is well located for the Latin-American trade, yet exploits it but little. A step in that direction is found in the recently developed inland waterways. From the Black Warrior River this waterway reaches the Gulf through Mobile by means of many locks and dams. Mobile possesses a spacious harbor. The inland waterways do not, as has been said, make Birmingham to all intents a seaport. The city, it must be remembered, is far inland; 270 miles from Mobile, and 354 from New Orleans. Since the iron plants are not located on river banks, rail carriage and transhipment are necessary. The waterways, however, afford transportation at about 80 per cent of prevailing railroad freight rates and in time may come to rival the Monongahela as a great carrier for barges of iron, steel, and coal. Alabama takes one of the first ranks among states with navigable waterways, possessing over 800 miles.

In spite of the favors of geography, the iron and steel industry in the South was slow in its beginnings and development. Like everything southern, the industry was retarded by lack of capital and technical skill. In 1870, Birmingham was a cotton field in which two railroads happened to cross. Railroad officials bought up the land, laid out a town, precipitated a boom, and watched it collapse. The foundations remained. In 1876 pig iron was first successfully made at the old Oxmoor furnaces with coke as a fuel. The Pratt mines of coking coal were first opened in 1879. In 1888 Birmingham saw its first ton of steel run through the furnaces of the Henderson Steel Company and burn out the crude furnace linings in the process. In 1899 the first open hearth steel was made in the area. In mining the first stage consisted of tracking the beds along the outcrops and mining from the open cut. The second stage followed the open cut down the incline with underground work. As Pittsburgh was synonymous with steel, Birmingham came to mean pig iron. For a long time with no local market available, Birmingham produced the cheapest pig iron in the country and sold it at ruinously low prices—ofttimes to competitors who promptly made it up into steel. The industry has, nevertheless, made Birmingham the largest city of equal age within the bounds of the old South. It did not, however, make the fortunes of the men who managed the industry nor did it conserve the professional reputation of its technical experts. For instance, while the production of pig iron in the United States, from 1902 to 1910, had increased 45 per cent, production in the South had remained practically at a standstill. A representative blast furnace at Pittsburgh produced 16,000 tons of steel a month, while one identical in size at Ensley was turning out but 10,000 tons. The coal in its fields was handled less cheaply than in other sections; the labor while cheap in many ways was dear in reality because of lack of skill; the steel was manufactured at too high a cost. Andrew Carnegie had told the officers: "You have coal and iron and dolomite all here in close proximity, but you cannot make steel." The period of ruinous competition and failures came to an end for the southern industry when the United States Steel Corporation took over the Tennessee Coal, Iron and Railroad Company in 1907.[35]

Since that date the industry has come to be regarded as national rather than sectional in its implications. The forward movement of the district under the guidance of George Gordon Crawford has served to accent the dire handicap of lack of capital and technical skill under which the industry previously labored. Crawford realized the inadequacies and obstacles inherent in the geographic and industrial situation, and described them honestly and frankly in technical journals.

If the factor of proximity were decisive Birmingham would no doubt stand higher. In the three decades 1910 to 1929 her iron output increased 25.7 per cent yet Alabama's share of the national production, never large, decreased from 8.5 per cent to 6.3 per cent,

[35] Edwin Mims, *The Advancing South,* pp. 94-95.

during this period. Certain disadvantages of the mining field account for the small part Birmingham plays in American steel. In spite of improved technology under United States Steel, the low grade of Alabama ore averaging less than 37 per cent in iron content, the necessity of mining ore, as contrasted with the advantage of stripping ore in the Great Lakes Region, and the distance from markets all operate to place Alabama at a comparative disadvantage.

The coal fields are badly disturbed geologically making the expense of mining very much higher, and the ore is nearly all hard ore, requiring to be drilled, blasted, and crushed. Further, the low iron content requires the use of about one and three quarters times or as much again of coke to make a ton of iron as compared with that coming from the Lake Superior district.

The high phosphorous content of southern pig iron prevents the use of the cheaper Bessemer process which is used on the low phosphorous pig iron of the northern district and the fact that no Bessemer steel industry exists in the South to furnish the scrap required in the straight open-hearth process prevents the economical use of this process in the South a disadvantage which does not exist in the North where scrap is available. Hence it is advisable to use a combination of the two processes, the iron being first bessemerized, then worked through the open-hearth furnace.[36]

This duplex process, of course, adds greatly to the cost of converting pig iron into steel.

Crawford thus found that the low price asked for pig iron at

TABLE XXXIII

SOUTHERN IRON OUTPUT

	Ore Mined (Thousand Tons)			Pig Iron Production (Thousand Tons)		
	1910	1928	1929	1910	1928	1929
North Carolina.................	65	.....	34	.....	.....	.....
Tennessee.....................	732	129	98	397	110	138
Georgia.......................	313	73	63	.....	.....	.....
Alabama......................	4,801	6,307	6,435	1,939	2,546	2,709
Total.....................	6,512	6,510	6,630	2,336	2,657	2,849
Total Southern States...........	6,923	6,537	6,630	3,272	3,917	4,014
The Nation....................	56,889	62,197	73,283	27,305	38,155	42,613

[36] Arundel Cotter, *United States Steel, a Corporation with a Soul*, pp. 81-82.

TABLE XXXIV

SOUTH'S COAL RESOURCES AND PRODUCTION, 1900-1929

STATE	Estimated Coal Land Area in Sq. Miles, 1924	Coal Reserves Exclusive of Lignite, Million Short Tons, 1924	COAL PRODUCTION			
			In Millions of Tons, 1900	In Millions of Tons, 1910	In Millions of Tons, 1928	In Millions of Tons, 1929
1. Virginia........	2,120	22,000	2.3	6.5	11.9	13.1
2. Kentucky......	16,000	123,000	5.3	14.6	61.8	60.5
3. North Carolina .	800	200	....	....	....	....
4. Tennessee......	4,400	25,500	3.5	7.1	5.6	5.7
5. South Carolina..	......	....	....	....	....	....
6. Georgia........	170	925	.3	.1	....	....
7. Florida.........	......	....	....	....	....	....
8. Alabama.......	8,500	67,500	8.3	16.1	17.6	17.7
9. Mississippi....	......	....	....	....	....	....
10. Arkansas.......	1,700	1,800	1.4	1.9	1.6	1.8
11. Louisiana......	......	....	....	....	....	....
12. Oklahoma......	15,000	55,000	1.9	2.6	5.6	5.7
13. Texas.........	11,000	8,000	.9	1.8	1.1	1.0
The South......	59,690	303,925	22.4	50.9	105.4	105.7
The Nation.....	496,776	1,518,212	269.6	501.3	576.0	608.9

Birmingham could be laid to bad bookkeeping and the practice of skimming the cream of the mine rather than to the efficiency in production.[37]   Labor-saving devices, efficiency systems, and a diversified industry for the utilization of by-products came to help solve the problems he met. The American Steel and Wire Company was organized for the manufacture of nails and wire fence. Coke oven plants were constructed to conserve such by-products as ammonia, tar, and gas.   Another plant transformed phosphatic slag into fertilizer.   Great water reservoirs, increased trackage and elevated railways, by-product plants, and plants for the manufacture of the finest grades of steel are among the results achieved. Moreover, in sanitary, health, and housing provisions the villages laid out at Fairfield are models of their kind.

A glance at the extent of the industry may well close this brief survey.   In the field of mining in 1925 Alabama produced coal valued at $42,422,000 and iron ore worth $14,134,677.   These two products amounted to over 75 per cent of the state's mineral products and yet it is noteworthy that they equalled only one fifth the value of its agricultural products.   The coal mines employed dur-

[37] Edwin Mims, op. cit., pp. 92-112.

ing 1924 27,956 workers an average of 220 days each. In iron mines during 1924 there were employed 7,156 men for 275 average days. Alabama ranks third in the United States in the number of blast furnaces. Their total output in 1925 was valued at $54,331,148. In the manufacture of cast iron pipe, Alabama leads the country with a total production of $46,185,000 out of $100,388,000. The state had in 1925, 27,500 workers engaged in all phases of iron and steel production, producing a total output valued at $194,000,000. In Alabama these developments are limited to Gadsden and Anniston, and in the Birmingham district the towns of Bessemer, Ensley, Fairfield, Oxmoor, North Birmingham, Thomas, and Woodward. In Tennessee the industry centering around Chattanooga employs more than 5,800 men credited with an output of over $26,500,000.[38]

Tobacco Manufacturing

Tobacco has performed an astounding economic somersault. Formerly of great importance agriculturally, it has become of much greater importance industrially. Once it supported a colonial economy and sustained the agricultural aristocracy of Virginia. Today its growers hardly receive returns for time and trouble invested. Industrially, however, the product has created half a dozen powerful corporations, accumulated capital reserves for the exploitation of southern resources, and lifted the first southern millionaires out of the dead level of post-war poverty. The industry may be regarded as the first phase of southern industrialism to rise out of the soil. Whereas cotton milling has to some extent been a migrant industry, moving from the North, tobacco manufacturing is indigenous to the region. Not so basically linked to the resources complex as water power or the steel industry, the industry finds its geographic foundation in nearness to the raw material of the bright tobacco belt. In more than one manufacturing plant it has demonstrated that keen business acumen in exploiting a native product could be developed in the South. The industry occupies the northern tip of the Piedmont Crescent centering the bright tobacco belt. North Carolina manufactures over half the cigarettes in the country, having more than three times the output of New York, its nearest rival. Its share of total tobaccos fabricated is slightly over one third.

[38] Hager, *Commercial Survey of the Southeast*, pp. 103, 132.

The greatest contribution of the industry has been in the field of management. It ranks among the highest in the value added to products by manufacturing. In few industries is there found so great a spread between the price of raw materials and that of the finished product. The industry moreover has shown itself among the least subject to cycles of business decline and depression. This stability extends both to employment and the payment of dividends. Not only have earnings been uniform; they have been uniformly high. A report by the Standard Statistics Company showed that for 849 railroad, public utility, and industrial corporations in 1924 the average returns were 6.25 per cent. For 22 representative tobacco companies they were 11 per cent and at no time between 1920 and 1924 did they fall below 10 per cent.[39] In the earlier days factories, small and scattered, were devoted to the preparation of cheap, black smoking tobacco and chewing plug. They added little to the value of the product, failed to produce a standardized grade and produced no famous brands. The finer smoking and plug tobaccos were imported from abroad. The art had not yet been acquired in the home of tobacco.

The consumption of tobacco is subject to shifting trends in intimate personal habits, and it is in attempting both to follow and to lead the vagaries of social psychology that management has shown itself most alert. The habit once begun is rarely stopped, so that the more significant trends have been found in the acquisition of new consumers and the shift among types and blends. From the beginning tobacco was used for pipe smoking. The habit of chewing developed among the colonists and caught the favor of sailors who spread it to all parts of the globe. The popularity of chewing tobacco appears to have reached its peak in 1897. Cigars first sprang into prominence at the beginning of the 19th century and appear to have reached their highest point in public favor during the period 1870 to 1905. The cigarette has long been smoked in Russia and Turkey whence it spread to France and England at the close of the Crimean War in 1856. The appeal of the cigarette spread to America around 1860 and the Civil War operated to diffuse the popularity of southern tobacco over the entire country. The story of the stripping by Sherman's soldiers of John R. Green's little factory near Durham, and of threatened ruin averted by floods of or-

[39] Charles D. Barney and Co., *The Tobacco Industry 1926*, pp. 23-25.

ders for that Durham smoking tobacco from the disbanded soldiers has often been recounted.[40]   Although at first hand-rolled by the consumer, the cigarette easily lent itself to machine production. Against a wave of taxation, prohibitory legislation, and agitation backed by many types of reformers, the industry made its way. Henry Ford for instance sponsored the publication of a pamphlet, *The Little White Slave,* and rumor that the paper wrapper was soaked in life-sapping chemicals could not be laid.   At one time the campaign against the cigarette reached such strength that James B. Duke was preparing to switch his factories to the making of little cigars on short notice.

The early discovery of the art of blending Turkish leaf with domestic tobacco increased the popularity of smoking.   About 80 per cent native to 20 per cent Turkish compose most of the blends, and over 75 per cent of the cigarettes are so made.   From 1900 to 1924 cigarette production increased twentyfold.   The World War stabilized the popularity of cigarettes.   The production of tax paid cigarettes which was less than 17 billion in 1914 jumped to 71 billion by 1924.   Smoking proved a diversion and solace to war-sick soldiers, and providing cigarettes furnished patriotic activity to earnest civilians.   Most of the increase since 1922 may be credited to an incoming army of women smokers.   Begun as a fad, continued as a habit, smoking among women has pushed over many old taboos and has been accepted as the index of a social movement. In the midst of these vagaries of changing personal taste management has used advertising in an attempt to ride and direct the waves of public favor.[41]   It has set new standards in sensational display in the use of placards, radio, billboards, newspapers, and testimonials from the "near great."   Restrictive legislation has retreated before the advance of public favor, but over-exploitation has "set in motion certain currents of antipathy which have ominous possibilities."   Large relative decreases in smoking, chewing, cigar, and snuff tobacco have represented transference of established tobacco habits to the cigarette.

The blend and the machine afford sufficient explanation to account for the success of the cigarette.   The process leading to

---

[40] See W. K. Boyd, *Story of Durham,* pp. 57-62.

[41] Charles D. Barney and Co., *The Tobacco Industry, 1924,* pp. 19-23; *1928,* p. 4.

the blend whether highly technical or not is carefully guarded. Between the harvest and the finished product the manufacturer keeps his tobacco in storage from one and a half to three years. Redistributed and reördered according to the classification demanded by blends, the leaf is passed into cooling chambers, packed into hogsheads under pressure and placed in great storage warehouses to age. There it remains two years, more or less, and undergoes two natural sweats each year. Before blending, the stems are removed and the leaf cleaned of dirt and grit, losing 30 per cent of their weight in the process. Blending, the process which imparts the distinctive flavor, is the most highly guarded of all trade secrets. After various type leaves are mixed in proper proportions they are conditioned for 24 hours, and then run through the cutting machines which reduce them to shreds. Ingenious machines at one operation wrap the shreds in paper in long tubes, cut, pack, seal, and stamp at the rate of 500 a minute. If the blend courts repeated sales by insuring a standardized flavor, it is the machine which has placed tobacco in the class of the billion dollar industries. The blend represented by a brand has become the weapon of warfare in competition. It must be established in public favor and kept there by advertising.

The cigarette manufacturing machine on the other hand has proved no less a weapon of competitive struggle. James Buchanan Duke, surrounded in the industry's early days by intense competition in producing smoking tobacco, found himself unable to stem the rival tide of Bull Durham's popularity and decided to go into a new field, cigarettes. Cigarette rolling was a handicraft unknown to the local workmen of North Carolina and skilled "rollers" had to be smuggled in from Russia where cigarette making was a government monopoly. Two brothers, Russian Jews, were imported by Duke to introduce the technique. It was a costly process, and, when James Bonsack of Virginia invented a cigarette machine for leasing to factories on a royalty basis, Duke was one of the first to take hold of it. Duke installed the machines and captured Bonsack's young Irish mechanic, O'Brien, in charge of the installation. O'Brien became the mechanical genius of the firm.[42] The machine, when it made cigarettes amenable to large scale centralized production by un-

[42] J. W. Jenkins, *James B. Duke, Master Builder, passim.*

skilled labor, reduced the cost of their manufacture from 80 cents a thousand to 39 cents. A comparison with cigars brings out significant contrasts. The value of output of cigarettes is much higher than that of cigars; cigar manufacturing, however, employs five times as many laborers. These workmen, being skilled, draw a higher average wage than those in cigarettes. Moreover, while a greater proportionate quantity of leaf is used in smoking tobacco and snuff, the total value of an equal bulk of cigarettes in the manufactured state is nearly twice as great.

The strategic position of the machine and the brand soon led to an attempt at monopoly. It is noteworthy that one of the first and most powerful of the "trusts" in America was engineered by a southern business man using southern capital in the exploitation of a southern product. J. B. Duke had out-distanced competitors by the use of an efficient machine and had cut the price of a package of cigarettes to five cents. There were on the market for sale or lease several machines, and retaliation inaugurated a period of strenuous competition. Duke set out to acquire the brands and business of competitors, and in 1890 effected the consolidation of five of the more powerful companies into the American Tobacco Company. Small independent manufacturers, unable to stand the strain of price-cutting, sold out. Their owners either retained their position with the company or agreed to retire from tobacco. By 1893 the corporation controlled 93 per cent of the cigarette output. By 1900 through a subsidiary company, the Continental Tobacco Company, it had extended its control over 63 per cent of the plug and 61 per cent of the pipe tobacco output. Another subsidiary, the American Snuff Company, enabled the combine to claim 67 per cent of the country's snuff production. By extension of its influence over other properties, the trust came to own the firms producing the licorice, tinfoil, and boxes used in the preparation and packing of tobacco. It was in the attempt to dominate the cigar industry, however, that Duke met failure. The combine was said never to have controlled more than 16 per cent. Small scattered units dependent upon skilled handwork rather than machine production did not prove amenable to the program of consolidation and overhead economies.

By 1907 the American Tobacco Company purchased 70 to 80 per cent of all tobacco grown in the United States; controlled 75 per cent of the cigarette trade, 70 per cent of the smoking tobacco, 81 per cent of the chewing, and 89 per cent of the little cigars.

The culture of tobacco had spread enormously, the price to farmers had fallen, sales had mounted skyward, and the combine, known and feared throughout the country, was growing rich. Under the Sherman Anti-Trust Law in 1907 the government opened suit against the company as a monopoly in restraint of trade. Its dissolution was ordered in 1911, and Duke assumed the burden of reorganization by distributing the various brands and segregating the stock among the component companies. The eggs were legally unscrambled, and yet the reorganization conserved the gains achieved in the years of the mergers. The brands, for example, were distributed among the various companies so that each corporation retained the relative share of the trade with which it entered the trust. Discrepancies have arisen since the dissolution as, for example, the rapid rise of Camels which has given the R. J. Reynolds corporation a disproportionate share of the cigarette trade.[43]

The tobacco industry of the Piedmont, concentrated in a few centers of Virginia, Kentucky, Tennessee, and North Carolina, furnishes its share of employment and capital to sustain the industrialization of the section. North Carolina is the first state in the fabrication of tobacco, producing one third of all the United States supplies. It accounts for over 60 per cent of the cigarette and one

TABLE XXXV

PRODUCTION OF TOBACCO IN THE SOUTH, 1929

1930	NUMBER OF FACTORIES MAKING			PRODUCTION 1929			
	Tobacco and Snuff	Cigars	Cigarettes	Tobacco Snuff (1,000 lbs.)	Cigars (Millions)		Cigarettes (Millions)*
					Large	Small	
Virginia..........	8	40	7	19,964	378.7	312.2	24,045.5
Kentucky.........	35	56	3	17,652	66.5	.....	3,706.0
North Carolina.....	12	19	7	127,353	11.3	36.1	75,135.4
Tennessee.........	17	29	..	20,032	78.7	.....	....
Florida...........	2	270	1	5	617.5	.....	3.7
Louisiana..........	1	46	1	89	70.9	.....	2.7
The South........	75	460	19	185,093	1,223.6	348.3	102,893.3
The Nation........	874	6,780	110	381,200	6,518.5	419.8	122,329.3
South's Per Cent...	8.5	6.9	17.2	48.8	18.7	82.9	84.0

*Does not include 9,952.000 large cigarettes.

[43] C. D. Barney, *op. cit., passim;* also Jenkins, *op. cit., passim.*

fourth of the smoking and chewing tobacco. It ranks as the third industry in the state in number of wage earners and size of payroll. In total value of products it ranks second. It has shown rapid and regular growth, and "compared with the textile industry on the whole supports a higher purchasing power."[44] The year 1925 registered a gain of about 16 per cent over 1923. Then 15,715 employees received $12,000,215 for the production of goods valued at $343,075,607. The 2,600-odd salaried employees received an additional six million dollars. The fact that the industry is comparatively unaffected by depression in other lines makes it important as a stabilizing influence in the business life of the Piedmont.

FURNITURE

The manufacture of furniture has come to rank third among North Carolina's industries, while High Point is the Piedmont synonym for Grand Rapids. In 1888 three young business men with a capital of $10,000 erected a plant at High Point to take advantage of the abundant hardwoods. They found labor plentiful but unskilled, and by 1890 the town boasted six small factories. By 1928 the state possessed 108 plants. In 1921 the South furnished 16.9 per cent of the nation's carload shipments, and by 1925 the section furnished the point of origin for 29.8 per cent of the national shipments of furniture. In a period during which the nation doubled its furniture output the South multiplied its production by four. In 1921 High Point completed at a cost of $1,200,000 its furniture exposition building of ten floors and 208,000 square feet of exhibition space, the second largest in the country. The production of High Point is classified as cheaper grades, 15 per cent, medium grades, 70 per cent, and fine grades, 15 per cent. There exists a trend to higher grades because of increasing skill of workers and increasing expense of materials in the Piedmont. Quantity production and low cost labor are coming to be supplemented by research in designing, in manufacturing processes, and in the study of public tastes. High Point with a population gain of 156 per cent in the decade 1920-30 possessed but 36,708 inhabitants in 1930. Its factories, however, draw hardwoods from the Mississippi Valley, mahogany from Africa, cane and rattan from Singapore and the Philippines, burlap from India, hardware and fabrics from

[44] Hager, *Commercial Survey of the Southeast,* pp. 130-32.

New England, and plate glass from the Pittsburgh district. In 1925, furniture making employed in North Carolina, Tennessee, and Georgia 26,610 workers who turned out products valued at $56,267,000. Of these North Carolina's 10,324 workers manufactured $40,073,000 worth of goods. The state now ranks sixth in the production of household furniture and eighth in the value of all furniture.

CHAPTER XIII

THE SOUTH MEETS THE WEST

FROM Coast to Piedmont across Highlands and Delta the South stalked to its last great frontier, the area of the Southwest. Differing from the South in many of its characteristics, the region was forced to capitulate as the newest province of the Cotton Kingdom. By its climate, its population elements, and its economy the South and the Southwest were fairly met. The adherence of Texas to the Confederacy further ratified its southern antecedents. The area's natural landscape is by no means a replica of that of the old South. The Southwest offers no such scheme for the physiographer as the valley section of the Southeast. Oklahoma and Texas together form a great inclined tableland sloping from an altitude of over four thousand feet, attained in the Panhandle, to the Gulf. Were it not for the fact that the majority of this area is prairie and plain this great expanse would lack any unifying physical factor. One writer says "It is impossible to lie about Texas. Tell a thousand contradictory things and if you seem to lie it is because you have told only a part of the truth." It is almost equally difficult to present a coherent picture of the physical regions of the Southwest.[1]

First comes the Coastal Prairies, a flat treeless area which fringes the Gulf and extends inland in a width varying from thirty to a hundred miles. It has a slope of about one foot to the mile and is broken in by peninsulas, deltas, and sand bar islands until it meets the sea. In the South the plain of the Rio Grande extends landward along the river course until it reaches the Edwards Plateau. Parallel to the Coastal Prairies come the Interior Flatwoods, a flat sandy soil covered with piney woods and joined on the north by the Interior Plains. Just to the west comes Texas' famous Black Waxy, covered with prairie grasses and underlaid with limestone. Beyond a long narrow strip of forest-bearing sandy soil called the

[1] See E. T. Dumble, *The Geology of Texas,* Rice Institute Pamphlets, III, 125-204

East Cross Timbers comes the Grand Prairie, hillier and drier than the Black Waxy. West of that comes a larger expanse of sandy soil covered with forests, the West Cross Timbers.

The limestone areas furnish a close-textured soil perfectly adapted for grass, the natural enemy of trees. The sandy soils on the other hand produce nothing so well as pine forests. Separated from the prairies by eastward-facing escarpments are the plateaus of West Texas, the Edwards Plateau, and the Staked Plains. These reach to Texas' highest mountain, El Capitan, of 8,690 feet altitude, a part of the Western Cordillera on the very borders of New Mexico. The contrast between these various regions is well marked in the case noted by J. Russell Smith of the Balcones Escarpment which divides Travis County with Austin in the center into two parts. One, the Black Waxy, "looks like the prairies of Illinois—cultivated, having good farm buildings, and worth from fifty to three hundred dollars per acre. In the Edwards Plateau the people have little patches of cleared lands in the valleys. Their cattle run in the woods and they make their money by hauling wood and charcoal to Austin. Many of these people are from southern Appalachia and live and think much as these more isolated mountaineers do."[2] The Panhandle, called Llano Estacado or Staked Plains by the Spaniards, "knows winters piercingly cold with northers, the rangers say, straight from the Pole broken only by barbed wire fences."[3] With their semi-arid climate these areas belong with the great Plains Region. It has been described as a country where one can look farthest and see less, possessed of more rivers and less water, more cows and less milk. "All hell needs is fine water and good society" is the way the cowboys expressed it. Another legend runs: "The temperature's a hundred and ten; too cold for the devil and too hot for men." The meridian of 98° longitude thus marks a transition line to a factor of greater importance for the Southwest than the area's topography of plain and prairie. West of this line the average yearly rainfall is less than twenty inches—oftentimes so much less as to imperil the section's whole settled area. Accordingly Texas still contains the largest undeveloped section in an area of equable climate in the United States.

[2] *North America*, pp. 247-48.
[3] George Clifton Edwards, "Texas, the Big Southwestern Specimen," in E. Gruenning (ed.), *These United States,* I, 307.

It has been the especial achievement of Professor Walter Prescott Webb to show that the entrance of settlers into this environment involved a change of institutions and culture. East of the Mississippi civilization stood on three legs—land, water, and timber; west of the 98th meridian not one but two of these legs were withdrawn—water and timber—and civilization was left on one leg—land.[4] The lack of timber abolished the old worm style split-rail fence, leaving nothing in its place to restrain wild cattle until the emergence of barbed wire. The replacement of tree lands by grass lands made the horse a paramount factor, an American ship of the steppes, and involved the change from the long rifle to the Colt six-shooter for rapid-fire work against galloping Indians. The scarcity of water led to dry-farming, ranching instead of agriculture, irrigation, wind mills, and fantastic attempts at rain making. It also changed the English common law of waters to the doctrine of prior appropriation.

Oklahoma lacks some of the variety of the Texas landscape. Of all the southern states it alone lacks navigable waters. Its area is mainly plains and prairies, and it is the most wind blown state in the Union. Southeastern Oklahoma is a part of the Southern Ozarks centering in Arkansas. To the West are the Eastern Oklahoma Prairies which with the Red Prairies make up most of the state. A small strip of Cross Timbers, a few sand hills along western rivers, some broken and eroded plains, and a touch of the Staked Plains complete the physical regions of this latest arrival in the Cotton Kingdom.

According to some analyses Arkansas and Louisiana are taken with Oklahoma and Texas to make up the section called the Southwest. In most respects, however, these easterly neighbors lack the distinctive aspects of Oklahoma and Texas. They have been settled longer and have thus long since passed through certain stages of the frontier and open range. Neither state touches on the Great Plains and thus they have always been more southern than western both in geography and culture. The eastern fringes of the two states and all of the New Orleans district belong with the Delta. Northern Arkansas belongs with the Ozarks. While Southern Louisiana possesses an enviable part of the port business of the Gulf, Arkansas takes rank along with Mississippi as the least indus-

[4] *The Great Plains*, p. 9.

trialized of the southern states. In their industries based on oil and natural gas the two states most resemble the Southwest, and the industry will be discussed in that connection. Ranching and the oil industry, together with the new type of cotton culture, make up the distinctive economic background of the Southwest.

From Frontier to Ranch

The transition from the frontier to the ranch offers the open sesame to much of the development of the Southwest. As long as it clung to the wooded valley slopes of the Eastern Coast the frontier remained a comparatively narrow belt. The frontier changed its ecology when it debouched from its wooded slopes upon the plains at the second tier of states beyond the Mississippi-Ohio system. Within a decade after the Civil War, as E. E. Dale has pointed out, the frontier expanded until it equalled the area of the agricultural region east of the Mississippi.[5] From this river to the Rockies and beyond stretched a new ranching area. Never had the American frontier loomed spatially so large.

The fundamental fact of geography is that the frontier here met grass lands rather than forests. Amid the tall grasses of the prairie and the short grasses of the plains it assumed a pastoral rather than a wilderness structure. The eastern squatters, establishing cowpens in the canebrakes or holding cornfield clearings against the encroaching wilderness, lived on a small scale. The herder, not the hunter, blazed the trail of the plains frontier. The sudden expansion of the fringe when it reached the region was simply the metamorphosis of the squatter into the rider of the open range. What has been called the problem of the "penetrability of the forest" no longer existed and the mode of life became a function of magnificent distances. For the hunted animals of the brush were substituted the domesticated animals of native pastures. The buffalo, the prairie fire, the less abundant rainfall and its seasonal distribution had stimulated the growth of grasses at the expense of forests. It only remained for the frontiersmen to take to horse.

The conquest of the plains by the frontier waited on the destruction of the region's equilibrium of native plants and animals. The extermination of the buffalo, completed for the southern herd

---

[5] "History of the Ranch Cattle Industry in Oklahoma," American Historical Association, *Report,* 1920, p. 307.

by 1875 and the northern herd by 1884, opened the way for the expansion of the open range. With the passing of free game the nomadism of the Plains Indian was at an end. It was thereafter a comparatively easy task for the government to hold the tribes herded on reservations and feed them on contractor's beef. With the Indian and the buffalo gone, the advancing emigrants substituted a pastoral for a hunting economy. In the place of the buffalo came the Longhorn, and for the buffalo hunt was substituted the round-up. The adobe hut in the limitless expanses took the place of the log hut in the clearing.

In Texas, the South met the West against a background of Spanish culture which was to lend color to the whole pastoral economy. Both the cattle and the ranch were a heritage from Spain and the Mexicans. Together they diverted what began as an advance of the Cotton Kingdom upon new plantations to an extension of the ranching frontier. Texas became the reservoir of cattle for the whole west. Early cleared of Indians, it possessed the stock brought in by the Spaniards as early as Coronado in 1540. Later in the seventeenth century Father King had introduced a form of ranching into Arizona with the labor performed by the Indians around his mission. Many horses and cattle escaped and bred wild, so that Louis St. Dennis in 1714 found cattle in abundance in parts of Texas. These small, half wild Spanish beasts which gave little milk and did not fatten well, were hardy and hustling. They were thus well-adapted to the range and were to leave as their descendants the Texas Longhorns, for a while the undisputed bovine masters of the plains.[6]

The western cowboy is a cultural descendant of the South American *gaucho* and the Mexican *vaquero*. For two centuries before our West the lasso and the branding iron had been the tools of the *vaquero's* trade on Mexican *haciendas*. When Austin framed a civil and criminal code for his American settlers, his Spanish political chief added only two articles. The first regulated the disposal of stray cattle, and the second provided for registering cattle brands. This action serves to show that ranching, already in Mexican economy, had not yet entered that of the American settlers.[7] In

[6] See Clara M. Love, "Cattle Industry of the Southwest," *Southwestern Historical Quarterly*, XIX, 370-99.

[7] Louis J. Wortham, *A History of Texas From Wilderness to Commonwealth*, V, 138.

the hundred mile strip between the Nueces and the Rio Grande the cattle business developed. Until Texas established her authority here at the close of the Mexican War the area remained a kind of no man's land where wild cattle multiplied to the point of saturation. James M. Cook in his *Fifty Years on the Old Frontier* tells of what it meant to capture those wild cattle. Here also developed the area of the first big cattle ranches, and in driving, roping, herding, and corralling these feral beasts the American cowboy learned his trade from the *vaquero*.[8]

At the time of annexation there existed no market for beef, and from the meagre trade in hides no one could have predicted the palmy days of ranching. So cheap was beef that the folkways of the range allowed a hungry wayfarer to kill a beef for his sustenance provided he turned the hide over to its owner. The Civil War left Texas the least injured of all the southern states. Cattle had increased rapidly, and the Texas soldier returned to find his cattle grown fat and numerous but with no market. At Christmas 1865, however, the Union Stockyards of Chicago opened for business.[9] The event which passed unnoticed on the plains was to open for Texas the era of the free range.

The interval between the passing of the Indian and the coming of legal private owners of the land was the era of the open range, "the golden age of the old time cattleman."[10] For an all too brief period there existed more grass than cattle, a period in which it was not necessary to own land to be a cattle king. Grass rights, range rights, water rights on a free prairie were unwritten laws with owners far away. Live and let-live policies prevailed. Ill-feeling, threats, bluffs, and fights were of small avail in keeping newcomers from crowding on the range. In an area of great expanses it was impossible to assert claims of ownership as the following story from California shows:

A man who came to the state with some cattle bought a large stock ranch. Other cattle ranged over it and he was helpless. He found that the cost was too great to fence it, and told his story thus: So, I just found a purchaser for my land, sold it to him and then purchased more cattle with the money I had thus obtained, and left my cattle to roam wherever

[8] *Ibid.*, V, 141-42.
[9] *Ibid.*, V, 157.
[10] H. Y. Benedict and John A. Lomax, *The Book of Texas*, pp. 166-88.

they pleased; and my whole herd continued, despite my purchaser's efforts, to roam just as much on this very land as they did whilst I owned it.[11]

Texas early worked out that unique adaptation of free land to private property in cattle which the movies and wild west thrillers have made known around the world. "The range," says an economic historian, "applies to the raising and fattening of cattle upon public lands or unfenced lands, generally where the herds of different proprietors are free to range and intermingle; whereas the ranch cattle business is carried on within the enclosure belonging to cattlemen on which their own cattle graze."[12] The land on which a cow was found offered no indication as to whom that cow belonged. Accordingly, property in brands as distinguishing marks on cattle came to be recognized by the ranching community, and these marks were registered in semi-official brand books.

The frontiersmen's method of organization arose. The Texas Cattle Raisers' Association, for example, turned back 80,000 head of stolen cattle and prevented the theft of thousands of others. The round-up, held for the purpose of branding the young calves each spring, thus had to be a joint affair. Everybody helped, and in the spring each outfit sent out its chuck wagon accompanied by a cook and five to thirty cow hands, with five or ten times as many horses. Each outfit aided in the process of "cutting out the stock" and then branded its own calves. In cutting out the stock they sorted cattle into smaller herds by brands, and thus each outfit shunted cattle nearer their home ranch. "A cow was often passed from round-up to round-up without her owner ever seeing her until she reached the home corral." If left unbranded, a calf became a "maverick," so named after a lawyer who neglected a herd he had accepted in payment of debt. The law of the range gave the maverick to whatever stockmen put a brand upon him. Thence grew cattle "rustling," which began as search for unherded cattle and became the clever changing of marks and the branding of the other stockgrowers' unweaned calves. "Your calves don't suck the right cows" was the frontier preacher's call to repentance which every old Texan appreciates.

[11] *Transactions,* California Agricultural Society, 1861, p. 153. Quoted by Love, *op. cit.,* pp. 376-77.
[12] Isaac Lippincott, *Economic Development of the United States,* p. 401.

Gold in California made one market for the live stock industry. The rise of Chicago as a meat packing center after the Civil War opened a greater. No longer could it be said in Texas that a man's poverty was measured by the number of cattle he owned. The number of cattle doubled almost every decade. As early as 1866 began the great drives to reach the nearest shipping points of the railroads creeping westward. It is estimated that in all five to six million head were driven north. Many herds went to the high plains and the fresh grasses of Montana and Wyoming so that Texas became known as the breeding ground and Montana the feeding ground. As the railroad came nearer, the trail for the long drives shortened, and the characteristic western cow towns, points of cattle shipment, saw their boom periods follow each other in rapid succession. Free grass and open markets had invited so many investors that prices reached $20 per head, range delivery. Men had seen great herds grow from small beginnings and had made money even when forced to borrow at extortionate rates.

The end of the open range was sudden and dramatic. The day of the stock ranch was ushered in by the invention of a "gadget" in the shape of barbed wire. The range had been overstocked so that grass was exhausted and destroyed, eaten and trampled underfoot before it could reseed. In 1886 came the year of the "great dies," and drought and hard winter followed. The panic of 1893 knocked the bottom out of cattle prices. Land began to assume value, provided it could be fenced from over-abundant cattle. The answer was at hand. John W. Gates, hardware salesman to an empire as it proved, had demonstrated barbed wire on the Alamo Plaza in San Antonio in 1875. Ranchers and cowmen who came to laugh at what Texas steers would do to a few strands of wire grew sober when the barbs held in the herds. They bought miles of it. The country was rapidly fenced, although posts had to be hauled in many instances as much as 200 miles. The wire was cheap, required but few posts, and held the herds. It made for conservation, for there no longer existed the race "to get grass while it lasted." Men were ruined in the transition as the land owner came into his own. Fences moved steadily across the open prairie, an unthinkable thing to many. The so-called "fence cutters' wars" ensued. The short struggle over the open range was succeeded by private control.

This revolution was officially dated when the Texas legislature met in special session in 1884 and made it a penitentiary offense to cut a wire fence. For the convenience of travelers it was decreed that a gate must be provided for every three miles. For a while in Texas the possesion of a pair of wire clippers cast more odium upon a man than the possession of a sixshooter ever had. "Next to the introduction of railroads," said Governor Roberts of Texas, "barbed wire has done most to develop the agricultural and pastoral pursuits of the state." Thus ownership of cattle and the land on which cattle grazed came to coalesce. A steer came to be marked by the place he stayed rather than by the brand he wore, and the days of the cowboy and the round-up receded.

Ranching in the Southwest is by no means a heritage of the past. Only 18 per cent of Texas' broad domain of 168,000,000 acres is under cultivation, while almost three times as much of her area is devoted to grazing as to agriculture. Texas has 5,700,000 of the 57,500,000 cattle in the United States and with Oklahoma possesses 12.9 per cent of the nation's stock. The "Nursery of American Ranches," the brush region between the Nueces and the Rio Grande, is still a ranching area where Mexican *vaqueros* work the range to-day.[13]   Great stretches of the coastal zone of post oak and piney woods are still grazed, while the Texas Panhandle south to the Texas and Pacific Railway is notable for its ranch holdings. While it is true that the world's largest ranch, the XIT, has been broken up, the day of large holdings has not passed. The land for this great ranch was deeded to a contracting company by the state in payment for the construction of the state capitol at Austin. One of the most efficiently managed, the XIT Ranch became popularly known as the Ten Counties in Texas. Its history has been recently written and adds a valuable page to the story of the development of the Panhandle.[14]   The King Ranch, however, still contains 1,000,000 acres while the Bill Jones Holdings aggregate 500,000 acres.

The old range conditions, however, have become a thing of the past. With the passing of the Longhorn, Texas cattle now cost "real money" and it takes capital to run a ranch. The great reduction in the number of cattle since 1890 has been accompanied by an improvement in quality. Recently the owner of a 250,000 acre ranch

[13] See J. Frank Dobie, "Ranch Mexicans," *Survey Graphic,* XIX, 167-70.

[14] J. E. Haley, *The XIT Ranch of Texas.*

aid $43,500 for 174 registered Hereford bulls. While the West
as graded up with Herefords and Shorthorns, districts near east-
rn cities have turned to dairying with Jerseys and Guernseys. A
on of cotton seed costs less than a steer, and will serve to keep
welve alive during a hard winter.

The cowboy is a changed man, for now he gives attention to
etty details his predecessors would have scorned. He must work
n foot, build fences and tanks, repair windmills, and even cultivate
attle feed. He is likely to be set the task of singeing the spines
ff cactus with a gasoline torch whereby a patient worker may make
ed available for twenty cattle. When they "work cattle," how-
ver, the cowboys resume their seats in the saddle. Life for the
ock hand on the isolated ranch is likely to be one of stark sim-
licity. The American who wants a Ford tends to leave his tasks
 the Mexican more satisfied with things of the soil. The pay of
le cowboy is from $30 to $60 a month with room and "grub" fur-
ished. If he boards himself he will receive $10 more. The Mex-
an cowhand draws $20 to $30 a month, the cook draws about $5
ore than a regular hand, while a horse breaker receives a bonus
n his work.[15]

The cowman, it is known, has regarded the aridity of West
'exas as his greatest ally against the encroaching farmer. It is
kely that ranching, however, will continue for a long time to
old a prominent place in Southwestern economy. There still re-
ain a few old cattle kings who can look back and say that a
w heifers and an uncrowded country made them; but, while
le range is gone, the ranch conducted on a business-like basis will
ontinue to hold a place in our economy. After passing through a
umber of remarkable evolutions, the ranch is prepared, no doubt,
 settle down as a permanent agricultural enterprise.

From Cattle to Cotton

It is hardly necessary to recall that Texas was settled by farmers
vho meant to carve out a new agricultural domain. Grass lands
nade their appeal to farmers no less than stockmen. Katherine
Coman writes:

he settler from the east of the Mississippi accustomed to the exhausting
abor of clearing the forests before plowing could begin, who had often

[15] Dobie, *loc. cit.*

seen the better part of man's life spent in reclaiming a few patches of cornfields which still remained encumbered by stumps and infected with malaria, rejoiced in the sunny open prairies where the soil seemed prepared by nature for the farmers' use.[16]

Texas' first crop was produced by Stephen F. Austin's colonist in 1822—a corn crop grown by the most primitive methods, which, except in the river bottoms, was nearly ruined by drought. Jared Groce established the state's first cotton plantation cultivated by slaves, and in 1825 set up Texas' first cotton gin on the banks of the Brazos. In 1833 Austin reported to the Mexican government 30 gins and a year's crop of 7,500 bales of cotton. The first cotton was exported across the Rio to Mexico on the backs of mules in bales of 150 pounds, two bales to the mule. In 1832 shipments were begun by water to New Orleans.[17] After statehood in 1845, the great influx of population made of Eastern Texas a new cotton belt by the outbreak of the Civil War.

The history of the farmers' advance on Oklahoma is illuminating. The advancing horde, for example, took the Cherokee strip of Oklahoma not from the Indians but from the ranchmen. The five civilized tribes did not till their lands; they rented them to stockmen and lived on the proceeds. Oklahoma thus offers a significant case of a sudden and complete change from a ranching to an agricultural economy effected through legislation and administration. E. E. Dale, in his "History of the Ranch Cattle Industry in Oklahoma," already cited, points out that Oklahoma had long stood as an island of sparsely settled land in the midst of the crowding surge of settlers which had advanced steadily westward on either side. Newspapers were established on its borders to "boom" Oklahoma and abuse the cattlemen. Efforts were made to settle the area in spite of the law. The Bureau of Indian Affairs had adopted the complaisant policy of neither allowing nor forbidding grazing leases from Indians to settlers. Accordingly in 1883, to stop irregular grazing, the Cherokee Strip Live Stock Association leased that area from the Cherokees for five years at $100,000 a year. Chartered under the laws of Kansas for the protection of the industry, this was the largest organization of its kind in the world. In the absence of laws, it protected property, held courts of arbitration, de-

[16] *Economic Beginnings of the Far West,* II, 103.
[17] Wortham, *op. cit.,* V, 118-19.

:ided both boundaries and precedents of cow custom. In the course of its life it held 300,000 cattle in the Cherokee strip, dealt justly with the Indians, and saw that no cattle owners grazed stock on their lands without paying fees. Forced by the relentless pressure of settlement, the government tried to buy the strip for the farmers but failed because the stockmen's lease paid the Cherokees more than the government offered. The government then invalidated the lease, drove the stockmen out, and after three years forced the Indians to accept $1.40 an acre in lieu of the $5.00 offered by the cattle syndicate.

In a struggle in which the Indians were helpless bystanders, the government opened the area to homestead, and thus by legal fiat replaced ranchmen by farmers. Populism in the Southwest owes much of its origin to a dislike of ranches. Ranchmen were regarded as wealthy monopolists, and a tradition of cattlemen as selfish, brutal, and domineering persisted. The industry disappeared in Oklahoma before it had a chance to live its reputation down. To this frontier struggle may be charged much of the political radicalism of the Southwest. An early Texas law forbade banks in the state. Oklahoma, it is noteworthy, placed more ordinary statute law in her constitution than any other state. The purpose of much of this law was to guarantee the *status quo* to the small farmer. Moreover, the state has acquired the tradition of impeaching its governors, because of mere impatience. The state finds it easy to impeach any governor it doesn't like, having developed a system of dismissing for incompetency rather than moral turpitude.

In most of the Southwest the replacement of ranching by homesteads was no less sure because it had more sobriety. It is difficult to realize that agriculture is hardly over sixty years old in most of Texas nor over thirty in Oklahoma. Many of the agricultural areas in the Southwest are, of course, much younger. With only 18 per cent of its immense area under cultivation, Texas has twice produced crops valued over one billion dollars. Texas was added to the list of United States cotton states by annexation in 1845 and by 1859 and 1869 it came to rank fifth in production. In 1890 the state assumed the leading position which it has since retained. Oklahoma was first opened to settlement in 1889 and made a state in 1907. The trans-Mississippi states first passed the cotton production of the eastern belt in 1920, due to the large increase in the acreage of the Southwest. Here then is the frontier of the cotton belt with its lands undepleted of fertility either by the continuous cropping or the leaching rains of the Southeast. The cotton fibre grows longer and stronger here than anywhere else except in the Delta. Texas now grows from 30 to 40 per cent of the nation's cotton supply, and half her population of 5,850,000 depends directly or indirectly on the crop for its livelihood.[18]

The east and the west here present strongly contrasted modes of cotton culture. Backed by similar physical conditions and a history of earlier settlement, eastern Texas has duplicated many of the conditions associated with the older South. If the Interior Coastal Plain resembles the Atlantic Coastal Plain, in some respects the Texas Black Waxy tends to duplicate conditions of other black land belts. Lacking the historical background of the plantation, the fertile black prairies have, by a rapid infiltration of unpropertied whites, reached a high percentage of tenancy. From 1890 to 1925 Texas increased her ratios of farm tenancy from 35.2 to 60.1 per cent. Starting at 0.7 per cent tenancy in 1890, Oklahoma's proportion of farm tenants increased from 43.8 per cent in 1900 to 58.6 in 1925. In the Interior Coastal Plain in 1910 one third of the improved land was in cotton and one half of the farms were operated by owners. In the Black Waxy 86 per cent of the land was in farms, 62 per cent improved, and 31.6 per cent planted to cotton. It was found that 55.7 per cent of the farms were run by white tenants and that 14.5 per cent were in plantations. In 1920 the percentage of Negro farmers in this belt was still as low as 15.9.

J. T. Sanders' study, made in 1919, of 368 farmers in six counties of the Black Waxy serves to show how socio-economic conditions approximate those of old cotton zones.[19] He found the total cost of family living for the year was $965 for share croppers, $1,243 for share tenants, and $1,742 for farm owners. The average size of families for the different groups was found to be about the same, so that the living cost of a cropper family can be estimated at 55 per cent and the average share tenant's living at 71 per cent of that of the owners'. Of all living expenses croppers average $262 fur-

[18] Ruel MacDonald, "Texas, An Empire State," *Current History*, XXXIV, 165-69.
[19] J. T. Sanders, "Farm Ownership and Tenancy in the Black Prairie of Texas," U. S. D. A., *Bulletin* 1068, 1922; Vance, *op. cit.*, pp. 231-33.

nished from the farm, share tenants $424, and owners $575. Thus with much lower money incomes, croppers receive only 41 per cent and share tenants 75 per cent as much family living from the farm as owners. Croppers buy the most groceries, $310, to $296 for tenants and $294 for owners.

The average amount spent for recreation, education, and advancement goods is strikingly small for all classes. Ten to fifteen dollars per family is spent for recreation. Few families of any tenure take vacations, and but few more patronize movies or theatres. About twice as much is spent for tobacco and similar personal expenses as for recreation. About one out of six croppers own cars, one out of two tenants, and three out of four owners. About one out of five croppers, half the tenants, and six out of seven owners have telephones. All owners read periodicals and daily papers, but 39 per cent of the croppers reported no periodicals whatever.

In school it was found that "the tenant's child is from six months to a year behind the owner's child in grade attainments." Ninety-six per cent of owner's daughters were promoted for the school year to 77.2 per cent of tenants' daughters, and 88.6 per cent of owners' sons to only 65.6 per cent of tenants' sons. The enrollment for cotton tenants' children always ranks lower than for any other group. This enrollment reaches its lowest stage during cotton picking time in October, November, and December. It "is due to the fact that tenants as a rule feel they cannot afford to hire their cotton picked and to the fact that the landlords expect and sometimes demand that renters' children be put into the cotton fields in order to rush picking as much as possible." The frequent moving of tenants also serves to cut down school enrollment. Such a study as this shows that eastern Texas has gone the full cycle and duplicates in almost every social detail the old cotton economy of the Southeast.

Not so of the West. In their Great Plain areas, Texas and Oklahoma have furnished the nation's newest and most rapidly expanding cotton areas—areas that promise a definite break with the South's traditional practices. Under the impression that the high, level, and semi-arid stretches of the Staked Plains would never be available for crops, stock raisers acquired the great ranches comprising thousands of acres. Though by 1885 it was realized that crops could be grown in the region, cotton was not seriously considered as late as 1910. The introduction of an adequate agriculture waited upon a substitute for corn which could not stand the dry hot weather. When this was found in the cultivation of kaffir corn, milo maize, and sudan grass the small farmer began to push his way into the midst of the ranching economy. Between 1919 and 1924 a million acres were added to cultivation, and by 1925 the decline of live stock values had conspired with rising prices for farm land practically to complete the removal of cattle raising from the region.[20] Moreover, "when once new land is plowed and put in cultivated crops, it rarely is used again for grazing as it does not become reset in the native grasses satisfactorily for many years."[21] Thus the land is kept in cotton or a competing crop.

From 1919 to 1926 Texas increased her cotton acreage from something over ten million to over eighteen million and her production from three million to almost six million bales. During the same period Oklahoma's acreage rose from approximately two and a half million to over four and a half, while her production increased from one to one and a half million bales. A section which possessed not a single mile of railroads before 1886 is now Texas' greatest cotton producing area. A Panhandle county such as Hale which in 1919 possessed not a single cotton gin, in 1930 operated twenty. From 1920 to 1930 the center of cotton production in Oklahoma shifted 125 miles to westward. During the same period the number of farms in southeast Oklahoma decreased by 11 per cent while the number in the southwest increased 27 per cent.[22] This expansion has occurred at a period when abandonment of cotton farms was going on rather rapidly in the easterly Gulf states and along the South Atlantic Coast. As to the future, it is estimated that in the Staked Plains as a whole over fifteen millions of acres in Texas and four and a half in New Mexico may be used for crops. With favorable market conditions it is likely that from 18 to 20 per cent of the region would be devoted to cotton, giving about 3,200,000 new acres.

The advantages of cotton culture in this area are based firmly

[20] E. O. Wooten, "Cotton in the Texas Plain Area," U. S. D. A. *Yearbook,* 1926, pp. 271-74.

[21] D. W. Watkins, "A Study of Cotton Growing in Texas Showing Influence on Cotton Production in South Carolina," Clemson College, *Bulletin* 75, p. 5.

[22] P. H. Stevens, "Mechanization of Cotton Farms," *Journal of Farm Economics,* Jan. 1931, pp. 27-31.

upon its geography. High altitude and a dry climate have so far kept the boll weevil in check and the necessity of continuously forcing cultivation ahead of insect depredation is not felt. This advantage is further aided by the absence of troublesome weeds which have gained foothold in the older cotton belt. Moreover, "the land above cap rock is generally level and gently rolling and the tillable soils are mostly light and easily worked when properly moist; hence cultivation of large fields with large equipment is easy. These new soils are now fertile; hence the application of fertilizers is not necessary at present and it is possible that on some of them it never will be."[23]

Level topography facilitates the riding-machine type of cultivation on large fields. Tractors are used more extensively than elsewhere in cotton. A farmer riding a two-row lister with a six-mule team and a set of fenders, knives, disks, and points can plow and plant the land at one operation. The average investment per farm in the new southwestern areas in 1929-30 was $50,000—more than ten times as great as in the older cotton areas of southeastern Oklahoma. Under climatic influence the plants tend to ripen at about the same time. Thus there has grown up the mechanized method of picking called "sledding." These sleds are dragged down the rows gathering the fruited fibers along with some unopened bolls. A study made in 1926 of 26 farmers who used the cotton sled shows that a man and two horses harvested an average of 4.4 acres or 1.8 bales a day at a cost of $2.78 a bale.[24] In the same area the cost for hand picking ranged from $12 to $15 a bale. Improvements in ginning, especially the boll extractor, have made it possible to process sledded cotton profitably. These improved gins return remarkably clean bales from sledded cotton. So much less labor is required of men and animals in the western plains that one farmer may cultivate a hundred acres in cotton.

In this new western belt farmers can produce cotton at a profit while eastern growers are selling below the cost of production. Fertile soil, low weevil damage, and mechanization place in constant jeopardy any economy based on twenty acres and a mule. The one supreme danger in the area is the recurring threat of drought.

[23] Wooten, *op. cit.*, p. 272.
[24] L. P. Gabbard and F. R. Jones, "Large Scale Cotton Production in Texas," *Bulletin* 302, Texas Agricultural Experiment Station.

The extent to which farmers realize profits in this transplanted economy is shown by studies made by the Department of Agriculture in Lubbock County, Texas, for 1924. The average net income per farm received for its operation by the family for the year, after paying all interest on borrowed capital (and including that part of the family living furnished directly by the farm as a part of the farm receipts) was, for 139 farms, over $3,000. Ten men lost money, 10 per cent made less than $1,000 but 13.5 per cent made over $5,000 and the remainder made between $1,000 and $5,000. These incomes were obtained on farms averaging 232 acres in size valued at $68 per acre with 37.6 per cent of the land in harvested cotton having a yield of 148 pounds of lint, selling at an average price of about 20 cents per pound. The average net worth of these farmers when they settled in the region was just over $5,000 per man and on March 1, 1925 the corresponding figure was $18,000, the difference having been made by the operation of the farm and its own increase in value in an average period of 5.84 years.[25]

The conditions in this county are typical of about eight others in the west Texas Plains.

Mechanization has combined with the expanse of new lands to place southwestern farming on a larger scale. To a southern average of 103.9 acres and a national average of 145.1, Oklahoma opposes an average farm of 156.7 acres while Texas reaches 235.5 acres. Some of the excess can be accounted for by the fact that the census does not segregate farms and ranches in its returns. Nevertheless, in the same year, 1925, the number of acres in crops averaged 63.8 and 80.3 for Texas and Oklahoma respectively compared to 38.7 and 61.4 averages for the South and nation. In values of the average farm, Oklahoma and Texas exceed the average for thirteen southern states by $2,586 and $3,286, 62.3 and 79.3 per cent. In total gross income per farm during the period from 1924 through 1928, Texas exceeded the South's average by $564, Oklahoma by $513, 44.8 and 40.7 per cent respectively. The Southwest with its departing ranches bids fair to return to cotton farming the expansiveness it lost through tenancy.

THE RIO GRANDE VALLEY

Smaller in expanse but equally startling in its development is the Southwest's rival to Florida, the lower Rio Grande Valley.

[25] Wooten, *op. cit.*, p. 274.

This valley lies between the Balcones Escarpment, the Uplands of Mexico, the Cotton Belt, and the sea. The climate is tropical and the scanty rainfall is reflected in a vegetation of brush, bunch grass, cactus, mesquite, and chaparral. The area's main use had been in grazing and as late as 1912 the valley possessed no more than a handful of American farmers. J. Russell Smith well says the Rio Grande is the Nile for this Egypt since with irrigation the zone can equal Florida for truck or the Delta for cotton.[26]

Irrigation has served to transform a combination of tropical jungle and semi-arid desert into a market garden area. As early as 1920 the combination of irrigation, new railroads, and land speculation brought the zone a typical land boom. On the whole, however, the valley has settled down to progressive development with some 150,000 inhabitants living in irrigation districts, dry farming areas, or in small thriving towns. The sub-division of old ranches, the removal of thorn bush vegetation, and the improvement of irrigation have proceeded apace.[27] Vegetables grown during the mild winter reach the early markets for the season's highest prices. The amount of vegetables shipped increased from 2,000 carloads in 1912 to 17,100 in 1928. The extensive plantings of citrus fruits are beginning to bear. In 1928, 1,183 cars of citrus fruits were shipped. In 1930 a total shipment of 29,000 carloads of vegetables and fruits left the valley. It is estimated that in 1930 there were 60,000 acres in the valley planted to citrus fruits.

The valley faces all the hazards of a trucking district plus those peculiar to irrigation areas. To guard against market gluts and limited demand the region will doubtless find it necessary, in Smith's opinion, to grow staples as well as specialties. The principal reasons for such failures as have occurred in the irrigated districts have been laid to "over-exploitation and lack of operating funds, want of experience in irrigation and tropical farming, poor management, lack of marketing organizations, high freight rates, the want of soil surveys and the failure to determine the crops best adapted to the various types of soil, the high cost of water, and under some of the irrigation systems the uncertainty of water

[26] *North America*, pp. 432-35.
[27] See William T. Chambers, "Lower Rio Grande Valley of Texas," *Economic Geography*, VI, 364-73.

supply."[28] Drainage of low lands to prevent rise of the water table and the accumulation of alkali salts deposited by the irrigation water also present problems. The region was so faced with flood dangers, that three counties had their state taxes remitted for 25 years that they might be applied to flood control. A system of levees and floodways was accordingly completed in 1928. The valley in spite of these difficulties comprises a prosperous, progressive section with promise of continued growth.

THE INDUSTRIAL SOUTHWEST

With the exception of comparatively isolated industrial development in Tennessee centers and New Orleans, the Southwest offers the first consistent break with an uninterrupted agricultural economy since the Piedmont. Texas with the lowest density of any southern state, 21.9 persons per square mile, ranks among the most highly urbanized with 41 per cent urban. Texas' billion dollar crops are exceeded by her manufactured products valued at $1,200,-000,000 in 1930, while Oklahoma has on occasion been able to rank eighth in agricultural and second in mineral production. Oklahoma is well supplied with reserves of coal, lead, and zinc, having led the nation in zinc production for the last decade. Moreover, the Texas Gulf Port area takes precedence in its exports of all the nation's shipping areas except the New York Port zone. Twenty-two per cent of the nation's mineral wealth comes from the South and three fifths of that production is found in fuels, coal and oil, the South's most exploited mineral wealth. It is her oil resources which furnish the basis of the emerging industrialism of the Southwest.

THE GULF COAST'S MONOPOLY OF SULPHUR

In the process of prospecting for oil were discovered a series of sulphur domes stretching along the southwest gulf coast from the mouth of the Mississippi to the mouth of the Rio Grande. While the geology of the area is favorable and the number of domes is large, only some five have yet proved of commercial value. Each dome consists of a salt core overlaid by porous cap rock through which the sulphur is distributed as seams, cavity fillings, impregnations, and disseminations. In depth these formations

---

[28] "Irrigation Development in the Lower Rio Grande Valley," Department of Interior, 1923. Cited by Smith, *op. cit.*, p. 434.

may vary from 300 to 1,200 feet, in thickness from a few feet to 250.[29]

The almost unlimited deposits of the gulf coast offered no competition to Sicily's monopoly of the world sulphur supply until the development of the Frasch Method. After having worked out a method of forcing up molten sulphur by piping super-heated steam underground, Herman Frasch formed in 1896 the Union Sulphur Company. Following a trade war in which the Sicilian product was practically forced out of the market by 1907, Frasch's concern came to supply practically all the nation's sulphur until war demands depleted the Louisiana deposits. Two Texas firms, working deposits estimated adequate for years to come, now supply over 95 per cent of the world's demand. No method of open cut or underground mining has proved as cheap as the Frasch process of extracting sulphur from 900 to 1,200 feet below the surface. By the use of this technique some 139 million long tons of sulphur valued at some 200 million dollars were extracted in 1929. Grading plants and refineries have been set up in the area; and the industry finds its greatest costs of production in fuel and piping. With the growing importance of sulphuric acid in the industrial arts, the region has proved to possess an essential resource.[30]

The Human Geography of Oil

The industrial and financial structure of the modern Southwest finds its most authentic interpretation in the human geography of oil. Oil, like the precious metals, has been a trail blazer on the map. Early in its history oil acquired the reputation of found wealth and easy money. However ill-deserved, this reputation has served to lead men on to new frontiers. The possibility of great returns from small investment has created the "wildcatter," who, corresponding to the prospector in mining, remains the hope and despair of the industry. If he discovers new resources for a waning industry, he also furnishes an ever-present threat of over-production. The production, distribution, and refining of oil early came under some measure of corporate control. The discovery of new supplies, however, remains pretty much an affair

[29] Walter H. Voskuil, *Minerals in Modern Society,* pp. 314-15.

[30] H. T. Warshow (ed.), *Representative Industries in the United States,* pp. 135-37.

of untrammelled individual initiative. The driller of test wells is the scout of the industry, making its initial contacts with nature. While the great oil companies stand ready to buy crude from the paying wells, it thus results that both the gains and the losses of prospecting are absorbed outside the industry. Often but not always the men who bring in new wells remain pioneers on the outside fringes of oildom while the industry's more settled habitués reap the great rewards.

The geology of oil creates this situation and serves to make it unique among natural resources. A complex mixture of hundreds of hydro-carbon compounds has resulted from the age-long imprisonment of minute marine organisms in a rock pocket. Oil saturates layers of porous rocks and moves upward until stopped between strata of impervious rock. In this pocket of rock, variously called an anticline, a dome, or fault, is found the oil pool. The geology of petroleum is thus the geology of rock structure in an area once covered by the ocean. Oil, however, is not likely to be found in mountainous areas because fissures, faults, and deep erosion allow leakage, leaving only dry holes. From the surface contours the oil prospector's problem is to ascertain the depth, incline, structure, and type of rock strata, masked as they are by hundreds of surface changes from erosion and sedimentation. Only as the results of drilling operations are recorded and accumulated can the geologist's surface findings be translated into three-dimensional knowledge. Such knowledge demands that logs be carefully recorded during drilling operations and transmitted to a central state Bureau of Mines or Geology where they are plotted on a peg model. This peg model is built to scale and serves as a three-dimensional diagram of the geology of an area. "As soon as a few wells have been driven in the given area the points on the various pegs where any given formation was encountered are connected by colored strings. In this manner the dip and strike of the series may be visualized and by the insertion of a peg at any given point the contact depth of any structure may be projected."[31]   One of the wastes of the competitive system in oil is that such data are often kept secret and thus not made available to check the losses attendant upon useless drilling and prospecting.

[31] Henry Mace Payne, *Undeveloped Mineral Resources of the South*, p. 74.

Its physical-chemical characteristics combine with the geological environment to give oil its unique characteristics of liquidity and pressure. The imprisoned crude, mainly a heavy liquid, runs the gamut from solids to gases. The natural gas which oil contains in occlusion furnishes the tremendous pressure that forces out a gusher. When exposure to the air is followed by distillation, the expelled gas is followed by the volatile gasoline, then by the more inert kerosene, next by the lubricating oils, leaving finally the solid base which may be either asphalt or paraffin. The highest type paraffin bases are found in Pennsylvania while the California oils are characteristically asphaltic.

Pressure and liquidity make the mining of oil a task both easy and baffling. Once the reservoir is tapped an oil dome proceeds to drain itself. Beyond this important fact it cannot be said that oil fits well into man-made laws of economics. An outcropping mineral deposit may be followed down its incline and the resource distributed in accordance with property lines drawn on its surface. Not so with oil. Oil is no man's property until it is drained off at the surface. American petroleum law is based on the English common law doctrine in regard to underground water: one must possess before one owns. The oil pool, however, is a geological unit and true to the law of liquids, a well on one lot may drain the oil resources under all neighboring tracts. This fact leads to competitive drilling and all the wastes of the industry which no amount of technical improvement has been able to halt.

The customary exploitation of an oil pool by a series of small unrelated holdings has of necessity established the industry on the principle of robbery. The aim of each producer is to drain the largest possible underground area in the shortest length of time before the oil is secured by a competitor.[32] Wells are drilled along boundary lines and each producer drills an offset opposite his competitor's well. Law can compel a driller to sink offset wells as protection to his lessee. Competition operates to lessen the amount of oil recovered and to raise the unit cost of recovery. This means waste by duplication in drilling where two wells do the work of one. Gas pressure forces oil up, but, because of the

[32] George Ward Stocking, *The Oil Industry*, pp. 140-41.

multitude of outlets, the gas pressure of an oil pool becomes exhausted long before the oil is recovered. It is estimated that from 40 to 90 per cent of the oil in pools remains underground when the field is abandoned. Further wastes in competitive drilling are found in loss of gasoline, in natural gas permitted to escape, in the flooding of oil sands by salt water, and the guarding of technical information. Of all natural resources oil seems to possess the greatest affinity for a monopolistic system of processing.

Here again it is noteworthy that the liquid nature of oil has helped to give it the measure of industrial control and direction it has attained. Organization in oil, begun at the transportation and refining ends, has crept closer and closer towards the fields of production. The nature of oil accounts for its unique transportation system, the pipe line. Pipe line mileage in the United States amounts to one eighth of that in railroads. As a matter of fact, the pipe line resembles nothing so much as a railroad system. It possesses its trunk lines, feeders, terminals, storage stations, switching systems, pumping stations, dispatchers, telegraphs and telephones by which the producing fields are linked with the refining centers. There were in 1932 operating in the United States some 100,000 miles of petroleum pipe lines. An investigation in 1916 by the Federal Trade Commission of a part of the line for Oklahoma to the Gulf Coast showed the cost of pipe line to be $6,389 a mile, of an average pumping station $126,810, and of telegraphs and telephones $312 a mile.

The first pipe lines threatened to lead to monopoly control in oil by allowing the great companies who laid their own lines to refuse the oil of independent producers. Such a threatened control of production through the means of transportation was blocked when the pipe lines were declared common carriers and thus forced to accept the oil of all producers on a *pro rata* basis Accordingly the large companies have left it to the wildcatter to find new supplies, and the pipe lines have followed him wherever he has found producing fields. It is noteworthy that wells may come and go, but the producing fields such as the Gulf and the Mid-Continent in the Southwest area remain pretty much the same. Thus, pipe lines and refining centers are not forced to migrate across the map, but serve to build up stable and settled cities.

The uncertainty of occurrence, the possibility of quick returns, and the transitory nature of the petroleum industry have given a whole section an adventurous and speculative tinge. This is the geographic complex that has conditioned the Texas and Oklahoma of today regardless of the extent to which science and business organization may come to control in the future. To the aid of the geologist pointing the way to scientific prospecting has come the seismograph, the torsion balance, and the radio step-up. It is now possible to set off a charge of dynamite, observe the earth's tremors, and plot the geological structure. The president of one company has computed that only five per cent of the wells located at random prove profitable, as compared with 85 per cent located on the basis of careful geological surveys. The geologist is about to live down the names of "ridge runner," "mud smeller," "rock hound," and "pebble peddler," thrown at him by the individualistic wildcatter. It cannot be said, however, that these improvements in technology have brought the industry any nearer a solution of over-competition, waste, and fluctuating production. Science has in fact made more severe the problems faced by business organizations in this speculative industry.

Oil has made for a mobile and dynamic industrial order in the Southwest. The petroleum sections have all the characteristics of a perpetual boom country. Poor men get rich and rich men go broke overnight. Social change is kaleidoscopic and the social ladder becomes an express elevator. Viewing the scene in 1922 Roderick Peattie remarked that many oil operators were ex-farmers, ex-bankers, and ex-roustabouts. The offices he found filled with men of action whose lined and sunburned faces told of lives in the open. They knew individual wells as they knew men and once having drilled and succeeded, they hoped to drill again. Every Oklahoma town, he felt, possessed its inhabitants who had struck it rich and retired to expensive homes to carry out their ideas of luxurious living. They may sit on front porches in stocking feet while their wives wear boudoir caps to town behind twelve cylinders, but they furnish the economic upper class of a new country.[33]

The drilling crews are organized for nomadism. To get men and materials to a new field ahead of time and competitors is the

[33] "Hunting Oil in Oklahoma," *Atlantic Monthly*, 129, pp. 630-41.

object. Sidelines to the main show are the geologist and his in-
strument man doing the prospecting, and behind him the "lease
hound" who sees that his company gets proportionate acreage in
any prospective field. Often the lease hound may operate on his
own with the hope of reselling his leases to the operators. At the
well, lowest on the ladder of promotion is the roustabout, a
greasy laborer on a twelve hour shift. Next comes the tool dresser
who tempers and sharpens the drills weighing hundreds of pounds.
The autocrat of the derrick is the driller, the boss of the rig and
its two crews. Then high enough to come into the white collar
class is the scout whose business it is to keep posted on the drilling
operations of his competitors as far as possible. Beyond one climbs
in the rank of the executives, the vice presidents, and the main
operators.

Such a natural landscape, in this case partly the invisible landscape of geology, has given rise to the cultural landscape of the
oil boom town. It is by a succession of booms that the Southwest
has grown. Ten of Texas' towns and cities of 3,000 population
and over listed by the 1930 Census did not exist in 1920. Twenty-
nine others possessed much less than 3,000 population in 1920.
Ellsworth Huntington has recounted the rise of a typical oil boom
town:

Some wildcat drillers brought in a well in the peaceful little township of
Desdemona, Texas, where fifty to a hundred people were raising pigs ten
miles from the railroad. There was no hotel, no telegraph line, and only
poor excuses for roads. But crowds of people poured in, rents soared,
wells were rapidly drilled, tanks and domes of earth were built to save
the oil that poured out, pipe lines were laid down in a rush, stores were
started in shacks. Soon the little hog-raising cross-roads had a thousand
derricks; ten thousand people were living in tents and walking on plank
walks; not enough of them had lived there six months to incorporate a
town. Trucks were still crawling in with loads of pipe and machinery;
nothing except the cemetery was sacred from the oil driller. Both the
state and Federal governments have tried to prevent waste in such cases
by a system of fines. But when people are making $12,000 for each
$100 investment, as happened in one case, they do not care how much is
wasted. In a Texas town 10,000 barrels per day were recently wasted.

Such rapid development stimulates business. There is a demand for
expensive machinery; the oil worker, the storekeeper, the extortionate

itney drivers, and every one else in the town must be supplied with food, helter, and clothing. Money is so abundant that prices rise to astonishing levels. The people who make fortunes are so extravagant that automobile makers say that such districts are among the best in the country or the sale of high priced cars. But the business stimulated by an oil oom as any other mining boom is not permanently valuable. It introduces wild speculation, a sudden demand along various lines and a udden change in the supply along others.[34]

Another case will show how a boom town rose in the once peaceful solitude of the old cow country of the Panhandle. A. P. Borger, an oil operator of Cromwell, Oklahoma, founded in February, 1926, Borger, Texas, thirty miles from the railroad. The oil ields started off with gushers, and the town started off with a bang. Overnight, grew up a "rootin', tootin', rip roaring, snorting, hell-aising place" with a main street two miles long. Every building on that street was a one-storied shack, appropriately called an ugly" in the boom country. In such a wilderness of hot dog tands, joints, chili parlours, rumbling trucks, and smelling oil anks, men are thick and happy while women are few and mis-rable. Gradually the rush and the hangers-on dissipate, and the tring of uglies changes into a new and respectable business dis-rict. Borger, reputed to have a population of 25,000 in 1927, ettled down to respectability with 6,530 people by the 1930 Census.[35]

In some respects, however, the discovery of new oil pools in parsely settled sections offers less of social incidence and change han the bringing in of gushers in settled territory. Oklahoma City found this out to her peril in the great discoveries of 1929 and 930. A half dozen terrific gushers blew in within dangerous istance of the state's capitol, and at one time seventy wells were rilling within the city limits. For sixty-six hours a gusher, Stout No. 1, blew wild with from 60,000 to 100,000 barrels of oil and 00,000,000 cubic feet of natural gas escaping every twenty-four ours. One eighth of the city was put under martial law, six chools closed, firemen and 200 state militia called, and all cook-ng fires and striking of matches forbidden. In spite of these

[34] In Davis, Barnes, *et al*, *Introduction to the Study of Sociology*, pp. 245-46.
[35] E. B. Garnett, "Oil is King in the Texas Panhandle," *World's Work*, LV, 58-74.

precautions the North Canadian River caught fire, burning several bridges, and 168 acres of vacant land were ignited before a thousand trained workers, wearing helmets and rubber coats, were able to cap the well. Drilled in the deepest field in oil history, these wells encountered rock pressure ranging from 2,000 to 3,000 pounds as compared with 800 to 1,800 pounds in other strata. No wonder the gushers blew, as a tool-dresser said, "like an exhaust pipe connected with hell." Some of these wells are fired by the friction of sand and pebbles against casing pipe. The problem of Oklahoma City was not the problem of the boom town. Her task was to halt by some legal means the near approach of a stupendous oil development which for a time threatened the very existence of the city. Until some *modus vivendi* was worked out with oil exploitation the city indeed stood in danger.[36]

In spite of its financial magnitude the industry especially in the Southwest has been opened by a series of runs and discoveries verging on stampedes as spectacular as they were unplanned. A glance at the industry's history bears this out.[37] By 1879 Texas was listed as an oil producing state with a yearly output of less than 500 barrels. A well was bored at Nacogdoches in 1866, only seven years after Drake's famous Pennsylvania strike. A well at Corsicana in 1895 produced 2½ barrels a day and served as the prelude to Spindle Top. In 1901 the famous Spindle Top pool near Beaumont blew in with a ten day gusher that opened the Gulf field once for all and definitely added Texas to the oil empire. Cattle kings became oil barons, and out of the Spindle Top came the four major companies that have since dominated Texas—the Gulf, the Texas, the Magnolia, and the Humble Oil corporations.

In 1906 a wildcatter well, dug at Kiefer near Tulsa under the jests of deriding cowboys, brought in the Glenn pool and opened the great Mid-Continent field for the Southwest. Kiefer became a wild town of excess, debauchery, promotion, and crime, just as Spindle Top had developed gigantic swindling schemes. Tulsa from a casual Indian trading post grew to 100,000 people almost within a decade. By 1911 a well on the Wagonner Ranch

[36] See Earl Sparling, "Oil Hells in Oklahoma," *Outlook and Independent*, Feb. 11, 1931, pp. 214-17.

[37] Isaac F. Marcosson, *The Black Golconda*, chs. vii, viii.

in North Central Texas opened a new pool and proved that the Mid-Continent field underlay West and Central Texas. Just a year later Oklahoma countered with the discovery of the famous Cushing field and thereby made the Osage Indians who occupied Creek County the richest collectivity in the world. Texas was ready to reply and by another series of lucky accidents opened the Ranger field of Central and North Texas in 1917 and the Burkburnett field of South Texas in 1918. Fort Worth then joined the parade, becoming the capital of the next oil promotion group. Nineteen-twenty saw E. W. Marland wildcat the famous Burbank pool for Oklahoma while Texas replied with the discovery of Mexia, the approach to the Powell pool and a return to the Gulf coast. Powell was brought in by 1923, the same year in which the Tankwa reservoir, also discovered by Marland, reached the peak of production for Oklahoma. In the meantime South Arkansas had joined the procession with a great gas well at El Dorado in 1922 and extended the pool to include a great oil producing field around Smackover in 1923. Renewed discoveries at lower depths in the Texas Panhandle, the Gulf, and near Oklahoma City have pushed the Southwest to its greatest production in history.

The figures on oil areas and production serve to indicate the predominance of the Southwest. In a classification that has stood unaltered for over twenty years the United States Geological Survey listed the nation's oil fields as Appalachian, Lima-Indiana, Illinois, Mid-Continent, Gulf Coast, Rocky Mountain, and California areas. The Mid-Continent formation underlies southern Kansas, Oklahoma, and Northern and Western Texas. The Gulf field, coextensive with that of Mexico, accounts for the producing wells of Arkansas, Louisiana, South and East Texas. Together with California they rank as the country's greatest producing fields, while Oklahoma, Texas, and California vie with each other for the position of the leading state. The extent of oil production varies in a large degree with the newness of the fields. While there are something over 300,000 producing wells in the United States, half the total product comes from some 6,900 wells. A recent year gave the following ratios: Pennsylvania with 25 per cent of all the wells produced less than two per cent of the country's oil. California with only four per cent of the wells produced almost 30 per cent of the year's supply. Oklahoma with 20 per cent of the wells produced 25 per cent of the supply, while Texas with 8 per cent accounted for 21 per cent of the crude.[8]

The statistics of oil reserves have proved too static for a dynamic industry, and practical oil men have ended by professing disregard for them. Figures of production, fluctuate as they will usually find the United States furnishing from 60 to 70 per cent of the world's total, and Oklahoma, Texas, and California taking turns at leadership. The result of the hectic activity recounted above has been to lift the production of petroleum in the South west from 1.3 per cent of the nation's output in 1900 to 32.3 per cent in 1910, 59.3 per cent in 1929, and 61.2 per cent in 1930. Table XXXVI also indicates that the Mid-Continent field finds its near

TABLE XXXVI

SOUTHERN PETROLEUM PRODUCTION
(In Barrels of 42 Gallons)

	1900	1910	1929	1930
Tennessee......................	....	....	19,000	19,000
Arkansas.......................	....	....	24,917,000	19,613,000
Louisiana......................	....	6,841,000	20,554,000	23,107,000
Oklahoma.....................	6,000	52,029,000	255,004,000	215,227,000
Texas.........................	836,000	8,899,000	296,876,000	289,965,000
South.........................	842,000	67,769,000	597,370,000	547,981,000
United States.................	63,620,000	209,556,000	1,007,323,000	896,268,000
South's Percentage............	1.3	32.3	59.3	61.2

PETROLEUM PRODUCTION BY FIELDS IN U. S.
(In Barrels of 42 Gallons)

	1928	1930
Appalachian..	31,454,000	34,262,000
Lima N. E. Indiana..	1,670,000	4,873,000
Michigan...	594,000	
Illinois S. W. Indiana......................................	7,425,000	6,638,000
Mid-Continent...	553,125,000	529,630,000
Gulf Coast...	46,591,000	69,505,000
Rocky Mountain...	29,199,000	23,258,000
California...	231,811,000	228,099,000
	901,474,000	896,265,000

[8] J. C. Welliver, "Oil, the New Industrial Giant," *Review of Reviews,* 76, pp. 177-86.

est competitor in the California field with less than half its output while the Gulf Coast is almost twice as productive as its nearest rival, the Appalachian field. Oil has been the most rapidly and ruthlessly exploited of all southern resources.

On the basis of the spectacular rise and fall of production from new and passing oil pools the industrialization of the Southwest has been erected. That the industry is basically a speculation is shown by the amazing figures on the number of dry holes. Up to 1924 four Oklahoma counties had counted 3,568 dry holes—each one marking the place where a small fortune had been sunk. A Bulletin of the American Association of Petroleum Geologists estimates, for example, that in 1922 the cost of drilling that year's 23,000 wells plus other costs of production was $59,000,000 in excess of the value of the oil secured. Twenty-four Oklahoma wells cost $8.14 per foot or $23,022 per average well to drill.[93] Let no one, however, doubt the compensations when the wildcatter strikes it rich. In 1922, for example, 37 oil producing counties paid 48 per cent of the Texas state property tax, leaving to the other 220 counties the task of completing the other 52 per cent. In 1917 before oil was found in the Rogers field the taxable property of Eastland County was a paltry 11 million. Three years later it had risen to 58 million dollars. Emphasis has been placed on royalties and profits, but the industry distributes in Texas well over $100,000,000 annually in wages.

Moreover, petroleum refining has reached a stage of permanence and stabilization possibly unattainable by migrating oil production. While one pool succeeds another with startling rapidity the general fields remain localized. Thus settled metropolitan centers have grown up to serve these areas as centers of refining, distribution, and export. Connected by railroads, highways, and pipe lines, with the hinterland of oil, there has developed on the strip of Coast between Corpus Christi and the Louisiana line one of the great refining and export centers of world commerce. Only the New York port area exceeds in volume and value the exports originating in the Gulf Port region of Texas, while only California at times exceeds Texas in the capacity of its refineries. Port Arthur can lay claim to serving as capital of

[39] Wortham, *op. cit.*, V, 178 ff.

the greatest oil refining district in the world. Single tank farms at both Beaumont and Port Arthur cover over a hundred acres. The Gulf Company, for example, owns a refinery at Port Arthur, covering 110 acres, which has run day and night for the last twenty-seven years. If, as Marcosson says, Tulsa is 75 per cent oil, Port Arthur is 100 per cent oil. The whole Southwest, if one includes Louisiana and Arkansas, possesses over 40 per cent of the country's refining plants with some 40 per cent of both the total crude and cracking capacity. In the adoption of cracking production to insure a higher return of gasoline, the Southwest has helped set the pace for the nation. Invented about 1912, the process subjects heavy oils to intense heat in stills built to withstand high internal pressure. As a direct consequence of its use, over 39 per cent of America's crude oil was converted into gasoline in 1929 as compared to only 5 per cent of Roumania's oil output. Table XXXVII serves to show the Southwest's comparative ranking in the refining industry.

TABLE XXXVII

PETROLEUM REFINING INDUSTRY, 1929

STATES	No. of Plants	No. of Plants Operating	Daily Crude Capacity in Bbls.	Plants with Cracking Production	Cracking Capacity
Arkansas	11	9	48,000	6	16,750
Louisiana	16	11	207,780	6	96,000
Oklahoma	64	44	313,900	29	117,050
Texas	110	81	813,700	38	494,950
Southwest	201	145	1,383,380	79	728,750
The Nation	479	362	3,721,360	186	1,705,299

Because of increasing improvement in technique, natural gas has long since ceased to rank as a comparatively unimportant by-product of the oil wells. Increasing quantities of wet gas are run to still and come out gasoline, while extensions of pipe lines have brought natural gas within reach of industrial and household consumers in urban areas outside the Southwest. The United States in 1931 possessed 65,000 miles of natural gas trunk lines, approximately one half originating in the Mid-Continent field. In 1928 the four states so denominated accounted for 55.4 per cent of the natural gas produced and marketed in the United States at a total value of over 363 millions of dollars. In 1930 two trillion cubic feet of gas worth one half billion dollars were consumed in the United States, and one fifth of this was manufactured gas. One giant pipe line system supplied the consumers of Birmingham and Atlanta from Shreveport; another leads from Aramillo to Chicago. In addition Louisiana has an important carbon black industry based on natural gas.

The Texas Gulf Port Area

In the Texas Gulf Port area is found the Southwest's most stable achievement toward industrialism. Two thirds of the tonnage leaving the Texas Gulf Ports is accounted for by oil and oil products.[40] Two thirds of its petroleum products are exported by tank steamers to Europe and our northeastern ports. But in spite of thousands of acres covered with refineries, storage tank farms, by-product plants, and shipping facilities, the value of petroleum exports is exceeded by cotton. Galveston and Houston have alternated as first and second cotton port of the world. Since Oklahoma and Texas are negligible in cotton manufacturing, practically the whole of the crop must be exported to eastern mills. High density compresses, superior terminal facilities, and low shipping rates attract practically the whole of the western crop through these ports. The situation is comparable in oil, for the pipe lines from Louisiana, Arkansas, Kansas, Wyoming, and Montana fields converge here. Moreover, every new discovery leads to the extension of existing pipe lines. Here the facilities are equally superior, and vessels carrying 75,000 to 125,000 barrels of oil can be loaded in 10 to 12 hours. Some sixty steamship lines serve Houston and Galveston and the trade of the combined port regions in 1925 comprised a tonnage of 31,819,624 valued at $1,919,002,237.

The extent of this development is all the more noteworthy when it is considered that not a single port is situated on a natural harbor. Man, not nature, made the Texas Gulf ports. From the shallow bays, tidal marshes, and sluggish bayous of a flat sand-bar coast have been dredged these excellent ship-channels making ports of inland cities from Corpus Christi to Lake Charles, Louisiana. Galveston, the only port situated on the ocean, in-

---

[40] See William T. Chambers' study, "The Gulf Port Region of Texas," *Economic Geography,* VII, 69-83.

creased her channels from their natural depth of 10 or 12 feet to 30 and 35 by dredging and jetties. The famous sea-wall and causeway completed the protection of her port. Houston, situated inland on a small stream, completed in 1914 a channel 50 miles long, 150 feet wide, and 28 feet deep, widened at the city to form a turning basin. Lake Charles is a port by virtue of a 30 mile channel to the sea. The Sabine Port District, including Orange, Beaumont, and Port Arthur, attained ocean transportation only by artificial ship channels finally completed in 1926. Of this group Houston, situated nearest the Black Waxy, has outdistanced all competitors having increased its population from 78,000 to 292,000 in the last twenty years. She is now the metropolis, and having vanquished Galveston, girds her loins for the struggle with New Orleans over the future of Gulf-borne commerce.

POPULATION ELEMENTS

In its population elements the Southwest differs considerably from the South. Not only does the section have less Negroes but Texas possesses a distinctive Mexican element while Oklahoma has its Indians. From Spanish origins came many things that make Texas culture distinctive. In this it can be approached by no southern state save Louisiana. With constant communication across the border, a steady stream of Mexican casual labor passes in and out of Texas. No one knows the number of Mexicans in the state but a recent estimate placed it at 249,652. Mexican immigration is increasing, a fact which adds weight to the characterization of the Southwest as a laboratory for social research.[41] Oklahoma is the last "permanent home of the Indians." The five civilized tribes, Cherokee, Creek, Seminole, Choctaw, and Chickasaw, were not wild Indians of the plains, nomadic and bloodthirsty. They were a quiet agricultural group, made up of small farmers and stock raisers.[42] Their land belonged to the tribe rather than the individual, and each group had a strong and intelligent tribal government. In 1920 these five tribes numbered 119,255 souls, held 19,551,890 acres of land to the value of more than $300,000,-

[41] J. J. and C. R. Rhyne, "The Southwest—Laboratory for Social Research," *Southwestern Political and Social Science Quarterly,* X, 33-41.

[42] Charles N. Gould, "Oklahoma, An Example of Arrested Development," *Economic Geography,* II, 426-50.

ooo, and received an income of nearly forty million dollars. In 1923 Indians as wards of the nation received the sum of $36,659,810 from royalties on gas and oil leases. The civilized tribes have largely taken over the white man's culture and have been practically assimilated into Oklahoma. They meet no prejudice, many have risen to positions of prominence, and many of the state's proudest families boast of Indian blood in their veins.

One cannot escape the feeling that the great Southwest repeats in scenery and stage properties much of the cultural landscape of the South. Originally meant as reinforcement of the ante bellum cotton kingdom, Texas has fulfilled her manifest destiny. From the close of the Civil War to 1900 it is estimated that Texas and the Southwest received some two million immigrants from the old Cotton Belt. The Black Waxy and the Grand Prairies furnish duplicates of the Cotton Belt, and Oklahoma not thirty years young has already attained its tenancy structure. This has been done, moreover, without an influx of Negro population at all proportionate to the ratios of older states. The main agricultural settlements of Texas were made after the abolition of slavery; and Oklahoma was settled on the run by a white pioneer yeomanry.

While a large proportion of the settlers of Oklahoma were southerners, an even larger part of the Texas immigration came from the South. East Texas comes nearest resembling the Old South while the plains to the west are truly western in population and spirit. The dust of their migrations is still on the population of the Southwest and the common greeting is "Where are you from?" Oklahoma is very much a young cosmopolite of North, South, East, and West. North Oklahoma is as full of Kansas Jayhawkers as Eastern Oklahoma is of Arkansawyers. One may guess the antecedents of an Oklahoma farmer from a simple culture trait. If he calls his cattle enclosure a barnyard, he is from the North; if he speaks of it as a cowpen, he hails from the South; if it is a corral, he comes from Texas.[43] While in the Southwest the frontier has lingered longest in the present, in Oklahoma it passed in a generation. In an industrial folder designed to lure immigration and investment the Oklahoma State Board of Agriculture has felt it necessary to reassure potential citizens that the frontier has passed:

[43] Charles N. Gould, loc. cit.

The traveler finds nothing particularly different here. He may ride on just as well equipped trains, put up at as modern hotels, eat as good food, transact business as expeditiously, in as attractive offices and with as keen minded men, find amusement at as good theatres or golf grounds, meet as refined and charming women, attend as good churches and hear as eloquent preachers, and in general live as pleasant and strenuous a life in Oklahoma as in other states.

Its naïve acceptance of values of the American business man should not blind us to the truth of the statement. In words that Americans understand: The Southwest, old cow country and contemporary frontier, has arrived. Its growing cities lift their new skyscrapers "like totem poles among the Baptists." Were it not for the Baptists and cotton the regionalist could not so boldly claim this area for the South.

CHAPTER XIV

THE SOUTHERN CLIME

THUS have passed in review the varied regions and resources of the South. Conditioning, integrating, dominating these diverse domains is the climate, called by W. G. Kendrew the most far-reaching of the natural elements that shape the destiny of man.[1] Human energy and efficiency, the type and extent of disease, the significance and bearing of regional diet, and the complexion of culture in the South no doubt carry certain gross as well as subtle imprints from sun, rain, and wind. This chapter attempts to delimit the southern climatic province, to discuss the biology of climate, and to ascertain how far the South suffers the handicaps of a sub-tropic climate. Succeeding chapters will show the relation of regional climate and efficiency to both disease and diet.

Certainly climate has not been neglected in the popular estimate of the South. It, in fact, has been regarded by many as the region's *raison d'etre*. Southern reactions to climate have been popularly estimated to range all the way from the forced importation of tropic laborers to a change in the Anglo-Saxon temperament and a lowering of biological adequacy similar to that encountered in tropic climes. Thus by some the southern United States is regarded as the scene of a geographical human experiment of great significance. In this area the white man has wagered against climate, and history and science are yet undecided as to whether he has won or lost. Thus the economic geographers, Jones and Whittlesey, can write: "The suitability of this climate for Europeans is in dispute as evidenced by the introduction of colored races into southern United States and Natal."[2] It may be admitted that in the usual course of things the European goes to the tropics and assumes the white man's burden by

[1] W. G. Kendrew, *Climate,* p. 1.
[2] W. D. Jones and D. S. Whittlesey, *An Introduction to Economic Geography,* p. 145.

[351]

organizing the native laborers under the plantation system for the production of such staples as tea, rubber, coffee, bananas, cotton or sugar cane. The plantation, as A. G. Keller has pointed out in his work on *Colonization,* is the mode agriculture assumes in the tropics.

While partly accounted for by imperialism and the European economic surplus for foreign investment, the plantation owes much of its actual structure to the influence of climate. To W. Z. Ripley "a colonial policy in the tropics means a permanent servile native population" largely because "one of the many things expressly forbidden to all colonists in the tropics is agricultural labor. It would be a waste of energy to give citations to prove this, for every work on acclimatization insists upon the necessity of this precaution."[3]

Now it is held the American South took an opposite course to the same end. The area itself partook of the nature of a colony. Possessing a subtropic climate, land in abundance, and a great scarcity of labor, the province imported both the plantation form and the servile labor to man it. Thus, in the course of time arose the nineteenth century superstition that no white man could work in southern fields and keep his health. It was contradicted at the time, needless to say, by thousands of yeoman farmers and their wives who tilled fields of cotton and corn alongside the plantation in its palmiest days. Then, as if to prove whether an agriculture so constructed could stand alone, the South saw its system of chattel slavery abolished.

Thus, one may claim that the whole South was organized around an attempt to escape the handicaps of a subtropic climate. The argument has been extended to claim a climatic change of temperament. For the first time in history, we are told, Nordics of the English, Teutonic, or Anglo-Saxon persuasion have lived below the 39th parallel. They have so lived, labored, and multiplied for nine generations. "Not elsewhere in the world over," writes E. N. Vallandingham, "have Englishmen dwelt continuously in large numbers under semi-tropical conditions for as much as three generations." The British official class in India have been constantly renewed from the homeland. Vallandingham, in 1907, saw the descendants of middle-class Englishmen in

[3] *Races of Europe,* pp. 586-87.

the process of becoming fiery Latins under the southern sun, and called the southerners "our men of the Midi." He saw the southerner taking on the characteristics and temperament of the European races that fringe the Mediterranean. Ardent in love, deadly in jealousy, fiery yet steady in physical courage, soft of speech and manner yet easily roused to flaming anger, provincial and supersensitive to outside criticism, the southerner had gained a warmth and color which made him seem to Vallandingham a different race from the Yankee. The impassive Englishman has been tempered by the southern sun with the tinge of the South European.[4] So runs the theory, and it is as neat as it is incapable of demonstration.

It would be folly to deny the great significance its climate bears to southern culture. Whether the introduction of the Negro as a slave was primarily an attempt to evade the consequences of climate rather than to remedy the labor shortage is more than doubtful. Certain it is that Virginia for three quarters of her first century relied on white labor. It is quite as doubtful that climate is molding racial temperament and disposition. Let us, however, attempt to reduce climate to its meteorological elements apart from its conditioning of food, clothing, habitation, and the content of culture. To delimit the South as a climatic province on the basis of temperature, humidity, and seasonal changes and to present its stable characteristics so that the region may be compared with similar areas would be a difficult first step. The next step, the determination, however roughly, of the bio-physics of a given regional complex of temperature, humidity, sun, and wind, has not yet been achieved by either biologist or climatologist. Then to trace the almost invisible margins where culture and climate impinge in the South would furnish further tasks. The attempt to chart climatic influences and adjustments has always proved the geographer's most elusive and difficult assignment. In our present state of knowledge it must be admitted these questions cannot be answered to our full satisfaction.

THE SOUTH AS CLIMATIC PROVINCE

The complex we call climate is composed of (1) temperature from solar radiation with the ratios of sunshine and cloudiness,

[4] "Our Men of the Midi," *Atlantic Monthly,* 99, pp. 848-56.

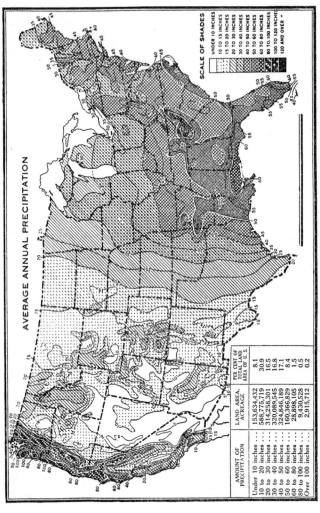

AMOUNT OF PRECIPITATION	LAND AREA, ACREAGE	PER CENT OF TOTAL LAND AREA OF U. S.
Under 10 inches	153,634,432	8.1
10 to 20 inches	588,775,719	30.9
20 to 30 inches	314,258,301	16.5
30 to 40 inches	320,089,545	16.8
40 to 50 inches	324,846,189	17.1
50 to 60 inches	160,366,829	8.4
60 to 80 inches	28,898,105	1.5
80 to 100 inches	9,430,528	0.5
Over 100 inches	2,915,712	0.2

SCALE OF SHADES

UNDER 10 INCHES
10 TO 15 INCHES
15 TO 20 INCHES
20 TO 30 INCHES
30 TO 40 INCHES
40 TO 50 INCHES
50 TO 60 INCHES
60 TO 80 INCHES
80 TO 100 INCHES
100 TO 120 INCHES
120 AND OVER "

AVERAGE ANNUAL PRECIPITATION

FIGURE 19.—Precipitation includes rain, melted snow, sleet, and hail. The map suggests why the United States should be divided agriculturally into an eastern and a western part. However, the division shown in Figure 1 does not follow a line of equal precipitation but advances diagonally across two of the precipitation zones from 14 inches in the northeastern portion of Montana to 24 inches on the south Texas coast, where, because the evaporation is much greater and the rainfall more torrential, more rainfall is required for crop production. (Courtesy of U. S. Department of Agriculture).

(2) precipitation with its functions of evaporation and humidity, and (3) the prevailing winds which bring changes in temperature. It is relative humidity that gives the feel of the air. High humidity in low temperatures means a "raw" climate, in high temperatures it means a "sultry" climate.[5] That for any area climate should be elusive is to be expected. Climate is no more than the long-time average of weather; and weather has long been the synonym of shifting uncertainty. Accordingly, as Kendrew points out, "no picture of climate is at all true unless it is painted in all the colors of the constant variation of weather and the changes of season."[6]

The South does not comprise a sharply defined climatic province. The topography of the United States possesses no great transverse mountain barrier from east to west, and the slowly graduated effect of latitude on solar heat is everywhere modified by wide plains left open to cold winds from Canada and warm moist winds from the Gulf.[7] While it is true that the United States may be divided roughly into a cold North, a warm South, a humid East, and an arid West, such division cannot do justice to the varied interplay of climatic factors. Both Köppen and Ward, however, have furnished classifications of climate from which we may compile a description of the types of climate met in the South. The picture, however, will not be as definite as that of the climate of southern California where the Pacific on the West and the mountains to the East sharply delimit a climatic zone, which can only be compared with the Riviera of southern Europe. The South is found in the east continental margins of the middle latitude, an area which Jones and Whittlesey assign to the humid subtropical zone.[8] In this they follow largely W. Köppen's classification.[9] In his analysis the South is practically coextensive with the East Coast Humid Mesothermal Province as developed in the United States. In the division of Robert De C. Ward all of the South falls within two climatic provinces, the Eastern and the Gulf. The Eastern province comprises most of the United States east of the High Plains. The Gulf prov-

[5] C. E. P. Brooks, *Climate*, p. 14.

[6] *Op. cit.*, p. 2.

[7] Robert De C. Ward, *The Climates of the United States*, p. 18.

[8] *Op. cit.*, pp. 142-45.

[9] *Die Klimäte der Erde*, Tafel I.

ince cuts into the area in the South, comprising all of Florida and Louisiana and the southern half of Georgia, Alabama, Mississippi, and south Texas. The world areas whose climates correspond most nearly to southern conditions are the southeast fringe of Australia, Natal, South Africa, southern Japan, southeastern China, and the pampas of Argentine.

The climate of the Gulf Coast is striking in that it is subject to sudden changes in temperature. The weather is warm because of the waters of the Gulf, but the interior is left wide open to the winds from the north which are neither broken by mountain ranges nor tempered by waters. Thus the winters are extremely variable but the cold spells are brief. The heat of summer while great is not oppressive. Sunstroke, for instance, is rare on the Gulf but frequent in northern interior states. Short days give the earth more time to cool, and Gulf breezes do the rest.[10]   The climate of Florida is subject to the same variations though they are not so striking. The range of temperature in Florida is about half that of the St. Lawrence Valley in a normal year. Maximum temperatures of 100° and over are not experienced in the peninsula of Florida or along the Gulf Coast. Nor has the Gulf Coast or the Atlantic Coast south of the Chesapeake Bay ever experienced a temperature below zero. This region possesses a high even temperature in a country whose range is from 130° in the Colorado desert of southern California to 50° below zero at Mount Washington, New Hampshire—the highest and lowest temperatures ever recorded in the United States.[11]

Eastern North America from Florida to Maine is distinctive for possessing one of the steepest temperature gradients for its length to be found in the world. It is noteworthy that this range in temperature is greatest in winter, to the benefit of the South. Ward explains lucidly: "A long journey from South to North in search of decidedly cooler summers gives far less change than the corresponding trip from North to South in winter in search of much warmer and balmier climates."[12]   For example, the annual average of temperature for North Carolina is about 15° above that of the Pennsylvania-Massachusetts section. The July nor-

[10] N. S. Shaler, *The United States*, I, 90.
[11] Bowman, *Forest Physiography of the United States*, p. 115.
[12] *Op. cit.*, p. 88.

mals for both regions are about the same while the January normal for North Carolina is around 15° to 20° above the New York normal for January.[13] According to monthly averages warmth seekers find the temperature increasing about 1.5° for every hour they travel southward in a fast express train.[14] "The products of tropical and polar lands are here separated by less distance than anywhere else in the world. At the same time communication between these districts of sharply contrasted climates and types of vegetation is easy."[15]

Miss Semple has pointed out the influence of this temperature gradient on the economic development of the thirteen colonies.

It gave New England commerce command of a nearly tropical trade in the West Indies, of subtropical products in the southern colonies in close proximity to all the contrasted products of a cold climate—dense forests for naval stores and lumber and an inexhaustible supply of fish from polar currents, which met a strong demand in Europe and the Antilles. The sudden southward drop of the O° C annual isothermal line toward the St. Lawrence and the Great Lakes brought the northwestern fur trade to the back gate of New York, where it opened on the Mohawk and upper Hudson, and brought prosperity to the young colony.[16]

Actually the South may be said to possess four climatic sub-regions, indicated roughly by the length of the growing season. Ulrich Phillips points out:

The growing season lasts on an average six months at Baltimore, Louisville, and Saint Louis; seven at Norfolk, Atlanta, and Memphis; eight at Columbia, Montgomery, and Dallas; and nine at Charleston, New Orleans, and Galveston. The climate has fostered the cultivation of tobacco in the first zone, cotton in the second and third, and rice and sugar cane in the fourth.[17]

Only in the fourth zone of South Florida and the Rio Grande Valley of Texas can the southern climate be called tropical. James J. Hill's rash dictum that no man on whom the snow does not fall can be worth a damn does not apply in its full force to the South, for frosts, freezes, and occasional snows occur on all but Gulf and

---

[13] S. H. Hobbs, Jr., *North Carolina Economic and Social*, p. 10.
[14] Ward, *op. cit.*, p. 83.
[15] *Ibid.*, p. 105.
[16] *Influence of Geographic Environment*, p. 618.
[17] *Life and Labor in the Old South*, p. 3.

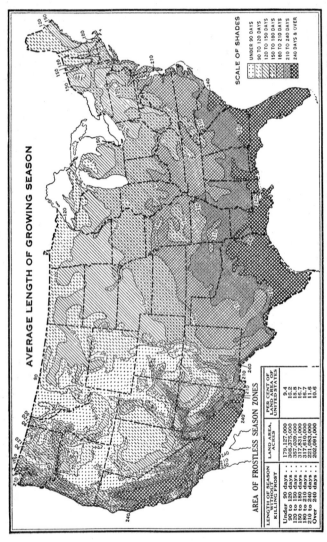

Figure 20.—Average length of the growing season. Map much reduced and generalized from a map prepared by the United States Weather Bureau and published in the Frost and Growing Season section of the Atlas of American Agriculture. (Courtesy of U. S. Department of Agriculture).

Coastal fringes. Nowhere is the growing season twelve months long and several times in each decade hard freezes grip the region, bringing death to perennial plants. Such were the Florida freezes of 1894 and 1896 which destroyed practically all the orange groves. On the other hand, the cold is normally neither severe nor protracted. Freezing temperatures anywhere in the South normally last no more than a few days at a time. The mean temperatures of the coldest months are likely to be over 32° F., nor is the soil frozen annually. Especially characteristic are the long warm summers of the deep South. The July mean is usually above 77° F. and the temperature can be trusted to ascend above 90° F. on fifty or more afternoons of every year. Moreover, its rainfall is well above the average of the country, with no pronounced dry season. Except west Texas, none of the South has an annual precipitation less than forty inches; Delta, Gulf, Coastal Fringe, and Mountains reach fifty or above. The whole region averages just about 48 inches. Accordingly, the relative humidity is high throughout the warm season. With only light daytime breezes, the change from day to night brings to the lower South the relief that saves it.

No one has more eloquently described the climate of the Deep South, that of the fourth zone, than a brilliant son of Alabama.

Those midday heats are often hard to bear. The sun's progress through the heavens is the hard march of a ruthless conqueror. The rank vegetation fairly chokes the earth. Insects buzz and sting and irritate. Serpents writhe to the surface of miasmous streams. Beasts palpitate and grow restless. Men brood and weary of the loneliness and long for excitement, for fierce deeds, battles, conquests. But with the sudden dropping of the sun in the west a swift change comes over the earth and beasts and men. There is the stillness of the wide level fields, snow-like with cotton; the softer, night-time noises of the woods and swamps; the splendor of the southern stars; the tinkling of banjos and the twinkling of lights in the Negro quarters; the white dresses of women and children; and the exquisite slow tones of human voices on the verandas of the great house. The rancor of the midday passes—eclipsed, overcome, atoned for, by the charmed sweetness of that dying hour.[18]

The comparison of mean annual temperature maxima and minima for the two sections gives the South certain definite ad-

[18] W. G. Brown, *The Lower South in American History*, pp. 48-49.

vantages over the North. Weather that in the North causes temperatures to fall from 10 below to 40 below zero rarely reaches zero in the South's middle zone or ten below in the upper range. Savannah, Georgia, for example, has a mean winter temperature equal to that of London in May. Moreover, it can readily be shown that the lowest possible temperature incident to an area is of much greater economic importance than the highest. Cheaper living costs, lower fuel costs, and unhampered transportation result from the South's climatic differential. The warmest temperatures for the whole United States are surprisingly uniform. Extreme temperature of 100° F. has been observed over all the United States except a few small and widely scattered areas. Excepting the winds of west Texas the southern United States possesses no counterpart to the "Zonda" of the Argentine pampas—that sultry wind from the north, feared because of the lassitude and disease it brings.

The whole advantage may be summed up by saying that while the South is largely free from the intensity of northern cold waves, the North is open to the periodic recurrence of hot waves. It is true that Texas has its norther, a rushing blast from the northwest known to bring at times a drop in temperature of 25° an hour. The cold waves of the North are, however, unique for their frequency and intensity.

According to Ward, the southern states have a somewhat different relation to hot waves. They naturally have prevailing higher summer temperatures. They are farther from the storm tracks. "Often, however, while warm, southerly and southwesterly winds are causing hot wave conditions over the central and northern sections, northerly and northeasterly winds are blowing across Florida and the northern Gulf Coast. Florida, with its winds coming directly from the Gulf, may then have decidedly lower temperatures than states much further north."[19] From the Mississippi and Ohio valleys to the eastern coast hot waves lasting over a week cause much suffering, prostration, and illness, especially in large cities. Neither sunstroke nor heat prostration is nearly so common in the South, and yet that area possesses cities which do not lack slum areas. Critics of the southern climate have to face the fact that in northern and eastern cities summers

[19] Ward, *op. cit.*, p. 388.

are likely to be more intolerable than in the South. Hot, moist winds blowing from southerly latitudes bring "sunstroke weather, epidemics of cholera infantum, spells of suffering in the crowded cities."[20]

The Biology of Climate

A regular dose of ultra-violet rays on the skin has perhaps a more important effect on the health of an individual than any single long-time factor except diet. With other factors equalized, the most healthful climate, Ward holds, is the one which permits and encourages its denizens to spend the maximum amount of time outdoors in open air and sun.[21] The South with 140 to 160 clear days a year is thus superior to the North and East with 100 to 120. In North Carolina, for example, winter days are about 50 minutes longer than in the New York-Massachusetts section, while in summer the days are 50 minutes shorter. This difference increases farther south. It is in summer that the sun's rays are enervating. Long winter days, however, are especially advantageous with the extra advantage they offer of exposure to the sun's rays.[22] This prevalence of sunshine reaches out into southern life in ways not yet analyzed. Despite poor food, housing, and sanitary conditions, southern rural Negroes often surprise observers with their sturdy physique and good health. It is no doubt partly because as children and adults they spend much time in the sun. Rickets in children, for instance, has been definitely related to lack of ultra-violet rays. In the absence of other data some have turned to athletic records as an indication of health and vigor reflecting climatic conditions. When southern football was at the bottom of the heap, practice in the debilitating heat of the southern autumn was taken to explain the players' comparative lack of stamina. Now that southerners hold their own or better in intersectional competition, such writers for the sporting press as George Trevor and Grantland Rice see reflections of the man building power of the climate. The greater exposure to ultra-violet rays is as fully a scientific explanation of the comparative rank of southern athletics, as heat and humidity.

The biological effects of extremes of heat and cold are known

[20] *Ibid.*, p. 49.
[21] *Ibid.*, p. 445.
[22] S. H. Hobbs, Jr., *op. cit.*, pp. 10-11.

and obvious, but to differentiate within temperate ranges such as those found in the United States is difficult. C. F. Brooks of Clark University has suggested that the scientific basis for classification of climate is in its effect on human comfort. The work of Huntington in attempting to ascertain the climatic optimum is well known.[23] It has tended to show the existence of a physical optimum for Europeans at a mean temperature of about 65° F. for day and night together, a relative humidity of about 80 per cent, and an interdiurnal variability averaging not far from 3° F. On these counts the optimum climate would show a midday summer temperature ranging from 70° to 75° F., winter nights frosty, air moist enough to form dew or frost at night, and storms frequent enough to cause weather variability of 3° F. daily. Southeastern England is the only area which approaches these conditions. Nowhere else does the white race, says Huntington, live under the optima of climate. The criteria by which Dr. Huntington attempts to establish these optima have been severely criticized in many quarters.[24]

Man is an adaptable animal, however, and no one is yet sure how far adaptation by habituation can go. It is readily pointed out that some two hundred degrees of temperature separate the coldest inhabited spot on earth from the hottest.[25] There is one folk saying which agrees with scientific fact. "It's not the heat but the humidity" is the plain statement of the fact that the temperature experienced by the body does not agree with that recorded by the dry bulb thermometer. If the thermometer had its bulb covered by a moist wick kept at the temperature of the body, 98° F., it would record sensible temperature—that felt by the body.

The incidence of climate on human activity was not fully understood until the researches of Dr. Leonard Hill, an English sanitary expert. Dr. Hill finds the rate at which heat is lost by the body the chief factor in comfort. Body heat is produced by oxidation regulated by types of food and muscular activity; it

[23] Ellsworth Huntington, *Civilization and Climate; World Power and Evolution.*

[24] Pitirim Sorokin, *Contemporary Sociological Theories,* pp. 137-59, 186-93. Also Stanley Stevens, "A Critique of the Climatic Hypothesis of Ellsworth Huntington," unpublished M.A. thesis, University of North Carolina, 1931. A. A. Goldenweiser, "Meteorological Magic," *New Review,* May 1916, pp. 164-65.

[25] E. E. Free and Travis Hoke, *Weather,* p. 287.

is lost by evaporation and radiation. High temperatures may be made tolerable by low humidity which increases evaporation of perspiration. Indeed the effect of humidity is to accent temperature extremes, since high relative humidity increases radiation of body heat in cold and decreases it in hot climates. That fat men feel the heat more than others is due to what has been called their insufficient radiating surface, the small proportion of skin area to body weight. Hill's "katathermometer" which he adapted to measure the rate at which heat is taken away from the body may come to be used for regulating temperatures in buildings. To hold, as does Huntington, that the optimum temperature for mental workers is some 25° F. lower than that for factory workers shows lack of appreciation of the bio-physics of heat loss. Because he is producing more bodily heat, the optimum for the manual laborer should be lower than that of the sedentary worker to promote a higher rate of heat loss. Moreover, the body gives off water as well as heat. In a factory perspiration of workers may raise the humidity and thus lower the rate of loss of heat.

In studying this problem Haughten, Yagloglou, and Miller devised experimental rooms in which any desired temperature and humidity might be obtained.[26] The subjects of the experiment were tested with varying temperatures and humidities and asked to record the stage at which they felt most comfortable. The following were found optimum for comfort:

1. 64° F when the air is saturated
2. 66° F with the air 80 per cent saturated
3. 69½° F with the air 50 per cent saturated
4. 72° F with the air 20 per cent saturated
5. 76° F with the air 45 per cent saturated and a breeze of 340 feet a minute blowing a gentle drift of air.

Comfort they defined as a "condition where the various physiological functions of the body are carried on with the greatest degree of efficiency and with the least strain so that the individual is not conscious of its existence."[27] This approaches very near the conditions of efficient work. These observations, it will be noted, were made by people in a state of inactivity, and accordingly come

[26] *Report of New York State Commission on Ventilation, 1923.*
[27] Ellsworth Huntington, *Pulse of Progress,* pp. 87-89.

nearer agreeing with conditions of mental rather than physical work.

The series of experiments showed that moderately high temperatures of 68° F. do not diminish ability to do mental work although an increase from 68° to 75° F. brought about a decrease of 15 per cent in *physical* efficiency. Temperature was shown to be more important than either the humidity or purity of the air, but cooler temperatures were shown to be more effective in regard to physical fitness. L. N. Hines found that school pupils did their best mental work at classroom temperatures between 60° and 70° F. and fell off below 60° F.[28] E. G. Dexter found clerical errors among bookkeepers and bank clerks least numerous not at 39° F. but at 58° F.[29] Only a temperature of above 77° F. seemed to be followed by appreciable increase of errors. Moreover, the evidence from biology leads one to conclude that the important factor in Huntington's mental work curves was not the outside temperature of 30° to 40° F., but the temperature inside. This, of course, could not so easily be measured, differing as it must have from room to room. Hence, the false impression of a temperature 24° lower than comfortable for physical work as conducive to the best mental efficiency.

The problem of life and labor in humid tropical regions seems, moreover, to reduce to a statement in bio-physics. The body should be regarded as a heat engine generating energy at various rates, depending on food and activity, in an environment which tends to retard the loss of heat. In some climates "muscular activity increases the heat output and thus for the sake of comfort and health is to be avoided."[30] This process of heat loss through the skin can best be shown by a study of recent experimental comparisons between the races. Dr. Eijkman, professor of hygiene and microbiology at the University of Utrecht, has done the best work in this field.[31] His experiments show that hard labor measured by oxygen consumption is performed less economically at high

[28] "Effect of Class Room Temperatures on Work of Pupils," *Psychological Clinic,* VIII, 1909.

[29] *Weather Influences,* ch. xiii.

[30] Glenn T. Trewartha, "Recent Thought on the Problem of White Acclimatization in the Wet Tropics," *Geographic Review,* 16, pp. 467-78.

[31] C. Eijkman, "Some Questions Concerning the Influence of the Tropics on Man," *The Lancet,* CCVI, 887-93.

temperatures. The research, moreover, indicates that man's body does not limit heat production in relation to external conditions in any automatic chemical way. His observations have also pointed out the biological foundation of the black man's climatic adaptation. The protective pigment of the Negro is immune to the effects of ultra-violet rays as in sunburn, and thus permit him to go unclothed for the full benefit of the cooling power of the air. Although black pigment leads to greater absorption of the sun's rays, increased dilation of the cutaneous capillaries follows and leads to greater loss of heat by conduction and radiation. Due to thicker epidermis the European is forced to lose more heat by evaporation. "The white man sweats profusely in the tropics; sweat literally drops from him, while the dark skin shows a fine velvet-like layer of perspiration, which permits the maximum in evaporation and acts as an efficient reflector of the sun's energy. The higher secretion of the white is useless, for it deprives the body of water and weakens it. Thus the brown man is superior to the white in his economy of sweating."[32]

Much of the biological evidence is thus directly against regarding the southern climate as tropic to the point of pathology. It is doubtful that the Australian studies of Sundstroem indicating a slight but systematic difference in the composition of the blood and general functioning of the system in tropic dwellers could be duplicated anywhere in the South. Nor is there any evidence to indicate the existence among southern people of that state of physiological stress, a nervous instability verging on neurasthenia, which life in the tropics tends to produce among Europeans.[33] Tropical dysentery, for which no therapeutic is known except immaculate sanitation on a regional scale, is comparatively unknown in the South. The supreme test of the pathology of climate is its effect on the birth rate. Long British experience in India and the shorter American experience in the Philippines seem to show beyond doubt that the ability of the white population to reproduce is reduced under tropical conditions. The maintenance of a vigorous and creative ruling class requires a constant stream of fresh migrants to replenish the European pop-

[32] *Ibid.*
[33] E. S. Sundstroem, "Contributions to Tropical Physiology," University of California, *Publications in Physiology*, VI, 1-216.

ulation. In Japan studies have shown that in September at the end of the long debilitating summer the conceptions which give rise to living children are but little over half as numerous as in June. No comparable effect of the southern climate on racial survival can be adduced. With practically no immigration, the native white birth rate in the southern states ranks highest in the nation. Neither death, sterility, nor migration has prevailed to weed out European types in the South.

Moreover, the record of the southern common soldier in the Civil War for forced marches and desperate combats should serve to contradict any theory that the climate had depleted vigor and vitality. Another tribute to the mild nature of the southern climate is paid by first settlers who found there no new and exotic diseases such as characterize the tropics. Southern dwelling Indians carried no infections with which the Europeans were not experienced. While malaria proved the greatest scourge, it had been known to Europeans for ages. On the other hand, it may be noted that the colonists brought over tuberculosis, measles, and smallpox, for which the Indians had acquired no natural immunity.

When we come to the biology of heat loss we find that the eighteenth century superstition that white men could not work in the fields in the South was never more than a superstition except as it served as a rationalized defense for slavery. So deep a hold on the popular mind had the eighteenth century superstition attained that many travelers felt impelled to contradict it. Olmsted has permitted himself a note of irony on this point.

Men born, nurtured, and trained in the South show no lack of strength or endurance when engaged in athletic exercise, which is immediately gratifying to their ambitions, passions, or their tastes. The climate prohibits no sort of labor, except such as would be generally productive of wealth, to the white man of the South.[34]

He took down the opinion of an Englishman who could do as much work in the South as in London. Those who drank much whiskey and cordials and kept old habits of eating just as if they were in England, he held, were the men who complained most of the climate, and who thought white men were not made to

[34] *Journey in the Back Country*, p. 299.

work in it. A New Yorker whom Olmsted questioned about this said: "I have worked steadily through the very hottest weather, steadily day after day and done more work than any three niggers in the state and been no worse for it. A man has only got to take some care of himself."[35]

Olmsted was led the more to agree because of the manual labor he witnessed. "I have in fact seen more white native American women at work in the hottest sunshine in a single month, and that near midsummer, in Mississippi and Alabama, than all my life in the free states, not on account of an emergency as in harvesting either, but in the regular cultivation of cotton and corn, chiefly of cotton."[36] Here he simply corroborates a fact known by almost all southerners that many families in various neighborhoods and places who never owned a slave did all their own work and left descendants among the most prosperous and healthy people in the South.

If before 1860 the dangerous effects of southern climate gained credence as rationalization for slavery, the vogue of the belief after the war was due to immigration. Foreign and northern immigrants, unaccustomed to the sun, took advantage of the longer days to accomplish more. Edward King was told in 1870 that many German immigrants had been ordered by organizations of native laborers not to work so much daily, since they were setting a dangerous example. King's informant, however, believed that almost any white man could do as much work as three Negroes.[37] It is still true that the northern farmer come South is likely to hit a midday summer pace that he cannot keep. The climate is no more dangerous than that of the midwest, however, and much less productive of sunstroke. The South today is sprinkled full of settlers from every part of Europe and the North who work with as great impunity and efficiency as either natives or Negroes. So passes the superstition. It belongs with Frederick Mayratt's view that the climate of America has caused a deterioration in the original physique of English settlers. Until further researches present facts now unknown, we are forced to the conclusion that any differential that exists in the southern

[35] *Journey in the Seaboard Slave States*, pp. 237-38.
[35] *Journey in the Back Country*, p. 298.
[37] Edward King, *The Great South*, p. 33.

climate is so slight that it cannot be proved by any of the biological criteria applied to the acclimatization of white races in the tropics. This is not to deny that man is forced to habituate himself to the southern climate, but to point out that such habituation is more a matter of personal routine and culture. The great test of biological adjustment must remain that of racial survival. This is a test the South meets without difficulty.

The Significance of Climate to the Culture of the South

That the bearing of climate extends beyond its biological relations into the field of culture goes without saying. This by no means implies that the culture is determined by the geographic complex nor that traits of culture of the South are adapted to its climate. Indeed an adequate method of demonstrating the significance of climate to a region would be to list the culture traits that are maladjusted to the climate. The contention of the human geographer is not that culture has developed in adjustment to its terrain but that these two complexes should become increasingly adjusted. The analysis of the South in this particular may serve to show that some of the so-called climatic handicaps are lodged in the culture rather than in the climate.

The very mildness of the climate, for example, has led to maladjustment in modes of life. Weather is not taken seriously enough, and ordinary health precautions are neglected. In mild autumn rains farmers travel for miles on horseback or in slow moving wagons without covering or raincoats. M. B. Hillyard wrote in the 1880's, "I have seen men by the score come to court in midwinter wet to the skin with a cold rain, after a ride of a dozen or twenty miles, and trust to fires and whiskey to dry and warm them."[38] Since then the open Ford has replaced many of the wagons but the habit remains.

Relying on mild weather, the southern farmer continues to work in dripping rain where his northern confrere would be forced much to his benefit to unhitch and go to the house. The same reliance on mild climate has left the common man no more careful of his beast than of himself. Cheap and open shelters rather than well constructed buildings and barns have prevailed. This has proved a heavy drain on the vitality of animals—pro-

---

[38] *The New South*, p. 279.

ucing a hardy native stock but handicapping the South with a
et of wrong practices in its treatment of imported blooded an-
mals.

Despite his rainy climate, the southern common man is less
kely to build the small fire needed to take the chill from rooms
1 early winter days. This trait is accelerated in Florida where a
light cold spell seems much colder because many householders
re not prepared for warming their houses. Hillyard feels that
1e northerner with his habitual precautions will benefit more
rom the characteristic southern weather than the too-accustomed
ative.

The architecture that has come to be associated with the planter
outh is a notable achievement in adjustment to weather—one
f the finest worked out on our continent. The verandas, the
vide high porches, set off by white columns, and the high ceil-
1gs did more than achieve a type of beauty. They protected
1e house from beating rains but more than that they shaded it
rom the sun's slanting rays. What if the hound dog, the cat,
nd the southern colonel with his mint julep followed the shade
round the veranda. The invasion of the South by an architecture
vithout porches is distinctly a step backward. The sun again be-
omes an enemy by heating the house too much during the day
or pleasant sleep at night, and southern summer rains necessitate
1e closing of windows during periods of greatest humidity.

If the common man lacked a colonial mansion, he too built in
ccordance with climate. The first houses built in Virginia, as
hillips reminds us, made use of sod and thatch. Not withstanding
1e rainy climate so well, they were replaced by the log house
dapted from Scandinavian practice,—all the more adjusted to
1e frontier because of its forests. A log house was of necessity
uilt like a crib. If two rooms were jointed with a floored space
etween, the result was the "dog-run" house—so called because
1e hounds scampered unobstructed through the hallway. With
1e emergence of the sawmill the house changed from log to
rame construction and added two rooms, one on each side.
uch houses came to dot the southern countryside wherever the
ommon man had his home. They, too, represented a valuable
atural adjustment. Like the dogs, the wind passed through the
all and on hot nights the place was excellent for sleeping. In like

manner, the winter winds and rains might blow through, and with increasing means the farmer was likely to board up the run for a hall. Thus he improved appearances at the expense of harmony with nature and suffered in loss of comfort. It is possible that he followed A. N. Lytle's farmer and weatherboarded the logs, added porches front and back, and ceiled the two half-story rooms.[39] In this case he was not left at such odds with his weather. The southern landscape still exhibits "dog-run" houses in many styles but they are a passing trait of our culture. Rather than slavishly copy modes from other regions, southern architecture should seek to incorporate the high veranda, the dog-run or open buildings. The principle of the inner court as used in Latin countries might even bear experiment among the more wealthy. Unless this is done the area may lose in comfort what it hopes to gain in beauty and adherence to style. The incompatibility of the porchless dwelling and the southern climate is recognizable, and it remains to be seen what Florida is to make of its modified Mediterranean architecture built of variegated stucco.

The open brush arbor and the gospel tent for the summer revival are both accommodations to the outdoor life conditioned by climate and slack labor routines. The midday siesta in the lower South has seemed as indigenous to the southern summer as to its Mediterranean home. In its humblest form it may be viewed in August noons on the front porch of Negro cabins in the Delta. In its higher reaches the siesta was once enjoyed by dignified business men of Charleston, Savannah, and New Orleans. In all three cities time has been when no business could be transacted with any figures of prominence for two or three hours after noon. Closely related are the cooling drinks and light clothing. Children can go barefooted in such a clime either from choice or necessity.

Southern people of a certain type have been held to possess the manners of leisure, a languid courtesy, perfection in the nice arts of life, and a contempt for manual labor. It is impossible either to compliment or indict a whole people but, in so far as the statements bear truth, they reflect some of the workings of climate. It is interesting to record that the leading historian of the South notes certain traits as climatic adjustments.

[39] *I'll Take My Stand*, p. 218.

Gastronomic resource is forced by the climate to stimulate appetites which the hot weather makes languid. Indeed most of the habits of life are affected. In the tedious heat work is hard, indolence easy; speech is likely to be slow and somewhat slurred; manners are soft; and except when tempers are hot the trend is toward easy-going practices even among healthy people.[40]

Ellsworth Huntington is fond of saying somewhat by way of a left-handed compliment that the climate is too good to the southern people. "The trouble is that people enjoy being too warm much better than they enjoy being too cold. Moreover, when they are too warm the easiest way to make themselves comfortable is to do as little work as possible, whereas when one is too cold the easiest way to be comfortable is to be active."

This statement of a simple human fact may be put alongside the geographic fact that the season best fitted for physical labor, the southern winter, is the very period of slack routine on cotton farms. Industrialization and the introduction of a new agriculture would serve to synchronize seasonal labor routines with periods of more abundant energy.

The trends of the cultural conditions of modern life, it is most important to note, favor the southern climate. Its climate demands a light vegetable, fruit, and milk diet, and that is the accelerating trend of the whole American people. It can no doubt, as a later chapter will show, be carried to a further extent to achieve greater efficiency in the South. Light clothing that does not bind and is open to sun and air reduces immediate humidity near the body and permits heat loss by circulation of air. This is the mode set by summer clothes for women and the trends now are for more sensible clothes for men. It needs but that these styles take a definite switch from women to men, from sports to business, to see efficiency under the southern sun take a sudden spurt upward. Moreover, the sun, once feared as the climate's most deadly weapon, is now openly courted. The South's denizens and visitors, once accommodated to heat and light, no longer dread it; and the ultra-violet rays no doubt tone up the whole system, effecting greater adjustment to climate. It may be that the climate will also be shown to allow far less reliance on distilled alcoholic liquors than permitted by colder climes. The South has

[40] Ulrich B. Phillips, *Life and Labor in the Old South*, p. 5.

long realized its effect on the Negro; and its partial commitment to a prohibition policy, antedating that of the rest of the nation, may be somewhat based upon such a recognition of its maladjustment. A trend either to complete disuse or to light wines as used by Mediterranean races would no doubt benefit the South. The South notably takes rank among the states having the fewest deaths from alcoholism.

With our emerging technology the time is not far distant when Huntington's strictures on the climate, if true, would apply only to field work. Factories are already scientifically controlled in winter as to temperature, lighting, ventilation, and humidity. The same control can be attained in summer. Humidity rather than temperature can as scientifically be taken as the control factor in mill work. By a system of freezing pipes, operated by electric refrigeration, the excess moisture can be condensed out of the air to give the humidity desired. With the degree of relative humidity regulated scientifically and ventilation controlled in accordance with changing temperatures, the factory can be made to yield the best climate for human energy. Neither the expense nor ingenuity should exceed that required in heating buildings by steam. As for intellectual work, the system can as easily be applied to dwellings and apartments as to movie theatres. Air conditioning devices have already appeared on the market. It cannot be emphasized too much that this is not a conquest of the tropics. Indeed the first application of controlled humidity for buildings is needed not in the South but in the treatment of northern cities to prevent the annual recurrence of deaths by heat prostration. When the machine age gives as good care and attention to its human resources as to its invested capital, the industrial invasion may be expected to bring those things South. It is not as much a matter of climate as of technology, business practice, and applying the knowledge we now possess.

HISTORICAL DEVELOPMENT

After biology, the next test of adjustment to climate may be historical. The best antidote against belief in the climate's determination of southern culture is the logic of events. A few examples will show this. Only a generation ago our most able human geographer assigned the American Negro his geographic doom in these words: "The catarrhal zone north of the fortieth parallel soon exterminates the Negro."[41] "Negroes," she explained, "meet a climatic barrier in America at the isotherm of 50° centigrade. They are found in New England and Nova Scotia generally with a large admixture of white blood; but there and farther north where the climate is moist as well as cold, they show a fatal tendency to pulmonary disease."[42]

The entry of the Negro into northern industry and the successful development of Negro communities as in Chicago and New York in the face of overwhelming prejudice has overthrown this cherished dogma. The Negro's accommodation to the North follows upon his attainment of housing hardly as adequate as that of the whites. Miss Semple, of course, hopelessly confused the cultural and the physical environments. Thus inexorably does the logic of history dispose of one-factor explanations.

Geographers have applied the same style of geographic determinism to account for the South's historic devotion to agriculture. This statement for example is but a generation old.

It is a climatic line [approximately 37° north latitude] which divides the urban north from the rural South, the area of abundant skilled white labor from the area of unreliable, unskilled Negro labor. Even when skilled workmen are imported from the north to some particularly favored center of industry in the South, an enervating climate makes their labor far more difficult and less efficient. Even the entrepreneur does not escape the paralyzing touch of heat and moisture.[43]

Again the trend of history contradicts a dogmatic climatic determinism. Research has shown that the Southeast led in certain phases in the early development of industry, and New England drew ahead only as cotton culture came to occupy first place in southern economy. The rise of a vigorous industrialism and an aggressive forward movement in literature, scholarship, and university life in the recent South has occurred in our day without change of climate.

Within the last half century there has occurred a shifting process in six industries. All of these industries have migrated further southward. The petroleum industry has moved from Penn-

[41] Ellen C. Semple, *Influence of Geographic Environment*, p. 37.
[42] *Ibid.*, p. 625.
[43] E. C. Semple, *American History and Its Geographic Conditions*, p. 346.

sylvania to the southwest, Louisiana, Texas, Oklahoma, Arkansas, and California. Cotton textiles have drifted from their century-old moorings in New England to the Piedmont of the South Atlantic states. Likewise the boot and shoe industry has changed its basis of operation from Boston to St. Louis. The lumber industry, it is true, has found a refuge in the Pacific northwest, but a more important section of the industry finds its locale in the Gulf states. Birmingham's development has drawn the center of gravity of iron and steel production nearer Dixie. In all these emerging industries the use of natural resources appears to have been retarded more by the socio-economic factors, such as lack of capital, technology, and trained labor, than the physical factor of climate.

In summary we have found, as might have been expected, no definite break between North and South in climate. The North, to be sure, is subject to the worst feature of the summer, the heat wave, while the South proves relatively free from the paralyzing extremes of cold visited on the North. There is no doubt, as Ward remarks, that the normal effect of a cold season which tends to stimulate and refresh is offset by the unfavorable effect of long winters on cultural routines, economic adjustment, and transportation.[44]

None of the evidence relating to the white man's inability to adjust himself to the tropics seems to have any bearing on the South. As far as the biology of the climate goes, the student may well agree with Sir Patrick Manson, author of *Tropical Diseases:* "Acclimatization is less an unconscious adaptation of the physiology of the individual than an intelligent adaptation of his habits." That is, while weather and climate may affect man directly, he may also change his water, his food, his clothing, his habitations and his surroundings, to fit climate. Climate can scarcely ever be considered by itself, and we are apt to enlarge the word to include much more than the meteorological elements. But clothing, food, drink, habitation, and physical artifacts go to make up man's culture. It is one thing to blame the climate; it is quite another to blame a culture that may be out of adjustment to the climate.

[44] See Robert De C. Ward, *Climate Considered Especially in Relation to Man, passim.*

CHAPTER XV

CLIMATE, HEALTH, AND ENERGY

THE GEOGRAPHY OF DISEASE

It has long been known that there exists what may be called a geography of disease. The prevalence of many diseases conforms to a spatial pattern, and the intensity of many diseases is completely seasonal. It can be shown that certain diseases in southern areas which carry over into social waste and economic efficiency are conditioned by geographic factors such as soil and climate. However, when each disease of temperate climes is traced, as Clemow has suggested, from the pole to the equator, it is not always found to become either more common or more severe.[1] The influence of climate is more likely to be found in the number and variety of disorders that occur than in a change in the frequency and intensity of each disease. While some diseases may grow milder as they approach the equator, the disease list is always larger in warm, moist regions. This observation can be shown to apply with justice to the semi-tropic parts of the South.

The seasonal variations in diseases do not entirely explain their geographic distribution. There exists a long list of diseases which prevail mostly in the cooler seasons of the year. These are mainly related to the respiratory passages—influenza, diphtheria, croup, whooping cough, pneumonia. On the other hand, many affections of the digestive system such as diarrhoea, dysentery, and cholera occur in the warmer seasons. Plague has proved a warm season disease in temperate climes and a cool season disease in the tropics.[2]

The geographic distribution of disease is something objective enough to be compared with the geography of animals or the ecology

[1] Frank G. Clemow, *The Geography of Disease,* pp. 16-17.
[2] *Ibid.,* p. 17.

of plants. The fact that the prevalence of certain diseases was restricted to hot, moist climates could not be satisfactorily explained until the life histories of minute organisms became known. These disorders, it was then shown, are caused by parasites which exist for long periods outside the human body, either in soil, water, or in the body of hosts. The geography of the disease is thus a biological fact, existing in the limitation by temperature and moisture of the range of the parasite. When the life cycle of the organism is dependent upon passage through the body of a host, as the malaria microbe depends on the anopheline mosquito, the distribution of the disease is determined largely by the geographic range of the host. The South has in its day possessed three such known disease organisms conditioned by climate; the yellow fever germ, the microbe of Texas Tick Fever and the malaria microbe. Moreover, the hookworm, while lacking an intermediary host, is responsive to climatic effects. It will be the purpose of this chapter to trace the geography of the human diseases affecting energy and efficiency in the South.

A brief glance at comparative death rates seems to confirm these trends in the geography of disease. The southern states tend to possess mortality rates higher than the mean for the nation. A glance at Table XXXVIII shows that from 1920 to 1929 Arkansas, Oklahoma, North Carolina, and Kentucky were the only southern states whose death rates consistently fell below the national death rate. Yet when the death rate for Negroes is excluded every southern state except Florida falls below both the white and rural death rates for the nation. To equalize the omission of Negroes from southern states it would probably be necessary to omit a comparable class, such as urban slum dwellers in the North. The death rate for Negroes is much higher in the northern areas.

Certain diseases reflect the incidence of the social as well as the geographic environment. In deaths from tuberculosis, typhoid, pellagra, influenza, childbirth, and in infant mortality, southern states uniformly exceed the national average. In fact, the first ten states in any of these particulars will be found overwhelmingly southern.

In brief, the reason is mainly that the South is too rural, too sparsely settled, and too poor to possess the best medical

TABLE XXXVIII

SOUTH'S COMPARATIVE DEATH RATES PER 1,000 POPULATION IN REGISTRATION
AREA BY STATES AND BY RACES, 1920-1929

STATES	RANK					RATES				
	1920	1925	1927	1928	1929	1920	1925	1927	1928	1929
Number of States in Area	34	40	42	44	46	(Adjusted)				
Alabama	..	20	14	25	29	....	11.6	10.5	12.3	12.4
White	..	..	..	..	..	....	9.5	8.7	10.0	10.2
Colored	..	..	..	..	..	....	15.2	13.7	16.2	16.2
Arkansas	..	..	8	11	10	....	....	10.0	10.9	10.5
White	..	..	..	..	..	....	....	8.8	9.7	9.4
Colored	..	..	..	..	..	....	....	13.4	14.3	13.8
Florida	24	37	38	40	33	13.4	13.6	13.6	13.7	12.7
White	..	..	..	..	..	11.4	11.9	11.7	11.8	10.8
Colored	..	..	..	..	..	17.6	17.4	17.9	18.2	17.1
Georgia	..	..	..	26	24	(1924)	12.0	....	12.4	12.2
White	..	..	..	..	..	....	10.1	....	10.3	10.0
Colored	..	..	..	..	..	....	14.8	....	15.9	15.8
Kentucky	8	16	16	19	22	11.7	11.3	10.6	11.8	12.0
White	..	..	..	.	..	10.9	10.4	9.8	10.9	11.1
Colored	..	..	..	..	..	19.5	20.2	19.3	20.8	21.3
Louisiana	23	30	27	23	21	13.3	12.8	11.8	12.2	11.9
White	..	..	..	..	..	10.9	10.0	9.4	10.0	9.7
Colored	..	..	..	..	..	17.5	17.3	15.8	15.9	15.7
Mississippi	25	21	29	35	35	13.4	11.6	11.9	13.1	13.0
White	..	..	..	..	..	9.7	8.8	9.2	10.5	10.3
Colored	..	..	..	..	..	16.8	14.3	14.5	15.6	15.5
North Carolina	26	15	18	18	19	13.4	11.3	10.9	11.8	11.8
White	..	..	..	..	..	11.6	9.7	9.4	10.4	10.2
Colored	..	..	..	..	..	17.7	14.9	14.6	15.1	15.2
Oklahoma	..	..	..	2	2	....	....	....	9.0	9.0
White	..	..	..	..	..	....	....	....	8.7	8.7
Colored	..	..	..	..	..	....	....	....	11.4	12.0
South Carolina	34	31	34	43	39	15.6	12.8	12.6	14.1	13.3
White	..	..	..	..	..	12.3	9.8	9.8	11.3	10.1
Colored	..	..	..	..	..	18.9	16.1	15.7	17.4	17.0
Tennessee	17	14	24	22	24	12.5	11.2	11.4	12.2	12.2
White	..	..	..	..	..	10.9	9.6	9.9	10.7	10.7
Colored	..	..	..	..	..	19.2	18.1	18.0	19.1	18.7
Virginia	29	26	32	31	35	13.6	12.4	12.0	12.6	13.0
White	..	..	..	..	..	11.4	10.3	10.1	10.6	11.0
Colored	..	..	..	..	..	18.9	17.6	17.0	17.9	18.2
United States Registration Area						13.1	11.8	11.4	12.0	11.9
White						12.7	11.4	10.9	11.5	11.3
Colored						18.3	17.6	16.5	17.1	16.9
Urban						14.0	12.6	12.4	13.3	13.0
Rural						12.2	10.9	10.4	11.0	10.9

facilities. If the states are ranked on the basis of the number
of physicians to the population six southern states will be found
among the lowest twelve; in ratio of number of people to each

dentist eight of the last ten states are southern; in percentage of counties having hospitals, and in the ratio of hospital beds to population the last ten are again southern. In the amount of public health expenditures per inhabitant in 1923 the South ranked around the median although five states were in the last ten. In the percentage of her rural population with health officers in 1927 the South did much better, with eight states among the first sixteen and none below twenty-six. By unweighted averaging of the diseases listed above with the general death rate Angoff and Mencken list as the worst fifteen Arizona, New Mexico, and the thirteen southern states.[3] The selection of degenerative rather than environmental diseases would have forced certain northern and eastern states into the lower positions. Improvement in this field in the South means raising the standards of the rural and Negro populations and is as much an economic as a health problem.

Again, in the geography of disease we must be careful not to regard the South as a unit. The Highland areas stand out in striking contrast to the rest. In the Appalachians and Ozarks the mortality and morbidity rates from pulmonary diseases are higher. In this, as in other aspects, these regions resemble colder temperate areas. Altitude, of course, has produced corresponding changes in climate. The effect of climate is, however, accentuated by social factors. Sparse population, scattered institutional and occupational centers, with poor avenues of transportation, have arranged matters so that mountain people as a matter of course walk long distances in bad weather. Children in going to school and men going to work often have to walk for miles.[4]

CLIMATE, HEALTH, AND ENERGY

The attempt to trace the relations of climate to human energy and resulting levels of economic efficiency in the American South has proved singularly ineffective. Not only has the question been encumbered with bias and opinion, but any measurement of human energy in terms of achievement in production of wealth is indissolubly bound up with natural resources and historical accidents. Furthermore, climate may yet be found to yield to

[3] See Charles Angoff and H. L. Mencken, "The Worst American State," Part II, *American Mercury*, XXIV, 175-88. S. H. Hobbs, Jr., *North Carolina Economic and Social*, p. 393.

[4] Campbell, *The Southern Highlands*, p. 211.

diet in affecting that form of biological adequacy which we term human energy. It is more than possible that bio-chemistry may demonstrate a maladjustment between warm climates and certain dietetic regimens. Where a maladjustment exists between climate and regional diet, the climatic factor must be regarded as secondary rather than primary.

As a matter of fact, the effect of climate on biological adequacy may in reality be twofold, psychological and biological. It is possible that an enervating climate lowers the drive or stimulus to effort without in any way impairing the ability of the human organism to function. On the other hand, it may be held that continued warm moist temperature lowers the level of healthful functioning of the human body. The first effect might be more evident in intellectual work but would also serve as lack of spur to any type of manual activity. The first concept is probably included in the commonsense application of the term lazy, with its moral implications considered as psychological. The second view considers the maladaptation to climate a mild pathological condition in which the psychological state is an effect of biological depletion. This no doubt has been the condition most often implied in critical comments on the inefficiency of the so-called "poor white" group in the South. The "nineteenth century superstition," often advanced as a defense for slavery, that white men could not work in the field in the South partakes of this view. The rise of modern medicine following the development of the germ theory of disease showed that economic inefficiency may be a pathological condition apart from the climate. "Laziness" thus may be actually due to a disease to which the climate is related as secondary rather than as a primary factor.

The seriousness of the rôle which a disease plays in a society is estimated most often by its rank in mortality tables. This is true because death of the breadwinner offers the greatest possible shock to family life and subtracts a member from the group. It is characteristic of many diseases which lead to biological depletion that they do not rank particularly high as causes of death. Being chronic they run no spectacular course and contribute to the death rate indirectly by weakening the resistance of the organism to other diseases which are finally reported as causes of death. A "concealed disease" in the statistical sense is one whose mortality rate offers no adequate index to its prevalence. If its recorded mortality bears but slight relation to its economic incidence the term concealed disease is doubly justified. In this sense both malaria and hookworm are concealed diseases. L. O. Howard has said: "A man may suffer from malaria throughout the greater part of his life and his productive capacity may be reduced from fifty to seventy-five per cent and yet ultimately he may die from some entirely different immediate cause."

Mortality records, where kept, offer no adequate index to the social effect of these diseases. Morbidity records, moreover, are discounted by prevailing attitudes. A lazy man, so runs the popular notion, is a lazy man by virtue of inherent depravity, and ignorance keeps a society which holds this view from suspecting that anything is wrong with its most inefficient members. Such views, it was found, were held by many communities of their hookworm victims before the discovery of hookworm disease. If the disease is both chronic and widely prevalent in an area, it comes to be regarded as one of the ills the flesh is heir to, accepted as something to be outgrown, worn off or endured. This has been a commonly accepted attitude toward chills and fevers. Being so common, they are not reported to doctors and do not find their way at full value into morbidity tables. This is especially true of malaria, in spite of the fact that it has long been a reportable disease. Allowances must be made for the South, however, because many of its states have only recently been included in the registration area of vital statistics. Mortality and morbidity rates of malaria and hookworm if fully available would be no index of the social and economic effect of those diseases. Accordingly, their importance has been underestimated. The condition due to their presence has been variously attributed to deficient heredity, climatic effects, and a lack of natural resources.

HOOKWORM AND THE SOUTH

It has long been said by certain critics of the South that at certain lower levels there existed biological strains not altogether adequate. An article by Joseph Pitt in 1808 described dirt-eating and anaemia among lower classes in the South and attributed these conditions to malnutrition. By some these strains were called "southern poor whites"—a fighting word anywhere south of the

Potomac. "In appearance," runs a typical description, "these people are usually most unprepossessing. Their skin is yellow, wrinkled, and waxy; their hair, dry and lustreless; their eyes, without color or sparkle; their expression, dull, stupid, and intensely melancholy." They are characterized by extreme emaciation. Perversions of appetite were said to prevail. Dirt-eating, snuff-dipping, tobacco-chewing, alcoholism, and resin-chewing have existed to an immoderate degree among the "sand hillers." All their troubles, and by their own account they have been many, were attributed by the pious to faults of character. The people themselves have called their ailment "the lazy sickness," "the big lazy," or malaria. Much nonsense, no doubt, has been written about the poor whites and the above description will appear to many as a caricature, but that certain strains and areas suffered a lowered biological efficiency need not be denied.

In Europe, hookworms have been known for 90 years. They were first recognized as human parasites in 1838 by an Italian physician, Angelo Dupino, who discovered them in the body of a peasant woman, dead of pneumonia. A later examination of a hundred bodies showed twenty infected with the parasites. Not until the techniques of hookworm ova count, demonstrated by Italian physicians in 1878, was there discovered a method of finding the disease other than by autopsy. Diseases in mines, the epidemic in the Saint Gothard Tunnel in 1880, the discovery of dermal infection, and the development of vermifuges were developments which served to keep the old-world species, *Ancylostoma duodenale,* before the European public.

The discovery of the parasite in the new world was reserved for a native of North Carolina, Dr. Charles Waddell Stiles, zoologist with the United States Bureau of Animal Industry. In his studies of parasites infecting animals he found hookworms extremely numerous in sheep and dogs in the South. These parasites, common to men and animals in southern Europe, he decided must also be found to infect the population of the southern states. His first expression of this view before a school of medicine in 1896 was allowed to go unnoticed. Dr. Stiles' examination of Sand Hill families of the down-and-out type, however, was rewarded with high counts of hookworm ova. Accordingly, on May 10, 1902, in a paper read before the Pan-American Sanitary Congress, he described the new species of hookworm which he named *Necator Americanus,* the American murderer. Dr. Stiles thought at the time he had discovered a new world species of the parasite, but it has since been shown that the American hookworm is a species from Africa, brought over by the Negro slaves. Not content with displaying a new zoölogical specimen, he had the boldness to point out the poor whites and attribute to this parasite the anaemia and inefficiency of certain low-level groups. The next morning the public was told by one New York newspaper that the "germ of laziness" had been discovered.[5] As was to have been expected, the reports raised both resentment and ridicule. Many of the people of the South took the matter as an assault upon southern prosperity. One southern newspaper carried an editorial in a dissenting voice.

We have known the poor whites for generations, and no one has ever explained their condition satisfactorily. Here is a man who claims that he has found the cause of their worthlessness and inefficiency. Now, in all fairness, do not let us go off the handle as some of our esteemed contemporaries have done, but let us hear him out. Perhaps he is a fool. Perhaps he is an Ananias. But, perhaps he is neither. It is just possible that he knows what he is talking about. In justice to the poor whites, let us hear what he has to say.[6]

In the meantime the first public health movement directed against the hookworm in the western hemisphere had been developing in Porto Rico under American auspices. After the American occupation Dr. Bailey K. Ashford of the United States Army was in charge of feeding a group of survivors of a cyclone disaster, threatened with starvation. He noted that anaemia persisted in spite of the efforts at relief. He carefully studied the patients, ascribed to the hookworm the cause of their condition, and wrote a detailed and accurate description of the disease, stressing its economic aspects. In 1902, after a complete study of 100 cases, he wrote an article charging that 30 per cent of the deaths in Porto Rico were due to this anaemia. His work bore fruit when in 1904 the legislature of the island appropriated $5,000 and

[5] See also Mark Sullivan, *Our Times,* III, ch. ix.

[6] Quoted by Francis M. Bjorkman, "The Cure for Two Million Sick," *World's Work,* May 1909, pp. 11607-11. See also "Hookworm Disease and Its Control," International Health Board, 1922.

appointed Doctors Ashford, King, and Guiteros to combat the disease. The appropriation was later renewed and increased and the direction gradually transferred to local authorities. In many ways this initial venture served as a model for the work that was to be done in the South.

In the development of public health the South lagged so noticeably behind the nation that, apart from the resentment aroused, any attack on the hookworm as a social handicap seemed remote indeed. No anti-hookworm campaign could be expected to originate as a popular movement, and the states were not prepared to organize such work. The appeal then must be to philanthropy. That such an appeal did not go unheeded was due to Dr. Stiles, Walter Hines Page, Dr. Wallace Butterick, and John D. Rockefeller. According to Burton Hendrick it came about in this way.[7] En route to a meeting of Roosevelt's Country Life Commission held at Raleigh, North Carolina, Page pointed out to Henry Wallace, as an example of the so-called dirt-eaters, a cadaverous tenant farmer who had boarded the train. Dr. Stiles broke in with the remark that he was merely an extreme case of hookworm disease and could be cured with fifty cents worth of drugs. Page quizzed Dr. Stiles in a long discussion and was told that two million people in the South were so affected. For the first time an intelligent and public-spirited southerner with influence accepted the "hookworm theory." At the hearing the next day Dr. Stiles, replying to a denial of the existence of hookworm in North Carolina, created a sensation by declaring that there were four cases of hookworm in the room at the moment. For their part in the discussion which followed, Page and Stiles, both North Carolinians, were accused in the newspaper of slandering their native region. Governor Glenn severely criticised the Commission for introducing the subject, and the *News and Observer* published pictures of Page's father and grandfather to show that they lived long, and *ergo* the country was perfectly healthy. Not all followed the crowd. The State Board of Health issued a public announcement that Dr. Stiles had underestimated the ravages of the disease in the state.

On October 26, 1909, the Rockefeller Commission for the Extermination of the Hookworm Disease was organized for a period

[7] *Training of an American*, pp. 370-73.

of five years with an initial gift of a million dollars by the philanthropist. Page had brought Dr. Stiles within the range of Dr. Buttrick's and Mr. Gates' knowledge and interest. The jokesmiths speculated as to how much of Epsom salts and thymol a million dollars would buy, and pictured the Commission on a junketing tour administering heavy doses to recalcitrant southerners. The campaign, however, was soon to make headway in public favor. The first task in hookworm control was undertaken early in 1910 in Richmond County, Virginia. The fund was supplied by the Commission, but the work was directed by the State Board of Health. Early in its course the Commission worked out a threefold procedure: (1) to conduct surveys to show the extent of the disease, (2) to cure the sufferers and (3) to stop soil pollution. It was the idea of the board that public health is a public function, and its ultimate aim was to transfer the direction and financial support of the movement to state and county governments. In 1910 two counties contributed $241 for the support of dispensaries; in 1913 there were 208 counties which contributed $43,649 for their support. In the period from 1910 to 1913, 556 counties in the South spent $110,000 in aiding the Rockefeller board. Surveys had shown the extent and prevalence of the disease, educational campaigns had been waged against soil pollution, and by March 31, 1914, 453 counties had completed the dispensary method of combating hookworm. Up to 1914, 548,992 rural children had been examined and 39 per cent found infected. On August 12, 1914, John D. Rockefeller announced the termination of the five year experimental period and created the International Health Board to carry on allied work all over the world. In May, 1921, the International Health Board transferred its part in the hookworm campaign to governmental authorities, and its policies are now administered as a part of county health programs.

The achievement was a social no less than a scientific triumph. A lack of interest and organization for public health was met and overcome. Although the South may not realize the debt, it is largely to the early Rockefeller campaigns that the section owes its present county public health organization. In overcoming the rather human resentment roused by the hookworm discussion, the Commission carried through a remarkable campaign of popular scientific education. In this task the scientific staffs owed much to the simple nature of the disease. As a Report of the Health Board stated:

There is probably no other disease which is so well understood in every detail and which can be so satisfactorily explained to a layman. Nor is there any other widely prevalent disease against which the lay community can so readily and surely protect itself by simple precaution. Its conquest virtually resolves itself into a problem of popular education against soil pollution.

The simplicity of the disease, Rockefeller millions, and the exact technique worked out by the scientific experts were factors in making the war on hookworms an impressive public health triumph. Re-surveys from 1918 to 1922 of 66 counties surveyed in the period 1910-1914, showed an average decrease in infection of 47.5 per cent. In Georgia, Grady County showed a decrease from 99.4 to 31.3 per cent infection, Pamlico in North Carolina fell from 62.9 to 9.3 per cent, and Lee County, Alabama, fell from 51.8 to 15.5 per cent. This decrease in numbers was accompanied by a proportionate decrease in severity of infection. Although the examination of drafted men from the South indicated that, depending on locality, 12 to 33 per cent of the adult males were infected, the majority of the cases were not severe. In its reports covering the year 1926 the International Health Board announced the virtual conquest of the disease in these words:

At the present time it is fair to say that hookworm disease has almost disappeared from the United States and is rapidly coming under control in many parts of the world. But the great achievement is not the social and economic rehabilitation of the more than six or seven million people who have been treated for the disease during the past ten or fifteen years; it is the development of administrative measures that will prevent millions yet unborn from ever suffering from its ravages.[8]

The reversal in public attitudes was no less an achievement. Dr. Stiles, who had narrowly missed becoming one of the martyrs of science, received at the hands of the University of North Carolina an honorary LL.D., and from the University of Richmond, an M.D. degree. Publicists like Gerald W. Johnson pointed out that the period of conquest of hookworm corresponded with the period of economic advance in the South. The most valuable

[8] P. 6.

single index of the change in attitude is found in the creation of full-time health departments in southern counties. "The evolution of simple hookworm posts," says a report, "into county agencies for conserving public health has been one of the gratifying developments in the Southern states."[9]   At the close of 1926 there existed in the United States 341 counties employing such services, and of these, 163 counties were found in twelve southern states. Representing local units, financed partly from local funds, employing local doctors, these organizations encountered less and less antagonism in their attack on hookworm and malaria. By January 1, 1928, the number of county health units for the twelve states had increased to 258, much over half of the 414 units in the whole United States. Only Ohio with 47 county health departments was leading nine southern states. A study of the map shows that the counties having health departments in the South are well distributed along coastal and alluvial lowlands and follow rather closely the distribution of malaria.

THE GEOGRAPHY OF THE HOOKWORM

In the course of its conquest a great many facts were gathered on the geography of hookworm disease. Climate affects distribution of hookworm by means of the relation which temperature bears to the development of larvae in the soil. Study of its world-wide distribution by the International Health Board narrowed hookworm disease to a climatic zone extending 36° north and 30° south of the equator and containing nine hundred million people, half of the world's population. Extensive investigations have shown that larvae in the infective stage are not to be found in the soil of southern Alabama between late October and early May. A minimum temperature of 40° F. at night is sufficiently low to check their development. Infection is thus shown to be acquired only during the summer.[10]   It is slowly acquired and as slowly lost. Frequent dry periods during the spring were also found to check hookworm development entirely.

The amount of rainfall thus proved another important geographic control in the distribution of hookworm disease. Texas, for example, can be divided into an eastern area of heavy rainfall,

[9] International Health Board, *Sixth Report,* 1919, p. 4.
[10] International Health Board, *Eleventh Report,* 1924, p. 112.

40 to 50 inches, a middle belt of 20 to 40 inches precipitation, and a West Texas with 10 to 20 inches rainfall. Hookworm infection is medium in the area of heavy rainfall, light in the middle area, and absent in the arid west. Regions along the coast, although characterized by heavy rainfall, are found to be areas of light infection if the soil is impregnated with salt.[11]

In the ecology of the disease, soil proved to have an importance hardly second to that of climate. Studies in the laboratory have demonstrated that humus, sand, loam, and clay have markedly different effects upon the number of hookworm larvae which develop to the infective stage. This has been demonstrated in the field by studies of two southern states, Alabama and Tennessee. Throughout these two regions the habits of rural sanitation, the temperature, and the rainfall are such that they affect the dissemination of hookworm infestation about equally. Of Tennessee's ten soil provinces the only areas of high infestation are Unaka Mountain Range and the Cumberland Plateau, both provinces with sandy soils. Of the six soil provinces into which Alabama is divided the great incidence of infection is found in the sandy Upper and Lower Coastal Plains. Children who had lived all their lives in regions of fine heavy clay soils failed to show heavy infestation. The efficiency of soil as a media for the culture of hookworm is thus found definitely related to texture of the top soil. An additional index to hookworm incidence is thus offered health officers in the South who can determine by culture methods what soils are favorable to hookworm development.[12]

Bio-Social Factors in Hookworm

Hookworm disease bears as close a relation to social factors as to geographic conditions. Standards of living, density of population, race, sex and age differences have been shown by various studies to operate in conditioning the spread and intensity of the infection. Negroes are hardly ever found so heavily infected that their condition approaches disease. Negro children "though

[11] *Sixth Report,* 1919, p. 59.

[12] E. R. Pickard and J. Austin Kerr, "The Incidence and Intensity of Hookworm Infestation in the Various Soil Provinces of Tennessee," *Journal of Preventive Medicine,* I, 185-203. Donald L. Augustine and Wilson G. Smillie, "The Relation of the Type of Soils of Alabama to the Distribution of Hookworm Disease," *American Journal of Hygiene,* VI, 36-62.

many of them were infected, as a rule had far fewer hookworms than white children living in a similar environment."[13] This partial immunity of the Negro to hookworm disease is a regularly observed phenomena and is apparently world-wide. It is attributed by Darling to slightly different sanitary customs, and by Payne to racial immunity. The condition still awaits adequate scientific explanation.

For the white group, living standards operate as might be expected. The wearing of shoes prevents the entrance of larvae through the pores in the soles of the feet. Soil pollution is found to be less prevalent in areas occupied by families whose higher standards include better habits of home sanitation. There exists, however, a significant rural-urban difference in infection rates which cannot be explained entirely on the basis of levels of living. Examinations have shown town children either negative or infected lightly as compared to heavy infection for country children of the same climatic and soil areas. Wearing of shoes is not a factor. Density of population operates to change customs. Where people live in close proximity, decency prevents promiscuous soil pollution, and village children have little opportunity to come in contact with larvae-infected soils.[14] Thus, like many things in the South, the prevalence of hookworm disease may be attributed to the survival of frontier conditions. Early in his studies, Dr. Stiles pointed out that children in mill villages in the South even when employed in the mills ranked higher in qualities of health than the child on the farm. Intensive study of 396 mill village children showed that hookworm disease was limited to those who had been in the village less than three years.

In none of the studies has sex been found to be a factor of importance. Age is a much more important consideration. Few children under five are found to be infected; and after eighteen the percentage and severity of the infection decrease. It must be remembered that the worms do not breed within the body, but on the contrary the ova must hatch in the soil from which the larvae find their way into the body. With the coming of adulthood, accordingly it is to be expected that changed habits of clothing and sanitation will decrease danger of infection from the soil and the

[13] *Twelfth Report*, 1925, p. 11, ff.
[14] *Eleventh Report*, 1924, p. 116.

previous infection will in the course of time be gradually eliminated. The percentage of hookworm infection on the basis of
age levels shows the following range:

Age	6-7	8-9	10-11	12-13	14-15	16-18
Per Cent	38.2	50.3	57.1	62.7	64.7	65.2

In its 1924 Report the International Health Board stated the
conclusion of its social studies. Severe hookworm infection in the
United States occurs only in children, rural, white, and of school
age in the southern states. While a far cry from the two million
sick souls of the first period of hookworm agitation, it seems
much nearer the scientific statement of fact.

Possibly the best summing up of the geography and the sociology
of hookworm is found in the formula of the application of its findings to social engineering. The following is the typical procedure
advised for the public health official in his attack on hookworm.

He should first inform himself of the mean yearly temperature and the
rainfall of the area to be worked. He should then study the types of
soil in the area to discover whether hookworm larvae can readily develop
in them to the infective stage. These preliminary observations, together
with a brief study of the sanitary habits of the inhabitants, will enable
him to estimate with considerable accuracy the economic importance of
hookworm infection to the community. His next step is the microscopic
examination of about 10 per cent of the total population to determine the
average intensity of the infection obtaining.

If the average hookworm index of the persons examined is less than 100
no treatment need be administered in the community, since no true hookworm disease exists there and sanitation and education will slowly and
gradually eliminate the light infections. If the average worm content is
found to be over 100, one standard treatment may be administered to all
moderately infected persons and two treatments to those having heavy
infections. This will reduce the infection of the community to the point
of economic cure. Only sanitation and education can permanently hold
it at this point. But reinfection is slowly acquired, and even though no
sanitary measures are instituted, some time will elapse before it becomes
necessary to give another course of treatment.

The relation that hookworm infection bears to general health
and to intellectual achievement has been indicated by a series
of studies. In the military cantonments during the World War

the incidence of pneumonia and its mortality rate were found to be much higher among southern than northern troops. Measles occurred more frequently (in the ratio of two and one half to one) among men who had hookworm disease. Measles patients who suffered also from hookworm were twice as susceptible to pneumonia and kindred diseases as men free from intestinal infection.[15]

The whole question of the relation of hookworm disease to mental retardation may be subjected to scrutiny by tests of the intelligence and achievement of groups living under the same climatic conditions. In one woman's college in the South the average standing of fifty-six infected students was 78 per cent compared to 89 per cent for students found free of infection. In a southern academy 25 infected boys averaged 64 per cent in their studies as compared with 86 per cent for the same number of boys found hookworm free. In the case of 10,000 men at Camp Travis, Texas, a comparison of the hookworm survey with the psychological tests showed that soldiers with hookworm disease ranked 33 per cent lower. A series of mental tests on Goddard's Revision of the Binet-Simon Scale of the school children of Queensland, Australia, showed lightly infected cases to be retarded 9.3 months while heavily infected cases were retarded 23.4 months. The longer the infection had persisted in the child the greater retardation was found to exist.[16]

MALARIA

It may be that some diseases exert a selective influence upon the race by weeding out the weak. Such cannot be said of either hookworm or malaria. Malaria "strongly resembles hookworm disease in its wide distribution and in the fact that it is an anaemia producing disease most prevalent among children and therefore preying upon the race most heavily during the period of physical and mental growth."[17] Dr. Andrew Balfour, director of the London School of Hygiene and Tropical Medicine, estimates the annual cost of sickness and death due to malaria in the British Empire at $300,000,000 and sets the world death rate from malaria at

---

[15] *Report of the Surgeon General*, U. S. Army, 1917, p. 131.

[16] Rockefeller Foundation, *Report*, 1918, p. 127. See also W. G. Smillie and C. R. Spence, "Mental Retardation in School Children Infested With Hookworms," *Journal of Educational Psychology*, XVII, 314-27.

[17] Rockefeller Foundation, *Annual Report*, 1915, p. 72.

2,000,000.[18]   Dr. Woods Hutchinson believes that malaria has probably killed more human beings than all the wars that have ever devastated the globe, while Dr. Henry R. Carter holds that it is the only disease capable of rendering a region uninhabitable. These two infections, hookworm and malaria, in the judgment of the International Health Board, "constitute what is probably the most serious obstacle to the development of civilization in the regions where they prevail."[19]

The history of malaria in America has been that of the frontier. It is a pestilence lurking on the outskirts of civilization, dogging the footsteps of the colonist, the pioneer, and the rural dweller. The first settlers of the tidewater South were indeed fortunate, according to T. J. Wertenbaker, if during the first year they escaped the "Virginia sickness."[20] The mortality of the early settlers on the James reached as high as 75 per cent at one time. "The low and marshy ground, the swarming mosquitoes, the hot sun, the unwholesome drinking water combined to produce an unending epidemic of dysentery and malaria." Of the Charleston district the Lords Proprietors wrote under date of May 13th, 1691:

Men will dye in Carolina for some time faster than they are borne or grow up, and if none come to you your numbers will by degrees bee so diminished that you will be easily cut off by the Indians or pyrats.[21]

A physician with several years experience in tidewater Virginia during colonial times wrote:

The acute diseases in these unhealthful parts of North America generally turn to intermittents, which are not mortal even in twenty months; but in a few months more they may bring on that cachexy, with an emaciated habit, a swelled belly, and a pale sallow complexion, which is the characteristic of the bad state of health in all the southern and maritime parts of North America.[22]

With time there came a type of acquired immunity which may have resulted in making the disease chronic rather than acute.

[18] International Health Board, *Twelfth Report*, pp. 71-72.
[19] *Fourth Annual Report*, p. 126.
[20] *The Planters of Colonial Virginia*, pp. 39-40.
[21] W. J. Rivers, *History of South Carolina*, p. 98.
[22] John Mitchell, M.D., *The Present Status of Great Britain and North America*, p. 191.

At least Governor Berkeley so held in 1671. "There is not oft seasoned hands (as we term them) that die now, whereas not one of five escaped the first year."[23] Much of the later improvements in conditions can be attributed to the introduction of Peruvian bark, as quinine was first called.

As settlement spread southward and westward this story could be repeated again and again though fortunately often in milder form. Frederick Law Olmsted reported graphically the death dealing effect of the miasma on the rice plantations of South Carolina.

"I would as soon stand fifty feet from the best Kentucky rifleman and be shot at by the hour, as to spend a night on my plantation in summer," a Charleston gentleman said to me. And the following two instances of the deadly work the miasma sometimes does were given to me by another: A party of six ladies and gentlemen went out of town to spend a day at the mansion of a rice-planter, on an island. By an accident to their boat, their return before night was prevented, and they went back and shut themselves within the house, had fires made, around which they sat all night, and took every other precaution to guard against the miasma. Nevertheless, four of them died from its effects, within a week; and the other two suffered severely. Two brothers owned a plantation on which they had spent the winter; one of them, as summer approached, was careful to go to another residence every night; the other delayed to do so until it was too late. One morning he was found to be ill; a physician could not be procured until late in the afternoon, by which time his recovery was hopeless. The sick man besought his brother not to hazard his own life by remaining with him; and he was obliged, before the sun set, to take the last farewell, and leave him with the servants, in whose care, in the course of the night, he died.[24]

The whole advancing fringe of the frontier was, in a phrase of Hutchinson's, colored with malarial tinge. In Hulbert's opinion, "chills and fevers" and "mylary" combined with limited diet to give the pioneer race a gauntness of frame and a sallow complexion. Even today, Campbell points out, a highlander in the Appalachians feels disgraced by a fat son. The literature left by travelers through the lowland South is full of descriptions of the inroads of malaria. Lowland fevers, said Amos Stoddard in his *Sketches of Louisiana,* were "induced by pestilential vapors which

[23] Cited by Wertenbaker, *op. cit.,* p. 39.
[24] *A Journey in the Seaboard Slave States,* II, 46.

arise from the rivers and from the decayed vegetable substances." The first settlers were dying "by inches of chills and fevers"; settlers from the North had to undergo a long period of acclimatization, but sooner or later "comes the fever."[25]

The sallow emaciated countenances that looked disturbed by the monstrous quantities of calomel they were accustomed to take, and the feeble and uncertain steps with which they went about their vocations betrayed how dearly they paid by the loss of health for the privilege they enjoyed of occupying a fertile soil.[26]

The South then had her frontier conditions augmented by climate and the low living standards of slaves. In the absence of statistics history can give us only impressions of the extent of diseases peculiar to the South. On the basis of existing records, however, their location can be assigned to hot, flat, and humid areas such as rich bottom lands. Old New Orleans possessed an estimated death rate three times that of London, New York, or Philadelphia and was called the graveyard of the Southwest. Life insurance companies charged one per cent more premium on southern risks. By 1817 Savannah with a population of 5,000 had begun to eliminate the rice fields in its vicinity. The municipality set aside $200,000 to recompense planters who abandoned the crop. Ten years after, the city's mortality rate, it was estimated, had dropped to half its former figure. By 1850 a Mr. J. C. Simmonds had calculated that death and illness cost New Orleans $45,000,000 annually. Strangely enough he used the value of slaves in estimating values of whites lost by disease. Cholera also took its sporadic toll in the old South. "The appearance of this scourge of nations was a truly terrifying phenomena. Overseers and slaves died within a few hours of the first appearance of symptoms." When cholera attacked Bishop Polk's plantation in 1849 there were 220 of his 356 Negroes who contracted the disease in two weeks and 70 died. Between strange tropical diseases and strange diseases of Negroes the South was much in need of medical skill. Between 1823 and 1844 there arose the Medical College of the State of South Carolina, the Medical Department of the University of Virginia, medical schools at Augusta, New Orleans, Richmond, and the Charity Hospital at New Orleans. Nevertheless,

[25] P. 231.
[26] George William Featherstonhaugh, *Excursions Through the Slave States*, I, 302.

the rapid extension of the frontier meant an insufficiency of doctors which gradually led to the abandonment of licensing by the states. By 1850 practically anyone who so desired was allowed to practice medicine. Many Negro slaves received the best of medical care, often on the contract basis. In spite of much talk on the subject southern medical colleges never introduced any courses dealing with the diseases of the South or the Negro.[27]

Malaria was the disease of the plantation, the frontier, and the scattered rural homes. Where sparse population gave way to cities in the South, yellow fever arose and appeared to drive before it the miasmatic fever. Dr. Josiah C. Nott of Mobile, a famous scientist of the old South, described this curious phenomenon.

Yellow fever is generated in crowded populations, perhaps exclusively; while bilious fever, on the contrary, is the indigenous product of southern soils. In fact, there would seem to be something antagonistic in the causes of these diseases. Generally, along the southern seaboard, when the forest is first leveled, and a town commenced, intermittents and remittents spring up, and in some places of a malignant and fatal type. As the population increases the town spreads, and draining and paving are introduced, yellow fever, the mighty monarch of the South, who scorns the rude field and forest, plants his sceptre in the centre, and drives all other fevers to the outskirts. As the town grows, the domain of yellow fever spreads, and the others recede. There is a middle ground where the two meet and struggle for supremacy. Here we see all imaginable grades, from the simple intermittent up to the most malignant yellow fever; but whenever they come in contact, intermittents and remittents are compelled to wear the livery of the master spirit.[28]

To Nott also belongs the honor of having, in the *New Orleans Medical and Surgical Journal* of March, 1848, offered for the first time the insect hypothesis of the transmission of yellow fever. When the biology of malaria and yellow fever became known it was found that many of the prejudices and half-lights of the frontiersman had excellent foundation in fact. Yellow fever and malaria did contend for mastery, with yellow fever ruling the town and malaria the plantation. Yellow fever was found to be

[27] R. H. Shryock, "Medical Practice in the Old South," *South Atlantic Quarterly,* XXIX, 160-71.

[28] "Value of Life in the South," J. D. B. DeBow, *Resources of the Southern States,* III, 86.

carried by *Aëdes aegypti,* a town mosquito. Originally a tree-hole breeder, it adapted itself to the gutters, barrels, cisterns, and tin cans of man so thoroughly that its entire life cycle may take place indoors. The *Anopheles,* carriers of malaria, are swamp mosquitoes noted for the extent and variety of their breeding places.[29] As the bayous of the frontier gave way to the gutters and cisterns of the southern city the phenomena described by Dr. Nott actually ensued.

The superstitious beliefs of the frontier were in many ways more than half truths.[30] If it was believed malaria was caused by tropic heat, the *Anopheles* possesses a range limited by climatic factors. If malaria was thought to be caused by decaying vegetable matter in stagnant swamps, at least such swamps are the breeding places of *Anopheles.* Mal-aria means bad air. Malaria, the pioneer held, was caused by the miasma which rises out of the marshy ground at night. Night air must be avoided to the extent of closing windows, stuffing keyholes, and building fires around the house. The answer was simple. After dark came the hour at which the malaria mosquito flies abroad. Sleepers in second and third story bed rooms did not so often acquire malaria because bad air did not rise to these heights. It was of course the mosquitoes and not the air which failed to rise so high. While the pioneers held that strong winds swept the miasma away, we substitute mosquitoes for miasma. Other alleged causes, such as bad drinking water, damp soils under the house, freshly plowed sod, all can be traced to their connection with stagnant pools.

Other baffling ways of malaria were to be explained by its biology. Without knowing how it operated, dwellers in the tropics had long realized that repeated doses of Peruvian bark repressed the attack of malaria. Another puzzling set of facts led to a fatalistic attitude toward the disease. Early in his illness a patient became resigned to the fact that he would have chills and fever every fourth day; another found his attacks came every second day; a third had irregular chills, while a fourth unhappy victim expected a paroxysm every day. The French surgeon, Laveran, with the army of occupation in Algeria, discovered in 1880 the clue to these mysteries. In the blood of all malarial sufferers he found

[29] *Use of Fish for Mosquito Control,* Rockefeller Foundation, 1924, p. 7.
[30] See Woods Hutchinson, *Preventable Disease,* pp. 297-99.

a microbe which burrowed in the red corpuscles. Every 48 hours a crop of spores ripened, burst out of the corpuscles, and by its effects on blood and tissue caused the famous two-day chills; another microbe hatched every fourth day; and another ripened intermittently. The poor victim of chills every day was found to be infected with two crops working turn about on an alternating schedule. Quinine, it was found, when administered in the traditional doses entered the blood stream sufficiently either to kill the spores or prevent sporalation.[31] After Gogli, Marchiafava, and Celli aided in establishing these facts, Ronald Ross working in India from 1897 to 1899 discovered that mosquitoes carried the microbes from bird to bird and from man to man.

Geography of the Disease

With the course of time malaria has become increasingly localized in the southern states. "Fifty years ago," says a public health expert, "the disease prevailed further north than it does now. The endemic area extended to the great Lakes and Canada. Ague was in this section the most common of ailments and quinine the most universal of household remedies."[32] Iowa, Minnesota, the Dakotas, Utah, Colorado, Montana, and Wyoming were also included in the infected areas. With the increase of knowledge and the advance of public health organizations, malaria is following the geographic trend and retreating to its most inaccessible strongholds.

Unfortunately for the South, topography and the waters of the land have aided climate in localizing malaria in that area. With the exception of the Pacific Coast and Great Lakes system the United States drains through the southern states. The great Mississippi system and the Atlantic and Gulf Coastal rivers meander sluggishly through level coastal plains on the slow route to the sea. A map of the wet lands which J. Russell Smith[33] terms enemy country, shows that 69.5 per cent of all swamp lands are in ten southern states. Only two states, Michigan and Minnesota, exceed any of these ten. Also 64.9 per cent of all the wet lands of any type are in the same ten states. Again only 25.5 per cent of all the land area in the United States has an average annual rainfall

---

[31] Woods Hutchinson, *op. cit.,* pp. 295-96.
[32] John W. Trask, "Malaria," *Public Health Reprint,* No. 382, 1916, p. 3.
[33] *North America,* p. 160.

of from 40 to 60 inches. With the exception of Texas and Oklahoma all southern states have that much precipitation. The areas of 50 to 60 inches precipitation, comprising 8.4 per cent of our land area, fall almost wholly within the limits of Tennessee, Alabama, Florida, Mississippi, Arkansas, Louisiana, and the southern highland area.[34] The climatic range of malaria is indicated by the comparative length of the growing season in the southern area: in the subtropic coast 240 days and more, in the coastal plains 210 days or more, and in the Uplands usually 180 days.[35]

The distribution of deaths from malaria as analyzed by the Public Health Service locates definitely the geography of the disease.[36] The whole South is in the endemic area, but certain "areas of high prevalence stand out as definite foci surrounded by large areas of moderate prevalence." Here is made the connection between death and geography for such areas are usually the "broad flats about the lower reaches of sluggish rivers." There are five such regions in the South: the Pamlico Sound region of North Carolina, the Savannah River between South Carolina and Georgia, the Flint River region of South Georgia, the coast of west Florida about the mouths of the Apalachicola and Suwannee rivers, and most important of all, the widely extending flood plain of the lower Mississippi with areas reaching up the valleys of its tributaries, the Tennessee, the Arkansas, the St. Francis, the Black and the Red rivers.[37] Again these figures show that malaria is essentially a rural disease. Prolonged and desperate cases tend to drift into city hospitals where death adds to urban mortality rates; but, in spite of this fact, there are six times as many deaths from malaria in the rural areas as in the cities of these regions.[38]

MALARIA AND SOCIAL RESOURCES

Mortality rates of malaria may be relied upon to show geographic distribution, but they afford insufficient index of the severity and far reaching influence of the disease. From 1904 to 1914, for example, there were in the army of continental United States 13,000 cases of malaria from which only two deaths re-

[34] *Ibid.,* p. 246.
[35] J. Russell Smith, *op. cit.,* map, p. 175.
[36] Kenneth F. Maxcy, "Distribution of Malaria in the United States" as indicated by Mortality Reports, *Reprint 839,* May 25, 1923, p. 5.
[37] *Ibid.,* pp. 8-9. [38] *Ibid.,* p. 11.

sulted.[39]   The case fatality rate in the United States has been shown to be among the lowest of diseases, about 0.5 per cent. The presence of a few cases of smallpox makes an epidemic with all the public health forces mobilized, while the continued presence of malaria in many southern states goes unnoticed. "Plague, leprosy, or typhus arouses to instant activity the press, the people, and the health authorities, while commoner diseases, though more destructive, receive far less consideration. To fear death and the disease associated with death and to give less consideration to the ailments which are not directly mortal are common characteristics."[40]

Mississippi is one state in the Union whose Health Department has for a long time consistently demanded morbidity reports from its physicians.   To the state's geography may be attributed its especially high malarial rate. "The returns constitute," says Frederick L. Hoffman, "the first reasonably complete morbidity index by counties available for any single American state at the present time." The trend of the statistics shows a marked progress toward the control of the disease. From the three year average for 1914-16 to that for 1928-30 the case rate of malaria per 10,000 white population decreased from 813.4 to 496.0, a decrease of 39 per cent. In the same period the morbidity rates for Negroes decreased from 788.9 to 338.4, a loss of 57 per cent. With an even greater decline in mortality has gone a decrease in the percentage of fatalities per case, from .71 per cent to .31 for whites and from 1.07 to .50 for colored. Negroes tend to have a fatality case rate almost twice as high as that of the whites. The following rates of mortality and morbidity per 100,000, white and colored, have been calculated from data furnished by Mississippi Public Health authorities:

The much greater importance of malaria morbidity is evident at a glance.   Contrary to common opinion the Negro is as susceptible to malaria as the Nordic.   Aldo Castellani, Professor of Tropical Medicine, Tulane University, writes: "In my experience the Negro is not immune to either malaria or yellow fever. In malarial countries adult Negroes may appear to be partially immune to malaria because they have had it when they were children."[41]

[39] John W. Trask, "Malaria," *Public Health Report* 38, 1916, p. 5.
[40] *Ibid.*, p. 2.
[41] Letter to writer, March 18, 1929.

TABLE XXXIX

MALARIA IN MISSISSIPPI, 1914-1930

	Total Morbidity Per 10,000 Population	WHITE			COLORED		
		Morbidity Per 10,000 Population	Mortality Per 10,000 Population	Percentage of Mortality	Morbidity Per 10,000 Population	Mortality Per 10,000 Population	Percentage of Mortality
1914.........	651.6	623.1	3.91	.67	679.3	7.30	1.07
1915.........	856.8	889.1	6.29	.71	833.9	10.10	1.21
1916.........	885.4	925.5	6.11	.66	854.7	9.63	1.12
1917.........	784.8	835.5	4.11	.49	743.1	6.87	.92
1918.........	590.3	601.3	2.41	.40	581.8	6.21	1.07
1919.........	628.3	625.3	2.44	.39	631.8	4.72	.75
1920.........	661.1	631.6	2.33	.37	687.8	5.67	.82
1921.........	668.7	654.6	3.69	.55	681.7	6.80	.99
1922.........	576.4	577.9	2.79	.50	375.1	4.97	.75
1923.........	512.9	524.6	2.09	.40	501.9	4.09	.81
1924.........	419.1	451.8	1.11	.25	397.5	2.73	.69
1925.........	374.3	398.8	1.15	.29	359.4	3.12	.87
1926.........	369.7	389.6	1.34	.34	358.8	2.87	.80
1927.........	449.1	462.2	1.36	.29	446.4	3.00	.67
1928.........	503.0	557.3	1.75	.31	449.9	3.53	.78
1929.........	458.0	529.5	1.22	.23	387.6	1.95	.50
1930.........	246.1	313.5	.96	.31	179.3	1.83	1.02

RELATION TO ENERGY AND EFFICIENCY

Malaria in the United States is of too mild a nature to permit of its accurate measurement by the death rate. In the same way it is doubtful if its effects upon human energy and output can be measured even by the ascertained rates of morbidity. "We have no idea," wrote an investigator in 1903, "of the loss occasioned by malaria in unfitting men for long or energetic hours of labor. Certainly there is no disease known to man that more insidiously undermines his constitution and lessens his ability to produce his full measure of wealth than malaria."[42] One death from pneumonia, it is known, ordinarily corresponds to about 125 sick days; typhoid fever equals 450 to 500 work days lost; tuberculosis amounts to more among whites, less among Negroes. A death from malaria, however, implies from 2,000 to 4,000 sick days.[43]

[42] Glenn W. Herrick, "The Relation of Malaria to Agriculture and Other Industries of the South," Popular Science, 62, p. 521.

[43] H. R. Carter, "The Malaria Problem of the South," Public Health Reprint No. 552, Aug. 22, 1919.

The relation of malaria to industrial efficiency may be aptly shown by field investigation in three different types of industry; a mill village in North Carolina, a railroad in the Mississippi Valley, and a Delta plantation.

Roanoke Rapids, N. C., is a mill village, or rather a group of mill villages, with a total of over 4,000 population. Prior to the malaria work the population was continually changing. Wages were good, work was abundant, and people came, but they developed malaria and would not stay. The mill managers estimated the efficiency of their employees at from 40 to 60 per cent during the four unhealthful months. During this time the machines were constantly idle. The mill physicians, who attended employees without charge, averaged during the summer months of 1912 and 1913, fifty calls per day for malaria. During 1914, the first year of malaria work (control of mosquitoes was depended on), there were still a few cases (33) of malaria, relapses from 1913. The efficiency rate rose to 90 or 95 per cent, and the average number of calls for the same months was three daily. In 1915 there was no question of efficiency to be considered—it was normal. The average of doctors' calls for malaria was one in three days. All these [sic] were newcomers and were believed to have been contracted [sic] elsewhere.

One of the millmen writes: "The money spent in your campaign against malaria here gave the quickest and most enormous returns I have ever known from any investment." It did pay in the first year from 100 to 400 per cent.

The cost here was 80 cents per head for the first year and 27 cents per head for the second year. The efficiency of the mill was raised from 50 to 100 per cent.[44]

On the Missouri Pacific lines south of St. Louis, malaria from 1900 to 1922 furnished 33 per cent of all hospital admissions and 45 per cent of all cases of illness. Moreover it was found that over 4,000 employees received out-patient treatment for malaria each year. A census taken in 1921 of the four southern divisions showed that only 18 per cent of those affected with malaria entered a hospital and only 68 per cent of those infected ever visited a doctor. Of all employees interviewed 32 per cent gave positive histories. Of various occupational groups the bridge and building crews and extra gangs had the highest hospital rate, 79.7 per cent, and the shopmen the lowest, 11 per cent. Statements from foremen indicated that malaria constitutes an enormous charge against the

[44] *Ibid.,* p. 7.

cost of operation by reducing the efficiency of labor, by producing a shortage of labor, and by creating a high labor turnover. Employees on malarious divisions are dissatisfied because of frequent sickness in the family and excessive expenditures for medical attention.[45]

One remarkable experiment has been conducted to ascertain the social and economic incidence of malaria in agriculture. Under the direction of D. L. Van Dine a controlled study was made of an entire plantation on the Mississippi near Vicksburg. With perfect coöperation between owner, physician, microscopist, and entomologist it was possible to secure a remarkable set of records. A complete collection of data relating to mosquito frequency, species, density, location, and direction of flight was secured and correlated with an admirable set of climatic data as to minimum temperature, humidity, rainfall, sunshine, cloudiness, and wind direction.

Next were gathered data on disease history of the human factors, recent malarial history, blood smears, fever duration, recent ingestion of quinine, use of chill tonics, and ultimate termination of the disease, recovery or death. In addition a complete survey included every house in relation to environmental conditions and mosquitoes. Data were gathered as to essential economic factors: the relation of the family to the plantation, length of residence, value of the land, the normal return per acre, and present return. Additional studies included labor requirements of cotton, corn, and oats. Finally the health and economic data were balanced in a study of losses to plantation and family from labor shortage, crop shortage, decreased efficiency, medical expenses, nursing, general ill health, and deaths. The information constitutes, as Hoffman has said, the most thorough collection of data on malaria in its social and economic relations extant. During 1914 the experiment had under observation 74 tenant families who cultivated 1,800 acres of land, of which 1,191 acres were under a tenant system and 609 acres under direct supervision of the plantation.

The tenants averaged 16 acres per family, and the 74 families included a total of 299 individuals. The crops grown consisted of 743 acres of cotton and 448 acres of corn under the tenant system and 80 acres of

[45] A. W. Fuchs, "Malaria Survey of the Missouri Pacific Railroad, 1922," *Public Health Bulletin 135*, May 1923.

cotton and 209 acres of corn, 200 acres of oats, 70 acres of cowpeas and 50 acres of lespedeza hay under the day-wage system. *All time was reduced to adult time, or man days of labor.* The time of a male over eighteen years of age was figured at full time, a male from twelve to eighteen years as one-half adult time, and from eight to twelve years as one-fourth. The time of a female was figured as one-half the time of a male. Reducing all the available labor on the plantation to adult time, the resulting equivalent labor was two adults to each of the 74 tenant families. The actual time lost through malaria consisted of 970 days for those treated by the plantation physician, 487 days representing cases not reported to the physician and 385 days lost by non-malarial members of the family in attending those who had the disease. There was a total loss of 1,842 days, which, reduced to adult time, and not taking account of illness in members of the families under eight years of age, amounted to 1,066 days of adult time, from May to October, inclusive. The time lost averaged 14.4 adult days for each family. There were 166 cases of malaria in 138 persons out of a total of 299 members of the tenant families. There was a loss of time equivalent to 6.42 adult days for each case of malaria.

In relating malaria morbidity to economic efficiency, the effect of the loss of time from work can be measured by the difference between the available labor and the labor requirements of the crops. When a surplus of labor exists over that required in cultivation, the losses from malaria may be charged against the family budget but not against the crops. During four months of the year the time lost from malaria falls at the period when there exists a deficiency of labor and the demands of the crops are greatest. In the cycle of cotton culture, the periods of chopping and hoeing, boll weevil control and picking fall during the months of greatest malaria incidence. By adjusting the seasonal cycle of malaria incidence to the labor cycle of cotton Mr. Van Dine was able to arrive at an estimate of the loss from malaria.

Each family cultivated an average of 16 acres. The plantation depended upon the tenants for labor to cultivate an average of 8.23 acres each on the day-wage basis. This amounted to a total of 24.23 acres to be cultivated by the labor represented in each tenant family, and equivalent to 13.51 acres of cotton. The total loss of time of 13.79 families is equivalent to that of the total crop on 186.3 acres of cotton. With an average yield of one-half of a bale of cotton per acre, this would equal a total loss of 93.15 bales of cotton. Allowing $70 a bale for the lint and seed, this would amount to $6,520.50.[46]

Climate as a bar to settlement and a handicap to the energy and industry conducive to a high state of civilization may thus be shown to resolve itself into innumerable factors of which diet, hookworm, and malaria are by no means least. Dr. Woods Hutchinson has said that when we hear much of climate as an obstacle to civilization we should read "malaria" for "climate." Some observers have professed to see subtle psychic influences arising from malaria infection. Dr. Hutchinson cites the singular apathy and indifference, numbing the moral sense of white colonists in the tropics, and alternating with outbursts of "tropical wrath." Remarkably enough he attributes "those wild outbursts of primitive ferocity in all classes" which take the form of white cap raids and lynching mobs "partly to the baneful, persistent influence of malaria, together with the hookworm disease."[47] Compared to Dr. Hutchinson's tropical rage, the listlessness of the chronic malarial patient is a very real thing. Its direct and indirect effect on the development of southern civilization has been incalculable.

Eradication of Malaria

A great many areas of potential resources in the South lie undeveloped because of malaria. Many cities and towns find their population ratios stationary or diminishing and their economic and civic affairs stagnant because of this disease in even its milder forms. As practical men of business often say, nothing puts a blight on real estate like malaria. However, if to malaria may be attributed much regional inefficiency formerly charged to climate, the strictures passed on the southern scene by critics like Huntington do not cut so deep. Diseases, it is suggested, may be eradicated though climate and weather persist unchanged. Writing in a caustic vein for a non-technical magazine an official of the public health service sees no easy road to eradication.

The major health problem of this desolate region is simple enough. . . . Drain all the swamps, sink holes and barrow pits, screen all the houses

[46] Frederick L. Hoffman, *The Malaria Problem in Peace and War*, pp. 34-36. See articles by D. L. Van Dine in *Scientific Monthly*, November, 1916, and *Southern Medical Journal*, March, 1915.

[47] *Preventable Diseases*, pp. 292-93.

and put shoes on thousands and then train them all to cleanly habits of living. In brief, the whole thing is as simple and easy as it would be for a one-armed man to empty the Great Lakes with a spoon.[48]

But it may be said that malaria statistics in even the worst areas afford a more cheering prospect. Mortality reports for the nation show that deaths from malaria from 1919 to 1928 were reduced by one third. The trying period from 1915 to 1930 saw reported morbidity in Mississippi fall from 153,707 to 49,538 cases. Delta counties witnessed a decline from 50,243 cases in 1915 to 27,222 in 1929 with a further fall to 7,580 in 1930. This last great decrease is, no doubt, partly due to a change in methods of reporting cases. Table XXXIX above shows the decreases in morbidity rates and the percentages of mortality for both races.

The problem in the South is to find whether methods of intensive attack, analogous to those which proved successful in the suppression of hookworm, can be applied to the control of malaria.[49] The change from men to mosquitoes and back again is necessary for the continued existence of the malaria parasite. This transition can be made the point of attack by one of four methods of control: (1) get rid of all *Anopheles* mosquitoes, (2) prevent their access to man, (3) free all persons in the community from malaria parasites, (4) by means of quinine protect all persons against infection.[50] Theoretically, then, the problem is relatively simple, but in practice the interaction of geography with the whole complex of socio-economic phenomena makes malaria control particularly baffling.

The advantages of eradication of all *Anopheles* are outstanding. The main work is done once for all when drainage is accomplished, and the upkeep is small. The work, moreover, is done with materials of earth and water and cannot be nullified by the carelessness or bad faith of refractory human factors. Unfortunately for many areas such a procedure is impossible. Geography and topography prevent ditching and drainage, as in the lower reaches of sluggish rivers and the Mississippi Delta. This, however, can be overcome in restricted districts, as, for example, cities in the Delta. It is not necessary to clean up a whole region in or-

[48] T. J. B. LeBlanc, "Malaria," *American Mercury,* III, 371.

[49] Rockefeller Foundation, *Annual Report,* 1915, p. 72.

[50] H. R. Carter, *op. cit.,* p. 6.

der to render it malaria free. The Canal Zone is regarded as a particularly happy experiment in malaria control, and yet only 10 per cent of the area, that surrounding cities, is mosquito free. War experience with southern cantonments showed that, when the expense involved is disregarded, any spot can be controlled regardless of the condition of the surrounding terrain.

Malaria control is after all a matter of getting public support, and here the elimination of only the *Anopheles* mosquito collides with popular psychology. "The average layman," writes a county health officer, "while willing to accept the mosquito-borne theory thinks you are splitting hairs too much in laying all the blame on one species of that family. As long as you have mosquitoes puncturing the hide of the average farmer you are going to do very little work in malaria control unless you go after the whole tribe."[51] It is possible, moreover, that freedom from the mosquito nuisance makes as strong an appeal to the normal community as the elimination of malaria. *Culex* control, however, often takes as much as 75 per cent of available funds and can hardly be regarded as a public health problem. It is thus almost impossible for public health officials to keep mosquito control to its scientific minimum and retain popular support.

Mosquito control in its final analysis will be found to depend upon what we may call social demography. A low density of population places limits on any fight that may be made against the mosquito. Again the rural South is at a disadvantage. "The expense of mosquito control in a community is roughly proportional to the area of breeding which lies within the limits of flight to the dwelling section of that community." As it has been stated by Dr. H. R. Carter, the expense per capita varies inversely as the population per unit of area.[52] In actual field work this has meant that feasible methods of exterminating the *Anopheles* can be used only in towns and cities.

The urban campaign against malaria in the Southern States got under way in 1917 in and about the army camps. Inside the camp the work was supervised by the army, outside the Public Health Service enlisted the assistance of state and community agencies. Smaller and poorer communities after 1918 hesitated

[51] International Health Board, *Ninth Report*, p. 114.
[52] *Op. cit.*, p. 7.

to carry on work begun as a war measure regardless of expense. The International Health Board, fresh from triumphs over hookworm, undertook with the Public Health Service and state and local agencies to demonstrate experimental methods of control.[53] The first step, the sanitary survey, is likely to be found encouraging in that it shows the existence of a limited number of foci of infection, irregularly distributed. Many foci of breeding are man-made, as fish ponds, mill ponds, barrow pits from highway construction and hydro-electric developments. Experiments have shown that with a careful preliminary survey a community may rid itself of infection at a per capita cost of from $0.45 to $1.00. In 1921 despite unfavorable climatic and financial conditions the International Health Board could report 225 square miles controlled and 228,740 persons protected.[54] In the new towns the per capita cost averaged $1.01. In thirty-five towns where measures were already established 25 cents was the average per capita cost of maintenance. Data from thirteen installation towns showed the main items of expense to average as follows: ditching $345.00 per mile, clearing streams $95.00 per mile, and oiling $3.00 per mile. The average cost of maintenance was $16.00 per mile. The reduction of malaria as measured in physicians' calls has reached as high as 90 per cent in some towns.

Experimental work has been done on many types of municipalities. Crossett, Arkansas, in 1918, was a lumbering town of 2,029 people, surrounded by swamps and sluggish streams. Malaria took 60 per cent of the time devoted to practice by all local physicians. A program of drainage, filling, and application of oil and larvacides effected within a year a reduction of physician's calls for malaria by 82.7 per cent. The cost was $2,505.90 or $1.23½ for each resident of the town. Four other towns in Arkansas, of distinct topographical types, have under supervision controlled malaria. Lake Village is in a level, low-lying area of buckshot soil with two miles of lake front and an extensive area of shallow swamps in the rear. Its 1,388 physicians' calls for malaria in 1917 for 975 people were reduced to 83 the next year, a decrease of 94.8 per cent at a per capita cost of $1.25. Dermott, with a population of 2,760, possessed abundant stagnant pools within its city limits

[53] *Tenth Report,* p. 54.
[54] *Eighth Report,* pp. 92-94.

because of the utter neglect of the elementary principles of drainage in the grading of two railroads and the streets of the town. An expenditure of forty-five cents per inhabitant reduced calls for malaria by 87.8 per cent. Monticello is a typical hill town, whose many clear streams with inadequate fall over stiff clay soil produced an abundant supply of mosquitoes. In 1917 its 3,023 people needed 1,271 doctor's visits for malaria. By an expenditure of 46 cents per inhabitant these calls were reduced by 89.8 per cent. Bauxite, a rambling mining community, covered a large area with its 2,500 people. Extensive hillside seepage and heavy flow of numerous small streams through sand beds offered ideal breeding conditions. In this difficult public health area a per capita expenditure of $1.11 accounted for a 78.4 per cent decrease in malaria, as measured by doctors' calls.[55]

Neither the Public Health Service nor the International Health Board can rid an area of malaria except as a demonstration. Legally the work remains under control of state and local authorities. The goal of these projects was achieved, therefore, when the towns took over the maintenance of malaria control. The above communities had been paying one and a half times as much for doctors' bills alone as the cost of the first year's operation. The cost of upkeep ranged from one fourth to one eighth of previous annual payments to physicians.[56]

Between 1920 and 1922 plans of control were carried out in over a hundred municipalities and their surrounding areas. From this experience was evolved a standard method applicable to any infected area of dense population and moderately high per capita income. Malaria control is now regarded as within the reach of any municipality in the South that is willing to pay for it. The Board accordingly withdrew from the urban demonstration and in its 1926 Report made the flat statement: "As a result of this work malaria has practically disappeared from the cities and towns of the republic."[57]

RURAL MALARIA CONTROL

The control of malaria in towns—even in small towns, as the Rockefeller Foundation well says, does not reach the heart of the

[55] *Report*, Rockefeller Foundation, 1918, pp. 186-93.
[56] *Ibid.*, p. 193.
[57] P. 119.

problem in the South.[58] It frankly remains a serious question as to whether in large rural areas mosquito control is practicable. Only in countries having full-time health service in areas where the disease possesses economic importance has it been found advisable to feature malaria control. Public health authorities must be resigned to the fact that in no rural area will the experimental work in control meet success so complete or spectacular as in the towns.[59]

Writing in 1919, a period of war-time prosperity in agriculture, Dr. Henry R. Carter felt that in many rural districts of the South there was not to be found one third of the malaria that existed in the 'eighties.[60] The reason he found in economic conditions, the rise in the price of cotton, and the fall in the price of quinine. Better economic conditions in agriculture lead to the clearing, drainage, and intensive cultivation of more land. Improved health results in greater energy and output of work which lead in time to prosperity. In course of time, also, economic advancement may be expected to go over into higher levels of culture, a complex which includes screening, knowledge of hygiene, and use of medicines. Improvement in a region's health remains, however, a factor of scientific direction no less than of economic cycles.

Several scientific discoveries in the biology of *Anopheles* have recently revived the hope that rural control is not impossible of achievement. M. Bruin Mitzmain of the Public Health Service discovered that the parasites of malaria do not live through the winter in the bodies of mosquitoes which hibernate in central Mississippi. Therefore, man is the winter carrier of malaria, and sterilization of carriers is a logical procedure. Rural *Anopheles* control is hardly possible, but it has been shown by H. R. Carter and confirmed by S. T. Darling that, of the three species of *Anopheles* found in the South, only one, the *A. quadrimaculatus,* carries parasites. Since its seasonal prevalence and preferential breeding places are known, these facts resolve malaria control into much simpler elements. A study of the range of this malaria mosquito proved that most were captured within a radius of three fourths of a mile from the breeding place. Some few were found

[58] *Annual Report,* 1918, p. 193.
[59] International Health Board, *Thirteenth Report,* p. 121.
[60] *Malaria Problem of the South,* p. 5.

within ranges from one to one and three fourths miles but none beyond. In 1921 Dr. M. A. Barber of the United States Public Health Service made the further discovery that Paris green makes an excellent larvaecide. One part mixed with 100 parts dust sprinkled on ponds kills *Anopheles* larvae with no dangers to man or beast.[61]

Mitzmain's discovery led to attempts to control by quinine sterilization all malaria carriers. Theoretically, it should be possible to stamp out malaria in America by freeing the blood stream of all individuals during the winter months. Actually the administration of standard quinine dosages under best control conditions possible has proved insufficient to prevent a large number of spring relapses. The method lessens the virulence of epidemics, reduces greatly the number of days lost through illness, but in many cases serves only to mask the symptoms.[62] A further handicap in the South has been the well-nigh universal consumption, in the form of chill tonics, of quinine solutions too weak to be effective. One valuable result which came from this type of demonstration was the adoption by physicians, public health workers, and the Malaria Commission of a standard dosage of ten grains of quinine daily for eight weeks.

It still remains possible that to prevent the access of mosquitoes to man is the most logical method of rural control. It is true that the rural population has never given screening an adequate trial. One county in Mississippi, surveyed in 1922, showed 44 per cent of rural homes well screened, 12 per cent partly screened, and 44 per cent not screened at all. A field experiment was conducted in 1916 on a group of cotton plantations with high *Anopheles* ratio and malaria incidence near Lake Village, Arkansas. The average cost of screening was $14.59 per house, the screens lasted two years, and the average per capita cost was $1.75. The method thus proved expensive as contrasted with municipal control, and the results doubtful.[63]

The countryside by all accounts is thus brought back to the problem of elimination of mosquitoes with the problem simplified but by no means solved. Science has shown that the quest

[61] International Health Board, *Report*, 1922, p. 114.
[62] *Twelfth Report*, 1925, p. 77.
[63] Rockefeller Foundation, *Report*, 1918, pp. 193-94.

may be limited to one species breeding in still waters, and that the time of the hunt may be limited from May to October. Some malariologists are willing to attribute the prevalence of the disease to a small number of fat, lazy, long-lived, house-loving female *anophelines* who carry the disease. Another group which feels that major drainage operations are necessary encounters on the other hand the advocates of the top minnow, Gambuscia, feeding upon wrigglers and aided by applications of Paris green. The per capita cost of application of this larvaecide has been comparatively slight, as low as 24 cents in a demonstration around Edenton, North Carolina. Still another school sees the source of infection in human carriers and advocates the compulsory dosing with quinine of the whole population.

The battle is slow and long. There still awaits a method, cheap, common-sense, and convincing. It may not be found. It is difficult to see how any effort short of Herculean can offer to control malaria in the tidal reaches, the plains of sluggish coastal rivers, the bayou swamps, and the cuts of the great Father of Waters meandering lazily through the deltas under his sway. Our last school of malariologists may be correct when they hold that malaria tends to disappear only when a people reach a comparatively high economic and cultural level.[64]

The conclusion of the chapter may be briefly stated. Much of the inefficiency and comparative lack of energy attributed to the climate of the South may be laid with justice at the door of the so-called concealed diseases. With their passing, no doubt, the so-called "poor whites" will pass into the realm of legend and myth. The position of Sir Patrick Manson in his *Tropical Diseases* is well taken in regard to hookworm and malaria in the South: "The more we learn about these diseases the less important in its bearing on their geographic distribution and as a direct pathogenic agency becomes the *rôle* of temperature *per se* and the more that of tropical fauna." As the parasites peculiar to the South are gradually brought under control we may expect a notable release of the energies of its population. As this results in higher cultural standards it will operate to speed the eradication of these concealed diseases.

[64] Rockefeller Foundation, *Report,* 1928, pp. 34-37.

CHAPTER XVI

CLIMATE, DIET, AND HUMAN ADEQUACY

THE GEOGRAPHY OF DIET

SOMEWHERE on the outer edge of the uncharted field of human geography lies an undeveloped sector, the geography of nutrition. The mapping of the world's dietary, province by province, would avail to show a functional relation with soil and plant and animal complexes. For basic diet men will, no doubt, continue to eat the products their lands will grow. In this the study resembles the geography of disease, for men tend to have the maladies transmitted by the minute organisms native to their regions. The second task of a proposed geography of nutrition transcends the first in difficulty and significance. The relation of diet to health and social efficiency represents the application of the ecology of diet to social adequacy. Any suggested analysis of regional diet, health, and efficiency was of necessity held in check to await the development of bio-chemistry.

The South has proved at the hands of the public health movement a great laboratory for testing the biology of disease. It may prove at the hands of the social scientist no less a laboratory for the study of the human geography of diet. It may be said to hold this position on several counts. An area especially prolific in plant and animal life has acquired a reputation for deficient diet. This diet is especially related to the characteristic pioneer stage through which the whole country passed and has been confirmed and established in the South by the plantation and the cotton system. Moreover, certain facts suggest that the diet is particularly maladapted to the climate and thus has more influence on the section's social characteristics than is generally realized.

The biochemistry of nutrition while making advances in the last decades in no sense ranks in scientific exactness with the biology of disease. In one instance, however, the two combine to

afford an enlightening index to dietetic regimens. Pellagra ac
cepted as a nutritional disease is of less importance in its own
right than as an index of dietary conditions. Nutritional disease
themselves are too occasional and sporadic to do more than indicate
the most flagrant dietary maladjustments. It is to the problem
of dietary regimens and human adequacy that the former specula
tions concerning diet and race must bow as of more pressing im
portance.[1]

THE SOUTH'S HERITAGE OF FOOD

Early travelers in America appear to have been torn between
amazement and despair at the food habits of its people. About
1800, Ashe, whom Henry Adams called an amusing and untrust-
worthy Englishman, said of Kentucky: "In a country then where
bacon and spirits form the favorite summer repast, it cannot be
just to attribute entirely the causes of infirmity to the climate.
No people on earth live with less regard to regimen. They eat
salt meat three times a day, seldom or never have any vegetables,
and drink ardent spirits from morn till night. They have not
only an aversion to fresh meat but a vulgar prejudice that it is
unwholesome. The truth is, their stomachs are depraved by burning liquors and they have no appetite for anything but what is
highly flavored and strongly impregnated by salt."[2]

Cooper in a novel describing American customs of 1784 had
a frontier mother say: "Give me the children that's raised on good
sound pork afore all the game in the country. Game's good as a
relish and so's bread; but pork is the staff of life. . . . My children
I calkulate to bring up on pork."[3]

No better regimen could have been invented for ruining the
health, said the traveler, Volney, than that of the Americans.
"They swallow, almost without chewing, hot bread half baked,
toast soaked in butter, cheese of the fattest kind, slices of salt or
briny beef and bacon. . . . At dinner they have boiled pastes under the name of puddings, and the fattest are esteemed the most
delicious; all their sauces even for roast beef are melted butter,
their turnips and potatoes swim in hog's lard, butter or fat; under

[1] As F. P. Armitage's attempts to associate salt and light pigmentation, diet and
cranial development, etc., in *Diet and Race*.

[2] Quoted in Henry Adams, *History of the United States, 1801-1805*, I, 43.

[3] *Chainbearer*, quoted by Adams, *op. cit.*

he name of pie or puddings their pastry is nothing but a greasy
paste never sufficiently baked. . . . As Castlelux says, the whole
day passes in heaping indigestions on one another; and to give
one to the poor, relaxed, and wearied stomach, they drink Madeira,
rum, French brandy, gin or malt spirits, which complete the ruin
of the nervous system."[4] Especially did the English traveler de-
test the American fondness for greasy foods. "The heavy diet
and the use of animal food at every meal was looked upon by the
English as the cause of many American diseases."[5] Poor teeth
among American women were often attributed to hot foods,
salted foods, sweets, and preserves.[6]

By 1850 the frontier had receded somewhat, but American diet
had not changed sufficiently to impress the critics. The newspapers were filled with advertisements of cures for indigestion, which
indicated that the stomachs of the nation were subject to great strain.
The three meals of the day were practically identical. "Meat was over
abundant and fresh vegetables were too few. This generation did indeed learn to eat tomatoes, but not to make salads. In the church
socials rivalry was keen in the production of cakes of elaboration
and succulence, and if sauces were few, as Talleyrand had earlier
remarked, relishes were many and recipes for them highly prized."[7]

William C. Duncan held the diet of Mississippi Valley settlers
in the fifties to be rich, varied, and abundant, consisting, however,
almost always of too much animal food in proportion to the
vegetable. "A common fault everywhere and one that ought to
be remedied," he wrote, "is bad cooking. Of the food thus ill-
prepared too much is eaten, and too hastily, to the great detriment
of health."[8]

The inevitable Olmsted, fresh from his tour of the South, believed that "wholesome water and wholesome fresh fruits are not
to be obtained by the traveler in the largest part of the United
States. Bacon, fat and salt, is the stock article of diet. He must
satisfy his appetite with this or with coarse or most indigestible
forms of bread. In either case he will have an unnatural thirst
and the only means ordinarily offered him at country houses for

[4] Quoted by Adams, op. cit., I, 44.
[5] Louise Jane Mesick, The English Traveler in America, 1785-1835, p. 59.
[6] Ibid., p. 90.
[7] Carl Russel Fish, Rise of the Common Man, 1830-1850, p. 140.
[8] In De Bow's Industrial Resources of the United States, I.

satisfying this, will be an exceedingly dirty and unpalatable decoction of coffee, of which the people usually consume an excessive quantity, or alcoholic liquor of the most fiery and pernicious description."[9]

Agreed as to the undesirability of alcohol, Governor Hammond of South Carolina defended the social efficiency of frontier diet for the South. "All the fermented and distilled liquors which in cold climates are in some sort necessaries are here uncalled for and injurious indulgences. Corn bread and bacon, as much as the epicure may sneer at them, with fresh meat only occasionally and a moderate use of garden vegetables will in this region at least give to the laborer greater strength of muscle and constitution, enable him to undergo more fatigue, and insure him longer life and more enjoyment of it than any other diet. And these indeed with coffee constitute the habitual food of the great body of southern people."[10] He proceeds to estimate 13 bushels of corn, 160 pounds of bacon, with sugar, coffee, and green vegetables, all amounting to $19 per year, as the annual cost per man of wholesome and palatable food purchased in the market.

In the 'eighties Edward King found the frontier diet the staff of life for the common man of the South especially in pioneer Texas. "The mass of people in the interior still have a hearty scorn for anything good to eat. The bitter coffee and the greasy pork or bacon as it is always called, still adorns the tables of most farmers." Whenever a luckless beefsteak found its way to the table it had been fried until not a particle of juice remained in its substance. "A railroad president inspecting a route in Northern Texas stopped at a little house for dinner. The old lady of the homestead, wishing to treat her guest with becoming dignity, inquired in the kindest manner after having spread the usual food before him 'Won't you have a little bacon fat to wallop your corn dodgers in now, won't ye?'" This was the acme of hospitality in that region. "Now and then . . . a housewife will venture a timid 'reckon ye don't think much of our home-made fare do ye?' when the visitor is a stranger and indeed he shows upon his face his wonder that a well-to-do farmer's stout sons and pretty daughters are satisfied with pork and molasses and clammy biscuits with

[9] Frederick Law Olmsted, *A Journey in the Seaboard Slave States*, II, 279-80.
[10] De Bow's *Resources of the South*, III, 31.

o vegetables whatever."[11]   Horace Greeley told the people of
'exas that their prime need was a thousand good cooks.   The in-
itation to hospitality in early Texas as reported by Olmsted was
gruff, "Sit up stranger and take some fry."   Sidney Andrews,
aveling in the South in 1866, said, "The southern consumption of
rease—of fat in one form or another would, I am sure, astonish
ven an Arctic explorer."[12]

Food habits become a thing of propriety and right, and a mark
f social and class distinctions.   There is more than a hint of the
ontier tradition in the address of a southern governor to his rural
udience: "If one of them high collared, fly-weight dudes of the
ast had sense enough to set down to a big dish of turnip greens,
oke sallet, and hog jowl he might sweat off enough of that talcum
owder to look like a man."   Comparable, of course, are the
poradic controversies concerning the advisability of "dunking"
orn pone in "pot-likker" with which southern governors some-
mes regale their constituencies.

One can hardly deny the semblance of truth to this running
escription of the diet of the common man in the South.   It is
picture that travelers and takers of social notes with few excep-
ons have conspired to paint.   For its existence reason can be
ound.   Such a diet is both a social heritage and an adjustment to
nvironment.

In the main the early American settler brought with him the
ood habits of the English common man including a great, if
ften unsatisfied, fondness for meats.   He found Indian maize an
ntegral part of the native plant complex and was early taught
s methods of culture by the Indians.   The frontier, because of its
aucity of resources, stripped this diet of whatever variety it pos-
essed and added corn which came to take the place held by wheat.
 reflective Tennessee pioneer has written:

uppose our fathers had had to depend on wheat for their bread.   It
ould have taken them a hundred years longer to reach the Rockies.
. . Corn will produce four times as much as wheat per acre and re-
uires only one tenth of the seed to seed it down and only one third of
e time from planting it till it can be used as food.   Wheat must have
repared soil, and be sown in the fall and watched and guarded for nine

[11] Edward King, *The Great South,* pp. 182-83.
[12] *The South Since the War,* pp. 181-82.

months before it is even ready to harvest; whereas a woman can take "sang hoe" in April and with a quart of seed plant a patch around cabin and in six weeks she and the children can begin to eat roasting ears; and when it [sic] gets too hard for that she can parch it. She need to gather only what she uses for the day, for it will stand all winter, well protected by its waterproof shuck. Not so with wheat. It must be all gathered at once when ripe, and thrashed, cleaned, and garnered. And even then it is hard to get bread out of it without a mill. But a small sack of parched corn with a bit of salt was an ample supply for a ten days' hunt with Jack Sevier after thieving Indians. Corn was King when I was a boy.[13]

Especially, because of the abundance of wild game and the strenuous life of the woodsmen, did the frontier accentuate the heritage of meat. The increasing scarcity of game as the frontier advanced ill comported with the climate and lack of preservatives. From fresh meat the frontiersman turned more and more to a salted diet. With a meat diet firmly entrenched, the docility and hardihood of the prolific porker fixed on the frontier the culture trait of salt pork. The immense early importance of salt mines and the salt trade in the back country is related to this complex of diet. Hogs thrive on corn and complete their growth in one season. It has been estimated that 24 per cent of the energy of grain consumed is recovered for human consumption in pork as compared with about 18 per cent in milk and 3.5 per cent in beef or mutton.[14] The drinking of distilled liquors, developed in the cold foggy climate of Britain and accepted as a part of the cultural heritage, proved more of a maladjustment on a semi-tropic southern frontier. It is likely, however, that so monotonous a diet could be made palatable only by strong coffee or strong waters—favorite beverages of frontier peoples. The southern climate made possible the easy cultivation of ribbon and sorghum cane so that early in its history the section supplemented the pioneer diet of pork and corn with a disproportionate consumption of molasses.

In the South, the transition from frontier to plantation saddled the minimum frontier regimen upon the slaves as their permanent staples of diet. A weekly allowance for each slave of three pounds of pork, a peck of corn, a pint of salt, and molasses in proportion

[13] Quoted by E. C. Brooks, *The Story of Corn*, p. 134.
[14] H. P. Armsby, "The Cost of Roast Pig," *Science*, XLVI, 160.

ecame standard for thousands of plantations. In winter a bushel
f sweet potatoes might be substituted for the corn meal. This
egimen fitted well with the close-paced routine of cotton culture
which left little time for variation. For the common man the
ransition from frontier to modern rural society was not so marked
s to cause a break in the food habits of the people. When a people
n the midst of a land capable of variety limit their diet to a few
taples they are in the grip of tradition. This heritage growing
ut of geographic adjustments has so conditioned food likes and
islikes that it determines both the growth and purchases of foods.
Moreover, since meat, meal, and molasses are cheap, the poverty of
 backward agriculture has further served to localize within the
outhern borders the basic diet of the frontier.

But out of this same transition from frontier to plantation arose
he South's tradition of good cooking. More than one chronicler
as doubted whether the preparation of appetizing foods has ever
een brought to higher perfection than by that scion of old Vir-
inia, Colonel Carter of Cartersville.[15]   Any number of old south-
rn cookbooks with recipes collected from people "who keep good
ables and use only southern cooking" may be assembled to testify
o this point. "A glance at the contents of this book," says one,
will, I am sure, recall to any Southerner the dishes of his child-
ood—Smithfield ham, chicken salad, rich cakes and puddings,
old drinks and fragrant coffee, from the days when the plantation
wners ate what they wanted and wanted good food."[16]   As pre-
ented by U. B. Phillips, the table regimen of the tidal and alluvial
ristocracy was variety, profusion, and repletion. The gastronomic
mbition of every southern host to the manor born was to keep
owing from the cookhouse a steady stream of hot breads—hot
nough to melt butter.[17]   The well-known southern devotion to
ot breads appears to have a frontier origin. In a society which
acked wheat flour, corn meal which cannot be made into a loaf
roved most palatable when served hot. When flour finally be-
ame available to a pioneer society accustomed to hot hoecakes, its

[15] See J. H. Beard, "The Gastronomy of Colonel Carter of Cartersville," *Scientific
Monthly*, 26, pp. 246-49.

[16] Mary D. Pretlow, *Old Southern Receipts*, foreword.

[17] U. B. Phillips, *Life and Labor in the Old South*, pp. 4, 336.

most obvious use was in the preparation of hot biscuits.[18] B
that as it may, the trait survives in many southern homes, wher
failure to provide hot biscuits three times a day almost vies wit
Scriptural grounds as sanction for divorce. "On the hottest evening
of summer women all over the South must fire up cookstoves t
prepare steaming grits, hot biscuits, fried ham and eggs."[19] I
the 'eighties, Edward King, who held that no northern travele
ever went South without returning to complain with great bitter
ness of the food, admitted that nowhere in the world might b
found better cooking or richer bills of fare than in Baltimore
Charleston, Savannah, and New Orleans.[20] Thus it happened, a
Dorothy Dickens points out, that alongside the common man din
ing daily off corn pone, salt pork, molasses, and coffee must b
placed his prosperous neighbor who fares sumptuously every da
on fried chicken, candied yams, gravy, and hot biscuits.[21]

The Biology of Diet

The shift from the table set by our pioneer forefathers to th
menus of our urban middle classes may be accounted one of th
notable triumphs of modern science. The adjustment of diet t
the needs of the organism and the region has possessed until re
cently no scientific criteria. Only within the last generation hav
the physical and biological sciences developed methods of researc
into the adequacy of human diet. Young as is the study, through th
investigations of Voit, Pettenhofer, Rubner, Atwater, Lusk, Ben
edict, Osborne, McCollum, and others, it has gone through severa
cycles of research and the end is not yet. First to be explored wa
the physics of diet. Measurement of the energy liberated by food
in combustion enabled students to estimate the number of calorie
afforded in the menu. To balance a meal was to ration foods ac
cording to their energy producing qualities; and in one chain o
restaurants at least the customer might take heed of his menu
The chemistry of diet had already arrived to point out the neces
sity for balance among the essential elements, fat, carbohydrates

[18] This suggestion comes from Emily Stevens Maclachlan in her M.A. thesis
"The South's Dietary Pattern," University of North Carolina, 1932, p. 29.

[19] *Ibid.*, p. 29.

[20] *The Great South*, p. 791.

[21] "A Study of Food Habits of White People in Two Contrasting Areas o
Mississippi," *Bulletin 245*, Mississippi A. and M., p. 3.

and protein. This balance could be measured in terms of calories, and beans and cheese since they contained protein might be substituted for meat. Of equal importance was the necessity of an adequate supply of mineral salts which go to make up tissues of muscle, bone, ligament, and new cells.

However, when E. V. McCollum fed chemically perfect rations to rats they wasted away and died.[22] Thus was investigated the biology of diet which discovered in milk, eggs, oranges, and tomatoes, glandular organs and leafy vegetables the vitamins. Of the six or seven found, one protects against scurvy, another rickets, one furthers growth, another protects against pellagra, another beri-beri, another governs fertility. "Retardation of growth in children, faulty posture, tendency to nervousness, defective teeth and faulty skeletal development," according to McCollum, result from lack of vitamins. "Five hundred persons suffering from arthritis, rheumatism, heart disease, diabetes, sick headaches, and other degenerative diseases who were tested by Dr. Lovell Loystroth of San Francisco, were found to be living on a diet consisting almost wholly of bread, meat, potatoes, sugar, and other food poor in vitamins. When their menus were changed to a protective diet consisting mainly of eggs, milk, fruit, and vegetables, 73 percent of the cases improved or recovered."[23]

The latest advance in dietetics is somewhat in debate. It has been indeterminately placed by the critics somewhere between food fads and science. It is based on the necessity of maintaining an alkaline reserve in the blood stream and is directed to correct conditions leading to acidosis. In order to rid the body of its acids they must be combined with alkaline elements. The acid-forming foods are meats, legumes, fats, starches, cereals, and proteins. Alkaline foods are most vegetables, fruits, and milk. Citrus fruits are alkaline in final reaction because of their large content of potash. The foundation of health is thus an alkaline blood stream in which the five alkaline elements, sodium, potassium, iron, magnesium, and calcium, overbalance the four acid elements, silicon, chlorine, sulphur, and phosphorus. Accordingly, from 60 to 80

[22] E. V. McCollum, *The New Knowledge of Nutrition, passim.*
[23] See article by Eunice Fuller Baird "In Food Also, A New Fashion Is Here," *New York Times Magazine,* May 4, 1930, p. 11.

per cent of the total food intake should be alkaline.[24] One need
not follow this theory to the last detail to find the diet of the South
indicted because of its devotion to meats, starches, fats, and cereals.
Conditions of acidity may be normally expected from such menus.

Each of the main contributions in the physics, the chemistry,
and the biology of diet—calories, mineral salts, vitamins, balancing
of carbohydrates, fats, and proteins, and of acid and alkaline
foods—have stood supplemented by the others. The need of rough-
age in diet, the necessity of preserving alkaline reserve in the blood,
the liver diet for pernicious anaemia, the sugarless diet for diabetes, and other specialized regimen have come, but the main
substructure of dietetic science seems to have been laid. A quart of
milk and a salad twice a day are Dr. McCollum's prescription for
the average adult. The standard agreed upon by nutritionists as
an adequate daily diet has been summed up as follows:[25]

Milk	One quart a day
Vegetables	
Potatoes (white or sweet)	Once a day
Others (preferably leafy)	Twice a day
Fruits	
Cooked	Once a day
Raw (or raw vegetables	Twice a day
or canned tomatoes)	
Eggs	Four times a week
Lean meat	Three or four times a week
Whole grain	Twice a day
cereal or breads	

THE SHIFTING AMERICAN DIET

The dictates of the laboratory have been followed by America's
upper and middle classes with amazing celerity and unanimity.
The increase in the consumption of oranges, grape fruit, milk, and
green vegetables has been unexpected and startling. New York
City consumes proportionately twice as much fruits and vegetables
as it did ten years ago; lettuce has increased in popularity in restaurants sevenfold. Cafeteria chains estimate that salad orders

[24] See Floyd W. Parsons, "What Shall We Eat?" *The World's Work,* July, 1927,
pp. 219-26.
[25] H. C. Sherman, *Chemistry of Food and Nutrition,* pp. 9, 325.

have doubled; dairy lunches and corner fruit stands have sprung up overnight. The dairy industry has grown much faster than the population, milk and ice cream have almost doubled their popularity, and in one national chain of restaurants dairy products make up 39 per cent of the food purchased.[26]

The social transition from frontier diet has been clearly pointed out by the Lynds in their study of Middletown.[27] This midwestern town like the rest of the country in 1890 lived on two diets: one for winter and one for summer. Provided she served meat three times a day, the housewife was at liberty to swap about in search of combinations of meats and starches. The repetition of steaks, roasts, macaroni, fish, sweet potatoes, turnips, fried apples, and stewed tomatoes was responsible for time spent in the kitchen on pickles, chow-chow, preserves, pies and cakes to add relish to meals. After the heavy winter diet came spring sickness. Spring tonics were urged upon people together with green garden stuff and sarsaparilla to alleviate the expected boils, thick blood, sluggishness, and spring fever.

Rule-of-thumb methods of cooking were passed down from mother to daughter, with the old doctor and cookbook owned by every family. It is safe to say that the old cookery broke down under the impact of the modern women's magazines. The latest discoveries in food chemistry, prepared in new dishes by domestic science experts, imposed on housewives new habits, new tastes, and new skills. Impetus was given the shift by flour millers, milkmen, cheesemakers, meat packers, orange growers, fruit and vegetable co-operatives organized to exploit to the utmost the facts given into their hands by science. Luscious, succulent dishes in colors came to dominate the advertising pages.

Raymond Pearl's analysis of the consumption of food in war time offers a Middletown of the national dietary.[28] In the total calories consumed in the United States he found that wheat contributed over 25 per cent, pork 15 per cent, dairy products 15, sugar 13, corn 7, and beef 5. Our frontier friend, the porker, has not been outmoded. "Approximately 40 per cent of the total fat in the nutri-

[26] Eunice Fuller Baird, *op. cit.*, p. 11.

[27] Robert S. and Helen M. Lynd, *Middletown*, pp. 156-57.

[28] Raymond Pearl, "Relative Contribution of the Staple Food Commodities to the National Food Consumption," *Proceedings*, American Philosophical Society, 1919, p. 209.

tional intake of this country comes from pork and its products. The hog is in a class by itself as a source of fat for human nutrition with the population of this country." Dairy products with $27\frac{1}{2}$ per cent, and oils and beef with 10 per cent of each follow. Thus when studies by the Department of Agriculture show that pork often amounts to 40 per cent of the value of all food consumed in southern rural homes, this trait can be put down as an accentuation of national trends.[29]

Finally we now have at hand statistical studies of changes in the nation's consumption of foodstuffs from 1898-1902 to 1922-1926 periods.[30]   Most astonishing have been the decline in the use of cereals; the annual consumption of wheat has fallen from 224 to 176 pounds and of corn from 126 to 46 pounds per person. Nor has the decreased use of breadstuffs been compensated in the use of beef and veal which taken together has remained stationary. For while beef has declined eight per cent the use of veal has doubled. Moreover, the consumption of mutton and lamb has shown a decline of 25 per cent. While chickens declined from 20 to 18 pounds, eggs remained at about the same annual level of consumption, 17 dozens annually per person.

It appears that bread and meat, the staff of life, have given way before fruits, vegetables, milk, and sugar. The one exception, strange to say, is the South's standby, pork and lard, whose consumption has increased from 77 to 84 pounds, reaching 90 pounds in the period, 1923-24. Although the fluctuating use of potatoes shows no permanent increase in consumption, the present-day American eats at least 15 per cent more vegetables. He has increased his eating of fruits from 173 to 178 pounds per year, but the great shift has come in milk and sugar. Whereas in 1900 he consumed 880 pounds of milk and its products, he now relishes 1,000 pounds a year. Moreover, the annual use of sugar lacks but little of doubling, having increased from 68 to 109 pounds per person. If the use of pork and sugar products have advanced, despite the nutrition experts, the consumption of milk, fruit, and vegetables shows that McCollum and his rats have sufficiently impressed the great American public so as to change that most cherished of habits—the choice of foods.

[29] H. W. Hawthorne, *et. al.,* "Farm Organization and Farm Management in Sumter County, Georgia," U. S. D. A. *Bulletin* 1034, p. 37.

[30] Summarized in O. E. Baker, "Do We Need More Farm Land?" Mimeographed Report, U. S. D. A., 1928, pp. 16-21.

The Southern Menu Today

The next question is as obvious as it is pertinent to our investigation: What is the diet of the present-day South? In an attempt to arrive at the food habits of its rural people I circularized the South's some eight hundred home demonstration agents. They were asked to give representative menus for the farm families of their counties according to two seasons and three social-economic levels. The two periods correspond to garden and non-garden seasons; the three levels to share tenants, small owners, and well-to-do farmers. One hundred and fifty agents replied. The tabulation of menus from 150 counties scattered from Virginia to Oklahoma and Texas was calculated to throw much light on the geography of diet.[31] For instance, it is worth while to show to what extent nutrition habits are a matter of geographic provinces, of levels of wealth, and of knowledge and training. Are there culture areas in diet corresponding to crop systems? What is the basic diet common to most of the type regions and classes in the South? If such a basic diet exists, exactly what variables are found to mark distinctions between croppers, small farmers, and well-to-do landowners. The theory underlying the work of home demonstration agents suggests that diet also depends on the skills and knowledge of homemakers. What changes actual and potential may be expected? How does the presence of the Negro rural groups complicate the picture? Tabulation of these menus was supplemented by comments of home demonstration workers and previous studies in selected areas to complete the picture.

The Share Tenant

For his winter breakfast the cropper and share tenant sits down to a meal of fried fat pork, molasses, biscuit, and coffee. For side meat he sometimes substitutes bacon, and supplements it with grits and gravy or sometimes butter. Only nine menus of the hundred and fifty contained milk and eggs, and only four cereals and fruit. In the spring and summer milk and eggs show a notable increase although grits remains the outstanding cereal. Only nine menus report fruit. While toast is altogether absent, cornbread appears six times.

For his noon meal in winter the board presents cornbread and fat

[31] These menus have been filed with the Institute for Research in Social Science, University of North Carolina.

pork boiled with a vegetable, preferably potatoes, dried beans or cow peas, turnips, or turnip greens, collards or cabbage. Baked sweet potatoes also rank fairly high, while boiled rice and canned tomatoes are less likely to be present. For beverage the tenant's first choice is water, his second coffee, with milk a lagging third. If he desires a dessert, the syrup pitcher sits on the table the three meals through and possesses first call. During the garden season he has more green vegetables, but cornbread and boiled pork remain the universal staple.

The evening meal follows one of two definite types. If eaten cold it is a replica of dinner; the left-overs of cold vegetables, cornbread, and boiled pork. If a hot meal must be prepared a replica of breakfast is presented—hot baking powder biscuits, coffee, fried meats, possibly grits and gravy and molasses. Strange enough the hot, fried meal almost as common in summer as in winter.

This is a fair and many will contend a generous picture of the nutritional regimen of a third of the rural South. The vast majority of Negroes and many more white people than commonly realized live the year around on such a diet. Before presenting the diet of other classes it will be well to analyze the import of these facts. It perhaps requires courage; but one should be frank enough to allow the comparison of this group with the Negro cropper. Happily Dorothy Dickens has studied carefully the nutrition of Negro croppers in the Yazoo-Mississippi Delta.[32]

The energy value of the Delta dietaries averaged 3,046 calories per man per day. This was lower than an Alabama study of 1895 which averaged 3,270 calories. The Alabama study, however, was not limited to tenants. Milk furnished only 8.7 per cent of the calories consumed and the diet registered low in protein, 62 grams per man per day. In spite of this fact planters say, "Our Negroes eat too much meat." This the Negroes admit. "Meat" refers, of course, to the ever-present salt pork which contributes to the fat rather than the protein group. Dickens has shown that in Mississippi both Negroes and whites consume more fats than their northern colleagues. Only 5.3 per cent of the calories consumed come from the fruit and vegetable group. This is less than half the minimum requirements of nutrition experts for the lowest cost dietaries. Much

[32] "A Nutritional Investigation of Negro Tenants in the Yazoo-Mississippi Delta," *Bulletin* 254, Mississippi Agricultural Experiment Station.

of the vegetable consumption was of Irish and sweet potatoes, conspicuous for starch content. These people live on a carbohydrate diet; more than one fourth of their calories come from the cereal group. In spite of "corn and cotton" the consumption of flour is higher than that of corn meal both for whites and blacks. The southerner likes his hot biscuits, and the sack of flour is a staple carried by every supply store. Less than one tenth of a pound of baker's bread was used by any family in the study, and not one made use of whole wheat flour.

The large proportion of calories furnished by sugar, purely a fuel food, was due to the amount of molasses used. The cropper in Mississippi, both white and black, lives on a diet of cereals, fats, and sugars. His supplies of meats, fruits, milk, and vegetables were low, thus producing deficiencies in protein, vitamins, and mineral salts. Out of 132 foods most commonly listed Negroes used flour, rice, corn meal, cane syrup, lard, salt pork, dry beans, cabbage, rabbit, and opossum to a greater extent than white farmers. For these Negro croppers the average cost of food per man per day was 21 cents, that is, $1.47 a week or $76.44 per year. Per family per year the cost was $330.14, which ranked higher than the $284.30 annual cost found for Negro croppers of Kentucky, Texas, and Tennessee by E. L. Kirkpatrick. Cash spent for food took 32 per cent of the Negro's income and 11 per cent of the white tenant's income.[33]

THE SMALL OWNER

When one turns to the breakfast table of the small farm owner he finds that biscuit and coffee reappear with characteristic unanimity, but fat pork has given way to more bacon. Eggs now appear on three fourths of the menus, milk, butter, and cereals on approximately half, while the ubiquitous molasses has declined from 80 to 40 per cent in frequency. A sprinkling of fruit is present but with only a bare mention of toast, white bread, and oatmeal. The summer menu shows a further fifty per cent decline in molasses, compensated by fruit for about half the families and slightly supplemented by jams, jellies, and preserves.

The noon meal continues to be an affair of cornbread and pork boiled either with dried beans, cow peas, Irish potatoes, collards, or greens. Biscuit shows an increase, while canned fruit and fried

[33] *Ibid.,* pp. 17-35.

meats break into the regimen of almost a third. Milk outstrips coffee two to one, although water is often drunk alone. Milk is used in about 60 per cent of the homes, while butter is consumed in only 30 per cent. Desserts also show greater prominence, pie or cake being served on almost 40 per cent of the menus. These menus are equally noteworthy for their omissions: beef, raw fruit, steak, kraut, carrots, spinach, veal, sea food, white bread, and meat-loaf each appear only once. Spring and summer show a decrease in fried meats and boiled pork and an increase in vegetables served on from 50 to 70 per cent of the menus. Fruits rise to 35 per cent and green beans, green peas, sliced tomatoes, new potatoes, and cabbage are served on from 30 to 50 per cent of the menus. Salads make their first appearance for about 20 per cent of the servings, and there is a slight sprinkling of lettuce, radishes, onions, slaw, etc.

Supper for the small farmer is his most slender meal. Milk is the most popular food, appearing in about 70 per cent of the dietaries, and milk and bread with cold left-over vegetables furnish the staples of nutrition. If no cold food remains, a replica of breakfast, consisting of hot breads, fried meats, and molasses and preserves is preferred.

Again we may use the work of Dorothy Dickens for comparison. She has studied the dietaries of white farmers in both the short-leaf pine and the brown loam areas of Mississippi.[34] Like the croppers these small farmers live on a diet of carbohydrates and fats, but unlike the tenants 95 per cent own cows. Where the diet of the urban dweller is built around meat, this diet is built around milk. As will be seen this is a much higher ratio than that found in our study. W. C. Funk holds that it is not unusual for the average sized southern family to consume 2,000 quarts of buttermilk a year.[35] The meat consumption was especially low; in fact salt pork was the only form of meat consumed by many families. For the nation nearly two thirds of the meat eaten on the farm is pork, amounting to some 500 pounds annually per family. All studies point to the fact that the protein intake is lower in the South than anywhere else in the nation. While the consumption of beef, for example, averages nearly 300 pounds per farmer family in the North and

[34] "A Study of Food Habits of White People in Two Contrasting Areas of Mississippi," *Bulletin* 245, Mississippi Agricultural and Mechanical College, 1927.

[35] W. C. Funk, "Home Supplies Furnished by the Farm," *Farmers' Bulletin* 1082, 1920, p. 4.

West, in the South it is less than 100 pounds.[36]   The egg consumption fell below the suggested standard of an egg per man per day, but the use of eggs was nearly as great as that of fresh meats, fish, and poultry combined.   Sixty-one per cent of the families preferred their eggs fried hard even for the children, 83 per cent chose meat fried, while 95 per cent wanted their vegetables cooked with salt pork.   Meats are fried to a greasy hardness in hog fat, and baking and broiling are comparatively unknown.   Plain or white gravy is much favored for grits or rice.   "Mississippi people like fats and use them excessively in cooking.   Many believe that people in warm climates require more fat."[37]

Again only seven per cent of the calories, about half the requirement for low cost dietaries, come from fruit and vegetables.   For the country as a whole vegetables constitute about eleven per cent of the volume of all foods of the farm family.   Fruits account for six per cent.[38]   Although many fruits and vegetables can be grown in Mississippi, comparatively few varieties were used.   There were more food dislikes found in the vegetable group than in any other.   Cabbage and turnips were most generally disliked and many people were found who disliked all vegetables except potatoes.   Vegetables were even more poorly prepared than meats, and much of the dislike may be laid to poor cooking.   In many homes vegetables are put on soon after breakfast and left to boil until noon.   Thus their natural juices are boiled away, they become impregnated with salt grease, develop a strong flavor and odor, and like cabbage bring all the flies in the neighborhood to the kitchen door.   Among the cereals corn retains its high place.   In the South the average annual consumption of corn meal is about 500 pounds per family as compared to about 50 pounds for northern families.[39]   The taste for sweets, especially molasses and cane syrup, is highly developed, and the consumption of sugar is high.   This may fairly account for vegetable dislikes.   If children are not taught to eat vegetables, highly flavored foods come to take their place.   The high consumption of sugar is as much a maladjustment in a warm climate as that of fat. It is not unusual for southern families to produce 10 to 25 gallons

[36] W. C. Funk, *op. cit.,* p. 7.

[37] Dickens, *op. cit.,* p. 13.

[38] Funk, *op. cit.,* pp. 7, 9.

[39] *Ibid.,* p. 11.

of syrup for home use. Negroes did not express the dislike for strong vegetables shown by white farmers.[40]

Milk is the life-saver in the Mississippi diet. Although coffee is used in a large number of these homes it was used by few children. Often coffee drinking was restricted to one or two adults, usually the father, while the rest of the family drank milk. Tea was used in only seven per cent of the homes and, as few rural dwellers purchase ice, iced tea remains an urban beverage. Milk cooled in a well or cistern furnished among other things 60 per cent of the calcium, 50 per cent of the phosphorus, and 15 per cent of the iron in this dietary. From milk rather than over-cooked vegetables comes much of the vitamin content, and that none of the subjects studied had pellagra was largely due to the use of milk in the diet. It must be added, too, that 53 per cent preferred their fruit raw rather than in pies. It is exceptional in the South to find 94 per cent of the farmers owning cows; and, however low in their standards in other respects, these Mississippi farmers stand out among dwellers in the Cotton Belt. Many areas in the various cotton and tobacco belts are found to rank exceedingly low in dairy animals.

The Well-to-Do Farmer

With the third group, the well-to-do farmer, one comes nearest the problem of repletion and the groaning board in southern diet. For breakfast, for example, cereals, coffee, eggs with bacon or ham, fruit, butter and milk, jams and preserves, all appear on over 70 per cent of the tables. Toast for the first time makes a showing, appearing on over 30 per cent of the menus. The summer finds an increase of toast, fresh fruits, berries, and melons with a proportionate decrease in bacon. If in the winter seven per cent report grapefruit, in the summer four per cent have chicken for breakfast.

For the noon meal the menu offers many interesting variations. Cornbread and Irish potatoes still lead, but fried meats outrank boiled pork in the ratio of four to three. Canned vegetables and fruit are found at half the meals. The proportion of desserts is double that in the menu of small farm owners and most significant; fruit and vegetable salads appear on almost 40 per cent of the tables. Roast beef for the first time gains an important place, appearing on the menu of 20 per cent, and is matched by fried chicken in the

[40] Dickens, *op. cit.,* p. 12.

same ratio. Although twenty-one vegetables are mentioned, only greens, beans, dried cow peas, Irish potatoes, and sweet potatoes are used in as many as 20 per cent of the meals. Summer lifts the percentage of salads to 55 per cent, and adds the use of raw fruits and vegetables. Cabbage and tomatoes play an important part as the list of vegetables is increased to twenty-seven. Surprisingly enough, the use of meat increases for summer, including, of course, fried chicken which appears on a third of the menus. This may be offset somewhat by a slight decrease in cooked desserts and an increase in raw fruits consumed. Milk is now used in about 75 per cent of well-to-do families, iced tea in not quite 30 per cent, while coffee falls to its lowest level in any menu, 12 per cent.

Supper in this group tends more to reproduce dinner. Hot breads, fried meats, and eggs are freshly prepared and serve to supplement the cold vegetables from noon.

This group comes nearest to the popular conception of southern cooking. "This being a southern county," writes an Oklahoma agent, "I find they are still holding to their 'southern' idea of serving rich foods, as meats and hot breads, etc." "The well-to-do Delta farmer," says a worker from Louisiana, "usually entertains extensively and during the winter months his table is supplied with duck, geese, quail, and deer. They usually do their shopping in town and it is not unusual to find the table graced with December strawberries." J. Russell Smith, a southerner and a geographer, finds the well-off southerner eats too much fried fish, fried chicken, fried meat for his climate. Walter Hines Page, as a North Carolina journalist, preached in and out of season, "The frying pan must go."

The menu, however, does not finish with the problem of nutrition. Over seventy-five per cent of the answers returned commented on children's eating between meals. The favorite foods are largely the same for all classes. Cold sweet potatoes, cornbread, bread and fried meat, bread and syrup furnish the child's favorite refreshment. In the upper classes preserves take the place of molasses and there are more cookies. In the more southern areas the chewing of sugar cane is a great between-meal pastime, while in the summer watermelons, berries, and fruits are eaten by all children with access to them. This trait, one of undisciplined childhood, cannot be expected to add either to health or efficiency, and its widespread prevalence makes the southern diet heavier than menus would indicate.

Culture Areas in Diet

Two generalizations emerge from this survey. First it is the South's basic diet of pork, fats, starches and sweets which reigns supreme throughout the great cotton and tobacco belts. Second a comparison of menus grouped by regions shows distinct traces of culture areas in diet. Often these areas retain the basic diet which they supplement by characteristic articles of food. For example, in the Delta and south of middle Georgia, a syrup made from the native sugar cane, superior both in minerals and vitamin content, decidedly improves the basic diet.

Outside the cotton belt, mountain and coastal diet areas are clearly marked. In the mountains corn furnishes the mainstay. On the coast, potatoes and green vegetables from trucking and sea food from fishing take its place. The coastal areas possess a great fondness for rice, a survival of the days when rice culture dominated the Carolina Tidewater. Coastal people have always known how to cook rice just so, and possess many ingenious recipes for its use, as chicken pilau. "Potatoes are raised in abundance and are served daily" writes an agent from the Pamlico Sound Country. The housewives also boil cornbread with vegetables making a kind of dumpling, called "corn dodger" because of the agility of the ball of meal in boiling water. As if to balance its comparative abundance of trucking vegetables, sea food, and farther South, citrus fruit, the southeast coast is greatly lacking in milk. "In this county," writes a home demonstration agent from Florida, "I find but little difference in the menus of the different classes, except in so far as the use of milk and butter is concerned. As a rule only the well-to-do or the better educated among the other classes, use milk to any extent. Only a few keep cows and, as milk sells for twenty-two to twenty-five cents a quart, many feel that it is extravagant to buy it."[41]

Trucking areas furnish a healthful, varied diet during off seasons. In Florida from the "month of October until June," writes an agent, "most rural folk have more or less citrus fruits, as nearly every home has a few trees even if there is not a grove. Also from December till June or July there is an abundance of one or more vegetables. Cabbage comes first, and about the time that is gone,

[41] Correspondence with home demonstration agents. Filed with Institute for Research in Social Science, University of North Carolina.

omatoes come into bearing, peppers, cucumbers, and eggplant fol-
ow, but these are gone by June first, and for the next two months
field peas and okra are the chief vegetables. During August and
September most of the homes have no fresh vegetables and depend
upon canned vegetables and rice for the menu. . . . There have been
very few home gardens . . . most of the families depending upon
truck growers and merchants for their supply of fresh vegetables.
. . . This method of obtaining vegetables tends to make a monotonous diet, but it is the usual practice in the majority of the homes
of the county." Strange enough, the need here is for the summer
rather than the winter garden.

It is an anomaly that the mountain dwellers of the Appalachians
and Ozarks who live at home more completely than any of their
contemporaries should in their domestic economy parallel so closely
the regimen of the cotton belt.[42]   Corn grows well on hillsides wa-
tered with mountain rains, while the roaming porkers once caught
are easily kept and cured. The usual mountain cow "has a lean
and hungry look. Her milk is thin and poor and her flesh tough
and hard. The keeping of sheep is far less frequent than in early
days, owing to the menace of dogs. Poultry is the only meat commonly used besides pork, and this is less common than the repute
of fried chicken would lead one to expect. Eggs are comparatively
cheap but do not form so great a factor in the diet as they should."[43]
For supplementing his diet the southern hill dweller depends not
on the towns but on an isolated country store. "Within a half dozen
miles of a railroad," writes Carl Sauer of the Ozarks, "few such
stores exist. Beyond that distance, however, they become increasingly numerous as the people find it more and more difficult to get
to a town."[44]   "Salt, vinegar, molasses, soda, coffee, sugar, white
flour, canned goods especially 'salmon,' tomatoes, peaches, salt pork,
soda crackers, and cheap candy make up the main articles of diet
kept in these stores."[45]   In return, eggs are received in barter, and
chicken and egg men make regular tours of the section collecting
produce.

The comparative diet of urban and rural groups in the South is

[42] See Lydia Roberts, "The Nutrition and Care of Children in a Mountain
County of Kentucky," Childrens' Bureau, *Publication 110*, 1922.
[43] Campbell, *Southern Highlander*, p. 199.
[44] *The Ozark Highlands*, p. 225.
[45] Campbell, *op. cit.*

as yet uncharted territory. A study in New York state shows that the town dwellers through their grocery stores are better supplied with vegetables than country dwellers. With superior climate the South finds itself in the same situation. Most northern towns are much better supplied with the product of southern vegetable trucking areas than southern towns of the same size. Rhyne in a cursory glance at the cookery of the mill village housewife holds her "an expert at the menus that include fried foods, large baking powder biscuits, and a little round of quickly prepared dishes."[46] "The mill family staples of diet are hot breads, fried meat with cake and pickles when possible." Company dinner is an elaboration of this menu. Lois McDonald cites, for example, a minister who reports the pattern of "company supper served him many times in the mill village as consisting of ham, steak, sausage, pickles, hot biscuits, black coffee, chocolate, coconut, and white icing cakes."[47] At least one home demonstration agent holds the farmer's standard lower. She writes from South Carolina: "I did welfare work in a mill village in this state for three years. It has been quite interesting to me to note the difference in the lives and modes of living in the village and that on the farm. Farm people are healthier due to their outdoor lives, but I believe as a whole mill people keep better tables than on [sic] tenant and small farms. Farmers will not give time and attention in the South (I am southern, from a farm in North Carolina) to the growing of gardens, poultry and dairy products. They spend too much time on larger crops—cotton, and feel they and teams are too busy to bother with these things. Therefore, they do not help the women to be in a position to do what they might along these lines."

Moreover, while there exists high-powered express and refrigeration service between southern trucking areas and northern metropolitan centers, town and county relations in Dixie remain halt and limping. In many towns the solitary farmer peddles his few green wares from back door to back door; in others he finds his huckster's privileges restricted by the green grocers acting through the town council. In surprisingly few southern towns and small cities does a curb market operate to the benefit of housewives and farmers. And yet the home demonstration movement realizes the force of

[46] J. J. Rhyne, *Some Southern Cotton Mill Workers and Their Villages*, p. 13.
[47] Lois McDonald, *Southern Mill Hills*, p. 94.

the principle: "If you want them to eat it, get them to grow it for sale." One reason why such limited variety is grown on southern farms is the limited facilities for city sale.

The South Deviates from Standards of Nutrition

That representative southern dietaries deviate from the best standards of nutrition more than those of other sections is hardly to be doubted. The extent of variation from adequate food requirements has been scientifically measured in many studies. Lydia Roberts studied the diet of 256 children from two to eleven years of age in 123 mountain families of Kentucky. She found that 28 per cent of the children had a diet which probably included all constituents necessary to nourish their bodies, 27 per cent had a diet clearly inadequate, and 45 per cent were in the doubtful or marginal zones.[48]

Susan J. Matthews found that the diet of 200 Georgia farm families composed of 1,323 persons showed close similarity to the Mississippi diets except that Georgia farmers consumed less than half as much milk. Comparison with accepted standards of nutrition showed a too liberal use of fats, starches, cereals, and sweets with a scarcity of lean meats, eggs, dairy products, fruits, and vegetables.[49] Her results may be tabulated as in Table XL.

TABLE XL

DEFICIENCIES IN DIET OF 200 GEORGIA FARM FAMILIES

Food Group	Per Cent Calories in Standard Diet	Per Cent Calories in Georgia Diet	Per Cent Excess	Per Cent Deficient
1. Meats, eggs, cheese..................	15	11.1	....	− 19
2. Milk, cream......................	12	9.2	....	− 23.3
3. Fats............................	17	24.7	+45.3	....
4. Sweets..........................	10	12.1	+21	....
5. Cereals (Starches).................	28	33.6	+20	....
6. Fruits, Vegetables.................	18	9.3	....	− 50

Separate tabulation of individual diets showed 44.7 per cent low in total calories, 37.8 per cent low in protein, 30.5 per cent short in calcium, 50.6 per cent deficient in phosphorus, and 77.4 per cent deficient in iron.[50]

[48] Op. cit., pp. 39-40.

[49] "Food Habits of Georgia Rural People," Georgia Experiment Station, Bulletin 159, 1929, pp. 27, 15-17.

[50] Ibid.

Sixteen authoritative food studies have been given a composite ranking by Emily Stevens Maclachlan according to variations from a standard dietary.[51] The basis was the percentage deviation from the standard number of calories furnished by the seven food groups averaged with the percentage deviation from standard mineral content. The extent to which southern families depart from the normal standards of nutrition is especially outstanding.

TABLE XLI

COMPARATIVE RANK OF DIET SURVEYS

Rank	Number Families Studied	Type Families	Average Deviation
1	178	Missouri farm families	7.75
2	12	Virginia prosperous farm families	9.05
3	406	Kansas farm families	9.85
4	224	Typical American families	14.62
5	950	Farm families in 14 states	15.50
6	27	Virginia prosperous urban	16.05
7	75	Mississippi white farm families	16.65
8	382	Ohio farm families	22.75
9	85	Virginia intermediate farm families	22.90
10	253	Georgia rural families	28.85
11	365	Kentucky farm families	31.25
12	40	Virginia poor farm families	37.62
13	78	Virginia intermediate urban families	37.80
14	11,900	Workingmen's families in 42 states	48.10
15	80	Mississippi Delta Negro cropper families	61.50
16	35	Virginia poor urban families	66.80

CULTURAL CHANGE IN FOOD HABITS

With regional deficiencies and inadequacies so clearly evident, the reader may well ask what social changes are being engineered to close up the dietary lag. It is noteworthy that the South, which furnishes the country a great area of need for cultural change to conform to geographic framework, has also furnished the nation machinery for change. Seaman Knapp originated farm demonstration work in the South in 1908; the southern states have led in the county health movement; North Carolina has a system of public welfare called by its name. In a similar manner, under the guidance of home demonstration agents, a significant cultural change is gaining momentum in the South. Food habits are being reformed under capable persuasion and demonstration.

[51] *Op. cit.*, p. 47. To the excesses and deficiencies in dietary regimen Mrs. Maclachlan applied the statistical technique of the standard deviation.

Through the formation of home demonstration clubs of farmers' wives these workers are teaching protective diets, home canning, the winter garden, and the preparation of salads from raw fruits and vegetables. One agent explains the technique of social change: "At several demonstrations to clubs last spring on salad making I used vegetables they carried me from their gardens, preparing the boiled salad dressing. They appeared astonished that so many delicious combinations were possible without using the things bought from the store. . . . At different 4 H canning parties I taught the girls how to make vegetable or cabbage slaw. They liked it but had never eaten any before. . . . At the girls' camp and also the women's camp we served salads for all dinners and suppers and a fruit for breakfast." Such are the slow inroads by which changes can be made in a traditional diet. Another agent writes that fourteen farm women in her Florida county kept accurate records of all vegetables and fruits eaten by their families in 1929. Still another from Florida trucking areas writes: "The average number of vegetables consumed per family last year was nine, while one girl had 45 varieties of vegetables throughout the year and another 43 varieties."

Many workers in the field have come to believe that adequate diet is not so much a matter of economic classes as of the mother's training. "Some poor people have better food than many well-to-do. . . . One entire club of ten women were renters' wives, yet each provided an adequate diet for her family. I once had occasion to have lunch with this club. Everything that should have been served to constitute an adequate diet was served neatly and well. The next day I had lunch with a well-to-do doctor's family in a small town. The housewife's menu consisted of biscuit, corn, potatoes, macaroni, rice, raw kraut, butter, a dessert of peach cobbler, nearly all dumplings. This was an all starch affair. Plenty of money but—"

"I note," writes another, "a wide departure from the old hog and hominy diet in this country, and this change has come among the poorer people with some intelligence. . . . There is a noticeable lessening of the use of coffee three times a day for everybody." From South Carolina a woman writes: "I have two hundred club women growing winter gardens. This has raised the standard of living a great deal."

In an Oklahoma county "more than 300 pressure cookers were

sold to farm women to be used in canning." From Texas one worker writes: "People in this county eat for health, and poverty is shown sooner by type of clothing than you will find it shown in diet." "I had occasion," writes another, "to cover a large area of South Carolina last January 1929 and I ate often in the homes of farm people. In counties where agents had worked a period of time there was a notable difference in diet than [sic] where they had been only a short time." One proudly affirms: "We have reached the point with salads where only a few men turn up their noses at them. This tells the story that salads now 'belong.'" A Georgia agent holds that variety has come to all through canning work in the budget plan. It is "even felt among the Negro population. Now nearly all crossroads' stores carry some vegetables in the winter." Another worker established a curb market and found that the townspeople's demands for fresh fruits and vegetables changed the crop plans of many farmers. Another in desperation has fallen back on that southern recourse, paternalism. "The county agent and I are trying to get some of the landlords to try out a plantation garden. If this plan is a success, the tenants will have vegetables all the year around." All agree with the South Carolina worker that "we have a wonderful climate and soil and there seems no excuse for all this poverty." The drought of 1929-30 caused the South to produce in 1931 one of the largest food and feed crops in history.

Regional Diet and Human Adequacy

With every advance of science in this field the evidence accumulates that the common man in the South has not yet made the transition from the temporary diet of the frontier. All primitive peoples who have survived to the present have through a process of trial and error succeeded in balancing their diet. A good example of this is found in the Chinese peasant who without milk has attained a balanced ration of rice and green vegetables. Jose Zozaya, brilliant young Mexican scientist, holds that the Mexican peasant has balanced his high intake of protein in corn and beans by the drinking of pulque, intoxicating but rich in vitamins.[52] Many meat eaters, according to McCollum and others, balance their diets by consuming the protective glandular organs.

Is there tangible evidence that unbalanced diet is telling on the

[52] Stuart Chase, *Mexico*, pp. 141-42.

South's population? No more pertinent question can be asked for the purposes of this investigation. The frequency of sallow complexions and gaunt frames, the protruding Adam's apple, the prevalence of risings, the vaguely denominated stomach troubles, tobacco chewing, snuff dipping, and the drinking of hard liquors may bear some relation to maladjusted diet. But just as the inertia, the apathy, the admission of "feeling poorly" of the common man was about to be resolved by science into an affair of the hookworm parasite a stranger and more disquieting malady flared up in the South. That pellagra existed long before it was brought into the open for recognition cannot be doubted. That it represents the whole extent and damage of unbalanced diet cannot be maintained. In fact the greatest importance of pellagra will be found in the fact that it has served as an index to nutrition deficiency for a whole region. It has cost and will cost high in its toll of disease and death, but it has served as nothing else to call to attention the hidden hunger and near-starvation for vital elements in southern diet.

In pellagra the nation was confronted with a disease, sinister in its implications, baffling in its diagnosis, sudden and startling in its appearance, comparable to old-world scourges like beri-beri and scurvy. Attention was first directed to the disease in the South by reports of its prevalence in an Alabama Negro asylum in 1907-08. Investigation showed the disease, long prevalent but unrecognized, and its "universal recognition made it seem like the outbreak of an epidemic." Gaspar Casal, a Spanish doctor, had first observed in 1738 the *mal de la rosa* (red spots) and regarded it as a combination of scurvy and leprosy. In northern Italy as early as 1755 the malady was known as Alpine scurvy, while in 1760 at Milan it was first described under the name pellagra. In New York in 1864 were isolated the first American cases to be recognized. Confined almost entirely to the South, it seemed governed by some mysterious principle of geography. So markedly did it follow the limits of the cotton belt that many thought it caused by spoiled corn meal of the "cotton and corn" complex. It seemed either contagious or infectious, for the disease broke out afresh each spring and summer in definite communities composed of people of the same level of living. Its occurrence in summer hinted at some relation with a pseudo-tropic climate and rendered obscure any connection with diet. Summer was the month of gardens and orchards; if pellagra were a nutritional disease it should by all means break out in the winter months. But there are three times as many deaths in mid-summer as in the midwinter. The effects of malnutrition are de-layed six months. Besides the malady occasionally occurred in the well-to-do families. Moreover the mental aberrations that often ac-company its later stages presented still more baffling symptoms.

It was left to Dr. Joseph Goldberger of the United States Public Health Service, alien to the South, to trace this hidden hunger to its source. He tested his long felt doubts of the theories of con-tagion and infection by well-planned experiments. With the per-mission of the governor of Mississippi and the men concerned, twelve life-term convicts had their diet over a long period limited to biscuit, cornbread, grits, fried mush, rice, gravy, syrup, sugar, and coffee. Infrequently they were given cabbage, sweet potatoes, and turnips, while all milk, butter, cheese, meats, eggs, fresh vegetables, and fruits were excluded. Six developed pellagra within six months, while no one in the control group living with the men under the same conditions, except for diet, contracted the disease.

In bulletins of the United States Public Health Service Gold-berger traced statistically the rise and fall of the disease cycle with the cycles of poverty and prosperity in the cotton belt. He publicly assigned the case of the malady to the "Three M diet"—meat, meal, and molasses, and despairing of any sudden improvement in lifting economic levels, worked out the palliative effects of yeast.[53] This knowledge was later to be used to good effect in the great Mississippi flood of 1927.

There is no denying that publicity concerning pellagra, just as that concerning hookworm, has been deeply resented by the South. On July 25, 1921, President Harding wrote to Surgeon General Cummings of the Public Health Service and Dr. Livingston Far-rand of the Red Cross asking for a survey of the pellagra situation in the South. He predicted, following the depression, 100,000 vic-tims of the disease, ten per cent of whom would die. Well or ill-advised, the move could have been prompted only by consideration for the welfare of the South. It was met, however, by a storm of abuse and reproof. Southern senators denounced the reports. Sen-

[53] See Paul de Kruif, *Hunger Fighters,* pp. 335-70. Joseph Goldberger, "Pellagra: Its Nature and Prevention," *Public Health Reprint,* 1174, 1927; "Pellagra in the Mississippi Flood Area," *Idem,* 1187, 1927.

ator Harris did not know of a single case in Georgia. The Georgia senate passed resolutions denouncing the report of an epidemic as damning. The Macon and Atlanta chambers of commerce wired protests. Eight state health officials took vigorous issue. Florida and Alabama claimed decreases; Tennessee reported nothing unusual; South Carolina admitted increase but no famine; Arkansas claimed "nothing alarming"; Mississippi admitted "twice as many as last year but no epidemic." All this in the face of the President's statement that it took six months for cases to develop. The survey was not made and in most southern states the rate of pellagra has been steadily on the increase. Dr. Charles Laughinghouse has shown that in North Carolina from 1928 to 1929 the pellagra death rate increased from eight to 30 per 100,000. The fatality rate is from five to ten per cent. Moreover, studies, as the one by the Public Health Service in seven cotton mill villages, show that the number of cases brought to the attention of the local physicians was slight compared to the ones found by house to house canvass.

It is not necessary to credit this resentment to any excessive provincialism. It is natural and to be expected in all diseases implying low social and economic standards. To say that an ailment indicates ignorance, filth, poverty, or undernourishment of an area has never been known to provoke a lively outpouring of gratitude. The controversy has died down. With the facts in, no intelligent southerner is disposed to deny the prevalence and consequences of pellagra. Mortality reports for 1929 show that ten southern states lead in deaths per 1,000 from pellagra ranging from .138 for Louisiana to .526 for South Carolina. Deaths from pellagra have shown a steady increase throughout the South. Reported deaths from pellagra in North Carolina, for example, have increased from 273 to 1,002 in seven years as follows:

1924	273
1925	398
1926	459
1927	712
1928	860
1929	953
1930	1,002

In the application of these findings to the South as a region one needs to go a step further. We will desire, of course, to apply the test of balance and protective content to southern diet. Beyond this stands the question of adaptability to climate. The sub-tropic climate of the South, it seems but safe to assume, must needs make special demands on the diet of its people. How well these demands are met can be measured in many instances by the general test of health. Its more subtle and widespread influences are to be found in the relative efficiency of the people. Efficiency may be thus a function of diet in relation to climate rather than of climate itself, as Ellsworth Huntington believes. Over-eating, the consumption of sugar, fats, and foods fried in grease, are particular maladjustments to warm climates. It remains strange that people in warm climates have not developed greater appetites for raw foods. Maladjusted diets are capable of effects on energy which, like those of energy-sapping diseases, are twofold. It robs one of ability to do work and it further saps one of inclination to do work of which he is capable. Experimental test of this could only be made on a large scale by, say, keeping the piece-work records of groups of operatives living on different diets under control conditions.

The conclusion seems forced by the data on hand that many of the so-called climatic handicaps of the South are assignable to other causes. One recalls an aphorism from the *Physiologie du Gout:* "La destinee des nations depend de la maniere dont elles se nourissent." E. V. McCollum holds that "students of mankind have hitherto failed to realize the importance of the selection of a food supply as an agency in the improvement of a race," and adds: "As a result of my many experimental observations, I have come to hold the view that animal experimentation, human geography, and history, all point in an all but conclusive manner to the diet as the principal cause of our health troubles in so far as these are not brought about by communicable diseases."[54]

Hot breads, sweets, fats and fried foods furnish a diet both heat producing and energy consuming in a climate noted for its summer heat. The lack of green salads, of milk and eggs, and the use of vegetables cooked until they lose the value of freshness completes a diet that even in winter creates a feeling of lassitude. "Several years of experience in the southern field," writes a North Carolina home demonstration agent, "convinces me that pork fat, starch, and sweets constitute the basis of diet at all seasons. Even in grow-

[54] *The Newer Knowledge of Nutrition*, pp. 415-16.

ing seasons vegetables are rendered more or less useless by fat and long cooking."

The monotony of a basic diet among the plain people—a diet that fills but does not satisfy or energize—is met with a plethora of good things in the upper dietary levels. It is enlightening to hear many a well-to-do farmer speak of Sunday as his hardest day. It is a further tribute to the insight of common men to find that many of them assign the cause to the prodigious Sunday dinner. While the higher level traditional southern cooking serves to show of what the region is capable in gastronomic wealth, it is by no means an ideal diet from the standpoint of biological efficiency. Overeating itself may be due to the hidden hunger of unbalanced diet.

The present generation has seen much so-called inherent southern backwardness dissolved with the fogs that once shrouded in ignorance the miseries of malaria and hookworm. The once neglected or ridiculed boils and risings, spring sickness, the feared rheumatism and the dreaded pellagra are, no doubt, indices of dietary maladjustment. As the diet imposed by the frontier and the cotton system recedes before the knowledge gained by science, we may expect a release of the energies of southern people comparable to that in sections which have conquered hookworm and malaria.

CHAPTER XVII

THE STRUCTURE OF A REGIONAL ECONOMY

THE SOUTH'S STATUS

THERE exists one fact which no regional analysis can escape. The statistical indices of wealth, education, cultural achievement, health, law and order reduced to a per capita basis combine in every instance to give the southern states the lowest rankings in the Union. One may take the *Statistical Abstract,* the *World Almanac,* the latest census, and manipulate the slide rule to his heart's content. The southern states always come out behind. Charles Angoff and H. L. Mencken after combining twenty-six tables ranking the states on per capita indices of wealth found twelve southern states at the bottom.[1] Their composite rankings on 63 items of wealth, health, culture, and education compared with the ranking of S. H. Hobbs, Jr. on 63 similar items show the South bringing up the rear guard of the states.

TABLE XLII

THE SOUTH'S STATUS

RANK	Angoff and Mencken*	S. H. Hobbs, Jr.†
34	Arizona	Florida
35	Oklahoma	Oklahoma
36	Florida	West Virginia
37	Virginia	Texas
38	Texas	New Mexico
39	New Mexico	Virginia
40	Kentucky	Kentucky
41	Louisiana	Louisiana
42	North Carolina	Tennessee
43	Tennessee	North Carolina
44	Arkansas	South Carolina
45	Georgia	Mississippi
46	South Carolina	Arkansas
47	Alabama	Georgia
48	Mississippi	Alabama

*"The Worst American State", *The American Mercury,* XXIV, 356.
†S. H. Hobbs, Ir. *North Carolina Economic and Social,* Table LIV, pp. 283-84.

[1] "The Worst American State," *The American Mercury,* XXIV, 8-9.

In Dr. Hobbs' tabulation, California, Nevada, Washington, New York, and Iowa rank among the first five; in the *American Mercury* article Massachusetts, Connecticut, New York, New Jersey, and California. Our concern here is not with the invidious distinctions of worst and best state but with the rank of the regions. On this basis southern states fall into distinct groupings. Florida with its mixed population of northern leisure class, southern "crackers," and its unique economic situation stands first among southern states. The newer Southwest of Texas and Oklahoma vies with the upper South of Virginia, Kentucky, Tennessee, and North Carolina for the next ranking position. Last in the nation comes the deep South. Georgia, Alabama, South Carolina, Arkansas, and Mississippi, areas of the old slave pattern, excessive ruralism, and devotion to cotton, compete for the last place. Louisiana alone is pulled out of this group by its natural resources of oil and the commercial supremacy of New Orleans.

REGIONAL RESOURCE AREAS

So rank the states of the American South. There is no denial of the fact that the modes of southern economy in wealth and welfare fall about one third short of national norms. Let us suppose, however, that lines are drawn to follow regional rather than state boundaries and the South's natural areas as we have presented them are ranked on the basis of resources and resource utilization. Such ratings will serve to inter-relate the areas and interpret the stance of the whole regional economy.

Because it has led in the coming of industry to the South, because its economy has been integrated, because its resources have been more adequately developed, the Piedmont Crescent ranks first. Coal, iron, and dolomite at Birmingham for rich and accessible mineral resources in unique juxtaposition; the textile industry for its importation of capital, equable regional distribution, and quantity of workers; furniture for skill of its labor and artistry of design; tobacco manufacturing for its accumulation of capital in value added by manufacturing; these are the industries and resources bound together in the Piedmont Crescent. Unified as to its energy resources by a most efficient utilization of water power, which is supplemented by readily accessible coal from Alabama and West Virginia, the area has found port outlets which range from Mobile Bay to the splendid facilities of the Hampton Roads area. Beyond the Appalachians appears the obverse and reciprocal development of another Piedmont in the emerging Tennessee Valley, stretching from Knoxville to Chattanooga, to Muscle Shoals, to its culminating point also at Birmingham. The returns to textile workers have not been high, the profits from tobacco manufacturing have suffered no wide distribution, the agriculture of the Piedmont is demoralized. Yet industry in the main has been deployed through the countryside without creating new urban slums. No super-cities have arisen; and the Negro has filled some of the highest skilled places in Birmingham. On performance and promise the Piedmont deserves its rank.

Next in the regional hierarchy is its newest comer, the Southwest, also emerging. If it lacks the Piedmont's diversity and integration of regional interests it possesses the gift of liquid minerals, petroleum. Here in Black Prairies, Rio Grande valleys, and the westward sweep of a new cotton culture, agriculture has aided rather than retarded regional growth. A ranching industry has been stabilized at a level lower than its earlier expansion. The tremendous oil industry of Texas and Oklahoma with pipe lines and the creation of deep sea harbors for Texas Gulf ports have furnished a basis of resource utilization. As reflected in the migration of population and the growth of large cities like Houston, Dallas, Fort Worth, Tulsa, and Oklahoma City the new Southwest deserves no lower than second place.

Third in the regional alignment of the South's resource areas fall certain agricultural sub-zones which possess in common only one main characteristic—they have remained outside the South's cotton economy. Only slightly supplemented by industrialism, these sub-regions have worked out diverse types of farming that place them in advance of the deep South. The balanced live stock and grain farming of the Kentucky Blue Grass, its supplement with apple orcharding in the Virginia Shenandoah give these belts high rank among the nation's farming systems. Trucking and orchard zones reaching from the Rio Grande Valley to the Virginia Eastern Shores belong also in this higher resource rating. This zone reaches its most notable development in Florida where its greatest crop, the tourists, flourish each winter to the value of some $200,000,000. Florida representing the sub-tropics and Virginia the Piedmont fringe may prove the first southern states to rejoin—in an economic sense—the Union.

Next must come the South's vast Cotton Belt. Its place, low as the economy has sunk, is based on the virtual monopoly of an important staple crop—a monopoly which no amount of subsidized foreign competition has yet served to topple from its position of producing 55 to 60 per cent of the world's crop annually. The ranking, however, must be qualified throughout by distinctions and differences. The Southeast ranks below, and the Southwest and the Delta rank above. In the old area tobacco complicates the problem; the differential costs of production are mounting, and farmers are leaving the soil. Moreover, the mixing of cotton seed in rural gins has led to the hybridization of cotton and the degeneration of staple in this area. If the new southwestern cotton lands be ranked first because of level topography, fertility, and freedom from the weevil, the Delta and alluvial lands of the great valley follow close behind. They possess the resources of soil that insure long staple. With the Delta goes the commercial economy of Memphis and New Orleans, the valley's historic metropolis and sea port. The Black Belts of Alabama and Georgia present a decadent economy, and in the uplands of Mississippi, Alabama, and Georgia, erosion further reduces the tillable holdings of farmers who farm meanly on too small a scale. In both areas the staple continues to grow shorter— a process which only South Carolina has appreciably arrested. Here in the old Cotton Belt the future of the industry seems most hazardous of all, and until new methods are found of utilizing that centuries old resource, the soil, only the most foolhardy can be optimistic.

For the lowest ranking region the Highlands yield to the Piney Woods because they possess more of a future. In its fertile plateaus and valleys the Appalachian Plateau can sustain a high type of agriculture. Mineral belts in Kentucky possess essential resources of coal, however disorganized the industry may be at present. More barren in resources, however, are the Highland's eroding ridge belts, an area maintaining the lowest level of backwoods farming in the United States today. Its resource foundation is being further undermined by the rapid depletion of timber.

The Piney Woods come last because they furnish a zone of fading resources. The naval stores and lumbering industry having swept the Carolinas clean, exploited most of the forest resources of Arkansas, Alabama, and Mississippi, the Piney Woods is now making its last stand in Georgia, Louisiana, and Florida. The area is now facing resource exhaustion with no concerted plans of re-forestation that yet appeal to private investors. Alternative uses of its sandy, infertile soil, seem neither needed nor desired in southern regional economy.

The Basis in Natural Resources

Such are the inter-related resource areas out of whose materials have been constructed the lowest economies in the nation. Their integration by commerce and manufacture has, of course, made such economies as here presented transcend state lines. But when it comes to cultural institutions supported by government—schools, for example—state lines are clearly lines of demarcation. Thus the crude oil of Oklahoma is a regional asset as an energy resource. But as a support for public education by means of the severance tax it serves to raise only the cultural status of Oklahoma above that of, say, Mississippi, which possesses hardly any mineral wealth. How far can the position of the South be attributed to a fundamental lack of natural resources? The question deserves as full and frank an answer as we are able to give it.

This rank of the South is not a recent thing, in fact the gaps between regional and national standards have been closing up. More-over, to offer the Civil War and Reconstruction as the persistent cause of the South's every regional difference is as if France should cite the War of 1870 as a plea for exemption from judgment on the basis of European standards. To account for the South's position in the United States of today requires an analysis of the pertinent data already offered in the discussion of regions and resources. This presentation may best be made in the light of a theory of resources, human energy, cultural equipment, and economic organization.

The starting point in our analysis is natural resources. The economist's concept of land as one of the three factors of produc-tion must be broken up by the geographer into various elements. These are gifts of nature, best called in the term of Erich W. Zim-mermann, the untransformed aspects of nature.[2] As outlined by C. C. Colby they are: position, area, relief, waters of land, oceans, coast lines, climate, soil, native vegetation, native animal life, and minerals.[3] How does the South stand on the geographic count of

[2] Unpublished lectures.

[3] *Source Book for Economic Geography of North America*, p. xi.

these gifts of nature? Its area is approximately one fourth that of the nation and its population likewise. Its position, favorable for contact with the densely settled East and with South America, is not so near Europe. Out of a nation's coast line 4,883 miles long, the South possesses 2,728 miles.

Relief, varied enough to account for regional diversity, has not offered excessive natural barriers. The southern areas isolated by topography are, it must be admitted, regarded by many as the most retarded in the nation. In the waters of the land, in ocean contact, and in coast lines, nature, as the South's history shows, has not been niggard either in quantity or quality. True enough, the South's natural harbors have given way before the man-made ports of Hampton Roads, New Orleans, and the Texas Gulf ports. Moreover, the area's greatest river has proved its greatest hazard. Nevertheless, the South's development has by no means been retarded by its water resources, surface, underground, or oceanic.

A region's soil is its greatest asset. Nowhere has the statement been truer than in the South. Nevertheless, it is difficult to rank the region on the basis of this important resource. Neither the best nor the worst soils are found here. In few places in cultivated agriculture are there found much poorer soils than the sub-tropic, leached, sandy flats of the pine barrens. Neither do many soils break away and erode faster than do Highlands and Mississippi Loessal Bluffs under southern rains. Both erosion and the excessive use of fertilizers in the Southeast can be charged to certain untoward cultural factors rather than wholly to the deficiency of nature. On the other hand, few soils outside the Corn Belt compare in natural fertility with the Bluegrass, Black Prairie, Mississippi alluvium, and Black Waxies. Other soils are tractable and under the mild climate may be guided into fertility by the culture of legumes. Even coastal flats become valuable truck lands with fertilization.

In native vegetation the South possesses a gift of forests equal to that of any comparable region. Here forests of greatest extent yield multiple resources—grazing, pulp wood, naval stores, turpentine, and yellow pine timber. That they have been so often exploited and wasted is not due to the niggardliness of nature. Moreover, forest resources renew themselves much faster in the South than elsewhere. In native animal life the region's coast offers considerable resources of fish, sea food, and sponges. In grasses the area has not been so fortunate, nor has it escaped many pestiferous weeds. In the negative aspects of animal life the area has suffered most, not from wild beasts but from insects. Prolific insect life, like the rapid growth of forests, is due to the South's climate.

With climate we come to the most debatable resource nature has furnished the South. Its value to resort areas such as Florida, and its effects on vegetation are beneficial and obvious. Equally positive are its harmful promotion of insect and parasitic spreaders of disease and of an ill-chosen diet. Very real is the area's relief from the handicaps which cold climes suffer in a shortened growing season and the blocking of transportation and other economic activities by snows and freezes. While the question of climatic effect on human energy still remains unanswered, the climate that allows the maximum outdoor life affords its devotees undeniable health benefits.

The question of mineral resources arises. Does the South as a region possess that abundance and high quality of structural metals and power fuels which have aided in giving America a high standard of material well-being? In 1928 the mineral production of the South was valued at 24.1 per cent of the nation's. The American states are listed 253 times as chief producers of the 85 most important minerals. Of the states so mentioned, southern states are listed 53 times or 20.9 per cent. Leading minerals, both metals and fuels, in the South are petroleum, coal, iron ore, zinc, natural gas, sulphur, bauxite, phosphate rock, feldspar, cement, clay products, Fuller's earth, stone, sand, gravel, and mineral waters. One survey lists 97 principal undeveloped mineral resources of the South. While none of the fuels is lacking, copper is possibly the greatest deficiency in metals. And it is the power fuels and structural metals on which modern industrial cultures are based.[4] Normally Oklahoma ranks second, Texas fourth, and Kentucky eighth in the value of minerals produced, while North Carolina, South Carolina, and Mississippi rank among the last twelve. The other southern states in 1928 ranged from 14 to 70 million dollars worth of minerals extracted.

Natural resources, however, may be differentiated on the basis of their adaptability to transport. Thus a region's soil and climate

[4] See E. W. Zimmermann, "The Resource Hierarchy of Modern World Economy," *Weltwirtshaftliches Archiv.*, XXXIII.

must be exploited on the site or not at all. Minerals, however, as well as the plant and animal products of the soil, can easily be transported. Accordingly, any point on the Mississippi River now possesses the possibility of securing cheap coal and iron by barge from Pittsburgh. Thus it happens that coal and oil are rarely used where found. Proximity counts less than economic organization, the state of the industrial arts, and capital accumulations in their development. Under modern pecuniary economy and absolute corporate ownership, location of resources may come, therefore, to mean little more than exploitation of an area by outside capitalists. The areas producing such resources will receive only the returns due to the unskilled labor, crude technology, and small capital of an extractive economy, while the larger values added by manufacturing and marketing will be absorbed in the area of skilled fabrication and stock ownership. This is due partly to the fact, embedded in our rate structure, that bulky goods of low value carry lower freight charges than finished products of high value. If the percentage of wastage of raw materials is not high, factories can more profitably be located near markets than near their sources of raw materials. Any economic retardation of the South related to minerals, it may be said in summary, is more likely to be due to a cultural deficiency than to lack of natural resources.

Conversely, lack of mineral resources will not handicap a region provided technology, capital, labor skill, and economic organization are so inter-related as to attract the raw materials into the area for processing. The value of finished aluminum is about 2,000 per cent of the value of the amount of bauxite from which it is made. Five tons of bauxite require 27 tons of other materials to produce one ton of aluminum. Bauxite areas receive only the wages paid to unskilled labor used in its extraction; other returns are absorbed in the region of its fabrication. We may sum up by saying that the position of the South has found no adequate explanation in terms of natural resources. If nature has not been prodigal, neither has she been niggard. If the South cannot be expected to rank with Pennsylvania in mineral resources nor with Iowa in soil, neither does the region rank with the poorest. Massachusetts, for example, possesses but three notable resources from the hand of nature, its fisheries, its water power, and its natural harbor at Boston. On many resource counts, as mineral and soil resources, the state ranks behind the median southern state; on power resources they are approximately equal; yet on the basis of economic and cultural indices Massachusetts ranks with the first while the southern group is at the bottom. The utilization of resources, not their bare presence, affords the explanation of regional status. And Massachusetts early accumulated the capital surplus with which to develop the resources of other areas.

The first point of departure in the analysis of the utilization of natural assets is the concept of modifiability of resources. Men collectively can determine, George Herbert Mead points out, what plant life and what animal life shall surround them and what shall be the immediate incidence of heat and cold upon their bodies. There exists no element of intractability in natural resources vouchsafed the South. Forests have been cleared, native weeds outlawed and pushed back to the fringes of cultivation. Animal and plant life, culturally preserved and propagated, have been introduced and have thrived. Grass and live stock can offer the only exception to the facile modifications of nature's products to man's use. Even here the handicaps are more cultural than inherent in the complex of nature.

TRANSPORTATION IN THE SOUTH

The modification of terrain through the telescoping of space relations, the convergence of location, and the conquest of relief by the utilization of natural waterways and artificial highways is the function of transportation. No analysis of the regional economy would be complete without consideration of the distinctive task which transportation has met in the modification and relocation of areal resources in the South.

In any consideration of the South's heritage of transportation it is difficult to over-emphasize the fact that the area developed as a coastal and river-bank civilization. Until 1850 the bulk of the South's export cotton, A. E. Parkins holds, was grown within ten miles of navigable streams. In the South Atlantic states, only 16.5 per cent of the land was improved, and in the new central south area the figure dropped to 10.1 per cent.[5] Here is the evidence of the South's upland frontier awaiting reclamation. This frontier remained undeveloped because an excellent network of waterways

[5] A. E. Parkins, "The Antebellum South: A Geographer's Interpretation," *Annals*, Association of American Geographers, XXI, 22.

reaching to seaports afforded competing areas means of ready transportation. An abundance of water courses meant tidewater plantations, family wharves, little sloops out of London or Bristol, but no coöperation of independent Virginia planters in building roads. In the hundred miles between Monticello and Washington, Jefferson had to cross eight rivers of which, he wrote, "five had neither bridges nor boats." In the succeeding steamboat era many rivers now regarded as unnavigable were used to a great extent. The Mississippi's fame has been recorded; but towns at the head of navigation in Georgia, Alabama, and other states became collecting points for goods going downstream and distributing points for goods coming up. Uplands and Piedmont, isolated from commerce, remained in the frontier, nor did the South discover her upland area until the railroad era. The South today possesses some 10,000 miles of navigable waterways to 7,000 for the rest of the nation. And even now many Chesapeake counties of Virginia and Maryland possess no railroads because boats perform the service usually done by trains.

In spite of these facts, however, the South is known to have led in early railroad construction. As early as 1836 a convention at Knoxville planned the Louisville, Cincinnati and Charleston Railroad. At one time the Charleston-Hamburg Railway was the longest in the world. Best Friend, one of the first locomotives built in the United States, was purchased in the early 1830's for a South Carolina road. It met a sad fate, for the engine was wrecked by a Negro who sat on a safety valve. Baltimore, failing of attaining a projected canal, undertook its famous railroad which as the Baltimore and Ohio had penetrated the Alleghenies by 1853.[6]

As elsewhere, the hue and cry for railroads reached untoward proportions. Transportation was seen as the cure for all southern ills. The section went through the craze for plank roads, canals, and even inclined planes. A caustic critic at the Memphis Commercial Convention said that every planter with a dozen Negroes wanted a railroad running in front of his house and every man who had fifty Negroes wanted one running by his house and another by his kitchen.[7]

Sparse population with few cities meant light passenger traffic. Each natural region produced the same great staples, a fact which

[6] Edward Ingle, *Southern Sidelights*, pp. 98-99.
[7] *Ibid.*, pp. 260-61.

obviated the necessity of regional interchange. These staples, however, demanded an outlet into world trade and commanded supplies in return. They were responsible, too, for a great rush to market after the harvest season with consequent lean traffic during spring and summer. These facts left the profits of southern railroads to be gained between September and January or not at all. Furthermore, there existed certain deficiencies in capital management and labor supply, due to the agricultural and the slavery system.[8] Transportation was almost the only field of endeavor open to white workingmen that was free from slave competition. "Commerce flooded the rivers from 1820 to 1860 with hundreds of steamboats plying the waterways of the Coastal Plain and the Mississippi Delta." For thirty years before the war the South kept persistently at construction, and by 1860 the section possessed 10,711 miles of railways, 32 per cent of the nation's trackage.[9] The effect of all this building was to extend the area devoted to the production of cotton. This lowered prices and consequently placed at tremendous disadvantage all cotton districts without railroads.

In the South the railroads were laid down with the idea of forming a system. Their goal, R. S. Cotterill has pointed out, was the commerce of the West. The passing of the center of cotton production to new lands of Georgia, Alabama, and Mississippi had seen the rise of New Orleans and the decline of Charleston and Savannah. These cities expected to direct this new commerce to their gates by railroads which would tap the stream of river-borne commerce at Nashville, Memphis, and Vicksburg. The roads were built, but the trade of Iowa, Wisconsin, and Illinois did not flow to Charleston. The South thought railroads would continue as auxiliaries of waterways. The idea of a railway system as an independent unit of transport did not occur until the demonstrated cost of transhipment from river to railway and from one road to another of different gauge proved the fallacy of attempting to divert commerce by merely tapping a waterway.[10] By that time northern

[8] B. H. Meyer, etc., *History of Transportation in the United States Before 1860.* Carnegie Institute Publication 215, pp. 214-15.

[9] A. E. Parkins, "The Antebellum South," *Annals,* Association of American Geographers, XXI, 13.

[10] R. S. Cotterill, "Southern Railroads and Western Trade," *Mississippi Valley Historical Review,* IV, 427-41.

roads had penetrated the heart of the old Northwest and were completing the diversion of traffic which the Erie Canal had begun.

To gain conciseness, it must suffice to say that after the blight of poverty left by war and reconstruction had begun to lift, railroad construction in the South did not vastly differ from that in the North. In 1870 over 1,200 miles were constructed, 1,000 miles in 1871, and over 1,300 miles in 1873. The main line trackage in the South increased from 19,171 miles in 1880 to 51,220 miles in 1900, then to 72,593 miles in 1910, and to 76,949 miles in 1929. Construction, consolidation, and integration of financial control have given the region four important trunk line systems. The Southern Railway spreads like a web over the whole South. Including nearly all strategic points on the border and the interior, it stretches to four important corners of the South: New Orleans, St. Louis, Norfolk, and Jacksonville. The Atlantic Coast Line, including the Louisville and Nashville system, equally extensive, reaches most of the important points served by the Southern, and adds a long line into Florida. The Seaboard Air Line serves the Coast reaching Atlanta, Birmingham, Montgomery, and Columbus with large trackage in Florida. The Illinois Central System furnishes the great Mississippi valley system, reaching to the Southeast through its subsidiary, the Central of Georgia.[11]

Mark Jefferson has classified the world's regions on the basis of their penetration by the civilizing rails. On maps of equal scale he has blocked in white all territory within ten miles of railways. On this basis he distinguishes between the railway web, the railway net, and the railway link. The web shows all the maps' area in white. Western Europe and the eastern United States thus find practically all their population and resources within ten miles of transportation. The second type shows a network fairly closely knit, with certain rather large isolated areas standing out. In this class are found Italy and the American South. Brazil is the type of net with open meshes, while Siberia, Africa, etc., possess only the outlying tentacles of transportation. "The first region with its closely knit fabric of transportation has no point out of reach of the locomotive for continuous hundreds of thousands of square miles. In

[11] Roland B. Eutsler, "Transportation Developments and Industrial Changes," *Coming of Industry to the South, Annals,* American Academy of Political and Social Science, pp. 204-5.

these regions people and goods move about with great facility, products are readily exchanged, and the inhabitants have a considerable acquaintance with each other."[12]

For 1925 the railway mileage for each 1,000 square miles of area ranged in the South from 121 for South Carolina to 60 for Texas, with the midpoint at 98. This compares with 283 for Pennsylvania, 215 for Illinois, 207 for Ohio, and 170 for New York.[13] The national index was some 84 miles of trackage per 1,000 square miles. With 28.5 per cent of the nation's area, the South in 1929 possessed 30.7 per cent of its railway mileage. When navigable waterways are added its total rises to 32.8 per cent of the nation's avenues of transportation. It is Eutsler's judgment that the adequacy of railroad facilities in the South is not to be questioned. There exists no seasonal congestion in the moving of agricultural products. Nor does regional consolidation present the problems to be found in other sections. If anything, the roads may have overdeveloped their facilities in an agricultural area of sparse population. Accordingly the chief task of consolidation here consists in the annexation of

TABLE XLIII

RAILWAY MAIN LINE TRACKAGE AND NAVIGABLE WATERWAYS IN THE SOUTH

STATE	1880	1900	1910	1928	1929	Navigable Waterways 1929	Total
Virginia	1,893	3,779	4,535	4,528	4,527	450	4,977
Kentucky	1,530	3,060	3,526	4,028	4,024	600	4,624
North Carolina	1,486	3,861	4,932	5,223	5,194	1,000	6,194
Tennessee	1,843	3,137	3,816	4,024	3,989	350	4,339
South Carolina	1,427	2,817	3,442	3,747	3,804	650	4,454
Georgia	2,439	5,652	7,056	6,835	6,835	700	7,535
Florida	518	3,299	4,432	5,730	5,740	1,200	6,940
Alabama	1,843	4,226	5,226	5,308	5,292	1,800	7,092
Mississippi	1,127	2,920	4,506	4,246	4,233	700	4,933
Arkansas	859	3,360	5,306	4,875	4,899	800	5,699
Louisiana	652	2,824	5,554	4,770	4,775	1,800	6,577
Oklahoma	289	2,399	5,980	6,622	6,708	.....	6,708
Texas	3,244	9,886	14,282	16,782	16,929	800	17,729
The South	19,170	51,220	72,593	76,725	76,949	+ 10,850	=87,799
The Nation	93,267	193,346	240,293	249,710	250,376	+ 17,675	=268,051
South's Percentage of the Nations Avenues of Transportation	25	27	30	31	31	60	33

[12] Mark Jefferson, "The Geography of Rolling Transportation," *Annals*, Association of American Geographers, XVIII, 64.

[13] Mark Jefferson, "The Civilizing Rails," *Economic Geography*, IV, 217-31.

weak and short lines to the large systems. The growth of industry has operated to distribute traffic evenly throughout the year and thus strengthen the position of the carriers.[14]

There remains to be considered the rate structure. The utilization of resources, the development of regions, the localization of industries in the nation and the South have all been greatly affected by early differentials in freight rates. Briefly, the two important interacting conditions affecting the development of the rate structure are the long and short haul clause and the competition of railways with water-borne commerce.

The growth of large cities and the concentration of industry in the East have depended to some extent on the rate structure, especially the precedence given to the long haul. What Malcolm Keir has to say of its effect on the Mid-West also applies to the South:

It was to the interest of the railroads, since they made their profits on the long rather than the short hauls, to keep manufacturing localized in the East where it first developed and to prevent wide decentralization of manufacturing in the western agricultural regions.

Rates were also adjusted so as to give undue favoritism to the large Eastern seaboard cities. . . . The result was a long haul for manufactured articles westward and a long haul of agricultural products eastward.

If rates were placed on the basis of service rendered—mileage charge plus charge for terminal facilities . . . there will be a rapid decentralization of manufacturing. Localization of industry will no longer be profitable. Nearness to raw materials and nearness to market will be enhanced.[15]

Like railway construction, the rate structure in the South developed in relation to waterways. Because of the competition from water-borne commerce between ports or parallel rail lines, cities on navigable waters were given low rates, while high rates were maintained to non-competing points. Forced by the Act of 1887 to adjust their long and short hauls, many railways blanketed their rates inland. Moreover, low rates over water routes were reflected in lower rates to such inland basing points as Atlanta, Chattanooga, and Birmingham. By such discrimination, industries were located, the

---

[14] Roland B. Eutsler, *loc. cit.,* p. 205.

[15] "Economic Factors in the Location of Manufacturing Industries," *Annals,* American Academy of Political and Social Science, 97, pp. 83-92.

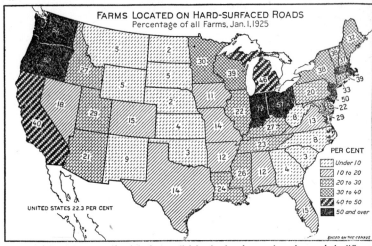

FIGURE 21.—The proportion of the farms adjoining hard-surface roads varies greatly in different portions of the United States. In Massachusetts, Ohio, Indiana, Oregon, and Washington 50 per cent or more of the farms were provided with such roads in 1925, but in most of the Great Plains region less than 5 per cent. In the region north of the Ohio and Potomac rivers from one-fourth to one-half of the farms are located on hard-surface roads. The quality of these roads varies greatly, however. In the lower Lakes region, Maryland, North Carolina, and California many farms are provided with concrete or brick roads, while in western Ohio, Indiana, Michigan, Minnesota, and parts of Kentucky, Tennessee, and Mississippi macadam or gravel roads are characteristic. (Courtesy of U. S. Department of Agriculture).

growth of certain southern cities promoted, and that of others retarded. Investigations of the Interstate Commerce Commission found that water competition had vanished on small streams and was decreasing elsewhere. Accordingly the tariffs put into effect in 1916 denied lower rates to interior basing points. After the 1920 Act this was followed by a complete revision of rates to a mileage basis. This supplanting of discriminatory low rates "eliminates one of the barriers to industrial and commercial diffusion. Thus, in the future, any concentration or localization of industrial activity in the South will be explainable in terms of other facts" than rate discrimination.[16]

Nor has the South's highway program lagged behind her railway development. In 1928 the 625,000 miles of surfaced highways in the nation represented 71 per cent more mileage than that of the railroads. Modern highways have done more than supplement railways; they have developed into a system of their own. Tourists

[16] Roland B. Eutsler, *loc. cit.*, pp. 205-9.

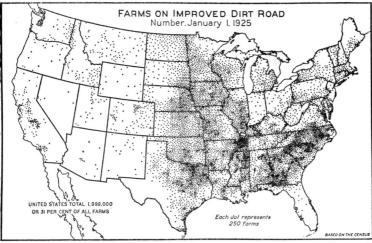

FIGURE 22.—More farms adjoin improved (graded) dirt roads in the South than in the North, partly because there are more farms (including cropper holdings) in the South and partly because there is a much smaller mileage of hard-surface road. A half or more of the farms adjoin improved dirt roads in several counties of the upper coastal plain of the Carolinas and Georgia, northeastern Mississippi, and western Tennessee, also in the upper piedmont and in northeastern Texas. Improved dirt road is the common kind in most of the prairie region, extending from Illinois westward to Oklahoma, Kansas, and North Dakota. Nearly a third of the farms of the United States are located on improved dirt roads. (Courtesy of U. S. Department of Agriculture).

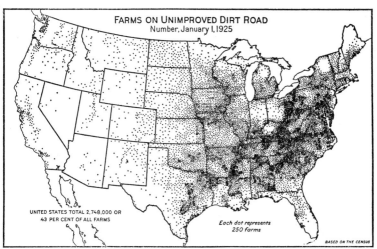

FIGURE 23.—Over two-fifths of the farms of the United States in 1925 were located on unimproved dirt roads. In New York, Pennsylvania, and New Jersey and in the South Atlantic States over half the farms were on such roads. Many of these farms are in districts that have rather poor soils or rough land surface, notably the upper Ohio Valley, eastern Kentucky, and the upper piedmont of Georgia and the Carolinas; but in other districts the soils are good, particularly in several counties of southeastern Pennsylvania. Note that in western Ohio, central Indiana, and the bluegrass district of Kentucky nearly every farm has been provided with a hard-surface road. (Courtesy of U. S. Department of Agriculture).

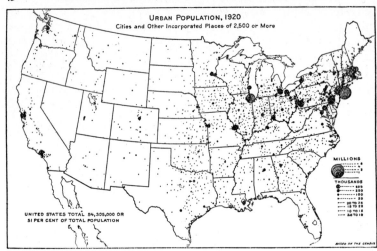

FIGURE 24.—By reference to figure 1 it will be noted that over half of the urban population in the United States resides in the agricultural region devoted to hay and dairying. Into this urbanized area the food and fibres of the West and South constantly move. The center of urban population in 1920 was located near Pigua, Ohio, whereas the center of agricultural production was over 400 miles to the west near Jefferson city, Missouri.(Courtesy of the U. S. Department of Agriculture).

and farmers, pleasure and business, buses and trucks find here new avenues. Because of its geography the South stood in especial need of the surfaced road. Slopes, swampy land, heavy rainfall, erosion, slick red clay combined to render dirt roads impassable and incapable of repair. When the level dirt roads in northern states remained frozen all winter the southern roads, unprotected from winter rains, either eroded beyond repair or sunk in the mud. Moreover, southern road construction has always faced large expenditures for grading in the highlands and swamps, along with the cost of bridging the numerous coastal streams.

In 1879 a convention of northern residents of the South passed among other resolutions the following about southern highways:

We find that no attention whatever has been given to roads or bridges in the South; that passage over many portions of the higher country is most difficult; that gullies and holes exist; and that frequently bridges have dangerous holes in them.[17]

After a slow start the South has begun to attain national standards in highway building. In 1929 the South possessed some 29

[17] "What Northern Men Say of the South," *Proceedings,* Convention of Northern Residents of the South, Charlotte, N. C., 1879, p. 15.

per cent of the nation's total surfaced mileage and 32.9 per cent of
the country's surfaced state highways. With 21.8 per cent of the
country's automobiles, the section applies 21.9 per cent of the nation's registration fees to its highways, and collects a total revenue
of $129,601,000 from gasoline taxes. State tax per gallon ranged
from four to six cents, with the section collecting 28.8 per cent
of the nation's revenue from gasoline. From 1904 to 1928 the section increased its annual expenditures on highways from $7,603,803
to $338,601,671, an increase of 5110 per cent as compared to a 2391
per cent increase for the nation. From 1914 to 1928, the South
increased its highway expenditures 845 per cent while for the country as a whole the increase was 592 per cent. In 1929, 54.4 per cent
of the section's expenditures on highways came from registration
and gasoline fees. Spurred by the desire to overcome geographic
handicaps and attain national standards, the section, in spite of
smaller comparative wealth and fewer automotive vehicles, has
fairly embarked on a vigorous program of construction. In 1928
the section accounted for 27.1 per cent of the nation's highway bill;

TABLE XLIV

HIGHWAY MILEAGE AND EXPENDITURES SOUTHERN STATES, JANUARY 1, 1929

STATE	State Highway System Mileage	Sur-faced Mileage	Local Roads Mileage	Total Sur-faced Mileage	EXPENDITURE STATE, COUNTY, AND FEDERAL AID FUNDS (In Thousand Dollars)			
					1904	1914	1928	1929 (esti-mated)
Virginia..........	6,932	4,722	56,766	7,175	$ 687	$3,224	$23,021	$25,000
Kentucky........	11,500	5,137	49,761	10,993	1,161	2,474	20,170	21,500
North Carolina...	7,137	6,390	63,392	21,995	624	5,215	44,289	30,500
Tennessee........	5,870	4,534	59,193	9,004	729	2,370	28,486	31,500
South Carolina ...	5,810	4,657	51,283	11,991	334	1,024	25,324	27,500
Georgia..........	6,253	3,776	93,284	10,198	894	3,688	26,626	27,300
Florida..........	6,414	3,234	23,326	10,784	437	2,280	44,556	48,500
Alabama.........	5,590	2,740	61,004	14,630	378	3,949	28,087	28,500
Mississippi.......	6,939	4,536	50,733	9,613	339	3,960	25,342	7,250
Arkansas.........	8,718	4,916	66,039	1,863	681	3,949	28,087	28,500
Louisiana........	9,003	6,287	26,440	4,444	345	1,777	18,081	23,200
Oklahoma........	6,142	1,995	114,485	1,716	447	2,112	25,307	26,100
Texas...........	18,728	10,749	169,836	14,666	2,543	9,920	51,210	53,000
Total South......	105,086	63,673	885,542	129,032	$9,603	$45,946	$388,601	$383,350
The Nation......	306,442	193,138	2,709,839	432,999	$59,527	$240,263	$1,423,870	$1,540,000
South's Percentage.....	34.6	32.9	32.6	29.0	16.1	19.9	27.1	24.9

Table XLV

Motor Vehicles, Registration, and Gasoline Tax Revenues, 1929

| STATE | Number Motor Vehicles | | | Registration, 1929 | | Gasoline Tax per Gallon, Cents | Total Revenue from Gas Tax (Thousand Dollars) |
	1912	1915	1929	Total Revenues (Thousand Dollars)	Applied to Highways (Thousand Dollars)		
Virginia.......	5,760	21,357	387,205	$6,145	$5,885	5	$10,510
Kentucky......	5,147	19,500	332,848	5,381	5,145	5	7,734
North Carolina.	6,178	21,000	483,602	7,045	6,745	5	11,983
Tennessee.....	12,490	26,000	368,431	4,288	4,181	5	9,250
South Carolina.	10,000	15,000	231,274	2,674	2,644	6	6,979
Georgia.......	19,120	25,000	358,905	4,568	4,403	6	10,264
Florida........	1,749	10,850	345,977	4,959	4,661	6	12,207
Alabama......	3,385	11,634	285,533	3,736	3,558	4	7,104
Mississippi.....	2,895	9,669	250,011	2,963	2,812	5	6,806
Arkansas......	2,250	8,021	233,128	4,212	4,127	5	6,730
Louisiana......	7,000	11,380	280,868	4,523	4,473	4	6,925
Oklahoma.....	6,524	25,032	570,791	6,964	6,749	4	10,929
Texas.........	35,187	40,000	1,348,107	20,418	19,622	4	22,180
Total South....	117,685	244,443	5,476,680	$74,917	$70,882	..	$129,601
The Nation....	1,010,399	2,445,666	25,501,443	$347,843	$323,337	..	$449,731
South's Percentage..	11.6	9.9	21.8	21.5	21.9	....	28.8

in 1929, 24.9 per cent. Incompetence in the fields of engineering taxation, and finance, coupled in some states with political mismanagement, has resulted in a considerable amount of loss and waste. Consequently highway policies have dominated local and state politics in the South for the last two decades, and some states have embarked on projects too ambitious for their exchequers. Other states, North Carolina notably, happen to have gotten the worth of their investments.[18]

In conclusion it can be pointed out that the different course of development the South has taken has not been due to lack of transportation facilities. True enough, reliance on waterways helped to keep the inland South in frontier condition until past the mid-century. Moreover, with adequate rail connections the rate structure favored to a certain extent the centralization of industry in the East

[18] The story of highway development in this state has recently been recounted much to the enlightenment of students of the South. The state has recently performed the unique experiment of taking all the county highways under state support and management. See Cecil K. Brown, *The State Highway System of North Carolina*.

and the growth of certain favored rate-basing points. Nevertheless, the South has long possessed transportation commensurate to the density of its population and its proportion of movable resources. The region has long retained a colonial economy, but with this colonial economy it developed transportation to a high degree—high enough it may be said to facilitate rather than retard the shift to a more industrialized economy. The transition to a mileage basis for the rate structure has affected the decentralization of industry, as the Piedmont proves. The combinations of rails, waterways, man-made harbors, and, in Texas, pipe lines, have given the South's transportation lanes three splendid terminals on the sea, the port area of Hampton Roads, New Orleans, and Texas Gulf ports. In between are scattered smaller but adequate facilities. Supplement these with the southern highways that have risen out of the mud, and it is safe to say that transportation in the future will not serve to perpetuate sectional differences, either economic or cultural.

Human Adequacy in Its Biological Aspects

Natural resources are transformed into articles fitted for the use of man by the application of human energy. Here is the point where the geographic and the biological factors meet in the process the economist calls production. Human labor has been further separated into human energy and human capacity to acquire and apply skills. Thus human labor, regarded as a force producing material changes in nature, runs the gamut from brawn to brain.

Wherever evident, aspects of cultural and material retardation in the South have usually been explained by citing deficiencies in the human elements. The biological interpretation of southern culture has assumed various forms, and from time to time has pointed an accusing finger at the indentured servant, the Negro, the "poor whites," and the loss of best stock in the decimation of the Civil War. For some reason a lower grade of humanity was consigned to the South; but blood will tell. Consequently, so runs the theory, the area can only be regarded as reaping the fruit of its biological deficiency in energy and capacity. This view has been widely accepted by southerners themselves, the more so because an early evolving tradition of aristocracy was coupled with the presence of a divergent race. It is only recently that explanations in terms of accumulated capital, culture, and conditioned responses have replaced among social scientists the old concepts of race capacity and deterministic instincts. It was not difficult then for the southern planter to impute to the Negro, the poor white, or the retarded frontiersman, an inferiority as innate as the natural depravity taught in his theology. Noble classes everywhere have confused, for example, the lack of good manners in their peasantries with the lack of capacity for good manners. We have no license here to anticipate scientific discoveries in a field in which bitter controversy still rages. The author may confess his bias, however, by saying that while he is disinclined to accept any of the biological theories about the South, he possesses no special knowledge with which to lay their ghosts.

The excess of land over labor and a supply of human energy inadequate to exploit the resources of the region, account for the admission to the South of both the indentured servant and the Negro slave. By the principle of indenture, a pauper laborer might arrange to pay his transportation to Virginia through his labor in a high wage society rather than in the low wage economy of densely populated England. As T. J. Wertenbaker points out, an indentured servant was by no means a slave, and the severity of the restrictions imposed during his term of labor were regarded a justifiable guarantee of repayment of passage money.[19] Transported felons and debtors also came. Whether or not their numbers have been exaggerated, there can be no doubt that in that brutal age of penology their crimes were exaggerated.

The same cause brought the Negro. Introduced to supply the area's striking deficiency in man power, he became, when the balance between resources and man power was reached, the assigned cause of a whole region's backwardness. He is the figure to which all southern apologists point in defense. The South cannot advance, it cannot reform its agriculture, it cannot develop industry, it cannot attain to national economic standards because the Negro comprises one fourth of its population, is lazy, is incapable, requires infinite direction in detail. The argument is obvious and hackneyed, but there can be no denial that the southern Negro ranks among the lowest in the nation in standards of living. It is his lack of per

[19] *Planters of Colonial Virginia, passim;* also *The First Americans, 1607-1690,* pp. 22-48.

capita wealth that brings down state averages. Admitted that, where congregated in large numbers, he pays but little taxes and offers a public burden, nevertheless, his labor furnishes the returns out of which taxes are paid. If the taxes are not sufficient it may be that some defect inheres in the system under which his labor is utilized. On the other hand, no race has come further against greater handicaps. A wild race, peremptorily shorn of its cultural heritage, became in three generations, N. S. Shaler pointed out, substantially comparable to the peasant classes of our western culture. That they have not entered into the general composition of all classes of the population as do the children of western peasants may be due mainly to contacts restricted by inescapable physical stigmata. Patient, enduring, laborious, tactful, they passed through slavery, survived the hiatus of abolition and economic reconstruction to find themselves inheriting the lowest rung of a disorganized but binding cotton economy. Blankly limited in cultural opportunities, encircled by race prejudice as by a barrier of fire, the Negro's rise to partial land ownership, to industrial position, and to a modicum of success in the arts and sciences is frankly a notable achievement for any race.

The South can enter no demurrer on the score of the Negro when it is realized that his toil hastened the opening of the section by some fifty to a hundred years. Suppose it be admitted that a portion of the race falls within a lower classification of capacities. Many nations have their retarded peasant or proletarian classes and yet reach a high general level of resources and material achievement. The South holds the Negro back; the Negro holds the South back; and both point in recrimination. In a field where doubts abound, let us make one sweeping statement. If biological inferiority of the whole Negro group were a proved fact, it would, nevertheless, be to the benefit of both white and black to behave as though it did not exist. Only in this way can the Section be sure of securing, in the economic sphere, the best of which both races are capable.

"Southern poor white," a fighting term south of the Potomac, has a connotation extending beyond poverty. The term implies some unspecified type of racial degeneracy and furnishes the second great item in the biological indictment of the South. To ante bellum travelers must go the credit of starting the poor white myth.[20] They

[20] In conversations with Dr. A. N. J. den Hollander in regard to his forthcoming monograph on this class.

came South expecting to see every member of the white race a
member of the plantation-owning aristocracy and found instead a
poverty-stricken frontier group dwelling in pine flats, sand hills, and
uplands. Here, then, was a new kind of poverty, a poverty that
implied inherent biological degeneracy. Their hereditary qualities
accordingly were traced back to transported felons and indentured
apprentices brought from England. But an indentured servant was
no more than a poor man who took this method of working out his
transportation, while to be a felon in those days of harsh penal
codes was no proof of degeneracy. T. J. Wertenbaker has well
shown that the Virginia aristocracy sprang not from the scions of
nobility but from the English middle class and a sprinkling of these
same indentured servants.[21] There is no denial that the interaction
of the frontier and plantation left stranded on infertile area a
poverty-stricken white yeomanry. It must be further pointed out
that their lot has been complicated by malaria, hookworm, climate,
poor diet, and ignorance of hygiene. These people were used in
ante bellum polemics as the horrible example of what slavery did to
a free white populace, a point no doubt well taken but much overplayed.

When John Forsythe of Mobile, in an article for the ante bellum
DeBow's Review, compared the unadulterated Yankee with the
unadulterated Cracker he, no doubt, thought he was comparing two
fundamental biological types of the human race. To the modern
sociologist he was pointing out the cumulative conditioning effect of
two cultural environments on human habits. Back of the Cracker
looms the frontier with its limited means of securing its limited
satisfactions. Back of the Yankee looms the diverse satisfactions of
a New England commercial town with the trim, punctual, well-
ordered methods of securing those satisfactions. Forsythe wrote:

One is slow and the other quick; one takes a minute to rise from his seat,
the other never sits at all except in pursuance of a calculation; one is not
without faculties but they all seem asleep, the other with all his wits
alive with sagacity, curiosity, invention. The one content to laze away
life with as little labor as possible and all the enjoyment compassable; his
log hut, wool hat, homespun suit, and cornbread and bacon the limit of
his desires for domicile, vesture, and food; loving his gun and his horse,
addicted to tobacco and strong drink, quick to anger, a dangerous enemy

---

[21] *Patrician and Plebian in Virginia, passim.*

and a fast friend. The other instinct with life, activity, intelligence, never satisfied with the present well-being while anything better is beyond to tempt his longings and his wits.[22]

The record of the southern common man as foot soldier in the campaigns of the Civil War should have, moreover, laid to rest this bogey of biological depletion. Forced marches, short rations, meager equipment, rugged terrain, inclement weather, and overwhelming odds found units like Jackson's "foot cavalry" giving an account of itself that paid tribute to stamina, endurance, and raw biological vitality. This was not the flourish of a well-fed aristocracy; it was the work of common men, yeomanry, non-slaveholders, poor whites, if you will. Nevertheless, the tradition has descended to the present to bedevil with the stigma of inherent defect three groups: the white tenant farmer, the "mountain whites," and the workers in mill villages. Nor has the success attending anti-malarial and hookworm campaigns in selected areas served to complete the obsequies of the bogey of poor white. The popular view discounts the environmental effect of mountain isolation, cotton system routine, and mill village status, and continues to accredit their lack of representation in *Who's Who* to the old poor white theory. This theory, as a matter of fact, has had much less respectable scientific support than the dogma that 45 per cent of American soldiery ranked under a mental age of twelve years, and it should have died an earlier death.

In its later presentation the biological theory assumed the depletion of the best stock of the South by the Civil War. This theory was given academic setting by a distinguished biologist and pacifist, David Starr Jordan, in *War's Aftermath*.[23] The volume assumes that the leading young men of the South in 1861 belonged to military companies, early went to war, and nearly all were lost. The war took only the physically fit and the best blood. Volunteers were better stock than conscripts, and exempts and deserters were worst of all. The upper classes accordingly left the smallest proportion of survivors, and the women of the upper class, both widows and virgins, either married below themselves or did not marry in large enough number to leave a proper proportion of descendants. Investigations of family records in five counties in Virginia and

[22] "The North and the South," *DeBow's Review*, XVII, 363.
[23] D. S. and H. E. Jordan, *War's Aftermath, passim.*

one each in Georgia, North Carolina, and Tennessee tended to confirm these conclusions. It has been pointed out more than once that many of the greatest lines of Virginia are near extinction. Douglass Freeman writes:

Not one name in ten that appeared in the list of those who entertained Lafayette or were the familiars of John Marshall or even of those on whom Jefferson Davis called when visiting in Virginia cities after the war is heard now at social functions. General Robert E. Lee had three sons and four daughters. There survive now only three grandchildren and two great-grandchildren. If three or four great families had not been extremely prolific and had not intermarried widely there would be no F. F. V.'s and Virginia genealogies. . . . Some of the old mansions remain, often inhabited by people ignorant of the history of the houses in which they dwell.[24]

The view advanced by David Starr Jordan presumes a greater stratification of class lines in the South than social historians have been able to show ever existed. It leaves out of account that the common man was often more of the professional fire-eater than aristocratic leaders. It ignores the question as to whether common foot soldiers did not suffer losses proportionate to those suffered by the officers. It passes over the exemptions allowed the owners of forty or more slaves and the early practice of hiring substitutes. Proportionately North Carolina sent more men to the front than any other state, more men than she possessed as legal voters, and North Carolina was not a planter aristocracy. Nor is it apparent that her tremendous losses threw her behind sister states in post-war recovery. Losses were great in the ranks of both groups, and the post-war eclipse suffered by the scions of planter aristocracy is undeniable. It was, however, due to the chaotic condition of southern agriculture, as much a matter of economic as of biological depletion. While the shift of leadership from the Confederate brigadiers may have shown the incompetence of the common man in the field of politics, it soon revealed his marked ability in neglected zones of industry, commerce, and finance.

But we may cease the examination. Certain it is that some well-informed students of the South's history as well as many practical men of affairs in daily contact with labor, both white and black, accept a theory of distinct biological inferiority. This is to be found,

---

[24] "Virginia," *These United States*, E. Gruenning, ed., I, 4-5.

they hold, either in inherent lack of biological vitality, inherent lack of muscular adaptability, or inherent unmodifiability of neural pathways. But as a basis for practical policy this view is passing even among the common folk. In place of the old deportation and colonization schemes for saving the South has come an emphasis on training, education, equalized opportunities, and public welfare policies in dealing with racial and underprivileged groups. Nor has the education and acculturation of mill population, southern highlanders, and poor whites involved an adoption of any of the methods of dealing with the feeble-minded. It has involved a task, no doubt more difficult, that of accumulating a new culture heritage on a community basis. Outside of reporters on the metropolitan dailies, no one at the Dayton trial imputed the Tennessee mountaineer's devotion to the first chapter of Genesis to his lack of native intelligence. This situation simply displayed a lack of knowledge, lack of cultural contacts and educational opportunities typical of much southern backwardness.

Social Adequacy and Economic Organization

In this discussion we seem surprisingly enough to have reached the conclusion that, without drastic changes in its natural resources or in its human elements, the South might have attained a much higher state of material well-being. After geography and biology, what factors remain to account for a region's economic position? There remains a great deal, as comparative history of the economic development of North and South, such as found in the volumes by the Beards, will go far to show.[25] The type of organization whereby resources and labor are brought together in the process of production, the development of invention, mechanization, and technology whereby the processes of production are short cut, the accumulation of working capital from the process of production, and the organization of credit whereby new resources are developed; these are the factors which placed, for example, an industrial revolution in England before France, in the North before the South.

The South, a Colonial Economy

From this point of view it must be pointed out that the South remains largely a colonial economy. The South's explanation is to

[25] Charles A. and Mary R. Beard, *The Rise of American Civilization*. See also James Truslow Adams, *The Epic of America*.

be sought in the colonial system under which it was founded, the frontier zone into which it expanded, the plantation system to which it passed, and the cotton system with its tenancy which prevailed after abolition.

It is not enough to dismiss the South as an agricultural economy. It is a peculiar agricultural economy, and it arrived at its present destination through a peculiar series of transitions. Like the rest of America it began as a colonial economy. Now the function of a region in colonial economy is to extract staple raw materials from its wealth of soils, forests, and minerals, export them to a mother country for fabrication, and then buy them back. Thus the high level of a complex commercial and industrialized culture is stabilized for the mother country, while the colony can support its increasing population based on an extractive economy only by fresh and continuous excursions into the storehouses of nature. Such exploitation means migration as the early areas are drained of their fertility by continuous cropping to staples. This migration creates the frontier in which, because of lack of markets, the staples are temporarily lost in the reversion to a self-sufficing backwoods economy. But while the frontier frees its denizens for a time from their dependence on the mother country, it does so at the cost of reversion to a lower level economy. That is, the first step out of the frontier is again to secure marketable staples and means for their transportation. This the South secured after the surprising emergence of cotton as a factor in the world's markets. Thus while the East was advancing after the Revolution out of colonial economy, the South was again wavering between the frontier and the staple of a colonial economy. It made little difference whether the region remained dependent on Europe or the East, it was still either behind or just coming up to the colonial economy. So much of the southern apologetic has been written around them that it is only necessary to mention here the tariff and the area's losing balance of trade.

It is perfectly obvious to point out that at its height this colonial economy supported a small upper class of distinctive charm and culture. It was the first to create an aristocracy out of the frontier, but at its best the staple-slave economy no doubt afforded its aristocracy more of leisure than of economic competence. The fluctuating price of cotton, the necessity of capitalizing the labor supply, the forced migrations to new frontiers of unexhausted soils operated here. Hinton Rowan Helper in his *Impending Crisis* flung in the face of the ante bellum South the devastating fact that the North's hay crop, which he ironically called a crop of dried grass, over a long period of time exceeded in value the South's boasted cotton crop.

The South had by this time already rationalized its agrarian mode of life. A writer in *DeBow's Review* for 1857, speaking of Virginia, used phrases that the whole South applied to itself:

By not developing manufacturers we have lost nothing, the world has gained a great deal, and we have fulfilled a mighty destiny in the moral and political field, greater than the achievements of trade and arts in the physics of other states. We have no cities but we have an ameliorated country populace, civilized in solitude, gracious in the amenities of life and refined and conservative in social habits. We have little associated but more individual wealth than any equal number of white population in the South.[26] "Those that labor in the earth," Jefferson had written in his *Notes on Virginia,* "are the chosen people of God, if ever He has a chosen people, whose breasts He has made His peculiar deposit for substantial and genuine virtues."

The colonial economy leads to the over-exploitation of natural resources without the accumulation of capital goods to take their place. Thus the fertility of the soil is expended in a desperate effort to maintain the balance of trade with industrial areas whence goods must be secured. The frontier results from the hopeless attempt to compensate by throwing open new lands and reaches the point of clearing new fields to take the place of exhausted soils. Moreover, the frontier further retards the acceptance of technology and the accumulation of capital.

The plantation with its post-war descendant, cotton tenancy, committed the area to a speculative staple whose one great value was that it offered the cash crop with which to escape from the frontier economy. When the frontier went over to the plantation, it abandoned its self-sufficiency and placed all its eggs in one basket. Here, then, was and is an extractive economy which out of its rich resources was not self-supplying. It fed neither itself nor its animals. Strangely enough, then, as the South emerged from frontier to staple economy, it placed its agriculture on the same basis

[26] Henry A. Wise, "Wealth, Resources and Hopes of Virginia," *DeBow's Review,* XXIII, 61.

of colonial economy on which its industry had long since rested. From this point of view its choice of a staple was doubly unfortunate. Cotton, with its price gyrating in the world market, led to cycles of over-production followed by low prices and consequent poverty. Acreage reduction and weather reduction operated to raise prices and start the cycle all over again. Consequently, starting from scratch, this cash-crop farming has never paid its debts nor gained a competence sufficient to raise the whole section from the credit basis. Credit for food and feed is proof sufficient of the colonial economy in which southern agriculture has long found itself.

For a colonial economy is a debtor economy. It begins as an investment on the part of the mother country; it accumulates little capital of its own; it lacks the organization of credit, and as economic opportunities arise on the frontier, they must be financed from outside the area. The surplus returns are exported as profits and interest to outside business men in command of capital. Thus the South has often turned the development of her basic resources—forestry, coal, iron, petroleum, and minerals—over to outside interests at rock bottom prices—all for lack of credit with which to finance development. The South capitalized its labor force under slavery, thus constricting its credit resources. The rise of textiles was largely financed by northern machinery manufacturers and commission merchants. That and the rise of tobacco manufacturing and power utilization marked in some respects the beginnings of the turn from a debtor economy. This explains the Chamber of Commerce emphasis in the New South—a movement not to attract new population, but capital and new industries. The South has been in the position of exporting leaders to the nation, importing investments, and exporting to other areas the dividends from this colonial economy.

Moreover, extractive industry, the world over, is the base line from which other industries count their gains. The world over, the economy of the peasant, the fisher, the forester draws a certain minimum return. The South thus finds itself in the world economy into whose bottom rungs may be fitted the Chinese and the Hindus. Here are vegetable rather than mineral civilizations. They make use of the energy resources of men and animals rather than the resources of industrial civilizations wherein each factory worker, as in the United States in 1927, has at his finger tips 4.65 average horsepower. Energy is not multiplied nor is time telescoped in a vegetable civilization. Nature's peasant, utilizing nature's force, waits nature's turn of the season to add its increment to the product of her fields. To the extent that mechanization has invaded agriculture, as in wheat farming, the tiller of soil has short cut the process and elevated himself above nature's peasantry with the cumulative returns from the machine. Thus rice growers, lowliest of the low in the Orient, conduct a capitalistic enterprise on the Louisiana coastal prairies.

Mechanized or unmechanized, the staple farmer, unlike his frontier brother, enters his product in the current of world prices. Here an extractive economy, because of its comparative inability to limit output, finds itself at a disadvantage with industrial society. Having attained nature's gifts at whatever cost, a staple economy finds itself unable to stem the flow of nature's prodigality. Overproduction in industry results in curtailment. The wheels are slowed down, output reduced, men are let off, and finally capital marked off or transferred. Thus a portion of the factories close their doors and a portion of the wage earners join the army of the unemployed, but the stream of shoes or autos to market is cut down somewhat nearer to demand. Agriculture chooses another way. It continues to over-produce, it accepts chronic agricultural surpluses with low prices for staples, and the whole economy endures a period of poverty.

In a rough way it is possible to measure the economic discrepancy between an industrial and extractive culture. In the thirteen southern states the capital invested in manufacturing in 1919 was 40 per cent of that returned for agriculture in 1924. The value of manufactured products for 1919, however, was over 181 per cent of the value of agricultural produce averaged for the years 1924-1928. Speaking in averages, a dollar invested in industry accounted for products selling at $1.38; invested in agriculture it returned goods valued at thirty cents. The ratio is 4.6 to 1 for industry. Again in the South the average value of products per wage earner in manufacturing in 1925 was $6,023; the average value of produce per agricultural producer in 1925 was $1,518. Here the ratio is 4 to 1 for industry.

By their habituation to unstabilized agricultural production, the business groups of the nation, before the depression of 1930, had become almost reconciled to a poverty status for the farmer in the midst of industrial prosperity. With a virtual monopoly on an essential staple the South has existed longer in a state of chronic overproduction and poverty than other agricultural areas of the nation.

A colonial economy retards both the accumulation of capital and the utilization of technology. In the presence of other natural resources than soil, the same principles apply. It is shown in the field of minerals by the early experience of Birmingham. Birmingham skimmed the cream of its ore deposits and exploited its labor to export cheap pig iron to other metallurgy centers—pig iron cheaper than they could produce it. This resource, by means of their improved technology, they fabricated into steel which sold so low on the market that it underbid all Birmingham's attempts at steel making. With her lack of capital and improved technology Birmingham's wealth of resources and labor served only to keep her out of the skilled steel industry. Not until the United States Steel Corporation brought capital, technology, and economic organization did the area reach the rank to which its resources had always entitled it. And then, no doubt, the area stopped selling the cream of its ore to competitors. Thus the colonial economy may dominate also in the utilization of minerals.

It is not at all difficult to make the point that the coming of industry to the South marks the transition from a colonial to a modern industrial economy. The colonial economy, with the high birth rates characteristic of the frontier and the low standards of living characteristic of a staple economy in a chronic state of over-production, offers a new resource to industry. That resource is to be found in the low-priced labor supply. Lest migration to crowded eastern centers raise living standards as well as living costs, this labor supply must be utilized, as the engineers say, at the point of origin. In spite of the fact that six southeastern states led the Union in increases in industrialization from 1919 to 1927, the proportion of their population employed in agriculture is double that of the nation, 56.6 per cent to 26.2 per cent. The proportion of southern population engaged in various occupations in 1920 compared with that of the nation in the following ratios: minerals, 1.3 to 2.6 per cent; manufacturing, 18.7 to 30.8 per cent; transportation, 4.9 to 7.4 per cent; trade, 6.1 to 10.3 per cent; public service, 3.2 to 5.1 per cent;

clerical, 2.9 to 7.5 per cent; and domestic, 8.5 to 8.2. The only ratio that seems out of harmony with the colonial economy, the higher percentage of domestic servants, is due to the presence of low wage Negro domestics.

Thus the South with 27.5 per cent of the nation's population possessed in 1927 about one fifth of its factories, produced about one sixth of the value of its total products, and received about one eighth of the total national wage. The Carolinas, it has been estimated, possess less than 4 wage earners per square mile to 50 for the Pennsylvania-New York area. In value of products turned out, the eastern centers are ten times as productive per square mile. For the South, 41.4 per cent of the value of these products was added by the process of manufacturing; for the rest of the nation, 44.3 per cent. In the South, the value added by manufacturing averaged $2,350 per wage earner, for the rest of the nation $3,474, giving the South a ratio of 67.6 per cent. The value added by manufacturing represents, among many factors, the skill of labor, the proportion of invested capital, the amount of technique employed, and thus the degree of finish and fabrication imparted to goods. When the low price of certain southern raw materials, as cotton and tobacco, are taken into account, the region's low values added by manufacturing again indicate that her industrialization is largely in the unskilled and less technical branches.

Clarence Heer, after surveying all the statistical evidence available on ten states of the Southeast, holds that southern incomes and wages range about two thirds of the norms for the rest of the nation.[27] Competition between the South's resource regions tends toward but never reaches a sectional plane. In the same way, competition between sections falls short of attaining a national plane of living. In a nation so characterized by mobility as ours, many workers, mainly Negroes, may move northward; some factories, mainly textile, may move South, but sectional differences in income persist. What is fundamentally competition between an extractive and an industrial economy is further complicated by the differences between occupations and economic classes within the section and the nation.

The twelve southerners who have recently issued a clarion call for the South to return to the agrarian way of life are, of course,

[27] Clarence Heer, *Incomes and Wages in the South*, p. 53.

aware that the South has never deserted agriculture.[28] In an area
but 32 per cent urban in 1930, agriculture represents the main source
of livelihood for nearly half the population. And it is agriculture
that sets the background for all other industries in the South. It
is in farming that the region's income differences with the rest
of the nation reach their greatest. Agriculture, Dr. Heer shows,
pays its southern farmer just about one half of what it pays its
followers elsewhere in this country. Here is where the cotton system, the tenancy system, and the credit system play their parts.
Moreover, many farms outside the Cotton Belt capable of sustaining
the backwoods mode of life of an earlier day can never be made to
yield the income sufficient for a modern standard of living.

The advance of industry into this region then partakes of the
nature, let us say it in all kindliness, of exploiting the natural resources and labor supply of a colonial economy. The occupations
in the South whose returns approach nearest to national standards
are those which have erected highest the barriers of skill against
raw recruits from the farm. The industries which have led the
exodus of factories to the South are mainly those in which the simple
skills required have permitted the tapping of the region's overflowing reservoir of labor reserves. Heer found very near the
country's average wage rate is paid in railroad shops, and the higher
mechanical and building trades. The cotton mill, while barred to
the Negro, lies especially open to invasion from the farms. Moreover, wages in textiles grow progressively lower the farther one
penetrates into the deep South from Virginia to Alabama. Thus
the threatening hordes on the farm assert themselves. In cold
figures Dr. Heer shows that returns from the 1927 Census of Manufactures assigned average annual earnings of $825 to southern non-
textile workers, $748 to laborers in lumber, $671 to cotton mill
operatives, while other figures assign $519 to southern farmers.[29]

Nor does the extractive colonial economy display bright opportunities for higher incomes in upper economic classes. The proportion of persons in the South with incomes large enough to require the filing of a Federal Income Tax return in 1926 was one
third as great as in the rest of the nation—1.43 to 4.01 per cent of
the population. Since great fortunes are averaged in the figures of

[28] *I'll Take My Stand.*
[29] *Incomes and Wages in the South,* pp. 42-56, 64-65.

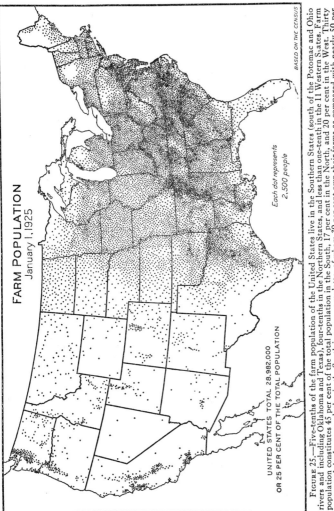

FARM POPULATION
January 1, 1925

UNITED STATES TOTAL 28,982,000
OR 25 PER CENT OF THE TOTAL POPULATION

Each dot represents
2,500 people

BASED ON THE CENSUS

FIGURE 25.—Five-tenths of the farm population of the United States live in the Southern States (south of the Potomac and Ohio rivers and including Oklahoma and Texas), four-tenths in the Northern States, and less than one-tenth in the 11 Western States. Farm population constitutes 45 per cent of the total population in the South, 17 per cent in the North, and 20 per cent in the West. Thirty per cent of the farm population in the South is negro or mulatto, of whom 30 per cent own their farms as compared with nearly 50 per cent for white farmers. In the North 70 per cent and in the West 75 per cent of the farm population consists of farm owner-operators and their families, nearly all white. (Courtesy of U. S. Department of Agriculture).

income per capita, they furnish rather striking comparison. From 1919 to 1921 income per capita for ten southern states ranged from 42 to 55 per cent of the figure for the rest of the country. In 1928 the average income per capita for the thirteen southern states was $1,736 to the nation's $3,473, a ratio of 49.9 per cent. The South's upper economic classes, supported as they are by an extractive economy, are not as large nor do they receive returns proportionate to the rest of the nation. Nor is the agrarian South yet prepared to support learned and professional classes at national standards. Comparative incomes in professional and clerical pursuits, Heer shows, give city school teachers in the South 67.6 per cent of the average incomes of those in the rest of the country, clergymen 73 per cent, college professors 87.7 per cent, and male clerks in manufacturing establishments 91 per cent. The consequent exportation of professional and business talent to other sections will go much further toward accounting for any comparative lack of leadership in the South than all the biological theories ever devised. It is estimated, for example, that between 1865 and 1900 some five million population left the South for the East, the North, the West and the Pacific. A million and a half settled in Texas and the Southwest.

Colonial Economy and Cultural Status

It may be well to close this chapter with a brief analysis of how the structure of regional economy affects the cultural status of the South. The frontier and the agricultural economy, for example, it can easily be shown, operate to give the South its low rating in education. The South is known to possess the highest birth rate in the nation, a fact which is often accounted for by citing its large Negro population. A comparison of racial birth rates, from 1920 to 1929 in the nation in Table XLVI as would seem to indicate that the South's birth rate is a matter of race and biology. A further analysis of the figures show, however, that, while southern Negroes possess a higher birth rate than northern Negroes, southern whites are highest of all. Exception must be made for Louisiana, Virginia, and North Carolina, while recently declining white birth rates show Negroes gaining in Florida, Georgia, and South Carolina. Every southern state except Oklahoma exceeds the national birth rate, and North Carolina leads the nation.

TABLE XLVI

South's Comparative Birth Rates per 1,000 by States and Races, 1920-1929

STATE	1920	1925	1927	1928	1929
Alabama.................	....	....	26.3	24.5	24.0
White.................	....	....	26.9	24.8	24.2
Colored...............	....	....	25.2	23.9	23.5
Arkansas................	....	....	22.1	20.8	20.2
White.................	....	....	23.3	21.9	21.0
Colored...............	....	....	18.6	17.8	17.8
Florida..................	....	23.8	25.6	21.5	18.8
White.................	....	23.7	25.7	21.3	18.2
Colored...............	....	24.0	25.4	22.0	20.1
Georgia.................	....	....	....	20.3	20.1
White.................	....	....	....	20.5	19.6
Colored...............	....	....	....	20.0	21.1
Kentucky...............	25.9	25.7	24.3	23.0	21.7
White.................	26.8	25.8	25.0	23.7	22.3
Colored...............	17.6	19.2	17.7	16.1	15.6
Louisiana...............	....	....	22.9	20.5	20.3
White.................	....	....	22.8	20.1	19.7
Colored...............	(1921)	....	23.0	21.1	21.2
Mississippi..............	25.8	23.7	25.3	24.4	22.9
White.................	27.6	23.7	25.3	24.3	22.3
Colored...............	24.1	23.6	25.2	24.6	23.4
North Carolina...........	31.4	29.0	27.7	26.4	24.7
White.................	31.6	28.5	27.3	25.8	24.2
Colored...............	31.1	30.2	28.8	27.7	25.9
Oklahoma...............	....	(1924)	....	18.4	16.8
South Carolina...........	28.3	27.8	....	25.0	22.7
White.................	28.9	27.6	....	23.4	20.9
Colored...............	27.8	27.9	....	26.9	24.9
Tennessee................	....	....	21.5	19.6	19.5
White.................	....	....	22.1	20.2	20.0
Colored...............	....	....	18.8	16.8	17.1
Virginia.................	28.4	25.8	24.3	23 5	22.4
White.................	27.8	24.9	23.6	22.9	21.7
Colored...............	29.8	28.0	26.1	25.2	24.2
United States Registration Area..........	23.7	21.5	20.6	19.8	18.9
White.................	23.4	21.2	20.4	19.5	18.6
Colored...............	26.9	25.4	23.6	22.2	21.3
Urban...................	23.9	21.9	21.0	20.1	19.4
Rural...................	23.5	21.0	20.3	19.5	18.4

In the excess of births over deaths every southern state except Florida ranks above the nation's rate of increase. A glance at Table XLVII indicates a white rate of increase often two or three times as great as that of the Negroes. In Tennessee and Kentucky, Negroes show an excess of deaths over births. Both races from 1925 through 1929 show a sharp decline of population increase in every southern

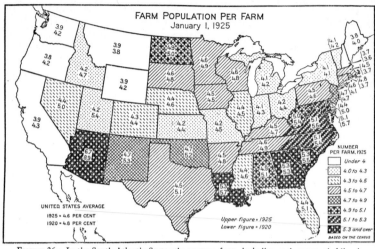

FIGURE 26.—In the South Atlantic States the average farm, including each cropper holding in a plantation as a separate farm, had over five people on January 1, 1925. This is true also in Louisiana, where there are many large sugar plantations worked by wage hands, and in Arizona, where there are a few large cattle ranches and cotton farms. On the other hand, in the Northeastern States there were only 3.7 to 4.7 persons per farm, including hired laborers, and in several far Western States only 3.9 persons. In almost every State the average number of persons per farm decreased between 1920 and 1925. The average decrease for the United States was from 4.8 to 4.6. (Courtesy of U. S. Department of Agriculture).

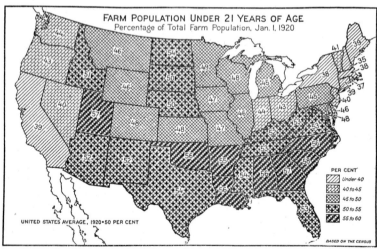

FIGURE 27.—The proportion of the farm population under 21 years of age, and more or less dependent on their elders for support, varies widely in the United States. In New England, excluding Vermont, less than 40 per cent of the farm population was under 21 years of age in 1925, whereas in Utah, Georgia, and South Carolina it was 57 or 58 per cent. Roughly three farm people had to support two minors in California and New England, whereas only a little over two farm people had to support nearly three minors in Utah and the Southeastern States. The burden of dependence, therefore, was twice as great in the latter States. From Illinois to Colorado and north about half the farm population are supporting the other half. (Courtesy of U. S. Department of Agriculture).

TABLE XLVII

EXCESS OF BIRTHS OVER DEATHS IN REGISTRATION AREA PER 1,000
POPULATION IN THE SOUTHERN STATES, 1925-1929

STATE	1925	1926	1927	1928	1929
Alabama..................	....	....	15.8	12.2	11.6
White.................	....	....	18.2	14.8	14.0
Colored...............	....	....	11.5	7.7	7.3
Arkansas.................	....	....	12.1	9.9	9.7
White.................	....	....	14.5	12.2	11.6
Colored...............	....	....	5.2	3.5	4.0
Florida..................	10.2	11.5	12.0	7.8	6.1
White.................	11.8	14.3	14.0	9.5	7.4
Colored...............	6.6	5.1	7.5	3.8	3.0
Georgia..................	....	....	....	7.9	7.9
White.................	....	....	....	10.2	9.6
Colored...............	....	....	....	4.1	5.3
Kentucky.................	13 9	12.0	13.7	11.2	9.7
White.................	15.4	13.5	15.2	12.8	11.2
Colored...............	-1.0	-2.9	-1.6	-4.7	-5.7
Louisiana................	....	....	11.1	8.3	8.4
White.................	....	....	13.4	10.1	10.0
Colored...............	....	....	7.2	5.2	5.5
Mississippi..............	12.1	14.0	13.4	11.3	9.9
White.................	14.9	16.6	16.1	13.8	12.0
Colored...............	9.3	11.6	10.7	9.0	7.9
North Carolina...........	17.7	16.2	16.8	14.6	12.9
White.................	18.8	17.2	17.9	15.4	14.0
Colored...............	15.3	13.2	14.2	12.6	10.4
Oklahoma.................	....	....	....	9.4	7.8
South Carolina...........	....	....	....	10.9	9.4
White.................	....	....	....	12.1	10.8
Colored...............	....	....	....	9.5	7.9
Tennessee................	....	....	10.1	7.4	7.3
White.................	....	....	12.2	9.5	9.3
Colored...............	....	....	.8	-2.3	-1.6
Virginia.................	13.4	11.4	12.3	10.9	9.4
White.................	14.6	12.5	13.5	12.3	10.7
Colored...............	10.4	8.3	9.1	7.3	6.0
United States............	9.7	8.5	9.2	7.8	7.0
White.................	9.8	8.6	9.5	8.0	7.3
Colored...............	7.8	6.8	7.1	5.1	4.4
Urban areas..............	9.2	8.1	8.6	6.8	6.4
Rural areas..............	10.1	8.9	9.9	8.5	7.5

state—a decline that will serve, if long continued, to bring these areas more in accord with national rates of population increase.

The birth rate of the area has been a response not to race and biology but to environment. Food supply, the frontier heritage, absence of industrial pressure, and lack of urban culture patterns, go to make up an environment favorable to large population increases.

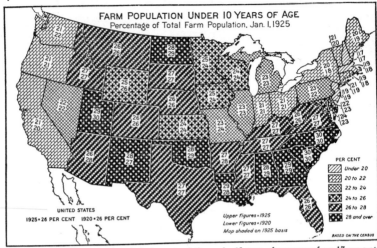

FIGURE 28.—The proportion of the farm population under 10 years of age ranges from 17 per cent in New Hampshire to 30 per cent in the Carolinas. It appears that the farm people of the South and of the Great Plains and Rocky Mountain regions are contributing 25 to 50 per cent more children proportionately to the Nation's need than are the farm people on the Pacific coast, the eastern Corn Belt, and the Northeastern States. In the case of the Great Plains and Rocky Mountain regions this greater contribution may be owing in part to a larger proportion of young married people in the population. The stationary ratio of children to adults since 1920 is largely attributable to the migration of many adults to the cities. (Courtesy of U. S. Department of Agriculture).

The population in the region is thus a young population with consequently greater tasks of education than other areas. While the South possesses 1,034 children under 15 years of age for every 1,000 adults, the North has only 782, and the Pacific Coast 599. Granted equal resources, the educational task per adult would remain much greater in the South. It is the farming environment which conditions a high birth rate, and a large majority of these children are on the farm. Moreover, the low density of an agricultural society operates to make the educational task more formidable. Eleven southern states, possessing one fourth of the nation's population, have and must educate one half of the nation's farm children. Fanny Wyche Dunn has made an interesting comparison between rural states in the North and South. Minnesota has 440,000 greater population than Alabama (1920) but Alabama has 312,000 more farm children. Wisconsin has 73,000 greater population than North Carolina but North Carolina has 405,000 more farm children. Indiana has 35,000 greater total population than Georgia, but Georgia has 565,000 more farm children. She adds: "It is very doubtful if the city schools of the South are significantly inferior to city schools the nation over, as it is doubtful if the rural schools of the South are strikingly inferior to rural schools in general."[30]   An exception may well be made for the Negro, but the statement is fundamentally valid.

For the same number of adults the cultural task of education is much greater in the South. Moreover, the low density of population attendant upon an agricultural society increases still further the regional differences. A school population sparsely settled in the open countryside may receive inferior training in the one-room, one-teacher school, or it may be transported at public expense to a consolidated school. In either case it stands to pay more for the same facilities than an urban community. Usually it pays less for inferior facilities. But we are not yet done. The bi-racial segregation of the South cuts across the institutional plane dividing the cultural institutions into two sets. Dual education then functions to lower the effective density of the population. Thus it happens that Mississippi ranks as the first state in the percentage of her population, 33.8, enrolled in schools, and the last in days of attendance at school, 98.1. Under this regional process aided by the restriction of foreign immigration, the South is in the position of rearing and educating, however imperfectly, the labor reserves for the rest of the nation. To low standards already existing will increasingly be added the enforced mobility characteristic of populations which have outstripped their resource structure. The alternative lies in the adjustment of a decreasing rate of population growth to an increasing utilization of regional resources.

[30] Wilson Gee (ed.), *The Country Life of the Nation*, p. 155.

CHAPTER XVIII

RECONSTRUCTING THE REGION

REGIONALISM AND REGIONAL PLANNING

REGIONAL RECONSTRUCTION falls in line with the best traditions of human geography. We have seen the old doctrinaire approach of geographic determinism yield to the point of view of man's mastery of his environment. The map may cradle man and mold him, but man is also shown remaking the map. The region which begins as a great complex of physical forces ends by being so re-shaped by the human groups which occupy it that it emerges as a cultural product. A brilliant American thinker of the 1880's, George Perkins Marsh, was among the first to point this out in a volume entitled *The Earth as Modified by Human Action*.

Man's modification of the earth, as when a mine is rifled or a forest is felled, may be called destructive exploitation. On the other hand, when an annual crop is harvested or the annual flow of water utilized, as in hydro-electric development, it may be called con-structive exploitation. The distinction is based on the difference between mining an unreplaceable store and reaping an annual "flow" of resources. One of the highest forms of regional planning consists of the transference of resources from the mining to the cropping economy accompanied by the orderly conservation of stored resources where this is not possible. Many resources as soils and forests fall so nearly between the two classifications that the mode of culture and the state of technology often determine the difference between a destructive and a constructive exploitation. An orderly resource flow may be achieved for an area, and yet the region may remain in the colonial-debtor economy. Accordingly, a second form of regional planning consists in the transition from absentee exploitation to self-contained development. Without this transition, resources may serve neither to accumulate capital nor to raise standards of living for a region. Thus the contention of human geography is not that man and natural environment have come to be in perfect accord by virtue of the determining force exercised by geography; it is rather that man's civilization must become better adapted to its terrain by means of conquest and mastery in the fields of techniques and economics.

Here then is the task for regional planning. Science is the pioneer, says Isaiah Bowman, in making things happen rather than waiting for them to happen. Regional planning may then be defined for our purpose as an attempt at coördination of all regional changes and readjustments toward a desirable goal. This goal is determined after a consideration of both natural and cultural forces. Patrick Geddes and Victor Branford have advocated in their studies a frank acceptance of the Utopian approach to regional planning. Thus a survey of the region-as-is is followed by a blue print of the region as it can be reconstructed. This plan is drawn with reference mainly to the possibilities of the area's natural features at the hands of the engineering arts. The practical task of the regionalist is to fill in step by step the gap between the survey and the plan. In its scientific aspects regional planning leans heavily on the engineering arts and techniques; in its policy making aspects it is part and parcel of the political process.

The call for science to furnish social guidance accordingly is only a half-truth. Of the two functions in social planning it is the policy making function which determines the rôle of science. Policy making is the task of statesmanship; it involves ofttimes the clash of interests; it finds roots deep in the historic, social, and political philosophies; and its goals must be defined through the traditional political processes. Science as technics or engineering is the handmaiden of policy. As the encompassing art it has the function of bringing to pass. The regional survey is a matter of science, cartographic, geographic, descriptive, statistical. The regional plan is a matter of applied science, technology, and engineering. Both carry out policies rather than determine them. Unfortunately political leadership notoriously lags far behind technical and scientific leadership. While engineering science is an achievement, political science remains a figure of speech.

It is apparent that the regional plan is the third step in a logical chain. Benton MacKaye calls it the conclusion in the regional syllogism.[1] The theory of regionalism is the major premise, the regional survey the minor premise, and the plan for the region comes at the end of the search. Strangely enough in this logical chain the greatest intellectual confusion will be found to center around the major premise of regionalism. Of regional and social plans, good, bad, and indifferent, there is no great lack. Many are proposed by engineers and technicians of undisputed competence. Of regional surveys there exist a gracious plenty. If the present volume be accepted as one example, it may be noted that for their purposes chambers of commerce turn out a certain type by the hundreds. But the formulation of regionalism as a social policy has not yet come into existence. The setting up of aims, ends, and goals, the definition of the situation in terms of relation of area to area, of industry to industry, of regional process to regional process; none of these has been attained. We do not practice regional housekeeping, we have no theory of regionalism; instead we trust to the invisible hand, beloved of Adam Smith, to guide our isolated activities.

Regionalism and the South

It has been the fate of frontier areas in colonial economy to undergo quick exploitation in a kind of resource skimming, much to their temporary prosperity and more to their long time retardation. Moreover, such areas too often arrive at a reasoned philosophy of regionalism only after exploitation has run its course. Thus areas work out adequate industrial codes after they have needlessly repeated the social horrors of an industrial revolution. Thus also a region launches conservation movements after much of its resources have been subject to destructive exploitation. The South stands at the entrance of a transitional period, in a position where wise planning may assure its orderly economic and cultural development. The transition finds the South an area of divided councils. Once set as a unit for the prosecution of a fratricidal war, the region cannot coördinate its leadership for guiding the social change from a colonial to an industrial economy.

To state that three philosophies of regionalism are at present contending for mastery in the South would, no doubt, ring of the

---

[1] In address before Round Table on Regionalism, University of Virginia, July 9, 1931, and elsewhere. See also his *The New Exploration: A Philosophy of Regional Planning*.

dramatic. It would not, however, ring as true as the statement that three attitudes toward regionalism are implicit in the position of three southern groups. That these groups are unevenly divided goes without saying; that certain factions are unaware that such a thing as regionalism exists is also obvious. Briefly these three groups may be characterized as the promoters of industrialism, the proponents of agrarianism, and a certain small sprinkling of liberals, technicians, and university scholars. We may well consider the position these three groups take with relation to regionalism and regional planning in the South.

THE CHAMBER OF COMMERCE MOVEMENT

Except that they have been kept longer from the flesh pots, the South's promotion agencies resemble those to be found anywhere in the nation. While state boards under varying titles of conservation, agriculture, development, and immigration play a part in the South as elsewhere, the chambers of commerce have taken the lead. It took the World War with its allocation of cantonments and essential industries, its methods of organizing immense financial drives, to make local section and cities progress-conscious. What the war began, the example of Florida clinched for the South. Those placed in charge of newly organized publicity and promotion agencies were often likable young men, more noted for their cheering speeches at dinner clubs than for any special qualifications for resource analysis, regional surveying, or city planning. Theirs was the task of policy making and their methods, worked out as they went along, were often more notable for general plausibility than for illuminating interpretations of the total layout of either a region or a particular industry.

Their drives, for such they may be called, are staged in a search for capital; they emphasize the attractions of the area for industry and tourists. Long ago her cities threw off the policy of seclusiveness attributed to the South and joined in the attempt to accelerate the progress of industrialization by advertising. Atlanta launched a publicity campaign pledged to spend a million dollars in three years, thus taking a place along the two leading booster cities of the Pacific Coast.[2] In two years New Orleans spent $130,000 in

[2] See Don E. Mowry, "Southeastern Communities Value Advertising," *Harpers,* May, 1930, Advertising Section.

advertising; Asheville in three years expended $144,000; Pinehurst possessed a national publicity layout that cost $200,000 in three years. In three campaigns Virginia purchased public notice to the value of $175,000; the Norfolk-Portsmouth area having spent $200,000 in the three years from 1927 to 1930 continued her program through 1931; Roanoke is credited with $28,000 in two years. Nor have the cities of the Southwest lagged behind.

Each area and each city thus advertises its wares of natural advantages, accessible resources, plentiful and therefore cheap labor, seeking to entice new industries and new capital from already developed areas. New establishments are measured in terms of capital invested, building expenditures, and total payrolls. They are offered the inducements of plant sites, local subscriptions for stock, tax exemptions, and at times a forthright bonus. The financial support for these chamber of commerce campaigns has come from the prominent local citizens who expect to profit from the rise in real estate values and business holdings attendant upon urbanization. This hope has been so often realized for fortunate individuals in growing cities inside and outside Dixie that the process needs no description.

In its transformation of the regional South it is possible to point out certain unfavorable aspects in this apparently inevitable movement. It has led in instances to overdevelopment and industrial demoralization. The invitation to more mills to join the textile procession has handicapped southern mills already on the ground by augmenting overproduction, by putting more capital into local units of an already overcapitalized industry, by exempting competitors from tax payments in what virtually amounted to government subsidy for a limited period. Because they have been motivated by local pride, because they have not been based on scientific surveys of regions as a whole, promotion activities have set community against community and section against section. What the Southeast has done to the textile centers of New England, the Texas chambers of commerce hope to do to the mill villages of the Piedmont. And what the South has done in the field of textiles, it hopes to accomplish in other industrial fields. Nor have the promotion activities based on the importation of outside capital always returned a profit to the progress-conscious natives who financed it. The failure of original owners to realize on the development of coal lands and virgin forests is well known. National chain stores, for example, have come in and taken part of the business local merchants thought they were creating for themselves. One result has been a resurgence of sectional feeling in blatant and futile anti-chain store campaigns conducted from a southern radio station. Clarence E. Cason has pointed out the comparative failure of United States Steel activity in Birmingham to bring expected prosperity to native boosters.[3] Outside interests have bought estates and directed development in their direction much to the benefit of land values. Such proceedings freeze out local interests and do much to dim the bright harmony of chamber of commerce co-operation. Certain it is in the developing of Elizabethton, Tennessee, that land values and rents were pushed to levels higher than mill workers could reach, thus fomenting labor disputes. In this connection the paternalism of mill villages has rarely been given the credit it deserves for keeping industrial housing out of the hands of real estate promotion. Wherever compared in the South, real estate development is found to furnish its industrial tenants much worse housing for much higher rents than the mill villages.

In many ways the naïve competitive theory of regionalism implicitly held by southern chambers of commerce has not been particularly happy. It has been accused of fostering an attitude of hurried skimming of natural resources and a selfish pride in docile 100 per cent Anglo-Saxon labor. It has set section against section, state against state, city against city. It lies back of many things from injunctions against population under-counts by the United States Census to tax wars between states determined to see how far they can go in attracting capital by relieving large incomes of the responsibility of supporting government. It has promoted a neo-mercantilism of the most local dimensions.

The greatest defect in the chamber of commerce style of development is its lack of unity. The South stands in especial need of the integrating influence of regionalism because it has lacked an empire builder. No Cecil Rhodes nor James J. Hill has left the permanent imprint of a regional policy on the South. Nearest to a figure of this stature has been James Buchanan Duke. Certain states, especially North Carolina, Alabama, and even Arkansas, have

[3] Clarence E. Cason, "Alabama Goes Industrial," *Virginia Quarterly Review,* VI, 161-70.

possessed notable developers of power resources. Railroads, as in Florida, have had their region builders on a small scale. Certain industries, notably tobacco manufacturing, have bid fair to show the nation an example in economic integration. Most of the South's fortunes have been accumulated in oil, textiles, power, and tobacco manufactures; but it is reasonable to believe that much of the section's financial talent potential to regional development has been frittered away in speculation in the cotton market. The business of oil production has partaken too much of the speculative to attain even the degree of integration that John D. Rockefeller introduced in the refining and distributing end. Certain it is that the textile industry has lacked a commanding genius to bring organization and integration out of competitive chaos. It has been too much an industry of small competitive units to attain a national plan; it has also, let it be whispered, been too much a business of the home folks to receive the social legislation one metes out to the interests. The point is that combination and integration often bring an industry nearer not only to stabilization but to social control. Be that as it may, the South's lack of the empire builder accents its need of regional planning.

It must be admitted, even by those to whom the chamber of commerce program has proved most distasteful, that certain values are implicit in its regional policies. It appeals frankly to the profit motive, and no regional economy can stand unless its pays its way. A planned economy is not an endowed economy. No section and no body of workers have any lease on economic life, nor can industries accumulate the right to a pension from the public. Thus this theory of regionalism recognizes the comparative advantage of one area over another for the localization of specific industries. Regionalism recognizes this and attempts to substitute scientific surveys for plausible guesses favorable to the home town. Unless a planned economy, partly by making use of comparative advantage, pays its way better than an unplanned economy, it has no economic reason for being. Thus for industries to go South and remain there can mean nothing except that certain economies of production are possible in that area. The chamber of commerce did not create these differences. The industrialization of the South would have occurred in time, no doubt, without their existence, but the fact remains that they were the region's representative planning agencies in the whole movement. And that movement toward industrialization has measured practically all the South's economic advance in a quarter century.

THE PROPONENTS OF AGRARIANISM

In the struggle centering around regional transition one is tempted to say that the industrialists like Eclipse are first and the rest are nowhere. In southern politics, true enough, the once dominant planters and country lawyers are being replaced by the business man and the corporation lawyer. Nevertheless, by virtue of mass and sheer inertia, the agrarians remain the strongest group in the South. Disorganized, demoralized in a losing business, the individualistic farmers of the Cotton Belt offer no leads to regional promoters, while through virtual helplessness they afford the greatest obstacle to orderly regional change. Irresponsive to efforts in his behalf, the southern farmer's marketing practices baffle the co-operatives, his food habits baffle home demonstration agents, his crop practices baffle farm extension workers. His one-time representatives, the planters, the agrarian bourbons, the country lawyers, have practically retired from the scene. The Tillman movement, the Grange, the Populist Party, Tom Watson, and the Farmers' Union all made their promises to the southern agrarian and passed off the stage in futility. The agrarian tradition of the South became inarticulate.

Just as the post-war bourbons, the Confederate Brigadiers, and the Moss-backs were being abandoned by southern liberals, the traditional agrarianism of the South became vocal. Driven to utterance by the encroachments of promotion and industrialization, the writers of *I'll Take My Stand* have given in the first coherent presentation of regionalism for the South a plea for return to agrarian aristocracy and isolation. The neo-Confederacy so far is a literary movement, but it attempts a cultural revival. Briefly it declares for a reversion to the civilization of the old South, mildly deplores the passing of slavery, and calls for a wall around the South that it may keep out industrial invaders. As an attitude of mind this was set at rest by Henry W. Grady and Walter Hines Page. As a practical program it has already fallen before the advancing enemy of industrialization; moreover, to return to an unreformed agrarianism is to return to an economic abyss. But, as an effective sentiment around which to rally a genuine regional movement, this nostalgia for the old South may prove of more avail than the formulae of technicians and the undifferentiated aspirations of southern liberals. It has all the latent potency of a slogan, a catchword, a flag. Moreover, there are certain values in the regional culture of the old South that may well be conserved. From any technical or economic angle the traditionalists have the least to present to regional planning; from the viewpoint of cultural ideals their gifts are greater.

In the meantime a thing most strange and most encouraging has happened in the South. The inarticulate, unresponsive agrarian folk, for whose cause literati appeared as spokesmen, have themselves displayed the first gropings toward policies of regional control and direction. Mistaken, stumbling, futile in its first reachings because of legal and constitutional restrictions, regionalism in the South has finally reared its head as a folk movement. Out of a great economic crisis, expressing themselves through the only means at hand, the political process, the common folk of the South have demanded that their state legislatures attempt to stabilize the cotton industry on a regional basis. There is not the space to recount the legislation passed by Louisiana, Texas, and South Carolina in the fall and winter of 1931-32. It is fitting that this movement should have been sponsored by a state governor who is both a folk product and a rabble rouser, a man who lives with his ear to the ground. This trial and error attempt, thwarted as it has been by our peculiar federal structure, our constitutional and legal commitments, even by the folk processes themselves, offers a challenge to technicians, academic leaders, and agricultural extension workers whose thinking it outruns. If any one rises to say that the common man of the agrarian South is not ready for regionalism and regional planning on the grand scale here is his answer. Moreover, it may well be pointed out that any legislative regulation of hours and conditions of industry must be regional in scope to be adequate. The challenge now passes to the liberal thinkers of the South. The technicians, the South's leaders, those who determine policies have here their call.

THE ECLECTIC TASKS OF REGIONALISM IN THE SOUTH

To the onlooker, southern policy, in so far as it exists, must appear caught between two groups of extremists. On the one side advocates of an extreme *laissez-faire* of the type that long since lost caste in England and New England call on the high gods to protect them in their inalienable rights to exploit cheap resources and cheap labor and to exploit them quick. Anything to attract new blocks of capital in the heedless rush pell-mell into an unplanned and chaotic industrialism is sacrosanct. On the other side one meets the advocacy of a return to the agrarian mode of life without an examination of the article, the presentation of an economic program without any attempted analysis of economic facts, an invitation to a whole section to live a life of high culture isolated in an economic vacuum. Neo-Mercantilism and the Neo-Confederacy are here met full tilt.

Yet neither of these extremes serves to plot the course taken by social planning. There exists a third group unassociated with either. For lack of a better one we shall make use of a much-abused term and call them the southern liberals. Few, scattered, non-aggressive, some have arisen in the universities, others have sprung from the more cultured of the industrialists, some from the inheritors of the old traditions. They range all the way from technicians and engineers to journalists, scholars, and artists. To cite but one example, their friendly yet critical spirit is well presented in a book like Howard W. Odum's *An American Epoch.* Much time have they wasted in fighting among themselves; some time, in repulsing attacks of those who regard them as dangerous to the South. The one thing on which they can unite is regional planning, for fundamental to all for which they strive is the social mastery of regional resources and processes. Their program will be eclectic. It will include both orderly industrial development and agricultural reform. It will seek to conserve certain regional values, yet will so far abandon sectionalism as to assume that any worthy national development may prove a worthy southern development. It will furnish the technical expert tasks worthy of his talents, and yet find a place for the artist and the theorist. It will see the task of regionalism as a whole, but will attack it piecemeal and by projects, that the whole may come to pass. It will visualize a regional planning broad enough to include groups now supposed to be working at cross purposes for the advancement of the South, yet not so broad as to be a colorless compromise.

Lest the reader rise at this point to challenge the concreteness of the discussion, it may be well to illustrate the concept of regional planning by an appeal to achievements, actual and under way. The concept will include, for example, the planning of individual corporations as the Bogalusa, Louisiana, Lumber Company's method of prolonging operation by regrowing its forest lands. It will include city planning done by the chamber of commerce in coöperation with industrial plants, so strikingly exemplified in the creation of Kingsport, Tennessee. Into the program of regional planning will fit any plan of a whole industry to set its house in order through research and economic stabilization, such as the Textile Institute may in a measure achieve for its industry. Here fits such a plan as C. T. Murchison's for the vertical integration of the textile industry.[4] In this frame of reference also falls any coöperative effort of an industry and the Federal Government to conserve natural resources and to stabilize production, a development hinted at by the creation of the Federal Petroleum Board.

In remaking the region there is a place for the great privately endowed foundations as leaders in engineering social change, as witness the experimental and demonstration work of the International Health Board in the mastery of disease. Here falls also the work of the Duke Endowment in extending the range of hospital services in the Carolinas.[5] Here fits also regional, state, and federal port development as at Hampton Roads, the Texas Gulf ports, and Alabama's development on the Warrior River from Birmingham to Mobile. Here also belongs, wherever efficiently administered, state activity in the construction of great highway systems. It also finds a place for Federal direction and unification of diverse regional interests as in the new Mississippi Flood Control. There exists also a place for state and federal coördination such as has been established by New Jersey, New York, and the United States in regulation of the Port of the City of New York. Moreover, local government has a part to play in the integration and increased efficiency that would follow from county consolidation. Thus the successful consolidation of Hamilton and James counties in 1919 gave impetus to a plan to merge Tennessee's 95 counties into 11 new units.[6]

[4] *King Cotton Is Sick.*

[5] W. S. Rankin, "A Million Dollars for Carolina Hospitals," *Review of Reviews,* 73, pp. 406-8.

[6] J. W. Manning, "County Consolidation in Tennessee," *National Municipal Review,* XVII, 511-13.

To the stabilization of industries and the remolding of the landscape, planning adds the increase of human adequacy by the changing of man's skills, habits, and organization. Here belong agricultural extension work which trains in farming as a technique and changes dietary habits of farm families. Planning thus includes the efforts of commodity coöperatives to regulate and stabilize the marketing of farm products. It will point to the South's recent strides in education, both public and university. Here will fall the efforts of mission churches and schools in the Highlands and the South's recent advances in the public welfare movement for its underprivileged. In is broadest scope regionalism can find a place for the factual studies in the realm of economic and social life, undertaken by disinterested and impartial university research groups, such as those already established at the Universities of North Carolina, Virginia, and Texas. Finally, many efforts will achieve synthesis in voluntary regional association, such as the recently organized Southeastern Economic Council.

Here then in bare mention have passed some of the trends and projects actively fostering regionalism in the South. Some of these plans and tendencies we have selected for more extended consideration.

The Reorganization of Southern Agriculture

The reorganization of agriculture—that primary gigantic task of the South—when it comes, may owe its appearance more to the pressure of economic crisis than to regional planning. Nevertheless, on the basis of facts already assembled by experts in the field we may attempt to chart the direction it will take. To break away from the traditional system, the region needs to incorporate live stock production in its staple cropping economy. This movement in its regional aspect waits upon the development and adoption of an adequate forage crop for the South, comparable to Timothy hay for northern areas. Food and live stock production may then be organized by means of vertical farming, supplemented by coöperative marketing for reaching urban markets. Finally must come the rationalization of the cotton system. Agricultural experimentation and extension may lead the way in these readjustments.

The Selma, Alabama, chamber of commerce has undertaken to develop and settle a tract of land. Colquitt County, Georgia, has worked out a widely advertised scheme of diversification which its farmers are following.[7]   The trend of development suggested by Hugh MacRae's farm colonies near Wilmington, North Carolina, Dr. E. C. Branson's work in rural-economics at the University of North Carolina, David R. Coker's seed farm near Hartsville, South Carolina, and the proposed farm colonies should be better known.   The land departments of certain southern railroads have coöperated.   The Central of Georgia in coöperation with the State College of Agriculture, for example, has guaranteed against loss a group of test farms which are to follow standardized plans of diversification.   It has also paid half the cost of establishing permanent test pastures.   One railroad has offered to carry lime free of charge to its farmer patrons.

It now seems probable that the South's primary need for an adaptable forage crop will be met by lespedeza.   The Kobe, the Korean, and Tennessee No. 76 seem at present writing the most promising.   Thirty thousand dollars appropriated by Congress to aid the search for a southern legume finally resulted in the development of these three varieties of Lespedeza *sricea*.   They have been successfully tested under experimental and field conditions.   J. Sidney Cates enthusiastically calls *sricea* "the long-dreamed-of perennial acid-soil legume, voracious in its feeding habits, camel-like in its drought resistance, omnivorous in its soil-type adaptation, and withal seeding so profusely over such a wide range of climate and soil that the cost for planting a farm need be only the charge for a cupful of seed for a start."[8]   Moreover, the plant returns fertility to the soil; in many tests it has tripled oat yields in three years.   It produces a forage which runs to over half leaves, palatable to all types of live stock.   In 1931 the South had some 250,000 acres planted to the three types, Kobe, Korean, and Tennessee No. 76.   Those who await the economic rehabilitation of the South may well keep an eye on this plant.

Let us turn next to the rationalization of the cotton system and attempt to take the long-time view of economic and technical change.   The cotton system should be considered first because it is

[7] J. P. Campbell, "A Coöperative Movement to Farm Financing Methods for the Development of a Safe Farming System," Georgia State College of Agriculture, *Extension Bulletin* 397, 1931.

[8] "The Plant That Stole the Show," *Country Gentleman,* February, 1932, p. 3.

basic to regional reconstruction for some six to eight million human beings. Moreover, the stabilization of cotton growing will meet not the hostility but the coöperation of most of the established interests in the South. It is basic to their prosperity. The greatest obstacle it will meet, and one that it may not overcome, is the apathy, the hopelessness, the ignorance, the inertia of its devotees, ossified in a routine beyond which they cannot see.

Without losing ourselves in the intricacies of technical economics, we may assume that the essential problem of the southern cotton grower is to so lower his costs of production that he may stabilize the volume of production at a fairly high level. Thus he can discourage foreign competition by a low price and yet receive adequate returns at that price level. This is no easy task and it may not be accomplished. There are those who say that, if the South possesses a natural monopoly, it is a monopoly not worth the retaining. The answer to this is that any purely live-at-home program finally reduces its farmers to a backwoods standard of living. What cash crop can the South find to substitute for its native cotton? To ask the question is to answer it. The cotton system may be rationalized, but no well-wisher of the South hopes to destroy it root and branch. The changes involved in the term rationalization of the cotton system may come in one of two ways; either as the result of individual and group planning or as an unplanned adjustment to a series of technical innovations started by scientific inventions. It has been suggested, for example, that the Department of Agriculture should unify its services to the cotton growers by the creation of a Cotton Industry Bureau.[9]

There is a method by which the yeoman farmer may live in the cotton system and yet isolate himself from many of its evils attendant upon price fluctuation, expensive credit, and soil exhaustion. It involves hard work, makes of farming a year-round business, but is not beyond the reach of the small farmer. Nor does it involve the abandonment of Dixie's supremacy to foreign competitors. Moreover, in its various phases it has been advocated by experiment stations and extension workers for many years. Briefly it runs as follows: (1) Plant the best land, a restricted fraction of the farm, to cotton and by intensive cultivation make it equal in productivity to the larger area. By this means the boll weevil is

[9] J. Sidney Cates, "Cotton at the Crossroads," *Country Gentleman*, 95, pp. 3-5.

beaten and the cost of production is lowered, for all figures tend to show that the higher the yield per acre the lower the cost of production per bale. (2) Diversify the area of the farm thus saved to produce not only feed for stock, food for family, occasional truck for cash but, if possible, one other staple for cash. This will serve as a reserve, or better as a balance wheel, to stabilize the family standards in the midst of gyrating cotton prices. Moreover, as part of the new crops are legumes and cover crops, the location of the cotton patch will be rotated from year to year, and the cost of fertilization obviated. Live stock is, of course, a part of the picture, and production for near-by urban markets. (3) Grow only long staple from prime seed. If necessary develop one variety cotton communities to preserve staple length, and deliver only to coöperatives which purchase and sell on the basis of carefully graded lots. Such a program insures lower costs of production, prevents acreage expansion, reduces the farmer's outside purchases and gives larger cash returns for the same quantity of cotton. Live stock, for example, divides with cotton the farm's overhead. Moreover, since it is not primarily aimed to reduce production, it does not stimulate foreign competition.

This program, like every other put forward for individual agricultural producers, lacks any element of compulsion by which it may become a universally accepted social policy. Compulsory restriction of acreage, if constitutional, might serve to enforce such a regional policy. As the situation now stands it remains a kind of individual insurance policy against fluctuating cotton prices. Unfortunately, the plan is not prosperity proof. A rise in cotton prices would as always increase cotton acreage and reduce acreage in "protective" crops.

The program makes no provision for plantation areas which possess specialized cotton lands, a labor supply trained to cotton routines and nothing else, and a business organization attuned only to cash crops. That is to say, in prosperous times the plantation has no aversion to supplying its tenants with food and feed at high interest charges. At no time could the plantation make returns on its investment by growing consumers' crops merely to raise the standard of living for its laborers. It must be remembered that these areas, especially in the Delta, have the comparative advantage in cotton production and would take any reduction of the cotton crops as a signal to expand plantings. A much needed form of regional planning may some day be done in this connection by agricultural experiment stations. By demonstration farms it may be possible to work out some other use of tenants than in the cotton system. An application of this system to general or specialized farming might serve as a transitional step out of tenancy. One group of plantations in Arkansas worked out uniform methods and set their tenants to the growing of spinach for the early market. Thus the plantation achieved another source of income, and the tenants were relieved of the necessity of taking up so much credit. Many planters throughout the South agree that the cropper's necessity of keeping his second-hand Ford on the road, coupled with his inability to part with any cash for repairs, had made of him a good mechanic. Thus when the plantation comes to mechanize it will find its Negro labor machine-conscious and able to make the transition.

The other possibility of rationalizing the cotton industry is bound up with technical changes. The invention of a practicable cotton-picker, often announced but never quite realized, will serve to lower the cost of production, extend acreage, consolidate holdings, and reduce the demand for labor. Corporation farming will prove the rule, and twenty acres, a Negro, and a mule will be forced out of the picture. The transitional period will find the South full of cotton tenants with no place to turn. Cotton will furnish higher returns to fewer men, and the tenants, once settled in shacks on the plantation, may be replaced by migratory workers as in wheat.

The other technical innovation has been suggested by the experiments of Professor Frank K. Cameron of the University of North Carolina.[10] Because of the large amount of cellulose in cotton, he proposes the utilization of the whole plant except the roots in the manufacture of rayon. Wood pulp is growing more expensive, while under the plan it has been shown by his assistant, Nicholas W. Dockery, that cotton can be sown broadcast and harvested by machines much in the manner of wheat. Here the desired quality is not staple length but a high percentage of lint and cellulose. Since cotton already has probably more cellulose than any other plant, it is naturally the most important plant to the rayon industry. Chemical research has also made sugar-cane waste, bagasse, available for rayon processing.

[10] Press releases, *Science Service* and Associated Press, December, 1931.

Here again the effect will be to dismiss laborers and raise the standards of the industry. There may also emerge two contrasting cotton regions: one developed on the basis of cellulose content for the rayon industry, another developed on the basis of staple lengths for the cotton goods industry. After preliminary experimentation with seeds, soils, and fertilizers, it may be found that the areas are non-competing, thus adding an element of stability to the industry.

SALVAGING THE MARGINAL HIGHLANDERS

Regional planning in the South will be forced to face sooner or later the task of salvaging marginal highlanders. There exist some areas so rugged, so infertile, so destitute of resources, actual and potential, that the most realistic thing agencies interested in the underprivileged of the mountains can do is "to advocate openly the abandonment of the most infertile soil even though it means the complete desolation of entire neighborhoods."[11] To attempt to build an adequate social life in such areas by means of community, health, and education work endowed from outside is futile. "Man must undo," writes Charles D. Lewis, "the process the past century has carried out, because it is destroying men, because it is providing breeding places for inferiority, for inefficiency, for lawlessness."[12] One survey of a mountain county in Kentucky found over 40 per cent of the land with a slope of over 20 per cent. Of the total area surveyed, only 23 per cent was land with a slope under 10 per cent and in good or fair condition. Under the most favorable plan of farm management that could be devised, over 43 per cent of the farms would be classified as submarginal.[13]

Heretofore the mill village and the tenancy system of the lowlands have been most accessible to the highland dwellers because they have demanded the minimum prerequisites of skill and capital. While southern farm areas have been losing black population, they have made some gains in white population. White farmers are coming down from the hills to more fertile lands of Delta and plantation belt. Bolivar County in the Mississippi Delta increased in white

[11] W. S. Anderson, "Future of the Mountain Home," *Mountain Life and Work*, January, 1931, p. 22.

[12] "Government Forests and the Mountain Problem," *Mountain Life and Work*, January, 1931, p. 6.

[13] L. C. Gray, "Objectives and Progress of the Economic and Social Survey of the Southern Appalachians," *Mountain Life and Work*, July, 1931, p. 132.

farm population threefold from 1920-30. Arthur Raper has pointed
out a general tendency for Negro families in the Georgia black
belt area to be replaced by white families from the hills. He
shows that fertile areas under the system of tenancy are first to be
abandoned in a population exodus, while near marginal land under
peasant proprietorship remains in cultivation.[14] The trend of
agricultural readjustment may turn more of the dwellers in Appalachia in this direction. Moreover, churches and schools, once established in the mountains to raise up community leaders for the area,
now recognize the right of the highland young people "to go where
they choose to go and now encourage them to engage in congenial
work wherever it can be found." For the submarginal areas, adds
Dr. W. S. Anderson, "the best thing the schools can do for mountain
boys and girls is to make them dissatisfied with the harsh conditions
under which they have been reared and inspire them to go where
normal life can be lived."[15]

It must be made clear to the branch water and cabin folks that
modern agriculture has no program to offer them. The high birth
rate on the ridges means that with every cleared slope, offered first
to the plow and then to erosion, living conditions will grow steadily
worse. "The more poverty-stricken the people, the more difficult it
is to get them to break away and seek better conditions. They are
afraid. They realize they know nothing of modern methods of
farm production; they are afraid to go out and meet strangers."[16]
But they face actual social demoralization for their children if they
remain. As for the submarginal regions themselves, they must be
returned, in the words of Lewis, to the one thing for which they
are fitted—forests. It would even benefit many southern states
if these sterile slopes were abandoned and allowed to reforest themselves—as they would in the course of time. But with the present
program of forest reserves and national parks this process may be
speeded up.

In the larger tracts an important step toward regrowing forests
has already been made. There are already 10,000 acres of national
forests in the highland areas of seven southern states. Possibly eight

[14] Arthur Raper, "Two Rural Black Belt Counties," unpublished doctor's dis-
sertation, University of North Carolina, 1931.
[15] W. S. Anderson, *loc. cit.*, p. 21.
[16] *Ibid.*

times this amount could advantageously be put into national forest reserves. Moreover, where large acreage is privately held for coal and mineral prospects as in Kentucky, surface rights could be secured for the government forest program. Regrowing forests is not yet a matter for individuals; only governments or corporations can live long enough to reap the profits. We do not yet have the facts well enough in hand to answer the question: How long does it take a forest to grow? R. B. Craig from tree borings in Kentucky mountains estimated that yellow poplar grows to the average diameter of 8 inches in fifteen years. In thirty years an acre will give a total production of 6,450 board feet of timber.[17] Such studies will answer one preliminary set of questions. Moreover, the economic and social survey of the southern Appalachians of the United States Department of Agriculture, in coöperation with the various State Agricultural Colleges under the direction of L. C. Gray, will show, among other things, just what are the submarginal areas. Mapping by the technique of aerial photography and determination of areal slopes will be followed by social and economic studies of selected areas to determine marginal limits of cultivation.[18]   And when these zones are definitely located, it will be the task of sound forestry and sound social engineering to further the transition from rural slum to scientifically regrown forest.

In the Piney Woods Belt, it may be added, reforestation may stand an even better chance of success by developing as a three level industry. The adoption of the technique of C. H. Herty and others to the processing of paper pulp from pitch pine will open new possibilities for southern forest planning. The management of turpentine stands has involved cupping operations for 15 to 20 years followed by timbering. With the increasing establishment of paper mills in the South it may prove possible to bridge the gap of about twenty years between the seeding and turpentining by a profitable removal of thinnings.[19] With the South as nature's forcing ground for trees and pine forestry as a triple-purpose industry, the new forestry may largely develop in the South.

[17] W. D. Nichols, "A Research Approach to the Problems of Appalachia," *Mountain Life and Work*, January, 1932, p. 7.

[18] See *Minutes* of Conference on Economics and Social Survey of the Southern Appalachian Highlands, Washington, February 24, 1930.

[19] S. F. Eldridge, "Management of Southern Pine for Naval Stores," *Journal of Forestry*, XXIX, 328-33.

The New Flood Control

It remained for the disaster of 1927 to give the lower Mississippi Valley a unified plan for flood control. From 1879 the federal government, under the fiction of aiding navigation, had acted with local levee boards through the agency of the Mississippi River Commission. Divided jurisdiction, divided support—approximately on a fifty-fifty basis—and irregular appropriations made the work of control halting and piecemeal. The state legislatures had given levee boards wide powers to issue bonds and float loans. On January 1, 1928, the total indebtedness of the levee districts amounted to $819,642,576, far exceeding the assessed property valuation of the districts. Moreover, the Commission in order to save its levee system as a unit had been forced to spend money, contrary to law, in building levees in districts unable to pay their allotments. The passage of the great flood of 1927 found many levee districts bonded to twice their assessed valuations with special district taxes exceeding $4.00 an acre annually. Interest payments had been defaulted and it was impossible to sell more bonds or raise further loans.[20]

Out of this chaos came federal control and support as embodied in the Jones-Reid Act of 1928. By a program extending over a period of ten years and estimated to cost $325,000,000, the greater part of the valley is to be protected against maximum flood heights.[21] The centers of population are to receive first consideration while protection of mere area will be secondary. As heretofore, levees are to be the main reliance, but for the first time spillways will be incorporated in the unified program. It is the feeling of engineers in charge that levees along the main stem have reached their ultimate heights, and the failure of a high levee is likely to invite more disaster than that of a low one.

In addition to coördinating the levee system in a way never done before, full advantage is to be taken of all advances in hydrographics and engineering science. The elimination of bends and turns will operate to increase channel capacity. Full use will be made of bank protection to protect levees from undercutting and caving at river bends. Revetments of concrete mattresses are to

[20] Arthur DeWitt Frank, *The Development of the Federal Program of Flood Control on the Mississippi River*, p. 237.

[21] L. Brown, "Flood Control Work on the Mississippi," *Scientific Monthly*, XXX, 481-99.

protect Memphis, Greenville, and New Orleans, as well as all strategic points along the levee system. Where existing levees cannot be so protected, they will be moved back. At a later point in the program, stage reservoirs are to be planned and constructed; but the most noteworthy departure from old methods is the introduction of spillways.

The Bonne Carré spillway was finished in 1931. Constructed twenty miles above New Orleans, it will divert at need one fifth of the river's flood waters in to Lake Pontchartrain where they will drain into the Gulf of Mexico, thus relieving pressure on the lower river. The huge flood canal is two miles wide, six miles long, and operated by a needle dam 7,700 feet wide, moving on a sill of masonry. With a drop of 24 feet to the Lake and a depth of 10 to 15 feet, the floodway is expected to give its waters a velocity of two to three and a half feet per second. Army engineers estimate that, with the spillway in operation, flood stage at New Orleans need not exceed twenty feet, while the Lake level will be raised only two feet. In conclusion, the success of the early stage of the unified plan may be suggested by the fact that the largest flood to occur without breaking a crevice flowed practically unnoticed to the Gulf in the winter of 1929.

The program is to be completed by the construction in certain areas of diversion channels, fuse-plug levees, and relatively uncontrolled riverside floodways according to the Jadwin plan. The fuse-plug is a purposely weakened section designed to break at a point three feet below the high level before the whole levee system is threatened. The plan of riverside floodways as at New Madrid, Missouri, proposes to lower the river bank levee some five feet, and five miles back to build up a stronger levee to retain the floodwater, thus relieving the system at other points. In spite of the fact that these proposals remain to be tested, the completion of the program set forth in the Jones-Reid bill will give the Delta greater protection than would have been necessary to hold the 1927 flood in check.[22]

The Florida Beautification Program

In every point the Florida boom of 1927 is at variance with regional planning; it may be taken, in fact, as the extreme type of real estate promotion and speculative activity to which a newly

[22] Frank, *op. cit.,* pp. 225, 252.

discovered frontier may be subject. It was boom run riot, California come south to inveigle a nation and wake a section into feverish activity. There is no need here to recount that episode in frenzied finance; as a chapter in social history it is doubtful if the story can be adequately written. It was planned, in so far as this Florida of the realtors' dream was planned, for a leisure class society—a society retired and ready to play. There had long, it seems, existed such a group at Palm Beach; now the world was informed it, too, might retire to a small Palm Beach of its own, a lot in Florida. Thousands lost their savings in Florida who never thought they belonged in America's leisure class. They hoped to get in on the gold rush, and, if they couldn't retire, they might sell to someone who could. Here, without any demonstrable basis in resources, signs informed the traveler, was to be the Chicago of the South, here the nation's second seaport. Along the highway, said leather-lunged announcers, was to stretch a solid city from West Palm Beach to Miami. Resources—the resources were to consist of other sections' population and other people's money. To buy as farms and to sell as lots is to pocket the profits of subdivision. Thus from the sale of lots one has enough to pay for city planning and city beautification which will sell more lots. Nobody stopped to figure the number of lots available to every man, woman, and child in America. The tourist congestion, freight embargo, the frenzied building activity, even the trek of tin can tourists added to the illusion that all the world sought Florida and its southern beauty.

It was not regional planning. It was America on the boom, on a southern boom for once. American speculation, exploitation, inflation at its most blatant and brazen. It burst and the echoes of its going were heard as far north as Asheville and throughout Georgia in the crash of a failing chain of banks. But the impetus of the movement has remained and will be permanent. It has shown, for example, of what grace and charm the southern shoreline is capable in landscaping and architecture. It has left some of the most beautiful and civilized spots in America. In the restless crowds that thronged Florida and in the minds of the promoters themselves might be found the same strange mixture of cupidity and love of beauty. George Merrick, by his insistence upon a unified type of modified Mediterranean architecture, succeeded in creating in Coral Gables a dream of earthly beauty—a contribution to

American architecture and landscape artistry in which he sincerely believed. At Hollywood, a plunger took pride in the fact that he had reclaimed a mangrove swamp for a beach resort and planned a city beautiful. Carl G. Fisher cut the trees and buried the mangrove swamps of Miami Beach under five feet of sand. Out of mangrove swamps and sandbars on the Bay of Biscayne and elsewhere was to rise the American Riviera, a hundred Venetian cities. Merrick went so far as to import gondolas and gondoliers from Venice to patrol the canals of Coral Gables. Chaotic, speculative, exploitative, profit-taking, the venture had as its basis the beauties of nature and man-made beauty in harmony.[23] There is much of charm and artistry that regional planning may learn from the plans of the ill-fated promoters of the Florida boom. A business magazine may carry the title, "Failure of Florida East Coast, the Story of a Wrong Guess," South Florida municipalities may be left saddled with well-nigh hopeless debts, but the core of development remains. Even high pressure salesmanship cannot permanently despoil the region of its natural charm.

Guiding the Urban Trend

It is to the growth of cities that chambers of commerce and Florida realtors point as the justification for their existence. From 1900 to 1920 the South gained 114 per cent in urban population, while the rest of the country advanced 71.6 per cent. For cities over 10,000, the South gained 132.4 per cent to an advance of 80.3 per cent for the rest of the country. The base for the South was lower, but the gains would be worthy of notice in any area. The 1930 census has shown an accelerated ratio of urban growth. From 1920 to 1930, 284 municipalities of over 3,000 doubled their population; approximately 40 per cent of these were in the South. In the procession of doubling cities California leads with 48, Texas follows with 44, Florida comes next with 25, and the Piedmont makes a notable showing. In the Gulf Southwest the decade has seen Tulsa grow from 72,075 to 141,258, Oklahoma City from 91,295 to 185,389, Dallas from 158,976 to 260,475, San Antonio from 161,379 to 231,542, and Houston from 138,276 to 292,352. In Florida it has watched West Palm Beach grow from 8,659 to 26,610, St. Petersburg from 14,237 to 40,425, Tampa from 51,608 to 101,161, and Miami from

[23] See Frederick Lewis Allen, *Only Yesterday*, pp. 270-89.

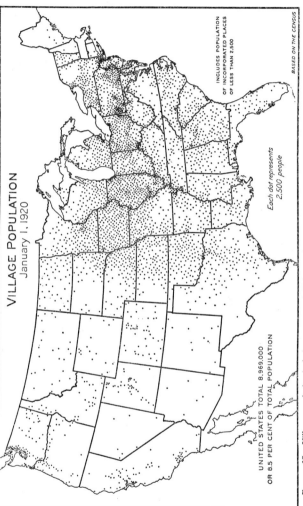

VILLAGE POPULATION
January 1, 1920

INCLUDES POPULATION
OF INCORPORATED PLACES
OF LESS THAN 2,500

BASED ON THE CENSUS

Each dot represents
2,500 people

UNITED STATES TOTAL 8,969,000
OR 8.5 PER CENT OF TOTAL POPULATION

FIGURE 29.—Village population includes many people living on farms within the village limits. This term includes population of incorporated places of less than 2,500. It includes also many retired farmers, especially in the Corn Belt, and in the South and West, and tradesmen who serve the farmer's needs. In the Northeast a considerable factory population resides in villages. The geographic distribution of village population in the Corn Belt and in the hay and dairy region is remarkably uniform, except near the cities and in New England. Whereas farm population is densest in the South and East, village population is densest in the Corn Belt and North-eastern States. It is also relatively dense in Utah, where many of the Mormon farmers live in villages. (Courtesy of U. S. Department of Agriculture).

29,571 to 110,637. In Piedmont Carolina it has witnessed the growth of High Point from 14,302 to 36,745, Asheville from 28,504 to 50,193, Durham from 21,719 to 52,037, Winston-Salem from 48,395 to 75,274, Charlotte from 46,338 to 82,675. These figures make a dull page, but they are the hymns the realtors and the chambers of commerce sing. Many of the Piedmont towns," wrote Harry M. Cassidy, "are raw and new. But they have the air of belonging to the Pacific Coast in boom days rather than to the old South."

Nevertheless the South has remained outside the area of high urbanization and great cities. No municipality in the South has yet gathered within its metes and bounds as many as half a million souls. Only two cities, Louisville and New Orleans, had in 1930 passed 300,000; 12 more have passed the 100,000 population mark; while 19 rank between 50,000 and 100,000. The total population of the South's 39 cities of over 50,000 amounted in 1930 to some 5,260,437, a million and a half less than the population of New York City. Fifty of the South's cities fall within the 20,000 to 50,000 grouping while 277 are in the 5,000 to 2,000 class. The South possesses some 666 municipalities of over 3,000; almost half of these, 45 per cent, have less than 5,000 population. Within the borders of the two Carolinas, Mississippi, and Arkansas will be found no city of over 100,000, while Mississippi fails to show a city of 50,000. Within the borders of the South is found only 16.7 per cent of the nation's municipalities of 5,000 and over. Over one fourth, 28.8 per cent, of all the South's cities of over 3,000 are found in the southwestern states, Texas and Oklahoma, while barely more than a third, 33.8 per cent, are found in the six states of Virginia, South Carolina, Tennessee, Mississippi, Alabama, and Arkansas.

What is the bearing of this statistical exhibit on the regional South? To promotion agencies with eyes glued on real estate values, it is a challenge to emulate, if possible, the urban agglomerations of the East. A cursory examination is sufficient to show, however, that the trend of the South is toward the growth of small cities rather than a few gigantic metropolises. Moreover, to the population movements from other sections in Texas and Florida has been added, as in the Piedmont, the migration of native country dwellers to cities of their immediate areas. Because urbanization has been delayed, because topography and transportation have given no overwhelming advantages to a few sites, the South has the opportunity to develop a metropolitan economy that shall escape the worst phases of congestion and crowding. The region's urbanization has been delayed until the perfection of the technology of transmitting electric power which permits a regional deployment of industry. The urbanization of eastern and northern centers occurred under the technical impetus of the steam engine where the economy of coal and iron forced industrial convergence and concentration. It is obvious, of course, that electricity is no economic substitute for coal in industries such as steel and brick making which require intense heat as well as power. Once established in concentration, cultural tradition has tended to perpetuate industrial congestion in the North. This is a tradition the South may escape.

The diffused pattern of urbanization now taking shape in the Piedmont has much to commend it to the regionalist. For the sake of its rural life the South should plan for a better balanced town and country relation. Farmers, of course, need near-by markets, and a large number of small cities spread economic opportunities over a wider area than one large metropolis. Only by the use of such markets, can many southern farmers ever hope to work out a diversified agriculture on a commercial basis. Moreover, for the urban dweller, it is probable that the small city has all the advantages of the great metropolis except certain cultural ones. While the South develops the small city, the medium city, and a few large cities, it need not produce the metropolis. Thus it may avoid traffic congestion, the creation of slum areas, the loss of time going to and from work, and the corrupt and inefficient municipal housekeeping almost inevitably attached to over-developed population centers. If such a program is possible, the South may finally attain many of the advantages of contemporary industrialization without suffering its accompanying deficiencies and maladjustments.

To get the best that urbanization has to offer, the South has remained too far outside the current of city planning. The Glynn County, Georgia, plan for orderly development of resort advantages along shore, of industrial and agricultural activities, of parks and boulevards has been called the first instance of regional planning in the South.[24] Atlanta, for example, has been allowed to grow up

[24] M. W. Weir, "Regional Planning in a Southern County," *American City,* XXXIX, 155-56.

with streets too narrow for a metropolis. Nevertheless, examples can be found. The speculative planning of Florida developers has been mentioned. Orangeburg, South Carolina, has created a most remarkable park system for a city of 15,000. While Kingsport has been mentioned, it may be noted that two rayon firms are creating for Happy Valley, between Elizabethton and Johnson City, Tennessee, a regional plan of industrial deployment, satellite towns and open spaces.[25]   Charleston, South Carolina, has provided for the expansion of its waterfront boulevard development in the direction of residences and recreation, shipping and industry by municipal ownership of adjacent marshes and flats.[26]   Moreover, attention has been called to the city's need for zoning and tax revision in order to encourage recent movement to preserve and restore the city's fine old architecture.[27]   While many other plans can no doubt be found, the South needs to realize that the time for city planning is while the city is in the process of growing.

A Folk Renaissance for the South

It would be a pleasant thing to believe the South is to achieve regionalism as a folk movement. The South possesses a traditionally inarticulate peasantry; it is developing an inferiority-conscious proletariat; it has the tradition of an aristocracy with leanings toward paternalism and *noblesse oblige;* it is growing a literary and artistic class. Such a configuration has meant regional and cultural revival for peasantries as underprivileged as the so-called southern poor whites. In our own day we have seen the peasantries of Denmark and Ireland recreated, as it were, in a new economy, a new culture, and a new state. Bishops turned farming experts and poets became agricultural economists to teach the farmer-folk bookkeeping and to set up coöperatives. After the same manner certain Victorian intellectuals, Ruskin, Kingsley, and Morris, attempted to give tone and direction to the English laboring classes when they were lacking in cultural guidance. They proved even more effective in making the movement respectable among the upper classes. It is largely due to this tradition, continued by the Fabians, that

[25] John Noles, "Regional Planning for Happy Valley, Tennessee," *City Planning,* IV, 199-205.

[26] *American City,* XXXVII, 741-44.

[27] *American City,* XLII, 134-35.

the English labor movement possesses a cultural strength and an intellectual prestige unknown to its American counterpart. In comparable situations, American college-bred leaders and intellectuals have established settlement houses in which to live in close cultural contact with our segregated immigrant masses in large cities.

It is easy to point out that any such movement, with and for the folk, in the South has faced the inevitable race dualism. While one can see that the Negro, the dweller in Highlands, the mill villagers are definitely regarded as missionary causes in certain northern circles, educational, religious, and labor, it is difficult to know how they are regarded by southern leaders. One knows that the rabble rousers look to what we shall call the southern peasantry for votes in large blocks, the church for members, the writers for local color, the academicians for source material. But nowhere is there genuine regional renaissance or a genuine folk movement; neither Ireland nor Denmark is being duplicated in Dixie.

The beginnings of such a movement were heralded over a generation ago by Edgar Gardiner Murphy, Joel Chandler Harris, Walter Hines Page, and Booker T. Washington. Those were the days when the South rang with talk of the forgotten man. The movement has, of course, been betrayed by innumerable cheap politicians who, sired of the common folk, have capitalized their vague unrest only to become spoilsmen in office or to drift with the tide. The one sure and definite exception, as H. C. Nixon points out, has been Governor Charles Brantley Aycock of North Carolina, who became the symbol of a people's aspiration for education. Only recently has the South nurtured a literary and artistic group of any prominence. It yet remains to be seen whether the southern intellectuals are to attain the close cultural contact with the folk that leaders of the Irish, Danish, and Victorian labor movements achieved. There may yet linger enough of certain traditions of aristocracy to bar the southern intellectual from such contacts. One of the contributors to *I'll Take My Stand* has written: "The inferior whether in life or education should exist only for the sake of the superior."[28] This statement not only leads one to wonder as to what purpose the superior exists; it casts doubt on the future of any regional movement.

[28] P. 119.

The program of such a movement must be eclectic; it cannot be sectional, doctrinaire, nor can it contradict natural and economic processes. It must accept these processes in an attempt to subject them to social guidance. If all that is needed be doubling cities and spreading industries, the process may be safely left to the southern birth rate and the southern realtors. There, however, clusters enough sentiment around the name of Dixie, there exists enough of public spirit, of love of native place and native folk in the nation and the region to rally men of intelligence around the banner of regionalism if its program rang true. Its program must be as wide and all-embracing as that of Victorian liberals, of Ireland, of Denmark. It must seek out southern peasants with talk of a reörganized agriculture. It must strive to lift southern mill operatives out of attitudes of inferiority and social isolation. The first task would not be disdained by George Russell, nor the second by Sherwood Anderson. We are told that the southern folk are spread more sparsely over a greater area than in Ireland or Denmark. But the South now has agencies of extension and demonstration that other areas did not have. The spread of the modern educational and leveling-up process is reducing illiteracy as a barrier to participation. What is needed is an adaptation of what we may call the technique of folk revival to the southern scene. The reader demands a concrete example. George Mitchell has suggested, to bring the mill folks into the stream of culture and to alleviate their sense of social inferiority, the establishment of a newspaper for all the mill people of the Piedmont. Edited by and for mill villagers it should, for example, play up the inventions of mill machinery—and there have been many—made by their number. It would create a feeling of solidarity, it might lead them to think of themselves in united political action for the ends of social welfare, but it would also mediate to them the world outside.

To lead the folk renaissance one might visualize the formation of a southern party—a party not in politics. A party with an emphasis more cultural than political, with a range intermediate between narrow state's rights and undifferentiated nationalism, with its motivation somewhere between quick individual profits and the old fire-eating sectionalism. Its ends will not be attained by the old hot-headed fighting of clique against clique and section against section. They will not be reached by a futile nostalgia for a South

that never was on land or sea. Nor will they be achieved by head-
long rushing into unplanned industrialization.

Here is nature and there stands the folk. Behind the folk stands
a tragic history. What we need to know is that, in spite of its
tragic history, the mold in which the South is to be fashioned is
only now being laid.

BIBLIOGRAPHY

Books

Abernethy, Thomas Perkins. *The Formative Period in Alabama, 1815-1828.* Alabama State Department of Archives and History. Montgomery: Brown Printing Company, 1922.

From Frontier to Plantation in Tennessee. Chapel Hill: University of North Carolina Press, 1932.

Adams, Henry. *History of the United States of America during the First Administration of Thomas Jefferson.* I. New York: C. Scribner's Sons, 1889.

Adams, James Truslow. *The American Epic.* Boston: Little, Brown, 1931.

Provincial Society, 1690-1763. New York: Macmillan, 1927.

Allen, Frederick Lewis. *Only Yesterday.* New York: Harpers, 1931.

Allen, William B. *A History of Kentucky, etc.* Louisville: Bradley and Gilbert, 1872.

Ambler, Charles Henry. *Sectionalism in Virginia from 1776-1861.* Chicago: University of Chicago Press, 1910.

Andrews, M. P. *Women of the South in War Times.* Baltimore: The Norman, Remington Co., 1920.

Andrews, Sidney. *The South Since the War.* Boston: Ticknor and Fields, 1866.

Annals of the American Academy of Political and Social Science. *The Agricultural Situation in the United States.* January, 1925.

American Waterways. XXXI, No. 1 (January, 1908), Philadelphia.

The Coming of Industry to the South. CLIII (January, 1931).

Farm Relief. CXLII (March, 1929).

Great Inland Waterway Projects. Part I, Mississippi Flood Control. CXXXV, 1-59 (June, 1928).

Anon. *The Old Pine Farm or Southern Ministerial Life.* Memphis: So. Baptist Publishing Society, 1860.

Armitage, F. P. *Diet and Race.* London: Longmans, 1922.

Arnett, A. M. *The Populist Movement in Georgia.* New York: Columbia University Studies, 1922.

Arnold, B. W., Jr. *The Tobacco Industry in Virginia Since 1860.* Baltimore: Johns Hopkins University Studies in Historical and Political Science. Series XV, Nos. I, II, 1897.

Arthur, John Preston. *Western North Carolina, A History (1730-1913).* Raleigh, N. C.: Edwards and Broughton Printing Co., 1914.

Avary, Myrta L. *Dixie After the War.* New York: Doubleday, Page & Company, 1906.

Bailey, L. H. *The Principles of Agriculture.* New York: Macmillan, 1919.

Baker, Ray S. *Following the Color Line.* New York: Doubleday, Page, 1908.

Baldwin, Joseph Y. *Flush Times in Alabama and Mississippi.* New York, 1853. Reprinted, Augusta, Ga.: Americus Book Co.

Banks, E. M. *Economics of Land Tenure in Georgia.* New York: Columbia University Studies, 1905.

Barbee, William J. *The Cotton Question.* New York: Metropolitan Record Office, 1866.

Barbour, G. M. *Florida for Tourists, Invalids and Settlers.* New York: D. Appleton & Co., 1882.

Barnes, Will C. *Western Grazing Grounds and the Forest Ranges.* Chicago: Breeder's Gazette, 1913.

Bartram, William. *Travels through North and South Carolina, Georgia, East and West Florida.* Philadelphia: James & Johnson, 1791.

Bassett, John Spencer. *Regulators in North Carolina.* American Historical Association Reports. Washington, 1894.

The Plantation Overseer as Revealed in His Letters. Printed for Smith College, Northampton, Mass., 1925.

Beal, W. J. *The Grasses of North America.* New York: Holt, 1887-96.

Beard, Charles A. and Mary R. *Rise of American Civilization.* 2 v. New York: Macmillan, 1927.

Benedict, H. Y., and Lomax, John A. *The Book of Texas.* New York: Doubleday, Page, 1916.

Berglund, Abraham, Starnes, G. T., de Vyver, F. T. *Labor in the Industrial South.* University, Virginia: Institute for Research in the Social Sciences, 1930.

Bowman, Isaiah. *Forest Physiography.* New York: Wiley, 1911.

Boyd, W. K. *Story of Durham.* Durham, N. C.: Duke University Press, 1925.

Boyd, W. K., and Brooks, Robert P. *Selected Bibliography and Syllabus on the History of the South, 1584-1876.* University of Georgia, Bulletin XVIII, 6. Athens, 1918.

Boynton, Henry Delano. *The Capitols of the South.* Washington: H. D. Boynton, 1917.

Brackenridge, H. W. *Views of Louisiana.* Baltimore: Schaeffer & Maund, 1817.

Branch, E. Douglass. *The Cowboy and His Interpreters.* New York: Appleton, 1926.

The Hunting of the Buffalo. New York: Appleton, 1929.

Westward: The Romance of the Frontier. New York: Appleton, 1930.

Brigham, Albert Perry. *Geographic Influences in American History.* Boston: Ginn, 1903.

The United States of America. Studies in Physical, Regional, and Human Geography. London: University of London Press, 1927.

Brochure de propagande. *Societe. Intern. de Science Sociale; L'orgine, le But et l'Organisation de la Societé.* Paris.

Brooks, C. E. P. *Climate through the Ages.* New York: Scribner's, 1930.

Brooks, E. C. *Story of Corn.* Chicago: Rand, McNally, 1916.

Story of Cotton. Chicago: Rand, McNally, 1911.

Brooks, John Graham. *As Others See Us.* New York: Macmillan, 1910.

Brooks, Robert Preston. *The Agrarian Revolution in Georgia, 1865-1912.* Madison: Wisconsin University Bulletin 639, Historical Series V, 1914.

Brown, Cecil K. *The State Highway System of North Carolina.* Chapel Hill: University of North Carolina Press, 1931.

Brown, Harry Bates. *Cotton.* New York: McGraw-Hill, 1927.

Brown, W. G. *The Lower South in American History.* New York: Macmillan, 1902.

Bruce, Phillip Alexander. *Economic History of Virgina in the Seventeenth Century.* New York and London: Macmillan, 1896.

Plantation Negro as Freedman. New York: Putnam, 1849.

Rise of the New South. Philadelphia: George Barrie & Sons, 1905.

Brues, Thomas. *Insects and Human Welfare.* Cambridge: Harvard University Press, 1920.

Brunhes, Jean. *Human Geography.* Chicago: Rand, McNally, 1920.

Brunhes, Jean, and Vallaux, Camille. *La Geographie de l'Histoire.* Paris: Alcan, 1921.

Brunner, Edmund de S. *Church Life in the Rural South.* New York: Doran, 1923.

Brunt, C. *Le Regionalisme.* Paris: Blaud et Cie, 1911.

Bryant, L. C. *Logging: The Principles and General Methods of Operation in the United States.* New York: Wiley, 1923.

Buchannan, J. S., and Dale, E. E. *A History of Oklahoma.* Chicago: Printed for the authors, 1924.

Buechel, Frederick A. *The Commerce of Agriculture.* New York: Wiley, 1926.

Buck, S. J. *The Granger Movement.* Cambridge: Harvard University Press, 1913.

The Agrarian Crusade. New Haven: Yale University Press, 1920.

Burkett, C. W., and Poe, C. H. *Cotton.* New York: Doubleday, Page, 1906.

Calhoun, A. W. *A Social History of the American Family.* 3 v. Cleveland: Arthur H. Clark Co., 1917.

Cameron, J. D. *A Sketch of the Tobacco Interests in North Carolina.* Oxford, N. C.: Davis, 1881.

Campbell, D. H. *On Outline of Plant Geography.* New York: Macmillan, 1926.

Campbell, John C. *The Southern Highlander and His Homeland.* New York: Russell Sage Foundation, 1921.

Cappon, Lester J. *Bibliography of Virginia History Since 1865.* University, Virginia: Institute for Research in the Social Sciences, 1930.

Carr, Lewis F. *America Challenged.* New York: Macmillan, 1929.

Carrier, Lyman. *Beginnings of Agriculture in America.* New York: McGraw-Hill, 1923.

Carson, W. W. *Agricultural Reconstruction in North Carolina After the Civil War.* Washington: American Hist. Assn. Reports, 1921.

Casson, H. N. *The Story of Artificial Silk.* London: Efficiency Magazine, 1928.

Chandler, J. A. C. *Representation in Virginia.* Baltimore: Johns Hopkins University Studies, XIV, 1896.

Chapman, A. W. *Flora of the Southern United States* (3d Ed.). New York: Ivison, Blakeman, Taylor & Co., 1897.

Chase, Stuart. *Mexico.* New York: Macmillan, 1931.

Chittenden, R. H. *The Nutrition of Man.* New York: F. A. Stokes, 1907.

Christy, David. *Cotton is King and Pro-Slavery Argument.* New York: Derby & Jackson, 1856.

Clark, John Bunyan. *Populism in Alabama.* Auburn, Ala.: Auburn Print., 1927.

Clark, V. S. *History of Manufactures in the United States.* New York: McGraw-Hill, 1929.

Clemen, R. A. *The American Livestock and Meat Industry.* New York: The Ronald Press, 1923.

Clemow, Frank G. *The Geography of Disease.* London: Cambridge University Press, 1903.

Cleveland, C. C. *The Great Revival in the West, 1797-1805.* Chicago: University of Chicago Press, 1916.

Clower, Ernest S. *Shipways to the Sea: Our Inland and Coastal Waterways.* Baltimore: Williams and Wilkins Co., 1929.

Colby, Charles C. *Source Book for the Economic Geography of North America.* Chicago: University of Chicago Press, 1921.

Coman, Katherine. *Economic Beginnings of the Far West,* 2 v. New York: Macmillan, 1912.

Combs, Josiah Henry. *The Kentucky Highlanders from a Native Mountaineer's Viewpoint.* Lexington, Kentucky: J. L. Richardson, 1913.

Compton, Wilson. *The Organization of the Lumber Industry.* Published by American Lumberman, 1916.

  Reforested America. Washington: National Lumber Manufacturers Association, 1929.

Connor, R. D. W. *History of North Carolina.* Chicago: Lewis Publishing Co., 1919.

Cooley, Charles Horton. *The Theory of Transportation.* Baltimore: Publications of the American Economic Association (Monograph), IX, No. 3, 1894.

Cotter, Arundel. *United States Steel: A Corporation with a Soul.* New York: Doubleday, 1921.

Craighead, James Geddes. *Scotch and Irish Seed in American Soil, etc.* Philadelphia: Presbyterian Board of Publication, 1878.

Cram, Mildred. *Old Seaport Towns of the South.* New York: Dodd, Mead and Co., 1917.

Crane, Verner W. *The Southern Frontier, 1670-1732.* Durham, N. C.: Duke University Press, 1929.

Craven, A. O. *Soil Exhaustion as a Factor in the Agricultural History of Virginia and Maryland, 1606-1860.* Urbana: University of Illinois Studies, xiii, I, 1926.

Crawford, M. D. C. *The Heritage of Cotton.* New York: Putnam's Sons, 1924.

Cromwell, A. D. *Agriculture and Life.* Philadelphia: Lippincott, 1915.

Daggett, Stuart. *Principles of Inland Transportation.* New York: Harper, 1928.

Dale, E. E. *History of the Range Cattle Industry in Oklahoma.* American Historical Association Reports, 1920.

Dana, W. B. *Cotton from Seed to Loom.* New York: Dana, 1878.

Davis, Jerome, and Barnes, H. E., et al. *Introduction to the Study of Sociology.* Boston: D. C. Heath, 1927.

Davis, W. M. *Physical Geography.* Boston: Ginn, 1902.

Davis, W. W. *The Civil War and Reconstruction in Florida.* New York: Columbia University Studies, 1913.

Dawley, Thomas R. *The Child that Toileth Not.* New York: Gracia, 1912.

Deadrick, W. H., and Thompson, L. O. *The Endemic Diseases of the Southern States.* Philadelphia: W. B. Saunders, 1916.

DeBow, J. P. B. *Industrial Resources of the Southern and Western States,* 3 v. New Orleans: Office of DeBow's Review, 1853.

De Cordova, Jacob. *Texas: Her Resources and Public Men.* Philadelphia: Lippincott, 1858.

De Tocquiville, Alexis. *Democracy in America.* 2 v. Cambridge: Sever and Francis, 1862.

Dexter, E. G. *Weather Influences.* New York: Macmillan, 1904.

Dinsmore, John Walker. *The Scotch-Irish in America, etc.* Chicago: Winona Pub. Co., 1906.

Dobie, J. Frank. *A Vaquero of the Brush Country, Partly from the Reminiscences of John Young.* Dallas: Southwest Press, 1929.

Dock, George, and Bass, C. C. *The Hookworm Disease.* St. Louis: 1910.

Dodd, William E. *The Cotton Kingdom.* New Haven: Yale University Press, 1921.

Doddridge, Joseph. *Notes on the Settlement and Indian Wars of the Western Parts of Virginia and Pennsylvania for the Year 1783.* Wellsburgh, Virginia: Printed at the Office at *The Gazette* for the author, 1824.

Douglass, H. Paul. *Christian Reconstruction in the South.* Boston: Pilgrim Press, 1909.

Doyle, J. O. *The English in America, Virginia, Maryland and the Carolinas.* London: Longmans, 1882.

Duggar, J. F. *Southern Field Crops.* New York: Macmillan, 1925.
Southern Forage Crops. New York: Macmillan, 1925.

Dunbar, Seymour. *A History of Travels in America.* 4 v. Indianapolis: Bobbs-Merrill, 1915.

Dunning, W. A. *Reconstruction: Political and Economic.* New York: Harpers, 1907.

Earle, F. S. *Southern Agriculture.* New York: Macmillan, 1908.

Ely, R. T. *et. al. The Foundations of National Prosperity.* New York: Macmillan, 1917.

Ely, R. T., and Morehouse, E. W. *Elements of Land Economics.* New York: Macmillan, 1924.

Elliott, J. R. *American Farms, Their Condition and Future.* New York: Putnam, 1890.

Emerson, Frederick V. *Agricultural Geology.* New York: Wiley, 1920.

Emerson, W. R. P. *Nutrition and Growth in Children.* New York: Appleton, 1922.

Enfield, R. R. *The Agricultural Crisis, 1920-1923.* New York: Longmans, 1924.

Engberg, R. G. *Industrial Prosperity and the Farmer.* Institute of Economics. New York: Macmillan, 1927.

Fagg, C. C., and Hutchings, S. E. *An Introduction to Regional Surveying.* London: Cambridge University Press, 1930.

Fairchild, G. T. *Rural Wealth and Welfare.* New York: Macmillan, 1900.

Fairholt, F. W. *Tobacco: Its History and Associations.* London: Chapman and Hall, 1859.

Faris, John Thomson. *Seeing the Sunny South.* Philadelphia: Lippincott, 1921.

Farrand, Livingston. *Basis of American History, 1500-1900.* New York: Harpers, 1904.

Faulkner, H. U. *American Economic History.* New York: Harpers, 1924.

Faust, Albert Bernhardt. *The German Element in the United States, etc.* Boston: Houghton Mifflin, 1909.

Featherstonhaugh, George William. *Excursions Through the Slave States.* London: J. Murray, 1844.

Febvre, Lucien. *A Geographical Introduction to History.* New York: Knopf, 1925.

Fernow, B. E. *A Brief History of Forestry in Europe, the United States and Other Countries.* Washington: American Forestry Association, 1913.

Fish, Carl Russel. *The Restoration of the Southern Railroads.* Madison: Wisconsin University Studies in Social Science and History, No. 2, 1919.

Rise of the Common Man, 1830-1850. New York: Macmillan, 1927.

Fiske, John. *Old Virginia and Her Neighbors.* Boston: Houghton Mifflin, 1898.

Fleming, Walter L. *Civil War and Reconstruction in Alabama.* New York: Columbia University Studies, 1905.

Documentary History of Reconstruction. 2 v. Cleveland: A. H. Clark, 1909.

The Sequel to Appomattox. New Haven: Yale University Press, 1919.

The Freedman's Savings Bank. Chapel Hill: University of North Carolina Press, 1927.

Flint, Timothy. *The Last Ten Years in the Valley of the Mississippi.* Boston: Hilliard and Company, 1826.

History and Geography of the Mississippi Valley. I. Cincinnati: E. H. Flint & L. R. Lincoln, 1832.

Ford, Henry Jones. *The Scotch-Irish in America.* Princeton: Princeton University Press, 1915.

Foreman, Grant. *Pioneer Days in the Southwest.* Cleveland: A. H. Clark, 1926.

Fox, Dixon Ryan. *Harper's Atlas of American History.* New York: Harpers, 1920.

Frank, Arthur DeWitt. *The Development of the Federal Program of Flood Control on the Mississippi River.* New York: Columbia University Press, 1930.

Free, E. E., and Hoke, Travis. *Weather.* New York: McBride, 1929.

Friedrick, C. J. *Alfred Weber's Theory of the Location of Industries.* Chicago: University of Chicago Press, 1929.

Fulton, M. G. *Southern Life in Southern Literature.* Boston: Ginn, 1917.

Gaines, Francis P. *The Southern Plantation.* New York: Columbia University Press, 1924.

Garrison, G. P. *Texas: A Contest of Civilizations.* Boston: Houghton Mifflin, 1903.

Geddes, Patrick, and Branford, Victor. *The Coming Polity.* London: Williams & N., 1919.

Gee, Wilson, and Carson, J. J., 3d. *Population Depletion in Certain Tidewater and Piedmont Areas of Virginia.* University, Virginia: Institute for Research in the Social Sciences, 1929.

A Statistical Study of Virginia. University, Virginia: Institute for Research in the Social Sciences, 1927.

Gennep, Arnold Van. *Traite Comparatif de Nationalites.* I. *Les Elements Exterieurs de la Nationalite.* Paris: Pogyat, 1922.

Gewehr, W. M. *The Great Awakening in Virginia, 1740-1790.* Durham, North Carolina: Duke University Press, 1930.

Giddings, Franklin Henry. *Civilization and Society*. Arranged and edited by Howard W. Odum. New York: Henry Holt and Co., 1932.

Gilbert, C. G., and Pogue, J. E. *America's Power Resources*. New York: Century, 1921.

Gillett, J. M. *Rural Sociology*. New York: Macmillan, 1925.

Goodwin, Cardinal. *The Trans-Mississippi West, 1803-1853*. New York: Appleton, 1922.

Grady, Henry W. *The New South*. New York: Bonner's Sons, 1890.

Graham, Stephen. *Children of the Slaves*. London: 1920.

Gras, N. S. B. *An Introduction to Economic History*. New York: Harpers, 1922.

A History of Agriculture in Europe and America. New York: F. S. Crofts, 1925.

Grattan, Thomas Calley. *Civilized America*. 2 v. London: Bradbury, 1861.

Gray, Lewis C. *Introduction to Agricultural Economics*. New York: Macmillan, 1924.

Greeley, A. W., *American Weather*. New York: Dodd, Mead, 1888.

Greene, Evarts Bontell. *Provincial America*. New York: Harpers, 1905.

Gruening, Ernest H. (ed). *These United States; A Symposium*. 2 v. New York: Boni and Liveright, 1923-24.

Haley, J. E. *The XIT Ranch of Texas*. Chicago: Lakeside Press, 1929.

Halle, Ernst von. *Baumwollproduktion und Pflanzugswirtschaft*. Leipzig: Duncker and H., 1897.

Hammond, Harry. *Handbook of South Carolina*. Columbia, South Carolina: Press of the State, 1883.

Hammond, M. B. *The Cotton Industry*. Publication of American Economic Association. New York: Macmillan, 1897.

Hann, Julius. *Handbuch der Klimologie*. 3 v., 3d ed. Stuttgart: 1908-11. English translation of 2d edition, Part I, by R. De C. Ward, New York: 1903.

Hanna, Charles A. *The Wilderness Trail*. 2 v. New York: Putnam's Sons, 1911.

Hardy, M. E. *The Geography of Plants*. Oxford: Clarendon Press, 1920.

Hart, Albert Bushnell. *The Southern South*. New York: Appleton, 1910.

Harwood, W. S. *The New Earth: A Record of the Triumphs of Modern Agriculture in America*. New York: Macmillan, 1906.

Hawk, F. L. *History of North Carolina.* Fayetteville, N. C.: E. J. Hale & Sons, 1857.

Heer, Clarence. *Income and Wages in the South.* Chapel Hill: University of North Carolina Press, 1930.

Helper, Hinton Rowan. *The Impending Crisis of the South: How to Meet It.* New York: Burdick Brothers, 1857.

Henderson, Archibald. *The Conquest of the Old Southwest.* New York: Century, 1920.

Herbertson, A. J., and F. D. *Man and His Work.* London: Black, 1904. *The Senior Geography.* 3 v. Oxford: The Clarendon Press, 1911.

Hibbard, B. H. *A History of the Public Land Policies.* New York: Macmillan, 1926.

Hilgard, E. W. *Agriculture and Geology of Mississippi.* Jackson: E. Barksdale, 1860. *Soils.* London: Macmillan, 1907.

Hill, Robert T. *Public Domain and Democracy.* New York: Columbia University Studies XXXVIII, 1910.

Hillyard, M. B. *The New South.* Baltimore: The Manufacturer's Record Company, 1887.

Hindehede, M. *Protein and Nutrition.* London: Ewart, Seymour, 1913.

Hirch, August. *Handbook of Geographical and Historical Pathology.* London: The New Sydenham Society, 1883.

History of State Agricultural and Mechanical Society of South Carolina from 1839-1916. Columbia: Bryan, 1916.

Hobbs, S. H., Jr. *North Carolina Economic and Social.* Chapel Hill: University of North Carolina Press, 1930.

Howard, L. O. *The Insect Menace.* New York: Century, 1931.

Howarth, J. R. *Climate and Geography.* Oxford: 1927.

Howath, Paul Leland. *George Washington, Gentleman Farmer.* Indianapolis: Bobbs-Merrill, 1925.

Hubbard, W. H. *Cotton and the Cotton Market.* New York: Appleton, 1927.

Huebner, Grover C. *Agricultural Commerce.* New York: Appleton, 1917.

Hulbert, Archer Butler. *Frontiers.* Boston: Little, Brown, 1929. *Historic Highways of America.* 11 v. Cleveland: Clark, 1902-1906. *Paths of Inland Commerce.* New Haven: Yale University Press, 1920. *Soil: Its Influence on American History.* New Haven: Yale University Press, 1930.

Hundley, D. R. *Social Relations in Our Southern States.* New York: Price, 1860.

Hunt, Thomas F. *The Cereals in America.* New York: Orange-Judd, 1904.

Huntington, C. C., and Carlson, F. A. *Environmental Basis of Social Geography*. New York: Prentice-Hall, 1929.

Huntington, Ellsworth. *Civilization and Climate*. 3d ed. New Haven: Yale University Press, 1924.

The Human Habitat. New York: Van Nostrand, 1927.

Pulse of Progress. New York: Scribner's, 1926.

The Red Man's Continent. New Haven: Yale University Press, 1919.

World Power and Evolution. New Haven: Yale University Press, 1919.

Huntington, Ellsworth, and Cushing, Sumner W. *Principles of Human Geography*. 3d ed. New York: Wiley, 1925.

Huntington, Ellsworth, and Williams, F. A. *Business Geography*. New York: Wiley, 1926.

Hutchinson, Woods. *Preventable Diseases*. Boston: Houghton Mifflin, 1909.

Imlay, Gilbert. *A Topographical Description of the Western Territory of North America, etc.* New York: Campbell, 1793.

Income in the United States; Its Amount and Distribution, 1909-1919. New York: National Bureau of Economic Research, 1922.

Industrial Conference Board, U. S. Chamber of Commerce. *The Condition of Agriculture in the United States and Measures for Its Improvement*. New York: 1927.

Ingle, Edward. *Southern Sidelights*. New York: Crowell, 1896.

Ise, John. *The United States Forest Policy*. New Haven: Yale University Press, 1924.

Jack, Theodore H. *Sectionalism and Party Politics in Alabama, 1819-1842*. Menasha, Wisconsin: George Banta, 1919.

Jacobstein, Meyer. *The Tobacco Industry*. New York: Columbia University Studies, XXVI, 3, 1907.

James, Harlean. *Land Planning in the United States*. New York: Macmillan, 1926.

Jefferson, Mark. *Principles of Geography*. New York: Harcourt, Brace, 1926.

Jenkins, John Wilbur. *James B. Duke, Master Builder*. New York: Doran, 1927.

Johnson, Clifton. *Highways and Byways of the South*. New York: Macmillan, 1904.

Johnson, Guion Griffis. *A Social History of the Sea Islands*. Chapel Hill: University of North Carolina Press, 1930.

Johnson, W. H. *Cotton and Its Production*. London and New York: Macmillan, 1926.

Johnston, Mary. *Pioneers of the Old South*. New Haven: Yale University Press, 1921.

Jones, C. C. *The Dead Towns of Georgia*. Savannah: Morning News Steam Printing House, 1878.

Jones, H. A., and Rosa, J. T. *Truck Crop Plants*. New York: McGraw-Hill, 1928.

Jones, L. Rodwell, and Bryan, P. W. *North America: An Historical, Economic, and Regional Geography*. New York: Dial Press, 1929.

Jones, Sarah L. [pseud Hopley, Catherine Cooper]. *Life in the South*. London: Chapman & Hall, 1863.

Jones, W. D., and Whittersley, D. S. *Economic Geography*. Chicago: University of Chicago Press, 1925.

Jordon, David Starr, and H. E. *War's Aftermath*. Boston: Houghton Mifflin, 1914.

Keir, R. M. *Manufacturing Industries*. New York: Ronald Press, 1920.

Kelley, William. *The Old South and the New*. New York: Putnam, 1888.

Kemble, Frances. *Journal of a Residence on a Georgia Plantation in 1838-1839*. New York: Harper, 1863.

Kendrew, W. A. *Climate: A Treatise on the Principles of Weather and Climate*. Oxford: Clarendon Press, 1930.

Climate of the Continents. Oxford: Oxford University Press, 1922.

Kendrick, Burton. *Training of an American*. New York: Doubleday, 1928.

Kephart, Horace. *Our Southern Highlanders*. New York: Macmillan, 1922.

Killebrew, J. B. *Tobacco Leaf—Its Culture and Cure, Marketing and Manufacture*. New York: Orange Judd Company, 1897.

Kimball, Fiske. *Domestic Architecture in the American Colonies and Early Republic*. New York: Scribner, 1922.

King, Edward. *The Great South*. Hartford: American Publishing Company, 1875.

Koller, A. H. *The Theory of Environment*. Menasha, Wis.: George Banta, 1918.

Koontz, Louis F. *The Virginia Frontier, 1754-1763*. Baltimore: Johns Hopkins University Studies, XLIII, No. 2, 1925.

Köppen, W. *Die Klimate der Erde*. Berlin: W. de Gruyter & Co., 1923.

Kruif, Paul de. *Hunger Fighters*. New York: Harcourt, 1928.

Leake, H. Martin. *Land Tenure and Agricultural Production in the Tropics*. Cambridge, England: W. Heffer & Sons, 1927.

Leigh, Frances B. *Ten Years on a Georgia Plantation Since the War.* London: Bentley, 1883.

Leith, C. K. *The Economic Aspects of Geology.* New York: Holt, 1923.

Lippincott, Isaac. *Economic Development of the United States.* New York: Appleton, 1923.

Livermore, T. L. *Numbers and Losses in the Civil War.* New York: Houghton Mifflin, 1901.

Livingston, B. E., and Shieve, Forrest. *The Distribution of Vegetation in the United States as Related to Climatic Conditions.* Washington: Carnegie Institution, 1921.

Long, Howard. *Kingsport.* Kingsport, Tennessee: Sevier Press, 1928.

Longstreet, A. B. *Georgia Scenes.* New York: Harper, 1871.

Lowie, R. H. *Culture and Ethnology.* New York: Smith, 1929.

Lusk, Graham. *The Elements of the Science of Nutrition.* Philadelphia: W. B. Saunders, 1928.

Lyell, Sir Charles. *A Second Visit to the United States.* New York: Harper, 1849.

Lynd, Robert S., and Helen M. *Middletown.* New York: Harcourt, Brace, 1929.

Lyon, T. L., Flippin, E. O., and Buckman, H. O. *Soils, Their Properties and Management.* New York: Macmillan, 1915.

Macdonald, Lois. *Southern Mill Hills.* New York: Hillman, 1928.

MacKaye, Benton. *The New Exploration: A Philosophy of Regional Planning.* New York: Harcourt, Brace, 1928.

Marcossin, Isaac F. *The Black Golconda.* New York: Harpers, 1924.

Marsh, George Perkins. *The Earth as Modified by Human Action.* Rev. ed. New York: Scribner, 1885.

Martin, William E. *Internal Improvements in Alabama.* Baltimore: Johns Hopkins University Studies, XX, No. 4, 1902.

Martineau, Harriett. *Society in America.* London: Saunders & Otley, 1837.

Mathews, John L. *Remaking the Mississippi.* Boston: Houghton Mifflin, 1909.

McCollum, E. V. *The Newer Knowledge of Nutrition.* New York: Macmillan, 1922.

McLendon, S. G. *History of the Public Domain in Georgia.* Atlanta: Foote and Davies, 1924.

Mesick, Jane Louise. *America as Viewed by British Travellers, 1785-1835.* New York: Columbia University Press, 1922.

Meyer, B. H. (ed.) with associates. *History of Transportation in the*

United States before 1860. Washington: Carnegie Institute Publication 25, 1917.

Miles, Emma B. *The Spirit of the Mountains.* New York: James Patt & Company, 1905.

Miller, George J., and Parkins, A. E. *Geography of North America.* New York: Wiley, 1928.

Mims, Edwin. *The Advancing South.* New York: Doubleday, Page, 1926.

Mitchell, Broadus. *Rise of Cotton Mills in the South.* Baltimore: Johns Hopkins University Press, 1921.

Mitchell, Broadus, and George, S. *The Industrial Revolution in the South.* Baltimore: Johns Hopkins University Press, 1931.

Monette, John Wesley. *History of the Discovery and Settlement of the Valley of the Mississippi.* New York: Harper, 1846.

Monks, William. *History of Southern Missouri and Northern Arkansas.* West Plains, Mo.: 1907.

Montgomery, Robert H. *The Coöperative Pattern in Cotton.* New York: Macmillan, 1929.

Moore, John M. *The South Today.* New York: Missionary Education Movement of the United States and Canada, 1916.

Morley, Margaret W. *The Carolina Mountains.* Boston: Houghton Mifflin, 1913.

Morris, Charles. *Old South and New.* Philadelphia: John C. Winston Co., 1907.

Mukerjee, R. *Regional Sociology.* New York: Century, 1926.

Murchison, Claudius T. *King Cotton is Sick.* Chapel Hill: University of North Carolina Press, 1930.

Murphy, Edgar Gardner. *Problems of the Present South.* New York: Macmillan, 1904.

Nevins, Allan. *American Social History as Recorded by British Travellers.* New York: Holt, 1923.

Newbigin, M. I. *Animal Geography.* Oxford: Clarendon, 1913.
Man and His Conquest of Nature. London: Black, 1912.
Modern Geography. New York: Holt, 1911.
Regional Geography of the World. New York: Harcourt, Brace, 1929.

Nordhoff, Charles. *The Cotton States in the Spring and Summer of 1875.* New York: Appleton, 1876.

Nourse, E. G. *Agricultural Economics.* Chicago: University of Chicago Press, 1916.

Oberholtzer, E. P. *History of the United States Since the Civil War.* New York: Macmillan, 1917-1931.

Odum, Howard W. *An American Epoch. Southern Portraiture in the National Picture.* New York: Holt, 1930.

(ed.) *Southern Pioneers in Social Interpretation.* Chapel Hill: University of North Carolina Press, 1925.

Olmsted, Frederick Law. *A Journey Through Texas.* New York: Dix, Edwards & Co., 1857.

Journey in the Back Country. New York: Mason Brothers, 1860.

A Journey in the Seaboard Slave States. In the Years 1853-56 With Remarks on Their Economy. 2 v. New York: Reprint by Putnam, 1904.

Osborn, Herbert. *Agricultural Entomology.* Philadelphia: Lea and Febiger, 1916.

Otken, C. H. *The Ills of the South.* New York: Putnam, 1894.

Page, Walter Hines. *Rebuilding of Old Commonwealths.* New York: Doubleday, 1902.

Paxton, F. L. *History of the American Frontier, 1713-1893.* Boston: Houghton Mifflin, 1926.

Payne, Henry Mace. *Undeveloped Mineral Resources of the South.* Washington: American Mining Congress, 1928.

Peake, R. J. *Cotton from Raw Material to Finished Product.* New York: Pitman & Sons, 1921.

Pearl, Raymond. *The Nation's Food.* Philadelphia: W. B. Saunders, 1920.

Phaser, D. L. *A Farmer's Book of Grasses.* Starksville, Mississippi: 1881.

Phillips, Ulrich B. *American Negro Slavery.* New York: Appleton, 1918.

Documents of the Plantation and Frontier. 2 v. Cleveland: A. H. Clark, 1910.

"Georgia and States Rights." *American Historical Association Reports,* II, 1901.

A History of Transportation in the Eastern Cotton Belt to 1860. New York: Macmillan, 1908.

Life and Labor in the Old South. Boston: Little, Brown, 1929.

Phillips, U. B., and James, David (editors). *Florida Plantation Records from the Papers of George Noble James.* St. Louis: Missouri Historical Society, 1927.

Powell, Lyman P. (ed.) *Historic Towns of the Southern States.* New York: Putnam, 1900.

Powell, W. J. *Physiographic Regions of the United States.* National Geographical Monograph No. 3. New York: American Book Company, 1896.

Pretlow, Mary D. *Old Southern Receipts.* New York: McBride, 1930.

Pringle, Elizabeth W. A. *A Woman Rice Planter.* [By] Patience Pennington [Pseud.]. New York: Macmillan, 1913.

Ralph, Julian. *Dixie, or Southern Scenes.* New York: Harper, 1896.

Ramsdell, C. W. *Reconstruction in Texas.* New York: Columbia University Studies, XXXVI, No. 1.

Randolph, Vance. *The Ozarks.* New York: Vanguard, 1930.

Reid, Whitlaw. *After the War: A Southern Tour.* Cincinnati: Land, Sampson, 1866.

Reynolds, J. S. *Reconstruction in South Carolina, 1865-1877.* Columbia, S. C.: State Company, 1905.

Ridgely, D. C. *Geographic Principles.* Boston: Houghton Mifflin, 1925.

Riegel, Robert. *America Moves West.* New York: Holt, 1930.

Ripley, W. Z. *Races of Europe.* New York: Appleton, 1899.

Rivers, W. J. *History of South Carolina.* Charleston: McCarter, 1856.

Roberts, Isaac P. *The Fertility of the Land.* New York: Macmillan, 1911.

Roosevelt, Theodore. *The Winning of the West.* 6 v. New York: G. Putnam's Sons, 1900.

Russel, Robert Royal. *Economic Aspects of Southern Sectionalism.* Urbana: University of Illinois, 1924.

Russell, Edward J. *Soil Conditions and Plant Growth.* London: Longmans, Green, 1917.

Russell, Israel C. *North America.* New York: Appleton, 1904.

Russell, J. H. *The Free Negro in Virginia, 1669-1865.* Johns Hopkins University Studies, III, No. 3, 1913.

Salisbury, Rollin D., Borrows, H. H., and Tower, W. S. *Modern Geography.* New York: Holt, 1913.

Sanderson, Dwight (ed.). *Farm Income and Farm Life.* Chicago: University of Chicago Press, 1928.

Sanford, A. H. *Story of American Agriculture.* Boston: Heath, 1916.

Sargent, C. S. *The Silva of North America.* 14 v. Boston: Houghton Mifflin, 1891-1902.

Sauer, Carl O. *The Geography of the Ozark Highlands.* Chicago: Geographic Society of Chicago, 1920.

Saxon, Lyle. *Father Mississippi.* New York: Century, 1928.

Schafer, William A. *Sectionalism and Representation in South Carolina.* Reports American Historical Association, I. Washington: 1900.

Scherer, James A. B. *Cotton as a World Power.* New York: Frederick A. Stokes, 1916.

Schimper, A. F. W. *Plant Geography upon a Physiological Basis.* Oxford: Clarendon Press, 1903.

Schlesinger, Arthur M. *Political and Social History of the United States, 1829-1925.* New York: Macmillan, 1925.

Schmidt, Louis Bernard, and Ross, Earle Dudley. *Readings in the Economic History of American Agriculture.* New York: Macmillan, 1925.

Scott, Emmett J. *Negro Migration During the War.* New York: Oxford University Press, 1920.

Selph, F. E. *South in American Life and History.* 5007 Michigan Avenue, Nashville, Tenn.: Author.

Semple, Ellen C. *American History and its Geographic Conditions.* Boston: Houghton Mifflin, 1903.

Influences of Geographical Environment. New York: Holt, 1911.

Shaler, N. S. *Nature and Man in America.* New York: Scribner, 1891.

The United States of America. I. New York: Appleton, 1894.

Shanahan, E. W. *Animal Foodstuffs.* London: Rutledge, 1920.

Shants, H. L., and Marbut, C. F. *Vegetation and Soils of Africa.* New York: American Geographical Society, 1923.

Sherman, H. C. *Chemistry of Foods and Nutrition.* New York: Macmillan, 1927.

Sherman, Wells A. *Merchandising Fruits and Vegetables.* New York: Shaw, 1928.

Shryock, R. H. *Georgia and the Union in 1850.* Durham, N. C.: Duke University Press, 1926.

Simkins, Frances Butler. *The Tillman Movement in South Carolina.* Durham, N. C.: Duke University Press, 1926.

Simkins, Frances Butler, and Woody, R. H. *South Carolina During Reconstruction.* Chapel Hill: University of North Carolina Press, 1932.

Skinner, Constance Lindsay. *Pioneers of the Old Southwest.* New Haven: Yale University Press, 1919.

Small, J. K. *Flora of the Southeastern United States.* New York: Author, 1903.

Smith, J. Russell. *Human Geography.* 3 v. Philadelphia: Winston, 1922.

North America. New York: Harcourt, Brace, 1925.

The Story of Iron and Steel. New York: Appleton, 1908.

Tree Crops. New York: Harcourt, Brace, 1929.

Sorokin, Pitirim. *Contemporary Sociological Theories.* New York: Harper, 1928.

South in the Building of the Nation, Economic History: 1607-1909, V, VI. Richmond: Southern History Publishing Co., 1909.

Southern Economic Problems. New York: American Economic Association Publications, 3d series, V, 1, 1904.

Spaulding, Arthur W. *The Men of the Mountains.* Nashville: Southern Publishing Company, 1915.

Spencer, Herbert. *Essays, Scientific, Political, and Speculative.* III. New York: Appleton, 1883.

Spillman, W. J. *Balancing the Farm Output.* New York: Orange Judd, 1928.

Farm Management. New York: Orange Judd, 1923.

Staples, T. S. *Reconstruction in Arkansas 1862-1874.* New York: Columbia University Studies, CIX, 1923.

Stewart, Charles L. *Tenant Farming in the United States with Special Reference to Illinois.* Urbana: University of Illinois Studies in the Social Sciences, V, No. 3.

Stocking, George Ward. *The Oil Industry.* Boston: Houghton Mifflin, 1925.

Stoddard, Amos. *Sketches of Louisiana.* Philadelphia: Carey, 1812.

Street, Julian. *American Adventures; A Second Trip Abroad at Home.* New York: Century, 1917.

Sullivan, Mark. *Our Times.* III. New York: Scribner's, 1931.

Surface, George Thomas. *Studies on the Geography of Virginia.* Philadelphia: Ph.D. Thesis University of Pennsylvania, 1907.

Tannenbaum, Frank. *Darker Phases of the South.* New York: Putnam, 1924.

Tanner, H. S. *Travelling Guide, A Map of the Roads, Canals and Steamboat Routes of the United States.* Philadelphia: The Author, 1825.

Tarr, Ralph S., and Von Englin, O. D. *New Physical Geography.* New York: Macmillan, 1926.

Taylor, Henry C. *Outlines of Agricultural Economics.* New York: Macmillan, 1919.

Teele, R. P. *The Economics of Land Reclamation in the United States.* Chicago: A. W. Shaw Co., 1927.

Thoburn, Joseph Bendfeld. *A Standard History of Oklahoma.* 5 v. Chicago and New York: American Historical Society, 1908.

Thomas, Franklin. *The Environmental Basis of Society.* New York: Century, 1925.

Thompson, C. Mildred. *Reconstruction in Georgia.* New York: Columbia University Studies, LXIV.

Thompson, Holland. *From Cotton Field to Cotton Mill*. New York: Macmillan, 1906.

   The New South. New Haven: Yale University Press, 1921.

Thompson, Samuel H. *The Highlanders of the South*. New York: Eaton and Mains, 1910.

Thompson, Warren S. *Population Problems*. New York: McGraw-Hill, 1930.

Todd, John A. *The World's Cotton Crops*. London: Black, 1924.

   The Cotton World. London: Pitman, 1927.

Tome, Philip. *Pioneer Life, or Thirty Years a Hunter*. Buffalo, 1854.

Tompkins, D. A. *Cotton and Cotton Oil*. Charlotte, North Carolina: D. A. Tompkins, 1903.

Trent, Paxon. *The National Land System, 1785-1820*. New York: E. B. Treat & Company, 1910.

Trowbridge, J. T. *The South*. Hartford: L. Stebbins, 1866.

Tuckerman, Henry T. *America and Her Commentators*. New York: Scribners, 1864.

Turner, F. J. *The Frontier in American History*. New York: Holt, 1921.

   The Rise of the New West. New York: Harper, 1906.

Turner, F. J., and Merk, F. *List of References on the History of the West*, rev. ed. Cambridge: Harvard University Press, 1922.

Turpin, Edna. *Cotton*. New York: American Book Company, 1924.

Twelve Southerners. *I'll Take My Stand*. New York: Harper, 1931.

Unstead, J. F., and Taylor, E. G. R. *General and Regional Geography*. London: G. Philips and Sons, 1911.

Vallaux, C. *Le Sol et L'etat*. Paris: Octave Dain et Fils, 1911.

Vance, Rupert B. *Human Factors in Cotton Culture*. Chapel Hill: University of North Carolina Press, 1929.

Van Dusen, John George. *Economic Bases of Disunion in South Carolina*. New York: Columbia University Studies, 305, 1928.

Van Hise, Charles R. *The Conservation of Natural Resources in the United States*. (Rev. ed. by L. Havemeyer, 1931.) New York: Macmillan, 1913.

Verhoeff, Mary. *The Kentucky Mountains, Transportation and Commerce, 1750 to 1911; a Study on the Economic History of a Coal Field*. Filson Club Publication 26. Louisville: J. P. Morton, 1911.

   The Kentucky River Navigation. Filson Club Publication 28. Louisville: John P. Morton, 1917.

Von Englin, O. D. *Inheriting the Earth, or The Geographic Factor in National Development*. New York: Macmillan, 1922.

Voorhees, Edward B. *Fertilizers*. New York: Macmillan, 1907.

Voskuil, Walter H. *The Economics of Water Power*. Chicago: A. W. Shaw, 1928.

Minerals in Modern Society. New York: John Wiley, 1930.

Walker, Cornelius I. *History of the Agricultural Society of South Carolina Founded August 24, 1785 at Charles Town*. Charleston, S. C., 1919.

Ward, Robert DeC. *Climate Considered Especially in Relation to Man*. New York: G. P. Putnam, 1918.

The Climates of the United States. Boston: Ginn, 1925.

Warren, C. D. *Studies in the South and West*. New York: Harper, 1889.

Warren, G. F. *Farm Management*. New York: Macmillan, 1919.

Warren, G. F., and Pearson, F. A. *The Agricultural Situation*. New York: Wiley, 1924.

Warshaw, H. T. (ed.). *Representative Industries in the United States*. New York: Holt, 1928.

Weaver, Charles Clinton. *Internal Improvements in North Carolina Previous to 1860*. Baltimore: Johns Hopkins Press, 1903.

Webb, Walter Prescott. *The Great Plains*. Boston: Ginn, 1931.

Weeden, W. B. *Economic and Social History of New England*. American Historical Association Reports, II, 860. 1891.

Wertenbaker, T. J. *The First Americans, 1607-1690*. New York: Macmillan, 1927.

Patrician and Plebian in Virginia. Charlottesville: Michie, 1910.

The Planters of Colonial Virginia. Princeton: Princeton University Press, 1922.

Wesley, Charles H. *Negro Labor in the United States*. New York: Vanguard, 1927.

White, George. *Statistics of Georgia*. Savannah: W. T. Williams, 1849.

Whitney, Milton. *Soil and Civilization*. New York: D. Van Nostrand, 1925.

Williams, Martha. *Dishes and Beverages of the Old South*. New York: Robert M. McBride, 1913.

Williams, S. C. *History of the Lost State of Franklin*. Johnson City, Tennessee, 1924.

Beginnings of West Tennessee. Johnson City, Tennessee, 1930.

Wilson, Samuel Tyndale. *The Southern Mountaineers*. New York: Literature Department, Presbyterian Home Missions, 1906.

Winsor, Justin. *The Westward Movement*. Boston: Houghton Mifflin, 1897.

Winston, G. T. *A Builder of the New South. D. A. Tompkins.* New York: Doubleday, Page, 1920.

Wolfanger, Louis A. *The Major Soil Divisions of the United States.* New York: Wiley, 1930.

Woofter, T. J., Jr. *Black Yeomanry.* New York: Holt, 1930.

Negro Migration. New York: Hillman, 1920.

The Plight of Cigarette Tobacco. Chapel Hill: University of North Carolina Press, 1931.

Wortham, Louis J. *A History of Texas from Wilderness to Commonwealth.* 5 v. Fort Worth: Wortham-Molyreaux, 1924.

Wright, Philip G. *Sugar in Relation to the Tariff.* New York: McGraw-Hill, 1924.

Zon, Raphael, and Sparhawk, William, *Forest Resources of the World.* New York: McGraw-Hill, 1923.

PERIODICALS

Adams, Ephraim Douglas. "The Point of View of the British Traveller in America." *Political Science Quarterly,* XXIX, 244-64 (June, 1914).

Adams, G. I. "Course of the Tennessee River and the Physiography of the Southern Appalachian Region." *Journal of Geology,* XXXVI, 481-93 (August, 1928).

Adams, S. H. "Battle of New Orleans Against the Mosquito." *McClure's,* XXVII, 178-92 (June, 1906).

Adams, Thomas. "The Social Objective in Regional Planning." *National Municipal Review,* XV, 79-87 (1926).

Adsit, C. G. "The Interconnected Power Systems of the Southeast." *Proceedings,* American Society of Civil Engineers, L, 1286-1302 (October, 1924); L, 1527-32 (November, 1924).

Albrecht, A. E. "Development of the American Rice Industry." *Journal of Geography,* XXI, 294-99 (November, 1922).

Allen, C. E. "Greater Agricultural Efficiency for the Black Belt of Alabama." *Annals,* American Academy of Political and Social Science, LXI, 187-98 (September, 1915).

Allen, J. A. "The Geographical Distribution of North American Animals." American Museum of Natural History, *Bulletin No. 1892.*

Anderson, W. S. "Future of the Mountain Home." *Mountain Life and Work,* VI, 20-23 (January, 1931).

Angoff, Charles, and Mencken, H. L. "The Worst American State." *American Mercury,* XXIV, 1-16; 175-88; 355-71 (September, October, November, 1931).

Armsby, H. P. "Cost of Roast Pig." *Science*, XLVI, 160-62 (August, 17, 1917).

Arnold, John J. "Financing of Cotton." *Annals*, American Academy of Political and Social Science, XXXVIII, 599-609 (September, 1911).

Ashe, W. W. "Forest Conditions in Southern States and Recommended Forest Policy." *South Atlantic Quarterly*, XXII, 295-303 (October, 1923).

"The Place of the Eastern National Forests in the National Economy." *Geographical Review*, XIII, 532-39 (October, 1923).

"Soil Erosion and Forest Cover in Relation to Water Power in the Southeast." *Engineering World*, XXIII, 73 (August, 1923).

"The Waste from Soil Erosion in the South." *Review of Reviews*, XXXIX, 439-43 (April, 1909).

Augustine, Donald L. "Hookworm Disease in Cotton Mill Villages of Alabama and Georgia." *Journal of Industrial Hygiene*, VIII, 382-91 (September, 1926).

Augustine, Donald L., and Smillie, Wilson G. "The Relation of the Types of Soils of Alabama to the Distribution of Hookworm Disease." *American Journal of Hygiene*, VI, 36-62 (March Supplement, 1926).

Aurouseau, M. "Recent Contributions to Urban Geography." *Geographical Review*, XIV, 444-55 (July, 1924).

Ayers, P. W. "Forest Preservation in the Eastern Mountains." *Review of Reviews*, LXI, 411-15 (April, 1920).

Bacot, D. Huger, Jr. "The South Carolina Up Country at the End of the Eighteenth Century." *American Historical Review*, XXVIII, 682-98 (July, 1923).

Baird, E. F. "In Food also a New Fashion is Here." *New York Times Sunday Magazine*, p. 10-11, (May 4, 1930).

Baker, O. E. "The Agricultural Regions of North America." *Economic Geography*, (October, 1926, January, July, October, 1927, January, October, 1928, January, 1929, April, 1930) II: 459-93; III: 50-86; 309-39; 447-65; IV: 44-73; 399-433; V: 36-69; VI: 166-90. With following installment titles: 1. The Basis of Classification; 2. The South; 3. The Middle Country Where South and North Meet; 4. The Corn Belt; 5. The Hog and Dairy Belt; 6. The Spring Wheat Region; 7. The Middle Atlantic Trucking Region; 8. The Pacific Subtropical Crops Region.

"The Agriculture of the Great Plains Region." *Annals*, Association of American Geographers, XIII, 109-67 (September, 1923).

"The Increasing Importance of Physical Conditions in Determining the Utilization of Land for Agricultural and Forest Production in the United States." *Annals,* Association of American Geographers, XI, 17-46 (1921).

"Land Utilization in the United States. Geographic Aspects of the Problem." *Geographical Review,* XIII, 1-26 (January, 1923).

"Population, Food Supply and American Agriculture." *Geographical Review,* XVIII, 353-73 (July, 1928).

See *Atlas of American Agriculture.*

Balfour, J. A. "Historical Aspects of Malaria." *Nature,* CXV, 17-20 (January 3, 1925).

Barrow, D. C. "A Georgia Plantation." *Scribner's Magazine,* XX, 830 (April, 1881).

Barrows, H. H. "Geography as Human Ecology." *Annals,* Assocation of American Geographers, XIII, 1-14 (1923).

Bean, L. H., and Stine, O. C. "Income from Agricultural Production." *Annals,* American Academy, CXVII, 27-34 (January, 1925).

Beard, J. H. "The Gastronomy of Colonel Carter of Cartersville. *Scientific Monthly,* XXVI, 246-49 (April, 1928).

Bennett, H. H. "The Increased Cost of Soil Erosion." *The Annals,* American Academy of Science, CXLII, 142 (March, 1929).

"Uncle Sam Spendthrift." *Scientific American,* CXXXVI, 237-39 (April, 1927).

"Soil Conservation." *Review of Reviews,* LXXV, 303-306 (March, 1927).

"Wasting Heritage of the Nation." *Scientific Monthly,* XXVII, 97-124 (August, 1928).

Bernard, L. L. "A Classification of Environments." *American Journal of Sociology,* XXXI, 318-32, (November, 1925).

Berry, Harriet. "Road to Fulfillment." *Mountain Life and Work,* III, 2-8 (January, 1928).

Berry, Katherine. "Differential Fertility According to Geographic Areas in the United States." *Quarterly Bulletin,* Milbank Memorial Fund, IX, 79-94 (July, 1931).

Bizzell, W. B. "Rural Housing and the Tenant Farmer." *Survey,* XLIV, 26-28 (April 3, 1920).

Bjorkman, Francis M. "The Cure for Two Million Sick." *World's Work,* XVIII, 11607-11 (May, 1909).

Blanchard, Raoul. "Geographical Conditions in Water Power Development." *Geographical Review,* XIV, 88-100 (January, 1924).

Blanchard, W. O. "Malaria as a Factor in Italian Environment." *Scientific Monthly*, XXVII, 172-76 (August, 1928).

Bogart, E. L. "The Bright Side of Tenancy Statistics." *Journal of Political Economy*, XVI, 201 (April, 1908).

Boucher, Chauncey Samuel. "The Ante-Bellum Attitude of South Carolina Towards Manufacturing and Agriculture." *Washington University Studies*, III, 243-70 (April, 1916).

Bowman, Isaiah. "Pioneer Fringe." *Foreign Affairs*, VI, 49-66 (October, 1927).

Bradley, Frances Sage. "A Survey of Conditions Affecting Children of Bradley County, Arkansas." *Social Forces*, I, 296-99 (March, 1923).

Brearley, H. C. "Homicides in South Carolina: A Regional Study." *Social Forces*, VIII, 218-21 (December, 1929).

Bretz, J. P. "Early Land Communication with the Lower Mississippi Valley." *Mississippi Valley Historical Review*, XIII, 3-29 (June, 1926).

Brigham, A. P. "Environment in the History of American Agriculture." *Journal of Geography*, XXI, 41-49 (February, 1922).

"The Eastern Gateway of the United States." *Geographical Journal*, XIII, 513-24 (May, 1899).

"The Great Roads Across the Appalachians." American Geographical Society, *Bulletin*, XXXVII, 321-339 (1905).

Brooks, Robert Preston. "The American Cotton Association." *South Atlantic Quarterly*, XIX, 97-108 (April, 1920).

Brown, L. "Flood Control Works on the Mississippi." *Scientific Monthly*, XXX, 481-99 (June, 1930).

Brown, Ralph H. "Muscle Shoals: A Study in the Utilization of Resources." *Journal of Geography*, XXIV, 30-34 (1925).

Brown, Robert M. "Cotton Manufacturing: North and South." *Economic Geography*, IV, 74-87 (January, 1926).

"The Mississippi River as a Trade Route." *Bulletin*, American Geographical Society, XXXVIII, 294-354 (1908).

"Our Waterway Requirements." *Geographical Review*, V, 119-26 (1918).

"The Protection of the Alluvial Basin of the Mississippi." *Popular Science Monthly*, LXIX, 248-56 (September, 1906).

Browne, W. A. "The Lower Mississippi as a Waterway." *Journal of Geography*, XXIX, 155-62 (April, 1930).

Bruere, Robert W. "Giant Power—Region Builder." *The Survey*, LIV, 161-64 (May 1, 1925).

Buck, P. H. "Poor Whites of the Old South." *American Historical Review*, XXX, 41-548 (October, 1924).

Burchard, E. F. "Alabama Ores Equal Lake Supply." *Iron Age*, CXIX, 847-50 (March 24, 1927).

Burton, Harley True. "A History of the J. A. Ranch." *Southwestern Historical Quarterly*, XXXI, 89-115, 221-60 (October, 1927, January, 1928).

Butler, Louise. "The Louisiana Planter and His Home." *Louisiana Historical Quarterly*, X, 355-63 (July, 1927).

Buttrick, P. L. "Forest Growth on Abandoned Agricultural Land." *Scientific Monthly*, V, 80-91 (July, 1917).

Bynum, Jefferson. "Piedmont North Carolina and Textile Production." *Economic Geography*, IV, 222-40 (July, 1928).

Callander, Guy S. "The Early Transportation and Banking Enterprises of the States in Relation to the Growth of Corporations." *Quarterly Journal of Economics*, XVII, 111-62 (November, 1902).

Campbell, Edna F. "New Orleans at the Time of the Louisiana Purchase." *Geographical Review*, XI, 414-25 (July, 1921).

Campbell, Marius R. "How Long Will the Coal Reserves of the United States Last?" *National Geographic Magazine*, XVIII, 129-138 (February, 1907).

Carney, F. "Springs as a Geographic Influence in Humid Climate." *Popular Science*, LXXII, 503-11 (June, 1908).

Carson, W. Wallace. "Transportation and Traffic on the Ohio and Mississippi Before the Steamboat." *Mississippi Valley Historical Review*, VII, 26-38 (June, 1920).

Carver, G. W. "Need of Scientific Agriculture in the South." *Review of Reviews*, XXV, 320-22 (March, 1902).

Cason, Clarence E. "Alabama Goes Industrial." *Virginia Quarterly Review*, VI, 161-70 (April, 1930).

Cates, J. Sidney. "Cotton at the Crossroads." *Country Gentleman*, XCV, 3-5 (August, 1930).

"The Plant That Stole the Show." *Country Gentleman*, CII, 3-5 (February, 1932).

Cauley, T. J. "The Cost of Marketing Texas Cattle in the Old Trail Days." *Journal of Farm Economics*, IX, 356-60 (July, 1927).

"Early Meat Packing Plants in Texas." *Southwest Political and Social Science Quarterly*, IX, 464-78 (March, 1929).

Cavanaugh, Frank J. "Financing the Cotton Farmer." *Acceptance Bulletin* 10 (September 29, 1928).

Chamberlin, T. C. "Soil Productivity." *Science,* XXXIII, 225-227 (February 10, 1911).

Chambers, William T. "Divisions of the Pine Forest Belt of East Texas." *Economic Geography,* VI, 94-103 (January, 1930).

"The Gulf Port Region of Texas." *Economic Geography,* VII, 69-83 (January, 1931).

"Lower Rio Grande Valley of Texas." *Economic Geography,* VI, 364-73 (October, 1930).

Chapman, H. H. "Why the Town of McNary Moved." *American Forestry,* XXX, 589-92 (October, 1924).

Cheyney, E. G. "Passing of an Industry: An Epic of the Great American Forest." *American Forestry,* XXVIII, 323-38 (June, 1922).

Chisholm, G. G. "Generalization in Geography, Especially Human Geography." *Scottish Geographical Magazine,* XXXII, 507-19 (1916).

"Is the Increasing Control of Man Over Nature Making Him Independent of Geographical Conditions?" *Scottish Geographical Magazine,* XXXII, 257-65 (1916).

Clark, D. T. "Live Stock Trade Between Kentucky and the South, 1840-1860." *Kentucky State Historical Society Register,* XXVII, 567-81 (September, 1929).

Clark, Ivan S. "An Isolated Industry: The Potteries of North Carolina." *Journal of Geography,* XXV, 222-28 (September, 1926).

Clark, N. M. "Birmingham, the Next Capitol of the Steel Age." *World's Work,* LIII, 536-45 (March, 1927).

Cleland, Herdman F. "Black Belt of Alabama." *The Geographical Review,* X, 375-87 (December, 1920).

Clonts, F. W. "Travel and Transportation in Colonial North Carolina." *North Carolina Historical Review,* III, 16-35 (January, 1926).

Cole, A. H. "American Rice Growing Industry: A Study in Comparative Advantage." *Quarterly Journal of Economics,* XLI, 595-643 (August, 1927).

Cooke, M. L. "Giant Power and Coal." *Annals,* American Academy of Political and Social Science, CXI, 212-18 (January, 1924).

Coman, Katherine. "The Negro as Peasant Farmer." American Statistical Association, *Publications,* IX, 39-54 (June, 1904).

Condra, G. E. "Opening of the Indian Territory." *Bulletin,* American Geographical Society, XXXIX, 321-40 (June, 1907).

Congressional Digest, "Muscle Shoals," II (1) (October, 1922); "Inland Waterways," III (12) (September, 1924); "Mississippi Flood Control," VII (2) (February, 1928).

Connor, L. G. "A Brief History of the Sheep Industry of the United States." *Annual Report,* American Historical Association, I, 97-197 (1918).

Connor, R. D. W. "The Rehabilitation of a Rural Commonwealth." *American Historical Review,* XXXVI, 44-62 (October, 1930).

Cope, J. A. "Progress Report on the Reseeding of Cut-Over Lands to Loblolly Pine." *Journal of Forestry,* XXII, 171-74 (February, 1924).

Cotterill, R. S. "The Beginnings of Railroads in the Southwest." *Mississippi Valley Historical Review,* VIII, 318-26 (March, 1927).

"The Natchez Trace." *Tennessee Historical Magazine,* VII, 27-35 (April, 1921).

"Southern Railroads and Western Trade." *Mississippi Valley Historical Review,* IV, 427-41 (March, 1917).

"Southern Railroads." *Mississippi Valley Historical Review,* X, 396-405 (March, 1924).

Cottle, H. J. "Studies in the Vegetation of Southwestern Texas." *Ecology,* XII, 105-55 (January, 1931).

Coulter, E. Merton. "A Century of a Georgia Plantation." *Agricultural History,* III, 159 (October, 1929).

Coulter, John Lee. "The Rural South." *Publications,* American Statistical Association, XIII, 54 (1914).

Cox, Alonzo B. "American Cotton in World Affairs." *Southwestern Social and Political Science Quarterly,* VI, 305-19 (March, 1926).

"New Cotton Areas for Old." *Southwestern Political and Social Science Quarterly,* VIII, 49-60 (June, 1927).

Cox, H. I. "Weather Conditions and Thermal Belts in the North Carolina Mountain Region." *Annals,* American Association of Geographers, X, 57 (1920).

Crane, C. R. "Some Aspects of the History of West and Northwest Texas Since 1845." *Southwestern Historical Quarterly,* XXVI, 30-43 (July, 1922).

Craven, A. O. "The Agricultural Reformers of the Ante Bellum South." *American Historical Review,* XXXIII, 302-14 (January, 1928).

Crawford, Bruce. "Whose Prosperity?" *Virginia Quarterly Review,* V, 325-35 (July, 1929).

Crittenden, Charles. "Bud Flat as a Type Area of River Flats on the Cumberland." Michigan Academy of Science, Arts, and Letters, *Papers,* X, 149-59 (1928).

Curlee, Abigail. "History of a Texas Slave Plantation, 1831-1863." *Southwestern Historical Quarterly,* XXVI, 79-127 (October, 1922).

Curtis, H. H. "Fertilizer: The World Supply." *Foreign Affairs*, II, 436-45 (March, 1924).

Dabney, T. E. "Economic Conditions in the Southern States." *Bankers' Monthly*, CII, 675-81 (April, 1921).

Dale, Edward Everett. "The Cherokee Strip Live Stock Association." Southwest Political and Social Science Association, *Proceedings*, V, 97-115 (1924).

"The Ranchman's Last Frontier." *Mississippi Valley Historical Review*, X, 34-46 (June, 1923).

Dale, F. A. "Dix River Hydro-Electric Development." *Electrical World*, LXXXVI, 939-42 (November 7, 1925).

Daniel, W. M. "Slave Plantation in Retrospect." *Atlantic Monthly*, CVII, 363-69 (March, 1911).

Darling, S. T. "Distribution of Hookworm in the Zoölogical Regions." *Science*, n. s., LIII, 323-24 (April 8, 1921).

Davidson, Philip G. "Industrialism in the Ante Bellum South." *South Atlantic Quarterly*, XXVII, 405-25 (October, 1928).

Davis, D. H. "The Blue Grass Region of Kentucky." *Journal of Geography*, XXV, 121-36 (April, 1926).

"The Changing Rôle of the Kentucky Mountains and the Passing of the Mountaineer." *Journal of Geography*, XXIV, 41-52 (February, 1925).

Davis, W. M. "The Progress of Geography in the United States." *Annals*, Association of American Geographers, XIV, 159-215 (December, 1924).

Dawson, C. A. "Population Areas and Physiographic Regions in Canada." *American Journal of Sociology*, XXXIII, 43-56 (July, 1927).

Dice, L. R. "Biotic Areas and Biological Habitats as Units for the Statement of Animal and Plant Distribution." *Science*, LV, 335-38 (March, 1922).

Dimock, A. W. "Southern Industrial Experiment." *Harper's*, III, 302-8 (July, 1905).

Dobie, J. Frank. "Ranch Mexicans." *Survey*, LXVI, 167-70 (May 1, 1931).

"The Mexican Vaquero of the Texas Border." *Southwest Political and Social Science Quarterly*, VIII, 15-26 (June, 1927).

Dodge, R. E. "Some Geographic Relations Illustrated in the Practice of Agriculture." *Bulletin*, American Geographical Society, XLIV, 277-82 (1912).

Dorris, Fern Ellison. "The Yazoo Basin in Mississippi." *Journal of Geography*, XXVIII, 72-79 (February, 1929).

Dowling, O. "Sociological Aspect of Hookworm Disease." *American Journal of Public Health*, X, 995-98 (July, 1920).

Dryer, Charles R. "Genetic Geography." *Annals*, Association of American Geographers, X, 3-16 (March, 1920).

"Regional Geography." *Journal of Geography*, XI, 73-75 (November, 1912).

Dupont, Charles H. "History of the Introduction and Culture of Cuba Tobacco in Florida." *Florida Historical Society Quarterly*, VI, 149-55 (January, 1928).

Eberling, Ernest J. "A Social Interpretation: Tennessee." *Social Forces*, V, 19-31 (September, 1926).

"Economic Future of the South." *Harper's Weekly*, LI, 795 (June 1, 1907).

Edmonds, R. H. "South's Resources: Their Development, Past, Present, and Future." *Review of Reviews*, LXXIII, 387-95 (April, 1926).

Edwards, Thomas J. "The Tenant System and Some Changes Since Emancipation." *Annals*, American Academy of Political and Social Science, XLIX, 38-46 (September, 1913).

Eldridge, S. F. "Management of Southern Pine for Naval Stores." *Journal of Forestry*, XXIX, 328-33 (March, 1931).

Eijkman, C. "Some Questions Concerning the Influence of the Tropics on Man." *The Lancet*, CCVI, 887-93 (1924).

Ekblaw, W. Elmer. "The Geographic Surveys of Kentucky." *Economic Geography*, IV, 385-98 (October, 1928).

Ellis, L. B. "Growth of the Sugar Industry in the South." *Bankers' Magazine*, LXXXII, 238-41 (February, 1911).

Emerson, F. V. "Geographic Influences in American Slavery." *Bulletin*, American Geographic Society, XLIII, 13-26, 166-118, 170-181 (1911).

"Geographic Influences in the Mississippi Valley." Mississippi Valley Historical Society, *Proceedings*, VIII, 289-96 (1914-15).

"Southern Long-Leaf Pine Belt." *Geographical Review*, VII, 81-90 (February, 1919).

Estabrook, Arthur H. "The Population of the Ozarks." *Mountain Life and Work*, V, 2-3, 25-28 (April, 1929).

"Is there a Mountain Problem? *Mountain Life and Work*, IV, 5-13 (April, 1928).

Eutsler, Roland B. "Transportation Developments and Industrial Changes." *Annals*, American Academy of Political and Social Science, CLIII, 202-9 (January, 1931).

Faris, Ellsworth. "The Origin of Punishment." *International Journal of Ethics*, XXV, 54-67 (October, 1914).

Farmer, Hallie. "The Economic Background of Frontier Populism."
Mississippi Valley Historical Review, X, 406-27 (March, 1924).

"The Economic Background of Southern Populism." *South Atlantic
Quarterly*, XXIX, 77-92 (January, 1930).

Fenneman, Nevin M. "The Circumference of Geography." *Geographical Review*, XII, 168-75 (1919).

"Physiographic Boundaries Within the United States." *Annals*, Association of American Geographers, IV, 84-134 (1914).

"Physiographic Divisions of the United States." *Annals*, Association
of American Geographers, VI, 19-98 (1916).

Fernow, B. E. "The Relation of Forests to Our Civilization." University of California, *Journal of Agriculture*, IV, 75-76 (1916).

Ferrell, J. A. "Challenge of Malaria in the South." *American Journal
of Public Health*, XX, 623-27 (June, 1930).

"The Trend of Preventive Medicine in the United States." Reprint
Journal of American Medical Association, LXXXI (September 20,
1922).

"North Carolina Campaign Against Hookworm." *South Atlantic
Quarterly*, XX, 276-97 (June, 1905).

Finley, W. W. "The Railroad's Work in the South." *World's Work*,
XIV, 8953-4 (July, 1907).

Flanders, Ralph B. "Two Plantations and a County of Ante Bellum
Georgia." *Georgia Historical Quarterly*, XII, 1-37 (March, 1928).

Fleming, W. L. "Immigration to Southern States." *Political Science
Quarterly*, XX, 276-97 (June, 1905).

"Industrial Reorganization in Alabama After the Civil War." *American Journal of Sociology*, X, 473-500 (January, 1905).

Florence, Howard. "Black Gold in Oklahoma." *Review of Reviews*,
LXXX, 142-44 (September, 1929).

Forbes, A. C. "Quality of Soils in Relation to Food and Timber Supply." *Nature*, CXXII, 54-55 (July 14, 1928).

Forbes, R. D. "The Passing of the Piney Woods." *American Forestry*,
XXIX, 131-36 (March, 1923).

Forsling, C. L. "Grazing in Pine Plantations." *Journal of Forestry*,
XXIII, 905-8 (November, 1925).

Forsyth, C. H. "Longevity in the Southern States." *Science*, n. s.
LVII, 490-93 (April 27, 1923).

Forsythe, John. "The North and the South." *De Bow's Review*, XVII,
361-78 (October, 1854).

Fort, Franklin W. "Decline in Purchasing Power of the American
Farmer Since 1900." *Proceedings*, Academy of Political and Social
Science, XII, 689-93 (1926-28).

Frankenfield, H. C. et al. "Floods of 1927 in the Mississippi Basin." *Monthly Weather Review,* Supplement No. 29.

Friday, David R. "The Course of Agricultural Income During the Last Twenty-five Years." *American Economic Review,* Supplement, March, 1923, pp. 147-58.

Frissell, Sidney D. "Southern Farmer Tries Coöperative Marketing." *Review of Reviews,* LXV, 59-63 (January, 1923).

Furches, M. J. "Crop Rotation in Relation to Southern Agriculture." *Journal,* American Society of Agronomy, XIX, 555-65 (June, 1927).

Gabbard, L. P. "Effect of Large Scale Production on Cotton Growing in Texas." *Journal of Farm Economics,* X, 211-24 (April, 1928).

Gamble, T. "Naval Stores Industry of the South." *Manufacturer's Record,* LXXXVI, Part II, 325-26 (December 11, 1924).

Garnett, E. B. "Oil is King in the Texas Panhandle." *World's Work,* LV, 168-74 (December, 1927).
"When the Oil Boom Hit the Panhandle." *World Today,* LI, 452-58 (March, 1928).

Geddes, Patrick. "Valley Plan of Civilization." *Survey,* LIV, 288-90 (June 1, 1925).

Geller, Carl. "Fewer Acres and More Dollars." *Commerce and Finance,* XVI, 123 (January 12, 1927).

Gemmill, Paul F. "Agriculture of the Eastern Shore Country." *Economic Geography,* II, 197-212 (April, 1926).

Gerry, E. "Naval Stores: Treasures of the Living Pines." *American Forestry,* XXIX, 72-74 (February, 1923).

Gibbons, Charles E. "Farm Children in Oklahoma." *Child Labor Bulletin* (May, 1918).

Giddings, F. H. "A Theory of Social Causation." *Publications,* American Economic Association, third series, Volume V, pp. 139-99, 1904.

GilFillan, S. C. "The Coldward Course of Progress." *Political Science Quarterly,* XXXV, 393-410 (September, 1920).

Gist, F. W. "Practical Crop Diversification in the Southern United States." *Commerce and Finance,* XVI, 115-7 (January 12, 1927).

Goldenweiser, A. A. "Meteorological Magic." *New Review,* 164-65 (May, 1916).

Gould, Charles N. "Oklahoma, an Example of Arrested Development." *Economic Geography,* II, 426-50 (July, 1926).

Grady, Henry W. "Cotton and Its Kingdom." *Harper's Magazine,* LXIII, 719-34 (October, 1881).
"Era of Speculation in the South." *New York Ledger* (1889).

Gras, N. S. B. "Regionalism and Nationalism." *Foreign Affairs*, VII, 454-67 (April, 1929).

Graves, L. M. "Interest and Taxes in Relation to Farm Income." *Annals*, American Academy of Political and Social Science, CXVII, 35-40 (January, 1925).

Graves, Ralph A. "Marching Through Georgia Sixty Years After." *National Geographic*, L, 259-311 (September, 1923).

Gray, John H. "The Dilemma of Giant Power Regulation." *Annals*, American Academy of Political and Social Science, CXXIX, 110-17 (January, 1927).

Gray, L. C. "Accumulation of Wealth by Farmers." *Proceedings*, American Economic Association, V, 158-78 (March, 1923).

"Objectives and Progress of the Economic and Social Survey of the Southeastern Appalachians." *Mountain Life and Work*, VI, 132 (July, 1931).

Greely, A. W. "Rainfall Types of the United States." *National Geographic Magazine*, V, 45-58 (April 29, 1893).

Greeley, W. B. "Economic Aspects of Forestry." *Journal of Land and Public Utility Economics*, I, 129-37 (April, 1925).

"The Relation of Geography to Timber Supply." *Economic Geography*, I, 1-14 (March, 1925).

Greene, S. W. "Forests that Fire Made: Longleaf Forests of the South." *American Forestry*, XXXVII, 583-84 (October, 1931).

Greever, G. "Southern Leadership Since the Civil War." *North American Review*, 192, pp. 264-72 (August, 1910).

Haas, W. H. "Mississippi River: Asset or Liability." *Economic Geography*, VII, 252-62 (July, 1931).

Halbrook, E. A. "The World's Present Fuel Resources." *Annals*, American Academy of Political and Social Science, CXI, 203-11 (January, 1924).

Halsey, F. M. "Southern Railway, Its Development and Future." *Moody's*, XIX, 245 (May, 1916).

Hamilton, J. G. de Roulhac. "Agricultural History Materials and Their Collection." *Agricultural History*, IV, 14-18 (January, 1930).

Hamilton, Peter J. "Early Southern Institutions." Southern Historical Association, *Publications*, II, 272 (1899).

Hamilton, S. A. "Poor Whites: New Race Question." *Arena*, XXVII, 352-58 (April, 1902).

Haney, Louis H. "Farm Credit Conditions in a Cotton State." *American Economic Review*, IV, 47-67 (March, 1914).

Harg, H. de H. "Rainfall and Civilization." *Discovery*, IV, 22-25 (January, 1923).

Harper, Charles M. "Cattle Trails of the Prairies." *Scribner's*, XI, 732-42 (June, 1892).

Harper, Roland M. "Agricultural Conditions in Florida in 1925." *Economic Geography*, III, 1-18 (July, 1927).

"Ante-Bellum Census Enumerations in Florida." *Florida Historical Quarterly*, VI, 42-52 (July, 1927).

"Development of Agriculture in Georgia." *Georgia Historical Quarterly*, VI, 3-27, 97-121, 211-32, 323-54 (March to December, 1922).

"Development of Agriculture in the Pine Barrens of the Southeastern United States." *Journal of Geography*, XV, 42-48 (October, 1916).

"Distribution of Illiteracy in Alabama." *Montgomery Advertiser* (April 9, 1922).

"Distribution of Illiteracy in Georgia." *High School Quarterly*, Athens, Ga., VII, 254-62 (July, 1919).

"The Forest Regions of Mississippi in Relation to the Lumber Industry." *Southern Lumberman*, LXX, No. 935 (August 23, 1913).

"The Forest Resources of Alabama." *American Forestry*, XIX, 657-70 (October, 1913).

"A Graphic Method of Measuring Civilization and Some of Its Applications." *Scientific Monthly*, X, 292-305 (March, 1920).

"A New Method of Mapping Complex Geographical Features Illustrated by Some Maps of Georgia." *School Science and Mathematics*, XVIII, 699-708 (1918).

"Per Capita Wealth in the United States." *Geographical Review*, XIV, 641-43 (October, 1924).

"The Population of Florida: Regional Composition and Growth as Influenced by Soil, Climate and Mineral Discoveries." *Geographical Review*, II, 361-67 (November, 1916).

"A Preliminary Soil Census of Alabama and West Florida." *Soil Science*, IV, 91-107 (August, 1917).

"Productivity of the Soil of Florida." *Quarterly Bulletin*, Florida Agricultural Department, XXX, 14-26 (October 1, 1920).

"The Regional Geography of South Carolina." *Journal*, Elisha Mitchell Scientific Society, XXXV, 105-12 (June, 1920).

"Rural Standards of Living in the South." *Social Forces*, II, 13-17, 253-65 (November, 1922 and January, 1923).

"Some Movements of State Centers of Population and Their Significance." *Journal of Geography*, XV, 227-31 (March, 1917).

"Some North Carolina Soil Statistics and Their Significance." *Journal*, Elisha Mitchell Scientific Society, XXXIII, 106-19 (November, 1917).

"Some Relations Between Soil, Climate and Civilization in the Southern Red Hills of Alabama." *South Atlantic Quarterly,* XIX, 201-15 (July, 1920).

"Some Vanishing Scenic Features of the Southeastern United States." *Natural History,* XIX, 192-204 (1919).

Harrison, Shelby M. "Community Participation in City and Regional Planning." *Publications,* American Sociological Society, XX, 177-187 (1926).

Hartshorne, Richard. "Iron and Steel Industry of the United States." *Journal of Geography,* XXVIII, 133-53 (April, 1929).

Haskell, S. B. "Fertilizer Use in the United States." *Annals,* The American Academy of Political and Social Science, CXVII, 265-70 (January, 1925).

Hayatt, J. B. "Story of Artificial Fertilizers." *Discovery,* VII, 213-14 (June, 1926).

Hayes, C. Willard, and Campbell, Marius R. "Geomorphology of the Southern Appalachian." *National Geographic Magazine,* VI, 63-126 (May, 1923).

Herrick, Glenn W. "The Relation of Malaria to Agriculture and Other Industries of the South." *Popular Science,* LXII, 521 (April, 1903).

Herring, Harriet L. "Early Industrial Development in the South." *Annals,* American Academy of Political and Social Science, CLIII, 1-10 (January, 1931).

Herty, H. C. "The Turpentine Industry in the Southern States." *Journal,* Franklin Institute, CLXXXI, 339-67 (March, 1916).

Hibbard, B. H. "Tenancy in the Southern States." *Quarterly Journal of Economics,* XXVII, 482-86 (May, 1913).

Hickman, W. C. "Weather and Crops in Arkansas 1819 to 1879." *U. S. Monthly Weather Review,* XLVIII, 447-51 (August, 1920).

Hicks, John D. "The Farmer's Alliance in North Carolina." *North Carolina Historical Review,* II, 162-87 (April, 1925).

Hines, L. N. "Effect of Class Room Temperatures on Work of Pupils." *Psychological Clinic,* VIII, (1909).

Hoffman, F. L. "The Malaria Record of 1927." *The Spectator* (November 15, 1928).

"Observations on the Malaria Problem of Today." *Southern Medical Journal,* XIX, 370-371 (May, 1926).

Hoffman, G. P. "Is the Trucking Industry in South Carolina at a Standstill?" *Market Growers' Journal,* XXXIV, 12 (January 1, 1924).

Holden, W. C. "West Texas Droughts." *Southwest Historical Quarterly,* XXXII, 103-23 (October, 1928).

Holt, Albert C. "The Economic and Social Beginnings of Tennessee." *Tennessee Historical Magazine,* VII, 194-230, 252-313 (October, 1921, January, 1922); VIII, 24-86 (April, 1923).

Howard, H. H. "Study in Hookworm Infestation in Jones County, Mississippi, 1924." *Southern Medical Journal,* XVIII, 668-72 (September, 1925).

Hoxmark, Guillerma. "The International Olympic Games as an Index to the Influence of Climate on Human Energy." *Ecology,* VI, 199-202 (July, 1925).

Hulbert, Archer B. "The Increasing Debt of History to Science." *Proceedings,* American Antiquarian Society, n. s. XXIX, 29-43 (1919).

Huntington, C. C. "What is Social Geography?" *Journal of Geography,* XXV, 90-96 (March, 1926).

Huntington, Ellsworth. "The Handicap of Poor Land." *Economic Geography,* XI, 335-57 (July, 1926).

Huntington, Ellsworth, and Cushing, S. W. "Rivalry Between Sugar Beet and Sugar Cane." *Journal of Geography,* XIX, 255-59 (October, 1920).

"Industrialization in the Southwest." *Southwestern Political and Social Science Quarterly,* X, 322 ff. (December, 1929).

James, Harlean. "The Cost of Regional Planning." *Journal of Land and Public Utility Economics,* V, 303-10 (August, 1929).

Jefferson, Mark. "Anthropography of Some Great Cities: A Study in the Distribution of Population." *Bulletin,* American Geographical Society, XLI, 537-66 (1909).

"The Anthropology of North America." *Bulletin,* American Geographical Society, XLV, 161-80 (1913).

"The Civilizing Rails." *Economic Geography,* IV, 217-31 (1928).

"The Geography of Rolling Transportation." *Annals,* Association of American Geographers, XVIII, 64 (1928).

"Some Considerations of the Geographic Provinces of the United States." *Annals,* Association of American Geographers, VII, 3-15 (1907).

Jeffers, D. S. "On the Trail of the Vanishing Spruce in the Southern Appalachians." *Scientific Monthly,* XX, 358-68 (April, 1925).

Jeffrey, E. "Our Household Heritage from the Old South." *Garden Magazine and Home Builder,* XLII, 209-12 (November, 1925).

Jernegan, M. W. "Slavery and Industrialism in the Colonies." *American Historical Review,* XXV, 220-40 (January, 1920).

Joerg, W. L. G. "The Subdivision of North America into Natural Regions: A Preliminary Inquiry." *Annals,* Association of American Geographers, IV, 36 (1914).

Johnson, Gerald W. "Cadets of New Market." *Harper's*, CLX, 111-19 (December, 1929).

"No More Excuses." *Harper's*, CLXII, 331-37 (February, 1931).

"South Takes the Offensive." *American Mercury*, II, 70-78 (May, 1924).

Jones, F. N. "Open Letter." *Dallas Morning News* (February 17, 1928).

Jones, Howard Mumford. "On Leaving the South." *Scribner's*, LXXXIX, 17-27 (January, 1931).

"The Southern Legend." *Scribner's*, LXXXV, 538-42 (May, 1929).

Keir, Malcolm. "Economic Factors in the Location of Manufacturing Industries." *Annals*, American Academy of Political and Social Science, XCVII, 83-92 (September, 1921).

Kemper, Charles E. "The Settlement of the Valley." *Virginia Magazine of History*, XXX, 169-82 (April, 1922).

Kendrick, Benjamin B. "Agrarian Discontent in the South, 1880-1900." *Report*, American Historical Association, Washington, I, 265-72 (1920).

Keys, C. M. "The Railroad Enterprizes of the South." *World's Work*, XIV, 954-58 (June, 1907).

Keyserling, Herman. "Genius Loci." *Atlantic Monthly*, 144, pp. 302-11 (September, 1929).

"The South: America's Hope." *Atlantic Monthly*, 144, pp. 605-8 (November, 1929).

Killebrew, J. B. "Tobacco." American Economic Association, *Publication*, V, 135-43 (1904).

Kincer, J. B. "The Relation of Climate to the Geographical Distribution of Crops in the United States." *Ecology*, III, 127-33 (April, 1922).

Lackey, E. E. "Classification and Use of Geographic Principles." *Journal of Geography*, XXVI, 64-71 (February, 1924).

Lacy, W. N. "Some Climatic Influences in American History." *Monthly Weather Review*, XXXVI, 169-73 (1908).

Lanier, R. S. "Revolution in Rice Farming." *Review of Reviews*, XXXIII, 716-9 (June, 1906).

Le Blanc, T. J. "Malaria." *American Mercury*, III, 366-71 (November, 1924).

Lewis, Charles D. "The Changing Mountains." *Mountain Life and Work*, IV, 14-20 (July, 1928).

"Government Forests and the Mountain Problem." *Mountain Life and Work*, VI, 2-9 (January, 1931).

Lippman, J. G. "Economic Significance of Commercial Fertilizer." *Annals,* American Academy of Political and Social Science, CXLII, 257-65 (March, 1929).

Lodge, Henry Cabot. "The Distribution of Ability in the United States." *Century Magazine,* XX, 687-94 (September, 1891).

Loewenthal, Louis C. "Power Generation." *Journal of the Franklin Institute,* CCI, 432 (April, 1926).

Lonn, E. "Fields for Research in Southern History After the Reconstruction." *Historical Outlook,* XIV, 14-20 (January, 1923).

Love, Clara M. "Cattle Industry of the Southwest." *Southwestern Historical Quarterly,* XIX, 370-99 (April, 1916).

Lovejoy, P. S. "Theory and Practice in Land Classification." *Journal of Land and Public Utility Economics,* I, 160-75 (April, 1925).

Lowdermilk, W. C., and Smith, J. Russell. "Notes on the Problem of Field Erosion." *The Geographical Review,* XVII, 226-235 (April, 1927).

MacClintock, S. S. "Kentucky Mountains and Their Feuds." *American Journal of Sociology,* VII, 1-28, 171-87 (July-September, 1901).

MacDonald, Ruel. "Texas, an Empire State." *Current History,* XXXIV, 165-69 (July, 1931).

Mack, B. "Oklahoma: Forty Years Young." *Review of Reviews,* LXXX, 132-40 (September, 1929).

Manning, J. W. "County Consolidation in Tennessee." *National Municipal Review,* XVII, 511-13 (September, 1928).

Marbut, C. F. "The Rise, Decline and Revival of Malthusionism in Relation to Geography and Character of Soils." *Annals,* Association of American Geographers, XV, 1-25 (March, 1925).

Martin, William. "Southern Frontier Life in Revolutionary Days." Southern Historical Association, *Publications,* IV, 443-68 (1900).

Matthews, J. H. "Fisheries of the South Atlantic and Gulf States." *Economic Geography,* IV, 323-48 (October, 1928).

Matthews, J. L. "Farmers' Union and the Tobacco Pool." *Atlantic Monthly,* CII, 482-91 (October, 1908).

Matthews, William H. "Geography and Southern Sectionalism in the Civil War." *Bulletin,* Geographical Society of Philadelphia, XXVI, 255-75 (October, 1928).

McCall, A. G. "The Development of Soil Science." *Agricultural History,* V, 43-56 (April, 1931).

McClarty, Julia. "Economic Opportunities in the Southern Appalachians." *Journal of Geography,* XX, 96-104 (March, 1921).

McCollum, E. V. "Nutrition and Physical Development." *Annals, American Academy of Political and Social Science,* XCVIII, 39 (November, 1921).

McCombs, C. A. "Present Status of Navigation of the Lower Mississippi." *Journal of Geography,* XXIV, 17-19 (January, 1925).

McConnell, John P. "Retardation of the Appalachian Region." *Mountain Life and Work,* V, 21-22 (April, 1929).

McDougall, Eric. "The Moisture Belts of North America." *Ecology,* VI, 325-32 (October, 1925).

McKenzie, H. B. "South, Cotton, and the Negro." *North American Review,* CCXIX, pp. 486-95 (April, 1924).

McKenzie, R. D. "The Scope of Human Ecology." *Journal of Applied Sociology,* X, 316-23 (March-April, 1926).

"The Ecological Approach to the Study of the Human Community." *American Journal of Sociology,* XXX, 287-301 (November, 1924).

McLaurin, J. L. "Commercial Democracy of the South." *North American Review,* 173, pp. 657-62 (November, 1901).

Mead, D. W. "Economics of Hydro-Electric Development." American Society of Civil Engineers *Proceedings,* L, 417-25 (April, 1924).

Mead, Ellwood. "Pygmies in the Earth: A Plea for Rural Reconstruction in the South." *Forum,* LXXIX, 209 (May, 1928).

Merriam, C. Hart. "The Geographical Distribution of Life in North America." Biological Society *Proceedings,* Washington, VII, 45-50 (April, 1892).

"Laws of Temperature Control of the Geographic Distribution of Terrestrial Animals and Plants." *National Geographic Magazine,* VI, 229-38 (December 29, 1894).

Miller, E. E. "Cotton a National Crop." *Review of Reviews,* LXXIV, 70-73 (July, 1926).

Milton, George Fort. "Can Cotton Be Controlled by Law?" *Independent,* CXVII, 531-32 (November 6, 1926).

Mims, Edwin. "Hartsville and Its Lessons." *World's Work,* XX, 149 (October, 1911).

"Redeemers of the Soil." "Remakers of Industry." *World's Work,* XXII, 14972-87; XXIII, 41-54 (October, November, 1911).

Mitchell, Broadus. "Fleshpots of the South." *Virginia Quarterly Review,* III, 161-76 (April, 1927).

"Growth of Manufactures in the South." *Annals,* American Academy of Political and Social Science, CLIII, 21-29 (January, 1931).

"The Industrial Revolution in the South." *American Labor Legislation Review,* XVIII, 16-25 (March, 1928).

"Three Southerners." *South Atlantic Quarterly,* XXI, 219-24 (July, 1922).

"Two Industrial Revolutions." *South Atlantic Quarterly,* XX, 287-303 (October, 1921).

"Why Cheap Labor Down South?" *Virginia Quarterly Review,* V, 481-91 (October, 1929).

Mitchell, W. E. "Interconnection of Power Systems in the Southeastern States." *Journal,* American Institute of Electrical Engineers, XLIII, 1150-53 (December, 1924).

Moody, Vernie Alton. "Slavery on Louisiana Plantations." *Louisiana Historical Quarterly,* VII, 191-301 (April, 1924).

Moore, Barrington. "The Scope of Ecology." *Ecology,* I, 3-5 (January, 1920).

Morrison, A. J. "Historical Farmer in America." *South Atlantic Quarterly,* XVII, 222-36 (July, 1918).

Morse, Josiah. "A Social Interpretation: South Carolina." *Social Forces,* IV, 690-701 (June, 1926).

Mowry, Don E. "Southeastern Communities Value Advertising." *Harper's,* Advertising Section (May, 1930).

Mumford, Lewis. "Regionalism and Irregionalism." *Sociological Review,* XIX, 217-88 (October, 1927).

"The Theory and Practice of Regionalism." *Sociological Review,* XX, 18-33 (January, 1928).

Murchison, C. T. "Southern Textile Manufacturing." *Annals,* American Academy of Political and Social Science, CLIII, 30-42 (January, 1931).

"Captains of Southern Industry." *Virginia Quarterly Review,* VII, 379-92 (July, 1931).

Murphy, Edgar Gardner. "Backward or Forward?" *South Atlantic Quarterly,* VIII, 19-38 (April, 1910).

Murphy, Raymond E. "Land Values in the Blue Grass and Nashville Basin." *Economic Geography,* VI, 191-203 (April, 1930).

Ness, H. "Distribution Limits of the Long-Leaf Pines and Their Possible Extension." *Journal of Forestry,* XXV, 825-27 (November, 1927).

Newbigin, M. I. "Human Geography: First Principles and Some Applications." *Nature,* CX, 339-404 (September 23, 1922).

Nichols, W. D. "A Research Approach to the Problems of Appalachia." *Mountain Life and Work,* VII, 5-8 (January, 1932).

Noles, John. "Regional Planning for Happy Valley, Tennessee." *City Planning,* IV, 199-205 (July, 1928).

Nott, Josiah C. *New Orleans Medical and Surgical Journal* (March, 1848).

Novakovsky, S. "Probable Effect of the Climate of the Russian Far East on Human Life and Activity." *Ecology,* III, 181-201 (July, 1922).

Oakman, W. G. "Condition of the South." *North American Review,* CLXXIII, 40-43 (July, 1901).

Odum, Howard W. "Folk and Regional Conflict as a Field of Sociological Study." *Publications* of the American Sociological Society, XXV, 1-17 (May, 1931).

"Notes on the Study of Regional and Folk Society." *Social Forces,* X, 164-175 (December, 1931).

Ogg, W. G. "Soil Classification and Soil Surveys." *Scottish Geographical Magazine,* XLIII, 193-203 (July, 1927).

Page, Arthur W. "The Cotton Mills and the People." *World's Work,* XIV, 8990-9002 (June, 1907).

Page, Walter Hines. "A Journey Through the Southern States." *World's Work,* XIV, 9002-38 (June, 1907).

Parkins, A. E. "The Ante Bellum South: A Geographer's Interpretation." *Annals,* Association of American Geographers, XXI, 1-34 (March, 1931).

"A Comparison of the Trans-Appalachian Railroads." *Journal of Geography,* IX, 113-18 (January, 1911).

Parr, Virgil Verser and G. S. Klemmedson. "An Economic Study of the Costs and Methods of Range Cattle Production of Forty Ranches in North Central Texas." *Cattleman,* XII, 9-11, 13-19, 21-23, 25 (September, 1925).

Parson, Floyd W. "What Shall We Eat?" *World's Work,* LIV, 219-26 (July, 1927).

Pearl, Raymond. "Relative Contribution of the Staple Food Commodities to the National Food Consumption." *Proceedings of the American Philosophical Society,* LVIII, 182-222. (1919).

Peattie, Roderick. "Hunting Oil in Oklahoma." *Atlantic Monthly,* CXXIX, 630-41 (May, 1922).

Pelzer, Louis. "A Cattleman's Commonwealth on the Western Range." *Mississippi Valley Historical Review,* XIII, 30-49 (June, 1926).

Peters, Iva L. "A Social Interpretation: Maryland." *Social Forces,* IV, 510-19 (March, 1926).

Peters, Mary Eleanor. "Texas Trails." *Proceedings,* Mississippi Valley Historical Association, VII, 55-66 (1913-14).

Phillips, M. Ogden. "Tung Oil: Florida's Infant Industry." *Economic Geography,* V, 348-57 (October, 1929).

Phillips, Ulrich B. "The Central Theme of Southern History." *The American Historical Review*, XXXIV, 30-43 (October, 1928).

"Conservatism and Progress in the Cotton Belt." *South Atlantic Quarterly*, III, 1-10 (January, 1904).

"Decadence of the Plantation." *Annals*, American Academy of Political and Social Science, XXXV, 738-53 (1910).

"The Economic Cost of Slaveholding in the Cotton Belt." *Political Science Quarterly*, XX, 257-75 (June, 1905).

"Economics of the Plantation." *South Atlantic Quarterly*, II, 231-36 (July, 1903).

"Origin and Growth of Southern Black Belts." *American Historical Review*, XI, 798-816 (July, 1906).

"Plantation as a Civilizing Factor." *Sewanee Review*, XII, 257-67 (July, 1904).

"Plantation with Slave Labor and Free." *American Historical Review*, XXX, 738-53 (July, 1925).

Phillips, V., and Howell, L. "Racial and Other Differences in Dietary Customs." *Journal of Home Economics*, XII, 396-411 (September, 1920).

Pickett, J. E. "World Against the Cotton Grower." *Pacific Rural Press*, (October 11, 1925).

Pitkin, Walter B. "Putting Old Man River to Work." *Survey*, LXI, 728-31 (March 1, 1929).

Poe, Clarence H. "Builders of An Agricultural Community." *South Atlantic Quarterly*, VIII, 1-11 (January, 1909).

"The Rebound of the Upland South." *World's Work*, XIV, 8961-78 (June, 1907).

Pool, R. J. "Our American Forests, Their Past, Present and Future." *Scientific Monthly*, XXIV, 74-80 (January, 1927).

Pope, J. D. "Issues Involved in Readjustment of Farm Organization in the Cotton Belt." *Journal of Farm Economics*, XI, 266-83 (April, 1929).

Pratt, Joseph Hyde. "Good Roads Movement in the South." *Annals*, American Academy of Political and Social Science, XXXV, 105-13 (January, 1910).

"Lumber and Forests Products Industry in the South." *Annals*, American Academy of Political and Social Science, CLIII, 70-71 (January, 1931).

Pressey, Henry A. "Water Power of the Southern States." *Forestry and Irrigation*, p. 32 (January, 1906).

Price, O. W. "Saving Our Southern Forests." *World's Work*, V, 3207-22 (March, 1903).

Prichard, Walter. "Routine on a Louisiana Sugar Plantation Under the Slavery Régime About 1850." *Mississippi Valley Historical Review,* XIV, 168-78 (September, 1927).

Prince, A. H. "Arkansas Rice Grower's Triumph." *Progressive Farmer,* LXI, 280 (March 6, 1926).

Putnam, George E. "Agricultural Credit Legislation and the Tenancy Problem." *American Economic Review,* V, 805-15 (December, 1915).

Rambo, Marian Y. "The Submerged Tenth Among the Southern Mountaineers." *Methodist Review,* 565-75 (July, 1905).

Rankin, W. S. "A Million Dollars for Carolina Hospitals." *Review of Reviews,* LXXIII, 406-8 (April, 1926).

Read, Opie. "Some Characters of the Old South." *Century,* XCVIII, 391-400 (July, 1919).

Redway, J. W. "Effects of Topography on Economic Development." *Gunton's,* XIX, 135-41 (August, 1900).

Reed, William G. "The Probable Growing Season." *Monthly Weather Review,* XLIV, 509-12 (September, 1916).

Reed, William G., and Folley, H. R. "Weather as a Business Risk in Farming." *Geographical Review,* II, 48-53 (July, 1916).

Rhyne, J. J. and C. R. "The Southwest—Laboratory for Social Research." *Southwest Political and Social Science Quarterly,* X, 33-41 (June, 1929).

Rich, J. L. "Cultural Features and the Physiographic Cycle." *Geographical Review,* IV, 297-308 (October, 1917).

"Notes on the Human Geography of an Oil Field." *Journal of Geography,* XIII, 185-90 (February, 1915).

Rickard, E. R., and Keer, J. Austin. "The Incidence and Intensity of Hookworm Infestation in the Various Soil Provinces of Tennessee." *Journal of Preventive Medicine,* I, 185-203 (November, 1926).

Ridgeway, W. "The Application of the Zoölogical Laws to Man." *Nature,* LXXVIII, (1908).

Ross, E. A. "Pocketed Americans." *New Republic,* XXXVII, 170-72; 224-26 (January 9, 23, 1924).

Roth, Lawrence V. "The Growth of American Cities." *Geographical Review,* V, 384-98 (May, 1918).

Roxby, P. M. "What is a Natural Region?" *Geographic Teacher,* IV (1907-8).

"The Scope and Aim of Human Geography." *Scottish Geographic Magazine,* XLVI, 276-89 (September, 1930).

Russel, Robert Royal. "Revaluation of the Period Before the Civil War: Railroads." *Mississippi Valley Historical Review*, XV, 341-54 (December, 1928).

Sauer, C. O. "Mapping the Utilization of Land." *Geographical Review*, VIII, 47-54 (July, 1919).

"The Economic Problem of the Ozark Highland." *Scientific Monthly*, XI, 215-27 (September, 1920).

"Notes on the Geographic Significance of Soils." *Journal of Geography*, XXI, 187-89 (May, 1922).

"The Survey Method in Geography and Its Objectives." *Annals*, Association of American Geographers, XIV, 17-34 (March, 1924).

Saville, Thorndike. "Power Situation in the Southern Power Province." *Annals*, American Academy of Political and Social Science, CLIII, 94-123 (January, 1931).

Scattergood, Margaret. "Facts About the South." *American Federationist*, XXXV, 826-29 (July, 1928).

Schmidt, L. B. "The Economic History of American Agriculture as a Field for Study." *Mississippi Valley Historical Review*, III, 39-49 (June, 1916).

"The Westward Movement of Corn Growing, etc." *Iowa Journal of History and Politics*, XXI, 112-141 (January, 1923).

"The Westward Movement of Wheat Growing, etc." *Iowa Journal of History and Politics*, VIII, 376-412 (July, 1926).

"Influence of Wheat and Cotton on Anglo-American Relations During the Civil War." *Iowa Journal of History and Politics*, XVI, 401-39 (July, 1918).

Shockel, B. H. "Changing Conditions in the Kentucky Mountains." *Scientific Monthly*, III, 105-31 (August, 1916).

Scroggs, William O. "Rural Life in the Lower Mississippi Valley About 1803." Mississippi Valley Historical Association, *Proceedings*, VIII, 262-77 (1914, 1915).

Sellers, J. L. "The Economic Incidence of the Civil War in the South." *Mississippi Valley Historical Review*, XIV, 179-91 (September, 1927).

"An Interpretation of Civil War Finance." *American Historical Review*, XXX, 282-97 (January, 1925).

Semple, Ellen C. "The Anglo-Saxons of the Kentucky Mountains: A Study in Anthropogeography." *Bulletin*, American Geographical Society, XLII, 561-94 (August, 1910).

"Mountain Passes: A Study in Anthropogeography." *Bulletin*, American Geographical Society, II and III (1901).

"Some Geographical Causes Determining the Location of Cities." *Journal of School Geography*, I, 225-31 (1897).

Shaffer, E. T. H. "New South: Boll Weevil Era." *Atlantic Monthly*, CXXIX, 116-23 (January, 1922).

"New South: Textile Development." *Atlantic Monthly*, CXXX, 562-68 (October, 1922).

"New South: Negro Migration." *Atlantic Monthly*, CXXXII, 403-9 (September, 1923).

Shaler, N. S. "The Peculiarities of the South." *North American Review*, CLI, 477-88 (October, 1890).

Shelby, Gertrude Mathews. "Florida Frenzy." *Harper's*, CLII, 177-86 (January, 1926).

Shemik, Bohumil. "The Pioneer and the Forest." Mississippi Valley Historical Association, *Proceedings*, III, 97-98 (1909-10).

Shryock, Richard H. "Medical Practice in the Old South." *South Atlantic Quarterly*, XXIX, 160-68 (April, 1930).

Shull, Charles A. "Some Changes in the Vegetation of Kentucky." *Ecology*, II, 120-24 (April, 1921).

Simkins, Frances Butler. "The Problems of South Carolina Agriculture after the Civil War." *North Carolina Historical Review*, VII, 46-77 (January, 1930).

"The Solution of Post-Bellum Agricultural Problems in South Carolina." *North Carolina Historical Review*, VII, 192-219 (April, 1930).

Simonds, Frederic William. "Geographic Influences in the Development of Texas." *Journal of Geography*, X, 277-84 (May, 1912).

Simplich, Frederick. "The Great Mississippi Flood of 1927." *National Geographic Magazine*, LII, 243-89 (September, 1927).

Smillie, W. G., and Augustine, D. L. "Intensity of Hookworm Infestation in Alabama: Its Relationship to Residence, Occupation, Age, Sex and Race." *Journal of the American Medical Association*, LXXXV, 1958-63 (December 19, 1925).

Smith, Bradford B. "Forecasting the Acreage of Cotton." *Journal of the American Statistical Association*, XX, 31-47 (March, 1925).

Smith, G. Otis. "A World of Power." *Economic Geography*, I, 133-42 (July, 1925).

Smith, Harriet. "Geographic Influences in the Settlement of the Black Prairies in Texas." XIX, 287-94 (November, 1920).

Smith, Herbert A. "Nature's Gifts to the South." *World's Work*, XIV, 8941-51 (June, 1907).

Smith, J. Russell. "The Elements of Geography and the Geographic Unit." *School and Society*, XVII, 617-28 (June 9, 1923).

"Farming Appalachia." *Review of Reviews*, LIII, 326-36 (March, 1916).

"Is This a Permanent Country?" *Survey*, LXI, 25-28 (October 1, 1928).

"Plan or Perish." *Survey*, LVIII, 370-77 (July 1, 1927).

"Wealth from Mississippi Mud." *Survey*, LIX, 127-31 (November 1, 1927).

Smith, J. Warren. "Effect of Weather on the Yield of Corn." *Monthly Weather Review*, XLII, 78-93 (February, 1914).

Smith, Z. F. "The Great Revival of 1800." *Register*, Kentucky Historical Society, VII, 19-35 (May, 1909).

Snider, S. C. "Petroleum Resources of the United States." Academy of Political Science, *Proceedings*, XII, 159-67 (July, 1926).

Snyder, Howard. "Negro Migration and the Cotton Crop." *North American Review*, 219, pp. 22-29 (July, 1924).

Soule, Andrew M. "Problem of the Cotton Growing Industry." *Commerce and Finance* (January 12, 1927).

Souissant, St. George L. "Memphis as Gateway to the West." *Tennessee Historical Magazine* (March-June, 1917).

A South Carolinian (*Pseud.*). "South Carolina Society." *Atlantic Monthly*, XXXIX, 670-84 (June, 1877).

Sparling, Earl. "Oil Hells in Oklahoma." *Outlook and Independent*, CLVII, 214-17 (February 11, 1931).

Splawn, M. W. "Financing Highways in Texas." *Southwest Political and Social Science Quarterly*, IV, 49-62 (June, 1923).

Stabler, Herman. "Nation's Water Power." *Economic Geography*, III, 434-42 (October, 1923).

Stephenson, L. W. "Major Features in the Geology of the Atlantic and Gulf Coast Plains." Washington Academy of Science, *Journal*, XVI, 460-68 (October 18, 1926).

Stevens, P. H. "Mechanization of Cotton Farms." *Journal of Farm Economics*, XIII, 27-36 (January, 1931).

Stiles, W. C. "Is the So-Called 'Cotton-Mill Anemia' of the Gulf-Atlantic States Due to Lint or Hookworms?" *Southern Medical Journal*, IV, 508 (1911).

Stone, A. H. "The Cotton Factorage System of the Southern States." *American Historical Review*, XX, 557-65 (April, 1915).

"Negro Labor and the Boll Weevil." *Annals*, American Academy of Political and Social Science, XXXIII, 391-8 (March, 1909).

"The Negro in the Yazoo-Mississippi Delta." American Economic Association, *Proceedings*, III, 235-78 (1902).

"Problems of Southern Economic History." *American Historical Review*, XIII, 779-97 (July, 1908).

Sulley, Daniel J. "Dawn of the Cotton Century." *Cosmopolitan*, XLVI, 408-17 (March, 1909).

"King Cotton's Impoverished Retinue." *Cosmopolitan*, XLVI, 253-63 (February, 1909).

Sumner, John D. "An Analysis of Mississippi River Traffic: 1918-1930." *Journal of Land and Public Utility Economics*, VII, 353-66 (November, 1931).

Sundstroem, E. S. "Contributions to Tropical Physiology." University of California, *Publications in Physiology*, VI, 1-216.

Surface, George Thomas. "Climate and Boundaries of Virginia." *Bulletin*, American Geographical Society, XXXIX, 92-102 (February, 1907).

"Geographic Influence on the Economic History of Virginia." *Bulletin*, American Geographical Society, XXXIX, 397-409 (July, 1907).

"Geography of Virginia." *Bulletin*, Geographic Society of Philadelphia, 211-60 (October, 1907).

"The Physiography of Virginia." *Bulletin*, American Geographical Society, XXXVIII, 741-53 (December, 1906).

"Racial and Regional Study of the Virginia Population." *Bulletin*, American Geographical Society, XXXIX, 285-91 (May, 1907).

"Rice in the United States." American Geographical Society, *Bulletin*, XLIII, 500-9 (July, 1911).

"Virginia Trade and Commerce." *Bulletin*, American Geographical Society, XXXIX, 463-72 (August, 1907).

Switzer, J. E. "A Trip to the Mississippi-Yazoo Flood District." *Journal of Geography*, XXVI, 293-99 (November, 1927).

Sydenstricker, Edgar, and Notstein, F. W. "Differential Fertility According to Social Class: A Study of 69,620 Native White Married Women under 45 Years of Age Based Upon Census Returns of 1910." *Journal of the American Statistical Association*, XXV, 9-32 (March, 1930).

Taylor, A. E. "After-the-War Economic Food Problem." *Journal of Home Economics*, XIII, 1-13 (January, 1921).

Taylor, R. H. "Commercial Fertilizers in South Carolina." *South Atlantic Quarterly*, XIX, 179-89 (April, 1930).

Taylor, W. P. "Emergence of the Biology of Forest and Range." *Science*, n. s., LXVI, 184-86 (August 26, 1927).

Taylor, W. P., and McGinnies, W. A. "Bio-ecology of Forest and Range." *Science Monthly*, XXVII, 177-82 (August, 1928).

Thomas, J. M. "Influence of Frontier Life on American Christianity." New Jersey Historical Society, *Proceedings*, XI, 1-18 (January, 1926).

Thompson, W. S. "Rural Demography." *Publications,* American Sociological Society, XIX, 150-60 (1925).

Titus, Harold. "Michigan Takes Stock." *The New Republic,* LX, 39-41 (August 28, 1929).

Tompkins, D. A. "The South's Vast Reserves." *World's Work,* XIV, 8951-52 (June, 1907).

Tower, W. S. "Geography of American Cities." *Bulletin,* American Geographical Society, XXXVII, 577-88 (1905).

"The Mississippi River Problem." *Bulletin,* Geographic Society of Philadelphia, VI, 83-100 (1908).

"Scientific Geography: The Relation of Its Content to Its Subdivisions." *Bulletin,* American Geographic Society, XLII, 801-25 (1910).

Townsend, C. W. "Grazing and Forests." *Scientific Monthly,* XXVI, 57-59 (January, 1928).

Trent, W. P. "Dominant Forces in Southern Life." *Atlantic Monthly,* LXXIX, 42-53 (January, 1897).

Trewartha, Glenn I. "Recent Thoughts on the Problem of White Acclimatization in the Wet Tropics." *Geographical Review,* XVI, 467-78 (1926).

Trimble, William J. "Historical Aspects of the Surplus Food Production of the United States, 1862-1902." *Annual Report,* American Historical Association, I, 223-39 (1918).

"Influence of the Passing of Public Lands." *Atlantic Monthly,* CXIII, 755-67 (June, 1914).

Trotter, S. "Atlantic Forest Regions of North America." *Popular Science,* LXXV, 370-92 (October, 1909).

Tryon, F. G. "Index Numbers of the Consumption of Fuels and Water Power." *Journal of the American Statistical Association,* XXVI (September, 1927).

Turnbull, Nichol. "The Beginnings of Cotton Cultivation in Georgia." *Georgia Historical Quarterly,* I, 39-45 (March, 1917).

Turner, F. J. "Children of the Pioneer." *Yale Review,* n. s., XV, 265-70 (July, 1926).

"Is Sectionalism in America Dying Away?" *American Journal of Sociology,* XIII, 661-75 (March, 1908).

"Report of the Conference on the Relation of Geography and History." American Historical Association *Reports,* I, 45-48 (1907).

"Sections and Nations." *Yale Review,* n. s., XII, 1-21 (October, 1922).

"Significance of the Section in American History." *Wisconsin Magazine of History*, VIII, 255-80 (March, 1925).

"South, 1820-1830." *American Historical Review*, XI, 559-73 (April, 1906).

Turner, Howard A. "Absentee Farm Ownership in the United States." *Journal of Land and Public Utility Economics*, III, 48-60 (February, 1927).

"The Share Renting of Farms in the United States." *International Review of Agricultural Economics*, I, 500-42 (October, 1923).

Tyler, M. C. "Wilson Dam—Its Cost and Value." *Electrical World*, LXXXVI, 739-43 (October 10, 1925).

Unstead, J. F. "Geography and Historical Geography." *Geographical Journal*, LIX, 55-59 (January, 1922).

Vallandingham, E. N. "Our Men of the Midi." *Atlantic Monthly*, XCIX, 848-56 (June, 1907).

Vanderblue, Homer B. "The Florida Land Boom." *Journal of Land and Public Utility Economics*, III, 113-31, 252-69 (May, August, 1927).

Van Dine, D. L. "Relation of Malaria to Crop Production." *Scientific Monthly*, III, 431-39 (November, 1916).

Vincent, G. E. "A Retarded Frontier: Kentucky." *American Journal of Sociology*, IV, 1-20 (July, 1898).

Viosca, Percy, Jr. "Louisiana Wet Lands and the Value of Their Wild Life and Fishery Resources." *Ecology*, IX, 216-29 (April, 1928).

Vishner, S. S. "Significance of the Biotic Area and of Biogeography." *Bulletin*, American Geographical Society, XLVII, 509-20 (1915).

"A Study of the Type of the Place of Birth and Occupation of the Fathers of Subjects in Who's Who." *American Journal of Sociology*, XXX, 551-57.

"Variations Among the States in Wealth." *Journal of Geography*, XXIV, 26-29 (January, 1925).

Voskuil, Walter H. "Utilization of Our Phosphate Resources." *Economic Geography*, I, 387-401 (October, 1925).

"Water-Power Situation in the United States." *Journal of Land and Public Utility Economics*, I, 89-101 (January, 1925).

Wallace, Henry C. "Forestry and Our Land Problem," *American Forestry*, XXIX, 15 (January, 1923).

Waller, A. E. "Crop Centers of the United States." *Journal*, American Society of Agronomy, X, 49-83 (1918).

Wang, Chi Che. "Is the Chinese Diet Adequate?" *Journal of Home Economics*, XII, 289-93 (July, 1920).

Ward, Robert De C. "Arable Land in the United States." *Geographical Review,* VIII, 55 (July, 1919).

"The Literature of Climatology." *Annals,* Association of American Geographers, XXI, 34-51 (March, 1931).

"A New Classification of Climates." *Geographical Review,* VIII, 188-91 (September, 1919).

Warren, G. F. "Agricultural Depression." *Quarterly Journal of Economics,* XXXVIII, 183-213 (February, 1924).

Way, R. B. "The Commerce of the Lower Mississippi in the Period 1830-1860." Mississippi Valley Historical Association, *Proceedings,* X, 57-58 (1918-1919).

Weatherly, U. G. "Habitation Areas and Interest Areas." *Journal of Applied Sociology,* X, 403-409 (May-June, 1926).

Wehrwein, George S. "Place of Tenancy in a System of Farm Land Tenure." *Journal of Land and Public Utility Economics,* I, 71-82 (January, 1925).

Weir, M. W. "Regional Planning in a Southern County." *American City,* XXXIX, 155-56 (September, 1928).

Welliver, J. C. "Oil, the New Industrial Giant." *Review of Reviews,* LXXVI, 177-86 (August, 1927).

Wernicke, O. H. L. "President Pine." *Review of Reviews,* LXXIV, 73-76 (July, 1926).

West, B. B., and Okey, R. "Cost and Nutritional Effect of Making an Institutional Diet Palatable." *Journal of Home Economics,* XXI, 254-60 (April, 1929).

Whitaker, J. Russell. "The Development of the Tobacco Industry in Kentucky, A Geographical Interpretation." *Bulletin,* Geographical Society of Philadelphia, XXVII, 15-42 (January, 1929).

Whitbeck, R. H. "Fact and Fiction in Geography by Natural Regions." *Journal of Geography,* XXII, 86-94 (March, 1923).

"Geographic Factors Affecting Growth of American Cities." *Journal of Geography,* XXI, 205-7 (September, 1922).

"Influence of Geographical Environment upon Religious Beliefs." *Geographical Review,* V, 317-23 (January-June, 1918).

White, Langdon. "Geography's Part in the Plant Cost of Iron and Steel Production at Pittsburg, Chicago, and Birmingham." *Economic Geography,* V, 327-33 (October, 1929).

"Iron and Steel Industry of the Birmingham, Alabama, District." *Economic Geography,* IV, 349-65 (October, 1928).

"Iron and Steel Industry of the Pittsburg District." *Economic Geography,* IV, 115-39 (April, 1928).

White, Melvin Johnson. "The Influence of Agricultural Conditions Upon Louisiana State Politics During the Nineties." *American Historical Association, Reports 1921*, 222, Washington (1926).

"Louisiana and the Succession Movement of the Early Fifties." *Mississippi Valley Historical Associations, Proceedings*, VIII, 278-88 (1914-15).

"Populism in Louisiana During the Nineties." *Mississippi Valley Historical Review*, V, 3-19 (June, 1918).

White, R. Clyde. "Cotton and Some Aspects of Southern Civilization." *Social Forces*, II, 651-54 (September, 1924).

Whittlesey, Derwent. "Sequent Occupance." *Annals, Association of American Geographers*, XIX, 162-65 (September, 1929).

Wickem, D. L. "Adjusting Southern Agriculture and Economic Changes." *Annals, American Academy of Political and Social Science*, CLIII, 193-201 (January, 1931).

Wilbur, Howard. "Cotton Manufacturing in the South." *Journal of Geography*, XXVI, 1-11 (1927).

Willey, D. A. "New Rice Farming in the South." *Review of Reviews*, XXVI, 177-82 (August, 1902).

Wise, L. E. "Our Oldest Industry." *American Forestry*, XXX, 404-407 (July, 1924).

Wolfanger, Louis A. "Abandoned Land in a Region of Land Abandonment." *Economic Geography*, VII, 166-76 (April, 1931).

"Economic Geography of the Gray-brownerths of the Eastern United States." *Geographical Review*, XXI, 276-96 (April, 1931).

"Major World Soil Groups and Some of Their Geographic Implications." *Geographical Review*, XIX, 95 (January, 1929).

Woods, J. B. "Problems of Southern Pine Lands." *American Forestry*, XXIX, 537-40 (September, 1923).

Wooley, R. W. "Development of our Gulf Ports." *Review of Reviews*, XXXIII, 190-99 (February, 1906).

"Lumbering Around Mobile, Alabama." *Review of Reviews*, XXXIII, 190-92 (1906).

"Yellow Fever and the South." *Independent*, LIX, 683-87 (September 21, 1905).

Youngman, Anna. "The Tobacco Pools of Kentucky and Tennessee." *Journal of Political Economy*, XVIII, 34-49 (January, 1910).

Zimmermann, C. C. "The Migration to Towns and Cities." *American Journal of Sociology*, XXXII, 450-55; XXXIII, 105-9; 237-41 (November, 1926; July, September, 1927).

Zimmermann, Erich W. "The Resource Hierarchy of Modern World Economy." *Weltwirtschaftliches Archiv*, XXXIII, 431-63 (April, 1931).

Zon, Raphael. "Forestry and the Agricultural Crisis." *Annals,* American Academy of Political and Social Science, CXLII, 70-76 (March, 1929).

"Forests and Human Progress." *Geographical Review,* X, 139-66 (1920).

PAMPHLETS, MONOGRAPHS, REPORTS, BULLETINS, AND FUGITIVE MATERIALS

Agelasto, A. M., Doyle, C. B., Meloy, G. S., and Stine, O. C. "The Cotton Situation." U. S. D. A. *Yearbook,* 1921, pp. 323-406 (Separate 879).

"The Agricultural Outlook for the Southern States, 1930-31." U. S. D. A. *Miscellaneous Publications, 102,* 1930.

"Agricultural Progress and Opportunities of South Mississippi." Mississippi Agricultural Experiment Station, U. S. D. A. *Joint Bulletin I,* May, 1926.

Ahern, George P. "Deforested America." *Senate Document 216,* 70th Congress, Second Session, Washington, 1929.

Allen, T. Warren, et al. "Highways and Highway Transportation." U. S. D. A., *Yearbook,* 1924, pp. 97-184 (Separate 914).

Alter, J. Cecil. "Crop Safety on Mountain Slopes." U. S. D. A., *Yearbook,* 1912, pp. 309-18.

American Red Cross. "The Mississippi Valley Flood Disaster of 1927." Washington, 1929.

"Relief Work in the Drought of 1930-31." Washington, 1930.

"Analysis of the Management of a Cotton Growing Enterprise." Federal Board for Vocational Education, *Bulletin 105, Agricultural Series 26,* 1926.

"Analysis of Migration of Population to and from Farms." Bureau of Agricultural Economics, October, 1927.

Andrews, Frank. "Railroads and Farming." U. S. D. A. Bureau of Statistics, *Bulletin 100.*

Arnold, J. H., and Montgomery, Frank. "Farming in the Blue Grass Region." U. S. D. A. *Bulletin 482.* 1917.

Ashley, Wm. E. "Immigration and the Material Development of the Southern States." Southern Inter-State Immigration Association, 1893.

Atwater, W. C. "Principles of Nutrition and Nutritive Value of Foods." U. S. D. A. *Farmers' Bulletin 142.*

Ayers, H. B. "Southern Appalachian Forests." U. S. Geological Survey. *Professional Paper, No. 37,* Washington, 1905.

BIBLIOGRAPHY 563

Bailey, J. W. "The Condition of the Farmers of North Carolina." A speech to the Farmers' Union of North Carolina in State Convention, Raleigh, November 16, 1921.

Baker, O. E. "Do We Need More Farm Land?" Address Agriculture Extension Conference, University of Minnesota, St. Paul. December 13 and 14, 1928. Issued in mimeographed form by U. S. Bureau of Agricultural Economics.

"A Graphic Summary of American Agriculture Based Largely on the Census." U. S. D. A. *Miscellaneous Publication 105,* 1931.

Baker, O. E., *et al. Seedtime and Harvest.* U. S. D. A. *Circular 183,* 1922.

Barney and Company, Charles D. "The Tobacco Industry." New York: Reports for 1924, 1928, 1929.

Baum, Frank G. *Atlas of U. S. A. Electric Power Industry.* New York: McGraw-Hill. 1923.

Bennett, Merrel K. "Farm Cost Studies in the United States." Food Research Institute, *Publication 4.*

Bentley, H. F. "Cattle Ranges of the Southwest—A History of the Exhaustion of the Pasturage and Suggestions for Its Restoration." U. S. D. A. *Farmers' Bulletin 72,* 1898.

Benton, Harmon. "A Successful Southern Hay Farm." U. S. D. A. *Farmers' Bulletin 312,* 1907.

Bivens, F. J. "The Farmer's Political Economy." Moultrie, Georgia: 1912.

Blue Book of Southern Progress. Annual Issues. 1920-1932. Baltimore: Manufacturers Record.

Boeger, E. A. and Goldenweiser, E. A. "Tenant System of Farming in Yazoo-Mississippi Delta." U. S. D. A. *Bulletin 337,* 1916.

Bonsteel, J. A. "Soils in the Vicinity of Savannah, Georgia." U. S. Bureau of Soils, *Circular 19,* 1909.

Brand, Charles J. "Improved Methods of Handling and Marketing Cotton." U. S. D. A. *Yearbook,* 1912, pp. 443-462. (Separate 605).

Brandes, E. W., *et al.* "Sugar." U. S. D. A. *Yearbook,* 1923, pp. 1-98. (Separate 893).

Brannen, C. O. "Relation of Land Tenure to Plantation Organization." U. S. D. A. *Bulletin 1269,* 1924.

Branson, E. C. (ed) "Home and Farm Ownership." North Carolina Club *Yearbook,* Chapel Hill, N. C., 1921-22.

Brodell, A. P. "Cost of Producing Virginia Dark and Light Tobacco and Incomes from Farming, 1922-25." Virginia Agricultural Experiment Station *Bulletin 255,* 1927.

Broune, D. F. "Progress of Agriculture." Commission of Patents *Annual Report,* 1857, pp. 1-50.

Burch, D. S. "Harnessing Heredity to Improve the Nation's Livestock." U. S. D. A. *Yearbook,* 1919, pp. 347-54.

Burchard, E. F. and Butts, C. "Iron Ores, Fuels and Fluxes of the Birmingham District, Alabama." U. S. Geol. Survey *Bulletin.* Washington, 1910.

Burmeister, C. A., *et al.* "Economic Factors Affecting the Beef Cattle Industry of Virginia." U. S. D. A. *Technical Bulletin 237,* 1931.

Byrne, Harriet A. "Child Labor in Representative Tobacco-Growing Areas." U. S. D. L. *Children's Bureau Publication 155.* Washington, 1926.

Caffey, G. N. "Study of the Soils of the United States." U. S. Bureau of Soils, *Bulletin 85,* 1913.

Campbell, John C. "Future of the Church and Independent Schools in Our Southern Highlands." New York: Russell Sage Foundation, 1917.

Campbell, John L., and Ruffner, W. H. "A Physical Survey in Georgia, Alabama and Mississippi along the Line of the Georgia Pacific Railway." New York, 1883.

Campbell, J. P. "A Coöperative Movement to Promote Farm Financing Methods for the Development of a Safe Farming System." Georgia State College of Agriculture, *Bulletin 397,* 1931.

Campbell, Olive D. "Southern Highland Schools Maintained by Denominational and Independent Agencies." New York: Russell Sage Foundation, 1920.

"The Cane Sugar Industry." U. S. D. C. *Miscellaneous Bulletin 53.* Washington, 1917.

Carlisle Independent. "History of Rice Development in Arkansas." Supplement Sixteenth Year, No. 7 (June 24, 1920) Carlisle, Ark.

Carson, W. J. "Financing the Production and Distribution of Cotton." Reprint from Federal Reserve *Bulletin,* 1923.

Carter, H. R. "The Malaria Problem of the South." *Public Health Reprint No. 552* (August 22, 1919).

Cassidy, Harry M. "The South and the Tariff." *Editorial Research Reports.* July 5, 1925.

Chapman, H. H. "Factors Determining Natural Reproduction of Longleaf Pine on Cut-over Lands in LaSalle Parish, Louisiana." New Haven: Yale University School of Forestry *Bulletin 16,* 1926.

"Child Labor and Work of Mothers on Gulf Truck Farms." U. S. D. L. *Children's Bureau Publication,* 1924.

Cline, Isaac Monroe. "Floods in the Lower Mississippi Valley." New Orleans Board of Trade, 1927.

Collins, Selwyn D. "Economic Status and Health—A Review and Study of the Relevant Morbidity and Mortality Data." *U. S. Public Health Bulletin 165.*

Cook, O. F. "Improvements in Cotton Production." U. S. D. A. *Circular 200,* 1921.

"One-Variety Cotton Communities." U. S. D. A. *Bulletin 1111,* 1922.

"Relation of Cotton Buying to Cotton Growing." U. S. D. A. *Bulletin 60,* 1914.

Cooper, M. R. and Park, J. W. "The Peach Situation in the Southern States." U. S. D. A. *Circular 420,* 1927.

Cooper, W. G. (ed.) "The Piedmont Region." *Southern Immigration and Improvement Company,* Atlanta, 1895.

"Corn and Its Uses as Food." U. S. D. A. *Farmers' Bulletin 1236,* 1924.

"The Cotton Plant," U. S. D. A. Experiment Station, *Bulletin 33,* 1896.

"Cotton Production and Distribution in the Gulf Southwest." *Domestic Commerce Series 49.* U. S. Dept. of Commerce, 1931.

"Cotton Section." *London Times Trade Supplement.* London, 1919.

Cowper, Mary O. "Cotton Cloth: A Type Study in the Social Process." MS. Institute for Research in Social Science, University of North Carolina, Chapel Hill, 1925.

Crawford, G. G. "The South's Part in American Exports." Address, Thirteenth National Foreign Trade Convention, Charleston, S. C., April 28-30, 1926.

Crawford, G. L. "Economic Study of the Dairy Industry in Texas." Texas Agricultural Experiment Station *Bulletin 358,* 1927.

Crosby, M. A. "An Example of Intensive Farming in the Cotton Belt." U. S. D. A. *Farmers' Bulletin 519,* 1913.

Crosby, M. A. and Jennings, R. D. "Systems of Livestock Farming in the Black Prarie Belt of Alabama and Mississippi." U. S. D. A. *Farmers' Bulletin 1546,* 1927.

Cut-Over Land Conference of the South, New Orleans, 1917.

Dabney, Charles W., Jr. "Progress of Southern Agriculture." U. S. D. A. *Circular 3,* 1896.

Dana, S. T. "Farms, Forests, and Erosion." U. S. D. A. *Yearbook,* 1916, pp. 107-34.

Daughtery, C. R. "The Development of Horsepower Equipment in the United States." U. S. Geological Survey, *Water Supply Paper 579.*

Davenport, W. R. "Growth of Water Power Development in the United States." U. S. Geological Survey, *Water Supply Paper 759.*

Davis, R. O. E. "Soil Erosion in the South." U. S. D. A. *Bulletin 180.*
  "Economic Waste From Soil Erosion."   U. S. D. A. *Yearbook,* 1913,
  pp. 207-20.

Delop, Simeon Alexander. "The Populist Party in North Carolina."
  Trinity College Historical Society, *Paper XIV,* pp. 40-74, 1922.

Denton, Virginia. "Social Economic Characteristics of the Mississippi
  Delta." Unpublished M. A. Thesis, University of North Carolina,
  1930.

Dervaux, R. C., Taylor, H. A., and Haas, T. D. "Malaria Control: A
  Report of Demonstration Studies Conducted in Urban and Rural Sections." *Public Health Bulletin No. 88,* September, 1917.

Dickens, Dorothy. "A Nutritional Investigation of Negro Tenants in
  the Yazoo-Mississippi Delta." Mississippi A. and M. College *Bulletin 254,* 1928.
  "A Study of Food Habits of White People in Two Contrasting Areas
  of Mississippi." Mississippi A. and M. College *Bulletin 245,* 1927.

Dixon, H. M. and Hawthorne, H. W. "An Economic Study of Farming
  in Sumter County, Georgia." U. S. D. A. *Bulletin 492,* 1917.

Doane, C. F., and Reed, A. J. "Cheesemaking Brings Prosperity to
  Farmers of Southern Mountains." U. S. D. A. *Yearbook,* 1917, pp.
  147-52. (Separate 737).

Drake, J. A. "Making Labor Go as Far as Possible." U. S. D. A.
  Farmers' Bulletin 614.

Du Bois, W. E. B. "Negro Landholders in Georgia." U. S. D. L.
  Bulletin 35.

Dumble, Edwin Theodore. "The Geology of Texas." *Rice Institute
  Pamphlets,* III, No. 2, pp. 125-206.

Dunlap, J. P. "Mineral Resources of the United States." U. S. Bureau
  of Mines, *Annual Reports on Secondary Metals,* 1930-31.

Dykes, A. W. "Sugar." *Blue Book of Southern Progress.* Baltimore:
  Manufacturers Record, 1929.

Edwards, E. E. "Bibliography of the History of Agriculture in the
  United States." U. S. D. A. *Miscellaneous Publication 84,* 1930.

Elliott, Howard, Roper, Daniel C., and Soule, George. "Report of the
  Special Advisers on Reclamation and Rural Development in the
  Southern States." *Bureau of Reclamation, Dept. of the Interior,*
  Washington, 1927.

Ellsworth, J. O., and Elliott, F. F. "Types of Farming in Oklahoma."
  Oklahoma Agricultural Experiment Station, *Bulletin 181.* Stillwater,
  1929.

Esdorf, R. H., von. "Malaria in the United States." *Public Health Reprint 277,* 1915.

Eutsler, Roland B. "Negro Agricultural Credit Conditions in North Carolina." Unpublished MS. Institute for Research in Social Science, University of North Carolina, Chapel Hill, N. C., 1927.

Fain, J. R., *et al.* "Survey of Livestock Production in Georgia." Georgia Agricultural College Experiment Station, *Bulletin 331,* 1927.

Farley, F. W. "Growth of the Beef-Cattle Industry in the South." U. S. D. A. *Yearbook,* 1917, pp. 327-40. (Separate 749).

Farley, F. W., and Greene, S. W. "The Cut-Over Pine Lands of the South for Beef-Cattle Production." U. S. D. A. *Bulletin 827,* 1921.

Faveau, Augustin L. "Rice Culture in South Carolina." U. S. D. A. *Report,* 1867.

Federal Trade Commission. "The Cotton Trade." *Senate Document 100,* Sixty-Eighth Congress, First Session, 1924.

Fernow, B. E. "Relation of Forests to Farms." U. S. D. A. *Yearbook,* 1895, pp. 333-40.

"The Fertilizer Problem in South Carolina." Clemson Agricultural College, *Circular 107.* Clemson, S. C., 1930.

"Floods, Forests and the Future." *The American Tree Association,* Washington, D. C., 1927.

Fox, John A. "Mississippi River Flood Problems." Memphis, Tennessee: Mississippi River Levee Association, 1915.

Fraley, J. W., and Smith, C. Beaman. "When Tenant Farming is Desirable." U. S. D. A. *Farmers' Bulletin, 437.*

Frayser, May A. "The Play and Recreation of Children and Youth in Selected Rural Areas of South Carolina." South Carolina Agricultural Experiment Station *Bulletin 275,* Clemson College, 1931.

Frost, Norman. "A Statistical Study of the Public Schools of the Appalachian Mountains." U. S. Bureau of Education, *Bulletin 11,* 1915.

Fuchs, A. W. "Malaria Survey of the Missouri Pacific Railroad, 1922." *Public Health Bulletin 135,* 1923.

Funk, W. C. "Home Supplies Furnished by the Farm." U. S. D. A. *Farmers' Bulletin 1082,* 1920.

"Value to Farm Families of Fuel, Food, and Use of House." U. S. D. A., *Bulletin 410,* 1916.

Gabbard, L. P., and Jones, F. R. "Large Scale Cotton Production in Texas." College Station, Texas: Texas Agricultural Experiment Station, *Bulletin 302.*

Garner, W. W. "Tobacco Curing." U. S. D. A. *Farmers' Bulletin 523,* 1928.

"Tobacco Culture." U. S. D. A. *Farmers' Bulletin 571,* 1922.

Garnett, W. R. "Rural Organization in Relation to Rural Life in Virginia." Virginia Agricultural Experiment Station, *Bulletin 256,* 1927.

Gatlin, G. O. "Coöperative Marketing of Cotton." U. S. D. A. *Bulletin 1392, 1926.*

Gerish, E. F. "Distribution of Dry Goods in the Gulf Southwest." *Domestic Commerce Series 43.* U. S. Dept. of Commerce, 1931.

Gilbert, C. G., and Pogue, J. E. "The Energy Resources of the United States: A Field for Reconstruction. U. S. National Museum, *Bulletin 102,* Smithsonian Institute, Washington, 1919.

Glenn, L. C. "The Physiographic Influences in the Development of Tennessee." The Resources of Tennessee. 1915.

"Denudation and Erosion in the Southern Appalachian Region and the Monongahela Basin." U. S. Geological Survey, *Professional Paper 72, 1911.*

Goodrich, C. L. "Factors that Make for Successful Farming in the South." U. S. D. A. *Farmers' Bulletin 1121, 1920.*

Gray, L. C., *et al.* "Farm Ownership and Tenancy." U. S. D. A. *Yearbook,* 1923, pp. 507-600. (Separate 897).

"The Utilization of Our Lands for Crops, Pasture, and Forests." U. S. D. A. *Yearbook,* 1923, pp. 415-506. (Separate 896).

Greeley, W. B., *et al.* "Timber: Mine or Crop?" U. S. D. A. *Yearbook,* 1922, pp. 83-180. (Separate 886).

"Growing Pine Timber for Profit in the South." U. S. D. A. *Miscellaneous Publication 24, 1928.*

Hager, John M. "Commercial Survey of the Southeast." *Domestic Commerce Series 19,* U. S. Dept. of Commerce, 1927.

Hall, B. M., and H. R. "Second Report on Water Powers of Alabama." Geological Survey of Alabama." *Bulletin 17, 1916.*

Hall, O. J. "Cost of Producing Rice in Arkansas in 1927." Arkansas Agricultural Experiment Station, *Bulletin 266, 1931.*

Haney, Lewis H., and Wehwein, George S. "Studies in the Industrial Resources of Texas." Texas University, *Bulletin 3,* Austin, 1915.

Harper, Roland M. "Economic Botany of Alabama." Geological Survey of Alabama, *Monograph 8, 1913.*

"The Forests of Alabama." Geological Survey of Alabama, *Special Report No. 8,* University of Alabama, 1913.

"The Geography and Vegetation of Northern Florida." *Sixth Annual Report,* Florida State Geological Survey, December, 1914, pp. 163-437.

"Geography of Central Florida." *Annual Report,* Florida Geological Survey, XIII, April, 1921, 71-307.

"The Natural Resources of Georgia." University of Georgia *Bulletin XXX,* 3, February, 1905.

"Resources of Southern Alabama." Alabama Geological Survey, *Special Report No. 11.* Montgomery, 1920.

Haskell, Chester G. "Irrigation Practices in Rice Growing." U. S. D. A. *Farmers' Bulletin 673,* 1915.

"Irrigation of Rice on the Coastal Prairies of Texas." Texas Department of Agriculture, *Bulletin 43,* pp. 88-116, 1915.

Hawthorne, H. W. "The Family Living from the Farm." U. S. D. A. *Bulletin 1338,* 1925.

Hawthorne, H. W., Dixon, H. M., and Montgomery, Frank. "Farm Organization and Farm Management in Sumter County, Georgia." U. S. D. A. *Bulletin 1034,* 1922.

Hemphill, J. C. "Climate, Soil, and Agricultural Capabilities of South Carolina and Georgia." U. S. D. A. *Special Report 47,* Washington, 1882.

Henry, A. J. "Climatology of the United States." *Bulletin Q,* U. S. D. A. *Bulletin,* Weather Bureau, 1906.

Henry, A. J., *et al.* "Weather and Agriculture." U. S. D. A. *Yearbook,* 1924, pp. 457-558. (Separate 918).

"Weather Forecasting in the United States." U. S. D. A. *Weather Bureau Publication 583,* 1916.

Henry, Walter Pickard. "Cotton and the Commission Merchant." Raleigh, N. C., 1883.

Hills, J. S., Wait, C. E., and White, H. C. "Dietary Studies in Rural Regions in Vermont, Tennessee, and Georgia." U. S. D. A. Office of Experiment Stations, *Bulletin 221,* 1909.

Hirsch, Joseph. "The Bankers' Effort to Improve Personal Credit in the South." Conference of Cotton State Bankers, New Orleans, December 6-7, 1915.

Hoffman, Frederick L. *The Malaria Problem in Peace and War.* Newark, N. J.: Prudential Press, 1918.

Holleman, O. T. *Is the South in the Grip of a Cotton Oligarchy?* Atlanta, Georgia, 1914.

Holmes, Francis S. "Phosphate Rocks of South Carolina and the Great Carolina Marl Bed together with a history of their Discovery and Developments." Charleston, 1870.

Holmes, George K. "Movement from City and Town to Farms." U. S. D. A. *Yearbook,* 1914, pp. 257-74.

"Progress of Agriculture in the United States." U. S. D. A. *Yearbook,* 1899, pp. 307-334.

"Supply and Wages of Farm Labor." U. S. D. A. *Yearbook,* 1910, pp. 189-200.

"Three Centuries of Tobacco Culture." U. S. D. A. *Yearbook,* 1919, pp. 151-75.

Holton, J. C. *Dairy Prosperity Dawns for Mississippi*. Leaflet, Mississippi Department of Agriculture, 1928.

"Hookworm Disease Among Cotton Mill Operatives." U. S. D. L. *Bulletin 175*. Women in Industry, No. 5, 1915, pp. 391-396.

"Hookworm Disease and Its Control." *International Health Board*, New York, 1922.

Howard, L. O. "The Economic Loss to the People of the United States Through Insects that Carry Disease." *Bulletin*, Bureau of Entomology, 1909.

Hunter, Arthur. *Blood Pressure: What Affects It*. New York: New York Life Insurance Company.

Hunter, W. D., and Coad, B. R. *The Boll Weevil Problem*. U. S. D. A. *Farmers' Bulletin 1329*, 1923.

Illick, J. S. "Southern Pine: What It Is, What It Is Used For." New Orleans: Southern Pine Association, 1923.

Jennings, R. D., and Crosby, M. A. "Economic Study of the Livestock Possibilities in the Southeastern Coastal Plain." U. S. D. A. *Technical Bulletin 127*, 1929.

Jesness, O. B. "Marketing of Tobacco." Kentucky Agricultural Experiment Station, *Bulletin 287*, 1928.

Johnson, L. A., *et al.* "An Investigation of Conditions in the Ragged Mountains of Virginia." Conducted by the Civic Club of the University of Virginia. Charlottesville, Va., January 1, 1912.

Juve, O. A. "Cost Data for Farm Products." U. S. D. A., *Yearbook*, 1921, pp. 805-45. (Separate 876).

Kentucky Geological Survey. Burroughs, W. A. *The Coal Fields*, 1927; *The Knobs*, 1926; Davis, D. H., *The Blue Grass*, 1927; *The Jackson Purchase*, 1923; *The Mountains*, 1924; Sauer, C. O., *The Pennyroyal*, 1929.

Killebrew, J. B. "Grasses and Forage Plants." *Bulletin*, Tennessee Agricultural Experiment Station, 1898.

"Report on the Culture and Curing of Tobacco in the United States." Washington: Department of the Interior, 1884.

Kincer, J. B. "Influence of Weather on Farm Work and Crop Yields." U. S. D. A. *Yearbook*, 1924, pp. 498-530.

King, W. R. "Water Resources of Tennessee." Nashville: Department of Education, Division of Geology, *Bulletin 34*, 1925.

Kirkpatrick, E. L. "The Farmer's Standard of Living." U. S. D. A. *Bulletin 1466*, 1926.

Kirkpatrick, E. L., and Saunder, J. T. "Relation Between Ability to Pay and the Standard of Living Among Farmers." U. S. D. A. *Bulletin 1382*, 1926.

Knapp, Bradford, and Creswell, Mary E. "The Effect of Home Demonstration Work on the Community and the County in the South." U. S. D. A. *Yearbook,* 1916, pp. 251-66. (Separate 710).

Knapp, Seaman A. "Causes of Southern Rural Conditions and the Small Farm as an Important Remedy." U. S. D. A. *Yearbook,* 1908, pp. 311-20.

"Rice Culture," U. S. D. A. *Farmers' Bulletin 417,* 1910.

Kyle, C. H. "Growing Corn in the Southeastern States." U. S. D. A. *Farmers' Bulletin 1149,* 1920.

Lane, F. K. "Conservation Through Engineering." U. S. D. I., Geological Survey, *Bulletin 705,* 1920.

Langsford, E. L., and Hutson, J. B. "Systems of Beef Cattle Farming for Southeastern Virginia." Virginia Agricultural Extension *Bulletin 258,* 1927.

Langworthy, C. F. "Food Customs and Diet in American Homes." U. S. D. A. Office of Experiment Stations, *Circular 110,* 1911.

Larson, C. W., *et al.* "The Dairy Industry." U. S. D. A. *Yearbook,* 1922, pp. 281-394. (Separate 897).

Lawson, Scribner F. "Economic Grasses." U. S. D. A. Division of Agronomy, *Bulletin 14,* 1898.

Lazor, J. T., and Currin, R. E. "Cultivation of Bright Tobacco." S. C. Agricultural Experiment Station, *Bulletin 92,* Clemson, S. C., 1928.

Leftwich, George J. "Some Main Traveled Roads, Including Cross Sections of Natchez Trace." *Publications,* Mississippi Historical Society Centenary Series. Jackson, 1916.

Leighty, C. E., Warburton, C. W., Stone, O. C., and Baker, O. E. "The Corn Crop." U. S. D. A. *Yearbook,* 1927, pp. 161-226. (Separate 872).

Long, L. E., and Kifer, R. S. "Systems of Farming for Hill Sections of Mississippi." Mississippi Agricultural Experiment Station *Bulletin 257,* September, 1928.

"Farm Practices in South Central Mississippi with Suggested Changes." Mississippi Agricultural Experiment Station, *Bulletin 273,* 1929.

Loring, F. W., and Atkinson, C. F. *Cotton Culture and the South Considered,* Boston: A. Williams and Co. 1869.

Lowe, E. N. Mississippi: Its Geology, Geography, Soils and Natural Resources." Mississippi Geological Survey, *Bulletin 12,* Jackson, 1915.

MacKaye, Benton. "Employment and Natural Resources." *Publication* U. S. D. L., 1919.

Maclachlan, Emily Stevens. "The South's Dietary Pattern." Unpublished M. A. Thesis, University of North Carolina, Chapel Hill, 1932.

Marbut, C. F., Bennett, H. H., Lapham, J. E., and Lapham, M. H. "Soils of the United States." U. S. D. A. Bureau of Soils, *Bulletin 96*, Washington, 1913.

Martin, Donald Frazier, Jr. "The Naval Stores Industry." Unpublished M. A. Thesis, University of North Carolina, Chapel Hill, 1931.

Matthews, Susan J. "Food Habits of Georgia Rural People." Georgia Agricultural Experiment Station, *Bulletin 159*, 1929.

Matthewson, E. H. "Intensive Methods and Systematic Rotation of Crops in Tobacco Culture." U. S. D. A. *Yearbook*, 1908, pp. 403-20.

Mattoon, W. R. "Forestry and Farm Income." U. S. D. A. *Farmers' Bulletin 1117*, 1920, pp. 1-34.

"Making Woodlands Profitable in the Southern States." U. S. D. A. *Farmers' Bulletin 1071*, 1926.

"Loblolly Pine Primer." U. S. D. A. *Farmers' Bulletin 1517*, 1926.

"Long-Leaf Pine Primer." U. S. D. A. *Farmers' Bulletin 1486*, 1926.

"Short-Leaf Pine Primer." U. S. D. A. *Farmers' Bulletin 1534*, 1927.

"Slash Pine Primer," U. S. D. A. *Farmers' Bulletin 1256*, 1922.

Maxcy, Kenneth L. "Distribution of Malaria in the United States." Reprint No. 839. *Public Health Report*, May 25, 1923.

McCallie, S. W., *et. al.* "Physical Geography of Georgia." Geological Survey of Georgia, *Bulletin 42*. Atlanta, 1925.

McConnell, O. J. "A Study of Cotton Market Conditions in North Carolina." U. S. D. A. *Bulletin 476*, 1917.

McCormick, E. B. "Housing the Worker on the Farm." U. S. D. A. *Yearbook*, 1918, pp. 347-56. (Separate 789).

McCutcheon, George. "The Case for Cotton. University of South Carolina *Bulletin*, 1915.

McGee, W. J. "Soil Erosion." U. S. D. A. Bureau of Soils, *Bulletin 71*, 1911.

McGill, Nettie P. "Children in Agriculture." U. S. D. L. *Children's Bureau Publication 187*, 1929.

McHatton, T. H. "History of Georgia Horticulture." University of Georgia, *Bulletin*, IX, 176-186, April, 1909.

McKee, E. R. "The French Turpentining System Applied to Long-Leaf Pine." U. S. D. A. *Circular 327*, 1924.

McNair, A. P. "Labor Requirements of Arkansas Crops." U. S. D. A. *Bulletin 1181*, 1924.

Meadows, William R. "Sea Island Cotton Industry." U. S. D. A. *Bulletin 146*, 1914.

Merriam, C. H. "Life Zones and Crop Zones of the United States." U. S. D. A. Division of Biology, *Bulletin 10*, 1898.

Merrill, I. C., Graves, N. C., Campbell, M. R. "Rational Review of Power Resources." Transactions of World Power Conference, London, 1924.

Message from the President of the United States transmitting a Report of the Secretary of Agriculture in relation to the Forests, Rivers, and Mountains of the Southern Appalachian Region. Washington, 1902.

Minutes of Conference on Economic and Social Survey of the Southern Appalachian Highlands. (Mimeographed). Washington, February 24, 1930.

Mohler, John R. "Texas or Tick Fever." U. S. D. A. *Farmers' Bulletin 569, November,* 1928.

Morgan, Alfred C. "Insect Enemies of Tobacco in the United States." U. S. D. A. *Yearbook,* 1910, pp. 281-96.

Morrill, Ark. "Floods of the Mississippi." Weather Bureau, Washington, D. C., 1897.

Mumford, H. W., and Hall, L. D. "Economic Factors in Cattle Feeding—A Review of Beef Production in the United States." Illinois Experiment Station, *Bulletin 169,* 1913.

Nason, Wayne, C. "Rural Hospital." U. S. D. A. *Farmers' Bulletin 1485,* 1926.

"Rural Planning: The Social Aspects." U. S. D. A. *Farmers' Bulletin 1325,* 1923.

"Rural Planning: The Village." U. S. D. A. *Farmers' Bulletin 1441,* 1925.

Nichols, W. D., *et al.* "Study of Farm Organization and Management in Mason and Fleming Counties." Kentucky Agricultural Experiment Station *Bulletin 253,* 1924.

"North Carolina Land Conditions and Problems." Report of State Land Commission appointed by the General Assembly, Raleigh, 1923.

Oemler, A. "Truck Farming." U. S. D. A. *Report,* 1885, pp. 583-627.

Parr, Virgil Vesser, *et al.* "Ranch Organization and Methods of Live Stock Production in the Southwest." U. S. D. A. *Technical Bulletin 68,* 1928.

Pertle, T. R. "Trend of the Dairy Cattle Industry in U. S., etc." U. S. D. A., *Circular 7,* 1919.

Piper, C. V., *et al.* "Growing Hay in the South for Market." U. S. D. A. *Farmers' Bulletin 677,* 1921.

"Hay." U. S. D. A. *Yearbook,* 1924, pp. 289-373. (Separate 916).

"Our Forage Resources." U. S. D. A. *Yearbook,* 1923, pp. 311-414. (Separate 895).

"The Poor Whites." *Virginia Political Pamphlets,* III, 7.

Poore, B. P. "History of Agriculture in the United States." Commission of Agriculture, *Annual Report for 1866*, pp. 498-527.

Price, O. W. "Influence of Forestry Upon the Lumber Industry." U. S. D. A. *Yearbook*, 1902, pp. 309-12.

Price, O. W., Kellogg, R. S., and Cox, W. T. "The Forests of the United States: Their Use." U. S. D. A. *Forest Service Circular 171*, 1909.

Proceedings, Annual Meeting of Southern Appalachian Water Power Conference, Knoxville, Tennessee, 1922.

Proceedings, Cotton Convention Held at Memphis, Tennessee, October 13, 1926.

Proceedings, Southern Forestry Congress, Chapel Hill, N. C., 1916-21.

Proceedings, Southwide Cotton Conference, New Orleans, La., January 11-12, 1928.

Quaintance, H. W. "Influence of Farm Machinery on Production and Labor." American Economic Association, *Publications*, Series 3, IV, No. 4, 1904.

Raper, Arthur. "Two Rural Black Belt Counties in Georgia." Unpublished Ph. D. Thesis, University of North Carolina, Chapel Hill, 1931.

"Rayon, A New Influence in the Textile Industry." New York: Metropolitan Life Insurance Company. n. d.

"Reclamation and Drainage of Central Florida." *Bulletin*, Atlantic Deeper Waterways Association, October, 1916.

"Report of Commission on Industrial Relations," *Senate Document 415*, IX, X, "The Land Question in the Southwest," 1916.

"Report of Committee on Nutritional Problems." 53 Meeting American Public Health Association, Detroit, October 1924. *American Journal of Public Health*, XIV, 1038-1040, December 1924.

Reports, International Health Board, New York: Rockefeller Foundation, 1913-32.

Report of National Conservation Congress. *Senate Document No. 676*, Sixtieth Congress, Second Session, 1907.

Report of New York State Commission on Ventilation. Albany, 1923.

Report of North Carolina Tax Commission, 1928. "Farm Income and Taxation in North Carolina." North Carolina State Agricultural Experiment Station, *Bulletin 267*, Raleigh, 1929.

Report of the Surgeon General United States Army. Washington, 1917.

Reynolds, R. V., and Pierson, A. H. "Lumber Cut of the United States, 1870-1920." U. S. D. A. *Bulletin 1119*, 1923.

Reynoldson, L. A. "Field and Crop Labor on Georgia Farms." (Coastal Plains Area). U. S. D. A . *Bulletin 1292*, 1925.

Rivers, C. D. *The Empire of Cotton.* Sandersville, Georgia, 1914.

Roberts, G. "Better Land Utilization in Kentucky." Kentucky Agricultural Extension *Circular 163,* 1924.

Roberts, John. "Food Animals and Meat Consumption in the United States." U. S. D. A. *Circular 241,* 1924.

Roberts, Lydia. "The Nutrition and Care of Children in a Mountain County of Kentucky." U. S. D. L. *Children's Bureau Publication,* 110, 1922.

Rommell, G. M. "The Function of Live Stock in Agriculture." U. S. D. A. *Yearbook,* 1916.

"Rural Children in Selected Counties of North Carolina." U. S. D. L. *Children's Bureau Publication 33,* 1918.

Russell, B. A. "Farm Power Utilization and Costs, South Carolina." South Carolina Agricultural Experiment Station, *Bulletin 280,* Clemson College, 1931.

Sally, Alexander Samuel, Jr. "The Introduction of Rice Culture Into South Carolina." South Carolina History Committee *Bulletin No. 6,* Columbia, 1919.

Sanders, J. T. "Farm Ownership and Tenancy in the Black Prairie of Texas." U. S. D. A. *Bulletin 1068,* 1922.

Saville, Thorndike. "The Water Power Situation in North Carolina." Water Resources Division, North Carolina Geological and Economical Survey, *Circular 6,* 1923.

Scarborough, W. S. "Tenancy and Ownership Among Negro Farmers in Southampton County, Virginia." U. S. D. A. *Bulletin 1404,* 1926.

Schorger, A. W., and Betts, H. S. "The Naval Stores Industry." U. S. D. A. *Bulletin 229,* 1915.

Semple, Arthur T. "Beef Production in the Cotton Belt." U. S. D. A. *Farmers' Bulletin 1379,* 1923.

Semple, A. T., *et al.* "Beef Production from Purebred, Grade and Native Cattle." U. S. D. A. *Technical Bulletin 203,* 1930.

Shaler, N. S. "The Origin and Nature of Soils." U. S. Geological Survey, *Twelfth Annual Report,* XCI, Pt. I, pp. 219-344.

"Sea Coast Swamps of the Eastern United States." U. S. Geological Survey, *Sixth Annual Report,* 1884-5, pp. 353-398.

Sherman, W. A., Taylor, Fred, and Brand, Charles, J. "Studies of Primary Market Conditions in Oklahoma." U. S. D. A. *Bulletin 36,* 1913.

"Short Term Farm Credit in Texas." Texas Agricultural Experiment Station, *Bulletin 351,* 1927.

Smedes, H. M. "Agricultural Graphics." University of North Carolina, *Extension Bulletin 42,* Chapel Hill, 1923.

Smillie, W. G. "Hookworm Disease." Reprint from *Nelson's Loose-Leaf Medicine*. New York: International Health Board, 1928.

Smith, G. Otis. "The People's Interest in Water Power Resources." U. S. Geological Survey. *Water Supply Paper 400-A*, 1916.

Snider, S. C., *et al*. "Geography of Oklahoma." Oklahoma Geographical Survey, *Bulletin 27*, Norman, Oklahoma, 1917.

Soil Survey, Field Book, U. S. Bureau of Soils, 1906.

Soussiat, St. George L. "Highway Legislation in Maryland and Its Influence on the Economic Development of the State." Maryland Geological Survey, III, 1899.

The South's Development: Fifty Years of Southern Progress. Baltimore: Manufacturer's Record, Pt. II, December 11, 1924.

Spafford, Russell R. "The Effect of Climate and Soil Upon Agriculture." *University of Nebraska Studies*, XVI, Nos. 1-2, pp. 91-113, Lincoln, 1916.

Spillman, W. J. "Distribution of Types of Farming in the United States." U. S. D. A. *Farmers' Bulletin, 1289*, 1923.

"Seasonal Distribution of Labor on the Farm." U. S. D. A. *Yearbook*, 1911, pp. 269-284.

Spillman, W. J., Crosby, M. A., Brodie, D. A., and Warburton, C. W. "Diversified Farming in the Cotton Belt." U. S. D. A. *Yearbook*, 1905.

Staple Cotton Review, Files of, Greenwood, Mississippi.

Statistical Abstract of the United States, 1920-1932.

Stevens, Stanley. "A Critique of the Climatic Hypothesis of Ellsworth Huntington." Unpublished M. A. Thesis, University of North Carolina, Chapel Hill, 1931.

Stevens, W. Mackenzie. "The Marketing and Distribution of American-Grown Onions." U. S. D. A. *Bulletin 1283*, 1926.

Stewart, C. L. "Farm Occupancy, Ownership, and Tenancy, and When Do Tenants Move." U. S. D. A. Division of Land Economics, Bureau of Agricultural Economics, April 1923.

Stiebling, H. K., and Birdseye, M. "Adequate Diets for Families with Limited Incomes." U. S. D. A. *Miscellaneous Publication 113*, 1931.

Stiles, W. C. "Economic Aspects of Hookworm Disease in the United States." *Transactions*, Fifteenth Conference of Hygiene and Demography, III, 757, Washington, 1913.

"The Story of the Cattle Fever Tick." U. S. D. A., 1922.

Strowbridge, J. W. "Origin and Distribution of the Commercial Potato Crop." U. S. D. A. *Technical Bulletin 7*, 1927.

Stuart, William. "Potato Production in the South." U. S. D. A. *Farmers' Bulletin 1205*, 1923.

Stubbs, W. C. "Sugar Cane: A Treatise in the History, Botany and Agriculture of Sugar Cane." Louisiana Bureau of Agriculture, 1897.

Swenson, Carl R., and Frank, W. C. "Economic Aspects of Citrus Fruit Growing in Polk County, Florida." U. S. D. A. *Bulletin 1435,* 1926.

Swift, W. H. "Child Welfare in North Carolina." National Child Labor Commission, 1918.

Switzer, J. A. "The Larger Undeveloped Water Power of Tennessee." Nashville: Dept. Education, Division of Geology, *Bulletin 20,* 1919.

Switzler, William F. "Report on the Internal Commerce of the United States." Washington: Government Printing Office, 1888.

Taylor, Carl C., and Zimmerman, C. C. "Economic and Social Conditions of North Carolina Farmers." State Tenancy Commission, Raleigh, 1922.

Taylor, Fred. "Relation Between Primary Market Price and Qualities of Cotton." U. S. D. A. *Bulletin 457,* 1916.

"Timber Depletion, Lumber Prices, Lumber Exports and Concentration of Timber Ownership." Public Document. *Capper Report on Senate Resolution 311,* 1920.

Tracy, S. M. "Forage for the Cotton Belt." U. S. D. A. *Farmers' Bulletin 1125,* 1920.

Trask, John W. "Malaria." *Public Health Reprint No. 382,* December 22, 1916.

Turner, Howard A. "Ownership of Tenant Farms in the United States." U. S. D. A. *Bulletin 432,* 1926.

Turner, Howard A., and Howell, L. D. "Condition of Farmers in a White-Farmer Area of the Cotton Piedmont, 1924-1926." U. S. D. A. *Circular 78,* 1929.

United States Bureau of the Census: *A Century of Population Growth 1790-1900.* Washington, 1909.

"Cotton Production." *Reports of Tenth Census 1880,* V. 5 and 6.

"Farm Population in the United States." *Census Monograph No. 6,* 1926.

"Growth of Manufacture, 1899-1923." *Census Monograph No. 8,* 1928.

"Negro Population 1790-1915." Washington: Government Printing Office, 1918.

"Plantation Farming in the United States." *Census Bulletin,* 1916.

"Plantations in the South." *Reports of the Thirteenth Census, 1910,* V, Ch. XII.

Report of the Fourteenth Census, 1920.

Report of Census of Agriculture, 1925.

Report of Fifteenth Census, 1930.

United States Department of Agriculture: *Atlas of American Agriculture*. (O. E. Baker, ed) 1918.

"Cotton." By C. Stine and O. E. Baker." (V, A) 1918.

"Frost and the Growing Season." By W. G. Reed (III) 1918.

"Natural Vegetation." By H. L. Shantz and Raphael Zon.

"Precipitation and Humidity." By J. B. Kincer (II A).

"Rural Population." By E. A. Goldenweiser (IX, I) 1919.

United States Food Administration, *Food and the War*. New York, 1918.

United States Tariff Commission. "Information Survey on Artificial Silk," Washington, 1925.

Use of Fish for Mosquito Control. New York: International Health Board, 1924.

Vasbury, E. D., and Roberts, T. R. "The Culture of Citrus Fruit in the Gulf States." U. S. D. A. *Farmers' Bulletin 1343, 1923*.

Vasey, George. "Agricultural Grasses and Forage Plants." U. S. D. A., Division of Botany, *Special Bulletin*, 1889.

Veatch, A. C. "Geology and Underground Water Resources of Northern Louisiana and Southern Arkansas." U. S. Geological Survey, *Bulletin 46*, 1906.

Wait, Charles E. "Dietary Studies at the University of Tennessee in 1895." U. S. D. A. *Bulletin 29*, 1896.

"Nutrition Investigations at the University of Tennessee in 1896 and 1897." U. S. D. A. *Bulletin 53*, 1898.

"The Waning Hardwood Supply and the Appalachian Forests." U. S. Forest Service, *Circular 16*, Washington, 1908.

Ward, Florence E. "The Farm Woman's Problem." U. S. D. A. *Circular 148*, November, 1920.

Ward, W. F. "Production of Beef in the South." U. S. D. A. *Yearbook*, 1913, pp. 259-282.

Warren, George M. "Tidal Marshes and Their Reclamation." U. S. D. A. *Bulletin 240*, Office of Experiment Station.

Watkins, D. W. "An Investigation of Cotton Growing in Texas, Showing the Influence on Cotton Production in South Carolina." South Carolina Agricultural Experiment Station, *Bulletin 75*, Clemson College.

"The Welfare of Children in Cotton-Growing Areas in Texas." U. S. D. L., *Children's Bureau Publication 134*, 1924.

Wernicke, O. L. H. "Growing Pine Timber for Profit in the South." U. S. D. A. *Miscellaneous Publication 24*, 1928.

"What Northern Men Say of the South." *Proceedings*, Convention of Northern Residents of the South, Charlotte, N. C., 1879.

White, Harry A. "The Grade and Staple of South Carolina's 1930 Cotton Crop." South Carolina Agricultural Experiment Station, *Circular 47*, Clemson College, 1931.

Whitney, Milton. "Some Physical Properties of Soils in Their Relation to Moisture and Crop Distribution." U. S. Weather Bureau *Bulletin 4*, 1892.

"The Use of Soils East of the Great Plains Region." U. S. D. A. Bureau of Soils, *Bulletin 78*, 1911.

"Why Grow Timber?" U. S. D. A. Forest Service, *Bulletin*, 1928.

William, J. O. "Mule Production." U. S. D. A. *Farmers' Bulletin 1341*, 1923.

Wood, Harriette. "The Kentucky Mountains." Unpublished M. A. Thesis, University of North Carolina, Chapel Hill, 1930.

Wooten, E. O. "Cotton in Texas Plain Area." U. S. D. A. *Yearbook*, 1926, pp. 271-74.

Wright, Sewall. "Corn and Hay Correlations." U. S. D. A. *Bulletin 1300*, 1925.

Yoder, F. R., Beardsley, H. S., and Honeycutt, A. J. "Farm Credit Conditions in North Carolina." North Carolina State College, *Bulletin*, 1923.

Young, E. C. "The Movement of Farm Population." Cornell University Experiment Station *Bulletin 426*.

Youngblood, Bonney. "An Economic Study of A Typical Ranching Area in the Edwards Plateau of Texas." Texas Agricultural Experiment Station, *Bulletin 297*, 1922.

INDEX

ABERNETHY, Thomas Perkins, 115
Acclimatization, 374
Adams, Henry, 49-50, 68, 412-13
Adams, James Truslow, 467
Advertising the South, 485-86
Aëdes aegypti mosquito, 395
Agrarianism in the South, attempted return to, 389-91
Agricultural development in southern highlands, 256-58
Agricultural extension and regional planning, 493
Agricultural regions in United States, 12-13
Agriculture, types of, 177-78; depression in, 178-79; characteristics of southern, 179-84; conditions favorable to South, 184-85; and Negro, 192-93; cotton and southern, 185-04; credit, 198-99; reorganization of southern, 494-98; live stock in, 494; Colquitt County (Georgia) plan, 493-94; forage in, 494; stabilization of cotton production, 494-98; see live stock, soil, cotton, tobacco, rice, sugar, trucking, etc.
Ahern, Major George P., 125, 137
Air conditioning and southern climate, 372
Alabama, 47, 49, 51, 53, 56, 75, 87, 90, 91, 97, 99, 108, 115, 121, 127, 150, 154, 161, 165, 167, 173, 196, 264, 275, 282, 284, 291, 301-07, 356, 385, 386, 387, 424, 437, 439, 443, 445, 451, 452, 488
Alcoholic drinks and southern climate, 371-72
Allen, Frederick Lewis, 504
Alluvial areas, see Delta
Alluvial soils, 87, 92
Anderson, Sherwood, 510
Anderson, W. S., 498-99
Andrews, Sidney, 415
Angoff, Charles, 378, 442-43

Anopheles mosquito, 395, 404-05, 408-09
Appalachian Highlands, as barrier to settlement, 47-48; diet in, 431; physiography of, 27-28; see southern highlands
Appalachian Valley, 27-28
Area, see Region
Architecture and southern climate, 369-70
Arkansas, 53, 90, 97, 141, 143, 150, 155, 161, 167, 173, 204, 215, 217, 229, 246, 259-60, 266, 269-70, 273, 318, 343, 346, 376, 397, 406-07, 409, 439, 443, 445, 487
Arkansas River Valley, 28-29
Arkwright, Preston S., 287
Armitage, F. P., 412
Armsby, H. P., 416
Arthur, John P., 65-66
Ashe, Thomas, 412
Ashe, W. W., 103-04, 120
Asheville, 486
Ashford, Bailey K., 382
Atlanta, 485, 507; site of, 38
Atlantic Coast Flatwoods, 89
Atlas of American Agriculture, 89, 89-92, 100, 111
Augusta, site of, 38
Augustine, Donald L., 387
Avram, M., 300
Aycock, Charles Brantley, 509

BAGASSE, rayon from, 497
Baird, Eunice Fuller, 419, 421
Baker, Oliver E., 12, 89, 135, 185, 186, 216, 217-18, 223, 227, 422
Balfour, Dr. Andrew, 390-91
Barbed wire, effect on ranching, 323-24
Barber, M. A., 409
Barney, Charles D., 309, 310, 311-13
Barrows, Harlan H., 4
Bassett, John Spencer, 46

Beard, Charles A.; Mary R., 467
Beard, J. H., 417
Benedict, H. Y., 321
Bennett, Hugh H., 83, 89, 102, 104, 106, 204
Berglund, Abraham, 131
Bernard, John, 69-70
Berry, Harriet, 255
Betts, H. S., 117
Biological factors in South's development, alleged deficiencies of, 461-62; indentured servants as, 462; Negro, 462-63; "poor whites," 464-65; Civil War depletes, 465-66; inferiority of, assessed, 467
Birmingham, 487
Birmingham ore district, 301-07
Birth rates, in South, 476-79; and climate, 365-66
Bjorkman, Francis M., 282
Black Prairie of Alabama, 91
Black Waxy Prairie of Texas, 91, 316-17; social-economies characteristics of, 328-29
Blair, Fred G., 227
Blanchard, Raoul, 282
Blue grass, Kentucky, 89, 90
Blue Ridge, soils of, 86-87, 90
Boom in petroleum production, 339-42
Borger, Texas, oil boom town, 341
Boutmy, Professor, 59
Bowman, Isaiah, 24, 25, 26, 27, 28, 29, 103, 242, 246, 356, 483
Boyd, W. K., 310
Branch, E. Douglass, 76
Brandes, E. W., 221, 222
Branford, Victor, 484
Brannen, C. O., 268
Branson, E. C., 494
Brearley, H. C., 14
Bretz, Julian P., 525
Brooks, C. E. P., 355
Brooks, C. F., 362
Brooks, E. C., 95, 415-16
Brown, Cecil K., 460
Brown, L., 501
Brown, Robert M., 291
Brown, W. G., 359
Bruere, Robert W., 17
Brunhes, Jean, 11-12
Buck, P. H., 75

Buckman, H. O., 81
Buffalo, effect of extermination, 319-20
Burroughs, W. G., 17
Butterick, Wallace, 383-84
Buttrick, P. L., 138, 139
Bynum, Jefferson, 277
Byrne, Harriet A., 212-13

CALIFORNIA, 321-22, 323, 343-45
Calvert, Benedict Leonard, 213
Cameron, Frank K., 497
Campbell, John C., 241, 378, 392, 431
Campbell, Mrs. John C.
Campbell, John L., 154, 156
Campbell, J. P., 493-94
Cance, A. E., 190, 192
Capital, invested in southern industry, 280; requirements in rayon, 299
Carlson, F. A., 84
Carnegie, Andrew, 305
Carolina tidewater, 34
Carr, Lewis F., 21, 154-55, 156, 157-58, 159
Carrier, Lyman, 145, 147, 154
Carter, Henry R., 391, 399, 400, 404, 405, 408
Casal, Gaspar, 437
Case fatality rate of malaria, 398-99
Cason, Clarence E., 487
Cassidy, Harry M., 506
Casson, N. H., 300
Castellani Aldo, 399
Castlelux, 413
Cates, J. Sidney, 494, 495
Cattle, introduction of, 145; raising on frontier, 146-50; raising on plantation, 150-52; pure bred, 151-52; pasturage for, in South, 152-59, 162-63; beef, 162, 163-65, 165-67; pasture requirements for, 173-76; trends in cattle raising, 173-76
Cattle drovers, 148-49
Central plain of Tennessee, 35-36
Century of Population Growth, 1790-1900, quoted, 51, 53, 57
Chamber of Commerce movement in the South, 485-89; drives of, 485-86; effects of, 486-87; theory of, 487, 490-91; lacks unity, 487; values in, 488-89; and Florida boom, 502-04
Chambers, William T., 333, 347-48

Chapman, H. H., 132

Charleston, 508

Charleston-Savannah, area of settlement, 46, 56

Chase, Stuart, 436

Cities, in Piedmont, 276; in the South, 504-09; growth of, 504-06; size of, 506; migration to, 507-08; diffused pattern of, 506-07

City planning, 492; in the South, 407-08

Civil War, effect on biological stock, 465-66

Clark, Evans, 178-79

Clark-McNary Bill, 137

Clay, Henry, introduces mules, 149; imports Herefords, 151

Clay Hills, 91

Clemow, Frank G., 375-76

Climate, action of on soils, 80-83; in cotton production, 185-86; in tobacco production, 205-07; in rice production, 215-17; in sugar production, 219-21; in trucking, 227, 229; social effects of, 351; significance to South, 351-53; and slavery, 351-52; effect on southern character, 352-53; definition of, 353, 355; of South, 355-61; zones of, 355-56; of Gulf Coast, 356; hot waves, 360-61; biological effect of, 361-68; optimum, 362; and humidity, 362; and efficiency, 363-67; racial adjustment, 364-65; and birth rate, 365-66; agricultural labor in South, 366-68; cultural adjustments to southern, 368-72; exposure to, 368-69; and southern architecture, 369-70; and dress, 371; and drink, 371-72; and air conditioning, 372; and the Negro, 372-73; and southern industry, 373-74; and human energy, 361-68, 378-83; and hookworm, 386-87; as natural resource, 448; see disease, diet, etc.

Climatic province, South as, 355-61

Coal and iron, in Birmingham area, 301-07; geology of, 301-03; factors of production, 303; juxtaposition of, 301, 303; transportation, 304; history of, 304-07; metallurgy of, 306; extent of industry, 307

Coast line of South, 41, 447

Coastal Plains, physiography of, 23-25; as economic region, 33-34; of Georgia, 37-38; soils of, 86, 89-91

Coker, David R., 494

Colby, C. C., 4, 446

Colonial economy, of South, 467-76; definition of, 468; and frontier, 468-69; rationalization of, 469; and plantation, 470; as debtor economy, 470; and extractive industry, 470-71; unmechanized, 471; and capital, 472; and technology, 472; and labor supply, 472-73; industry in, 473; agriculture in, 473-74; wages in, 474-76; and educational status, 480-81; and regional planning, 482, 484

Columbus (Georgia), site of, 38

Coman, Katherine, 325-26

Connor, R. D. W., 43

Continental margin, 24

Cook, James M., 321

Cooper, James Fenimore, 412

Coöperation, on the frontier, 69

Corporation planning, 492

Corson, J. J., Jr., 57

Corson, W. J., 268-69

Cotter, Arundel, 306

Cotterill, R. S., 452

Cotton belt and live stock, 152, 154; dairying in, 167-71; resources of, 445

Cotton culture complex, 200-04

Cotton culture in Southwest, 326-32; beginnings, 326; replaces ranching, 327; social-economic characteristics of Black Waxy, 328-29; of Plains area, 329-32; mechanization of, 331-32

Cotton production, and soils, 99-100; geography of, 185-86; history of, 186-90; and the plantation, 186-87; and tenancy, 187, 190-92; and Negro, 192-93; system of, 193-99; cycle of, 194-96; diversification, lack of, 196-97; unmechanized, 197-98; labor in, 197-98; credit in, 198-99; over-expansion in, 199; social-economic aspects, 200-04; mobility in, 201-02

Cotton restriction legislation, 490

Cotton system, rationalization of, 494-98; problem of, 495; and small farmer, 495-96; and plantation areas, 496-97; technical changes in, 497-98

Cotton Textile Industry, in the Southeast, 289-98; historical development of, 289-90; geographic distribution, 291-92; proximity to markets, 292; proximity to raw materials, 292; factors of location, 292-96; labor in, 293-96; growth of, 296; disorganization in, 297-98

Cotton Textile Institute, 298

Coulter, E. Merton, 278

Coves of Appalachian Mountains, 28

Covington, Leonard, 54

Cowboy, 320-21; of today, 325

Cowpens, 147-48

Cracking process in petroleum refining, 346

Craig, R. B., 499

Craven, Avery O., 61, 62, 93-94, 105, 116

Crawford, George Gordon, 305-06

Culex mosquito, 405

Cultural areas, in United States, 14-15; of the South, 30-39

Cultural factors of the region, 10-18

Cultural lag of frontier, 62

Cultural landscape, 12, 14; of oil boom area, 340-41

Cultural rank of the South, 442-43, 446

Cultural succession on frontier, 63

Culture, factors of American, 3

Culture pattern of frontier, 60-62

Cumberland Plateau, 90; as cultural area, 35

Cummings, Surgeon General, 438

Cushing oil field, 343

Cut-over lands, in the South, 133-44; extent of, 133; agriculture on, 135-36; stock raising on, 136, 140-42; reforestation of, 136-43; reseeding of, 138-39

DAIRYING, in South, 167-71; and plantation, 167-68; and urban markets, 168; secondary markets in, 168; development of, in Mississippi, 168-71; and processing of milk, 169, 171; trends in, 175-76

Dale, Edward Everett, 319, 326-27

Darling, S. T., 388, 408

Davis, D. H., 17, 245, 253

Davis, R. O. E., 102

Davis, William M., 7, 23

Dawson, C. A., 5

DeBow, J. D. B. (ed.), 70, 119, 146, 413, 414

DeBow's Review, quoted, 72, 464-65, 469

De Cordova, Jacob, 151

De Kruif, Paul, 438

De la Blache, Paul Vidal, 10

De Long, Ethel, 247

Delta of the Mississippi, soils of, 87, 92; metropolis of, 262-63; commerce of, 263-66; agriculture in, 266-67; plantations in, 267-69; social-economic characteristics of, 269-71; floods in, 271-74

Den Hollander, A. N. J., 463

Density of frontier settlement, 60

Denton, Virginia, 269-70

De Tocqueville, Alexis, 75

Dexter, E. G., 264

Dice, L. R., 8

Dickens, Dorothy, 418, 424-25, 426-28

Diet, in the South, 411-41; the geography of, 411-12; and the frontier, 412-16; corn in, 415; salt pork in, 412-16; and the plantation, 416-18; hot breads in, 417-18; bio-chemistry of, 418-20; calories in, 418-19; vitamins in, 419; alkaline balance in, 419-20; trends in American, 420-22; of rural South, 423-36; of share tenants, 423-25; of Negroes, 424-25; of small owners, 425-28; of well-to-do farmers, 428-29; culture areas in, 430-31; of urban South, 432; South deviates from standard, 433-34; changes in southern, 434-36; and human adequacy, 436-38, 440-41; and climate, 440; see pellagra.

Difficulties of settlement, 49-50

Disease, and the South, 375-10; geography of, 375-78; seasonal distribution of, 375-76; and social environment, 376-78; and human energy, 379-81; "concealed," 379-81; history of, 391-92, 393-95; see hookworm, malaria, pellagra

Doane, C. F., 257-58

Dobie, J. Frank, 324, 325

Dockery, Nicholas W., 497

Doddridge's Notes, quoted, 70-71

"Dog-run" house, 369-70

Domestic economy of frontier, 64, 65-66; of southern highlands, 247-48

Dorris, Fern Ellison, 266

Dress, frontier, 65; and southern climate, 371

Duke, James Buchanan, 284, 310, 311-13, 487

Dumble, E. T., 316

Duncan, William C., 55, 413

Dunn, Fanny Wyche, 480-81

Dupino, Angelo, 381

Dykes, A. W., 225

EASTERN Oklahoma prairies, 92

Economic planning, see regional planning

Education in Appalachians, 254-55; in the South, 480-81

Edwards, George Clifton, 317

Edwards Plateau, 92, 316-17

Eijkman, C., 364-65

Eldridge, S. F., 500

Elizabethton, Tenn., 487

Emerson, F. V., 111, 126-27, 130, 135

Empire builder, South lacks, 487-88

Environment, organic, 5; inorganic, 4-5; see geography, culture, etc.

Equilibrium of nature, 6

Eradication of malaria in the South, 403-10; methods, 404, 409-10; *Anopheles* control in, 404-05, 408-09; in cities, 405-07; costs of, 406-07, 409; in rural areas, 408-10

Erosion, of soil, 85, 99-104; effect on soil formation, 85; human geography of, 104-06; remedies for, 106-08; as natural process, 100-02; form of, 102-03; effects of, 102-04; and leaching, 102; effect of, on water table, 102; sheet, 101-02; gully, 101-02; and hydro-electric power, 102; and tree crops, 107; and frontier, 104-05; and plantation, 105-06

Estabrook, Arthur H., 241, 245-46, 259

Eutsler, Roland B., 453, 454, 455, 456

Everglades, drainage of, 26

FALL LINE, 26, 275-76; and textiles, 291

Family on the frontier, 67

Farley, F. W., 135-36, 151, 162-63, 165

Farm tenancy, and cotton, 187, 190-92; social economic aspects of, 200-04

Farrand, Livingston, 40, 438

Featherstonhaugh, George William, 393

Fenneman, Nevin N., 7

Ferris, E. B., 163

Fertilizers, commercial use of, in South, 95-97

Feuds in Southern Highlands, 250-55

Fish, Carl Russell, 413

Fisher, Carl G., 504

Fisher, Russell T., 294

Fishing, in South, 236-39; on Atlantic coast, 236-37; Gulf coast, 237-38; social, economics of, 238; laborers in, 239

Fiske, John, 43, 244

Flint, Timothy, 55

Flippin, E. O., 81

Floods along Mississippi, 271-74

Flood control, on Mississippi, 301-02; levees, 501-02; revetments, 501-02; spillways, 501-02; riverside floodways, 502

Flood hazards in Rio Grande Valley, 333-34

Florida, 25-26, 55, 56, 75, 84, 89, 90, 97, 109, 121, 145, 161, 164, 165, 173, 174, 177, 227, 230, 232, 233, 237-38, 239, 356, 357, 360, 369, 376, 397, 430-31, 435, 439, 443, 444, 446, 477, 485, 488, 502-04

Florida boom, 502-04

Florida Flatwoods, 89

Florida, physiography of, 25-26

Florida program of city "beautification," 503-04

Folk renaissance, in the South, 490, 508-10

Forage and hay in South, 155-59; timothy, 155; alfalfa, 156; clover, 156; cowpeas, 158; lack of improved pastures, 173-74 see grasses

Forbes, R. D., 131, 132, 133, 138

Forests, of North America, 109-11; distribution of, in United States, 9

Forsythe, John, 464-65

Foundations in regional planning, 492

Fox, Dixon Ryan, 51

Fox, John A., 272

Frank, Arthur De Witt, 501-02

Frasch method in mining sulphur, 335

Free, E. E., 262
Freeman, Douglass, 466
French Hugenots, 43
Friedrick, C. J., 292
Frissell, Sidney D., 34
Frontier, American, 11; in 1790, 51; and migration, 53-54; settlement in 1820, 1840, 53; dress, 66; housing, 66-67; family, 67; as stage of settlement, 59-60; Indian as element in, 60; adjustment of culture traits to, 60-61; in the South, 61-62; stages of, 62-63; as process, 62-64; traits of southern, 65-70; occupational types in, 70-71; farm, 64, 71; and poor whites, 75; and plantation systems, 74-75; and soil exhaustion, 104-05; conflict with plantation, 71-75; heritage of, 62, 75-76; trials of, 68; coöperation on, 69; hospitality on, 69-70; commerce of, 70-71; and live stock, 146-50; and forests, 313-16, 319; and grasslands, 319-20; and the buffalo, 320; passing of, in southwest, 349-50
Frost, President, of Berea, 247
Furniture manufacturing, in the southeast, 314-15
Fuchs, A. W., 400-01
Funk, W. C., 426, 427, 428

GABBARD, L. P., 331
Gariel, Georges, 11
Garner, W. W., 210
Garnett, E. B., 341
Gates, John W., 323
Geddes, Patrick, 29-31, 484
Gee, Wilson, 57, 482
Geller, Carl, 195
Geography, field of, 14; elements of, 4-5; interaction in, 5-6; regional, 6-7; of tobacco, 205-07; of rice production, 215-17; see human geography, climate, soil, agriculture, etc.
Geographic conditioning, 11
Geographic determinism, 482-83
Geology, of soil formation, 80-83; of petroleum, 336-37
Georgia, 24, 37-38, 44, 46, 50, 51, 52, 53, 56, 57, 75, 84, 89, 90, 91, 97, 99, 111, 115, 120, 121, 139, 150, 161, 173, 186, 196, 200-01, 202, 204, 208, 209, 211, 214, 216, 217, 229, 233, 237, 254, 275, 278, 282, 291, 292, 293, 297, 315, 356, 360, 385, 430, 433-34, 436, 439, 443, 445, 446, 451, 452, 466, 476, 480-81, 493-94, 499, 503, 507
Georgia, regional distribution of population in, 37-38
Germans, 42, 43
Gilbert, C. G., 283
Gilbert, L. D., 141-42
Glenn, Governor, of North Carolina, 383
Glenn, L. C., 34-37, 130
Glenn oil pool, 342
Glynn County, Georgia, 507
Goldberger, Joseph, 438
Goldenweiser, A. A., 362
Gould, Charles N., 348-49
Grady, Henry W., 275, 489
Gras, N. S. B., 16
Grasses, of the South, 154-59; geography of, 154-55; Johnson, 155-56; crab, 155; Bermuda, 156-57; Lespedeza, 157-58, 494; wire grass, 162; carpet grass, 162-63; see forage
Gratton, Thomas Calley, 59
Gray, L. C., 498, 500
Great Plains region, 317-18; cultural adjustment in, 318, 319-20
Great Valley as avenue of settlement, 45-46; in Tennessee, 35
Greeley, Horace, 415
Greeley, General W. A., 9-10
Greeley, W. B., 111, 123, 124, 129, 130, 143
Greene, Evarts Boutell, 46
Greene, S. W., 133, 135-36, 139-41, 162-63, 165
Growth of cities in the South, 506-07
Gulf Coastal Prairies, 316
Gulf oil field, 342-43
Gulf Plain, physiography of, 25; of Tennessee as cultural area, 36

HAGER, John M., 112-13, 121, 122, 131, 136, 233, 282, 307, 314
Haley, J. E., 324
Hammond, Governor, of South Carolina, 414
Harding, Warren G., 438
Harper, Roland M., 78
Harris, Joel Chandler, 509

Hartshorne, Richard, 303
Hawks, F. L., 65
Hawthorne, H. W., 422
Heer, Clarence, 182, 293, 473-75
Henderson, Archibald, 63, 66
Henderson, Judge Richard, 48
Hendrick, Burton, 383
Herrick, Glenn W., 399
Herring, Harriet L., 289
Herty, Charles H., 120, 130, 501
Hess, R. H., 59
Heyward, Du Bose, 248
Highlands, see southern highlands
Highland Rim, of Tennessee, 91
Highways in South, need of, 458; development of, 456, 459-60; in Appalachians, 255-56
Hilgard, E. W., 89, 112
Hill, James J., 263-64, 357, 487
Hill, Leonard, 362-63
Hillyard, M. B., 368-69
Hines, L. N., 364
Hobbs, S. H., Jr., 32-33, 356-57, 361, 378, 442-43
Hoffman, Frederick L., 398-99, 403
Hoke, Travis, 262
Holmes, George K., 192
Holton, J. C., 169
Home demonstration agents, quoted, 435-36
Hookworm disease, and the South, 380-90; and biological adequacy, 380-81; history of, 381-83; discovery of parasite, 381-82; eradication of, 382-85; and public opinion, 382, 383, 384-85; geography of, 386-87; and climate, 386-87; and soil, 387; social factors in, 387-88; and living standards, 388-89; sex and age differences, 388-89; and mental retardation, 390; method of attack on, 389
Horses in the South, 145, 151-52
Hospitality on the frontier, 69-70
Hot waves, in the South, 360
Housing, frontier, 65-66
Howell, L. D., 200-01
Howard, L. O., 380
Hulbert, Archer B., 50, 61, 68, 70, 71, 74, 97-98, 147-48, 261-62
Human geography, approach to, 4, 6;

scope of, 11; as science of distribution, 29-31; of erosion, 104-06
Humidity, 362; in textiles, 277
Huntington, C. C., 84
Huntington, Ellsworth, 86, 129, 139, 177, 178, 340-41, 362, 363-64, 371, 372, 403, 440
Hutchinson, Woods, 391, 392, 395-96, 403
Hydro-electric power, in Southeast, 281-89; cycle in development of, 281; geography of, 283; development of, 281-86; super-power zone, 286-87; rural electrification, 287-88

INDENTURED servants in South, 462
Indian culture on frontier, 60
Indian trader, 62-63, 70
Industrialization, of the Southeast, 275-315; see textiles, tobacco, steel, furniture, hydro-electric power, mining, etc.; in Southern Highlands, 251-53; in Southwest, 334; see petroleum
Ingle, Edward, 451
International Health Board, 384-90, 391, 404-10
Interior Coastal Plain, 91
Interior Flatwoods, 91, 316
Irrigation in Rio Grande Valley, 333-34
Iron ore in Birmingham field, 302-03
Isolation in Southern Highlands, 246-47
Isothermal lines, in relation to migration, 52-53

JACOBSTEIN, Meyer, 211-12
James River, 44-45
Jefferson, Mark, 453-54
Jefferson, Thomas, 469
Jenkins, J. W., 311-13
Jillson, W. R., 17
Joerg, W. L., 7
Johnson, Gerald W., 385
Johnson, J. K., 143
Jones, F. R., 331
Jones, Howard Mumford, 243
Jones, W. D., 262-63, 351, 355
Jones-Reid Act, 501
Jordan, David Starr, 455-56

KATATHERMOMETER, 363
Keller, Albert G., 352

Kendall, Henry P., 294
Kendrew, W. G., 351
Kentucky, 17, 31, 44, 48, 51, 56, 63, 84, 89, 90, 98-99, 108, 111, 146, 149, 151-52, 134, 161, 174, 205, 206, 208, 209, 212, 245, 248, 251-52, 254, 255, 314, 376, 425, 433, 443, 444, 445, 448, 477, 498
Kentucky Bluegrass, cultural succession in, 63
Kentucky, regional survey of, 17
Kephart, Horace, 242-43
Kerr, J. Austin, 387
Keyserling, Herman, 14-15
Kier, Malcolm, 455
Killebrew, J. B., 205, 207
Kincer, J. B., 10
King, Edward, 271, 367, 413-14, 418
Kingsley, Charles, 508
Kingsport, Tennessee, 258-59
Kirkpatrick, E. L., 425
Knapp, Seaman A., 216, 217-18, 434
Köppen, W., 8, 355

LABOR, in tobacco, 208-09, 212-13; in southern industry, 279-81; in southern textiles, 293-96; wages of, 293-96
La Forge, Lawrence, 37, 38
Land, desire for, 49
Lapham, J. E., 83
Lapham, M. H., 83
Laterites, 86
Laughinghouse, Charles, 439
Laveran, 395-96
Lay, Captain W. P., 284
Leadership, in southern industry, 278-79
Le Blanc, T. J. B., 403-04
Lee, W. S., 284
Le Play, P. G. F., 11, 14, 30
Lespedeza sericea, 157-58, 494
Levees, fuse plug, 502
Lewis, Charles D., 242, 252, 255-56, 499-500
Liberalism in the South, 491-92
Limestone valleys, soils of, 87-88, 90-91
Lincecum, Gideon, 54
Lippincott, Isaac, 322
Live stock, on pine lands, 140-42; in the South, 145-76; early development, 145-46; and the frontier, 146-50; and Indians, 146, 147; in the cowpens, 147-48; on the plantation, 150-52; effect of Civil War on, 152; units in cotton belt, 152, 154; and grass, 152-59; and tick fever, 159-62; and native pastures, 162; cut-over lands, 136, 140-42, 162-63; biological factors in, 163-65; improving breed, 164-65; markets, 165-67; South's disparity in, 173-75; ratios in South, 175; in Southwest, 320-27; see dairying, ranch, and range
Loblolly pine, 111-12, 113
Local governments, consolidation of, 492
Loess soils, 87, 91
Lomax, John A., 321
Long, Howard, 258-59
Longhorn cattle, 320; passing of, 324-25
Long hunter, 63
Long-leaf pine, 111-12
Louisiana, 25, 44, 52, 53, 55, 72, 91, 109, 121, 132, 138, 143, 150, 161, 167, 173, 177, 204, 215, 217, 218, 220-24, 229, 262, 264, 266, 269-70, 318, 335, 345, 346, 347, 397, 439, 443, 446, 476, 490, 492, 501-02
Love, Clara M., 320, 321-22
Lovejoy, P. S., 17
Lowe, E. N., 87, 101
Lumber camps, 129
Lumber industry, in United States, 122-25; production, 125-26; technology of, 126-29; methods of development in South, 126-28; and wood pulp, 129-30; characteristics of, in South, 130-32; economics of, 132
Lumber towns, 130-32
Lyell, Sir Charles, 52-53, 75
Lyon, T. L., 81
Lynd, Robert S. and Helen M., 421
Lyttle, A. L., 370

MACLACHLAN, Emily Stevens, 418, 434
Macon, site of, 38
McCollum, E. V., 419, 420, 422, 436, 440
McCombs, C. A., 265
McConnell, John P., 245
McDonald, Lois, 432
McDonald, Ruel, 328
McDonald, Silar, 247
McGee, W. J., 101

MacKaye, Benton, 483-84
McRae, Hugh, 494
Malaria, in the South, 390-10; significance of, 390-91, 392; history of, 391-95; on the frontier, 392, 394; and yellow fever, 394-95; folk beliefs about, 395-96; medical discoveries, 395-96; geography of, 396-97; mortality and morbidity, 397-99; and the Negro, 399; and efficiency, 399-03; and industry, 400-01; and agriculture, 401-03; decline in, 404; see eradication of malaria
Malinowski, Bronislaw, 62
Manning, J. W., 492
Manson, Sir Patrick, 374, 410
Manufacturing industries in the Southeast, 275-15; progress in, 280-81; see cotton textiles, steel, furniture, hydroelectric power, mining, tobacco, rayon, etc.
Marbut, C. F., 77-78, 80, 83, 86
Marcosson, Isaac F., 342-43, 346
Marketing, of tobacco, 210-12
Marland, E. W., 343
Marsh, George Perkins, 5, 483
Martineau, Harriett, 49
Maryland, 54, 213, 233-34
Mason, D. L., 137
Matoon, W. A., 113
Matthews, J. H., 236-37, 238, 239
Matthews, Susan J., 433
Maxcy, Kenneth F., 397
Mayratt, Frederick, 367
Mead, George Herbert, 450
Mechanization of cotton production, 497-98; in southwest, 331-32
Medical facilities of the old South, 376-78
Mencken, H. L., 378, 442-43
Meredith, Secretary, 121
Merriam, C. Hart, 9
Merrick, George, 503-04
Mesick, Louise Jane, 413
Metropolitan economy, of the South, 506-08
Metropolitan regionalism, 16-17
Meyer, B. H., 452
Michigan land economic survey, 17-18
Mid-continent oil field, 342-43
Middle Coastal Plains, 90

Migration, avenues of, in South, 41-56; forces in, 48-49; and isothermal lines, 52-53; process of, 44, 48-49, 53-54, 56-58
Miller, E. E., 35, 36
Mill villages, 510
Mims, Edwin, 120, 305-06
Mineral resources of South, 448-49
Mining, in Southern Highlands, 251-53; in Birmingham area, 301-07
Mississippi, 24-25, 44, 49, 50, 51, 53, 54, 55, 75, 83, 87, 89, 91, 92, 103, 104, 108, 109, 111, 121, 150, 158, 161, 169-71, 173, 174, 196, 200, 262, 264, 266, 267, 269-70, 273, 318, 356, 398-99, 401-03, 404, 409, 422-25, 426-28, 439, 443, 445, 446, 448, 451, 481, 498-99, 501-02
Mississippi Alluvial Valley, 24-25
Mississippi Bluffs, 91
Mississippi Flatwoods, 89
Mississippi River, geography of, 261-62; as artery of commerce, 263-66; steamboats on, 264-65; Erie Canal, effect on, 265; floods on, 271-74; flood control on, 501-02; see Delta of the Mississippi
Mississippi Valley, in 1850, 55; in 1860, 56
Missouri, 52, 62, 149, 255, 259
Mitchell, Broadus, 275, 279, 280-81, 289, 296
Mitchell, George, 289, 511
Mitchell, John, 54, 391
Mitzmain, M. Bruin, 408, 409
Mobility and cotton culture, 201-02
Mohler, John R., 159
Mohr, Charles, collect grasses, 154
Monette, John Wesley, 66-67
Montana, 323
Montgomery, Robert H., 193, 195-96
Moonshining in Southern Highlands, 249
Moore, Bishop John M., 244
Morris, Robert, 508
Mosquitoes in the South, 395, 404-05, 408-09
Mountain passes as avenues of settlement, 50-51
Mowry, Don E., 485-86
Mukerjee, Radhakamal, 14

Mules, introduction of, 149; suited to South, 151

Murchison, Claudius T., 290, 296, 298

Murphy, Edgar Gardner, 509

NASHVILLE, 48

Natchez Trace, 51

National forests in Southern Highlands, 499-500

National Industrial Conference Board, quoted, 778-79

Natural gas in Southwest, 346-47

Natural life area, 7-8

Natural region, concept of, 10

Natural resources of the South, 446-50; modifiability of, 449-50

Natural vegetation areas, 8

Nature, human conquest of, 6

Naval stores, 117-22; statistics of production, 120-22

Negro, distribution of, in relation to soils, 99; in southern agriculture, 192-93; and climate, 372-73; as retarding factor, 462-63

Newbigin, Marion, 22-23, 39

New Orleans, 51, 485; metropolis of Delta, 262-63; site of, 262; municipal engineering in, 263

Nolen, John, 258, 508

Norfolk, 486

North Carolina, 31-34, 43, 45-46, 52, 56, 64, 65, 75, 89, 90, 94-95, 97, 117, 120, 121, 123, 146-47, 150, 154, 161, 173, 174, 186, 201-02, 205, 206, 207, 208, 209, 215, 232, 236-37, 241, 247-48, 254, 255, 257, 275, 282, 289, 291, 292, 293, 297, 299, 308-14, 314-15, 356, 361, 376, 385, 397, 400, 430, 432, 439, 440, 443, 445, 433, 460, 466, 476, 480, 487, 492, 493, 422

North Carolina, sequence of regions in, 31-34

Northern, Governor W. J., 192

Nott, Josiah C., 394-95

Nicholas, W. D., 500

Nixon, H. C., 509

ODUM, Howard W., 19, 491

Oklahoma, 92, 104, 155, 161, 259, 316, 318, 324, 326-32, 334, 338-46, 347-50, 376, 429, 435-36, 443, 444, 446, 448, 476

Oklahoma City, 341-42

Olmsted, Frederick Law, 72, 73, 75-76, 151, 208, 446-67, 392, 413-14, 415

Oil, see petroleum; oil pools, geology of, 336; exploitation of, 337-38; in southwest, 342-43

Orangeburg, South Carolina, 508

Orchard crops, 232-33

Ozark-Ouachita Highlands, 90; phyiography of, 28-29; soils of, 28; area, 259-60; population, 259; mining, 259; fruit culture, 260; diet in, 430-31

PACK-HORSE trade, 70-71

Page, Walter Hines, 278, 383-84, 429, 490, 510

Parkins, A. E., 450, 452

Parsons, Floyd W., 420

Pathways of settlement, 42

Payne, Henry Mace, 336

Pearl, Raymond, 421-22

Pease, Dr. T., describes tick fever, 159

Peattie, Roderick, 339

Peck's New Guide to the West, cited, 63-64

Pedalfers, soil group, 84-85

Pedocals, soil group, 84-85

Peg-model in petroleum prospecting, 336

Pellagra, a deficiency disease, 437, 438; history of, 437-38; research on, 438; public reaction to, 438-39; deaths from, 439

Petroleum industry of Southwest, human geography of, 335-42; geology of, 336-37, 339; prospecting in, 335-36, 339; physical and chemical characteristics of, 337-38; laws of, 337; drilling for, 337-38, 339-40; wastes of competition, 337-38, 340; transportation and pipe lines, 338, 345-48; speculative industry, 339-42, 345; hazards of, 341-42; history of discoveries, 342-43; fields, 343; production, 343-45; refining in, 345-46

Physiographic areas of the South, 22-29

Physiography, influence on population movements, 40-41

Phillips, Ulrich B., 41, 45, 46, 47, 53,

54, 55, 56, 71, 72, 86, 89, 115, 186, 357, 370-71, 417
Pickard, E. R., 387
Piedmont, as fringe belt, 275-81; cities in, 276; resources of, 276-77, 443-44; nearness to markets, 277; labor in, 279-81; development of industry in, 287; see hydro-electric power, textiles, tobacco, furniture, iron
Piedmont Plateau, physiography of, 26-27; as economic region, 32-33; of Georgia, 37-38; settlement of, 46-47; soils of, 86-87, 90
Pierson, Albert H., 124, 128
Pinchot, Gifford, 116, 118, 120
Pine Barrens, barrier to settlement, 46-47
Pine forests, of the South, 109-44; location, 111; description, 111; species of pines in, 111-13; rate of growth, 113; turpentining the, 117-22; naval stores in, 177-22; lumbering in, 122-33; classification of, 125; and wood pulp industry, 129-30; lumber towns in, 130-32; cut-over lands of, 133-44; reseeding of, 138-39; see reforestation
Pine, uses of, 121
Pinehurst, 486
Pine Institute, 142
Piney Woods, 445-46
Pinkerton, John, 146-47
Pioneer squatters, 63
Pioneer migrations, 63-64
Pipe line system in petroleum, 338; in natural gas, 347
Pitt, Joseph, 380
Place-work-folk formula, 11
Plains and agriculture, 325-26
Plant areas, effect of temperature and rainfall on, 8-9
Plantation, characteristics of, 61; competition with frontier, 71-75; distinct social classes in, 72; economies of large scale production, 73; expansion of, 74; and soil exhaustion, 74; and live stock, 150-52; and cotton, 186-90; of Mississippi Delta, 267-71
Planters, and frontiersmen, 73-74
Pogue, J. E., 287
Political geography, of Tennessee, 36-37; and soils of Kentucky, 98-99
"Poor Whites," distribution of, in Old

South, 75; and frontier, 75; hookworm, 380-81, 383; as retarding factor, 463-65
Population depletion in tidewater South, 56-57
Population, distribution in South, 1790, 51; 1820, 53; 1840, 53; 1860, 55-56; in Georgia, 37-38; elements, of southwest, 348-49; Negroes, 348-49; Mexicans, 348-49; Indians, 348-49; white settlers, 349; movements in the early South, 40-56
Port development and regional planning, 492
Porto Rico, 382-83
Prairie soils in South, 91, 92
Pratt, J. H., 129
Precipitation, areas of, in United States, 9-10
Pressey, Henry A., 283
Pretlow, Mary D., 417
Price, O. W., 118, 128
Prospecting for petroleum, 335-36, 339
Public health movement and hookworm disease, 382-85; method of attack, 389
Pudgin, M. A., 120
Pulp wood, thinning for, 142

RACE and climate, 364-65
Race differences and susceptibility to malaria, 399
Racial elements in settlement of South, 42-43
Railways, in South, early construction, 451-52; system, 453; network, 453-54; adequacy of, 454; rate structure of, 455-56; coöperate in agricultural reform, 494
Rainfall, distribution in United States, 9-10
Rambo, Marion G., 244
Ranching, Spanish heritage, 320; and free range, 321-22; transition to, 323; present economy, 324-25; replaced by farming, 326-27
Randolph, Vance, 259
Range, the open, first area of, 320-21; era of, 321-22; definition of, 322; round up on, 322; cattle drivers on, 323; end of, 323
Ranger oil pool, 343

Rankin, W. S., 492

Raper, Arthur, 499

Rayon industry, in Southeast, 299-300; capital requirements in, 299; production costs in, 299; location factors in, 299-300; effect on cotton industry, 300

Rayon, from cotton plant, 497-98; from bagasse, 497

Red Prairies of Oklahoma-Texas, 92

Reed, A. J., 257-58

Reforestation, attitude toward, 136-37; economics of, 137-38; a natural process, 138-39; advantages of South for, 139-43; and grazing, 140-42; in Piney Woods, 500

Region, physical factors of, 4-10; as environmental type, 7; physiographic, 7; rainfall, 9-10; biotic, 10; concept of natural, 10; of human use, 10-11; agricultural, in United States, 12-13; economic and financial, 16-17; cultural factors of, 10-18; sequence of South's, 29-39; relation of, to types of culture, 29-31

Regional geography, field of, 29

Regional economy, see colonial economy

Regional planning, scope of, 482; definition, 483; place of science in, 483-84; social policy in, 483-84; regional survey in, 483-84; in the South, 488-93; tasks of, 491-02, 504-11; and cotton system, 495-98; and marginal highlanders, 498-01; flood control as, 501-02

Regional research, 7, 18

Regionalism, in American literature, 15-16; metropolitan, 16-17; theory of, 482-84; and the South, 484-93; integrating effect of, 487-88; see Chamber of Commerce, agrarianism

Religion in southern highlands, 249-50

Resource areas of South, 443-46

Resources of South, attract migration, 41; destructive exploitation of, 482-83; constructive exploitation of, 482-83

Revetments on Mississippi, 501-02

Reynolds, R. V., 124, 128

Rhodes, Cecil, 487

Rhyne, Jennings J., 432; and Clyde R., 348

Rice, in the South, 214-19; area of production, 215-16; discovery of area, 215-16; geography of, 216-17; culture of, 217; mechanization in, 217-18; consumption of, 218-19

Rice, Grantland, 361

Riegel, Robert, 43

Rio Grande Valley, 316, 332-34; trucking in, 333; irrigation in, 333-34; flood hazards in, 333-34

Ripley, W. Z., 352

Rivers, W. J., 391

Rivers, of the southeast, 41; as avenues of settlement, 44-46; through Appalachians, 50; trade of frontier, 71; and soil, 85-86

Roanoke, 486

Roberts, Governor, of Texas, 324

Roberts, Lydia, 431, 433

Robertson, James, 48

Rockefeller, John D., 383-84, 484

Romans, Bernard, 154

Ross, Edward A., 242, 248, 250, 251

Ross, Ronald, 396

Round-up, 322

Ruffner, W. H., 154, 156

Rural electrification, 287-88

Rural traits, relation to frontier, 61-62

Ruskin, John, 508

Russell, Edward J., 79

Russell, George, 510

Salmon, Dr. D. E., draws quarantine lines against tick fever, 159

St. Helena Island, survey of, 18

Sand Hills, 90; as barriers to settlement, 46-47

Sanders, J. T., 328-29

Sanderson, Dwight, 192, 201

Sanford, A. H., 62

Sauer, Carl O., 7, 17, 20-21, 29, 44, 63, 106, 149, 253, 431

Saunders, Colonel Lewis, introduces shorthorns, 151

Savannah, site of, 38

Saville, Thorndyke, 282

Scattergood, Margaret, 293

Schaper, W. A., 3, 41, 46

Schaub, Dean I. O., 106

Schenck, C. A., 138

Scherer, James A. B., 199

Science, in regional planning, 483

Schorger, A. W., 117

Scotch highlanders, 43

Scotch-Irish, 42-43

Seasons, routine of, 14; effect on disease, 375-76

Seasonal distribution of homicides in South Carolina, 14

Semple, Arthur T., 163

Semple, Ellen C., 41, 44, 45, 47-48, 50, 51, 53, 99, 264-65, 276, 357, 372-73

Settlement, process of, 44, 48-49; difficulties of, 49-50; see population movements

Shaler, N. S., 25, 47, 48, 77, 98-99, 101, 356, 463

Shannonhouse, F. M., 190

Shemik, Bohumil, 114-15

Sheriff, Patrick, 77

Sherman, H. C., 420

Sherman, Wells A., 230, 231-32, 234-35, 236

Short-leaf pine, 111-12

Shryock, Richard H., 393-94

Siesta, 370

Simmonds, J. C., 393

Skinner, Constance Lindsay, 43

Slash pine, 111-12, 113

Slavery, and plantation, 71-75; reaction of yeomanry to, 73-74; and climate, 351-53

"Sledding" cotton, 331

Smedes, Henrietta R., 150, 196

Smillie, Wilson G., 387, 390

Smith, Adam, 484

Smith and Kilborne, work on tick fever, 160

Smith, J. Russell, 10, 85-86, 104, 107, 113, 207, 230, 251, 252, 261, 271, 301, 317, 333, 396-97, 429

Social Science Research Council, 18

Soils, in geography of the South, 77-108; native fertility of, 77-78; cycles in development of, 78, 80; structure of, 78; physics of, 78-80; circulation of water in, 78-79; particles, size of, 79; clay in, 79; humus in, 79; as organism, 79-80; origin of, 80-83; and climate, 80-83; profile, 81, 84; factors in classification of, 81; and geological factors, 80-83, 85-86; areas of United States, 83-85; areas of South, 83-92;

horizons, 84; lime in, 84; stream action on, 85-86; of Coastal Plains, 86; of Piedmont, 86-87; of Blue Ridge, 86; of river "bottoms," 87; of Limestone Valleys, 87-88; of Loess Belt, 87; human geography of, 93-99; exhaustion, 93-97; fertilization of, 95-97; and politics, 98-99; and population, 99; and cotton culture, 99-100; in tobacco production, 205-07; in rice production, 215-17; in sugar production, 220-21; in trucking, 227, 229, 232; and hookworm disease, 387; of South as natural resource, 447; see erosion

Soil exhaustion, effect of plantation on, 47

South in Building of the Nation, quoted, 149, 150, 151, 152

South, in literature, 15-16; as region, 20-21; physiographic areas of, 22-29; as colonial economy, 467-76

South Carolina, 14, 18, 24, 44, 46, 51, 52, 56, 57, 75, 89, 90, 94-95, 97, 117, 120, 121, 123, 150, 154, 161, 173, 174, 175, 196, 209, 212, 215, 216, 217, 232, 237, 275, 282, 289, 291, 292, 293, 295, 297, 397, 432, 435, 436, 439, 443, 445, 448, 451, 476, 490, 492, 494, 508

Southeast, 275-15; survey of, 18

Southeastern Economic Council, 493

Southern Forestry Congress, *Proceedings,* 140-41, 141-42

Southern Highlands, as cultural area, 32, 35; contrast with Delta, 240-41; physiography of, 241-42; topography effect of, 242-43; soil type of, 243-44; biological stocks of, 244-45; social economic conditions, 245-51; isolation in, 246-47; culture of, 247-56; domestic economy of, 247-48; place of women, 248-49; moonshining, 249; religion, 249-50; feuds, 250-51; mining in, 251-53; towns in, 253-54, 258-59; education in, 254-55; highways, 255-56; agricultural developments in, 256-58; cheese-making in, 257-58; resources of, 445; migration from, 498-99; agriculture in marginal, 499; national forests in, 499-500; salvaging marginal, 498-500; see Appalachians, Cumberlands, Ozarks, etc.

Southwest, 316-50; topography of, 316-17; extent of, 318-19; population elements of, 348-49; passing of frontier, 349-50; and the South, 349-50; resources, 444; see range, ranching, petroleum, sulphur, Texas gulf ports, etc.

Sparling, Earl, 341-42

Spence, C. R., 390

Spencer, Herbert, 3

Spillman, W. J., 12, 135

Spillways on Mississippi, 501-02

Spindle Top Oil Pool, 342

Spottswood, Governor, 244

Stabler, Herman, 283

Staked Plains, 92, 317

Staple length of upland cotton, 292

Steel production in Alabama, 301-07

Stevens, C. M., 137, 138

Stevens, P. H., 330

Stevens, Stanley, 362

Stevens, W. Mackenzie, 234, 235

Stiles, Charles Waddell, 381-83, 385, 388

Stine, O. C., 185-86

Stocking, George Ward, 337

Stock raising, see live stock

Stoddard, Amos, 392-93

"Stringtown" mode of settlement, 45, 49

Stuart, William, 227

Sugar cane, varieties, 224-25; P. J. O., 225

Sugar production in South, 219-25; geography of, 220-21; labor in, 221-23; organization of, 222-23; by-product in, 224-25

Sullivan, Mark, 282

Sulphur mining in Southwest, 334-35

Sundstroem, E. S., 365

Super-power zone, southeastern, 286-87

Surveys, regional, 17-18, 483-84

Swine, in South, introduction of, 145; decline in, 173-74

Taxation and lumber industry, 132-33

Taylor, Carl C., 201-02

Taylor, R. H., 94-95

Temperature gradient, 356-57

Tenancy, in Southeast, 186-90, 193-99; in Delta, 267-71; in Southwest, 328-29

Tennessee, 34-37, 44, 48, 51, 56, 84, 89, 90, 91, 108, 111, 150, 161, 174, 186, 205, 229, 241, 245, 255, 258-59, 282, 284, 295, 299, 307, 313, 315, 387, 425, 439, 443, 466, 467, 477, 492, 508; sequence of regions in, 34-37

Tennessee River system, 282, 284, 285

Texas, 15, 25, 53, 54, 56, 83, 89, 91, 92, 97, 99, 104, 106, 108, 109, 113, 135, 141-42, 145, 150, 151, 152, 155, 161, 167, 177, 195-96, 215, 239, 297, 316, 317, 318, 320-30, 332-35, 340-46, 347-49, 356, 357, 359, 360, 386-87, 390, 425, 436, 443, 444, 448, 461, 486, 490, 493, 504

Texas, gulf port area, 347-48; exports of, 347; cultural harbor of, 347-48

Textiles, and humidity, 277; labor in, 279-81, 293-96; and rayon, 300; see cotton textile industry

Textile industry, proposed integration of, 492

Thompson, Holland, 22

Thompson, Samuel H., 246-47

Tick fever, biology of, 159; causes of, discovered, 159-60; quarantine against, 159, 160-61

Tidewater areas, population depletion in, 56-57; settlement of, 44-47

Timber, supply of, 123-26; stands of, 124-26; and types of sawmills, 126-29; and transportation, 126-29

Titus, Harold, 18

Tobacco, consumption of, 309-10; growing in the South, 205-14; geography of, 205-07; introduction of bright, 206-07; social-economic characteristics of culture, 207-08, 213-14; labor in, 208-09, 212-13; curing, 210; marketing, 210-12; bright, 206-07, 208, 209; dark, 206, 208; burley, 206, 208; manufacturing, in southeast, 307-14; location, 308; management in, 309; blending in, 310; mechanization in, 310-12; brand, 312; monopoly in, 312-13; earnings, 313-14

Tompkins, D. A., 279, 295-96

Topography, of Southern Highlands, 241-43; see physiography

Towns in Appalachians, 253-54, 258-59

Tracy, S. M., 155-56, 157, 158

Trails, to Kentucky, 50-51; to lower Mississippi valley, 51-52
Trask, John W., 396, 398
Transportation in the South, 450-62; waterways, 450-57; network, 453-54; effect of, 460-61; see railways, highways, etc.
Trevor, George, 361
Trewartha, Glenn L., 364-65
Trucking, in the South, 225-36; areas, 225-27; geography of, 227, 229; transportation, 229-30; economics of, 230-32; hazards of, 230-31; expansion in, 231; specialization in, 232; and orchard crops, 232-33; and canning, 233-34; marketing, 234-36; grading, 235-36; in Rio Grande Valley, 333
Turpentining, the pine forests, 117-22; methods of, 119-20; "ahead of the cut," 121
Turner, Frederick J., 11, 42, 59, 60, 63-64, 69, 74, 147, 149
Turner, Howard A., 200-01

ULTRA-VIOLET rays, effect of, 361
University research and regional planning, 493
Upper Coastal Plain, 90
Urbanization of the South, 504-08; diffused pattern of, 507
Urmstone, Rev. John, 65

VALLANDINGHAM, E. N., 352-53
Vallaux, Camille, 11
Valley section, 30-39; definition, 30; zones, 30-31; of North Carolina, 31-34; of Tennessee, 34-37; and distribution of population through Georgia, 37-38
Van Dine, D. L., 401-03
Vaquero, 320-21, 324
Vegetation of South as a natural resource, 447-48
Verhoeff, Mary, 252-53
Virginia, 15, 42-44, 45, 47, 49, 51, 55-56, 57, 69-70, 84, 89, 93-94, 106, 108, 117, 123, 145-46, 150, 151, 152, 154, 161, 174, 205, 207, 208, 212, 213, 227, 232, 234, 245, 255, 257, 275, 299, 313, 353, 384, 443, 444, 451, 462, 464, 465-66, 469, 476, 493
Volney, 412
Voskuil, Walter H., 283, 286, 335

WAGES of labor, in southern textiles, 293-95
Wallace, Henry C., 139, 383
Ward, Robert De C., 355, 356-57, 360-61, 374
Ward, W. F., 159, 163
Warshaw, H. T., 335
Washington, Booker T., 509
Washington, George, introduces mules, 149
Water, circulation of, in soil, 78-79
Water power, reservoirs and erosion, 102-03; see hydro-electric power
Watkins, D. W., 330
Watzek, J. W., 143
Webb, Walter Prescott, 318
Weber, Alfred, 292
Welliver, J. C., 344
Weeden, W. B., 67
Weir, M. W., 507
Wertenbaker, T. J., 391, 392, 462, 464
Wernicke, O. L. H., 142
West Virginia, 245, 257
Whitbeck, R. H., 5, 7
White, Langdon, 362-63
Whitner, M. C., 284
Whitney, Milton, 79-80, 227, 229
Whittlesey, D. S., 262-63, 351
"Wild catter" in petroleum production, 335-36
Williams, F. E., 86, 129, 139, 177, 178
Williams, John L., 105
Williams, J. C., 143
Wilson, Secretary James, 194
Windsor, Justin, 42
Winston, George T., 295-96
Wise, Henry A., 469
Wolfanger, Louis A., 78, 84
Women, place of, in Southern Highlands, 248-49
Women on frontier, domestic routine, 65-66; dress, 66
Wood, Hariette, 248-49
Woods, J. B., 135
Woofter, T. J., Jr., 18, 212

Woolley, R. W., 127
Wooten, E. O., 330-32
Wortham, Louis J., 320, 321, 326, 345
Wright, Philip G., 220
Wyoming, 323

Xit Ranch, 324

Yellow fever, in old South, 394-95
Yeomanry and planters, 73-74

Zimmerman, C. C., 202
Zimmermann, Erich W., 232-33, 446, 448
Zozaya, Jose, 436